Gender and American Law
The Impact of the Law on the Lives of Women

Series Editor
Karen J. Maschke

GARLAND PUBLISHING, INC.
New York & London
1997

Contents of the Series

Pornography, Sex Work, and Hate Speech

Edited with introductions by
Karen J. Maschke

GARLAND PUBLISHING, INC.
New York & London
1997

Library of Congress Cataloging-in-Publication Data

Pornography, sex work, and hate speech / edited with introductions by
    Karen J. Maschke.
        p.   cm. — (Gender and American law ; 6)
    Includes bibliographical references.
    ISBN 0-8153-2520-7 (alk. paper)
        1. Prostitution—United States. 2. Pornography—United States.
    3. Obscenity (Law)—United States. 4. Women—Crimes against—
    United States. I. Maschke, Karen J. II. Series.
    KF9448.A75P67 1997
    346.7301'34—dc21   96-51517
                                                                CIP

Printed on acid-free, 250-year-life paper
Manufactured in the United States of America

Contents

Series Introduction

From colonial times to the present, the law has been used to both expand and contract the rights of women. Over the last two decades, a body of literature has emerged that examines the ways in which the law has had an impact on the lives of women in the United States. The topics covered in this series include the historical development of women's legal rights, matters surrounding reproduction, sexuality and the family, equal employment opportunity, educational equity, violence against women, pornography, sex work, hate speech, and developments in feminist legal thought. The articles represent multidisciplinary approaches in examining women's experiences with the law and provide theoretical insights about the nature of gender equality.

A unifying theme in these articles is that women have been constructed historically as "different," and that this characterization "has had implications in regard to the way in which women are understood as objects and subjects of law" (Fineman 1992, p. 1). Biological differences between women and men and assumptions about the different "nature" of women and men have provided the basis for legal restrictions on women's ownership of property, guardianship of their children, ability to control their reproduction, and access to the workplace and educational institutions.

Even though women have more legal rights now than at any other time in history, many of the articles show that the law can both eradicate and reinforce women's subordination. Nineteenth-century child custody law is a telling example. While "judges granted women new legal power in family affairs," they also placed "severe limits on married women's overall legal rights" (Grossberg 1983, p. 235). On the one hand, by claiming the authority to determine which parent should be granted custody, judges dismantled the practice of fathers possessing unquestioned domain over matters of child custody and guardianship. Yet judges also "ensured that women's domestic powers did not translate into extensive external political and economic authority" (Grossberg 1983, p. 237).

The limitations of legal reform are also revealed by contemporary attempts to achieve gender equality. For example, in the 1970s many local governments adopted comparable worth wage policies. Such policies were "designed to correct historically discriminatory wages of female- and minority-dominated jobs" (Evans and Nelson 1989, p. 172). However, when some local communities were forced to raise women's wages to correct discriminatory practices, they eliminated or modified various jobs and social programs. Many of these programs, such as after school latchkey programs, were developed in response to the needs of two-paycheck and female-headed families. "In other words," note Evans and Nelson, "local governments are reacting to comparable worth with threats to renege on the emerging social commitment to policies addressing what have been traditionally defined as *women's* problems" (Evans and Nelson 1989, p. 183).

Other articles provide additional evidence of how legal reforms may actually disadvantage women in ways that are unanticipated. Furthermore, they reveal the problems in employing the model of equality as a basis for achieving gender justice. The emerging "difference theories" in feminist legal thought focus on the ways in which women and men live "gendered lives," and the ways in which legal and social institutions are shaped and operate according to gendered constructs (Fineman 1992).

The articles in this series also show how the law affects women in different ways. Women of color, poor women, and single mothers may experience the power of the law in ways that are different from the experiences of white, middle-class women. Poverty reform discourses are laden with images of single mothers as "bad" and often lump these women together "with drug addicts, criminals, and other socially-defined 'degenerates' in the newly-coined category of 'underclass'" (Fineman 1992, p. 283). Consequently, current welfare policies are not designed so much to help single mothers as they are to punish them for their bad behavior.

Several authors show how in the legal matters concerning male violence against women, "the experiences of women of color are frequently the product of intersecting patterns of racism and sexism" (Crenshaw 1991, p. 1243). These authors contend that theories of gender oppression must acknowledge the intersection of race and sex, the ways in which women have contributed to the social construction of race, and the oppression of black women. They also point out that the analyses of the law's role in women's oppression must take account of the intersectional identities of women and of how the law responds to, reinforces, and stigmatizes those identities.

The articles in this series bring together an outstanding selection from a growing body of work that examines how the law treats women and gender difference. They represent some of the most intriguing theoretical writing on the subject and reflect the strong multidisciplinary character of contemporary research on women and the legal order.

Notes

Cited works are contained in volumes five, three, seven, and two, respectively.

Crenshaw, Kimberle. 1991. Mapping the Margins: Intersectionality, Identity Politics, and Violence Against Women of Color. *Stanford Law Review* 43:1241–99.

Evans, Sara M. and Barbara J. Nelson. 1989. Comparable Worth: The Paradox of Technocratic Reform. *Feminist Studies* 15:171–90.

Fineman, Martha. 1992. Feminist Theory in Law: The Difference it Makes. *Columbia Journal of Gender and Law* 2:1–23.

Grossberg, Michael. 1983. Who Gets the Child? Custody, Guardianship, and the Rise of a Judicial Patriarchy in Nineteenth-Century America. *Feminist Studies* 9:235–60.

Volume Introduction

As Belinda Cooper has noted, "[P]rostitution poses a particularly thorny issue for feminists" (Cooper 1989, p. 112). So too does the issue of pornography. Feminists are divided over whether prostitution and pornography are forms of male oppression or whether women who choose to be involved in these activities are asserting control over their own sexuality. They also disagree whether prostitutes can ever freely consent to sell their services in a society that is male defined and male centered and that objectifies women through sexuality (Freeman 1989–90). The issue of pornography has drawn attention in recent years from some feminists who have promoted stronger governmental restrictions on the development, sale, and distribution of pornography.

Pornography is a multibillion-dollar-a-year, worldwide industry. Films, magazines, books, videos (and now the Internet) depict women in a variety of sexual acts, from erotic lovemaking to activities in which they are being "disintegrated, dismembered, or disoriented by destructive sexual forces" (Tong 1984, p. 10). Many believe pornography should be prohibited, while others contend that any form of anti-pornography censorship is unacceptable. At issue in the debate over pornography is whether it harms women.

According to Catharine MacKinnon, "[P]ornography, in the feminist view is a form of forced sex, a practice of sexual politics, an institution of gender inequality" (MacKinnon 1987, p. 148). She also contends that pornography "eroticizes hierarchy, it sexualizes inequality. It makes dominance and submission into sex" (p. 172). In 1983 MacKinnon and Andrea Dworkin drafted legislation for the City Council of Minneapolis that defined pornography as a form of sex discrimination. Approved by the city council, the legislation was vetoed by the mayor. A more moderate version was passed by the City of Indianapolis. The Indianapolis ordinance was held to be unconstitutional by a federal district court and by the Seventh Circuit Court of Appeals.

The MacKinnon/Dworkin ordinance was based on the view that pornography harms women. According to MacKinnon, the "harm of pornography, broadly speaking, is the harm of the civil inequality of the sexes made invisible as harm because it has become accepted as the sex difference" (MacKinnon 1987, p. 178). In specific terms, women are harmed from beatings, rape, torture, and the psychological intimidation they undergo while being filmed and photographed. They also are harmed by the negative and threatening conditions of their physical environment when pornography is concentrated in or near their neighborhoods. MacKinnon and others also argue that some rapes and other physical assaults against women are the direct result of pornography (1987).

In response to the MacKinnon/Dworkin ordinance, several feminists formed the Feminist Anti-Censorship Taskforce (FACT). These feminists argued that censorship of pornography violated the First Amendment right of freedom of speech. Some of the anticensorship feminists also argued that women have a right to sexually express themselves through engaging in or viewing pornography. The themes of freedom of sexual expression and male dominance in the pornography debate are also present in the debate over prostitution.

In early America prostitution was a common-law offense; it was not until the 19th century that statutes were passed criminalizing prostitution (Kandel 1992). There are two general feminist approaches to prostitution: a liberal feminist approach and a radical feminist approach. The liberal feminist approach contends that women can freely consent to engage in sex work for pay. This view is supported by prostitutes' rights groups such as Cast Off Your Old Tired Ethics (COYOTE) and the National Task Force on Prostitution. The vision of these groups is that women should have "equal access to an equality defined and perpetuated by men." They do not view women as a class of sexual subordinates or believe structural change is needed with regard to the sex trade (Freeman 1988–89). Consequently, they argue that women are free to give their consent to work as prostitutes.

On the other side of the debate are feminists who argue that consent is not possible because prostitution is a "microcosm of gender hierarchy" (Freeman 1988–89, p. 93). "Radical feminists," says Freeman, "reject the notion that women are empowered by fulfilling male desire, and they see the desire for prostitution as male" (p. 92). Consequently, prostitution perpetuates the "objectification of women through sexuality" (p. 93).

Unlike matters involving pornography, women connected with prostitution often come into contact with the criminal justice system. They are more likely than the men who purchase sex, or the pimps for whom they work, to be arrested, prosecuted, and incarcerated for their activities. Furthermore, it is prostitutes, and not the men they service or work for, who are subjected to a variety of social control practices.

Minouche Kandel's study of the experiences of prostitutes in the Boston criminal justice system shows that they end up being the victims of the "crime" of prostitution. She found that the police regularly arrest women for prostitution-related offenses, yet rarely arrest their pimps or the johns who purchase their services. While Boston judges tend to dismiss cases or give prostitutes suspended sentences, they dismiss more charges against male prostitutes than charges against female prostitutes. Judges also believe that arresting and incarcerating prostitutes is often desirable to protect prostitutes from the risk of AIDS and to provide them with a safe haven from violence and drugs (Kandel 1992). Kandel argues that such judicial intervention does not serve an "effective protective, rehabilitative or deterrent function" (p. 351). Hence, she supports the decriminalization of prostitution.

Decriminalization is not the same as legalization. If prostitution were decriminalized, there would be no legal restraints on commercial sex. Legalization, which has only occurred in some counties in Nevada, "carries with it a full regime of government regulations and controls" (Kandel 1992, p. 331). Prostitutes in these localities are usually required to work in brothels and are subjected to various regulatory measures. Consequently, legal prostitution "simply sanctions the concept of readily available sexual satisfaction for men by women," rather than representing the "liberal ideal of freedom and sexual equality" for women (Cooper 1989, p. 111).

Many feminists argue that "women in prostitution are primary victims of pornography" (Baldwin 1989, p. 116). Yet there continues to be widespread resistance to prohibiting the production and distribution of pornographic materials. One recent proposal aimed at eliminating pornography would involve applying the prostitution statutes to the pornography industry. Under this proposal, pornographic filmmaking would be prosecuted as a form of prostitution. As Sarah Garb explains, [W]omen acting in pornographic films are being paid—legally—to have sex, while women who are paid for sex *outside* the scope of film are deemed prostitutes, who by definition, break the law." Defining pornographic film as a form of prostitution would ensure that the "pornography industry no longer profits from the exploitation and trafficking of women, but rather is penalized for that very thing" (Garb 1995, p. 301).

Given the extraordinary amount of money that is generated by the pornography industry, it is unlikely that any one statutory scheme will eliminate pornography. Nor is it likely that decriminalization or legalization of prostitution will protect all prostitutes from the many hazards they face in the sex trade. What we can hope and work for is a society in which women are valued as full human beings rather than as sexual objects men want to dominate, violate, and possess.

Notes

Articles marked with an asterisk (*) are included in this volume.

*Baldwin, Margaret A. 1989. Pornography and the Traffic in Women: Brief on Behalf of Trudee Able-Peterson, et al., *Amici Curiae* in Support of Defendant and Intervenor-Defendants, *Village Books* v. *City of Bellingham. Yale Journal of Law and Feminism* 1:111–55.
Cooper, Belinda. 1989. Prostitution: A Feminist Analysis. *Women's Rights Law Reporter* 11:99–119.
*Freeman, Jody. 1989–90. The Feminist Debate Over Prostitution Reform: Prostitutes' Rights Groups, Radical Feminists, and the (Im)possibility of Consent. *Berkeley Women's Law Journal* 5:75–109.
Garb, Sarah H. 1995. Sex for Money Is Sex for Money: The Illegality of Pornographic Film as Prostitution. *Law and Inequality* 13:281–301.
*Kandel, Minouch. 1992. Whores in Court: Judicial Processing of Prostitutes in the Boston Municipal Court in 1990. *Yale Journal of Law and Feminism* 4:329–52.
*MacKinnon, Catherine A. 1987. Not a Moral Issue. In *Feminism Unmodified.* Cambridge: Harvard University Press.
Tong, Rosemarie. 1984. *Women, Sex, and the Law.* Totowa, New Jersey: Rowman and Allanheld.

Pornography, Sex Work, and Hate Speech

Not a Moral Issue
(1983)

Pornosec, the subsection of the Fiction Department which turned out cheap pornography for distribution among the proles . . . nicknamed Muck House by the people who worked in it . . . produce[d] booklets in sealed packets with titles like *Spanking Stories* or *One Night in a Girls' School*, to be bought furtively by proletarian youths who were under the impression that they were buying something illegal.

George Orwell, *Nineteen Eighty-four* (1949)

A critique of pornography[1] is to feminism what its defense is to male supremacy. Central to the institutionalization of male dominance, pornography cannot be reformed or suppressed or banned. It can only be changed. The legal doctrine of obscenity, the state's closest approximation to addressing the pornography question, has made the First Amendment[2] into a barrier to this process. This is partly because the pornographers' lawyers have persuasively presented First Amendment absolutism,[3] their advocacy position, as a legal fact, which it never has been. But they have gotten away with this (to the extent they have) in part because the abstractness of obscenity as a concept, situated within an equally abstract approach to freedom of speech embodied in First Amendment doctrine, has made the indistinguishability of the pornographers' speech from everyone else's speech, their freedom from our freedom, appear credible, appealing, necessary, inevitable, *principled*.[4] To expose the absence of a critique of gender[5] in this area of law is to expose both the enforced silence of women and the limits of liberalism.

This brief preliminary commentary focuses on the obscenity standard in order to explore some of the larger implications of a feminist critique of pornography for First Amendment theory. This is the ar-

This speech was originally delivered to the Morality Colloquium, University of Minnesota, Feb. 23, 1983. These ideas were also discussed at the National Conference on Women and the Law, Apr. 4, 1983, and at the Conference on Media Violence and Pornography, Ontario Institute for Studies in Education, Feb. 4, 1984. The title is a play on "Not a Love Story," a 1983 anti-pornography film by the Canadian Film Board.

146

2

gument. Obscenity law is concerned with morality, specifically morals from the male point of view, meaning the standpoint of male dominance. The feminist critique of pornography is a politics, specifically politics from women's point of view, meaning the standpoint of the subordination of women to men.[6] Morality here means good and evil; politics means power and powerlessness. Obscenity is a moral idea; pornography is a political practice. Obscenity is abstract; pornography is concrete. The two concepts represent two entirely different things. Nudity, explicitness, excess of candor, arousal or excitement, prurience, unnaturalness—these qualities bother obscenity law when sex is depicted or portrayed. Abortion, birth control information, and treatments for "restoring sexual virility" (whose, do you suppose?) have also been included.[7] Sex forced on real women so that it can be sold at a profit to be forced on other real women; women's bodies trussed and maimed and raped and made into things to be hurt and obtained and accessed, and this presented as the nature of women; the coercion that is visible and the coercion that has become invisible—this and more bothers feminists about pornography. Obscenity as such probably does little harm;[8] pornography causes attitudes and behaviors of violence and discrimination that define the treatment and status of half of the population.[9] To make the legal and philosophical consequences of this distinction clear, I will describe the feminist critique of pornography, criticize the law of obscenity in terms of it, then discuss the criticism that pornography "dehumanizes" women to distinguish the male morality of liberalism and obscenity law from a feminist political critique of pornography.[10]

This inquiry is part of a larger project that attempts to account for gender inequality in the socially constructed relationship between power—the political—on the one hand and the knowledge of truth and reality—the epistemological—on the other.[11] For example, the candid description Justice Stewart once offered of his obscenity standard, "I know it when I see it,"[12] becomes even more revealing than it is usually understood to be if taken as a statement that connects epistemology with power. If I ask, from the point of view of women's experience, does he know what I know when I see what I see, I find that I doubt it, given what's on the newsstands. How does his point of view keep what is there, there? To liberal critics, his admission exposed the obscenity standard's relativity, its partiality, its insufficient abstractness. Not to be emptily universal, to leave your concreteness showing, is a sin among men. Their problem with Justice Stewart's formulation is that it implies that anything, capriciously, could be suppressed. They are only right by half. My problem is more the other half: the meaning of what his view permits, which, as it turns out, is anything but capricious. In fact, it is entirely systematic and determinate. To me, his statement is precisely descriptively accurate; its candor is why it has drawn so much criticism.[13] Justice Stewart got in so much trouble because he said out loud what is actually done all the time; in so doing, he both *did it* and gave it the stature of doctrine, even if only dictum. That is, the obscenity standard—in this it is not unique—*is* built on what the male standpoint sees. My point is: *so is pornography.* In this way the law of obscenity reproduces the pornographic point of view on women on the level of Constitutional jurisprudence.

·　　　　　　·　　　　　　·

Pornography, in the feminist view, is a form of forced sex, a practice of sexual politics, an institution of gender inequality. In this perspective, pornography is not harmless fantasy or a corrupt and confused misrepresentation of an otherwise natural and healthy sexuality. Along with the rape and prostitution in which it participates, pornography institutionalizes the sexuality of male supremacy, which fuses the erotization of dominance and submission with the social construction of male and female.[14] Gender is sexual. Pornography constitutes the meaning of that sexuality. Men treat women as who they see women as being. Pornography constructs who that is. Men's power over women means that the way men see women defines who women can be. Pornography is that way.

In pornography, women desire dispossession and cruelty. Men, permitted to put words (and other things) in women's mouths, create scenes in which women desperately want to be bound, battered, tortured, humiliated, and killed. Or merely taken and used. This is erotic to the male point of view. Subjection itself, with self-determination ecstatically relinquished, is the content of women's sexual desire and desirability. Women are there to be violated and possessed, men to violate and possess them, either on screen or by camera or pen, on behalf of the viewer.

One can be for or against this pornography without getting beyond liberalism. The critical yet formally liberal view of Susan Griffin, for example, conceptualizes eroticism as natural and healthy but corrupted and confused by "the pornographic mind."[15] Pornography distorts Eros, which preexists and persists, despite male culture's pornographic "revenge" upon it. Eros is, unaccountably, *still there.*

148

Pornography mis-takes it, mis-images it, mis-represents it. There is no critique of *reality* here, only objections to how it is seen; no critique of that reality that pornography imposes on women's real lives, those lives that are so seamlessly *consistent* with the pornography that pornography can be credibly defended by saying it is only a mirror of reality.

Contrast this view with the feminist analysis of Andrea Dworkin, in which sexuality itself is a social construct, gendered to the ground. Male dominance here is not an artificial overlay upon an underlying inalterable substratum of uncorrupted essential sexual being. Sexuality free of male dominance will require *change*, not reconceptualization, transcendence, or excavation. Pornography is not imagery in some relation to a reality elsewhere constructed. It is not a distortion, reflection, projection, expression, fantasy, representation, or symbol either. It is sexual reality. Dworkin's *Pornography: Men Possessing Women*[16] presents a sexual theory of gender inequality of which pornography is a core constitutive practice. The way pornography produces its meaning constructs and defines men and women as such. Gender is what gender means.[17] It has no basis in anything other than the social reality its hegemony constructs. The process that gives sexuality its male supremacist meaning is therefore the process through which gender inequality becomes socially real.

In this analysis the liberal defense of pornography as human sexual liberation, as derepression—whether by feminists, lawyers, or neo-Freudians[18]—is a defense not only of force and sexual terrorism, but of the subordination of women. Sexual liberation in the liberal sense frees male sexual aggression in the feminist sense. What looks like love and romance in the liberal view looks a lot like hatred and torture in the feminist view. Pleasure and eroticism become violation. Desire appears as lust for dominance and submission. The vulnerability of women's projected sexual availability—that acting we are allowed: asking to be acted upon—is victimization. Play conforms to scripted roles, fantasy expresses ideology—is not exempt from it—and admiration of natural physical beauty becomes objectification.

The experience of the (overwhelmingly) male audiences who consume pornography[19] is therefore not fantasy or simulation or catharsis[20] but sexual reality: the level of reality on which sex itself largely operates. To understand this, one does not have to notice that pornography models are real women to whom something real is being done,[21] nor does one have to inquire into the systematic infliction of pornographic sexuality upon women,[22] although it helps.

149

5

Pornography

The aesthetic of pornography itself, the *way* it provides what those who consume it want, is itself the evidence. When uncensored explicit—that is, the most pornographic—pornography tells all, all means what a distanced detached observer would report about who did what to whom. This is the turn-on. Why does observing sex objectively presented cause the male viewer to experience his own sexuality? Because his eroticism is, socially, a watched thing.

If objectivity is the epistemological stance of which objectification is the social process,[23] the way a perceptual posture is embodied as a social form of power, the most sexually potent depictions and descriptions *would* be the most objective blow-by-blow re-presentations. Pornography participates in its audience's eroticism because it creates an accessible sexual object, the possession and consumption of which *is* male sexuality, to be consumed and possessed as which *is* female sexuality. In this sense, sex in life is no less mediated than it is in art. Men *have sex* with their *image* of a woman. Escalating explicitness, "exceeding the bounds of candor,"[24] is the aesthetic of pornography not because the materials depict objectified sex but because they create the experience of a sexuality that is itself objectified. It is not that life and art imitate each other; in sexuality, they *are* each other.

• • •

The law of obscenity,[25] the state's primary approach[26] to its version of the pornography question, has literally nothing in common with this feminist critique. Their obscenity is not our pornography. One commentator has said, "Obscenity is not suppressed primarily for the protection of others. Much of it is suppressed for the purity of the 'community.' Obscenity, at bottom, is not a crime. Obscenity is a sin."[27] This is, on one level, literally accurate. Men are turned on by obscenity, including its suppression, the same way they are by sin. Animated by morality from the male standpoint, in which violation—of women and rules—is eroticized, obscenity law can be seen to proceed according to the interest of male power, robed in gender-neutral good and evil.

Morality in its specifically liberal form (although, as with most dimensions of male dominance, the distinction between left and right is more formal than substantive) revolves around a set of parallel distinctions that can be consistently traced through obscenity law. Even though the approach this law takes to the problem it envisions has shifted over time, its fundamental norms remain consistent: public is

150

opposed to private, in parallel with ethics and morality, and factual is opposed to valued determinations. Under male supremacy, these distinctions are gender-based: female is private, moral, valued, subjective; male is public, ethical, factual, objective.[28] If such gendered concepts are constructs of the male experience, imposed from the male standpoint on society as a whole, liberal morality expresses male supremacist politics. That is, discourse conducted in terms of good and evil that does not expose the gendered foundations of these concepts proceeds oblivious to—and serves to disguise—the position of power that underlies, and is furthered by, that discourse.

For example, obscenity law proposes to control what and how sex can be publicly shown. In practice, its standard centers upon the same features feminism identifies as key to male sexuality: the erect penis and penetration.[29] Historically, obscenity law was vexed by restricting such portrayals while protecting great literature. (Nobody considered protecting women.) Having solved this by exempting works of perceived value from obscenity restrictions,[30] the subsequent relaxation—some might say collapse—of obscenity restrictions in the last decade reveals a significant shift. The old private rules have become the new public rules. The old law governing pornography was that it would be publicly repudiated while being privately consumed and actualized: do anything to women with impunity in private behind a veil of public denial and civility. Now pornography is publicly celebrated.[31] This victory for Freudian derepression theory probably did not alter the actual treatment of women all that much. Women were sex and still are sex. Greater efforts of brutality have become necessary to eroticize the tabooed—each taboo being a hierarchy in disguise—since the frontier of the tabooed keeps vanishing as one crosses it. Put another way, more and more violence has become necessary to keep the progressively desensitized consumer aroused to the illusion that sex is (and he is) daring and dangerous. Making sex with the powerless "not allowed" is a way of defining "getting it" as an act of power, an assertion of hierarchy. In addition, pornography has become ubiquitous. Sexual terrorism has become democratized. Crucially, pornography has become truly available to women for the first time in history. Show me an atrocity to women, I'll show it to you eroticized in the pornography. This central mechanism of sexual subordination, this means of systematizing the definition of women as a sexual class, has now become available to its victims for scrutiny and analysis as an open public system, not just as a private secret abuse.[32] Hopefully, this was a mistake.

151

7

Pornography

Reexamining the law of obscenity in light of the feminist critique of pornography that has become possible, it becomes clear that male morality sees as good that which maintains its power and sees as evil that which undermines or qualifies it or questions its absoluteness. Differences in the law over time—such as the liberalization of obscenity doctrine—reflect either changes in the group of men in power or shifts in their perceptions of the best strategy for maintaining male supremacy—probably some of both. But it must be made to work. The outcome, descriptively analyzed, is that obscenity law prohibits what it sees as immoral, which from a feminist standpoint tends to be relatively harmless, while protecting what it sees as moral, which from a feminist standpoint is often that which is damaging to women. So it, too, is a politics, only covertly so. What male morality finds evil, meaning threatening to its power, feminist politics tends to find comparatively harmless. What feminist politics identifies as central in our subordination—the erotization of dominance and submission—male morality tends to find comparatively harmless or defends as affirmatively valuable, hence protected speech.

In 1973 obscenity under law came to mean that which "'the average person applying contemporary community standards' would find that, . . . taken as a whole, appeals to the prurient interest . . . [which] depicts or describes, in a patently offensive way, sexual conduct specifically defined by the applicable state law; and [which], taken as a whole, lacks serious literary, artistic, political, or scientific value."[33] Feminism doubts whether the average person, gender neutral, exists; has more questions about the content and process of definition of community standards than about deviations from them; wonders why prurience counts but powerlessness doesn't; why sensibilities are better protected from offense than women are from exploitation; defines sexuality, hence its violation and expropriation, more broadly than does any state law and wonders why a body of law that can't in practice tell rape from intercourse should be entrusted with telling pornography from anything less. The law of obscenity says that intercourse on street corners is not legitimized by the fact that the persons are "simultaneously engaged in a valid political dialogue."[34] But, in a feminist light, one sees that the requirement that a work be considered "as a whole" legitimizes something very like that on the level of publications like *Playboy*.[35] Experimental evidence is beginning to support what victims have long known: legitimate settings diminish the injury perceived as done to the women whose trivialization and objectification it contextualizes.[36] Besides, if

152

a woman is subjected, why should it matter that the work has other value?[37] Perhaps what redeems a work's value among men *enhances* its injury to women. Existing standards of literature, art, science, and politics are, in feminist light, remarkably consonant with pornography's mode, meaning, and message. Finally and foremost, a feminist approach reveals that although the content and dynamic of pornography are about women—about the sexuality of women, about women as sexuality—in the same way that the vast majority of "obscenities" refer specifically to women's bodies, our invisibility has been such that the law of obscenity has *never even considered pornography a women's issue.*[38]

To appeal to "prurient interest"[39] means, I believe, to give a man an erection. Men are scared to make it possible for some men to tell other men what they can and cannot have sexual access to because men have power. If you don't let them have theirs, they might not let you have yours. This is why the *indefinability* of pornography, all the "one man's this is another man's that,"[40] is so central to pornography's *definition.* It is not because they are such great liberals, but because some men might be able to do to them whatever they can do to those other men, and this is more why the liberal principle is what it is. Because the fought-over are invisible in this, it obscures the fact that the fight over a definition of obscenity is a fight among men over the best means to guarantee male power as a system. The question is, whose sexual practices threaten this system that can afford to be sacrificed to its maintenance for the rest? Public sexual access by men to anything other than women is less likely to be protected speech. This is not to say that male sexual access to anything—children, other men, women with women, objects, animals—is not the real system. The issue is *how public* that system will be; the obscenity laws, their definition and patterns of enforcement, have a major role in regulating that. The bind of the "prurient interest" standard here is that, to find it as a fact, someone has to admit that they are sexually aroused by the materials,[41] but male sexual arousal signals the importance of protecting them. They put themselves in this bind and then wonder why they cannot agree. Sometimes I think that what is ultimately found obscene is what does *not* turn on the Supreme Court, or what revolts them more, which is rare, since revulsion is eroticized; sometimes I think that what is obscene is what turns on those men the men in power think they can afford to ignore; sometimes I think that part of it is that what looks obscene to them is what makes them see themselves as potential targets of male sexual aggression, even if

153

9

only momentarily; sometimes I think that the real issue is how male sexuality is presented, so that anything can be done to a woman, but obscenity is sex that makes male sexuality look bad.[42]

The difficulties courts have in framing workable standards to separate "prurient" from other sexual interest, commercial exploitation from art or advertising, sexual speech from sexual conduct, and obscenity from great literature make the feminist point. These lines have proven elusive in law because they do not exist in life. Commercial sex resembles art because both exploit women's sexuality. The liberal's slippery slope is the feminist totality. Whatever obscenity may do, pornography converges with more conventionally acceptable depictions and descriptions just as rape converges with intercourse because both express the same power relation. Just as it is difficult to distinguish literature or art against a background, a standard, of objectification, it is difficult to discern sexual freedom against a background, a standard, of sexual coercion. This does not mean it cannot be done. It means that legal standards will be practically unenforceable, will reproduce this problem rather than solve it, until they address its fundamental issue—gender inequality—directly.

To define the pornographic as the "patently offensive" further misconstrues its harm. Pornography is not bad manners or poor choice of audience; obscenity is. Pornography is also not an idea; obscenity is. The legal fiction whereby the obscene is "not speech"[43] has deceived few; it *has* effectively avoided the need to adjudicate pornography's social etiology. But obscenity law got one thing right: pornography is more actlike than thoughtlike. The fact that pornography, in a feminist view, furthers the idea of the sexual inferiority of women, a political idea, does not make the pornography itself a political idea. That one can express the idea a practice embodies does not make that practice into an idea. Pornography is not an idea any more than segregation is an idea, although both institutionalize the idea of the inferiority of one group to another. The law considers obscenity deviant, antisocial. If it causes harm, it causes antisocial acts, acts against the social order.[44] In a feminist perspective, pornography is the essence of a sexist social order, its quintessential social act.

If pornography is an act of male supremacy, its harm is the harm of male supremacy made difficult to see because of its pervasiveness, potency, and success in making the world a pornographic place. Specifically, the harm cannot be discerned from the objective standpoint because it *is* so much of "what is." Women live in the world pornography creates. We live its lie as reality. As Naomi Scheman has said,

154

10

"Lies are what we have lived, not just what we have told, and no story about correspondence to what is real will enable us to distinguish the truth from the lie."[45] So the issue is not whether pornography is harmful, but how the harm of pornography is to become visible. As compared with what? To the extent pornography succeeds in constructing social reality, it becomes *invisible as harm*. Any perception of the success, therefore the harm, of pornography, I will argue, is precluded by liberalism and so has been defined out of the customary approach taken to, and dominant values underlying, the First Amendment.

The theory of the First Amendment under which most pornography is protected from governmental restriction proceeds from liberal assumptions[46] that do not apply to the situation of women. First Amendment theory, like virtually all liberal legal theory, presumes the validity of the distinction between public and private: the "role of law [is] to mark and guard the line between the sphere of social power, organized in the form of the state, and the area of private right."[47] On this basis, courts distinguish between obscenity in public (which can be regulated, even if some attempts founder, seemingly in part *because* the presentations are public)[48] and the private possession of obscenity in the home.[49] The problem is that not only the public but also the private *is* a "sphere of social power" of sexism. On paper and in life pornography is thrust upon unwilling women in their homes.[50] The distinction between public and private does not cut the same for women as for men.[51] It is men's right to inflict pornography upon women in private that is protected.

The liberal theory underlying First Amendment law further believes that free speech, including pornography, helps discover truth. Censorship restricts society to partial truths. So why are we now— with more pornography available than ever before—buried in all these lies? Laissez faire might be an adequate theory of the social preconditions for knowledge in a nonhierarchical society. But in a society of gender inequality, the speech of the powerful impresses its view upon the world, concealing the truth of powerlessness under that despairing acquiescence that provides the appearance of consent and makes protest inaudible as well as rare. Pornography can invent women because it has the power to make its vision into reality, which then passes, objectively, for truth. So while the First Amendment supports pornography, believing that consensus and progress are facilitated by allowing all views, however divergent and unorthodox, it fails to notice that pornography (like the racism, in which I include

155

11

anti-Semitism, of the Nazis and the Klan) is not at all divergent or unorthodox. It is the ruling ideology. Feminism, the dissenting view, is suppressed by pornography. Thus, while defenders of pornography argue that allowing all speech, including pornography, frees the mind to fulfill itself, pornography freely enslaves women's minds and bodies inseparably, normalizing the terror that enforces silence from women's point of view.

To liberals, speech must never be sacrificed for other social goals.[52] But liberalism has never understood that the free speech of men silences the free speech of women. It is the same social goal, just other *people.* This is what a real inequality, a real conflict, a real disparity in social power looks like. The law of the First Amendment comprehends that freedom of expression, in the abstract, is a system, but it fails to comprehend that sexism (and racism), *in the concrete,* are also systems. That pornography chills women's expression is difficult to demonstrate empirically because silence is not eloquent. Yet on no more of the same kind of evidence, the argument that suppressing pornography might chill legitimate speech has supported its protection.

First Amendment logic, like nearly all legal reasoning, has difficulty grasping harm that is not linearly caused in the "John hit Mary" sense. The idea is that words or pictures can be harmful only if they produce harm in a form that is considered an action. Words work in the province of attitudes, actions in the realm of behavior. Words cannot constitute harm in themselves—never mind libel, invasion of privacy, blackmail, bribery, conspiracy or most sexual harassment. But which is saying "kill" to a trained guard dog, a word or an act? Which is its training? How about a sign that reads "Whites only"? Is that the idea or the practice of segregation? Is a woman raped by an attitude or a behavior? Which is sexual arousal? Notice that the specific idea of causality used in obscenity law dates from around the time that it was first "proved" that it is impossible to prove that pornography causes harm.[53] Instead of the more complex causality implicit in the above examples, the view became that pornography must cause harm the way negligence causes car accidents or its effects are not cognizable as harm. The trouble with this individuated, atomistic, linear, isolated, tortlike—in a word, positivistic—conception of injury is that the way pornography targets and defines women for abuse and discrimination does not work like this. It does hurt individuals, not *as* individuals in a one-at-a-time sense, but as members of the group "women." Harm is caused to one individual woman rather than another essentially the way one number rather than another is caused in roulette. But on a group basis, as women, the selection process is absolutely selective and systematic. Its causality is essentially collective and totalistic and contextual. To reassert atomistic linear causality as a sine qua non of injury—you cannot be harmed unless you are harmed through this etiology—is to refuse to respond to the true nature of this specific kind of harm. Such a refusal calls for explanation. Morton Horowitz says that the issue of causality in tort law is "one of the pivotal ideas in a system of legal thought that sought to separate private law from politics and to insulate the legal system from the threat of redistribution."[54] Perhaps causality in the pornography issue is an attempt to privatize the injury pornography does to women in order to insulate the same system from the threat of gender equality, also a form of redistribution.

Women are known to be brutally coerced into pornographic performances.[55] But so far it is only with children, usually male children, that courts consider that the speech of pornographers was once someone else's *life*.[56] Courts and commissions and legislatures and researchers have searched and re-searched, largely in vain, for the injury of pornography in the mind of the (male) consumer or in "society," or in empirical correlations between variations in levels of "antisocial" acts and liberalization in obscenity laws.[57] Speech can be regulated "in the interests of unwilling viewers, captive audiences, young children, and beleaguered neighborhoods,"[58] but the normal level of sexual force—force that is not seen as force because it is inflicted on women and called sex—has never been a policy issue. Until the last few years experimental research never approached the question of whether pornographic stimuli might support *sexual* aggression against women[59] or whether violence might be sexually stimulating or have sexual sequelae.[60] Only in the last few months have laboratory researchers begun to learn the consequences for women of so-called consensual sexual depictions that show normal dominance and submission.[61] We still don't have this kind of data on the impact of female-only nudity or of depictions of specific acts like penetration or even of mutual sex in a social context of gender inequality.

The most basic assumption underlying First Amendment adjudication is that, socially, speech is free. The First Amendment says, "Congress shall not abridge *the freedom of speech*." Free speech exists. The problem for government is to avoid constraining that which, if unconstrained by government, *is* free. This tends to presuppose that whole segments of the population are not systematically silenced *so-*

157

13

cially, prior to government action. The place of pornography in the inequality of the sexes makes such a presupposition untenable and makes any approach to *our* freedom of expression so based worse than useless. For women, the urgent issue of freedom of speech is not primarily the avoidance of state intervention as such, but finding an affirmative means to get access to speech for those to whom it has been denied.

•   •   •

Beyond offensiveness or prurience, to say that pornography is "dehumanizing" is an attempt to articulate its harm. But "human being" is a social concept with many possible meanings. Here I will criticize some liberal moral meanings of personhood through a feminist political analysis of what pornography does to women, showing how the inadequacy of the liberal dehumanization critique reflects the inadequacy of its concept of person. In a feminist perspective, pornography dehumanizes women in a culturally specific and empirically descriptive—not liberal moral—sense. Pornography dispossesses women of the power of which, in the same act, it possesses men: the power of sexual, hence gender, definition. Perhaps a human being, for gender purposes, is someone who controls the social definition of sexuality.

A person, in one Kantian view, is a free and rational agent whose existence is an end in itself, as opposed to instrumental.[62] In pornography women exist to the *end* of male pleasure. Kant sees human as characterized by universal abstract rationality, with no component of individual or group differences, and as a "bundle of rights."[63] Pornography purports to define what a woman *is.* It does this on a group basis, including when it raises individual qualities to sexual stereotypes, as in the strategy of *Playboy's* "Playmate of the Month." I also think that pornography derives much of its sexual power, as well as part of its justification, from the implicit assumption that the Kantian notion of person actually describes the condition of women in this society. According to that assumption, if we are there, we are freely and rationally there, when the fact is that women—in pornography and in part because of pornography—have no such rights.

Other views of the person include one of Wittgenstein's, who says that the best picture of the human soul is the human body.[64] I guess this depends upon what picture of the human body you have in mind. Marx's work offers various concepts of personhood deducible

158

from his critique of various forms of productive organization. A person is defined by whatever material conditions the society values; in a bourgeois society, a person might be a property owner.[65] The problem here is that women *are* the property that constitutes the personhood, the masculinity, of men under capitalism. Thinking further in marxian theoretical terms, I have wondered whether women in pornography are more properly conceived as fetishes or objects. Does pornography more attribute lifelikeness to that which is dead—as in fetishism—or make deathlike that which is alive—as in objectification? I guess it depends upon whether, socially speaking, women are more alive than dead.

In Hume's concept of a person as a bundle or collection of sense perceptions, such that the feeling of self-identity over time is a persistent illusion,[66] we finally have a view of the human that coincides with the view of women in pornography. That is, the empiricist view of person is the pornographic view of women. No critique of dominance or subjection, certainly not of objectification, can be grounded in a vision of reality in which all sense perceptions are just sense perceptions. This is one way an objectivist epistemology supports the unequal holding and wielding of power in a society in which the persistent illusion of selfhood of one half of the population is materially supported and maintained at the expense of the other half. What I'm saying is that those who are socially allowed a self are also allowed the luxury of postulating its illusoriness and having that called a philosophical position. Whatever self they ineluctably have, they don't lose by saying it is an illusion. Even if it is not particularly explanatory, such male ideology, if taken as such, is often highly descriptive. Thus Hume defines the human in the same terms feminism uses to define women's dehumanization: for women in pornography, the self is, precisely, a persistent illusion.

Contemporary ordinary language philosopher Bernard Williams says "person" ordinarily means things like valuing self-respect and feeling pain.[67] How self is defined, what respect attaches to, stimuli of pleasure and to an extent stimuli and thresholds of pain, are cultural variables. Women in pornography are turned on by being put down and feel pain as pleasure. We want it; we beg for it; we get it. To argue that this is dehumanizing need not mean to take respect as an ahistorical absolute or to treat the social meaning of pain as invariant or uniformly negative. Rather, it is to argue that it is the acceptance of the social definition of these values—the acceptance of self-

159

15

respect and the avoidance of pain as values—that permits the erotization of their negative—debasement and torture—in pornography. It is only to the extent that each of these values is *accepted as human* that their negation becomes a quality of, and is eroticized in and as,, woman. Only when self-respect is accepted as human does debasement become sexy and female; only when the avoidance of pain is accepted as human does torture become sexy and female. In this way, women's sexuality as expressed in pornography precisely negates her status as human. But there is more: exactly what is defined as degrading to a human being, *however* that is socially defined, is exactly what is sexually arousing to the male point of view in pornography, just as the one to whom it is done is the girl regardless of sex. In this way, it is specifically women whom pornography identifies with and by sexuality, as the erotic is equated with the dehumanizing.

To define the pornographic as that which is violent, not sexual, as liberal moral analyses tend to, is to trivialize and evade the essence of this critique, while seeming to express it. As with rape, where the issue is not the presence or absence of force but what sex *is* as distinct from coercion,[68] the question for pornography is what eroticism *is* as distinct from the subordination of women. This is not a rhetorical question. Under male dominance, whatever sexually arouses a man is sex. In pornography the violence *is* the sex. The inequality is the sex. Pornography does not work sexually without hierarchy. If there is no inequality, no violation, no dominance, no force, there is no sexual arousal.[69] Obscenity law does the pornographers a real favor by clouding this, pornography's central dynamic, under the coy gender-neutral abstraction of "prurient interest." Obscenity law also adds the attraction of state prohibition, a tool of dominance, to whatever the law of obscenity is seen to encompass.

Calling rape and pornography violent, not sexual, the banner of much antirape and antipornography organizing,[70] is an attempt to protest that women do not find rape pleasurable or pornography stimulating while avoiding claiming this rejection as *women's* point of view. The concession to the objective stance, the attempt to achieve credibility by covering up the specificity of one's viewpoint, not only abstracts from our experience, it lies about it. Women and men know men find rape sexual and pornography erotic. It therefore *is*. We also know that sexuality is commonly violent without being any the less sexual. To deny this sets up the situation so that when women are aroused by sexual violation, meaning we experience it *as* our sexuality, the feminist analysis is seen to be contradicted. But it is not contradicted, it is *proved*. The male supremacist definition of female sexuality as lust for self-annihilation has won. It would be surprising, feminist analysis would be wrong, and sexism would be trivial, if this were merely exceptional. (One might ask at this point, not why some women embrace explicit sadomasochism, but why any women do not.) To reject forced sex in the name of women's point of view requires an account of women's experience of being violated by the same acts both sexes have learned as natural and fulfilling and erotic, since no critique, no alternatives, and few transgressions have been permitted.

The depersonalization critique, with the "violence not sex" critique, exposes pornography's double standard but does not attack the masculinity of the standards for personhood and for sex that pornography sets. The critiques are thus useful, to some extent deconstructive, but beg the deeper questions of the place of pornography in sexuality and of sexuality in the construction of women's definition and status, because they act as if women can be "persons" by interpretation, as if the concept is not, in every socially real way, defined by and in terms of and reserved for men and as if sexuality is not itself a construct of male power. To do this is to act as if pornography did not exist or were impotent. Deeper than the personhood question or the violence question is the question of the mechanism of social causation by which pornography *constructs* women and sex, defines what "woman" means and what sexuality is, in terms of each other.

The law of obscenity at times says that sexual expression is only talk, therefore cannot be intrinsically harmful. Yet somehow pornographic talk is vital to protect. If pornography is a practice of the ideology[71] of gender inequality, and gender *is an ideology,* if pornography is sex and gender is sexual, the question of the relation between pornography and life is nothing less than the question of the dynamic of the subordination of women to men. If "objectification . . . is never trivial,"[72] girls *are* ruined by books.[73] To comprehend this process will require an entirely new theory of social causality—of ideology in life, of the dynamic of mind and body in social power—that connects point of view with politics. The development of such an analysis has been stymied equally by fear of repressive state use of any critique of any form of expression, by the power of pornography to create women in its image of use, and by the power of pornographers to create a climate hostile to inquiry into their power and profits.

. . .

I said all that in order to say this: the law of obscenity has the same surface theme and the same underlying theme as pornography itself. Superficially both involve morality: rules made and transgressed for purposes of sexual arousal. Actually, both are about power, about the equation between the erotic and the control of women by men: *women* made and transgressed for purposes of sexual arousal. It seems essential to the kick of pornography that it be to some degree against the rules, but it is never truly unavailable or truly illegitimate. Thus obscenity law, like the law of rape, preserves the value of, without restricting the ability to get, that which it purports to both devalue and to prohibit. Obscenity law helps keep pornography sexy by putting state power—force, hierarchy—behind its purported prohibition on what men can have sexual access to. The law of obscenity is to pornography as pornography is to sex: a map that purports to be a mirror, a legitimization and authorization and set of directions and guiding controls that project themselves onto social reality while claiming merely to reflect the image of what is already there. Pornography presents itself as fantasy or illusion or idea, which can be good or bad as it is accurate or inaccurate, while it actually, *hence accurately,* distributes power. Liberal morality cannot deal with illusions that *constitute* reality because its theory of reality, lacking a substantive critique of the distribution of social power, cannot get behind the empirical world, truth by correspondence. On the surface, both pornography and the law of obscenity are about sex. In fact, it is the status of women that is at stake.

18

Not a Moral Issue

Many of the ideas in this essay were developed and refined in close collaboration with Andrea Dworkin. It is difficult at times to distinguish the contribution of each of us to a body of work that—through shared teaching, writing, speaking, organizing, and political action on every level—has been created together. I have tried to credit specific contributions that I am aware are distinctly hers. This text is mine; she does not necessarily agree with everything in it.

1. This speech as a whole is intended to communicate what I mean by pornography. The key work on the subject is Andrea Dworkin, *Pornography: Men Possessing Women* (1981). No definition can convey the meaning of a word as well as its use in context can. However, what Andrea Dworkin and I mean by pornography is rather well captured in our legal definition: "Pornography is the graphic sexually explicit subordination of women, whether in pictures or in words, that also includes one or more of the following: (i) women are presented dehumanized as sexual objects, things or commodities; or (ii) women are presented as sexual objects who enjoy pain or humiliation; or (iii) women are presented as sexual objects who experience sexual pleasure in being raped; or (iv) women are presented as sexual objects tied up or cut up or mutilated or bruised or physically hurt; or (v) women are presented in postures of sexual submission, servility or display; or (vi) women's body parts—including but not limited to vaginas, breasts, and buttocks—are exhibited, such that women are reduced to those parts; or (vii) women are presented as whores by nature; or (viii) women are presented being penetrated by objects or animals; or (ix) women are presented in scenarios of degradation, injury, torture, shown as filthy or inferior, bleeding, bruised, or hurt in a context that makes these conditions sexual." Pornography also includes "the use of men, children or transsexuals in the place of women." Pornography, thus defined, is discrimination on the basis of sex and, as such, a civil rights violation. This definition is a slightly modified version of the one passed by the Minneapolis City Council on December 30, 1983. Minneapolis, Minn., Ordinance amending tit. 7, chs. 139 and 141, Minneapolis Code of Ordinances Relating to Civil Rights (Dec. 30, 1983). The ordinance was vetoed by the mayor, reintroduced, passed again, and vetoed again in 1984. *See* "Francis Biddle's Sister" for subsequent developments.

2. "Congress shall make no law . . . abridging the freedom of speech, or of the press . . ." U.S. Const. amend. I.

3. Justice Black, at times joined by Justice Douglas, took the position that the Bill of Rights, including the First Amendment, was "absolute." Hugo Black, "The Bill of Rights," 35 *New York University Law Review* 865, 867 (1960);

262

Edmund Cahn, "Justice Black and First Amendment 'Absolutes': A Public Interview," 37 *New York University Law Review* 549 (1962). For a discussion, see Harry Kalven, "Upon Rereading Mr. Justice Black on the First Amendment," 14 *UCLA Law Review* 428 (1967). For one exchange in the controversy surrounding the "absolute" approach to the First Amendment, as opposed to the "balancing" approach, *see, e.g.*, W. Mendelson, "On the Meaning of the First Amendment: Absolutes in the Balance," 50 *California Law Review* 821 (1962); L. Frantz, "The First Amendment in the Balance," 71 *Yale Law Journal* 1424 (1962); Frantz, "Is the First Amendment Law?—A Reply to Professor Mendelson," 51 *California Law Review* 729 (1963); Mendelson, "The First Amendment and the Judicial Process: A Reply to Mr. Frantz," 17 *Vanderbilt Law Review* 479 (1964). In the pornography context, *see e.g.*, Roth v. United States, 354 U.S. 476, 514 (1957) (Douglas, J., joined by Black, J., dissenting); Smith v. California, 361 U.S. 147, 155 (1959) (Black, J., concurring); Miller v. California, 413 U.S. 15, 37 (1973) (Douglas, J., dissenting). The purpose of this discourse is not to present a critique of absolutism as such, but rather to identify and criticize some widely and deeply shared implicit beliefs that underlie both the absolutist view and the more mainstream flexible approaches.

4. The history of obscenity law can be read as a failed attempt to make this separation, with the failure becoming ever more apparent from the *Redrup* decision forward. Redrup v. New York, 386 U.S. 767 (1967). For a summary of cases exemplifying such a trend, see the dissent by Justice Brennan in Paris Adult Theatre I v. Slaton, 413 U.S. 49, 73 (1973).

5. Much has been made of the distinction between sex and gender. Sex is thought the more biological, gender the more social. The relation of sexuality to each varies. *See, e.g.*, Robert Stoller, *Sex and Gender* 9–10 (1974). Since I think that the importance of biology to the condition of women is the social meaning attributed to it, biology *is* its social meaning for purposes of analyzing the inequality of the sexes, a political condition. I therefore tend to use sex and gender relatively interchangeably.

6. The sense in which I mean women's perspective as different from men's is like that of Virginia Woolf's reference to "the difference of view, the difference of standard" in her "George Eliot," 1 *Collected Essays* 204 (1966). Neither of us uses the notion of a gender difference to refer to something biological or natural or transcendental or existential. Perspective parallels standards because the social experience of gender is confined by gender. *See* Catharine A. MacKinnon, *Sexual Harassment of Working Women* 107–41 (1979), and the articles mentioned in note 11, below; Virginia Woolf, *Three Guineas* (1938); *see also* Andrea Dworkin, "The Root Cause," in *Our Blood: Essays and Discourses on Sexual Politics* 96 (1976). I do not refer to the gender difference here descriptively, leaving its roots and implications unspecified, so they could be biological, existential, transcendental, in any sense inherent, or social but necessary. I mean "point of view" as a view, hence a standard, that is imposed on women by force of sex inequality, which is a political condition. "Male," which is an adjective here, is a social and political concept, not

263

20

a biological attribute; it is a status socially conferred upon a person because of a condition of birth. As I use "male," it has nothing whatever to do with inherency, preexistence, nature, inevitability, or body as such. Because it is in the interest of men to be male in the system we live under (male being powerful as well as human), they seldom question its rewards or even see it as a status at all.

7. Criminal Code, Can. Rev. Stat. chap. c-34, § 159(2)(c) and (d) (1970). People v. Sanger, 222 N.Y. 192, 118 N.E. 637 (1918).

8. *The Report of the Commission on Obscenity and Pornography* (1970) (majority report). The accuracy of the commission's findings is called into question by: (1) widespread criticism of the commission's methodology from a variety of perspectives, *e.g.*, L. Sunderland, *Obscenity—The Court, the Congress and the President's Commission* (1975); Edward Donnerstein, "Pornography Commission Revisited: Aggression—Erotica and Violence against Women," 39 *Journal of Personality and Social Psychology* 269 (1980); Ann Garry, "Pornography and Respect for Women," 4 *Social Theory and Practice* 395 (Summer 1978); Irene Diamond, "Pornography and Repression," 5 *Signs: A Journal of Women in Culture and Society* 686 (1980); Victor Cline, "Another View: Pornography Effects, the State of the Art," in *Where Do You Draw the Line?* (V. B. Cline ed. 1974); Pauline Bart and Margaret Jozsa, "Dirty Books, Dirty Films, and Dirty Data," in *Take Back the Night: Women on Pornography* 204 (Laura Lederer ed. 1982); (2) the commission's tendency to minimize the significance of its own findings, *e.g.*, those by Donald Mosher on the differential effects of exposure by gender; and (3) the design of the commission's research. The commission did not focus on questions about gender, did its best to eliminate "violence" from its materials (so as not to overlap with the Violence Commission), and propounded unscientific theories such as Puritan guilt to explain women's negative responses to the materials.

Further, scientific causality is unnecessary to legally validate an obscenity regulation: "But, it is argued, there is no scientific data which conclusively demonstrate that exposure to obscene materials adversely affects men and women or their society. It is [urged] that, absent such a demonstration, any kind of state regulation is 'impermissible.' *We reject this argument*. It is not for us to resolve empirical uncertainties underlying state legislation, save in the exceptional case where that legislation plainly impinges upon rights protected by the Constitution itself . . . Although there is no conclusive proof of a connection between antisocial behavior and obscene material, the legislature of Georgia could quite reasonably determine that such a connection does or might exist." Paris Adult Theatre I v. Slaton, 413 U.S. 49, 60–61 (1973) (Burger, J., for the majority) (emphasis added); see also Roth v. U.S., 354 U.S. 476, 501 (1957).

9. Some of the harm of pornography to women, as defined in note 1 above, and as discussed in this talk, has been documented in empirical studies. Recent studies have found that exposure to pornography increases the willingness of normal men to aggress against women under laboratory conditions; makes both women and men substantially less able to perceive ac-

264

counts of rape as accounts of rape; makes normal men more closely resemble convicted rapists psychologically; increases attitudinal measures that are known to correlate with rape, such as hostility toward women, propensity to rape, condoning rape, and predictions that one would rape or force sex on a woman if one knew one would not get caught; and produces other attitude changes in men, such as increasing the extent of their trivialization, dehumanization, and objectification of women. Diana E. H. Russell, "Pornography and Violence: What Does the New Research Say?" in Lederer, note 8 above, at 216; Neil M. Malamuth and Edward Donnerstein (eds.), *Pornography and Sexual Aggression* (1984); Dolph Zillman, *The Connection between Sex and Aggression* (1984); J. V. P. Check, N. Malamuth, and R. Stille, "Hostility to Women Scale" (1983) (unpublished manuscript); Edward Donnerstein, "Pornography: Its Effects on Violence against Women," in Malamuth and Donnerstein, eds., *Pornography and Sexual Aggression* (1984); Neil M. Malamuth and J. V. P. Check, "The Effects of Mass Media Exposure on Acceptance of Violence against Women: A Field Experiment," 15 *Journal of Research in Personality* 436 (1981); Neil M. Malamuth, "Rape Proclivities among Males," 37 *Journal of Social Issues* 138 (1981); Neil M. Malamuth and Barry Spinner, "A Longitudinal Content Analysis of Sexual Violence in the Best-Selling Erotic Magazines," 16 *Journal of Sex Research* 226 (1980); Mosher, "Sex Callousness Towards Women," in 8 *Technical Report of the Commission on Obscenity and Pornography* 313 (1971); Dolph Zillman and J. Bryant, "Effects of Massive Exposure to Pornography," in Malamuth and Donnerstein, eds., *Pornography and Sexual Aggression* (1984).

10. The following are illustrative, not exhaustive, of the body of work I term the "feminist critique of pornography." Andrea Dworkin, note 1 above; Dorchen Leidholdt, "Where Pornography Meets Fascism," *Win*, Mar. 15, 1983, at 18; George Steiner, "Night Words," in *The Case Against Pornography* 227 (D. Holbrook ed. 1973); Susan Brownmiller, *Against Our Will: Men, Women and Rape* 394 (1975); Robin Morgan, "Pornography and Rape: Theory and Practice," in *Going Too Far* 165 (Robin Morgan ed. 1977); Kathleen Barry, *Female Sexual Slavery* (1979); *Against Sado-Masochism: A Radical Feminist Analysis* (R. R. Linden, D. R. Pagano, D. E. H. Russell, and S. L. Star eds. 1982), especially chapters by Ti-Grace Atkinson, Judy Butler, Andrea Dworkin, Alice Walker, John Stoltenberg, Audre Lorde, and Susan Leigh Star; Alice Walker, "Coming Apart," in Lederer, *Take Back the Night*, note 8 above, and other articles in that volume with the exception of the legal ones; Gore Vidal, "Women's Liberation Meets the Miller-Mailer-Manson Man," in *Homage to Daniel Shays: Collected Essays 1952–1972* 389 (1972); Linda Lovelace and Michael McGrady, *Ordeal* (1980). Works basic to the perspective taken here are Kate Millett, *Sexual Politics* (1969) and Florence Rush, *The Best-Kept Secret: Sexual Abuse of Children* (1980). "Violent Pornography: Degradation of Women versus Right of Free Speech," 8 *New York University Review of Law and Social Change* 181 (1978) contains both feminist and nonfeminist arguments.

11. For more extensive discussions of this subject, *see* my prior work, especially "Feminism, Marxism, Method and the State: An Agenda for Theory,"

7 *Signs: Journal of Women in Culture and Society* 515 (1982) [hereinafter cited as *Signs* I]; "Feminism, Marxism, Method and the State: Toward Feminist Jurisprudence," 8 *Signs: Journal of Women in Culture and Society* 635 (1983) [hereinafter cited as *Signs* II].

12. Jacobellis v. Ohio, 378 U.S. 184, 197 (1964) (Stewart, J., concurring).

13. Justice Stewart is said to have complained that this single line was more quoted and remembered than anything else he ever said.

14. See *Signs* I, note 11 above.

15. Susan Griffin, *Pornography and Silence: Culture's Revenge Against Nature* 2–4, 251–65 (1981).

16. Dworkin, note 1 above.

17. *See also* Dworkin, note 6 above.

18. The position that pornography is sex—that whatever you think of sex you think of pornography—underlies nearly every treatment of the subject. In particular, nearly every nonfeminist treatment proceeds on the implicit or explicit assumption, argument, criticism, or suspicion that pornography is sexually liberating in some way, a position unifying an otherwise diverse literature. *See, e.g.,* D. H. Lawrence, "Pornography and Obscenity," in his *Sex, Literature and Censorship* 64 (1959); Hugh Hefner, "The Playboy Philosophy," *Playboy*, December 1962, at 73, and *Playboy*, February 1963, at 43; Henry Miller, "Obscenity and the Law of Reflection," in his *Remember to Remember* 274, 286 (1947); Deirdre English, "The Politics of Porn: Can Feminists Walk the Line?" *Mother Jones*, Apr. 1980, at 20; Jean Bethke Elshtain, "The Victim Syndrome: A Troubling Turn in Feminism," *The Progressive*, June 1982, at 42. To choose an example at random: "In opposition to the Victorian view that narrowly defines proper sexual function in a rigid way that is analogous to ideas of excremental regularity and moderation, pornography builds a model of plastic variety and joyful excess in sexuality. In opposition to the sorrowing Catholic dismissal of sexuality as an unfortunate and spiritually superficial concomitant of propagation, pornography affords the alternative idea of the independent status of sexuality as a profound and shattering ecstasy." David Richards, "Free Speech and Obscenity Law: Toward a Moral Theory of the First Amendment," 123 *University of Pennsylvania Law Review* 45, 81 (1974) (footnotes omitted). *See also* F. Schauer, "Response: Pornography and the First Amendment," 40 *University of Pittsburgh Law Review* 605, 616 (1979).

19. Spending time around adult bookstores, attending pornographic movies, and talking with pornographers (who, like all smart pimps, do some form of market research), as well as analyzing the pornography itself in sex/gender terms, all confirm that pornography is for men. That women may attend or otherwise consume it does not make it any less for men, any more than the observation that mostly men consume pornography means that pornography does not harm women. *See* Martha Langelan, "The Political Economy of Pornography," *Aegis: Magazine on Ending Violence against Women*, Autumn 1981, at 5; J. Cook, "The X-Rated Economy," *Forbes*, Sept. 18, 1978, at 60. Personal observation reveals that most women tend to avoid pornography as much as possible—which is not very much, as it turns out.

266

20. The "fantasy" and "catharsis" hypotheses, together, assert that pornography cathects sexuality on the level of fantasy fulfillment. The work of Edward Donnerstein, particularly, shows that the opposite is true. The more pornography is viewed, the *more* pornography—and the more brutal pornography—is both wanted and required for sexual arousal. What occurs is not catharsis, but desensitization, requiring progressively more potent stimulation. See works cited note 9 above; Murray Straus, "Leveling, Civility, and Violence in the Family," 36 *Journal of Marriage & The Family* 13 (1974).

21. Lovelace and McGrady, note 10 above, provides an account by one coerced pornography model. *See also* Andrea Dworkin, "Pornography's 'Exquisite Volunteers,' *Ms.*, March 1981, at 65.

22. However, for one such inquiry, see Russell, note 9 above, at 228: a random sample of 930 San Francisco households found that 10 percent of women had at least once "been upset by anyone trying to get you to do what they'd seen in pornographic pictures, movies or books." Obviously, this figure could only include those who knew that the pornography was the source of the sex, so this finding is conservative. *See also* Diana E. H. Russell, *Rape in Marriage* 27–41 (1983) (discussing the data base). The hearings Andrea Dworkin and I held for the Minneapolis City Council on the ordinance cited in note 1 produced many accounts of the use of pornography to force sex on women and children. *Public Hearings on Ordinances to Add Pornography as Discrimination against Women*, Committee on Government Operations, City Council, Minneapolis, Minn., Dec. 12–13, 1983. (Hereinafter cited as *Hearings*).

23. *See Signs* I; *see also* Susan Sontag, "The Pornographic Imagination," 34 *Partisan Review* 181 (1977).

24. "Explicitness" of accounts is a central issue in both obscenity adjudications and audience access standards adopted voluntarily by self-regulated industries or by boards of censor. *See, e.g.,* Grove Press v. Christenberry, 175 F. Supp. 488, 489 (S.D.N.Y. 1959) (discussion of "candor" and "realism"); Grove Press v. Christenberry, 276 F.2d 433, 438 (2d Cir. 1960) ("directness"); Mitchum v. State, 251 So.2d 298, 302 (Fla. Dist. Ct. App. 1971) ("show it all"); Kaplan v. California, 413 U.S. 115, 118 (1973). How *much* sex the depiction shows is implicitly thereby correlated with how *sexual* (that is, how sexually arousing to the male) the material is. *See, e.g.,* Memoirs v. Massachusetts, 383 U.S. 413, 460 (1966) (White, J., dissenting); Richard Heffner, "What G, PG, R and X Really Means," 126 *Cong. Rec.* 172 (daily ed. Dec. 8, 1980); *Report of the Committee on Obscenity and Film Censorship* (the Williams Report) (1981). Andrea Dworkin brilliantly gives the reader the experience of this aesthetic in her account of the pornography. Dworkin, note 1 above, at 25–47.

25. To the body of law ably encompassed and footnoted by William Lockhart and Robert McClure, "Literature, the Law of Obscenity and the Constitution," 38 *Minnesota Law Review* 295 (1954) and "Censorship of Obscenity," 45 *Minnesota Law Review* 5 (1960), I add only the most important cases since then: Stanley v. Georgia, 394 U.S. 557 (1969); U.S. v. Reidel, 402 U.S. 351 (1970); Miller v. California, 413 U.S. 15 (1973); Paris Adult Theatre I v. Slaton,

267

24

413 U.S. 49 (1973); Hamling v. U.S., 418 U.S. 87 (1973); Jenkins v. Georgia, 418 U.S. 153 (1973); U.S. v. 12 200-Ft. Reels of Super 8mm Film, 413 U.S. 123 (1973); Erznoznik v. City of Jacksonville, 422 U.S. 205 (1975); Splawn v. California, 431 U.S. 595 (1976); Ward v. Illinois, 431 U.S. 767 (1976); Lovisi v. Slayton, 539 F.2d 349 (4th Cir. 1976). *See also* New York v. Ferber, 458 U.S. 747 (1982).

26. For a discussion of the role of the law of privacy in supporting the existence of pornography, see Ruth Colker, "Pornography and Privacy: Towards the Development of a Group Based Theory for Sex Based Intrusions of Privacy," 1 *Law and Inequality: A Journal of Theory and Practice* 191 (1983).

27. Louis Henkin, "Morals and the Constitution: The Sin of Obscenity," 63 *Columbia Law Review* 391, 395 (1963).

28. These parallels are discussed more fully in *Signs* II. It may seem odd to denominate "moral" as *female* here, since this article discusses male morality. Under male supremacy, men define things; I am describing that. Men define women *as* "moral." This is the male view of women. My analysis, a feminist critique of the male standpoint, terms "moral" the concept that pornography is about good and evil. This is *my* analysis of *them*, as contrasted with their attributions to women.

29. A reading of case law supports the reports in Robert Woodward and Scott Armstrong, *The Brethren* 194 (1979), to the effect that this is a "bottom line" criterion for at least some justices. The interesting question becomes why the tactics of male supremacy would change from keeping the penis hidden, covertly glorified, to having it everywhere on display, overtly glorified. This suggests at least that a major shift from private terrorism to public terrorism has occurred. What used to be perceived as a danger to male power, the exposure of the penis, has now become a strategy in maintaining it.

30. One possible reading of Lockhart and McClure, note 25 above, is that this was their agenda, and that their approach was substantially adopted in the third prong of the *Miller* doctrine. For the law's leading attempt to grapple with this issue, *see* Memoirs v. Massachusetts, 383 U.S. 413 (1966), *overruled in part*, Miller v. California, 413 U.S. 15 (1973). *See also* U.S. v. Ulysses, 5 F. Supp. 182 (S.D.N.Y. 1933), *aff'd* 72 F.2d 705 (2d Cir. 1934).

31. Andrea Dworkin and I developed this analysis in our class "Pornography" at the University of Minnesota Law School, Fall 1983. *See also* Dworkin, "Why So-Called Radical Men Love and Need Pornography," in Lederer, note 8 above, at 141 (the issue of pornography is an issue of sexual access to women, hence involves a fight among men).

32. Those termed "fathers" and "sons" in Dworkin's article, note 31 above, we came to call "the old boys," whose strategy for male dominance involves keeping pornography and the abuse of women private, and "the new boys," whose strategy for male dominance involves making pornography and the abuse of women public. In my view Freud and the popularization of his de-repression hypothesis figure centrally in "the new boys'" approach and success. To conclude, as some have, that women have benefited from the public

268

25

availability of pornography and hence should be grateful for and have a stake in its continuing availability is to say that the merits of open condoned oppression relative to covert condoned oppression warrant its continuation. This reasoning obscures the possibility of *ending* the oppression. The benefit of pornography's open availability, it seems to me, is that women can know who and what we are dealing with in order to end it. How, is the question.

33. Miller v. California, 413 U.S. 15, 24 (1973).

34. Paris Adult Theatre I v. Slaton, 413 U.S. 49, 67 (1973). *See also* Miller v. California, 413 U.S. 15, 25 n.7 ("A quotation from Voltaire in the flyleaf of a book will not constitutionally redeem an otherwise obscene publication," quoting Kois v. Wisconsin, 408 U.S. 229, 231 [1972]).

35. Penthouse International v. McAuliffe, 610 F.2d 1353, 1362–73 (5th Cir. 1980). For a study in enforcement, *see* Coble v. City of Birmingham, 389 So.2d 527 (Ala. Ct. App. 1980).

36. Malamuth and Spinner, note 9 above (". . . the portrayal of sexual aggression within such 'legitimate' magazines as *Playboy* and *Penthouse* may have a greater impact than similar portrayals in hard-core pornography"); Neil M. Malamuth and Edward Donnerstein, "The Effects of Aggressive-Pornographic Mass Media Stimuli," 15 *Advances in Experimental Social Psychology* 103, 130 (1982).

37. Some courts, under the obscenity rubric, seem to have understood that the quality of artistry does not undo the damage. People v. Mature Enterprises, 343 N.Y.S.2d 911, 925 n.14 (N.Y. Sup. 1973) ("This court will not adopt a rule of law which states that obscenity is suppressible but that well-written or technically well produced obscenity is not," quoting, in part, People v. Fritch, 13 N.Y.2d 119, 126, 243 N.Y.S.2d 1, 7, 192 N.E.2d 713 [1963]). More to the point of my argument here is Justice O'Connor's observation that "[t]he compelling interests identified in today's opinion . . . suggest that the Constitution might in fact permit New York to ban knowing distribution of works depicting minors engaged in explicit sexual conduct, regardless of the social value of the depictions. For example, a 12-year-old child photographed while masturbating surely suffers the same psychological harm whether the community labels the photograph 'edifying' or 'tasteless.' The audience's appreciation of the depiction is simply irrelevant to New York's asserted interest in protecting children from psychological, emotional, and mental harm." New York v. Ferber, 458 U.S. 747, 774–75 (1982) (concurring). Put another way, how does it make a harmed child *not harmed* that what was produced by harming him is great art?

38. Women typically get mentioned in obscenity law only in the phrase, "women and men," used as a synonym for "people." At the same time, exactly who the victim of pornography is, has long been a great mystery. The few references to "exploitation" in obscenity litigation do not evoke a woman victim. For example, one reference to "a system of commercial exploitation of people with sadomasochistic sexual aberrations" concerned the customers of women dominatrixes, all of whom were men. State v. Von Cleef, 102 N.J. Super. 104, 245 A.2d 495, 505 (1968). The children at issue in *Ferber* were boys.

269

Similarly, Justice Frankfurter invoked the "sordid exploitation of man's nature and impulses" in discussing his conception of pornography in Kingsley Pictures Corp. v. Regents, 360 U.S. 684, 692 (1958).

39. Miller v. California, 413 U.S. 15, 24 (1973).

40. *See, e.g.,* Miller v. California, id. at 40–41 (Douglas, J., dissenting) ("What shocks me may be sustenance for my neighbors"); U.S. v. 12 200-Ft. Reels of Super 8mm Film, 413 U.S. 123, 137 (1972) (Douglas, J., dissenting) ("[W]hat may be trash to me may be prized by others"); Cohen v. California, 403 U.S. 15, 25 (1970) (Harlan, J.) ("One man's vulgarity is another's lyric"); Winters v. New York, 333 U.S. 507, 510 (1947) ("What is one man's amusement, teaches another's doctrine"); Lawrence, note 18 above, at 195 ("What is pornography to one man is the laughter of genius to another"); Ginzburg v. United States, 383 U.S. 463, 489 (1966) (Douglas, J., dissenting) ("Some like Chopin, others like 'rock and roll'"). As one man, the pimp who forced Linda Lovelace into pornography, said to another: "I don't tell you how to write your column. Don't tell me how to treat my broads." (Quoted in Gloria Steinem, "The Real Linda Lovelace," in *Outrageous Acts and Everyday Rebellions* 243, 252 [1983].)

41. For the resolution of this issue for nonconventional sexuality, *see* Mishkin v. New York, 383 U.S. 502, 508 (1966).

42. None of this is intended as a comment about the personal sexuality or principles of any judicial individual; it is rather a series of analytic observations that emerge from a feminist attempt to interpret the deep social structure of a vast body of case law on the basis of a critique of gender. Further research should systematically analyze the contents of the pornography involved in the cases. For instance, with respect to the last hypothesis in the text above, is it just chance that the first film to be found obscene by a state supreme court depicts male masturbation? Landau v. Fording, 245 C.A.2d 820, 54 Cal. Rptr. 177 (1966). Given the ubiquity of the infantilization of women and the sexualization of little girls, would *Ferber* have been decided the same way if it had shown twelve-year-old girls masturbating? Did works like *Lady Chatterley's Lover* and *Tropic of Cancer* get in trouble because male sexuality is depicted in a way that men think is dangerous for women and children to see?

43. Roth v. U.S., 354 U.S. 476 (1957), but cf. Stanley v. Georgia, 394 U.S. 557 (1969), in which the right to private possession of obscene materials is protected as a First Amendment *speech* right. *See* 67 *Landmark Briefs and Arguments of the Supreme Court of the United States: Constitutional Law* 850 (P. Kurland and G. Casper eds. 1975).

44. *E.g., The Report of the Commission on Obscenity and Pornography,* note 8 above, at 1, charges the commission to study "[t]he effect of obscenity and pornography upon the public and particularly minors and its relation to crime and other antisocial behavior."

45. Naomi Scheman, "Making it All Up," transcript of speech, January 1982, at 7.

46. This body of work is usually taken to be diverse. Thomas I. Emerson,

Toward a General Theory of the First Amendment (1966); Emerson, *The System of Freedom of Expression* (1970); Alexander Meiklejohn, *Free Speech and Its Relation to Self-Government* (1948); Whitney v. California, 274 U.S. 357, 375 (1927) (Brandeis, J., concurring, joined by Holmes, J.); T. Scanlon, "A Theory of Free Expression," 1 *Philosophy and Public Affairs* 204 (1972); John Hart Ely, "Flag Desecration: A Case Study in the Roles of Categorization and Balancing in First Amendment Analysis," 88 *Harvard Law Review* 1482 (1975); Zechariah Chafee, *Free Speech in the United States* 245 (1948). This literature is ably summarized and anatomized by Ed Baker, who proposes an interpretative theory that goes far toward responding to my objections here, without really altering the basic assumptions I criticize. *See* C. E. Baker, "Scope of the First Amendment Freedom of Speech," 25 *UCLA Law Review* 964 (1978) and "The Process of Change and the Liberty Theory of the First Amendment," 55 *Southern California Law Review* 293 (1982).

47. Emerson, *Toward a General Theory of the First Amendment*, note 46 above, at 28.

48. *See* Erznoznik v. City of Jacksonville, 422 U.S. 205 (1975); Breard v. Alexandria, 341 U.S. 622, 641–45 (1951); Kovacs v. Cooper, 336 U.S. 77, 87–89 (1949).

49. Stanley v. Georgia, 394 U.S. 557 (1969).

50. *See* Walker, "Coming Apart," in Lederer, note 8 above, at 85; Russell, note 9 above; *Hearings. Cf.* Paris Adult Theatre I v. Slaton, 413 U.S. 49, 71 (1973) (Douglas, J., dissenting) ("[In] a life that has not been short, I have yet to be trapped into seeing or reading something that would offend me"). He probably hadn't.

51. *See* "Privacy v. Equality" in Part II for a fuller discussion of this point.

52. Emerson, *Toward a General Theory of the First Amendment*, note 46 above, at 16–25. *See also* Emerson, *The System of Freedom of Expression*, note 46 above, at 17.

53. The essentially scientific notion of causality did not *first* appear in this law at this time, however. *See, e.g.*, U.S. v. Roth, 237 F.2d 796, 812–17 (2d Cir. 1956) (Frank, J., concurring) ("According to Judge Bok, an obscenity statute may be validly enforced when there is proof of a causal relation between a particular book and undesirable conduct. Almost surely, such proof cannot ever be adduced." Id., 826 n.70).

Werner Heisenberg, criticizing old ideas of atomic physics in light of Einstein's theory of relativity, states what conditions must exist for a causal relation to make sense: "To coordinate a definite cause to a definite effect has sense only when both can be observed without introducing a foreign element disturbing their interrelation. The law of causality, because of its very nature, can only be defined for isolated systems." Werner Heisenberg, *The Physical Principles of the Quantum Theory* 63 (1930). Among the influences that disturb the isolation of systems are observers. Underlying the adoption of a causality standard in obscenity law is a rather hasty analogy between the regularities of physical and of social systems, an analogy that has seldom been explicitly justified or even updated as the physical sciences have questioned their own

271

epistemological foundations. This kind of scientific causality may not be readily susceptible to measurement in social systems for the simple reason that social systems are not isolated systems; experimental research (which is where it *has* been shown that pornography causes harm) can only minimize the influence of what will always be "foreign elements." Pornography and harm may not be two definite events anyway; perhaps pornography *is* a harm. Moreover, if the effects of pornography are systematic, they may not be isolable from the system in which they exist. This would not mean that no harm exists. Rather, it would mean that because the harm is so pervasive, it cannot be sufficiently isolated to be *perceived* as existing according to this causal model. In other words, if pornography is seen as harmful only if it causes harm by this model, and if it exists socially only in ways that cannot be isolated from society itself, its harm will not be perceived to exist. I think this describes the conceptual situation in which we find ourselves.

54. Morton Horowitz, "The Doctrine of Objective Causation," in *The Politics of Law* 201 (David Kairys ed. 1982). The pervasiveness of the objectification of women has been treated as a reason why pandering should not be constitutionally restricted: "The advertisements of our best magazines are chock-full of thighs, ankles, calves, bosoms, eyes, and hair, to draw the potential buyer's attention to lotions, tires, food, liquor, clothing, autos, and even insurance policies." Ginzburg v. U.S., 383 U.S. 463, 482 (1966) (Douglas, J., dissenting). Justice Douglas thereby illustrated, apparently without noticing, that *somebody* knows that associating sex, that is, women's bodies, with things causes people to *act* on that association.

55. *See* Lovelace and McGrady, note 10 above.

56. Two boys masturbating with no showing of explicit force demonstrates the harm of child pornography in New York v. Ferber, 458 U.S. 747 (1982), while shoving money up a woman's vagina, among other acts, raises serious questions of "regulation of 'conduct' having a communicative element" in live sex adjudications, California v. LaRue, 409 U.S. 109, 113 (1972) (live sex can be regulated by a state in connection with serving alcoholic beverages). "Snuff" films, in which a woman is actually murdered to produce a film for sexual entertainment, are known to exist. People v. Douglas and Hernandez, Felony Complaint No. NF8300382, Municipal Court, North Judicial District, Orange County, Calif., Aug. 5, 1983, alleges the murder of two young girls to make a pornographic film. Hernandez turned state's evidence; Douglas was convicted of first-degree murder in November 1984. No snuff film was found. (Conversation with Tony Rackackaus, district attorney, Sept. 3, 1986.)

57. Both Griffin, note 15 above, and the oldest Anglo-Saxon obscenity cases locate the harm of pornography in the mind of the consumer. *See, e.g.,* Regina v. Hicklin, 3 L.R-Q.B. 360, 371 (1868) ("tendency . . . to deprave and corrupt those whose minds are open to such immoral influences and into whose hands a publication of this sort may fall"). The data of John Court and Berl Kutchinsky, both correlational, reach contrary conclusions on the relation of pornography's availability to crime statistics. Kutchinsky, "Towards

272

an Explanation of the Decrease in Registered Sex Crimes in Copenhagen," 7 *Technical Report of the Commission on Obscenity and Pornography* 263 (1971); Kutchinsky, "The Effect of Easy Availability of Pornography on the Incidence of Sex Crimes: The Danish Experience," 29 *Journal of Social Issues* 163 (1973); *cf.* Court, "Pornography and Sex Crimes: A Re-Evaluation in the Light of Recent Trends around the World," 5 *International Journal of Criminology and Penology* 129 (1977). More recent investigations into correlations focused on rape in the United States have reached still other conclusions. Larry Baron and Murray Straus have found a strong correlation between state-to-state variations in the rate of reported rape and the aggregate circulation rate of popular men's sex magazines, including *Playboy* and *Hustler*. "Sexual Stratification, Pornography, and Rape," Family Research Laboratory and Department of Sociology, University of New Hampshire, Durham, N.H., Nov. 18, 1983 (manuscript). The authors conclude that "the findings suggest that the combination of a society which is characterized by a struggle to secure equal rights for women, by a high readership of sex magazines which depict women in ways which may legitimize violence, and by a context in which there is a high level of non-sexual violence, constitutes a mix of societal characteristics which precipitate rape" at 16. *See also* the "Williams Report," note 24 above, and the opinions of Justice Harlan on the injury to "society" as a permissible basis for legislative judgments in this area. Roth v. U.S., 354 U.S. 476, 501–02 (1957) (concurring in companion case, Alberts v. California).

58. Laurence Tribe, *American Constitutional Law* 662 (1978).

59. I am conceiving rape as *sexual* aggression. On the connection between pornography and rape, *see* Neil M. Malamuth, "Rape Proclivity among Men," 37 *Journal of Social Issues* 138 (1981); Neil M. Malamuth, "Rape Fantasies as a Function of Exposure to Violent Sexual Stimuli," 10 *Archives of Sexual Behavior* 33 (1981); Scott Haber and Seymour Feshbach, "Testing Hypotheses Regarding Rape: Exposure to Sexual Violence, Sex Differences, and the 'Normality' of Rapists," 14 *Journal of Research in Personality* 121 (1980); Maggie Heim and Seymour Feshbach, "Sexual Responsiveness of College Students to Rape Depictions: Inhibitory and Disinhibitory Effects," 38 *Journal of Personality and Social Psychology* 399 (1980). *See also* works by Malamuth, note 9 above. Of course, there are difficulties in measuring rape as a direct consequence of laboratory experiments, difficulties that have led researchers to substitute other measures of willingness to aggress, such as electric shocks.

60. Apparently, it may be impossible to *make* a film for experimental purposes that portrays violence or aggression by a man against a woman that a substantial number of male experimental subjects do not perceive as sexual. *See Hearings*, at 31 (testimony of Edward Donnerstein).

61. *See* works of Zillman, note 9 above.

62. Immanuel Kant, *Fundamental Principles of the Metaphysics of Morals* (T. Abbott trans. 1969); Arthur Danto, "Persons," in 6 *Encyclopedia of Philosophy* 10 (P. Edwards ed. 1967); Margaret Radin, "Property and Personhood," 34 *Stanford Law Review* 957 (1982).

63. *See* Kant, note 62 above; Danto, note 62 above; Radin, note 62 above.

See also the "original position" of John Rawls, *A Theory of Justice* (1971), and Rawls, "Kantian Constructivism in Moral Theory," 9 *Journal of Philosophy* 515, 533–35 (1980).

64. Ludwig Wittgenstein, *Philosophical Investigations* 178 (G. Anscombe trans. 3d ed. 1958).

65. Karl Marx's critique of capitalist society is epitomized in *Capital* chap. 1 (1867). His concept of the "fetishism of commodities" in which "relations between men [assume], *in their eyes,* the fantastic form of a relation between things" (emphasis added) is presented in the 1970 edition at 72.

66. David Hume, "Of Personal Identity," in *A Treatise of Human Nature* bk. I, pt. IV, § VI (1888).

67. Bernard Williams, "Are Persons Bodies? Personal Identity and Individualization" and "Bodily Continuity and Personal Identity," in his *Problems of the Self* 1, 64 (1973). Bernard Williams was principal author of the "Williams Report," note 24 above, Britain's equivalent of the U.S. Commission on Obscenity and Pornography, in which none of his values of "persons" were noticed lacking in, or women deprived of them by, pornography.

68. *See Signs* I and II.

69. I have come to this conclusion from my analysis of all the empirical data available to date, the pornography itself, and personal observations.

70. Brownmiller, note 10 above, is widely considered to present the view that rape is an act of violence, not sex. Women Against Pornography, a New York based antipornography group, has argued that pornography is violence against women, not sex. This has been almost universally taken as *the* feminist position on the issue. For an indication of possible change, *see* 4 *NCASA News* 19–21 (May 1984).

71. This, again, does not mean that it is an *idea.* A new theory of ideology, prefigured in Dworkin, note 1 above, will be needed to conceptualize the role of pornography in constructing the condition of women.

72. Dworkin, note 1 above, at 115.

73. "Echoing Macaulay, 'Jimmy' Walker remarked that he had never heard of a woman seduced by a book." U.S. v. Roth, 237 F.2d 796, 812 (1956) (appendix to concurrence of Frank, J.) What is classically called seduction, I expect feminists might interpret as rape or forced sex.

274

The White Slave Traffic Act: Historical Impact of a Federal Crime Policy on Women

Marlene D. Beckman

ABSTRACT. When Congress passed the White Slave Traffic Act, legislators were strongly influenced by early twentieth century progressive era reformers, who sought to rid the country of commercial prostitution. The statute was directed at the elimination of the business of securing women and girls and selling them outright or exploiting them for immoral purposes. Instead, it was used to prosecute the voluntary and ordinary immoralities of people and to punish the women "victims" whom the law was designed to protect.

On June 25, 1910, Congress passed the White Slave Traffic Act, known as the Mann Act. Progressive era reformers used the catchwords "white slavery" to promote the vision of women held in bondage against their will, of mysterious druggings and abductions of helpless young girls, and of unexplained disappearances of innocent and naive immigrants forced into lives of prostitution and vice. Yet, just several years later, law enforcement officials relied on the White Slave Traffic Act to arrest, prosecute and send to prison a man and a woman who traveled from Jersey City to spend the weekend in New York.

This paper will show how the White Slave Traffic Act was misapplied. The Mann Act was to be directed at the elimination of the business of securing women and girls and selling them outright or exploiting them for immoral purposes. Instead, it was used to prose-

Marlene D. Beckman, U.S. Department of Justice, Washington, D.C. I acknowledge Dr. Claudine SchWeber, Criminal Justice Department, State University College at Buffalo, for getting me started and Wendy Williams, Georgetown University Law Center, for keeping me going.

cute the voluntary and ordinary immoralities of people and to punish the women "victims" whom the law was designed to protect.

DEVELOPMENT AND EXPANSION
OF THE WHITE SLAVE TRAFFIC ACT

The White Slave Traffic Act made it a federal crime to engage in prostitution in interstate commerce. The act provided heavy penalties for transporting or in any way aiding, abetting or causing the transporting in interstate or foreign commerce of "any woman or girl for the purpose of prostitution or debauchery, or for any other immoral purpose."[1]

In more than one sense, the name "White Slave Traffic Act" remains a misnomer.[2] First, the act makes no distinction as to the race or the color of the female whose transportation is a violation of the law. Second, in many instances the "victims" willingly consented to the practices in which they were engaged. Nonetheless, Congress gave the act its name because the central purpose of it was to halt what many believed was a serious and widespread practice: foreign-born commercial procurers taking innocent young girls and women by force and holding them captive with threats to their lives, a practice held to resemble black servitude in its exploitative and barbarous nature.

The legislators were influenced by what was taking place in the country. In no period of U.S. history did the custodians of morality direct more serious attention to the eradication of prostitution than during the first two decades of the twentieth century known as the progressive era.[3] The energetic outburst against white slave traffic grew out of the progressive's view that women were naturally chaste and virtuous, and no woman became a whore unless she had first been raped, seduced, drugged or deserted. The image of the prostitute, developed by reformers, was of a lonely and confused female. In the search for explanations of what could have led girls so to degrade and ultimately destroy themselves, the progressive formula maintained that female prostitutes were passive victims of social disequilibrium and the brutality of men. This conception of female weakness and male domination left no room for the possibility that prostitutes might consciously or aggressively choose their activities.[4]

A review of the historical development of the Mann Act reveals two themes. First, Congress intended the act to apply only to commercial vice and those cases where there was evidence of coercion.[5] Second, the act was not intended to apply to ordinary prostitution, control of which remained within the police powers of the states.[6] Instead, Congress intended to supplement local authority by reaching interstate transportation for commercial purposes. Despite this clear congressional intent, inclusion in the statute of the words "any other immoral purpose" had an unforeseen effect: the prosecution of noncommercial sex as a federal crime.

In the 1917 case, *Caminetti* v. *United States*, the U.S. Supreme Court first upheld convictions under the act where there was no evidence that the women were prostitutes, that their actions were involuntary, or that the defendants derived any profit except their own pleasure. In *Caminetti* two men voluntarily accompanied by two women traveled from California to Reno, Nevada, for the weekend. The five-justice majority, relying on the plain meaning of the words "any other immoral purpose," upheld the convictions on the grounds the Mann Act applied to voluntary acts of immorality, even when no commercial intention or business profit was shown.[7]

While opportunities to overrule *Caminetti* subsequently presented themselves, the Court continued to rely on this landmark case. In 1946 it reaffirmed the *Caminetti* holding in *Cleveland* v. *United States* by finding that "other immoral purposes" applied to a Morman who, in practicing polygamy, had frequently transported his wives across state lines.[8] Cases such as *Cleveland* show that the clause "any other immoral purpose" was so broad, it could be used to reach any conduct that fell within the popular understanding of immorality. For a time, the federal courts relied on the controversial immoral status concept to become a censor of the nation's sexual morals. The term "other immoral acts" was held to apply to the interstate transportaton of a woman to work as a chorus girl in a theatre where the woman was exposed to smoking, drinking and cursing;[9] a dentist who met his young lover in a neighboring state and shared a hotel room to discuss her pregnancy;[10] two students at the University of Puerto Rico who had sexual intercourse on the way home from a date;[11] and a man and woman who lived together for four years and traveled around the country as man and wife while the man sold securities.[12]

The activity prohibited by the Mann Act was transportation of "any woman or girl" in interstate commerce. On a plain reading of the act, Congress intended the woman who was to engage in sexual conduct to be treated as the person "transported" and the persons who accompanied her or assisted in her transportation were to be prosecuted as "transporters." Only the latter were targeted by the act's criminal sanctions. The courts, however, went beyond the law's objectives.

While two early cases established that a woman could not be an "accomplice" to the offense of transporting herself from one state to another for immoral purposes, the Court held that the woman may be indicted for *conspiracy*.[13] A woman could have conspired to "commit an offense against the United States" within the meaning of the federal statute, although the objective of the conspiracy was her own transportation in interstate commerce for the purpose of prostitution. The extension of the law of conspiracy to include the woman would, the Court reasoned in the 1915 case of *United States* v. *Holte*, prevent victimization of men. The spectre of blackmail, whereby a woman would lure a man to cross a state line with her and then, by threatening to notify authorities, extort money from him, moved the Court to find a way to prosecute the woman, the language of the act notwithstanding. The woman could now be punished for blackmail or for malicious prosecution. Justice Holmes, writing for the majority in *Holte*, made clear the Court's position:

> We think that it would be going too far to say that the defendant could not be guilty in this case. Suppose, for instance, that a professional prostitute, as well able to look out for herself as was the man, should suggest and carry out a journey within the Act of 1910 in the hope of blackmailing the man, and should buy the railroad tickets, or should pay the fare from Jersey City to New York, she would be within the letter of the Act of 1910, and we see no reason why the act should not be held to apply. We see equally little reason for not treating the preliminary agreement as a conspiracy that the law can reach, if we *abandon the illusion that the woman always is the victim.*[14]

In the 1932 case of *Gebardi* v. *United States*, the Court looked again at this issue and held that for the woman to fall within the ban of the Mann Act, she must at least aid or assist someone else in transporting or procuring transportation for her, and such aid and assistance must be more active than mere acquiescence.[15] This retreat from the broader implications of the earlier *Holte* decision may be explained on the ground that the *Gebardi* Court was confronted with a woman whose only immoral action was acquiescence to interstate transportation, as opposed to the situation in *Holte* in which the woman was actually a prostitute. The facts of *Gebardi* made the need for establishing limits to the *Holte* principle apparent. In fact, the *Gebardi* Court's conclusion was consistent with the contemporary view that women's criminality was due primarily to their economic and psychological dependence on men. It was also more attuned to the act's original philosophy than was the *Holte* decision.

ENFORCEMENT OF THE MANN ACT

In 1969 William Seagle, a commentator on the Mann Act, asserted that the critics of the Mann Act who had made a "bogey law" out of its sweeping potentialities had failed to consider the selectivity that prosecuting officials exercised in the enforcement of the act. Seagle maintained that although the decisions of the courts had allowed wide latitude to law enforcement authorities, U.S. Attorneys had taken little advantage of this latitude; rather, absent commercial vice, they prosecuted only those cases involving highly aggravated circumstances.[16] The evidence, however, contradicts the Seagle theory. Official circulars issued by the U.S. Department of Justice reveal that the Attorney General, concerned about "federal courts allowing themselves to be turned into ordinary police courts," cautioned prosecutors to use their discretion in noncommercial cases. Nevertheless, my review of the official files of individuals convicted under this law suggests that U.S. Attorneys did not exercise the desired restraint.[17] F.B.I. statistics obtained for this project also confirm the finding.[18]

After *Caminetti* established, in 1917, that commercialism was not an essential element of a Mann Act violation, the Attorney General issued a circular outlining the elements of aggravation required for prosecution in noncommercial cases. The guidelines restricted prosecution in noncommercial cases to "those cases involving a fraudulent overreaching, or involving previously chaste, or very young women or girls, or (when State laws are inadequate) involving married women (with young children) then living with their husbands . . . ." The guidelines further provided "that blackmail cases should, so far as possible, be avoided; and that whenever the women herself voluntarily and without any overreaching, has consented to the criminal arrangement she, too, if the case shall seem to demand it, may be prosecuted as a conspirator.'' These guidelines represented a significant departure from the congressional intent, articulated in the legislative history, to punish only the procuror or transporter of an unwilling victim of commercial vice.[19]

These instructions were re-issued every year from 1917 to 1932.[20] During the 15-year period, the U.S. Attorneys continued to prosecute individuals engaged in strictly personal sexual escapades that in no way involved either commercial gain or exploitation of innocent victims. The evidence presented here cannot be explained by an occasional error on the part of federal prosecutors in judging the circumstances of a particular case to be "aggravated."

A more likely explanation for this overzealous enforcement was the emergence, at the same time, of the Federal Bureau of Investigation (F.B.I.) as a national police force. As one of the first laws to create a "federal" crime, the Mann Act allowed the new crime-fighting office to prove its mettle. F.B.I. agents were encouraged to present to U.S. Attorneys for a decision on prosecution those complaints which alleged interstate transportation but failed to indicate the existence of prostitution.[21] Further, agents actually filed complaints against victims charging them with conspiracy in order to keep them in custody. If the victim later cooperated, she was not prosecuted on a charge of conspiracy because U.S. Attorneys viewed her as a valuable witness. Arrests of women were thus used to induce them to testify against their male "transporters."[22]

In 1932, one month after the *Gebardi* case was decided, the Attorney General altered the guidelines for prosecution for the first time since *Caminetti*. The Attorney General advised that as a result of the *Gebardi* decision, "a woman, by consenting to go and voluntarily going from one state to another with a man, with a view to immoral relations with him, does not violate the conspiracy statute." He instructed U.S. Attorneys to drop from their list of priorities the prosecution of "the woman herself who voluntarily and without any overreaching has consented to the criminal arrangement."[23] Thus, although before *Gebardi* U.S. Attorneys prosecuted women for conspiracy under the Mann Act whether commercial prostitution was involved, the only cases indicting women after *Gebardi* did involve prostitution, albeit sometimes only on an extremely limited scale. Women engaged in prostitution for a short time in order to earn a few dollars for support could hardly be considered models of the commercial vice that concerned Congress when it passed the Mann Act in 1910.[24]

THE WOMEN IN ALDERSON

After 1927, female violators of the Mann Act were sent to the Federal Industrial Institution for Women in Alderson, West Virginia, which was opened that year as the first and only federal prison exclusively for women. Prior to 1927, female federal prisoners were housed in state correctional facilities. Early records of the women incarcerated for Mann Act violations support the hypothesis that the objectives of the White Slave Traffic Act were thwarted in two ways: 1) by prosecuting individuals who were not involved in commercial vice, but rather engaging in ordinary sexual behavior and 2) by prosecuting the female "victims" of a law designed to "protect" women.

The author examined the records of 156 women committed to Alderson for Mann Act violations between the years 1927 and 1937. This sample represents 87% of the total number of women committed for Mann Act violations during this period.[25] The women were divided into four groups based on the extent of commercial vice associated with their offense.[26]

1. Group one consists of those women with no prostitution or commercial activity of any kind connected with their arrest (n=36, 23%). For the most part, these women were traveling with men across state lines, and either one or both of them was married to someone else. One predominant pattern involved single women traveling with men they loved and hoped to marry, but who turned out to be already married; both the woman and the man were arrested as co-conspirators when the man's wife turned them in.

2. Group two includes those women whose prostitution was incidental to their interstate travels with a man, who was sometimes their husband (n=25, 16%). A common pattern here involved a woman who, at the man's insistence, engaged in isolated instances of prostitution to earn enough money so that they could complete their journey.

3. Group three is composed of women involved in commercial prostitution (n=23, 15%). Typically, such women worked in a brothel or house of ill-repute, and were arrested when they solicited at a hotel, and in so doing crossed the state line. These women had become prostitutes to earn enough money to support themselves.

39

4. Group four is comprised of women who, themselves often prostitutes, were arrested for aiding or securing transportation for another woman to cross state lines for prostitution (n=72, 46%). At one extreme was the madame who actually ran the brothel and recruited new workers; at the other was the woman who wrote a letter to a friend back home suggesting that she might do well to come north and join her in her illegal activity. In one case, a woman was sentenced to 18 months because she gave a friend's name to her boyfriend for this purpose. A factor in this indictment may also have been the fact the woman and her boyfriend were, at the time of the arrest, living together as man and wife.

The women in group one were not involved in commercialized vice and further did not fit the profile of the "aggravated" noncommercial cases that had been established by the Attorney General as targets for federal prosecution. On the contrary, most of these cases contain no hint of commercialism nor of the aggravating circumstances required by the prosecution guidelines. Excerpts from the personal history files of two women in group one are illustrative.

Viola had known Blake since she was eight years old—he owned a tin shop and she worked in his office, sending out bills and answering the phone. A friend of his came to the shop by the name of Thomas. He was 24 years old and married, but not living with his wife. Viola became infatuated with Thomas. Her family objected to her working for Blake and she finally left home. Blake told her that he was going to close his shop and go away with Loretta and suggested that she go along with Thomas. Viola agreed and they left Pittsburgh and went as far as Fredericksburg, Virginia where they stayed all night, Loretta and Blake registering as man and wife, and Viola and Thomas as man and wife. The next two days they took turns driving and sleeping. The fourth day they decided to separate; she had had quite enough of the trip and wanted to go home. While the two men were willing to send the girls home, Loretta didn't want to be discarded, so she telephoned the police and reported that they were being beaten. All four were arrested and charged with Mann Act violations.

When Elizabeth was 15, she secured employment as a domestic in order to get away from an unhappy home. There were nine children in all, and as long as Elizabeth stayed at home, she had to wash, iron and cook for her brothers and sisters only to get unkind words in repay for her efforts. Elizabeth left home and went to live with a maternal aunt who sympathized with her. While she was staying with this aunt, she met and fell in love with a man named Steve. He proposed to her but postponed the date of marriage. Steve asked Elizabeth to accompany him on his business trips to deliver liquor. She did and stayed with him at a hotel as his wife. They made 11 trips until they were both arrested on the road in Fairmont, West Virginia. It was then that Elizabeth first learned that Steve was married and that his wife had turned them in.

Overall, the women in group one cannot be described as fitting the profile of aggravated noncommercial cases. Fifteen of the 36 women are under 20 years of age, 14 are in their 20s, and 7 others are in their 30s. The majority, or 25 of the 36 women, had been married at an earlier time. Only 9, however, were married and living with their husbands at the time of their offense; 13 were separated and 3 were divorced. Only 14 had any children at all and, in 2 of those cases, the children were grown and no longer dependents.[27]

This prosecutorial "indiscretion" in noncommercial cases slowed down only after 1932 when the Attorney General directed U.S. Attorneys to drop women as targets in noncommercial cases. As indicated in Figure 1, after *Gebardi*, women were committed in only five noncommercial cases; in three instances the man involved left behind a wife and children; in the fourth case the woman had an illegitimate child with the man; and in the fifth case, the couple were prosecuted for Mann Act violations only after they were apprehended for holding up a gas station. Women in group two—those women to whom prostitution was incidental to their interstate travels—were still being sent to prison but also in smaller numbers. Eighteen of the 25 in this group were convicted before *Gebardi*, while 7 were convicted following *Gebardi*.[28]

Across all 4 groups, the average age is 28 years with the most pronounced age cluster in the 24 to 30 year old bracket. This is a significant departure from the progressive era stereotype of prostitutes as girls whose youthfulness, naivete and inexperience with the world betrayed them. Also, extending across the entire sample, 107 (69%) were not living with a husband; the majority were separated or divorced. Significantly, few of the women had any dependent

41

TABLE 1a - DESCRIPTION OF MANN ACT VIOLATORS BY *NUMBER* AND GROUP FOR YEARS 1927-1937

Group	Marital Status[1] S	M	Div	Age 16-19	20-29	30+	Race W	Blk	Citizenship USA	Other	Education None-8th	9th+	IQ[2] 50-75	76+	Children[3] 0	1-2	3+	Prior[4] Convictions None	1+	Sentence (Yrs) 1-1½	2-5	Region Where[5] Prosecuted South	Midwest	Other
1(N=36)	11	9	16	15	14	7	35	1	36	0	32	4	25	11	22	8	6	33	3	28	8	27	7	2
2(N=25)	7	6	12	5	18	2	25	0	24	1	15	10	13	12	17	7	1	19	6	20	5	19	6	0
3(N=23)	7	7	9	2	19	2	22	1	23	0	16	7	17	6	22	1	0	16	7	18	5	17	3	3
4(N=72)	13	27	32	2	28	42	68	4	67	5	59	13	47	25	42	26	4	38	34	35	37	28	22	22
Total (N=156)	38	49	69	24	79	53	150	6	150	6	122	34	102	54	103	42	11	106	50	101	55	91	38	27

TABLE 1b - DESCRIPTION OF MANN ACT VIOLATORS BY *PERCENT* AND GROUP FOR YEARS 1927-1937

Group	Marital Status[1] S	M	Div	Age 16-19	20-29	30+	Race W	Blk	Citizenship USA	Other	Education None-8th	9th+	IQ[2] 50-75	76+	Children[3] 0	1-2	3+	Prior[4] Convictions None	1+	Sentence (Yrs) 1-1½	2-5	Region Where[5] Prosecuted South	Midwest	Other
1(N=36)	31	25	44	42	39	19	97	3	100	—	89	11	69	31	61	22	17	92	8	78	22	75	19	6
2(N=25)	28	24	48	20	72	8	100	—	96	4	60	40	52	48	68	28	4	76	24	80	20	76	24	—
3(N=23)	30	30	40	9	82	9	96	4	100	—	70	30	74	26	96	4	—	70	30	78	22	74	13	13
4(N=72)	18	38	44	3	39	58	94	6	93	7	82	18	65	35	58	36	6	53	47	49	51	38	31	31
Total (N=156)	24	31	45	15	51	34	96	4	96	4	79	21	65	35	66	27	7	68	32	65	35	58	24	17

1. Women separated and widowed were counted in divorced category.
2. Women whose IQ was too low to test were counted in 50-75 category.
3. Children were often not dependent on their mother at time of her arrest, i.e., grown-up, living with father, living with other relatives. The number of women with any dependent children included: Group 1-12. Group 2-6. Group 3-1. and Group 4-19.
4. Prior convictions were usually for such related offenses as prostitution, running a house of prostitution, liquor law violations, and vagrancy.
5. States counted in southern region: Alabama, Arkansas, Florida, Georgia, Louisiana, Mississippi, North Carolina, South Carolina, Tennessee, Texas, Virginia, and West Virginia. Midwestern states included: Illinois, Indiana, Iowa, Michigan, Minnesota, Missouri, Ohio, and Wisconsin.

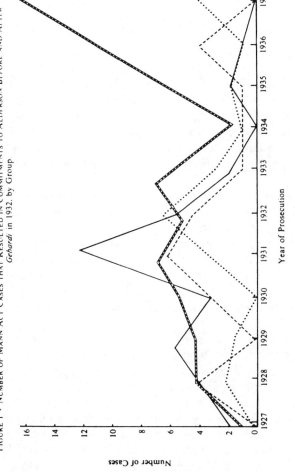

FIGURE 1 - NUMBER OF MANN ACT CASES THAT RESULTED IN COMMITMENTS TO ALDERSON BEFORE AND AFTER *Gebhardi* in 1932. by Group

——— Group 1 - No prostitution or commercial activity
------- Group 2 - Prostitution as incidental
·········· Group 3 - Commercial prostitution
▬▬▬▬ Group 4 - Madames and procurers

Year of Prosecution

Number of Cases

43

children. Of the total 156 women, only 38 had dependent children at the time of their arrest; aside from 9 with 3 or more dependents, 8 had 2 dependent children, and the remaining 21 had 1 dependent child. Almost all these women received low scores on the Binet Simon IQ test routinely administered by prison officials with 102 (65%) scoring below 76. Thirty-four (21%) went beyond the eighth grade in school.[29]

In contrast to the disproportionately black prison population in this country today, 150 (96%) of the women in the sample are white. Of the six black women, one became infatuated with a white fireman who took her from Montgomery, Alabama, to Columbus, Ohio, where they lived as man and wife until they were arrested. The second was the illegitimate daughter of a white prostitute mother and black father; she too became a prostitute to support her lover. The remaining four black women were madames—one was 63 years old.[30]

Despite the anxiety over "widespread prostitution by alien women," only six women were not U.S. citizens and of those, five were procurers. The sixth was a Mexican woman who most closely resembles the lawmakers stereotype of a "victim." The woman did not speak a word of English and was forced to commit acts of prostitution by her boyfriend, who held her captive by pocketing the money she earned and in return gave her gifts of inexpensive jewelry. Not only did this woman receive a prison sentence, she was also deported.[31]

Overall, the family histories of these women reveal deprived life experiences. Typically, the woman left home at an early age (i.e., 13 or 14) to enter a bad marriage or take on a menial job in the city. She sought to escape abusive parents who had forced her to quit school, or desolate rural surroundings. In many cases, her father or mother died when she was very young, and she had to take care of the surviving parent and a large number of even younger siblings. Most of these women were unskilled and had little education. They were, for the most part, law-abiding individuals. Only 16 women of a total of 84 in the first 3 groups had any prior convictions.[32] The following three case histories exemplify this pattern:

> When Leota's father became deputy sheriff in 1926, he began to drink liquor, deserted his family several times and repeatedly beat his wife and children. Leota's mother did washing, ironing and sewing in order to support herself and

the children. Leota made good grades and wanted to complete high school, but her father would not allow her to continue school after she was fourteen. Leota did the housework and took care of her younger brother and sister while her mother worked. Several times her father left the family without food and money and would be gone for weeks at a time. In 1928 he lost his position and took work now and then on the highway. He would come home at all hours and if supper was not ready, he would threaten to kill his wife. One night Leota heard her father threaten to kill her mother if she didn't get the salt shaker for him. After her mother got it, he threw his plate full of hot food at her. Leota ran to a neighbor's house and called the police who came and put her father in jail. When he was released on bond, he beat Leota and the other children everytime he came home from work. When Leota's sweetheart came and found her in tears, he begged her to marry him. She consented and left for Louisiana to get married since it took several days to get a license in Texas. Leota admits having immoral relations on the road. As soon as Leota's father learned that she was going to get married, he notified the police. She was arrested two weeks later.

Betty is the 7th of 15 children. Her childhood was very unhappy due to the family's poverty and her father's drinking liquor. Three siblings starved to death when they were infants. The father was never very ambitious and never provided a good home. Her parents and their five small children live in a one room shack and are considered "white trash." Betty finished the 5th grade and then ran away from home because her father was drunk and beat her often. She went to a tourist camp and worked for $10.00/week making beds and running errands. She sent this money to her mother and prostituted for her spending money. Betty has prostituted since she was 12 years of age. She was only 16 years old at the time of this arrest.

Ruby's mother died in childbirth when Ruby's father refused to call a doctor. He seemed repentant for a short while, then deserted the children. Ruby and her two young brothers shifted for themselves. Ruby had been going with a man by the name of Elmer. He was married, but separated from his wife and was expecting to divorce. After Ruby's father deserted the children, Ruby completed the 8th grade by living with Elmer's

45

mother and working for her room and board. Elmer asked her to take a trip with him to Stubenville, Ohio promising that they would be gone only a few days. His mother thought it was okay for Ruby to go. Ruby had immoral relations with Elmer and lived with him for several days. When Elmer's wife learned that Elmer had taken Ruby across the state line, she reported it to the F.B.I. and they were both arrested for Mann Act violations.

In sum, the evidence shows that the women committed to Alderson for Mann Act violations were neither the helpless, naive, exploited "white slaves" of the Progressive Era imagination nor the independent, economically sophisticated, self-determining women the *Holte* Court believed them to be. The truth is somewhere in between. In reality, the female "violators" of the Mann Act were "victims" of their own hard lives and the morals of the time.

THE PRESENT STATUS OF THE MANN ACT

Law enforcement authorities have become less enthusiastic about enforcing a law which has grown increasingly unpopular with changes in sexual mores over the years. The U.S. National Archives and Records Service has prepared a historical narrative of the White Slave Traffic Act, based on extensive review of F.B.I. headquarters records. The narrative reports that:

> In 1962 the Department of Justice prohibited U.S. Attorneys from prosecuting noncommercial cases without express approval of the Criminal Division. The F.B.I. followed suit relying on local authorities to handle routine cases and concentrating on "organized commercialized prostitution." It is currently a low priority in F.B.I. field offices.[33]

Nonetheless, men and women are still being sent to prison for Mann Act violations. According to federal prison system records, 439 defendants were committed to federal prisons between 1970 and 1982 for violations of the act, 35 of whom are women. Although a review of the records of all 35 women most recently convicted is beyond the scope of this paper, it is reasonable to assume from post-*Gebardi* trends that these women more closely resemble the violators whom Congress had in mind when the statute was enacted. While these women are more likely to be madames or procurers of other women for prostition, they are not any more likely than their predecessors to be part of an organized white slave ring. Moreover, even though the Mann Act has decreased in use as a penal law, Congress has breathed new life into it. In 1978 the act was amended to make the interstate transportation of minor boys for sexual purposes a crime.[34] Whether this recent expression of legislative intent to protect young males will result in the same kinds of distortions by courts and enforcement agencies remains to be seen.

REFERENCES

1. The White Slave Traffic Act, ch. 395, 36 Stat. 825 (1910) (codified as amended at 18 U.S.C. §§ 2421-2424 (1976 and Supp. V 1981), includes this provision: "That any person who shall knowingly transport or cause to be transported, or aid or assist in obtaining transportation for, or in transporting, in interstate or foreign commerce . . . any woman or girl for the purpose of prostitution or debauchery, or for any other immoral purpose, or with the intent and purpose to induce, entice, or compel such woman or girl to become a prostitute or to give herself up to debauchery, or to engage in any other immoral practice; . . . shall be deemed guilty of a felony, and upon conviction thereof shall be punished by a fine not exceeding five thousand dollars, or by imprisonment of not more than five years; or by both such fine and imprisonment, in the discretion of the court."

2. According to Vern and Bonnie Bullough, *Prostitution: An Illustrated Social History* (New York: Crown Publishers, Inc., 1978), p. 245, the term "White Slavery" is often attributed to Clifford G. Roe, an Assistant State's Attorney in Illinois and a leader in the fight against involuntary prostitution. Roe supposedly used the term at the beginning of the twentieth century when he became involved in a case in which a girl had thrown a note from a house of prostitution. She had written: "Help me—I am held captive as a white slave." The incident may have occurred, but the term predated Roe's use. The term also comes from the English translation of the French term, "Traite des Blanches," trade in whites, used in Paris in 1902 at a conference of 15 European nations to discuss the problem of international trade in women and children. At an earlier international conference on the Negro slave trade, the French had used the phrase "Traite des Noires," trade in blacks, and the reference to white trade was used to contrast the later conference with the earlier one. The British Government translated the French term as "White Slave Traffic or Trade," and in the United States, this translation was usually abbreviated to "White Slavery."

3. E. Feldman, "Prostitution, the Alien Woman and the Progressive Imagination," *American Quarterly* 19 Summer (1967) 2, part I: 200, reports that between 1890 and 1900 the *Reader's Guide to Periodical Literature* lists 36 entries under the separate subject of "Prostitution"; between the years 1910 and 1914 entries climbed sharply to 156 and then dropped to 41, 1915-1924.

4. Alan Block, "Aw! Your Mother's in the Mafia: Women Criminals in Progressive New York," in *The Criminology of Deviant Women*, ed. Freda Adler and Rita Simon (Boston: Houghton, Mifflin, 1979), p. 180.

5. On December 10, 1909, the immigration commissioner made a personal appearance before Congress to testify about the prosecutions initiated by immigration agents against pimps and procurers. In his introduction the Commissioner referred to the importing and harboring of alien women and girls for immoral purposes and the practice of prostitution or the

so-called "white slave traffic" as the most pitiful and revolting phase of the immigration problem. The commissioner painted a lurid picture of the capture of young girls who were subsequently forced into lives of squalor and prostitution.

Eleven days after the commissioner's testimony, Representative Mann reported from committee the bill that Congress subsequently enacted as the White Slave Traffic Act. The purpose of the bill as stated in the House report includes the following: "[The Act] does not attempt to regulate the practice of voluntary prostitution, but aims solely to prevent panders and procurers from compelling thousands of women and girls against their will and desire to enter and continue in a life of prostitution." Representative Mann defined the term "white slave" to include "only those women and girls who are literally slaves—those women who are owned and held as property and chattels. . . those women and girls who, if given a fair chance, would, in all human probability, have been good wives and mothers and useful citizens."

6. Representative Mann emphasized that the intent of Congress was "not to interfere with or usurp in any way the police powers of the states." He stated that "the punishment of the practice of prostitution or the keeping of houses of ill-fame, or other immoral places, in the several states, are matters wholly within the powers of the states. . . . " This distinction made by Representative Mann between the aims of the act and "ordinary prostitution" was an important one. Power to enact this legislation was derived from the commerce clause and extended only to interstate criminal activity. Mann and others justified this early interstate crime by analogizing the transportation of women (who, if the rhetoric is to be taken at face value, were viewed as passive, nonvolitional victims) to the interstate transportation of goods for commercial purposes.

7. 242 U.S. 470, 485 (1917). Factors unique to the circumstances of *Caminetti* may have led to the prosecution and conviction of the defendants. First, the interstate weekend was not a casual affair, but rather the culmination of the seduction of two young women, aged 19 and 20, by married men in a situation not entirely free from coercion. The men had apparently concealed their marital and parental status from the women. When the women discovered the truth, the men allegedly induced the women to take the trip to Reno by telling them that their wives would prosecute them in the juvenile court if they were found out. Second, the case had political overtones. Representative Mann and his Republican colleagues were eager to direct national attention to the fact that one of the seducers was Drew Caminetti, the son of the Democratic commissioner of immigration.

8. 329 U.S. 14 (1946).

9. *Athanasaw* v. *United States*, 227 U.S. 326 (1913).

10. *Carey* v. *United States*, 265 F. 515 (8th Cir. 1920).

11. *Jarabo* v. *United States*, 158 F.2d 509 (1st Cir. 1946).

12. *MacKreth* v. *United States*, 103 F.2d 495 (5th Cir. 1939).

13. *United States* v. *Holte*, 236 U.S. 140 (1915); *Diggs* v. *United States*, 220 F. 545 (1915).

14. *Holte* at 145 (emphasis added).

15. 287 U.S. 112 (1932). The *Gebardi* Court left open the question of just how much activity over and above mere acquiescence would bring the woman's conduct within the ban of the statute.

16. William Seagle, "The Twilight of the Mann Act," 55 *American Bar Association Journal* 643 (1969).

17. U.S., Department of Justice Circular No. 647, issued January 26, 1917. From the beginning, the department has advised district attorneys: "As to specific cases, the Department must rely upon the discretion of the District Attorneys who have firsthand knowledge of the facts, and opportunity for personal interviews with the witnesses, and who will thus be able to ascertain what circumstances of aggravation, if any, attend the offense, the age and relative interest of the parties, the motives of those urging prosecution, and what reasons, if any, exist for thinking the ends of justice will be better served by a prosecution under Federal law than under the laws of the State having jurisdiction."

18. 1939 and 1940 are the only years for which conviction statistics contain a breakdown

of defendants and victims by both age and sex and whether commercial activity was involved. Fiscal year 1939 data show that out of a total of 425 cases, 88 did not involve commercial interstate activity. In 1940, the total cases numbered 415, of which 106 were not commercial interstate situations.

19. U.S., Department of Justice Circular No. 647, issued January 26, 1917.

20. For example, U.S., Department of Justice Circular No. 986, issued August 5, 1919; U.S., Department of Justice Circular No. 2027, issued April 19, 1929.

21. F.B.I. Policy Memorandum No. 66-6200-31 issued September 15, 1949, and titled "Policy and Procedure: White Slave Traffic Act," p. 10.

22. *Ibid*. at 41.

23. U.S., Department of Justice Circular No. 2347, issued December 14, 1932.

24. With regard to convictions of women F.B.I. data show that in fiscal year 1939 of a total of 429 defendants *committed* for commercial trafficking, 93 were female; out of 88 defendants *committed* where there was no evidence of commercialism, 6 were women. In 1949, of the 357 defendants *committed* for commercial trafficking, 49 were female, and out of 106 defendants committed where there was no commercialism, none were female. No sex comparison data is available for the years prior to the *Gebardi* decision.

25. This particular 10-year span was selected because of the special interest in noting the after-effects of the 1932 *Gebardi* case on subsequent convictions of women. There were a total of 179 Mann Act commitments to Alderson during this period. Twenty-three records were unavailable (i.e., missing or incomplete); therefore the study deals with the 156 cases for which information is available.

26. Although this information is self-reported, there are two checks on accuracy. First, the inmate had already been sentenced and was incarcerated and therefore had little to gain by being untruthful to institutional social workers. Second, the information reported was corroborated by a description of the circumstances of the offense completed by the prosecuting official and included in the inmate's file for later determination of parole eligibility.

27. U.S., National Archives, Department of Justice, Bureau of Prisons, Record Group Number 129, Alderson Inmate Case Files, 1927-1940.

28. *Ibid*.

29. *Ibid*.

30. *Ibid*.

31. *Ibid*.

32. *Ibid*.

33. Brief for Plaintiff at Appendix X, Vol. II, Category 31, n.p., *American Friends Service* v. *Webster*, No. 79-1655 (D.D.C., Appendix filed Jan. 8, 1982). This appendix is an appraisal of the records of the F.B.I. submitted to the court by the National Archives and Records Service.

34. Pub. L. No. 95-225, § 3, 92 Stat. 7, 8-9 (1978) (codified at 18 U.S.C. § 2423 (1982)).

New York State's Prostitution Statute: Case Study of the Discriminatory Application of a Gender Neutral Law

Frances P. Bernat

ABSTRACT. In 1978, New York State upgraded its "patronizing a prostitute" statute from a violation to a misdemeanor offense. It was expected that upgrading the law would accomplish essentially two goals: deter prostitution by giving the police incentive to arrest patrons, and end the disparity that existed between the prostitution and patronizing statutes, as prostitution had been a misdemeanor offense since 1969. These goals were not accomplished. An analysis of prostitution arrest information from Buffalo, New York, for the years 1977 through 1980, shows that the Buffalo city police arrest practices did not change despite the 1978 reform of the prostitution statute. In particular, women continued to be singled out for prostitution arrests more often than men. In addition, despite constitutional prohibition of gender based discrimination, New York State courts have not been persuaded to find unconstitutional the differential enforcement practices of the prostitution statute. One Buffalo criminal court, for example, approved gender based discrimination on the basis of insufficient police staffing. The end result was that while the new statute was to be gender neutral, the application of the law was not; police nonenforcement of patron activity perpetuated discrimination against women.

PART I: INTRODUCTION

Prostitution is a crime in almost every area of the United States,[1] and will most likely continue to be criminalized. In New York State, prostitution constitutes an offense when a "person engages or agrees or offers to engage in sexual conduct with another person in

Frances P. Bernat, J.D., is Assistant Professor of Political Science, Criminal Justice Program, Washington, State University at Pullman, 99164-4880. Special thanks are extended to Ms. Lee Gagnon, Director of the Buffalo City Court Records Room, who provided me with access to the records utilized in this study.

return for a fee.''[2] Both women and men can be, and have been, arrested for prostitution. In addition to proscribing prostitution, New York State also prohibits patronizing a prostitute;[3] patronizing constitutes an offense when a person engages or agrees or offers to engage in sexual conduct with another person, or a third party, in return for paying a fee.[4]

Reform of the prostitution statute occurred in 1967, 1969 and 1978. The reforms were designed to penalize prostitution and patronizing in order to deter prostitution.

Prior to September 1, 1967, prostitution and patronizing a prostitute were incorporated into the vagrancy statute as violations, or noncriminal offenses. At that time, vagrancy was punishable by a sentence of up to six months of imprisonment.[5] Subsequently, following a penal law revision in 1967, both prostitution and patronizing were separately classified as violations, punishable by a maximum of 15 days imprisonment.[6]

For the next one and one/half years, law enforcement officials and prosecutors intensively lobbied the state legislature to reform the prostitution law.[7] The lobbying efforts focused on increasing penalties for prostitution, not patronizing. Lobbyists argued that if prostitution was not criminalized as a class A misdemeanor, the most serious misdemeanor offense, prostitution would run rampant in the large cities within the state and that the statute would have little deterrent effect.[8] However, the penal law review committee, the New York State's Senate Committee on Codes, decided otherwise. In 1969, the legislature made prostitution a class B misdemeanor for three reasons:

> First, the Committee believed that the Penal Law Commission's decision to make prostitution a violation had been well-considered and that the Law had been in effect too short a time for any group to be able to evaluate its effectiveness. Second, the Committee feared that giving prostitutes one year sentences would overcrowd the jails. Third, the senators on the Committee did not believe that the act of prostitution warranted a one year jail sentence.[9]

With respect to patronizing, lobbyists did not argue against proscribing patronizing as a violation.[10] On September 1, 1969, prostitution was made a class B misdemeanor,[11] while patronizing a prostitute remained as a violation.[12] As a result, prostitutes faced a maximum of three months imprisonment[13] while patrons faced a maximum of 15 days imprisonment.[14] Prostitutes were imprisoned for a longer period of time than patrons for essentially the same conduct.

During the years after the 1969 penal law reform, great pressure was brought on the New York State legislature by women's groups seeking to end the disparity in penalties between the prostitute and patron. It was asserted that the disparity existed between females and males because mostly females were arrested and, therefore, subjected to the harsher penalties of the prostitution statute. Almost a decade later, the legislature, responding to the pressure, reformed the law proscribing patron activity. On September 1, 1978, patronizing was upgraded from a violation to a class B misdemeanor.[15] In addition, the legislature enacted several other penal code sections which were designed to progressively increase the severity of the patron offense when young prostitutes were patronized.[16] In general, however, the statutory reform was designed to provide the same penalties for prostitution and for patronizing.

Since patronizing a prostitute is a crime, the 1978 reform of the patronizing law might have given law enforcement officials the incentive to arrest patrons as well as prostitutes to curb prostitution. This paper focuses on the 1978 criminal law revision of the prostitution statute to ascertain whether the objectives of the reform reflected the actual results of the reform. Specifically, this paper will analyze the legal parameters of prostitution and patronizing activity, and the distinctions made between conduct committed by females and that committed by males. It is expected that despite the statutory change in 1978, law enforcement officers did not alter their arrest practices and continued to arrest female prostitutes more often than male patrons. I argue that such an enforcement practice is unconstitutional. This study addresses law enforcement of the prostitution statute in Buffalo, New York, for the years 1977, 1978, 1979 and 1980.[17] Buffalo was selected as the location of the study for three reasons. First, it is the second largest urban area in New York State. Second, arrest records were available. Finally, there were court challenges to the constitutionality of the prostitution statute and its enforcement. Besides the data collected, court decisions which focused on the issue of selective enforcement of the prostitution statute will be analyzed.

PART II: BUFFALO LAW ENFORCEMENT OF THE NEW YORK STATE PROSTITUTION STATUTE

Over the past few years, the judicial system in New York State has been asked to determine the constitutionality of the state's enforcement practice of its prostitution laws. A state's enforcement practice is unconstitutional if it violates equal protection principles.[18] To show an unconstitutional enforcement practice, such as selective enforcement of a law, a criminal defendant must prove that: 1) the statute was not applied to others who were similarly situated with the defendant; and 2) the enforcement practice was based on impermissable criteria.[19] When alleging selective enforcement, part of the defendant's burden of proof within the first criteria of such an allegation is to prove that "conscious, intentional discrimination" exists.[20] Intentional discrimination against a particular group may be shown by statistical evidence "of a grossly disproportionate incidence of nonenforcement against others similarly situated. . . ."[21] As indicated above, this paper focuses on the arrest practices in Buffalo, New York, after the 1978 reform equalized the penalties, to determine if the statute was selectively enforced against prostitutes as opposed to patrons. Two categories of persons arrested for prostitution activity will be discussed: female prostitute arrestees and male patron arrestees.

An analysis of whether the Buffalo police selectively enforced the prostitution statute must concentrate on the differences, if any, between females arrested for prostitution and males arrested for patronizing, rather than between females and males arrested for prostitution. This is because a very small number of male prostitutes "work the streets," while there are larger numbers of female prostitutes and male patrons.[22] A conservative estimate of the number of prostitute to patron arrestees should be one to three, because it is estimated that prostitutes could generally service three customers each night. This estimate was obtained by looking at the number of arrests of males for patronizing made by Buffalo's vice squad on nights when the squad performed "Operation Johnny." "Operation Johnny" was a police undercover operation. A female police officer posed as a prostitute to effectuate the arrest of potential patrons of prostitutes. From 1977 through 1980, two or three female decoy officers were staked out for two or three hours a night about once a month. Despite the limited amount of time put into "Operation Johnny" by the Buffalo vice squad, the female officers were each able to arrest about three customers each night. In fact, almost all the arrests of patrons in Buffalo, from 1977 through 1980, occurred during the vice squad's "Operation Johnny."

When the nature of prostitution is considered, we should expect to find more patrons than prostitutes. Prostitutes service areas where the greatest number of patrons are likely to be located. Their objective is to service a patron quickly, return to the street and quickly attract another customer. This objective is motivated by both the need to make money and the desire not to be arrested for loitering.

As Table 1 shows, between 1977 and 1980, the majority of those arrested under the prostitution statute were women. Women prostitutes comprised 72.08% of the arrests in 1977, 76.90% in 1978, 81.54% in 1979, and 75.62% in 1980.[23] Male patrons comprised 22.84% of the arrests in 1977, 12.87% in 1978, 7.71% in 1979, and 14.69% in 1980. Overall, from 1977 through 1980, female prostitute arrestees comprised 77.39% of the arrests for prostitution activity. Male patron arrestees comprised 13.13% of the arrests in Buffalo between 1977 and 1980. These figures show that the Buffalo police focused their enforcement of the sex neutral prostitution statute primarily against women.

Even these figures may be a faulty indicator of the actual arrest percentage difference between female prostitute arrestees and male

TABLE 1

NUMBER AND PERCENT OF ARRESTS FOR PROSTITUTION ACTIVITY
IN BUFFALO, NEW YORK (BY SEX AND YEAR) *

Year	Female Prostitution (NYPL §230.00)		Male Prostitution (NYPL §230.00)		Male Patronizing a Prostitute (NYPL §230.00)		Total
	N	%	N	%	N	%	N
1977	142	72.08	10	5.08	45	22.84	197
1978	263	76.90	35	10.23	44	12.87	342
1979	349	81.54	46	10.75	33	7.71	428
1980	242	75.26	31	9.69	47	14.69	320
Total	996	77.39	122	9.48	169	13.13	1287

Source: Buffalo Police Department Cell Block and City Court Record Sheets: 1977-1980.
*Female Patrons, 0 throughout.

patron arrestees because the police in Buffalo also arrested persons for "loitering for the purposes of prostitution."[24] A person may be arrested for "loitering for the purposes of prostitution" if that person "remains or wanders about in a public place and repeatedly beckons to, or repeatedly stops, or repeatedly attempts to stop motor vehicles, or repeatedly interferes with the free passage of other persons, for the purpose of prostitution, or of patronizing a prostitute. . ."[25] An analysis of persons arrested for prostitution offenses, together with persons arrested for the "loitering" offense would provide a better indication of the differences between the percentage of women as compared to men who were arrested for prostitution activity. The combination of arrest statistics would show whether women were singled out for prostitution arrests regardless of the form—prostitution or loitering—taken by the prostitution activity. (Table 2.)

TABLE 2

NUMBER AND PERCENT OF COMBINED ARRESTS FOR PROSTITUTION ACTIVITY AND
LOITERING FOR THE PURPOSES OF PROSTITUTION
IN BUFFALO, NEW YORK (BY SEX AND YEAR)

Year	Female Prostitution and Female Loitering for the Purposes of Prostitution (N.Y.P.L $$230.00, 240.37)		Male Patronizing a Prostitute and Male Loitering for the Purposes of Prostitution* (N.Y.P.L. $$230.03, 240.37)		Total
	N	%	N	%	N
1977	355	84.52	65	15.48	420
1978	626	86.58	97	13.42	723
1979	583	90.67	60	9.33	643
1980	357	84.20	67	15.80	424
Total	1921	86.92	289	13.08	2210

Source: Buffalo Police Department Cell Block and City Court Record Sheets: 1977-1980.

*The number of male patrons is overestimated because the loitering arrests ($240.37) listed on the Cell Block Sheets make no indication whether the male was engaging in patron or prostitution activity. Since females were not arrested for patron activity during the period studies, it is assumed that the loitering females were arrested for prostitution activity rather than patron activity.

Arrest figures show that women were arrested for the combined offenses of prostitution and loitering 84.52% of the time in 1977, 86.58% of the time in 1978, 90.67% of the time in 1979, and 84.20% of the time in 1980. In contrast, the arrest figures show that male patrons were arrested for combined activities of patronizing and loitering 15.48% of the time in 1977, 13.42% of the time in 1978, 9.33% of the time in 1979, and 15.80% of the time in 1980.[27] Overall, we can see that women comprised 86.92% of the combined offense arrests, while men comprised 13.08% of such arrests between 1977 and 1980. Once again, despite the fact there are believed to be greater numbers of patrons than prostitutes, prostitution laws were almost always enforced against women rather than men.

All the above findings are disturbing. They show a disproportionate percentage of women arrested for prostitution activity, and also that the new patron statute did not alter enforcement practices of the police. When police resources are scarce, as they were in Buffalo, concentration on criminal activity takes precedence over noncriminal activity. After the promulgation of the upgraded patron statute in 1978, one might have expected to find an increase in the proportion of men arrested for patronizing, because police would have had more incentive to arrest patrons for a crime than for a violation.[28] This expectation proved incorrect. Instead, the percentage of men arrested for patronizing in 1978 and 1979 decreased from 1977, while the percentage of women arrested for prostitution increased for the same period.

The increased arrests for patrons in 1980 is misleading for two reasons: 1) during the summer of 1980, when enforcement of the prostitution statute was constitutionally challenged in Buffalo City Court in *People* v *Burton*[29] pressure was placed on Buffalo police to enforce the patron law; and 2) during the end of 1980, the Buffalo police overall instituted a work slow-down which appears to have affected the number of arrests for female prostitution throughout the last months of the year.

In the *Burton* case, Burton, a criminal defendant, was arrested for "loitering for the purposes of prostitution." Her patron was not arrested. The court in *People* v *Burton*, 1980, was asked to determine whether the Buffalo police were selectively enforcing the prostitution statute against women, despite reform of the law proscribing patron activity. In June 1980, the court held a hearing on the selective enforcement issue. In addition to the factual circumstances sur-

57

rounding her arrest, Burton presented statistical evidence of the disproportionate number and percentage of women arrested for prostitution and for "loitering for the purposes of prostitution" in Buffalo from 1977 through June 1980.[30] On September 12, 1980, the *Burton* court handed down its decision, holding the unequal enforcement of the statute to be constitutional.[31]

To determine if the hearing placed pressure on local enforcement of the prostitution statute, one must review the number of arrests for patronizing a prostitute. The patron arrest data reveals that of a total of 47 men arrested in the year 1980, 31 of these arrests (66%) occurred between June and September, the time period when the local criminal court in Buffalo was conducting its hearing and decided the selective enforcement issue. It is, therefore, conceivable that the court case placed immediate pressure on the police to maintain a high number of patronizing arrests.

Also, during the last few months of 1980, an internal dispute arose between police officers and the Buffalo Police Department and city. The police officers' contract with the city was under negotiation. Unhappy with the way labor negotiations were progressing, officers instituted a work slow-down. The slow-down resulted in fewer women arrested for prostitution during the last quarter, September through December, of 1980. If we compare the number of arrests of female prostitutes during September through December for each of the years discussed in this paper, 1977 - 1980, we find that significantly fewer women were arrested during the work slow-down time period in 1980. Specifically, in 1977, 68 women were arrested for prostitution in the September through December time period, 97 women in 1978, 91 women in 1979, and 47 women in 1980. Had the slow-down not occurred, one would have expected that the pattern of the previous three years would continue and more women, possibly twice as many, would have been arrested during the last quarter of 1980.

The slow-down did not effect the number of men arrested for patronizing during the last quarter of 1980. Specifically, in 1977, 45 men (all of the patron arrests for 1977) were arrested for patronizing in the September through December time period, 16 men in 1978, 10 men in 1979, and 12 men in 1980. With the exception of 1977, the number of arrests remained more or less constant. Arguably, the *Burton* case might have effected the number of patron arrests during the last quarter of 1980. As indicated above, the Buffalo police effectuated most of their arrests in 1980 during the June through

September time period. However, even if the number of arrests for patronizing during the last quarter of each year studied excluded the month of September, the police went about their business as usual. Specifically, in 1977, 17 men were arrested for patronizing in the October through December time period, 4 men in 1978, 1 man in 1979, and 1 man in 1980. Again, with the exception of 1977, the number of arrests for patronizing remained more or less constant.

In light of these two factors, the court case and the police work slow-down, the percentage of women as compared to men arrested under the prostitution statute in 1980 should be viewed as an anomaly, since both operated to inflate the percentage of males arrested for patronizing while deflating the percentage of females arrested for prostitution.

If the differences between the number and percentage of prostitution and patronizing arrests are to be compared by a court which has been asked to determine the constitutionality of the state's enforcement practice, the court must determine, or acknowledge, that prostitutes and patrons are similarly situated groups. If the groups are not similarly situated, then further constitutional review would be inappropriate, regardless of any statistical difference between the two groups' arrest rates. While the court in *People* v *Burton*, 1980, did not explicitly indicate that the two groups, prostitutes and patrons, were similarly situated, the court did allow a pre-trial hearing on the issue of selective enforcement of the prostitution statute against females and did compare the difference in arrest practices by the Buffalo police in regard to prostitutes and patrons. In addition, the court analyzed whether the state's reasons for the gross disparity between the percentage of prostitute and patron arrests were "good and sufficient."[32] Because such an analysis can occur only after the state has had an opportunity to rebut proof presented by a defendant in support of her/his claim, the court in *Burton* tacitly acknowledged that the categories are comparable.

Another criminal court in Syracuse, New York, explicitly held in 1980 in *People* v *Nelson*[33] that prostitutes and patrons are similarly situated groups. This holding, as to whether prostitutes can be compared with patrons by a court determining if there is unconstitutional enforcement of the prostitute statute, should have put to rest the issue of the statute's sections comparability; but, both the *Burton*, 1980, and *Nelson*, 1980, decisions can be contrasted with a New York appellate court decision, *In re Dora P.*,[34] 1979. In *In re Dora P.*, the court ruled that equal protection was not violated by the selective enforcement practices of the New York City police because the prostitution statute delineated the offense of prostitution and patronizing into two separate sections, N.Y.P.L. §230.00 and §230.03, respectively. The court, in *In re Dora P.*, held that two "separate crimes" could not be compared when an individual is alleging disparate treatment because the crimes require "separate acts. . . to affect their commission."[35] Local criminal courts in Buffalo are not required to follow the opinion in *In re Dora P.*, as it was not decided by the appellate division reviewing lower court decisions from Western New York. In 1981, however, a Buffalo criminal court adopted the analysis found in *In re Dora P.* and also held that prostitutes and patrons are not similarly situated persons.[36]

The court in *In re Dora P.* appears to argue that since two separate sections for prostitution and patronizing are provided by the prostitution law, they are not comparable. Yet, the "loitering for the purposes of prostitution" statute, defined above, does not separate the activity of patrons and prostitutes, as both acts are proscribed within a single statutory section. If the appellate court's concerns in *In re Dora P.* were appropriate or correct, then proscription of patronizing and prostitution could not be contained together within the single section of the loitering statute. Therefore, it is possible that the prostitution and patronizing sections of the prostitution statute could have been contained within a single statutory section, as the state legislature designed the loitering statute,[38] and may be comparable in a constitutional review.

To determine whether the two classes of people, prostitutes and patrons, are similarly situated, an understanding of the two sections of the prostitution statute is essential. Perhaps the only rational consideration for finding that the two sections are not comparable would be that the sections are dissimilar because they have different purposes and proscribe different acts. Historically, the New York legislature has repeatedly indicated that the purpose of proscribing prostitution and patronizing is to deter prostitution activity by reaching both the source, prostitutes, and the demand, patrons.

The issue as to whether the sections proscribe the same acts is much more difficult to answer. As argued above, the mere fact that the statute has separate sections does not necessarily mean that the sections are not comparable. Common sense indicates that while the prostitute and patron have different roles to be carried out when committing prostitution, the nature of the activity, commercial sex, is the same. The court in *People* v *Nelson*, 1980, specifically found that:

> The court in *Matter of Dora P.* also based its conclusion on its consideration of the "separate acts necessary to effect their commission," but did not mention what those separate acts were. If we compare §230.00 (prostitution) with §230.02 (patronizing a prostitute; definitions), we find that the only significant difference in the proscribed behavior is that the prostitute sells sex and the patron buys it. Neither gender nor solicitation is a differentiating factor.[37]

While a differentiation between the responsibilities and liabilities of sellers and buyers may occur when analyzing some crimes, the distinction is not easily made in regard to "sellers" and "buyers" of prostitution. For example, criminal liability usually falls heavier on sellers of narcotics than buyers because the seller is perceived to constitute a greater threat to the community. However, the New York legislature upgraded the patron law to acknowledge that patrons and prostitutes present similar, or the same, threats to the community. Prostitution activity by patrons and prostitutes may interfere with the free flow of traffic, or may involve the harassment of persons who are not prostitutes or their patrons. Because the activity of patrons and prostitutes might be described as a joint commercial venture with comparable or the same community consequences, such groups may be similarly situated.

By showing that the police in Buffalo were disproportionately arresting women for prostitution, and that prostitutes and patrons may be similarly situated groups, a case for gender based discrimination can be made. If the state cannot justify its enforcement practice, then such a practice is unconstitutional. In gender based discrimination situations, the state must prove that the enforcement practice bears a fair and *substantial relationship*, which is in the public interest, to an important state objective.[39] The heightened scrutiny test is the middle-tier of equal protection doctrine and makes it difficult for a state to justify semi-suspect classifications based on gender groups.

In *People* v *Burton*, 1980, the Buffalo court's findings of fact and law appear to be logical and just by balancing the defendant's allegation of discrimination with the state's reasons for its existence.

However, in constitutional analysis, the court did not utilize the substantial relationship test. Instead, the court considered whether the state had "good and sufficient reasons" for the unequal treatment of women.[41] In this regard, the *Burton* court specifically found:

> For one thing, the Buffalo Police Department is short of manpower in general, laboring under budgetary restrictions, which cannot be easily corrected, since they are due to a shrinking tax base and other problems common to older cities. For another, the police department is guilty of engaging in discriminatory hiring practices of women in the past, it has very few women on its force, and it is now under a federal court mandate to increase the number of women in the force. Therefore, when police decoys are needed (to arrest patrons of prostitutes), they must be obtained from other bureaus in the department outside the vice squad because they do not mesh with the other related duties of this squad, such as the prosecution of male prostitution, and of gambling and liquor law violations. Also, the use of police decoys requires additional manpower because the policewomen have to be guarded from prostitutes on the street where they are staked out and they must have additional back-up support to arrest sometimes panicky "Johns." For these reasons, police decoys are not as readily employed against male customers as male decoys or officers are against female prostitutes. For these reasons and others, it is more efficient to use police manpower to arrest female prostitutes than their male customers.[42]

The police enforcement practice of the state's prostitution statute was upheld in *Burton*, at least for the time being,[43] because of staffing problems. These practices were not found unconstitutional on the basis of gender discrimination.

A "good and sufficient reasons" test of constitutionality is a less strict standard of review than the substantial relationship test applied to cases of racial discrimination. A careful analysis of the *Burton* court's rationale for its decision would indicate that the court's reasons would not withstand the heightened scrutiny test.

The city's budgetary problems resulted in "manpower" shortages on the police force. In economically hard times, a police department has to effectively allocate its funds and resources so that the greater number of persons who commit crimes are apprehended. Which offenders the police should focus attention upon, prostitutes or patrons, is not easily answered. Prostitutes repeatedly return to the streets to service patrons, even after they are arrested and released on bail or bond. Because patrons do not return to the streets after they engaged the services of a prostitute, or are arrested, the choice might be to arrest the female. However, time and again, it has been found that police attempts to "sweep the streets" of prostitution by arresting prostitutes did not stop or deter prostitution.[44] Such police crackdowns only served to move prostitution to other locations in a city. The legislature, by enacting the patron law, has acknowledged that by attacking the demand, patronizing, cities might be better able to stop or deter prostitution. Simply stated, if there is no demand, there is no service. The patron law, as indicated above, is designed to give police incentive to arrest males in the battle against prostitution. If a male knows that police are arresting patrons, he might not want to risk the consequences stemming from an arrest. These consequences might be more than punishment for commission of a crime. In Buffalo during "Operation Johnny," for example, the names of patrons were published in local newspapers. Since males arrested for patron activity are usually white, middle class family men, it was hoped that men would not patronize prostitutes if they knew they, or their families, might be subject to public ridicule.[45]

The *Burton* court indicated that as a result of "manpower" shortages, difficulties arose in assigning female officers to the vice squad. These difficulties, according to the court, were due to employment discrimination in hiring practices, the inability of female officers to "mesh" with other vice squad duties, and the need for back-up support for female officers. These justifications stem from "archaic and overbroad" generalizations about the capabilities of women who perform police work. The equal protection clause is designed to curtail misconceptions "concerning females in the home rather than in the 'marketplace and world of ideas.' "[46]

Studies of the history of women in policing have shown that substantial discrimination did not end as more women were hired into the police ranks. For example, according to Clarice Feinman:

> In departments containing more than one precinct, women have to prove themselves over and over again in each precinct

to which they are assigned. . . Because there are so few
women in each department, women tend to be transferred
from one tour of duty or special assignment or precinct to another more frequently than men. Each time a woman is transferred she again has to go through the lonely process of proving her ability by working harder than men.[47]

Any temporary assignment of women for decoys to the vice squad,
operated as a continual prohibitive factor to the acceptance of
women on the squad. Women officers would be continually thought
unable to fit into vice squad work, even if they were capable of performing these duties. Further, most male officers work with partners and, in Buffalo, vice squad officers working undercover as a
"lone" patron in a car almost always have another officer waiting
nearby to aid in the effectuation of the arrest. While some patrons do
become "panicky," so, too, do some prostitutes. This back-up support for male decoy officers does not solve the problem of alleged
"manpower" shortages. In addition, policewomen assigned to a
decoy operation when one police department began a crackdown on
prostitution in 1974 were physically able to defend themselves and
effectuate arrests without any help.[48] Of more crucial importance,
the *Burton* court's analysis appears to state that existing conditions,
sexual discrimination against female police officers, justified the
discrimination against another group of women, prostitutes.

As the court's scrutiny is intended to prevent the perpetuation of
gender discrimination, courts should not allow a state's law enforcement practices to perpetuate it. A finding that "manpower" problems justified the disparity in arrests between women and men
(prostitutes and patrons) should not be upheld.

PART III: CONCLUSION

In New York State, prostitution and patronizing a prostitute are
crimes of equal severity, class B misdemeanors. Prior to September, 1978, patronizing was a non-criminal offense, a violation; prostitution has been a crime since 1969. In 1978, the state legislature
upgraded the patron offense: Both prostitutes and patrons of prostitutes were to be treated alike by state enforcement officials in efforts
to deter prostitution. This paper has analyzed whether enforcement
of the New York State prostitution statute in one major city, Buffalo, was selective despite reform of the prostitution statute.

This inquiry consisted of analysis of two issues: whether the enforcement practice was selective, and whether the enforcement practice was based upon an impermissable criterion, gender. An enforcement practice may be constitutionally impermissible if it intentionally treats similar situated groups differently. It has been shown that a disproportionate percentage of women, as compared to men, were arrested for prostitution. If the party alleging selective enforcement does not prove intentional discrimination, then the state practice would presumably be found constitutional. Additionally, it was argued that prostitutes and patrons are similarly situated groups because the two sections of the prostitution statute have the same purpose and proscribe the same acts.

Gender is a classification that will receive heightened scrutiny if harmful gender based discrimination has been alleged. To date, no New York court has utilized the appropriate test when determining if the state's prostitution enforcement practice has been constitutional. A state practice based on gender must bear a fair and substantial relationship to a legitimate state interest, and must be in the public interest. Once intentional discrimination is proved, such a test can make it difficult for a state to defend selective enforcement practices. The state's argument that it has "manpower" problems hindering its enforcement in Buffalo of the prostitution statute seems unlikely to pass constitutional muster. The Buffalo police were basically operating as if the old patron law were in effect. Regardless of increased incentive to arrest persons committing a criminal offense, as opposed to those engaging in noncriminal behavior, the Buffalo police concentrated arrest efforts on females, the prostitutes. Because in *Burton* the Buffalo City Court did not hold unconstitutional the selective enforcement practice, gender based discrimination was perpetuated. Women were thereby placed in a double bind. Because there was discrimination in hiring women onto the police force and no women were assigned to the vice squad, the police were allowed to focus their arrests on female prostitution. Although there was a gender neutral prostitution statute in New York State, there was no gender neutral enforcement of the statute. Because selective enforcement of the prostitution statute kept women in a vulnerable position, a continued assessment of prostitution arrest practices by the police in Buffalo, or elsewhere, is essential. Although Buffalo is the only city in New York State where prostitution arrest data have been collected,[49] similar enforcement practices may exist in other cities. The objective of penal law reform may be to end past inequities, but deeply ingrained practices of gender based discrimination are difficult to curtail.

REFERENCES

1. The State of Nevada allows prostitution in unincorporated areas (less than 200,000 population). Nev. Rev. Stats. §269.175 (1979).

2. N.Y.P.L. §230.00 (McKinney 1980).

3. N.Y.P.L. §§230.03, 230.04, 230.05, 230.06 (McKinney 1980).

4. N.Y.P.L. §230.02 (McKinney 1980)

5. Former Code of Criminal Procedure §887(4) (McKinney Practice Commentary, N.Y.P.L. §230.00, 1980); *People* v *Bailey*, 432 N.Y.S. 2d 789 (N.Y. City Crim. Ct., 1980).

6. N.Y.P.L. §230.00 (McKinney Practice Commentary 1980).

7. Pamela Roby, "Politics and Criminal Law: Revision of the New York State Penal Law and Prostitution," *Social Problems* 17 (Summer 1969): 102-03.

8. N.Y.P.L. §230.00 (McKinney Practice Commentary 1980).

9. Roby, "Politics and the Criminal Law," p. 103.

10. Ibid., p. 101.

11. N.Y.P.L. §230.00 (McKinney 1980).

12. N.Y.P.L. §230.03 (McKinney 1980).

13. N.Y.P.L. §70.15 (2) (McKinney 1980).

14. N.Y.P.L. §70.15 (4) (McKinney 1980).

15. N.Y.P.L. §230.03 (McKinney 1980).

16. N.Y.P.L. §230.04 (McKinney 1980) is a class A misdemeanor; N.Y.P.L. §230.05 (McKinney 1980) is a class E felony; N.Y.P.L. §230.06 (McKinney 1980) is a class D felony. In Buffalo, where this study was carried out, there were no arrests of patrons of minor prostitutes for the time period studied. Additionally, a defense to such a charge is that the patron did not know the age of the minor prostitute, N.Y.P.L. §230.07 (McKinney 1980). Therefore, it seems doubtful that these patron sections will effectively deter patrons from seeking young women for hire.

17. Data found earlier than 1977 were not retrieved by this researcher because they were not stored in an accessible manner. The data that were collected include one and one/half years of pre-patron statutory reform and one and one/half years of post-patron statutory reform.

18. In New York State, equal protection of the laws is guaranteed by the Fourteenth Amendment to the U.S. Constitution and by Article 1, §11 of the state constitution.

19. *People* v *Goodman*, 338 N.Y.S. 2d 97 (1972).

20. *People* v *Nelson*, 427 N.Y.S. 2d 194 (1980).

21. 427 N.Y.S. 2d 194, 198.

22. This author reviewed the arrest sheets on everyone arrested in the city of Buffalo from 1977 through 1980. Persons arrested for a prostitution related offense were identified by McKinney's N.Y.P.L. section numbers; i.e., an arrested person was spotted by a §230.00 penal code designation. Date of arrest, sex and charge were recorded.

Although it is difficult to give an exact number of the male and female prostitutes working in Buffalo from 1977 through 1980, an overall total of 996 arrests of women (89.09%), as opposed to a total of 122 arrests of men (10.91%), for prostitution occurred during that period. That fewer men than women were arrested for prostitution may be attributed to the fact there are not as many male as female prostitutes in the Buffalo area [*People* v *Burton*, 432 N.Y.S. 2d 312, 314 (1980)]. Therefore, male prostitution arrestees did not make up a large percentage of arrests overall. By year, in 1977, male arrestees comprised 5.08% of the arrests, in 1978, 10.23%; in 1979, 10.75%; and, in 1980, 9.69% of the arrests. These male prostitute arrests were effected by undercover male police officers.

The male prostitution arrestee percentages roughly reflect the same increase/decrease trends indicated for female prostitution arrests. That is, between 1977 and 1979, prostitution arrests increased; but in 1980, prostitution arrests decreased.

23. There were no arrests for females patronizing a prostitute. This fact might be due to the scarcity of women patronizing prostitutes in the Buffalo, New York, area, or it might be due to the police's failure to focus on such activity.

24. N.Y.P.L. §240.37 (McKinney 1980).

25. N.Y.P.L. §240.37 (McKinney 1980); cited in *People* v *Smith*, 407 N.Y.S. 2d 462, 464-5 (1978).

26. Arrest data for males and females who were charged with "loitering for the purposes of prostitution" were collected in the same fashion as data collected on prostitution arrests: See footnote 22.

27. The combined male patron arrest figures may be inflated because arrest records utilized for the "loitering for the purpose of prostitution" offense made no distinction between male prostitution and male patron offenses. Thus, the combined male patron figures in Table 2 probably include male prostitution arrests.

28. Interview, Chief of Operations Robert Ford of the Erie County Sheriff's Department, Summer 1979.

29. 432 N.Y.S. 2d 312.

30. The statistical evidence presented a comparison of the number and percentage of males and females arrested for prostitution and loitering for the purposes of prostitution from 1977 to June 1980; basically, my data are presented in Tables 1 and 2.

31. Because of the complex legal issues involved, the decision will be analyzed in detail later in the text. In general, however, the court found that "although the circumstances of the defendant's arrest and the fact that almost all of the people arrested in Buffalo for prostitution-related offenses are women would seem to suggest that the defendant and other women are victims of bias, a comprehensive view satisfies this court that there are good and sufficient reasons . . . to justify . . ." the enforcement practice, 432 N.Y.S. 2d 312, 315.

32. 432 N.Y.S. 2d 312, 315 (1980).

33. 427 N.Y.S. 2d 194.

34. *In re Dora P.*, 418 N.Y.S. 2d 597 (1979).

35. 418 N.Y.S. 2d 597, 604.

36. *People* v *Simms*, No. 2C-50775, Buffalo City Court, Filed April 1, 1981.

37. 427 N.Y.S. 2d 194, 197.

38. Some states do proscribe patronizing and prostitution within the same statute: Fla. Stats. Ann. §796.07 a, b, e (1978 and 1982 Supp.); Iowa §725.1 (1979); Minn. Stats. Ann. §609.324 (1982 Supp.); N.J. Stats Ann. §26:34-1 a, e (West 1982); Ore. Rev. Stats. §167.007 (1981); Penn. Stats Ann. §18-5902 a, e (Purdon 1973).

39. *Craig* v *Boren*, 97 S. Ct. 451, 458 (1976); *California* v *Goldfarb*, 97 S. Ct. 1021 (1977); *Orr* v *Orr*, 99 S. Ct. 1102 (1979); *Mississippi University for Women* v *Hogan*, 102 S. Ct. 1422 (1982).

40. 432 N.Y.S. 2d 312, 314-315.

41. 432 N.Y.S. 2d 312, 315.

42. 432 N.Y.S. 2d 312, 315.

43. 432 N.Y.S. 2d 312. The *Burton* court did warn that "what may be good and sufficient reasons today will not suffice tomorrow when there are many more women available in the police ranks," at 315.

44. Jacqueline Boles and Charlotte Sadro, "Legal and Extra-Legal Methods of Controlling Female Prostitution: Cross-Cultural Comparison," *International Journal of Comparative and Applied Criminal Justice* 2 (Spring 1978) pp. 78-80; Holcome B. Noble, "A Return to the Old Morality Puts New Pressure on City Police," *Police Magazine* 2 (March 1979) pp. 55-56.

45. Frances P. Bernat, "Gender Disparity in the Setting of Bail: Prostitution Offenses in Buffalo, N.Y.: 1977-1979," *Journal of Offender Counseling, Services and Rehabilitation* 9 (forthcoming 1984).

46. *Craig* v *Boren*, 97 S. Ct. 451, 457-458 (1976). Also, *Califano* v *Goldfarb*, 97 S. Ct. 1021, 1029 (1977).

47. Clarice Feinman, *Women in the Criminal Justice System* (New York: Praeger, 1980), p. 79.

48. Susan Martin, *Breaking and Entering: Policewomen on Patrol* (Berkeley: University of California Press, 1980).

49. In *People* v *Nelson*, 427 N.Y.S. 2d 194, (1980), the court refused to allow the defendant access to the city's arrest records, thereby making it impossible for the defendant to prove selective enforcement of the prostitution statute in Syracuse, New York.

AGAINST THE MALE FLOOD:
CENSORSHIP, PORNOGRAPHY, AND EQUALITY

ANDREA DWORKIN*

Editor's Note: Andrea Dworkin's *Against the Male Flood: Censorship, Pornography, and Equality* is not a traditional law journal article; it is a political essay. Her goal, in this as well as in her other works, is to change not only what people think, but also the way they think.

Dworkin is a creator and one of the leading exponents of the feminist analysis of pornography. She is the author of several books, including *Woman Hating* (1974); *Pornography: Men Possessing Women* (1981); and *Right-wing Women* (1983). With Catharine A. MacKinnon, she authored the anti-pornography ordinances recently enacted in Minneapolis and Indianapolis. These ordinances declare pornography to be a form of discrimination against women and provide a civil remedy for its harms. Dworkin and MacKinnon have also drafted a model anti-pornography law, which is reproduced as Appendix A to this Essay.

Against the Male Flood presents the feminist ideas and goals that underlie the anti-pornography laws. It is thus a crucial addition

* Copyright © 1985 by Andrea Dworkin.

I thank all of the women who talked to me about how pornography has been used on them all over the years when there was nothing we could do. I thank Jeanne Barkey in particular for her stunning work in organizing the first Minneapolis hearings on pornography; and Charlee Hoyt, for being the driving force behind getting the legislation written and enacted. I thank Van White for co-sponsoring the bill and conducting the hearings. I thank everyone who testified in behalf of the legislation at the first hearings and later in subsequent hearings, and also those who talked to the press about sexual abuse at great cost to themselves. I thank the people who organized and now run the Pornography Resource Center in Minneapolis, especially for their work in organizing victims. I especially thank Therese Stanton for her extraordinary personal courage in testifying at the first Minneapolis hearings and for her untiring work in behalf of victims. I thank Steve Jevning for his tenacity, courage, and astuteness in working for the legislation, and for initiating the political process that led to both the legislation and a new kind of grassroots organizing. I especially thank my colleague, Catharine MacKinnon, for the honor of the intellectual and political dialogue we have had in conceiving and drafting the legislation, and for her indomitable will to stop the pornographers from hurting women. I thank John Stoltenberg for his many contributions to the politics of equality on which the legislation and this essay are built. All of these people contributed in both knowledge and faith to the writing of this essay. I dedicate this essay to all those resolute and brave people who worked to accomplish the passage of the first Minneapolis anti-pornography civil rights bill. Thank you.

to the current literature on the harms of pornography and the attempts to redress those harms through law. An equally important contribution is MacKinnon, *Pornography, Civil Rights, and Speech*, 20 Harv. C.R.-C.L. L. Rev. 1 (1985). In addition, Dworkin has compiled a selected bibliography of literature on pornography, which is included as Appendix B.

To say what one thought—that was my little problem—against the prodigious Current; to find a sentence that could hold its own against the male flood.   —VIRGINIA WOOLF

I want to say right here, that those well-meaning friends on the outside who say that we have suffered these horrors of prison, of hunger strikes and forcible feeding, because we desired to martyrise ourselves for the cause, are absolutely and entirely mistaken. We never went to prison in order to be martyrs. We went there in order that we might obtain the rights of citizenship. We were willing to break laws that we might force men to give us the right to make laws.   —EMMELINE PANKHURST

I. CENSORSHIP

Censorship is a real thing, not an abstract idea or a word that can be used to mean anything at all.

In ancient Rome, a censor was a magistrate who took the census (a count of the male population and an evaluation of property for the purpose of taxation done every fifth year), assessed taxes, and inspected morals and conduct. His power over conduct came from his power to tax. For instance, in 403 B.C., the censors Camillus and Postimius heavily fined elderly bachelors for not marrying. The power to tax, then as now, was the power to destroy. The censor, using the police and judicial powers of the state, regulated social behavior.

At its origins, then, censorship had nothing to do with striking down ideas as such; it had to do with acts. In my view, real state censorship still does. In South Africa and the Soviet Union, for instance, writing is treated entirely as an act, and writers are viewed as persons who engage in an act (writing) that by its very nature is dangerous to the continued existence of the state. The police in these countries do not try to suppress ideas. They are more specific, more concrete, more realistic. They go after books and manuscripts (writing) and destroy them. They go after writers as persons who have done something that they will do again and they persecute, punish, or kill them. They do not worry about what people think—not, at least, as we use the word *think*: a mental event, entirely internal, abstract. They worry about what people do: and writing, speaking, even as evidence that thinking is going on, are seen as things people *do*. There is a quality of immediacy and reality in what writing is taken to be. Where police power is used against writers systematically, writers are seen as people who by writing do something socially real and significant, not contemplative or dithering. Therefore, writing is never peripheral or beside the point. It is serious and easily seditious. I am offering no brief for police states when I say that virtually all great writers, crossculturally and transhistorically, share this view of what writing is. In countries like ours, controlled by a bourgeoisie to whom the police are accountable, writing is easier to do and valued less. It has less impact. It is more abundant and cheaper. Less is at stake for reader and writer both. The writer may hold writing to be a life-or-death matter, but the police and society do not. Writing is seen to be a personal choice, not a social, political, or esthetic necessity fraught with danger and meaning. The general view in these pleasant places* is that writers think up ideas or words and then other people read them and all this happens in the head, a vast cavern somewhere north of the eyes. It is all air, except for the paper and ink, which are simply banal. Nothing happens.

Police in police states and most great writers throughout time see writing as act, not air—as act, not idea; concrete, specific, real, not insubstantial blather on a dead page. Censorship goes after the act and the actor: the book and the writer. It needs to

---

* "Well, you know, it amazes me . . . ," says dissident South African writer Nadine Gordimer in an interview. "I come to America, I go to England, I go to France . . . nobody's at risk. They're afraid of getting cancer, losing a lover, losing their jobs, being insecure . . . . It's only in my own country that I find people who voluntarily choose to put everything at risk—in their personal life." *Nadine Gordimer*, WRITERS AT WORK: THE PARIS REVIEW INTERVIEWS 261 (G. Plimpton ed. 6th ser. 1984).

destroy both. The cost in human lives is staggering, and it is perhaps essential to say that human lives destroyed must count more in the weighing of horror than books burned. This is my personal view, and I love books more than I love people.

Censorship is deeply misunderstood in the United States, because the fairly spoiled, privileged, frivolous people who are the literate citizens of this country think that censorship is some foggy effort to suppress ideas. For them, censorship is not something in itself—an act of police power with discernible consequences to hunted people; instead, it is about something abstract—the suppressing or controlling of ideas. Censorship, like writing itself, is no longer an act. Because it is no longer the blatant exercise of police power against writers or books because of what they do, what they accomplish in the real world, it becomes vague, hard to find, except perhaps as an attitude. It gets used to mean unpleasant, even angry frowns of disapproval or critiques delivered in harsh tones; it means social disapproval or small retaliations by outraged citizens where the book is still available and the writer is entirely unharmed, even if insulted. It hangs in the air, ominous, like the threat of drizzle. It gets to be, in silly countries like this one, whatever people say it is, separate from any material definition, separate from police power, separate from state repression (jail, banning, exile, death), separate from devastating consequences to real people (jail, banning, exile, death). It is something that people who eat fine food and wear fine clothes worry about frenetically, trying to find it, anticipating it with great anxiety, arguing it down as if—if it were real—an argument would make it go away; not knowing that it has a clear, simple, unavoidable momentum and meaning in a cruel world of police power that their privilege cannot comprehend.

II. OBSCENITY

In the nineteenth and twentieth centuries, in most of Western Europe, England, and the United States, more often than not (time-out for Franco, for instance), writing has been most consistently viewed as an act warranting prosecution when the writing is construed to be obscene.

The republics, democracies, and constitutional monarchies of the West, now and then, do not smother writers in police violence; they prefer to pick off writers who annoy and irritate selectively with fairly token prosecutions. The list of writers so harassed is elegant, white, male (therefore the pronoun "he" is used throughout this discussion), and remarkably small. Being among them is more than a ceremonial honor. As Flaubert wrote his brother in 1857:

My persecution has brought me widespread sympathy. If my book is bad, that will serve to make it seem better. If, on the other hand, it has lasting qualities, that will build a foundation for it. There you are!

I am hourly awaiting the official document which will name the day when I am to take my seat (for the crime of having written in French) in the dock in the company of thieves and homosexuals.[1]

A few months later that same year, Baudelaire was fined 300 francs for publishing six obscene poems. They also had to be removed from future editions of his book. In harder, earlier days, Jean-Jacques Rousseau spent eight years as a fugitive after his *Émile* was banned and a warrant was issued for his arrest. English censors criminally prosecuted Swinburne's *Poems and Ballads* in 1866. They were particularly piqued at Zola, even in translation, so his English publisher, seventy years old, went to jail for three months. In 1898, a bookseller was arrested for selling Havelock Ellis' work and received a suspended sentence. This list is representative, not exhaustive. While prosecutions of writers under obscenity laws have created great difficulties for writers already plagued with them (as most writers are), criminal prosecutions under obscenity law in Europe and the United States are notable for how narrowly they reach writers, how sanguine writers tend to be about the consequences to themselves, and how little is paid in the writer's life-blood to what D.H. Lawrence (who paid more than most modern Western writers) called the "censor-moron."[2] In South Africa, one would hardly be so flip.

---

[1] G. FLAUBERT, LETTERS 94 (J.M. Cohen trans. 1950).

[2] Letter from D.H. Lawrence to Morris Ernst, *quoted in* H. Moore, *Introduction* to D.H. LAWRENCE, SEX, LITERATURE AND CENSORSHIP 9 (1959).

In our world, the writer gets harassed, as Lawrence did; the writer may be poor or not—the injury is considerably worse if he is; but the writer is not terrorized or tortured, and writers do not live under a reign of terror as writers, because of what they *do*. The potshot application of criminal law for writing is not good, nice, or right; but it is important to recognize the relatively narrow scope and marginal character of criminal prosecution under obscenity law in particular—especially compared with the scope and character of police-state censorship. Resisting obscenity law does not require hyperbolic renderings of what it is and how it has been used. It can be fought or repudiated on its own terms.

The use of obscenity laws against writers, however haphazard or insistent, is censorship and it does hold writing to be an act. This is a unique perception of what writing is, taking place, as it does, in a liberal context in which writing is held to be ideas. It is the obscene quality of the writing, the obscenity itself, that is seen to turn writing from idea into act. Writing of any kind or quality is idea, except for obscene writing, which is act. Writing is censored, even in our own happy little land of Oz, as act, not idea.

What is obscenity, such that it turns writing, when obscene, into something that actually happens—changes it from internal wind somewhere in the elevated mind into a genuinely offensive and utterly real fart, noticed, rude, occasioning pinched fingers on the nose?

There is the legal answer and the artistic answer. Artists have been consistently pushing on the boundaries of obscenity because great writers see writing as an act, and in liberal culture, only obscene writing has that social standing, that quality of dynamism and heroism. Great writers tend to experience writing as an intense and disruptive act; in the West, it is only recognized as such when the writing itself is experienced as obscene. In liberal culture, the writer has needed obscenity to be perceived as socially real.

What is it that obscenity does? The writer uses what the society deems to be obscene because the society then reacts to the writing the way the writer values the writing: as if it does something. But obscenity itself is socially constructed; the writer does not invent it or in any sense originate it. He finds it, knowing that it is what society hides. He looks under rocks and in dark corners.

There are two possible derivations of the word *obscenity*: the discredited one, *what is concealed*; and the accepted one, *filth*. Animals bury their filth, hide it, cover it, leave it behind, separate it from themselves: so do we, going way way back. Filth is excrement: from down there. We bury it or hide it; also, we hide where it comes from. Under male rule, menstrual blood is also filth, so women are twice dirty. Filth is where the sexual organs are and because women are seen primarily as sex, existing to provide sex, women have to be covered: our naked bodies being obscene.

Obscenity law uses both possible root meanings of *obscene* intertwined: it typically condemns nudity, public display, lewd exhibition, exposed genitals or buttocks or pubic areas, sodomy, masturbation, sexual intercourse, excretion. Obscenity law is applied to pictures and words: the artifact itself exposes what should be hidden; it shows dirt. The human body and all sex and excretory acts are the domain of obscenity law.

But being in the domain of obscenity law is not enough. One must feel alive there. To be obscene, the representations must arouse prurient interest. *Prurient* means *itching* or *itch*; it is related to the Sanskrit for *he burns*. It means sexual arousal. Judges, lawmakers, and juries have been, until very recently, entirely male: empirically, *prurient* means *causes erection*. Theologians have called this same quality of obscenity "venereal pleasure," holding that

> if a work is to be called obscene it must, of its nature, be such as actually to arouse or calculated to arouse in the viewer or reader such venereal pleasure. If the work is *not* of such a kind, it may, indeed, be vulgar, disgusting, crude, unpleasant, what you will—but it will *not* be, in the strict sense which Canon Law obliges us to apply, obscene.[3]

A secular philosopher of pornography isolated the same quality when he wrote: "Obscenity is our name for the uneasiness which upsets the physical state associated with self-possession . . . ."[4]

---

[3] H. Gardiner, Catholic Viewpoint on Censorship 65 (1958).

[4] G. Bataille, Death and Sensuality 12 (1969).

Throughout history, the male has been the standard for obscenity law: erection is his venereal pleasure or the uneasiness which upsets the physical state associated with his self-possession. It is not surprising, then, that in the same period when women became jurors, lawyers, and judges—but especially jurors, women having been summarily excluded from most juries until perhaps a decade ago—obscenity law fell into disuse and disregard. In order for obscenity law to have retained social and legal coherence, it would have had to recognize as part of its standard women's sexual arousal, a more subjective standard than erection. It would also have had to use the standard of penile erection in a social environment that was no longer sex-segregated, an environment in which male sexual arousal would be subjected to female scrutiny. In my view, the presence of women in the public sphere of legal decision-making has done more to undermine the efficacy of obscenity law than any self-conscious movement against it.

The act that obscenity recognizes is erection, and whatever writing produces erection is seen to be obscene—act, not idea—because of what it makes happen. The male sexual response is seen to be involuntary, so there is no experientially explicable division between the material that causes erection and the erection itself. That is the logic of obscenity law used against important writers who have pushed against the borders of the socially defined obscene, because they wanted writing to have that very quality of being a socially recognized act. They wanted the inevitability of the response—the social response. The erection makes the writing socially real from the society's point of view, not from the writer's. What the writer needs is to be taken seriously, by any means necessary. In liberal societies, only obscenity law comprehends writing as an act. It defines the nature and quality of the act narrowly—not writing itself, but producing erections. Flaubert apparently did produce them; so did Baudelaire, Zola, Rousseau, Lawrence, Joyce, and Nabokov. It's that simple.

What is at stake in obscenity law is always erection: under what conditions, in what circumstances, how, by whom, by what materials men want it produced in themselves. Men have made this public policy. Why they want to regulate their own erections through law is a question of endless interest and importance to feminists. Nevertheless, that they do persist in this regulation is simple fact. There are civil and social conflicts over how best to regulate erection through law, especially when caused by words or pictures. Arguments among men notwithstanding, high culture is phallocentric. It is also, using the civilized criteria of jurisprudence, not infrequently obscene.

Most important writers have insisted that their own uses of the obscene as socially defined are not pornography. As D.H. Lawrence wrote: "But even I would censor genuine pornography, rigorously. It would not be very difficult . . . . [Y]ou can recognize it by the insult it offers, invariably, to sex, and to the human spirit."[5] It was also, he pointed out, produced by the underworld. Nabokov saw in pornography "mediocrity, commercialism, and certain strict rules of narration . . . . [A]ction has to be limited to the copulation of clichés. Style, structure, imagery should never distract the reader from his tepid lust."[6] They knew that what they did was different from pornography, but they did not entirely know what the difference was. They missed the heart of an empirical distinction because writing was indeed real to them but women were not.

The insult pornography offers, invariably, to sex is accomplished in the active subordination of women: the creation of a sexual dynamic in which the putting-down of women, the suppression of women, and ultimately the brutalization of women, *is* what sex is taken to be. Obscenity in law, and in what it does socially, is erection. Law recognizes the act in this. Pornography, however, is a broader, more comprehensive act, because it crushes a whole class of people through violence and subjugation: and sex is the vehicle that does the crushing. The penis is not the test, as it is in obscenity. Instead, the status of women is the issue. Erection is implicated in the subordinating, but who it reaches and how are the pressing legal and social questions. Pornography, unlike obscenity, is a discrete, identifiable system of sexual exploitation that hurts women as a class by creating inequality and abuse. This is a new legal idea, but it is the recognition and naming of an old and cruel injury to a dispossessed and coerced underclass. It is the sound of women's words breaking the longest silence.

---

[5] D.H. LAWRENCE, *supra* note 2, at 69.
[6] V. NABOKOV, *Afterword* to LOLITA 284 (1977).

III. PORNOGRAPHY

In the United States, it is an $8-billion trade in sexual exploitation.

It is women turned into subhumans, beaver, pussy, body parts, genitals exposed, buttocks, breasts, mouths opened and throats penetrated, covered in semen, pissed on, shitted on, hung from light fixtures, tortured, maimed, bleeding, disemboweled, killed.

It is some creature called female, used.

It is scissors poised at the vagina and objects stuck in it, a smile on the woman's face, her tongue hanging out.

It is a woman being fucked by dogs, horses, snakes.

It is every torture in every prison cell in the world, done to women and sold as sexual entertainment.

It is rape and gang rape and anal rape and throat rape: and it is the woman raped, asking for more.

It is the woman in the picture to whom it is really happening and the women against whom the picture is used, to make them do what the woman in the picture is doing.

It is the power men have over women turned into sexual acts men do to women, because pornography is the power and the act.

It is the conditioning of erection and orgasm in men to the powerlessness of women: our inferiority, humiliation, pain, torment; to us as objects, things, or commodities for use in sex as servants.

It sexualizes inequality and in doing so creates discrimination as a sex-based practice.

It permeates the political condition of women in society by being the substance of our inequality however located—in jobs, in education, in marriage, *in life*.

It is women, kept a sexual underclass, kept available for rape and battery and incest and prostitution.

It is what we are under male domination; it is what we are for under male domination.

It is the heretofore hidden (from us) system of subordination that women have been told is just life.

Under male supremacy, it is the synonym for what being a woman is.

It is access to our bodies as a birthright to men: the grant, the gift, the permission, the license, the proof, the promise, the method, how-to; it is us accessible, no matter what the law pretends to say, no matter what we pretend to say.

It is physical injury and physical humiliation and physical pain: to the women against whom it is used after it is made; to the women used to make it.

As words alone, or words and pictures, moving or still, it creates systematic harm to women in the form of discrimination and physical hurt. It creates harm inevitably by its nature because of what it is and what it does. The harm will occur as long as it is made and used. The name of the next victim is unknown, but everything else is known.

Because of it—because it is the subordination of women perfectly achieved—the abuse done to us by any human standard is perceived as using us for what we are by nature: women are whores; women want to be raped; she provoked it; women like to be hurt; she says no but means yes because she wants to be taken against her will which is not really her will because what she wants underneath is to have anything done to her that violates or humiliates or hurts her; she wants it, because she is a woman, no matter what it is, because she is a woman; that is how women are, what women are, what women are for. This view is institutionally expressed in law. So much for equal protection.

If it were being done to human beings, it would be reckoned an atrocity. It is being done to women. It is reckoned fun, pleasure, entertainment, sex, somebody's (not something's) civil liberty no less.

What do you want to be when you grow up? *Doggie Girl? Gestapo Sex Slave? Black Bitch in Bondage?* Pet, bunny, beaver? In dreams begin responsibilities,[7] whether one is the dreamer or the dreamed.

IV. PORNOGRAPHERS

Most of them are small-time pimps or big-time pimps. They sell women: the real flesh-and-blood women in the pictures. They

---

[7] The actual line is "In dreams begins responsibility," quoted by Yeats as an epigram to a collection of his poetry. W.B. YEATS, RESPONSIBILITIES AND OTHER POEMS (1916).

like the excitement of domination; they are greedy for profit; they are sadistic in their exploitation of women; they hate women, and the pornography they make is the distillation of that hate. The photographs are what they have created live, for themselves, for their own enjoyment. The exchanges of women among them are part of the fun, too: so that the fictional creature "Linda Lovelace," who was the real woman Linda Marchiano, was forced to "deep-throat" every pornographer her owner-pornographer wanted to impress. Of course, it was the woman, not the fiction, who had to be hypnotized so that the men could penetrate to the bottom of her throat, and who had to be beaten and terrorized to get her compliance at all. The finding of new and terrible things to do to women is part of the challenge of the vocation: so the inventor of "Linda Lovelace" and "deep-throating" is a genius in the field, a pioneer. Or, as Al Goldstein, a colleague, referred to him in an interview with him in *Screw* several years ago: a pimp's pimp.

Even with written pornography, there has never been the distinction between making pornography and the sexual abuse of live women that is taken as a truism by those who approach pornography as if it were an intellectual phenomenon. The Marquis de Sade, as the world's foremost literary pornographer, is archetypal. His sexual practice was the persistent sexual abuse of women and girls, with occasional excursions into the abuse of boys. As an aristocrat in a feudal society, he preyed with near impunity on prostitutes and servants. The pornography he wrote was an urgent part of the sexual abuse he practiced: not only because he did what he wrote, but also because the intense hatred of women that fueled the one also fueled the other: not two separate engines, but one engine running on the same tank. The acts of pornography and the acts of rape were waves on the same sea: that sea, becoming for its victims however it reached them, a tidal wave of destruction. Pornographers who use words know that what they are doing is both aggressive and destructive: sometimes they philosophize about how sex inevitably ends in death, the death of a woman being a thing of sexual beauty as well as excitement. Pornography, even when written, is sex because of the dynamism of the sexual hatred in it; and for pornographers, the sexual abuse of women as commonly understood and pornography are both acts of sexual predation, which is how they live.

One reason that stopping pornographers and pornography is not censorship is that pornographers are more like the police in police states than they are like the writers in police states. They are the instruments of terror, not its victims. What police do to the powerless in police states is what pornographers do to women, except that it is entertainment for the masses, not dignified as political. Writers do not do what pornographers do. Secret police do. Torturers do. What pornographers do to women is more like what police do to political prisoners than it is like anything else: except for the fact that it is watched with so much pleasure by so many. Intervening in a system of terror where it is vulnerable to public scrutiny to stop it is not censorship; it is the system of terror that stops speech and creates abuse and despair. The pornographers are the secret police of male supremacy: keeping women subordinate through intimidation and assault.

V. SUBORDINATION

In the amendment to the Human Rights Ordinance of the City of Minneapolis written by Catharine A. MacKinnon and myself,* pornography is defined as the graphic, sexually explicit subordi-

---

* *Editor's note:* The first anti-pornography law drafted by Dworkin and MacKinnon was proposed as an amendment to Minneapolis, Minn., Code of Ordinances Relating to Civil Rights tit. 7, chs. 139 & 141. Extensive hearings on the proposed bill, which included testimony from expert witnesses and victims of sexual abuse, were held on December 12 and 13, 1983. The Minneapolis City Council passed the ordinance on December 30, 1983; Mayor Donald Fraser vetoed it on January 5, 1984. The City Council, with several newly elected members, passed a slightly revised form of the bill on July 13, 1984, and Mayor Fraser again vetoed it.

The Indianapolis City Council passed a similar bill on April 23, 1984; it was signed into law by Mayor William H. Hudnut, III. Gen'l Ordinance No. 24 (May 1, 1984) (amending Indianapolis & Marion County, Ind., Code ch. 16). The ordinance was later amended by Gen'l Ordinance No. 35 (June 15, 1984), to bring it into closer conformity with the Minneapolis prototype.

The Indianapolis ordinance was immediately challenged on first amendment grounds by media trade groups with support from civil liberties organizations. On November 19, 1984, Judge Sarah Evans Barker held the ordinance unconstitutional. *See* American Booksellers Ass'n, Inc. v. Hudnut, 598 F. Supp. 1316 (S.D. Ind. 1984), *appeal docketed*, No. 84-3147 (7th Cir. Dec. 21, 1984).

nation of women whether in pictures or in words that also includes one or more of the following: women are presented dehumanized as sexual objects, things or commodities; or women are presented as sexual objects who enjoy pain or humiliation; or women are presented as sexual objects who experience sexual pleasure in being raped; or women are presented as sexual objects tied up or cut up or mutilated or bruised or physically hurt; or women are presented in postures of sexual submission; or women's body parts are exhibited, such that women are reduced to those parts; or women are presented being penetrated by objects or animals; or women are presented in scenarios of degradation, injury, abasement, torture, shown as filthy or inferior, bleeding, bruised, or hurt in a context that makes these conditions sexual.

This statutory definition is an objectively accurate definition of what pornography is, based on an analysis of the material produced by the $8-billion-a-year industry, and also on extensive study of the whole range of pornography extant from other eras and other cultures. Given the fact that women's oppression has an ahistorical character—a sameness across time and cultures expressed in rape, battery, incest, and prostitution—it is no surprise that pornography, a central phenomenon in that oppression, has precisely that quality of sameness. It does not significantly change in what it is, what it does, what is in it, or how it works, whether it is, for instance, classical or feudal or modern, Western or Asian; whether the method of manufacture is words, photographs, or video. What has changed is the public availability of pornography and the numbers of live women used in it because of new technologies: not its nature. Many people note what seems to them a qualitative change in pornography—that it has gotten more violent, even grotesquely violent, over the last two decades. The change is only in what is publicly visible: not in the range or preponderance of violent pornography (e.g., the place of rape in pornography stays constant and central, no matter where, when, or how the pornography is produced); not in the character, quality, or content of what the pornographers actually produce; not in the harm caused; not in the valuation of women in it, or the metaphysical definition of what women are; not in the sexual abuse promoted, including rape, battery, and incest; not in the centrality of its role in subordinating women. Until recently, pornography operated in private, where most abuse of women takes place.

The oppression of women occurs through sexual subordination. It is the use of sex as the medium of oppression that makes the subordination of women so distinct from racism or prejudice against a group based on religion or national origin. Social inequality is created in many different ways. In my view, the radical responsibility is to isolate the material means of creating the inequality so that material remedies can be found for it.

This is particularly difficult with respect to women's inequality because that inequality is achieved through sex. Sex as desired by the class that dominates women is held by that class to be elemental, urgent, necessary, even if or even though it appears to *require* the repudiation of any claim women might have to full human standing. In the subordination of women, inequality itself is sexualized: made into the experience of sexual pleasure, essential to sexual desire. Pornography is the material means of sexualizing inequality; and that is why pornography is a central practice in the subordination of women.

Subordination itself is a broad, deep, systematic dynamic discernible in any persecution based on race or sex. Social subordination has four main parts. First, there is *hierarchy*, a group on top and a group on the bottom. For women, this hierarchy is experienced both socially and sexually, publicly and privately. Women are physically integrated into the society in which we are held to be inferior, and our low status is both put in place and maintained in the sexual usage of us by men; and so women's experience of hierarchy is incredibly intimate and wounding.

Second, subordination is *objectification*. Objectification occurs when a human being, through social means, is made less than human, turned into a thing or commodity, bought and sold. When objectification occurs, a person is depersonalized, so that no individuality or integrity is available socially or in what is an extremely circumscribed privacy (because those who dominate determine its boundaries). Objectification is an injury right at the heart of discrimination: those who can be used as if they are not fully human are no longer fully human in social terms; their humanity is hurt by being diminished.

Third, subordination is *submission*. A person is at the bottom of a hierarchy because of a condition of birth; a person on the bottom is dehumanized, an object or commodity; inevitably, the situation of that person requires obedience and compliance. That diminished person is expected to be submissive; there is no longer any right to self-determination, because there is no basis in equality for any such right to exist. In a condition of inferiority and objectification, submission is usually essential for survival. Oppressed groups are known for their abilities to anticipate the orders and desires of those who have power over them, to comply with an obsequiousness that is then used by the dominant group to justify its own dominance: the master, not able to imagine a human like himself in such degrading servility, thinks the servility is proof that the hierarchy is natural and that the objectification simply amounts to seeing these lesser creatures for what they are. The submission forced on inferior, objectified groups precisely by hierarchy and objectification is taken to be the proof of inherent inferiority and subhuman capacities.

Fourth, subordination is *violence.* The violence is systematic, endemic enough to be unremarkable and normative, usually taken as an implicit right of the one committing the violence. In my view, hierarchy, objectification, and submission are the preconditions for systematic social violence against any group targeted because of a condition of birth. If violence against a group is both socially pervasive and socially normal, then hierarchy, objectification, and submission are already solidly in place.

The role of violence in subordinating women has one special characteristic congruent with sex as the instrumentality of subordination: the violence is supposed to be sex for the woman too—what women want and like as part of our sexual nature; it is supposed to give women pleasure (as in rape); it is supposed to mean love to a woman from her point of view (as in battery). The violence against women is seen to be done not just in accord with something compliant in women, but in response to something active in and basic to women's nature.

Pornography uses each component of social subordination. Its particular medium is sex. Hierarchy, objectification, submission, and violence all become alive with sexual energy and sexual meaning. A hierarchy, for instance, can have a static quality; but pornography, by sexualizing it, makes it dynamic, almost carnivorous, so that men keep imposing it for the sake of their own sexual pleasure—for the sexual pleasure it gives them to impose it. In pornography, each element of subordination is conveyed through the sexually explicit usage of women: pornography in fact is what women are and what women are for and how women are used in a society premised on the inferiority of women. It is a metaphysics of women's subjugation: our existence delineated in a definition of our nature; our status in society predetermined by the uses to which we are put. The woman's body is what is materially subordinated. Sex is the material means through which the subordination is accomplished. Pornography is the institution of male dominance that sexualizes hierarchy, objectification, submission, and violence. As such, pornography creates inequality, not as artifact but as a system of social reality; it creates the necessity for and the actual behaviors that constitute sex inequality.

VI. SPEECH

Subordination can be so deep that those who are hurt by it are utterly silent. Subordination can create a silence quieter than death. The women flattened out on the page are deathly still, except for *hurt me*. *Hurt me* is not women's speech. It is the speech imposed on women by pimps to cover the awful, condemning silence. The Three Marias of Portugal went to jail for writing this: "Let no one tell me that silence gives consent, because whoever is silent dissents."[8] The women say the pimp's words: the language is another element of the rape; the language is part of the humiliation; the language is part of the forced sex. Real silence might signify dissent, for those reared to understand its sad discourse. The pimps cannot tolerate literal silence—it is too eloquent as testimony—so they force the words out of the woman's mouth. The women say pimp's words: which is worse than silence. The silence of the women not in the picture, outside the pages, hurt but silent, used but silent, is staggering in how deep and wide it goes. It is a silence over centuries: an exile into speechlessness. One is shut up by the inferiority and the abuse. One is shut up by the threat and the injury. In her memoir of the

---

[8] M.I. Barreno, M.T. Horta & M. Velho da Costa, The Three Marias: New Portuguese Letters 291 (H.R. Lane trans. 1976).

Stalin period, *Hope Against Hope*, Nadezha Mandelstam wrote that screaming

> is a man's way of leaving a trace, of telling people how he lived and died. By his screams he asserts his right to live, sends a message to the outside world demanding help and calling for resistance. If nothing else is left, one must scream. Silence is the real crime against humanity.[9]

Screaming is a man's way of leaving a trace. The scream of a man is never misunderstood as a scream of pleasure by passers-by or politicians or historians, nor by the tormentor. A man's scream is a call for resistance. A man's scream asserts his right to live, sends a message; he leaves a trace. A woman's scream is the sound of her female will and her female pleasure in doing what the pornographers say she is for. Her scream is a sound of celebration to those who overhear. Women's way of leaving a trace is the silence, centuries' worth: the entirely inhuman silence that surely one day will be noticed, someone will say that something is wrong, some sound is missing, some voice is lost; the entirely inhuman silence that will be a clue to human hope denied, a shard of evidence that a crime has occurred, the crime that created the silence; the entirely inhuman silence that is a cold, cold condemnation of hurt sustained in speechlessness, a cold, cold condemnation of what those who speak have done to those who do not.

But there is more than the *hurt me* forced out of us, and the silence in which it lies. The pornographers actually use our bodies as their language. Our bodies are the building blocks of their sentences. What they do to us, called speech, is not unlike what Kafka's Harrow machine—"'The needles are set in like the teeth of a harrow and the whole thing works something like a harrow, although its action is limited to one place and contrived with much more artistic skill'"[10]—did to the condemned in *In the Penal Colony*:

---

[9] N. MANDELSTAM, HOPE AGAINST HOPE 42–43 (M. Hayward trans. 1978).
[10] F. KAFKA, *In the Penal Colony*, in THE PENAL COLONY 194 (W. Muir & E. Muir trans. 1965).

"Our sentence does not sound severe. Whatever commandment the prisoner has disobeyed is written upon his body
by the Harrow. This prisoner, for instance"—the officer
indicated the man—"will have written on his body: HONOR
THY SUPERIORS!"[11]

. . .
". . . The Harrow is beginning to write; when it finishes
the first draft of the inscription on the man's back, the layer
of cotton wool begins to roll and slowly turns the body over,
to give the Harrow fresh space for writing . . . . So it keeps
on writing deeper and deeper . . . ."[12]

Asked if the prisoner knows his sentence, the officer replies:
"'There would be no point in telling him. He'll learn it on his
body.'"[13]

This is the so-called speech of the pornographers, protected
now by law.

Protecting what they "say" means protecting what they do to
us, how they do it. It means protecting their sadism on our bodies,
because that is how they write: not like a writer at all; like a
torturer. Protecting what they "say" means protecting sexual
exploitation, because they cannot "say" anything without diminishing, hurting, or destroying us. Their rights of speech express
their rights over us. Their rights of speech require our inferiority:
and that we be powerless in relation to them. Their rights of
speech mean that *hurt me* is accepted as the real speech of
women, not speech forced on us as part of the sex forced on us
but originating with us because we are what the pornographers
"say" we are.

If what we want to say is not *hurt me*, we have the real social
power only to use silence as eloquent dissent. Silence is what
women have instead of speech. Silence is our dissent during rape
unless the rapist, like the pornographer, prefers *hurt me*, in which
case we have no dissent. Silence is our moving, persuasive dissent during battery unless the batterer, like the pornographer,
prefers *hurt me*. Silence is a fine dissent during incest and for all
the long years after.

---

[11] *Id.* at 197.
[12] *Id.* at 203.
[13] *Id.* at 197.

Silence is not speech. We have silence, not speech. We fight rape, battery, incest, and prostitution with it. We lose. But someday someone will notice: that people called women were buried in a long silence that meant dissent and that the pornographers— with needles set in like the teeth of a harrow—chattered on.

VII. EQUALITY

To get that word, male, out of the Constitution, cost the women of this country fifty-two years of pauseless campaign; 56 state referendum campaigns; 480 legislative campaigns to get state suffrage amendments submitted; 47 state constitutional convention campaigns; 277 state party convention campaigns; 30 national party convention campaigns to get suffrage planks in the party platforms; 19 campaigns with 19 successive Congresses to get the federal amendment submitted, and the final ratification campaign.

Millions of dollars were raised, mostly in small sums, and spent with economic care. Hundreds of women gave the accumulated possibilities of an entire lifetime, thousands gave years of their lives, hundreds of thousands gave constant interest and such aid as they could. It was a continuous and seemingly endless chain of activity. Young suffragists who helped forge the last links of that chain were not born when it began. Old suffragists who helped forge the first links were dead when it ended.

—CARRIE CHAPMAN CATT

Feminists have wanted equality. Radicals and reformists have different ideas of what equality would be, but it has been the wisdom of feminism to value equality as a political goal with social integrity and complex meaning. The Jacobins also wanted equality, and the French Revolution was fought to accomplish it. Conservatism as a modern political movement actually developed to resist social and political movements for equality, beginning with the egalitarian imperatives of the French Revolution.

Women have had to prove human status, before having any claim to equality. But equality has been impossible to achieve, perhaps because, really, women have not been able to prove human status. The burden of proof is on the victim.

Not one inch of change has been easy or cheap. We have fought so hard and so long for so little. The vote did not change the status of women. The changes in women's lives that we can see on the surface do not change the status of women. By the year 2000, women are expected to be one hundred percent of this nation's poor.* We are raped, battered, and prostituted: these acts against us are in the fabric of social life. As children, we are raped, physically abused, and prostituted. The country enjoys the injuries done to us, and spends $8 billion a year on the pleasure of watching us being hurt (exploitation as well as torture constituting substantive harm). The subordination gets deeper: we keep getting pushed down further. Rape is an entertainment. The contempt for us in that fact is immeasurable; yet we live under the weight of it. Discrimination is a euphemism for what happens to us.

It has plagued us to try to understand why the status of women does not change. Those who hate the politics of equality say they know: we are biologically destined for rape; God made us to be submissive unto our husbands. We change, but our status does not change. Laws change, but our status stays fixed. We move into the marketplace, only to face there classic sexual exploitation, now called sexual harassment. Rape, battery, prostitution, and incest stay the same in that they keep happening to us as part of what life is: even though we name the crimes against us as such and try to keep the victims from being destroyed by what we cannot stop from happening to them. And the silence stays in place too, however much we try to dislodge it with our truths. We say what has happened to us, but newspapers, governments, the culture that excludes us as fully human participants, wipe us out, wipe out our speech: by refusing to hear it. We are the tree falling in the desert. Should it matter: they are the desert.

The cost of trying to shatter the silence is astonishing to those who do it: the women, raped, battered, prostituted, who have something to say and say it. They stand there, even as they are erased. Governments turn from them; courts ignore them; this country disavows and dispossesses them. Men ridicule, threaten,

---

* For a comprehensive analysis of how the feminization of poverty brutally impacts on people of color in the United States, see *The Coming Gynocide*, in A. DWORKIN, RIGHT-WING WOMEN 147, 162–73 (1983).

or hurt them. Women jeopardized by them—silence being safer than speech—betray them. It is ugly to watch the complacent destroy the brave. It is horrible to watch power win.

Still, equality is what we want, and we are going to get it. What we understand about it now is that it cannot be proclaimed; it must be created. It has to take the place of subordination in human experience: physically replace it. Equality does not co-exist with subordination, as if it were a little pocket located somewhere within it. Equality has to win. Subordination has to lose. The subordination of women has not even been knocked loose, and equality has not materially advanced, at least in part because the pornography has been creating sexualized inequality in hiding, in private, where the abuses occur on a massive scale.

Equality for women requires material remedies for pornography, whether pornography is central to the inequality of women or only one cause of it. Pornography's antagonism to civil equality, integrity, and self-determination for women is absolute; and it is effective in making that antagonism socially real and socially determining.

The law that Catharine A. MacKinnon and I wrote making pornography a violation of women's civil rights recognizes the injury that pornography does: how it hurts women's rights of citizenship through sexual exploitation and sexual torture both.

The civil rights law empowers women by allowing women to civilly sue those who hurt us through pornography by trafficking in it, coercing people into it, forcing it on people, and assaulting people directly because of a specific piece of it.

The civil rights law does not force the pornography back underground. There is no prior restraint or police power to make arrests, which would then result in a revivified black market. This respects the reach of the first amendment, but it also keeps the pornography from getting sexier—hidden, forbidden, dirty, happily back in the land of the obscene, sexy slime oozing on great books. Wanting to cover the pornography up, hide it, is the first response of those who need pornography to the civil rights law. If pornography is hidden, it is still accessible to men as a male right of access to women; its injuries to the status of women are safe and secure in those hidden rooms, behind those opaque covers; the abuses of women are sustained as a private right supported by public policy. The civil rights law puts a flood of light on the pornography, what it is, how it is used, what it does, those who are hurt by it.

The civil rights law changes the power relationship between pornographers and women: it stops the pornographers from producing discrimination with the total impunity they now enjoy, and gives women a legal standing resembling equality from which to repudiate the subordination itself. The secret-police power of the pornographers suddenly has to confront a modest amount of due process.

The civil rights law undermines the subordination of women in society by confronting the pornography, which is the systematic sexualization of that subordination. Pornography is inequality. The civil rights law would allow women to advance equality by removing this concrete discrimination and hurting economically those who make, sell, distribute, or exhibit it. The pornography, being power, has a right to exist that we are not allowed to challenge under this system of law. After it hurts us by being what it is and doing what it does, the civil rights law would allow us to hurt it back. Women, not being power, do not have a right to exist equal to the right the pornography has. If we did, the pornographers would be precluded from exercising their rights at the expense of ours, and since they cannot exercise them any other way, they would be precluded period. We come to the legal system beggars: though in the public dialogue around the passage of this civil rights law we have the satisfaction of being regarded as thieves.

The civil rights law is women's speech. It defines an injury to us from our point of view. It is premised on a repudiation of sexual subordination which is born of our experience of it. It breaks the silence. It is a sentence that can hold its own against the male flood. It is a sentence on which we can build a paragraph, then a page.

It is my view, learned largely from Catharine MacKinnon, that women have a right to be effective. The pornographers, of course, do not think so, nor do other male supremacists; and it is hard for women to think so. We have been told to educate people on the evils of pornography: before the development of this civil rights law, we were told just to keep quiet about pornography altogether; but now that we have a law we want to use, we are encouraged to educate and stop there. Law educates. This law educates. It also allows women to *do* something. In hurting the pornography back, we gain ground in making equality more likely, more possible—someday it will be real. We have a means to fight the pornographers' trade in women. We have a means to get at the torture and the terror. We have a means with which to challenge the pornography's efficacy in making exploitation and inferiority the bedrock of women's social status. The civil rights law introduces into the public consciousness an analysis: of what pornography is, what sexual subordination is, what equality might be. The civil rights law introduces a new legal standard: these things are not done to citizens of this country. The civil rights law introduces a new political standard: these things are not done to human beings. The civil rights law provides a new mode of action for women through which we can pursue equality and because of which *our* speech will have social meaning. The civil rights law gives us back what the pornographers have taken from us: hope rooted in real possibility.

APPENDIX A
MODEL ANTI-PORNOGRAPHY LAW

Section 1. STATEMENT OF POLICY

Pornography is sex discrimination. It exists in [PLACE], posing a substantial threat to the health, safety, peace, welfare, and equality of citizens in the community. Existing [state and] federal laws are inadequate to solve these problems in [PLACE].

Pornography is a systematic practice of exploitation and subordination based on sex that differentially harms women. The harm of pornography includes dehumanization, sexual exploitation, forced sex, forced prostitution, physical injury, and social and sexual terrorism and inferiority presented as entertainment. The bigotry and contempt it promotes, with the acts of aggression it fosters, diminish opportunities for equality of rights in employment, education, property, public accommodations and public services; create public and private harassment, persecution and denigration; promote injury and degradation such as rape, battery, child sexual abuse, and prostitution and inhibit just enforcement of laws against these acts; contribute significantly to restricting women in particular from full exercise of citizenship and participation in public life, including in neighborhoods; damage relations between the sexes; and undermine women's equal exercise of rights to speech and action guaranteed to all citizens under the Constitutions and laws of the United States and [PLACE, INCLUDING STATE].

Section 2. DEFINITIONS

1. *Pornography* is the graphic sexually explicit subordination of women through pictures and/or words that also includes one or more of the following: (i) women are presented dehumanized as sexual objects, things, or commodities; or (ii) women are presented as sexual objects who enjoy pain or humiliation; or (iii) women are presented as sexual objects who experience sexual pleasure in being raped; or (iv) women are presented as sexual objects tied up or cut up or mutilated or bruised or physically hurt; or (v) women are presented in postures or positions of sexual submission, servility, or display; or (vi) women's body parts—including but not limited to vaginas, breasts, or buttocks— are exhibited such that women are reduced to those parts; or (vii) women are presented as whores by nature; or (viii) women are presented being penetrated by objects or animals; or (ix) women are presented in scenarios of degradation, injury, torture, shown as filthy or inferior, bleeding, bruised, or hurt in a context that makes these conditions sexual.

2. The use of men, children, or transsexuals in the place of women in (1) above is pornography for purposes of this law.

Section 3. UNLAWFUL PRACTICES

1. *Coercion into pornography*: It shall be sex discrimination to coerce, intimidate, or fraudulently induce (hereafter, "coerce") any person, including transsexual, into performing for pornography, which injury may date from any appearance or sale of any product(s) of such performance(s). The maker(s), seller(s), exhibitor(s), and/or distributor(s) of said pornography may be sued for damages and for an injunction, including to eliminate the product(s) of the performance(s) from the public view.

Proof of one or more of the following facts or conditions shall not, without more, negate a finding of coercion: (i) that the person is a woman; or (ii) that the person is or has been a prostitute; or (iii) that the person has attained the age of majority; or (iv) that the person is connected by blood or marriage to anyone involved in or related to the making of the pornography; or (v) that the person has previously had, or been thought to have had, sexual relations with anyone, including anyone involved in or related to the making of the pornography; or (vi) that the person has previously posed for sexually explicit pictures with or for anyone, including anyone involved in or related to the making of the pornography at issue; or (vii) that anyone else, including a spouse or other relative, has given permission on the person's behalf; or (viii) that the person actually consented to a use of the performance that is changed into pornography; or (ix) that the person knew that the purpose of the acts or events in question was to make pornography; or (x) that the person showed no resistance or appeared to cooperate actively in the photographic sessions or in the events that produced the pornography; or (xi) that the person signed a contract, or made statements affirming a willingness to cooperate in the production of pornography; or (xii) that no physical force, threats, or weapons were used in the making of the pornography; or (xiii) that the person was paid or otherwise compensated.

2. *Trafficking in pornography*: It shall be sex discrimination to produce, sell, exhibit, or distribute pornography, including through private clubs.

(i) City, state, and federally funded public libraries or private and public university and college libraries in which pornography is available for study, including on open shelves but excluding special display presentations, shall not be construed to be trafficking in pornography.

(ii) Isolated passages or isolated parts shall not be actionable under this section.

(iii) Any woman has a claim hereunder as a woman acting against the subordination of women. Any man, child, or transsexual who alleges injury by pornography in the way women are injured by it also has a claim.

3. *Forcing pornography on a person*: It shall be sex discrimination to force pornography on a person, including a child or transsexual, in any place of employment, education, home, or

public place. Only the perpetrator of the force or responsible institution may be sued.

4. *Assault of physical attack due to pornography*: It shall be sex discrimination to assault, physically attack, or injure any person, including child or transsexual, in a way that is directly caused by specific pornography. The perpetrator of the assault or attack may be sued for damages and enjoined where appropriate. The maker(s), distributor(s), seller(s), and/or exhibitor(s) may also be sued for damages and for an injunction against the specific pornography's further exhibition, distribution, or sale.

Section 4. DEFENSES

1. It shall not be a defense that the defendant in an action under this law did not know or intend that the materials were pornography or sex discrimination.

2. No damages or compensation for losses shall be recoverable under Sec. 3(2) or other than against the perpetrator of the assault or attack in Sec. 3(4) unless the defendant knew or had reason to know that the materials were pornography.

3. In actions under Sec. 3(2) or other than against the perpetrator of the assault or attack in Sec. 3(4), no damages or compensation for losses shall be recoverable against maker(s) for pornography made, against distributor(s) for pornography distributed, against seller(s) for pornography sold, or against exhibitor(s) for pornography exhibited, prior to the effective date of this law.

Section 5. ENFORCEMENT*

1. *Civil action*: Any person aggrieved by violations of this law may enforce its provisions by means of a civil action. No criminal penalties shall attach for any violation of the provisions of this law. Relief for violation of this act may include reasonable attorney's fees.

---

* In the event that this law is amended to a preexisting human-rights law, the complaint would first be made to a Civil Rights Commission. Any injunction issued under Sec. 3(2), the trafficking provision, would require trial *de novo* (a full court trial after the administrative hearing).

2. *Injunction*: Any person who violates this law may be enjoined except that:

(i) In actions under Sec. 3(2), and other than against the perpetrator of the assault or attack under Sec. 3(4), no temporary or permanent injunction shall issue prior to a final judicial determination that the challenged activities constitute a violation of this law.

(ii) No temporary or permanent injunction shall extend beyond such material(s) that, having been described with reasonable specificity by the injunction, have been determined to be validly proscribed under this law.

Section 6. SEVERABILITY

Should any part(s) of this law be found legally invalid, the remaining part(s) remains valid. A judicial declaration that any part(s) of this law cannot be applied validly in a particular manner or to a particular case or category of cases shall not affect the validity of that part(s) as otherwise applied, unless such other application would clearly frustrate the [LEGISLATIVE BODY'S] intent in adopting this law.

Section 7. LIMITATION OF ACTION

Actions under this law must be filed within one year of the alleged discriminatory acts.

APPENDIX B
SELECTED BIBLIOGRAPHY

Able-Peterson, Trudee. Children of the Evening (1981).
Armstrong, Louise. Kiss Daddy Goodnight (1982).
Barry, Kathleen. Female Sexual Slavery (1981).
Blakely, Mary Kay. *Who Were the Men?*, Ms. (July 1983).
Bogdanovitch, Peter. The Killing of the Unicorn: Dorothy Stratton, 1960–1980 (1984).
Brady, Katherine. Father's Days: A True Story of Incest (1981).
Brownmiller, Susan. Against Our Will: Men, Women, and Rape (1976).
Daly, Mary. Gyn/Ecology (1979).

Dworkin, Andrea. *The Root Cause*, in Our Blood: Prophecies and Discourses on Sexual Politics (1976).
——. Pornography: Men Possessing Women (1981).
——. Woman Hating (1974).
Griffin, Susan. Pornography and Silence (1981).
Hite, Shere. The Hite Report on Male Sexuality (1982).
Lederer, Laura, ed. Take Back the Night (1980).
Linden, Robin Ruth, et al., eds. Against Sadomasochism (1981).
Lovelace, Linda with Mike McGrady. Ordeal (1983).
MacKinnon, Catharine. Sexual Harassment of Working Women (1979).
Morgan, Robin. *The Stake in the Heart*, in The Anatomy of Freedom (1984).
Steinem, Gloria. *Erotica vs. Pornography*, in Outrageous Acts and Everyday Rebellions (1983).
——. *I Was a Playboy Bunny, id.*
——. *The Real Linda Lovelace, id.*

PANDORA'S BOX: AN ESSAY REVIEW OF AMERICAN LAW AND LITERATURE ON PROSTITUTION

*Anita L. Morse**

"So, if she has been called a woman of the town, a tart, a bawd, a wanton, a bawdy-basket, a bird-of-the-game, a bit of stuff, a buttered bun, a cockatrice, a cock-chafer, a cow, a crack, a cunt, a daughter of Eve, a gay girl, a gobble-prick, a high-flyer, a high-roller, a hussy, a hurry-whore, a jill, a jude, a judy, a jug, laced mutton, lift-skirts, light o'love, merry legs, minx, moll, moon-lighter, morsel, mount, mutton-bro-ker, nestcock, night-bird, night-piece, night-walker, nymph of darkness, nymph of the pavement, petticoat pick-up, piece, pillow-mate, pinch-prick, pole-climber prancer, quail, quiet mouse, or even Queen—it is not surprising."[1]

I. PROSTITUTION IN LAW AND LITERATURE

A. *Introduction*

Erica Jong's introduction to her story of Fanny Hackabout-Jones is

---

* Professor of Law and Law Library Director, University of New Mexico School of Law.

I wish to give thanks to Hendrik Hartog and Willard Hurst of the University of Wisconsin Law School for all of their assistance and encouragement; to Christian Fritz of the University of New Mexico School of Law for his suggestions; and to my research assistants, Julie Brewer of the Auraria Library of the University of Colorado and Maha Khoury of the University of New Mexico School of Law.

In Hesiod's THEOGONY, Pandora introduces sexuality into the world (opens her "box") and destroys the golden age when men were free from work, sickness, and old age. In his WORK AND DAYS, Pandora is perilous temptation sent by Zeus to ruin men. Pandora, like Eve, carries the stigma of all sexual responsibility and is responsible for the fall of man. In Genesis, Chapter 3, Adam, too, is tempted by Eve who offers him fruit from the tree of knowledge of good and evil. When God asks Adam why he disobeyed God's commandment not to eat of the fruit of the forbidden tree, Adam places all responsibility on Eve. God says to Eve: "I will multiply thy sorrow, and thy conceptions: in sorrow shalt thou bring forth children, and thou shalt be under thy husband's power, and he shall have dominion over thee." In both stories, the tempter is a god, the woman takes the rap, and the man is held blameless for his fall.

1. E. JONG, FANNY: BEING THE TRUE HISTORY OF THE ADVENTURES OF FANNY HACKABOUT - JONES, 448-453, 490-95 (1980). (FANNY is the feminist retelling of J. Cleland - FANNY HILL OR MEMOIRS OF A WOMAN OF PLEASURE, (1748-49 Penguin ed. 1985), in which Fanny becomes an initiator of her own actions. She both recognizes her debased status in the patriarchal system and works to substitute a communal version of power sharing. Fanny never denies the humanity of men but, rather, recognizes the inhu-manity of patriarchal oppression. Fanny transcends modern feminists by expressing the life of every woman, recognizing the existence of sexuality, accepting her own complex nature, and truly entering into the universal sisterhood).

a feminist scholar's ironic comment on prostitution and female sexuality in a society that equates power with gender. Catherine MacKinnon argues that gender is not a biological difference but a social construct of male domination over women. Sex roles and sexuality, MacKinnon asserts, are both defined by men for women. Sexuality is what men want as erotic gratification and, therefore, how women must define their sexuality. Sex roles are the circumscribed social roles that women are given in a male-dominated society. "Gender is an inequality of power, a social status based on who is permitted to do what to whom."[2]

The literature I survey in this essay shows that the United States created its own version of prostitution. This version told a story of a public sphere for men's political and economic power and a private sphere for women's domesticity. Prostitution became a marketplace version of women's sexuality and sex role, controlled by men. By labelling the fate of a woman who did not conform to norms of sexual behavior and sex role, prostitution defined the legitimate domestic role of acceptable women in the private, domestic sphere.

The sanctions against prostitution were overt suppression and covert control. Suppression upheld the norm of acceptable female sexuality and sex role. Control maintained the reality of economic and political male power in the marketplace to buy or sell women as sexual objects. The stories about prostitution justified the social and legal norms as well as behavior. Historians and economists asserted prostitution was the oldest profession. Politicians considered prostitution a necessary evil. Medical reformers called prostitution the social evil. Churchmen denounced prostitutes as scarlet women. New abolitionists said prostitutes were white slaves. Behind each of these statements was a story about women and the patriarchy they lived in. They were explicit statements of social and legal norms; whereas the statement, unlike slaves, the wife could usually deny her sexual favors to her husband, was an implicit assertion of the status and role of women, who, under male control, were only able to act through passive resistance.[3]

Indeed prostitution is one of the oldest professions, if by that we mean it is an accepted trade. What type of trade it is, however, has been viewed in many ways. The earliest recordings of legal codes include prostitution as another set of property relationships among men. The discourse created on this topic views prostitution as another aspect of the role of women as property—subjects of exchange, barter, and slavery—which

---

2. C. MacKinnon, Feminism Unmodified 6-10, quotation at 8 (1987) *See* R. Bleier, Science and Gender 80 (1984) (". . .gender is, in fact, a social construction or accomplishment, and gender attributions differ across cultures. Science, however, in the form of gender-difference and gender role (sex-difference and sex-role) research, views these attributions as 'natural' categories for which biological explanations are appropriate and even necessary.").

3. V. Bullough & B. Bullough, The History of Prostitution (1964); The Image of the Prostitute in Modern Literature, at 1-17 (1984).

was regulated by legal codes, customs, and taboos.[4] Prostitution can just as easily be analyzed under a modern market economy theory: prostitution as a business relationship, a market transaction which should be regulated by appropriate zoning, tax, health, safety, and fair advertising laws.[5]

Each story about prostitution was created in the context of patriarchal society in different historical settings. Since each story has a distinct origin which includes a cultural and political setting with its own legal norms and cultural explanations, each can be used as a fundamental analysis of the nature of that patriarchal society.[6] Necessary evil is at least as old as the Old Testament, Plato, Aristotle, and St. Paul.[7] Social evil is a product of the near-plague conditions brought about by the spread of syphilis in the sixteenth and seventeenth centuries.[8] White slavery caught the fervid attention of old and new abolitionists, suffragettes, and the social purity movement in late nineteenth century America as well as of nativists who could then blame immigration and degenerate races for the growth of urban crime and poverty.[9]

The purpose of each story has been to explain prostitution as a product of women's irrational nature and to justify the social and legal regulation of all women. Prostitution describes the final degradation of women through their sexuality which permits men to place women in a subservient status.

B. Theories of Regulation

The justifications for legal regulation of prostitution are numerous and not mutually contradictory. The primary reason given for controlling prostitution is preservation of the family. The family serves as a means of enforcing wider socializing controls by the state. The state, in turn, regulates prostitution in order to protect the family. Women are treated as property controlled by father, brother, husband, and state.[10]

Other reasons for regulation include medical regulation to prevent

---

4. V. BULLOUGH & B. BULLOUGH, *supra* note 2, at 17 states the Hammurubi Code (c. 1404-1162 b.c.) regulated the position of prostitutes. *See generally*, G. LERNER, THE CREATION OF PATRIARCHY (1986).

5. *See, e.g.*, C. WINNICK & P. KINSIE, THE LIVELY COMMERCE: PROSTITUTION IN THE UNITED STATES (1971); J. DECKER, PROSTITUTION: REGULATION AND CONTROL (1979).

6. C. SMITH-ROSENBERG, DISORDERLY CONDUCT: VISIONS OF GENDER IN THE UNITED STATES 18 (1985); *See generally*, G. LERNER, *supra* note 4.

7. K. HARRIS, SEX, IDEOLOGY, AND RELIGION (1984); THE INTERPRETERS DICTIONARY OF THE BIBLE 963-66 (Supp. 1976); E. STANTON, THE ORIGINAL FEMINIST ATTACK ON THE BIBLE; THE WOMEN'S BIBLE (Arno Reprint ed. 1974).

8. V. BULLOUGH & B. BULLOUGH, *supra* note 2, at 127-144.

9. W. RECKLESS, VICE IN CHICAGO (1933); G. KNEELAND, COMMERCIALIZED PROSTITUTION IN NEW YORK CITY (1913).

10. E. MORGAN, THE PURITAN FAMILY: RELIGION AND DOMESTIC RELATIONS IN SEVENTEENTH CENTURY NEW ENGLAND (Rev. ed. 1966); S. DITZION, MARRIAGE, MORALS, AND SEX IN AMERICA (Rev. ed. 1969).

the spread of disease, protection of minors and victimized women, protection of property values, prevention of official corruption and the regulation of organized crime. Both Carol Smith-Rosenberg and G.J. Barker-Benfield see the imposition of strict medical and social controls over female sexuality in nineteenth century America as attempts during a period of great social disorganization to reinforce patriarchy. Gerda Lerner cautions researchers, however, to place the controls over women into a larger context of class and gender controls.[11]

Nineteenth century America created its own special theory of gender, stressing the need for male self-control and female passivity. The justification advanced for control over female sexuality was a belief in women's inferiority. Caesar Lombroso,[12] a major figure in nineteenth century criminal anthropology, began his study of female offenders by quoting the biblical condemnation of Eve and then set forth his assumption that women are by nature primitive, intellectually underdeveloped, lacking in compassion (an intellectual trait), and emotive. Male criminality arose either because of evolutionary differentiation (property crimes) or aggressive personality traits (violent crimes). Women were criminal because of their underdeveloped natures which permitted them to be led into crime. Prostitutes were normally mentally defective. But all women were of lesser intelligence and incapable of intellectual development and would become totally atavistic if led into crime. Thus nineteenth century theories of criminal responsibility and penal reform did not apply to women since they could do nothing about their underdeveloped natures or change their inferior status.[13] The Supreme Court opinion in *Buck v. Bell*[14] upholding

---

11. C. SMITH-ROSENBERG, *supra* note 6 at 22-24, 182-244, *The Cycle of Femininity in Nineteenth Century America, The Hysterical Woman: Sex Roles and Role Conflict in Nineteenth Century America, The Abortion Movement and the AMA, 1850-1880*; G. BARKER-BENFIELD, THE HORRORS OF THE HALF-KNOWN LIFE: MALE ATTITUDES TOWARD WOMEN AND SEXUALITY IN NINETEENTH CENTURY AMERICA (1976); G. LERNER, THE MAJORITY FINDS ITS PAST: PLACING WOMEN IN HISTORY 3-14, 169-180 (1979).
12. C. LOMBROSO & W. FERRERO, THE FEMALE OFFENDER xi, xv, 109-113 (1903, trans. 1915).
13. *Id.*; C. SMITH-ROSENBERG, *supra* note 6, at 24-26; E. FREEDMAN, THEIR SISTERS' KEEPERS: WOMEN'S PRISON REFORM IN AMERICA, 1830-1930, at 18-21, 111-116 (1981).
14. 274 U.S. 200 (1927) "It is better for all the world, if instead of waiting to execute the degenerate offspring for crime, or to let them starve for their imbecility, society can prevent those who are manifestly unfit for continuing their kind . . . Three generations of imbeciles are enough." *Id.* at 207. *See* S. GOULD, THE FLAMINGO'S SMILE: REFLECTIONS IN HISTORY 306-318 (1985) for the story of Carrie Buck. Dr. K. Ray Nelson, director of the Lynchburg Hospital, where Carrie was sterilized, researched the records of more than 4,000 sterilizations performed at the institution, the last in 1972. He found Carrie and her sister, Doris, who was also sterilized under the same law. Carrie was a woman of normal intelligence. She was committed on the testimony of her foster parents whom she continued to live with as an adult, doing chores around the house. Carrie was raped by a relative of her foster parents and then blamed for the rape. She was sent away to have an illegitimate child. Carrie was a sexual deviant, not a mental deviant.

state laws on sterilization of delinquent women placed a great reliance on these new theories of scientific criminology.

In general, criminology classed delinquent women with the insane and children, assigning them to indeterminate sentences and "protection" by the state, which meant controls but not rights. Women were not afforded the constitutional protections given to men under criminal jurisprudence. The fourth amendment did not protect suspected prostitutes against medical inspections and enforced medical procedures. The fourteenth amendment did not protect women against lack of due process or unequal protection when laws discriminated between prostitutes and their male customers on the basis of sex. Vagrancy laws were indiscriminately applied to unescorted women on the streets.

The irony of social controls over prostitution is best seen in the double standard of enforcement. Male customers of prostitutes were very seldom arrested because male purchase of sex was acceptable legal and social behavior. The moral justifications for the legal control of prostitution were justifications for control, called protection, of women.[15]

The legal and cultural history of prostitution in nineteenth and twentieth century America offers us the opportunity to review attitudes towards female sexuality and sex roles, and the legal controls placed on women to control their sexuality and sex roles. The literature shows that America stood apart from Europe in its statements of values and norms, if not its treatment, of prostitution. We created a sacred vision of the American family as a counterpart to our secular vision of individualism. The legal control of women was perceived as essential to this vision because she was the upholder of virtue in a nation of opportunistic individualism.[16]

II. LITERATURE OF POPULAR CULTURE REFLECTING ATTITUDES TOWARDS SEXUALITY AND PROSTITUTION

A. Literature of Women's Sexuality and Prostitution

Until recently, there had been little interest in the lives of working women in early America; historical and intellectual accounts dealt primarily with the middle and upper classes. What is written about servants and

---

15. B.M. HOBSON, UNEASY VIRTUE: THE POLITICS OF PROSTITUTION AND THE AMERICAN REFORM TRADITION 172-175 (1987): P. ROBY, POLITICS AND PROSTITUTION: A CASE STUDY OF THE FORMULATION, ENFORCEMENT AND JUDICIAL ADMINISTRATION OF THE NEW YORK STATE PENAL LAWS ON PROSTITUTION, 1870-1970 (1971); H. WOOLSTON, PROSTITUTION IN THE UNITED STATES: VOL. I. PRIOR TO THE ENTRANCE OF THE UNITED STATES INTO THE WORLD WAR (1921, reprint 1969).

16. See Cott, Passionless: An Interpretation of Victorian Sexual Ideology, 1790-1850, at 162-181; Lerner, The Lady and the Mill Girl: Changes in the Status of Women in the Age of Jackson, 1800-1840, at 182-196; Smith-Rosenberg, Beauty, the Beast, and the Militant Woman: A Case Study in Sex Roles and Social Stress in Jacksonian America, at 197-221 in N. COTT & E. PLECK, A HERITAGE OF HER OWN: TOWARD A NEW SOCIAL HISTORY OF AMERICAN WOMEN (1979).

common laborers is about their control by masters and by the state. But it should be understood that control over all women was a part of life in early America. The male family head was the governing institution and the larger family was the state. The head of the family—the father—was expected to train, discipline, and manage his wife, children, and servants. If he failed in this responsibility, then the state intervened.[17]

American writers maintained the primacy of the father in decision-making but advised wisdom in accepting his children's choices as essential to a sound marriage. The religious reform background of America tempered its attitude towards the marriage as a romantic rather than a business transaction. Marriage itself, however, was a sacred institution and sexuality outside of marriage was forbidden. Early American ideology did not countenance a double standard of sexuality, and the Puritan communities used communal shaming to both rehabilitate sinners and to illustrate that the state would not condone transgressions.[18]

The writings of seventeenth and eighteenth century church and political leaders show continuing movement towards a growing tolerance of increased female participation in education and public life. Yet, there was a desire to place strict limits on women's activities outside the home. On the one hand, social conditions in America often required the woman to manage her husband's business affairs and to train her children and domestics in his absence. On the other hand, women in public life would destroy the stratified role women must play in upholding family values, and a clear line was drawn between education for private and for public spheres.[19]

Charles Brockden Brown's gothic romance, *Ormond*, set in Philadelphia during the plague of the 1790's, illustrates this dichotomy. Constantia Dudley was unable to support her sick and destitute father because he trained her in mathematics and the classics rather than in domestic skills; she was not suitable to be a governess for young ladies. Despite her pov-

---

17. E. MORGAN, *supra* note 10; *See*, M.S. BENSON, WOMEN IN EIGHTEENTH CENTURY AMERICA: A STUDY OF OPINION AND SOCIAL CHANGE (1935) is a study of the middle and upper class family. For a study on working class communities of women, see T. DUBLIN, WOMEN AT WORK: THE TRANSFORMATION OF WORK AND COMMUNITY IN LOWELL, MASSACHUSETTS, 1826-1860 (1979), and Basch, *The Emerging Legal History of Women in the United States: Property, Divorce, and the Constitution*, 12 Signs: J. of Women and Culture in Soc. 97-117 (1986) (for new research on working class women in early American history).

18. *See*, Hartog, *The Public Law of a County Court: Judicial Government in Eighteenth Century Massachusetts*, 20 AM. J. OF LEGAL HISTORY 282, 298-308 (1976) (a study of fornication cases in local courts that shows the change from moral use of the courts to enforcing support obligations for illegitimate offsprings). *See also*, M. HINDUS, PRISON AND PLANTATION: CRIME, JUSTICE AND AUTHORITY IN MASSACHUSETTS AND SOUTH CAROLINA, 1767-1878 (1980).

19. Smith, *The Study of the Family in Early America: Trends, Problems, and Prospects*, 39 WILLIAM AND MARY Q. 3-28 (1982 3d Ser.) (an excellent review of the literature on post revolutionary changes in women's status); M.S. BENSON, *supra* note 17, at 131-178.

erty Constantia, educated to make her own decisions and maintain her integrity, resisted the advances of the evil Ormond. Her foil, the orphaned Helena, had no other choice than to become a fallen woman, the mistress of the evil Ormond, because her wealthy father educated her only in dancing music and romantic novels, the domestic skills. She had no mind of her own, no ethical basis to withstand the destruction of her moral purity.

Brown was the exception, however, in presenting a cultural counterpoint in his novels and in *Alcuin*, a polemical essay about the subjugation of women.[20] All other sermons, essays, and popular literature of his time confirmed the legal and religious concept of male authority over the family and in the state. They all set the standard for a carefully restricted education for women based on useful domestic skills.[21]

Popular literature reinforced the need for restrictions over women. The stories portrayed passive, sublimated, and domestically skilled women. Their foils were romantic, flighty, and ungovernable, and the result was downfall and damnation. There was no redemption for the fallen woman but death, even if the seduction was not her fault. The lesson of these stories was that sin weighed equally on both male and female. The female, however, received the greater punishment since she had the greater responsibility for falling into original sin and since the fall of the male was attributed to her sexual attractions. Each story was a recreation of Adam and Eve.[22]

In "Images of Women in Early American Literature,"[23] Ann Stanford discusses early stories which stressed the Puritan concept of male and female duties. A favorite story was the "captivity theme" where a woman prevailed among her Indian captors through belief in God.[24] But later eighteenth century narratives and fiction began to indicate a growing dis-

20. C.B. BROWN, ORMOND OR THE SECRET WITNESS (1887 ed.); *The Problem of Origination in Brown's Ormond*, 126-141, Davidson, *The Matter and Manner of Charles Brockden Brown's Alcuin*, 71-86, Baym, *A Minority Rendering of Wieland*, 87-103, in B. ROSENTHAL, CRITICAL ESSAYS ON CHARLES BROCKDEN BROWN (1980); C.B. BROWN, ALCUIN, Parts I and II were published in 1798 and Parts III and IV were published in 1815, in W. DUNLAP, THE LIFE OF CHARLES BROCKDEN BROWN.

21. M.S. BENSON, *supra* note 17, at 101-171, citing E. HITCHCOCK, MEMOIRS OF THE BLOOM GROVE FAMILY (2 vol. Boston, 1790); BENJAMIN FRANKLIN, REFLECTIONS ON COURTSHIP AND MARRIAGE; C. MATHER, ORNAMENTS FOR THE DAUGHTERS OF ZION (1692); B. RUSH, THOUGHTS UPON FEMALE EDUCATION (Philadelphia 1787).

22. S.H. ROWSON, CHARLOTTE TEMPLE: A TALE OF TRUTH (1794, reprint 1986); W.H. BROWN, THE POWER OF SYMPATHY (1798, reprint 1970); *see* N. BAYM, WOMEN'S FICTION: A GUIDE TO NOVELS BY AND ABOUT WOMEN IN AMERICA, 1820-1870 (1978); Welter, *The Cult of True Womanhood*; 1820-1860, 18 Am. Q. 151-174 (1966).

23. Stanford, *Images of Women in Early American Literature*, 184-234 in WHAT MANNER OF WOMAN: ESSAYS ON ENGLISH AND AMERICAN LIFE AND LITERATURE (1977).

24. M. ROWLANDSON, THE SOVEREIGNTY AND GOODNESS OF GOD (1682); C. MATHER, HUMILIATIONS FOLLOW'D WITH DELIVERANCES (1697) LUCTUOSUM (1699) are examples cited in Kolodny, *Turning the Lens on "The Panther Captivity": A Feminist Exercise in Practical Criticism*, in WRITING AND SEXUAL DIFFERENCE (1980).

content among women in their appointed roles and a fear in men of the changes. The literature ranged from satirical pieces about uppity women by Benjamin Franklin in "The Courant" (a New England periodical) and John Turnbull's satire on women, *The Progress of Dullness* (1792) to epistolary novels such as William Hill Brown's *The Power of Sympathy* which warns young women against seduction and betrayal. In Brown's novel, the theme of sexuality as a form of female insanity is fully developed.

Stanford notes that the gothic tale of seduction coincided with a rise in premarital conception and served as a moral caution of the dire consequences of sexual incontinence. Early writers linked premarital pregnancy with a change of controls over marriage property settlement and the advent of romantic marriage, but recent studies indicate that more to the point was a loss of control over the lower social classes.[25] Morality was still rigid in the middle classes where property and status were maintained, but the rural to urban migration of villagers to industrial settings increased premarital cohabitation among the propertyless classes. Or, at least, it reduced the former pattern in villages of enforced marriage after conception of a child out of wedlock.[26]

Cathy N. Davidson[27] explains the sentimental and gothic American novels of post-revolutionary America as setting forth a story of women's oppression within a myth of freedom. Although most critics see Charles Brockden Brown's protagonists as predecessors to the heroic tradition of James Fenimore Cooper, Nathaniel Hawthorne, and Herman Melville, Davidson places Brockden Brown in the earlier tradition of William Hill Brown's *The Power of Sympathy* and Susanna Rawson's *Charlotte Temple*. Both novels were based on recent scandals involving the seduction and betrayal of a young woman by a wealthy married man, and her subsequent suicide. The authors tell the reader they are not writing romantic novels but, rather, setting forth cautionary moral tales to inspire young women to purity.[28]

Charlotte Temple became a cult novel of the 1800's, with its sentimentalization of death as the consequences of romantic love. On one level it could be read as a moral lesson teaching the need to stay on the straight and narrow path of true womanhood, but it also contrasted the oppressed and servile status of women in the new republic with male freedom to

---

25. Stanford, *supra* note 23; V. BULLOUGH & B. BULLOUGH, *supra* note 3, at 187-198; Freedman, *Sexuality in Nineteenth Century America: Behavior, Ideology, and Politics*, 10 Rev. in Amer. Hist. 196-215 197-201 (1982).

26. Stanford *supra* note 23; Smith, and Hindus, *Premarital Pregnancy in America 1640-1971: An Overview and Interpretation*, J. of Interdisciplinary History 537-570 (1975); Shorter, *Female Emancipation, Birth Control, and Fertility in European History*, 78 Am. Hist. Rev. 605-640 (1973); Shorter, *Illegitimacy, Sexual Revolution, and Social Change in Modern Europe*, J. of Interdisciplinary History 237-272 (1971).

27. C. DAVIDSON, REVOLUTION AND THE WORD: THE RISE OF THE NOVEL IN AMERICA (1986).

28. *Id.* at 95-109.

quest for self-fulfillment. Not only were women depicted as sexually enslaved by men, it was also clear that men were free to seek sexual gratification without fear of punishment whereas women were ruined by any indiscretion.[29]

Perhaps the most representative popular novelist of mid-nineteenth century America was James Fenimore Cooper, who romanticized the aristocratic ideal of arcadian America and decried the onslaught of revolutionary America in his *Leatherstocking Tales*.[30] In *The Ways of the Hours*, Cooper attacked two legal reforms of nineteenth century America: the jury system and women's property rights. In the novel, Mary Munson (Mildred de Larocheforte nee Millington) was a wealthy young matron, educated and married in France to a dissolute aristocrat. She abandoned him and secluded herself in the house of a poor, upstate New York farm couple, the wife, a harridan and the husband, a drunkard. A fire caused the couple's deaths, and Mary was accused of arson, murder, and theft.

Exotic Mary was contrasted to pale Anna Updyke, the submissive young woman betrothed to Jack Wilmeter, one of Mary's defending attorneys. Jack was sexually attracted to Mary, but Anna cleaved faithfully to his side and dutifully supported his belief in Mary's innocence. Mr. Thomas Dunscomb was Mary's senior attorney, and, as the story unfolds, we learn that he was jilted by Mary's mother. Attorney Dunscomb is convinced that instability and recklessness, now allowed to run amuck by women's property rights, were endemic in the family. What else could account for women's actions? Certainly not men's actions towards women or a woman's rational choice.

Mary managed to escape the clutches of a biased local jury and a prosecutor out to win an election through victory in this trial, but then showed her "moral insanity." Thereafter her affairs were firmly managed by her "friends." The dissolute husband was, of course, sympathetically treated by Attorney Dunscomb as a rightful claimant to Mary and handsomely paid off with Mary's funds. Attorney Dunscomb lectured Mary,

"Your return to America has, I fear, been most inopportune. Among other innovations that are making on every side of us, even to the verge of the dissolution of civilized society, comes the liberty of woman. Need I

---

29. *Id.* at 110-150. *See also,* C. PEARSON & K. POPE, THE FEMALE HERO IN AMERICAN AND BRITISH LITERATURE 1-49, 260-70, Bibliography 297-305 (1981) (A study of male and female images of self-worth in literature. Males can be independent questors. Females, the authors assert, are expected to emulate the dependent prefallen virgin. Any deviation from this ideal form is accompanied by suffering. The only way most female writers could transcend the dilemma created by independence being related to female failure was to portray a total selflessness that is experienced in a new respiritualized community.).

30. THE LEATHERSTOCKING TALES (Reprint 1985) include THE PIONEERS (1823), THE LAST OF THE MOHICANS (1826), THE PRAIRIE (1827), THE PATHFINDER (1840) THE DEERSLAYER (1841); *See* J. TOMPKINS, SENSATIONAL DESIGNS: THE CULTURAL WORK OF AMERICAN FICTION, 1790-1860, at 94-121 (1985) (on the cultural history in James Fenimore Cooper).

tell you, what will be the next step in this downward career? Her licentiousness. No woman can throw off the most sacred of all her earthly duties, in this reckless manner, and hope to escape from the doom of her sex."[31]

Nina Baym notes that male heroic literature of the nineteenth century did not deal with women as characters but rather used them as symbolic representations of the ideal and the soul, or the soul and the real. Cooper's good women were domesticated pillars of society. Poe created oppressive relationships between lovers and mistresses or wives and husbands as a counterfoil to the male's heroic search for self. Melville sought self-identity in freedom from female destiny. Although Hawthorne's women were more fully developed than other authors of his time they were still symbols. But women in Hawthorne's stories were symbols of values of creativity and sincerity while men were portrayed as repressed and conventional.[32]

Hester in *The Scarlett Letter* (1850) and Zenobia in *The Blithesdale Romance* (1852) were strong, passionate women who transgressed social standards and were punished by society. Hawthorne portrayed the women in these novels as powerless to show the plight of the individual in a repressive society and to illustrate problems of choosing between self and society's moral order. Hester represents choosing oneself while Dimmesdale is constrained by a morality imposed on him by society. But literary criticism of *The Scarlet Letter* elevated Dimmesdale's choice: Dimmesdale's remorse was greater than Hester's because his was based on the ideal he has degraded whereas Hester's repentance was based on love. Hester, as woman, was able to seek redemption in loving absolution. Dimmesdale could only be redeemed through confession and deliverance from sin in death.[33]

Male writers used women as symbols of lightness and darkness. Some were the writers of moral tales who sought to maintain social control through cautionary tales of evil brought about by female transgression. Others were more aspirational and wrote about the heroic quest in which female represented social organization and male represented freedom and ideal. Hawthorne and Brockden Brown portrayed sympathetic pictures of strong women who were labelled deviant but who actually rep-

---

31. J.F. COOPER, THE WAYS OF THE HOUR: A TALE, at 491 (1968) (1850).

32. Baym, *Portrayals of Women in American Literature, 1790-1870*, 211-234 in WHAT MANNER OF WOMAN, *supra* note 23.

33. Munger, *Notes on the Scarlet Letter*, 93 ATLANTIC 521-535 (April 1904); Baym, *Portrayal of Women in American Literature, 1790-1870* 211-234, in WHAT MANNER OF WOMAN *supra* note 23; D.B. DAVIS, HOMICIDE IN AMERICAN FICTION, 1798-1860, at 169, 205-206 (1957) (stating that popular literature assigned different moral natures to men and women. Men were rational beings, capable of freedom and responsibility, but a woman's nature was based on her sexuality. A fallen woman, even though seduced, embodies positive evil that must be condemned. Hester, therefore, had to repent for the guilt she shared with all women of having corrupted natural man through her sexuality. Back to Pandora and Eve.).

resented freedom and moral will opposed to a repressive society. On the whole, however, the popular literary culture was dominated by the gothic tale of seduction and abandonment.[34]

Women writers used masks of conformity to hide their assertions of individualism and their rebellion against dependence. Emily Dickinson's poetry and Harriet Beecher Stowe's and Louisa Mae Alcott's fiction used the domestic realm of a dependent woman's separate sphere to adjust to a male world. Thus domestic reality became the realm by which they measured their quest. They still used the patriarchal definitions of the status of women and the roles women should play. Women who did not adjust to domesticity were social transgressors, fallen women. Sexuality and nonconformity were sinful. Therefore, the only way to gain independence within these definitions was to withdraw from sexuality. The nineteenth century literary portrait by women of women was an attempt to gain a realistic independence through asexuality. A separate domestic sphere based on higher ideals could be maintained.[35]

B. The Counter Culture Movement and Popular Advice Literature

In the nineteenth century sexual immorality became the target of the commonly held fears that the established social order was disintegrating. Industrialization and the rise of individualism tended to reduce the socializing control of nuclear family organizations.[36]

Counter-culture reactions to nineteenth century industrialization present a vivid picture of the fear about family disintegration and loss of patriarchal control. The Mormons, Shakers, and Oneida Perfectionists were just three contemporary examples of evangelical, communal movement; each one included rigid control over female sexuality, reproduction, and child rearing. The movements were, in fact, well-ordered brothels as well as well-ordered houses. Although they advocated a new moral regime, their way of life was but a transparent parallel to the greater world where the well-ordered house and the well-ordered brothel existed side by side.[37]

---

34. Baym, supra note 32; J. HART, THE POPULAR BOOK: A HISTORY OF AMERICA'S LITERARY TASTES, at 68-73 (1950).

35. N. AUERBACH, COMMUNITIES OF WOMEN: AN IDEA IN FICTION, 11, 55-73 (1978); See, e.g., BEHIND A MASK: THE UNKNOWN THRILLERS OF LOUISA MAY AL-COTT (1975). (Alcott's gothic romances were published in the popular press such as Frank Leslie's "Illustrated Newspaper" and "The Flag of Our Union" and in the Ten Cent Novelette series. Although the plots were typically based on the seduced and abandoned theme, the dark ladies are interesting women who sometimes are victorious, like Jean Muir in BEHIND A MASK, OR A WOMAN'S POWER.) See also, J. DONOVAN, NEW ENG-LAND LOCAL COLOR LITERATURE: A WOMEN'S TRADITION (1983).

36. M. GROSSBERG, GOVERNING THE HEARTH: LAW AND THE FAMILY IN NINE-TEENTH-CENTURY AMERICA (1985).

37. L. KERN, AN ORDERED LOVE: SEX ROLES AND SEXUALITY IN VICTORIAN UTOPIAS: THE SHAKERS, THE MORMONS, AND THE ONEIDA COMMUNITY (1981).

John Humphrey Noyes, the leader of the Oneida Perfectionists, discussed this sexual tendency of revivalism:

> Revivals lead to religious love, religious love excites the passions; the converts, finding themselves in theocratic liberty, begin to look about for their mates and their paradise. Here begins the divergence. If women have to lead, the feminine idea that ordinary wedded love is carnal and unholy rises and becomes the leading principle. Mating on the spiritual plan, with all the heights and depths of sentimental love, become the order of the day. Then, if a prudent Mother Ann (The Shakers) is at the head of affairs, the sexes are fenced off from each other, and carry on their Platonic intercourse through the grating.
>
> On the other hand, if the leaders are men, the theocratic impulse takes the opposite direction, and polygamy in some form is the result. Thus Mormonism is the masculine form, as Shakerism is the feminine form, of the more morbid product of Revival.
>
> Our Oneida Socialism, too, is a masculine product of the great revival.[38]

By mid-century, America, in the eyes of many contemporary commentators, was perceived as suffering from social disorganization that threatened to destroy the basic family control mechanism. Republican ideals of individualism were turning into a license for licentiousness. Both the sectarian revivalists and the middle class establishment were struggling against the same problems created by industrialization, immigration, and urban poverty. The radical fringe characterized the establishment as the problem and wanted total reorganization of the economy and the family. The establishment viewed the revivalists as destructive of modernization and existing modes of social organization. The American establishment, however, had sown the seeds of its own destruction with the revolutionary concepts of individual salvation, romantic love, and republican government.[39]

America attempted to encourage modernization without social disintegration by imposing a system of rigid social controls on men and women. Men were to be trained to be entrepreneurial actors who were independent and self-actuated but socialized into a regulated economic order. Women were responsible for maintaining the domestic aspects of this well-regulated system. Although women were not allowed to be a part of the public order, they were an essential part of the economy, the private order which nurtured children, managed the domestic sphere, and tended the spiritual ideals of the country. Men dealt with production and women with reproduction.[40]

---

38. Noyes, *Essay on Scientific Propagation*, at 145 reprinted in R. WALTERS, PRIMERS FOR PRUDERY: SEXUAL ADVICE TO VICTORIAN AMERICA (1974).

39. L. KERN, *supra* note 37, at 20-33.

40. C. DEGLER, AT ODDS: WOMEN AND THE FAMILY IN AMERICA FROM THE REVOLUTION TO THE PRESENT 26-110 (1980); Degler, *What Ought To Be and What*

The popular advice literature of the day and the popular magazine story of the day repeated these lessons. Women were taught to be submissive but strong, managerial yet dependent, and, above all, chaste—a clean bill of goods on the marriage market. Men were taught to be independent but self-controlled, entrepreneurial but socialized, and self-sufficient in business but a part of a family organization. Advice literature combined health, religion, education, and science to create a new ideology of an American secular religion. Its mainstream theologians were not too far removed from their revivalist brothers and sisters of communal societies. Dr. Graham and Dr. Kellogg, popular medical health experts, wrote and lectured to young men on diet, sexual self-restraint, and the terrors of onanism while Robert Dale Owens, founder of the communal colony at New Harmony, wrote on birth control and self restraint. Catherine Beecher and Harriet Beecher Stowe lectured and wrote for young women on the same delicate subjects.[41]

All of the writers were particularly distressed about the vices of city life. Middle class young men were admonished to marry late when economically able and adjured to refrain from visiting houses of prostitution. The prevailing scientific theory was that men were biologically controlled by sexual energy which must be diverted to other purposes. One theory was that sexual energy expended on fornication would deplete the bodily resources needed for successful commercial enterprise thus the literature was filled with dire warning of the effects of masturbation, which included insanity, epilepsy, consumption, lassitude, bashfulness, baldness, and lower back pain.[42]

An important aspect of this campaign for moral control was the new science of early childhood development which held that adolescence was a time when minds and bodies should be trained for life. Earlier theory had viewed children as miniature adults, and seventeenth and eighteenth century law provided for early indentures and rigid religious instruction.[43] The creation of adolescence was instrumental in raising the level of female

---

Was: Women's Sexuality in the Nineteenth Century, 79 Am. Hist. Rev. 1467-1490 (1974).

41. R. WALTERS *supra* note 38 at 19-31 citing examples of writings from S. GRAHAM, *Chastity*, in A COURSE OF LECTURES TO YOUNG MEN: INTENDED ALSO, FOR THE SERIOUS CONSIDERATION OF PARENTS AND GUARDIANS (n.d.); C. BEECHER & H. B. STOWE, THE AMERICAN WOMAN'S HOME: OR, PRINCIPLES OF DOMESTIC SCIENCE, BEING A GUIDE TO THE FORMATION AND MAINTENANCE OF ECONOMICAL, HEALTHFUL, BEAUTIFUL, AND CHRISTIAN HOMES (1869); R.D. OWEN, MORAL PHYSIOLOGY OR A BRIEF AND PLAIN TREATISE ON THE POPULATION QUESTION (1841).

42. R. WALTERS, *supra* note 38, at 32-48 citing examples of writings from W. ALCOTT, THE YOUNG MAN'S GUIDE (16th ed. 1846); J. KELLOGG, PLAIN FACTS FOR OLD AND YOUNG (1974) (1st ed. 1877); M. LAZARUS, INVOLUNTARY SEMINAL LOSSES: THEIR CAUSES, EFFECTS, AND CURE (1852); H. BEECHER, TWELVE LECTURES TO YOUNG MEN ON VARIOUS IMPORTANT SUBJECTS (rev. ed. 1879).

43. J. HAWES, CHILDREN IN URBAN SOCIETY: JUVENILE DELINQUENCY IN 19TH CENTURY AMERICA, at 12-26 (1971); Reinier, *Rearing the Republican Child: Attitudes and Practices in Post-Revolutionary Philadephia*, 34 WILLIAM AND MARY Q. 150-163 (3d Ser. 1982).

education in order that women be prepared for their nurturing roles in the domestic sphere, since the family was so important in determining the outcome of a child's life. The campaign also played a major role in allowing state intervention in the control of juveniles.[44]

At the same time that the importance of early childhood training became accepted practice, America experienced the new problem of a mass or urban, destitute children who were falling into crime and delinquency. Reformers set out to save these children through institutionalization and socialization into middle class values. The state took the place of the family in social control.[45] Delinquent girls, however, fell victim to the prevailing practice of abandonment by the society. They were no longer fit for their domestic roles. Fallen girls were believed to be totally depraved due to their weak natural constitutions; delinquent girls were not educated but only placed in detention homes where they would not corrupt young men.[46]

Medical science also contributed to the control of women's sexuality. Dr. William W. Sanger made the first major investigation of prostitution in America in 1858. He attempted to present a realistic picture of the reasons for young women entering prostitution, the duration of most prostitute's work life, and their chances of leaving prostitution for marriage or other work.[47] In his interviews of prostitutes, the majority of respondents talked of deprivation and family conflict. But he noted that even in the case of those who gave inclination as a reason there were few alternatives to prostitution available.[48]

Dr. Sanger was unusual, however; others in the medical profession offered more radical solutions to female sexuality. Charles D. Meigs[49] treated "nymphomania" in a nine-year old female by applying nitrate of silver to her clitoris, which burned the tissues and nerve endings. He then gave her opium enemas. Joseph W. Howe advised amputation of the clitoris of sexually excitable female adolescents and thought blondes between the ages of sixteen to twenty-five were most susceptible to nymphomania. G.J. Barker-Benfield catalogues "gynecological history" in the United States and asserts that both psychology and medicine were used to enforce controls over women and separate the sexes in society. Gynecologists advocated sexual control of both men and women by placing on women the

---

44. C. SMITH-ROSENBERG, *supra* note 6, at 167-181; E. BLACKWELL, COUNSEL TO PARENT ON THE MORAL EDUCATION OF THEIR CHILDREN (1879); S. WELLS, WEDLOCK: OR, THE RIGHT RELATIONS OF THE SEXES: DISCLOSING THE LAWS OF CONJUGAL SELECTION, AND SHOWING WHO MAY, AND WHO MAY NOT MARRY (1869).

45. J. HAWES, *supra* note 43, at 12-31.

46. *Id.* at 39, 179.

47. R. WALTERS, *supra* note 38, at 75; W. SANGER, THE HISTORY OF PROSTITUTION: ITS EXTENT, CAUSES, AND EFFECTS THROUGHOUT THE WORLD, at 488-89 (1858, reprint 1976).

48. W. SANGER, *supra* note 47, at 488-489.

49. C MEIGS, WOMAN: HER DISEASES AND REMEDIES. A SERIES OF LETTERS TO HIS CLASS, at 151-52 (1859).

burden of preserving male energy for more noble purposes than sex as essential to a woman's role in maintaining the family.[50]

By applying these same restrictive definitions of female sexuality, women reformers, both liberal and purity reformers, also blamed prostitutes for much of the social disintegration of the times. They adhered to the philosophy of training females to asexuality and used it in their struggle for women's rights. They believed that women should preserve the social ideal of the Christian home against natural predatory male instincts which led to war and political corruption. It was necessary, therefore, to condemn the prostitute as not fulfilling women's higher moral role in order to advance the greater cause of women.[51]

A few women reformers began to see prostitution as a problem of social class and as a problem of the status of women. In 1879, Elizabeth Blackwell wrote of the use of the poor by the rich, and the translation of that use for women into prostitution. Although Blackwell still accepted the theory that a fallen woman was no longer fitted for her natural domestic role, she did recognize that prostitutes were not inherently evil. She noted the competition between prostitutes and virtuous young women brought about by the commercialism and display of modern life. Blackwell set the stage for the literary uses of that glitter and glamour of urban life invoked by Theodore Dreiser and Stephen Crane in their tragic tales of Maggie and Carrie.[52]

C. Social Realism at the Turn of the Century

Dreiser wrote the novel, *Sister Carrie* in 1899. Like much of his work, it was based on what he saw and read: His sister, Emma, had run away to New York with a cashier in a tavern who, like Hurstwood, the character in *Sister Carrie*, absconded with his employer's funds. Dreiser turned his sister's story into a story of fatalistic destiny; he rejected placing the responsibility for their own actions on his characters. Instead, Dreiser blamed the corruption of the big city wealth, which benefitted only a few, and the poverty of the working class and migrants, rural or foreign, who settled for mere existence. Carrie and Emma wanted something more and did not settle for less.[53]

---

50. J. Howe, Excessive Venery, Masturbation, And Continence, at 108-11 (1883); G. Barker-Benfield, *supra* note 11, at 37-57, 83.

51. C. Smith-Rosenberg *supra* note 6, at 109-128, 167-181; L. Gordon, Woman's Body, Woman's Right: A Social History of Birth Control In America, at 95-135 (1976).

52. E. Blackwell, *supra* note 44, at 105; Elizabeth Cady Stanton, however, challenged the indissoluble marriage contract and championed a view of marriage as contract rather than status. But Stanton's views on marriage and divorce were shared by only a small group of feminists. *See* E. Clark, Matrimonial Bonds: Slavery, Contract And The Law Of Divorce In Nineteenth Century America, at 2-3, 18-33 (1987) (working paper, available at the Institute for Legal Studies, University of Wisconsin Law School).

53. T. Dreiser, Sister Carrie, at vii-viii (1900, Penguin ed. 1981).

Dreiser vividly portrayed the difference between Carrie, a rural farm migrant who fled to Chicago, and flashy Druet, a not very intelligent but successful salesman. Carrie was relegated to sweat shops where employers wanted sex in trade for jobs. She could only aspire to working for less than $5.00 a week in a department store, spending her pay on the clothes demanded for the job and on board and room. This was respectability for the working woman. Druet could better himself in the new profession of salesman and make enough money to impress Carrie with the glitter and glamour of theaters and restaurants. Why should Carrie not have accepted Druet's offer for a comfortable life, even if, in the eyes of society, she was a fallen woman, a concubine, a mistress, a prostitute? What did society offer to her except decent poverty?

Jane Addams, social worker and founder of Hull House in Chicago, set forth in her essays published in *A New Conscience and an Ancient Evil*[54] true stories of the plight of young working women like Carrie. Addams noted that economic deprivation, ". . .ventures to capitalize a virtuous girl at much less than one who has yielded to temptation, and it may well hold itself responsible for the precarious position into which, year after year, a multitude of frail girls is placed."[55] The factory or shop worker earns $6.00 per week, the bar girl earns $21.00 per week, the prostitute earns $25.00 per week.[56]

She called for reform, education, rehabilitation, and better working conditions to save young women from prostitution. She noted that "thousands of women are so set aside as outcasts from decent society that it is considered an impropriety to speak the very word which designates them."[57] She compared the existence of commercial bondage and traffic in women with pre-Civil War slavery.[58] She spoke of the political corruption that deprived these women of basic rights.[59]

But Addams still believed that sin was personal weakness based on love of pleasure or the influence of evil companions, and that reform and rehabilitation were the answers to the social evil: increased social control over women was her solution.[60] Indeed, public opinion supported the theory of blaming the victim of poverty. If we were a country of unlimited opportunity, then failure must be the fault of the poor.[61] Critics labelled Carrie a trite, heartless, deviant woman and warned parents not to permit tender minds to read such unnecessarily vulgar prose.[62] The sympathetic

---

54. J. ADDAMS, A NEW CONSCIENCE AND AN ANCIENT EVIL (1912 Arno Press ed. 1972).
55. *Id.* at 57.
56. *Id.* at 58.
57. *Id.* at 1.
58. *Id.* at 2-13.
59. *Id.* at 13-57.
60. *Id.* at 59, 181-219.
61. *See, e.g.*, Chase, *Toward a Legal Theory of Popular Culture*, 1986 Wis. L. Rev. 527, 549-550 (an analysis of the blaming the victim psychology of the popular media).
62. J. SALZMAN, THEODORE DREISER: THE CRITICAL RECEPTION, at 1-54 (1972).

treatment Dreiser gave to Carrie violated the American myth of female respectability. To most reviewers, Carrie became just another Eve, responsible for the fall and punished by eternal damnation.

Stephen Crane's earlier novel, *Maggie Girl of the Streets*[63] was also rejected by critics as too brutal. Crane finally privately published the novel under the pseudonym, Johnston Smith. Although it failed in sales, Hamlin Garland, novelist and critic, responded favorably, comparing Maggie to Emile Zola's *Nana*.[64] Garland, however, felt that Crane's portrayal of Maggie's family as the "worst elements of the alley" was unrealistic and that Crane should write of families living "lives of heroic purity and hopeless hardship."[65]

Maggie's family was real. Maggie, herself, had none of the complexity of character of Carrie; rather, Maggie was the Victorian ideal of the pure lily who rises from the muck. Her innocence caused her seduction and fall, and she chose death rather than the dishonor of prostitution. It was the pattern story of the slums, celebrating innate purity. The triumph of the book was its vivid description of the culture of poverty that could destroy family life and push young people into the street. It stands out as a cry against the refusal of polite, Victorian America to look at itself and wonder whether its moral vision was secure.[66]

The novel that was successful was Reginald Wright Kauffman's *The House of Bondage*,[67] a polemical tract on white slavery. Kauffman, editor of a muckraking magazine and prominent reform leader, presented a vivid portrait of rural and foreign immigrant women in the big city, downtrodden by low wages, lack of security, and a corrupt political and legal system. His characters are closer to Crane's lily whites and villains than to Drieser's complex human beings. He trades on the standard prejudices of the day, portraying the villainous white slave traders and pimps as foreign Jews and Italians. But the ironic picture of the wealthy social reformer whose family owns the very business that exploits women and pushes them into prostitution rings true. It is doubly ironic that the appendix to the book is a Presentment of a New York City Grand Jury by the foreman, John D. Rockefeller, Jr. on the trade in women for immoral purposes.[68]

---

63. S. Crane, Bowery Tales: Maggie And George's Mother (Univ. of Va. Press ed. 1969).

64. E. Zola, Nana (1880) (A novel about a woman who becomes a prostitute. The novel's themes stressed both transmission of traits through heredity and the influence of environment on people's lives.).

65. S. Crane *supra* note 63, at xxxviii-xl; Garland, *An Ambitious French Novel and A Modest American Story*, VIII Arena xi-xii (June, 1893).

66. S. Crane *supra* note 63, at xliii-lii.

67. R. Kauffman, The House of Bondage (1910), (The Gregg Press ed. 1968).

68. *Id.* at 466-480. Riegel, *Changing American Attitudes Towards Prostitution, 1800-1920*, 29 J. of Hist. of Ideas 437-452, 450 (1968) (stating that by 1900 many people saw prostitution as big business, the Standard Oil of vice).

D. *The Purity Movement*

Social realism fell to the censors. Purity reformers were guarding the family against knowledge of the streets. Paul Boyer in his study of late nineteenth and twentieth century censorship notes that the purity movement was supported by feminists, social reformers, and progressives who saw literature as having a national spirit which would form our ideals and morals. The Comstock Law, which prohibited obscene materials from being sent through the mails, was the legal means of censorship, but publishers enforced their own internal censorship as well. Prestigious organizations such as the New England Watch and Ward Society were backed by prominent literary families, and fear of both moral and legal retribution was sufficient to deter publication by reputable firms.[69]

David Pivar[70] in his study of the purity crusade against prostitution, pornography, and alcohol notes that the movement was able to unite temperance, political reform, social hygiene, white slavery abolition, and women's rights movements because of its emphasis on reconstructing America through children and the family.[71] There was an obvious conflict in the goals of rehabilitation and protection. The crusade sought the protection of children and rehabilitation of fallen women. In order to be rehabilitated, the "fallen woman" had to be reintegrated into society to some extent, but her presence in society would taint the "purity" of the family and bring home the very elements from which children needed protection. *The House of Bondage* neatly portrays the conflict when Miriam, the socialite reformer, won't let Violet, a teenager rescued from a house of prostitution, attend the girls' club classes. Violet cannot be allowed to corrupt pure young girls.[72]

America's emphasis on purity necessitated rejecting European based models of regulation and medical reform of prostitution as a legal trade. The proponents of this model felt that the public would be protected but that prostitutes would be free from legal harrassment and able to re-enter society. But regulation, medical or otherwise, would entail acceptance of a trade reformers sought to suppress. The mere existence of prostitution, however, was antithetical to the philosophy of family protection. Post-Civil War purity crusade efforts to resist medical regulationists were led by the old abolitionists, temperance leaders, and suffragettes, who saw women as leading the country to a new moral standard.[73]

Purity and political reformers as well as business leaders wanted to socialize urban working class women and saw the problem of prostitution as one created by corrupt city politicians who profited from controlling

---

69. P. Boyer, Purity In Print: The Vice-Society Movement and Book Censorship In America, at 5-17 (1968).

70. D. Pivar, Purity Crusade: Sexual Morality and Social Control, 1868-1900 (1973).

71. *Id.* at 7-9.

72. R. Kauffman *supra* note 67, at 336.

73. D. Pivar, *supra* note 70, at 50-73, 157-74; B. Hobson, *supra* note 15, at 6-7.

vice traffic. Business leaders refused to acknowledge the problem of prostitution as one of low economic status, even though novels like *Sister Carrie* and *The House of Bondage* vividly portrayed the city department store and the garment factories which depended on low-paid women. Study after study reported that employers deliberately paid women low wages, assuming they would live as family dependents, working on a short-term basis before marriage. The reality was that many women were the sole support of families or of themselves.[74]

The purity crusade grew out of a perception of social disorganization and brought together many disparate groups, all looking for a new vision of America—or an old myth of America—as family. Pivar believe that the crusade channelled the women's movement into conservative social objectives and buried the freedom of women in the greater reform movements. The adoption of the purity crusade by reformers of the political system led to secularization of purity reform because of reliance on government to control our social environment. The purity reformers were Puritans, but the political reformers were pragmatists who fell in line with political, economic, and social theories of the moment.

As new theories of sex education, population control, and family planning supplanted earlier programs of strict censorship and sexual continence, purity reformers lost control of the movement. Changing theories of economic and social deprivation altered the treatment of juveniles and women in the criminal justice system. Changing economic and social circumstances, and the dislocations brought about by world war altered attitudes to censorship and social control.[75] Publishers and writers began to have second thoughts about being the literary censors of America and retreated from their earlier support of thought control. Paul Boyer's *Purity in Print* documents the strong support anti-vice activists received from publishers, writers, and librarians which then turned to opposition as censorship critics recognized the government was gaining the ability to control freedom of expression.[76]

E. *The Literature of the Cult of True Womanhood*

The struggle against vice did not end, but the players and the goals changed. In the 1930's and 1940's sexuality became a symbol of true American womanhood and manhood. Cultural exploitation of sexuality replaced censorship as an economic and political goal.[77] Several commen-

---

74. D. Pivar, *supra* note 70, at 204-227; F. Cordasco & T. Pitkin, The White Slave Trade And The Immigrants: A Chapter In American Social History (1981) (Appendix, Sen. Rep. No. 196, 61st Cong., 2d. Sess. 1909, Importing Women for Immoral Purposes).

75. D. Pivar, *supra* note 70, at 257-267; B. Hobson, *supra* note 15, at 163-183.

76. P. Boyer *supra* note 69, at 207-221, 249-273.

77. Butler, Flora, *The Passive Female: Her Comparative Image by Class and Culture in Women's Magazine Fiction*, 33 J. of Marriage and the Family 435-44 (1971); K. Fishburn, Women In Popular Culture, at 125-135 (1982); Hearth And

tators have pointed to the use of mass media magazines and television to create a cult of femininity through advertisements, fiction, nonfiction fashion and "how to" become or stay married stories (themselves advertisements in another form). The stories all stressed women as passive sex objects defined by male values. The most telling controversy over sexuality in the 1950's was the attempted censorship of a book that portrayed the sexual commercialization of American girl children and women as the reality of the modern cult of the family.

The controversy over Vladimir Nabokov's *Lolita* was representative of the new morality. *Lolita* was a symbol of the so-called sexual revolution: the commercialization of female sexuality from childhood to womenhood. Nabokov later noted how four American publishers were shocked by *Lolita* and refused publication,[78] when in fact, the novel was free from lewd descriptions of sex that peppered pulp novels of the same era. George Baker in "Saturday Review" noted that readers would be disappointed if they wanted obscenity; rather, the book was filled with comic horror.[79] Even the U.S. Customs Office found the book, finally published in Paris, unobjectionable. Although some journals (e.g., "The Chicago Tribune" and "The Christian Science Monitor") refused to review *Lolita*, most critics were obsessive in finding high literary content hidden in the text.[80] Some saw it as a myth of decadent Europe disappointed in immature America. Others saw it as a satire on America's commercialism.[81]

Most of the reviewers were interested in the male seducer's psyche and not in the adolescent girl's victimization, even to the point of finding her juvenile sexual experiments proof of her fallen status and Eve-like depravity.[82] Many reviewers thought the book was a comic spoof on American life. A few critics, however, saw the reality that comic horror allows us to experience. Donald Malcolm noted this quality and compared Nabokov's approach to Mark Twain. Malcolm said the book was not "wonderfully or wildly funny".[83] The reader should be horrified by a scene where, knowing the captive sexual relationship Humbert holds Lolita in, we hear the school principal talking to Humbert of the school goals to educate girls to adjust to dating, sex, and marriage.

HOME: IMAGES OF WOMEN IN THE MASS MEDIA, at 19-20, (including on annot. bib. on television and women,) at 275-319 (1978).

   78. V. NABOKOV, LOLITA, at mcmlv (1955, Greenwich House ed. 1982).

   79. Baker, *'Lolita': Pornography or Literature*, 40 SAT. REV. 18 (June 22, 1957).

   80. Rolo, *The Reader's Choice*, 202 ATLANTIC 78-80 (Sept. 1958).

   81. Hicks, *Lolita and Her Problems*, 41 SAT. REV. 12, 38 (Aug. 16, 1958).

   82. Molnar, *Matter-of-Fact Confession of a Non-Penitent*, 69 THE COMMONWEALTH 102 (Oct. 24, 1958). *See* J. HART, THE CONCISE OXFORD COMPANION TO AMERICAN LITERATURE, at 231 (1986) (where this same table of male innocence still holds true; Professor Hart states that Humbert plans to seduce Lolita "only to be seduced by her, for she is no longer a virgin.").

   83. Which was the viewpoint of the reviewer in *The Lolita Case*, TIME 102 (Nov. 17, 1958); *Lolita In Tunbridge Wells*, TIME 72 (March 2, 1959).

Anyone who tried to label Lolita the nymphet Eve, should have been silenced by Humbert's confession that,

> "At the hotel we had separate rooms, but in the middle of the night she came sobbing into mine, and we made it up very gently. You see, she had absolutely nowhere else to go."[84]

Like Carrie and Maggie, Lolita had nowhere else to go.

Malcolm noted that Nabokov's style allowed the reader to approach the narrative with human sympathy and then be horrified by a world where the narrator can say,

> "Unless it can be proven to me - to me as I am now, today, with my heart and my beard, and my putrefaction - that in the infinite run it does not matter a jot that a North American girl-child named Dolores Haze [Lolita] had been deprived of her childhood by a maniac, unless this can be proven (and if it can, then life is a joke), I see nothing for the treatment of my misery but the melancholy and very local palliative of articulate art."[85]

What, then, is the truth about the moral revolution that changed our views of sexuality? Why did *Lolita* both upset and titillate the public? Granville Hicks thought it was the purity reformers at work again, protecting our culture by demanding silence about what we all know about.[86] A "New Republic" editorial may be more to the point in saying that comic horror fails in its purpose when the critics and the public take it as simply comic satire and overlook the real Lolita who exist in darkness all of their lives.[87] But the controversy over *Lolita* is the question of what does the modern sexual revolution mean for women? A new way to control women by making their sexuality a subject of films, ads, and books which create a role for women as sales items?[88]

F. *Feminist Response to the Sexual Revolution*

Feminist literature in the 1980's stresses the interaction of pornography, prostitution, and rape as constituting violence and subjugation of women. The entrepreneur can now increase sales with cigarette ads of women swathed in gold lame or in classic prostitute poses of the billowing, short skirt, stiletto heels propped up against a tenement wall. Pornographic films and magazines feature sadomasochism, child abuse and male physical dominance over women. And although the sexual revolution supposedly decreased the social need for commercial prostitution, the literature reveals that prostitution still flourishes under new and ever more op-

---

84. Malcolm, *Lo, The Poor Nymphet*, THE NEW YORKER, Nov. 8, 1958, at 196.
85. *Id.* at 199.
86. Hicks, *supra* note 81, at 38.
87. *Lolita and the Critics*, NEW REPUBLIC, Oct. 27, 1958, at 3.
88. M. FERGUSON, FOREVER FEMININE: WOMEN'S MAGAZINES AND THE CULT OF FEMININITY 7-14, 187-88 (1983).

pressive conditions. In many instances, it has become an outlet for aggressive abuse and, as labelled by one writer, cultural sadism.[89] Kate Millett argues that the so-called "sexual revolution" means women have been given the freedom to cooperate in their own sexual subjugation.[90]

Many feminists have warned, however, that recent political reform activity against pornography and for supporting the decriminalization or legalization of prostitution seems to mirror the past. Commercialized vice is perceived as just one part of the larger issue of male control over female sexuality. Male degradation of women is seen as the issue.[91] But the difference between earlier female critics of the treatment of prostitution in America and today's critics is the former group's faith in government as a positive force for reform. Today's skeptical feminists recognize that discrimination in the justice system is a product of inequality in our culture and that equality through government is only as successful as the regulators want it to be.[92]

Those feminists reformers who seek more restrictive state control over prostitution or male exploitation of women may fall into the trap of their predecessors. On the one hand, all feminist critics of inequality see the cultural perception of women's passive role as a yoke which enforces stereotypical roles in law and society and thus seek freedom from sexual repression in gender specific laws (e.g., prostitution, homosexuality, etc.) But the critics of inequality who look to governmental interference to protect women from male exploitation of female sexuality may find that if the government, like society, operates by the same old stereotypes it cannot truly protect much less free women from this yoke. The same repression that resulted from earlier social purity movements may well destroy current reform efforts.[93]

---

89. L. LEDERER, TAKE BACK THE NIGHT: WOMEN ON PORNOGRAPHY 15-20 (1980), *see*, e.g. Lederer, *An Interview with a Former Pornographic Model*, 57-70, and Rush, *Child Pornography*, 71-82; K. BARRY, FEMALE SEXUAL SLAVERY (1979); Snitow, *Mass Market Romance: Pornography for Women is Different*, 245-263, in A. B. SNITOW, C. STANSELL, AND S. THOMPSON, eds. POWERS OF DESIRE: THE POLITICS OF SEXUALITY (1983).

90. K. MILLETT, SEXUAL POLITICS 23-58 (1970). V. GORNICK AND B. MORAN, WOMAN IN SEXIST SOCIETY: STUDIES IN POWER AND POWERLESSNESS (1971).

91. K. MILLETT *supra* note 90, at 3-22 (discusses the uses of images of inferiority of women, domination over women, and cruelty to women as being sexual in the novels of Norman Mailer and Henry Miller. She relates this to the history of male attitudes towards women as sexual objects of gratification). C. MACKINNON, *supra* note 2, at 127-228. (The MacKinnon/Dworkin antipornography ordinance, which was struck down in *American Booksellers Ass'n v. Hudnut*, 598 F. Supp. 1316 (S.D. Ind. 1984), aff'd, 771 F.2d 323 (7th Cir. 1985), aff'd mem. 106 S. Ct. 1172, rh'g denied, 106 S. Ct. 1664 (1986) defined pornography as "the sexually explicit subordination of women, graphically depicted, whether in pictures or words," which depicted women as "sexual objects," "commodities," in "postures of submission," or as "whores by nature".

92. Musheno and Seeley, *Prostitution Policy and the Women's Movement: Historical Analysis of Feminist Thought and Organization*, 10 CONTEMPORARY CRISES 237-255 (1986).

93. Walkowitz, *The Politics of Prostitution*, 6 SIGNS: JOURNAL OF WOMEN IN CUL-

III. The Use of Law to Control Women's Sexuality and Sex Roles

A. Early American Controls

Colonial America was settled by a diverse group of European migrants. We associate New England and Mid-Atlantic migration with religious reform and moral puritanism. The Southeastern colonies were established as economic ventures, but legal codes still emphasized strict social and moral controls. Most of the colonists equated moral law, based on the strictures of biblical sources, with the secular legal system.[94]

David Flaherty in his discussion of law and morals in early America asserts the main contribution of moral law to secular codes was equating sin with crime. Fornication was labeled both as a crime in the community and a shameful sin.[95] The colonists, however, resisted English ecclesiastical courts of the established church and left the enforcement of morals up to civil government.[96]

Although both religious and secular authorities believed in the ideal moral order, they were all too aware of lapses in behavior. Moral wrongdoers were likely to be forced into marriage or required to support an illegitimate offspring. Only a married woman was subject to severe penalty for sexual intercourse outside of marriage; a married man was punished for the lesser offense of fornication, unless it was with a married woman who was not his wife. Flaherty sees an increasing indifference on the part of the public despite official attempts to improve behavior as the reason for a shift from enforcement of morals to protection of the public purse. But that does not explain why authorities continued to use the same laws to punish women for their moral transgessions.[97]

The rationale behind moral regulation began to change in eighteenth century America from moral to social control over the lower classes. Secular authorities were concerned about the behavior of the growing number of indentured servants and laborers imported to the United States. The structure of America was changing from colonists seeking a new moral order to immigrants and settlers seeking commercial success and the pleasures they had known in Europe. Statutes either specifically referred to occupations and classes or enforcement was limited to the working class.[98]

TURE AND SOCIETY 123 (1980).

94. DAVID H. FLAHERTY, ed., ESSAYS IN THE HISTORY OF EARLY AMERICAN LAW (1969); *See also*, Smith, *supra* note 19; Moran and Vinovskis, *The Puritan Family: A Critical Reappraisal*, 39 William & Mary Q. 29-63 (3d Ser. 1982).

95. Flaherty, *Law and the Enforcement of Morals in Early America*, 5 PERSPECTIVES IN AMERICAN HISTORY 203, 208 (1971).

96. *Id.* at 209.

97. *Id.* at 214; Cott, *Eighteenth Century Family and Social Life Revealed in Massachusetts Divorce Records*, at 107-135, in N. COTT AND E. PLECK, *supra* note 16.

98. Flaherty, *supra* note 95, at 216-217, *citing* C. Van Doren, BENJAMIN FRANKLIN (1938); L. B. WRIGHT AND M. TINLING, eds., THE SECRET DIARY OF WILLIAM BYRD

Legal norms and actual behavior differed between the upper and lower classes.[99] Social customs in the southern slave states openly permitted illicit relationships between masters and slaves. Enforcement of moral codes in the South was limited to interracial relationships between free black and indentured white servants. In these cases, punishment was severe and could include substantial periods of servitude.[100] But, on the whole, the law in the eighteenth century was turning away from punishing immorality as a moral harm to the community towards punishing bastardy as an economic loss to the public coffers. In most cases, prosecution was not undertaken if a source of support was available.[101]

This is not to say that there were not frequent moral revivals which attempted to use the law to enforce morals. In the seventeenth century, Cotton Mather sought to destroy whorehouses in Boston.[102] The Puritans created tythingmen in the mid-1670's as a neighborhood moral watch, but the system quickly died from lack of enforcement.[103] Law, however, turned away from enforcing private morality, and most commentators see this time as a major shift from an identification of sin with crime to the protection of property.[104]

Flaherty notes that Thomas Jefferson argued that "the legislative powers of government extend to such acts only as injurious to others."[105] This statement, of course, simply leads to the original problem of what does the social order believe is injurious to others? Early Puritans believed sin was visited on the community. Victorian America conceived of property as the subject of legal protection. Both equated control over women and women's sexuality as grounded in the necessity to protect the community, whether the reason was to prevent sin or to protect property. Thus Jefferson's conception of law as the prevention of harm to others did little

---

OF WESTOVER, 1709-1712 (1941), and THE LONDON DIARY 1712-1721, AND OTHER WRITINGS (1958); Cott, *supra* note 16, at 170, (states that a content analysis of nine New England magazines between 1777-1794 shows that, although the characters advocated male punishment for illicit sexual relationships, it was always the female who was ostracized and punished).

99. Flaherty, *supra* note 95, at 214-234.

100. *Id.* at 237-240; W. D. JORDON, WHITE OVER BLACK: AMERICAN ATTITUDES TOWARDS THE NEGRO, 1550-1812, at 136-78 (1968); C. Degler, *supra* note 40, at 111-143, *Under Stress: Families of Afro-Americans and Immigrants*, G. Lerner *supra* note 11, at 63-82, *Black Women in the United States: A Problem in Historiography and Interpretation*, and 94-111, *Black and White Women in Interaction and Confrontation*.

101. Flaherty, *supra* note 95, at 230, 246-49.

102. *Id.* 235, *citing* W. C. FORD, ed., DIARY OF COTTON MATHER, Massachusetts Historical Society Collections, 7th Ser., VII-VIII (Boston, 1911-12).

103. Flaherty, *supra* note 95, at 221-225.

104. Nelson, *Emerging Notions of Modern Criminal Law in the Revolutionary Era: An Historical Perspective*, 42 N.Y.U. L. REV. 450, 455-457, 461-462 (1967); Riegel, *supra* note 68, at 437-52, 437-39.

105. Flaherty, *supra* note 95, *citing*, T. JEFFERSON, NOTES ON THE STATE OF VIRGINIA, 159-61 (W. Penden ed. 1955).

to change the social mores; it only relabelled or redefined the reasons for control.

B. Nineteenth Century Reform of Family Law

Reformers sought not only the podium and print to enforce their standards of social control but also the law. Nineteenth century America saw a tightening of moral strictures both on the legislative and judicial levels. Ironically, it was the use of the state to promote individual rights in commerce, property, and labor that began the rural to urban migration and a loss of small town social control over individuals. Moreover, in many instances, the social purity reformers and the advocates for women's rights, abolition of slavery, and economic freedom were the same individuals. Studies of the major individuals associated with various reform groups reveal a surprising cross-fertilization among anti-pornography, pro-women's rights, and business interests.[106]

A review of major nineteenth century legal change that took place in the law of the family is important to any study of women's sexuality and sex role, because the concept of the family governed American institutional life, and the law was intended to maintain family control. In the quest for individual rights, early republican theory had moved away from imposing a subservient status on family dependents.[107] But mid-century legal commentators attempted to move marriage and family back to a status relationship. Legislatures might pronounce marriage to be a civil contract, but courts and commentators maintained its sacred social status as essential to the balance of Victorian separate spheres.[108]

1. Marriage Reform

Reformers sought to legislate their vision of public and private morality through marriage and the family. Since adolescence was now con-

---

106. C. Smith-Rosenberg, *supra* note 6, at 78-89; M. Connelly, the Response to Prostitution in the Progressive Era (1980); D. Pivar, *supra* note 70, at 281-298.

107. M. Grossberg, *supra* note 36, at 19; M.B. Norton, Liberty's Daughters, the Revolutionary Experiences of American Women, 1750-1800, at 234-235 (1980); Gundersen and Gampel, *Married Women's Legal Status in Eighteenth Century New York and Virginia*, 39 William & Mary Q. 114-134 (3d. Ser. 1982). Boylan, The Law of the Hearth; Grossberg, *Governing the Hearth: Law and the Family in Nineteenth Century America*, 14 Revs. in Amer. Hist. 382-86 (1986).

108. M. Grossberg, *supra* note 36, at 20-21; N. Basch, in the Eyes of the. Law: Women, Marriage and Property in Nineteenth Century New York 120-121, 222-227 (1982) (notes that married women's property reform support came from male advocates of debtor reform, members of the new middle class seeking protection of property rights, and foes of the old equity trust system which was perceived as a tool of the wealthy. These same supporters were careful to note that political rights were not involved and that the basic unity of the family would remain intact. Basch also notes that the courts consistently narrowed the application of the reform statutes to restrict rights given to women under the Married Women's Property Acts).

sidered the time that young men and women should be educated for successful performance of their public or private role, reformers advocated against early marriage. Early nineteenth century law permitted, in most cases, marriage at twelve for girls and fourteen for boys. Even though legislative reform to increase the age for marriage was successful, the courts upheld common law policy against legislative attempts to restrict marital freedom. Real social practice was an increase in the age of middle class marriage and a continuance of young marriages or cohabitation for the lower classes. Critics of early marriages were finally successful in the beginning of the twentieth century when youthful indiscretion was linked with the campaign against white slavery and prostitution and the need for family control and state protection of the young.[109]

The campaign against nonmonogamous marital practices was a much more successful campaign for a cultural and legal definition of the family. Mormons were condemned as destructive of America; polygamy was called slavery. The Mormons fled to Utah to escape what they saw as religious persecution, but Congress declared polygamy illegal in American territories. Finally the Supreme Court held that religious freedom did not include the right to destroy the American way. Chief Justice Waite called polygamy an odious practice, holding the U.S. could outlaw and punish seditious acts whether or not labelled as religion. Justice Waite denied any claim of first amendment religious freedom and held the civil government had the right to determine the social life of the people under its control. Religious freedom could not subvert the law of the land.[110]

The Edwards Act of 1882 which punished multiple cohabitation as well as multiple marriage was upheld in *Cannon v. United States*.[111] The final blow against the Mormons was the Edwards-Tucker Act which an-

---

109. M. GROSSBERG, *supra* note 36, at 105-107.

110. M. GROSSBERG, *supra* note 36, at 120-129; *U.S. v. Reynolds*, 1 Utah 226 (1874); 1 Utah 319 (1876); *Reynolds v. U.S.*, 98 U.S. 145, 162-67 (1878). (Chief Justice Waite explored the history of the first amendment, which he traced to Jefferson's Act for Establishing Religious Freedom passed by the Virginia legislature (12 Hennings' Stat. 84.) Chief Justice Waite stated, for what responsibilities property belong to church and state. ". . .[T]hat to suffer the civil magistrate to intrude his powers into the field of opinion, and to restrain the profession or propagation of principles on supposition of their ill tendency, is a dangerous fallacy, which at once destroys all religious liberty," and, "that it is time enough for the rightful purposes of civil government for its officers to interfere when principles break out into overt acts against peace and good order." Chief Justice Waite noted that polygamy had been punished as an offense against society under the common law, and that by the statute of 1 James I (c. 11) the offense was punishable in the civil courts by death, which was reenacted in Virginia, after the act establishing religious freedom and after Virginia recommended a similar amendment to the United States Constitution (12 Hennings' Stat. 691). Polygamy had been an offense against society in every state in the Union since that time. There could be no doubt in the mind of the Court that the constitutional guarantee of religious freedom was not intended to prohibit legislation regarding marriage).

111. 116 U.S. 55, 68 (1885). (The statute legitimated all children born of polygamous marriages prior to January 1, 1883 and authorized amnesty to all offenders for acts prior to its enactment).

nulled the Mormon articles of incorporation and confiscated their property.[112] Finally Utah, the Mormon stronghold, was admitted as a state in 1894 with a constitutional provision prohibiting polygamy. Thus the full force of the law—federal legislature and judiciary—was employed to uphold the American concept of the family as one husband, one wife, and their children.[113]

2. Reproductive Control

Nineteenth century theories of separate public and private spheres divided male and female roles into production and reproduction, respectively. The battle over abortion was a part of the campaign to control female sexuality and women's reproductive rights. Abortion was first perceived as a threat when it moved from being a practice of lower class women to the middle class. It caused fear among the purity reformers because it threatened to shift traditional male control of the family into the hands of women. Early legislation and court decisions were ambivalent over the use of abortion in early term and as a therapeutic measure; moreover, women, unlike the abortionists, were not seen as criminally responsible but as passive instruments of doctors or quacks. Recent commentators on the history of abortion argue that the criminalization of abortion was spearheaded by physicians as an attack on medical quackery, but social purity reformers took the opportunity to advocate control over women as well as punishment for the abortionist.[114]

Contraception also fell to the reforms of the 1860's social purity groups. The Comstock Law of 1873, which prohibited the circulation and importation of obscene materials through the mail, became the major weapon of purity reformers over the next several decades. Anthony Comstock, a lobbyist and advocate for social purity groups, was appointed a special postal agent. Several state legislatures passed statutes explicitly barring the sale, advertisement and manufacturing of contraceptives. Connecticut banned the use of contraceptives as well.[115] The federal courts upheld prosecution for the distribution of contraceptives. Such distribution was found to be obscene and therefore against the law. The Supreme Court upheld the Comstock Law as the right of Congress to use the federal regulatory power to "refuse its facilities for the distribution of matter deemed injurious to public morals."[116]

---

112. *The Late Corporation of the Church of Jesus Christ of Latter-Day Saints v. United States*, 136 U.S. 1 (1890). (Upholding the constitutional power of Congress over its territories (Art. 4, Sec. 3, cl. 2) to abrogate the corporate charter of the Church of the Latter-Day Saints and confiscate property granted under that charter).

113. M. GROSSBERG, *supra* note 36, at 125.

114. G.J. BARKER-BENFIELD, *supra* note 11, at 61-90; M. GROSSBERG, *supra* note 36, at 157-195.

115. L. GORDON, *supra* note 51, at 47-71. M. GROSSBERG, *supra* note 36, at 175-178.

116. *U.S. v. Popper*, 98 F. 423 (N.D. Cal. 1899); M. GROSSBERG, *supra* note 36, at

3.   Moral Reform

The reform campaigns against prostitution and pornography, which were seen as stemming from the growing laxity of moral standards resulting in male incontinence and female freedom outside of the home, were equally vigorous. The medical profession initiated a battle against prostitution based on its growing understanding of the cause of venereal disease. Moral reformers, however, were appalled by medical efforts to regulate the activities of prostitutes through health measures and demanded the total suppression of prostitution. Contraception, abortion, obscenity, and prostitution were seen as part and parcel of a growing wave of moral corruption infecting America.

Numerous commentators have discussed the connection among the old abolitionists and the new purity reformers and between supporters of censorship, temperance, suppression of prostitution, reform of the juvenile justice system, women's rights, and family purity. They have also noted the willingness of industrialists and philanthropists to advocate moral reform and social control of the working classes rather than deal with the economic reasons for social disintegration and urban poverty. At the turn of the century, middle class America was distraught over increased immigration, wide-spread political corruption, and the increase of organized crime in the cities. The middle class were beneficiaries of entrepreneurial individualism but were unwilling to admit there were major problems in America of economic inequality and social injustice.[117]

Women's rights groups were active in the struggle. They viewed temperance and purity as part of the higher ideal of a new world where women held their rightful place as upholders of American values.[118] The women's rights groups were unanimous in resisting legal regulation of prostitution and demanded programs of suppression and reform. But they differed over legislative and judicial control of family planning. Consequently women were divided over issues of contraception, abortion, and the use of obscenity laws to ban use or distribution of family planning materials.[119]

The male-dominated reform groups continued to perceive women's sexuality as a negative force and women as inherently incapable of independent development. All women's rights movement rejected this theory and advocated reforms based on education, economic reform, and rehabili-

---

188-195.

117. Freedman, *Sexuality in Nineteenth Century America: Behavior, Ideology, and Politics*, 10 REVS. IN AM. HIST. 196-215 (1982); D. Pivar, *supra* note 70, at 169-180.

118. Walkowitz, *The Politics of Prostitution*, 6 SIGNS: J. OF WOMEN AND CULTURE IN SOC. 123-135 (1980).

119. L. GORDON, *supra* note 51, at 186-245; Conway, *Women Reformers and American Culture, 1870-1930*, 5 J. OF SOC. HIS. 164-177 (1971-72), (comments that the separate spheres theory of women reformers created a stereotype of female inequality. Reform efforts were accepted as preserving the family and female domesticity and making no changes in women's equality).

tation. But both male and female dominated groups joined in advocating for legislative and judicial controls to end urban political corruption, to prevent juvenile delinquency and the white slave traffic, and to protect the family as the ideal American social organization. The reform movement reflected an imperfect amalgamation of cultural and moral concepts of reform.

C. The Criminal Justice System

1. The Vice Reform Movement

Uniting to combat what they perceived as a single force destroying the social fabric of America, some quite disparate groups joined together in the campaign to destroy prostitution and save family institutions. The campaign included reform of corrupt urban politics, control of population through restrictive immigration laws, and stabilization of the family through education, juvenile law reform, as well as, if needed, substitution of the government or private agencies for the family. The advocates of reform ranged from liberal urban progressives seeking better government to settlement house workers. The movement was supported by Comstockers and temperance advocates who saw in commercialized vice the outlets for liquor and printed filth as the cause of social impurity. Influential churchmen and corporation heads saw the need for capturing control of urban political power and for ameliorating the plight of industrial workers in urban ghettoes.[120]

For all of these groups, social purity and the suppression of commercial vice became a major focus of agreement. For conservative groups, it represented family stability because it focused on the plight of dependent females driven into prostitution. They thought that if prostitution could be eliminated then their goals could be more easily realized. The women's rights groups, with their vision of women as bringing a higher order of morality to American life, were also attracted by the idea that the plight of prostitutes was a product of their economic dependency.

It fit in with the racist theories of nativists who labelled recent immigrants as degenerates, even though the reports on commercialized vice showed that the majority of prostitutes were native to America, not foreigners. Moreover, entry into prostitution was not usually a product of organized crime but more often a choice between low wage jobs at long hours in unhealthy conditions and a chance for some degree of luxury. As Theodore Dreiser portrayed the world of *Sister Carrie* in Chicago, it was drudgery versus a chance to share in the American dream.[121]

Ruth Rosen, in her study of prostitution and the progressives, asserts that the effect of suppression of a previously open trade was merely to place prostitution in the hands of organized crime and remove it from the

---

120. B. M. HOBSON, *supra* note 15, at 139-54.
121. J. ADDAMS, *supra* note 54; W. RECKLESS, *supra* note 9, at 189-192.

control of women. Although the early studies of parlor houses managed by women seem to indicate more absentee male landlord control of prostitution than Rosen's theory would warrant, the general assertion does appear to be valid. The outcomes of reform were to further degrade a prostitute by increasing her dependency on pimps and police protection and diverting women into a gender-biased criminal justice system.[122]

2. Women, Crime, and Justice

Women in the criminal justice system were not a significant issue until late nineteenth century America. Recent criminology literature explains the reason for this neglect was a cultural conception of women as biologically different, inherently less criminal than men and socially conditioned to conformity.[123] Whether the causes were biological or social, it was believed that women had a lower participation in crime and lived on a higher level of morality than men. Deviation from this higher level of morality provided a subcategory of crimes applicable only to women.[124] Francis Lieber, in his introduction to de Beaumont and De Tocqueville's *On the Penitentiary System*, stated that men's crimes were more rational than women's crimes. A fallen woman had denied her own pure nature and would sink to the depths of sinfulness. Prostitution was labelled the woman's crime.[125] For the female, sexual activity outside of marriage

---

122. R. ROSEN, THE LOST SISTERHOOD: PROSTITUTION IN AMERICA, 1900-1918, (1982); R. ROSEN AND S. DAVIDSON, eds., THE MAIMIE PAPERS (1977).

123. Provine, *Gender, Crime, and Criminal Justice: Edward's Women on Trial*, AM. BAR FOUNDATION RESEARCH J. 571-583 (1986); C. LOMBROSO AND W. FERRERO, *supra* note 16, at xi, xv, and 109-113 (was the major European exponent of biological or social explanation for delinquency. Lombroso and his followers advocated different sentencing of males and females for the same offense because of their inherently different natures. Women, he believed, were less developed than men on the evolutionary scale and, thus, more atavistic. They tended to be conformists, and, since men usually refuse to breed with deformed women, women did not tend to differentiate through time. Women were, therefore, occasional criminals rather than habitual criminals. Their crimes were associated with hysteria, passion and insanity. Prostitution was the classic female crime because it was the result of degenerative atavism. The prostitute was a primitive, undeveloped human). *Also see*, Klein, *The Etiology of Female Crime: A Review of the Literature*, in L. CRITES, ed, THE FEMALE OFFENDER 5-31 (1976).

124. O. POLLACK, THE CRIMINALITY OF WOMEN at xvi-xvii, 58-76, 120-148 (1950). *Also* Bibliography, at 162-175. (The theories in the United States have mixed biological and social conditioning. The biological theorists see masculine traits in women as leading to criminality. The social theorists posit that lack of opportunity, social conditioning, and nature of occupations are responsible for low crime participation and say that women's entry into the workforce and women's liberation have led to greater participation in crime). E. FREEDMAN, *supra* note 13, at 13-14 (notes that higher crime rates for women from the 1860's onward reflected the transformation of the economy from family to market and rural or overseas migration to urban areas which resulted in loss of control of traditional institutions of church, family, and community. But women's crimes reflected the limited economic opportunities available to them and their sexual role in the community).

125. B.M. HOBSON, *supra* note 15, at 110, citing F. LIEBER, INTRODUCTION TO

meant deviance and is prohibited by the state. What for the male was normal was for the female deviant and criminal.[126]

3. The Treatment of Female Juveniles in Criminal Law

In the twentieth century, the emphasis in criminology changed from detention to preventative social services. Reformers stressed the difference between male and female natures and sought specialized treatment for female offenders. In many states, specialized courts were created for women and for juveniles. The treatment of females in juvenile courts explicitly dealt with their sexuality as a special offense applicable only to women. Girls were referred to juvenile courts for running away, ungovernability, larceny and sex offenses. On the contrary, boys were committed for larceny, burglary and theft.[127]

Juvenile law, in efforts to socialize the young into good citizenship, covers both criminal and noncriminal behavior that is socially disapproved and includes a moral judgment about behavior.[128] Reformers in the early 1900's who crusaded for juvenile courts and protective custody relied heavily on the biological theories of sexual differentiation, labelling the female offender as an unadjusted, amoral delinquent.[129]

In 1923, W.I. Thomas published *The Unadjusted Girl*, a pioneer study in the psychology of women who failed to adapt to socially acceptable behavior. Thomas stated that, "Civilized societies. . .have endowed the young girl with a character of social sacredness. . . 'Virginity' and

---

GUSTAVE DE BEAUMONT AND ALEXIS DE TOCQUEVILLE, ON THE PENITENTIARY SYSTEM IN THE UNITED STATES, AND ITS APPLICATION IN FRANCE xiv-xvi (1833). E. FREEDMAN, *supra* note 13, at 14-21 (asserts that nineteenth century sexual ideology cast the fallen woman as a pariah. Women imprisoned for sexual offenses were crowded together, abused, and isolated to prevent communication with male prisoners. Male prison reformers explained the differential treatment to be a result of women's sexual natures).

126. E. SCHUR, LABELING WOMEN DEVIANT: GENDER, STIGMA, AND SOCIAL CONTROL 5 (1984). (In William Acton's seminal study of prostitution, male reasons for sex outside of marriage were perceived as normal, biological, and based on trends toward late marriages in Victorian England. Female prostitutes were mental and moral degenerates from whom males needed medical protection. Because there would always be a demand, Acton was a proponent of regulation of prostitution, although he preferred early marriage, better sex education, and continency). *See*, W. ACTON, PROSTITUTION CONSIDERED IN ITS MORAL, SOCIAL AND SANITARY ASPECTS (1857, 1969); E. FREEDMAN, *supra* note 13, (states that a few women reformers attempted to discredit the Lombrosian theories of criminal types but, at the same time, new theories of hereditary defects that caused delinquency became popular explanations for crime and prostitution).

127. C. VEDDER AND D. SOMMERVILLE, THE DELINQUENT GIRL 16-18 (1970).

128. *Id.* at 31-32; E. FREEDMAN, *supra* note 13, at 110-111.

129. W.I. THOMAS, THE UNADJUSTED GIRL 98 (1923, Torchbooks 1967 ed.). (This theory has been propounded by many criminologists. All theorists, whether they rely on biological or social explanation label male delinquency as aggressive and female delinquency as sexual, passive, and self-destructive). C. GILLIGAN, IN A DIFFERENT VOICE: PSYCHOLOGICAL THEORY AND WOMEN'S DEVELOPMENT 5-23 (1982) (notes that Freudian theorists from Piaget to Erickson have followed this theory in describing child development).

'Purity' have almost a magical value. . .The girl as a child does not know she has any particular value until she learns it from others, but if she is regarded with adoration she correspondingly respects herself and tends to become what is expected of her. And so she has in fact a greater value. She makes a better marriage and reflects recognition on her family."[130]

Thomas saw female sexuality as female "capital" used in exchange for obtaining other wishes.[131] He wrote that prostitution was becoming an individualized and transitory occupation, which was contrary to the nineteenth century view of prostitution as destroying women's lives and the early twentieth century view of prostitutes as white slaves. Rather Thomas saw casual prostitution as the major problem of social disorganization.[132]

Female demoralization was considered to be a product of family disorganization. Thus the solution was to remove these delinquent girls from their parents to institutions where societal rules would be enforced. But Thomas did not see this solution as responsive to the problems facing America in terms of changes in social and economic structures and values and the growing trend towards individualization rather than social cohesion. In short, no longer were there good girls and fallen women, only individuals making choices on how to use their capital.[133]

---

130. W.I. THOMAS, *supra* note 129, at 98 and Introduction by Michael Parenti at ix.

131. *Id.* at 98-108. M. DOUGLAS, PURITY AND DANGER: AN ANALYSIS OF CONCEPTIONS OF POLLUTION AND TABOO (1966) (discusses impurity taboos of primitive cultures in relation to their sexual customs. She notes that purity and control of female sexuality is especially important in societies that make a commodity of sex through sale of the female in marriage, slavery, or concubinage as a part of inter or intra tribal relations. There is, indeed, small difference between the sale of property in women through marriage or slavery and the sale of women through sexual intercourse). *See generally* Davis, *The Sociology of Prostitution*, 2 AM. SOC. REV. 744 (1935) (Modern feminists have asserted that the only difference between prostitutes and respectable women is hypocrisy). *See*, Millett, *Prostitution: A Quartet for Female Voices*, at 60-125 in V. GORNICK AND B. MORAN, eds., *supra* note 90. G. LERNER, *supra* note 4, (traces the history of early societies in which women were an important commodity of trade and barter and thus subject to strict regulation in order to protect their value).

132. W.I. THOMAS, *supra* note 129, at 109. (Thomas believed that human behavior was guided by four "wishes":
1. The desire for new experience.
2. The desire for security.
3. The desire for response.
4. The desire for recognition.
Thomas accepted the theory of women's passive sexuality).

133. *Id.* at 116-125, 230. (Thomas gave an insightful review of the Chicago Vice Commission Report on Prostitution). *See* CHICAGO VICE COMMISSION, THE SOCIAL EVIL IN CHICAGO: (Reprint ed. 1970). (The report clearly stated it would make no discoveries nor recommendations that did not conform to society's standards, "[the Commission] has kept constantly in mind that to offer a contribution of any value such an offering must be, first, moral; second, reasonable and practical; third, possible under constitutional powers of our courts; fourth, that which will square with the public conscience of the American people." But Thomas noted that the method sought to enforce and justify a stated norm

The prevailing mood of American public policy towards female juveniles was the dependency stereotype which permitted preventive intervention and coercive supervision. Reformatories for girls began in the mid 1800's. They were primarily run by philanthropic organizations and focussed on the wayward girl or the fallen woman. The late 1870's saw a growth of girl's clubs, YWCA activities, and settlement houses aimed at providing wholesome activities for the newly emerging factory populations of urban areas. The juvenile court was a product of the Progressive Era reform, intended to remove for re-education delinquent youth from bad families and socially impoverished communities. Delinquent girls were sexually deviant, and the courts acted to control social norms and protect young males by removing deviant females from society.[134]

Girls were never perceived as tractable in adolescence. Prevailing theory held that boys could be shaped in adolescence for economic independence through appropriate training, whereas girls were completely developed at puberty. Female reformatories isolated sexually deviant women. They retrained and conditioned the inmates in skills of domesticity and prepared the juvenile for entry into the "marriage market" or, at least, domestic employment. There was little or no effort to train women for the economic market place: domesticity, not economic independence, was the countervailing value to deviance.[135]

One rather frightening goal of the reformatories was discouraging or preventing further procreation by "unfit races." The eugenics movement was a prominent part of the Progressive Reform movement, and many leading Progressive Reformers were equally active in birth control, juvenile court reform, vice control, and eugenics. Permanent institutionalization or sterilization of the unfit was a stated goal of the eugenicists.[136] This point is somewhat ironic since the original impetus for the women's movement on prostitution was to fight the medical community who advocated regulation and inspection of prostitutes rather than prohibition.

---

and ignored the ongoing social evolution).

134. Schlossman and Wallach, *The Crime of Precocious Sexuality: Female Juvenile Delinquency in the Progressive Era.* 48 HARV. ED. REV. 69-79 (1978); E. FREEDMAN, *supra* note 13, at 129-30; (states that juvenile courts and women's courts usually had no jury trials. In most women's courts, physical inspection was mandatory, no complaint was filed until after arrest, and the case was postponed pending the results of the physical examination).

135. Schlossman and Wallach, *supra* note 134, at 72-73. (In Chicago 59% of boys and 37% of girls were placed on probation and one half of girl delinquents as opposed to one fifth of boy delinquents were sent to reformatories. In Milwaukee twice as many girls as boys were incarcerated. This was despite the fact that girls were usually sent to court for status offenses while boys were there for criminal charges).

136. *Id.* at 75-84. (Girls were not given probation because prevailing theory of adolescence held women were weak, impressionable and emotional. They were thus less susceptible to informal change mechanisms. Adolescence for boys was a testing time but girls were formed at puberty. Moreover family degeneracy was usually blamed for sexual deviance, and domesticity was deemed essential to rehabilitation). *See also,* Black and Reiss, *Police Control of Juveniles,* 35 AM. SOC. REV. 63 (1970).

Early women's rights advocates saw medical regulation of prostitutes as a rights infringement only perpetrated upon women because of their status as nonpersons under the Constitution. Twentieth century reformers were more enthralled by pseudoscientific theories of race degeneracy and thus able to justify intrusion into the individual's privacy in order to save society.

The goals of the progressive reformers ignored Thomas' insights on social evolution. Progressive reformers accepted the stereotype of passive dependency and thus created a myth of innocent white slaves, preyed upon by mercenary immigrants. This myth appealed both to Victorian morality and nativist fears of new immigrants. The women reformers pointed to economic impoverishment, but they did not make any connection between reform of the system and the sale of women as a commodity. Rather they joined with corporation heads and churchmen to link economic deprivation to being easily preyed upon by men. Reformers did not look at social disorganization and wonder how to meet new conditions, instead they tried to step backwards in time and recreate the myth of small town, homogeneous America through social purity, political reform, and placing women in the higher moral sphere essential for correct family development.[137]

D.   The Sexual Revolution

The modern trend in legal literature is to oppose the criminalization of prostitution; however, opinion differs on whether legalization or decriminalization is preferable. Feminist critics of existing law assert that legalization is only another means of official oppression of women and decriminalization is the only alternative. Legalization entails registration, segregation, possible police harassment, and commercial exploitation of women. Nevada is a case in point where prostitution is permitted on a local option basis. The regulation includes redlight zoning, medical inspection, and licensing. Here it is once again taken out of women's control and turned into a major tourist trade operated by the state and big business.[138]

Decriminalization, it is asserted, would free women of police harassment and, at the same time, make it unnecessary for women to seek unofficial protection from pimps and police. It would also permit women to leave prostitution without the fear of a police record which could prevent them from obtaining another job.[139] To the contrary, proponents of legali-

---

137. D. Pivar, supra note 70.

138. Symanski, Prostitution in Nevada, at 126-154, in L. Bowker, ed., Women and Crime in America (1981).

139. Bennetts, Prostitution: A Non-Victim Crime? Women Endorsing Decriminalization, 8 Issues in Criminology 137-162 (1973); Milman, New Rules for the Oldest Profession: Should We Change Our Prostitution Laws? 3 Harv. Women's L.J. 1-82 (1980); Millett, supra note 131. (Kate Millett's attempts to link the plight of the oppressed and prostitutes may be misplaced. At the same time prostitutes are labelling their status as a

zation argue that prostitution should be regulated because of the public health issues, which now include AIDS as well as venereal diseases; the relationship between prostitution and other crimes; and the threat to property values caused by streetwalkers and houses of prostitution, although evidence linking crime and prostitution is not substantial.

Public opinion, however, continues to support legal suppression of prostitution.[140] There has not been a significant change in public or judicial attitudes towards prostitution since the beginning of the twentieth century when the Supreme Court upheld statutes criminalizing prostitution and interstate transportation of prostitutes as essential to stamp out a major social evil, dangerous to the family.[141] Prostitution statutes have survived equal protection and privacy attacks in the face of a sexual revolution where legislation banning contraceptive devices, abortion, and obscene materials has been struck down as unconstitutional infringement of our right to privacy.[142] The statutory offense of prostitution is usually defined as the exchange or barter of sexual services.[143] Soliciting, pandering, and pimping are offenses associated with males, but most courts have held that males cannot be convicted of hiring a prostitute, although the sale is a two-way contract.[144] Even when laws have been reformed to penalize both the buyer and the seller, studies show that arrests of male

---

business, feminists are seeking to expose the underlying patriarchy that creates commodization of the female body. It is probably unrealistic to expect solidarity on this issue. Once again middle class America seeks to impose its understanding of the world on its less-well endowed inhabitants). *See* e.g., B. HOBSON *supra* note 15, at 215-223 (on prostitute's organizations in the United States and in Europe). Boyle and Noonan, *Prostitution and Pornography: Beyond Formal Equality*, 10 DALHOUSIE L. J. 226 (1986).

140. Roenbleet and Pariente, *The Prostitution of the Criminal Law*, 11 AM. CRIM. L. REV. 373-427 (1973).

141. *United States v. Bitty*, 208 U.S. 393, 401 (1908) (Upheld statute prohibiting importation of any girl or woman for purposes of prostitution); *L'Hote v. New Orleans*, 177 U.S. 587 (1900) (Upheld city ordinance prescribing redlight district outside of which no women of "lewd character" could live). *See*, B. M. HOBSON, *supra* note 15, at 211-214. (Hobson notes that cases that have upheld gender as being an appropriate classification in prostitution laws are based on a false dichotomy of private sexual acts (pornography) which are held to be constitutionally protected and public sexual acts (prostitution) which are not). *See*, *e.g.*, *Hawaii v. Kam*, 56 U.S.L.W. 2429 (Hawaii Sup. Ct. 11861, 1/8/88), (Striking down Hawaii statute banning sale of pornography as infringing right of privacy, in which the court stated, "*Hawaii v. Mueller*, 671 P.2d 1351 (1983) is distinguishable. Mueller upheld the legislature's authority to prohibit prostitution even in the privacy of one's home. It resolved that inasmuch as the right to privacy does not protect prostitution, the state was not required to show a compelling state interest").

142. *Griswold v. Connecticut*, 381 U.S. 479 (1965) (Invalidated statute prohibiting use and prescription of contraceptive drugs of devices as violation of right of privacy); *Eisenstadt v. Baird*, 405 U.S 438 (1972) (Invalidated statute prohibiting distribution of contraceptives to unmarried individuals); *Roe v. Wade*, 410 U.S. 113 (1973) (Invalidated Texas abortion statute); *Stanley v. Georgia*, 394 U.S. 557 (1968) (Invalidated Georgia obscenity statute which intruded in individual's privacy in own home).

143. Milman, *supra* note 139, at 2. For a listing of state statutes *see*, Erbe, *Prostitutes: Victims of Men's Exploitation and Abuse*, 2 LAW & INEQUALITY 609, 624 (1984).

144. E. SCHUR, *supra* note 12, at 164-167.

buyers do not rise appreciably. Cultural perceptions still guide official actions.[145]

But, perhaps, this continuing stigma of commercialized sex represents an ambivalence in our attitudes toward the real meaning of sexual revolution for women. We fail to acknowledge the parallel between commercialized prostitution and other forms of sexual service.

E. Sex Roles, Sexuality, and the Sexual Marketplace

Prostitution is but one species of sexual services. In an essay on market inalienability, Margaret Radin analyzes the sale of sexual services as part of the classic liberal view of all rights as property, transferrable in the marketplace.[146] Our society, however, does not permit certain rights of personhood to be commodified. We express moral or social intolerance to the marketability of body organs, children, or sexual services, which are associated with cultural values such as marriage or family. What the legal economists refer to as externalities.[147]

Radin looks at the prophylactic reasons for prohibiting alienability of personhood as applied to prostitution, baby selling, and surrogate mothering and suggests that although inalienability oppresses women who are not otherwise able to increase their wealth as market traders, commodification legitimates and enforces gender oppression.[148] She suggests a partial solution of incomplete commodification of prostitution, similar to regulation of labor, through decriminalization of the sale of sexual services but prohibition of an organized market by banning brokerage, recruitment, and advertisement. The solution might lower potential sales but maintains sexuality as an inalienable right of personhood.[149]

The analyses of surrogate mothering and baby sales point up some difficulties of such partial solutions. In baby sales, the problem is commodification of the child as opposed to the right of the mother and father to alienate their own reproductive rights. In the surrogate mothering contract, one legal theory espoused is that the mother is selling sexual services, not the child, and the father is the owner of the child. The surrogate transaction is commodification and gender hierarchy.[150] Even incomplete

---

145. C. VEDDER AND D. SOMMERVILLE, supra note 127.

146. Radin, *Market-Inalienability*, 100 HARV. L. REV. 1849 (1987).

147. *Id.* at 1863-1870.

148. *Id.* at 1915-1921.

149. *Id.* at 1921-1925. *See* e.g., B.M. HOBSON, *supra* note 15, at 235-36, ("To view prostitutes as working women is an indictment of the hypocrisy in a society that charges with a criminal offense prostitutes in a multimillion dollar, visible industry . . . A society that institutionalizes prostitution as a work option for the poor makes a statement about its position on inequality . . . Changing the course of prostitution history will require beginning with a recognition that prostitution is not a private contract between consenting adults but an issue that is intrinsically bound up with long-term agendas for social and sexual equality").

150. *In re Baby M*, 13 FAM. L. REP. (BNA) 2001, 2018 (N.J. Super. Ct. Ch. Div.) (discussed *infra* note 163 and accompanying text. The ABA Family Law Section passed a

commodification by permitting each party to rescind the surrogate contract does not change the fact that women are marketed as reproduction machines and children can be traded or abandoned in the marketplace. These half-way solutions of an imperfect society only point up the reality of class and gender oppression that cannot be changed by attempted fixes of just one part of the existing legal and cultural system.[151]

Kingsley Davis asks why prostitution is so thoroughly disapproved of in western society and yet so vital an institution and answers,

> The basic element in what we actually call prostitution—the employment of sex for non-sexual ends within a competitive-authoritative system—characterizes not simply prostitution itself but all of our institutions in which sex is involved, notably courtship and wedlock. Prostitution therefore resembles, from one point of view, behavior found in our most respectable institutions. It is one end of a long sequence or gradation of essentially similar phenomena that stretches at the other end to such approved patterns as engagement and marriage. What, then, is the difference between prostitution and these other institutions involving sex?
>
> The difference rests at bottom upon the functional relation between society and sexual institutions. It is through these institutions that erotic gratification is made dependent on, and subservient to, certain cooperative performances inherently necessary to societal continuity. The sexual institutions are distinguished by the fact that though they all provide gratification, they do not all tie it to the same social functions. This explains why they are differently evaluated in the eye of the mores.
>
> Of the numerous functions which sexual institutions subserve, the most vital relate to the physical and social reproduction of the next generation. If we ask, then, which sexual institutions in a society receive the greatest support from law and mores, we must point to those which facilitate the task of procreating and socializing the young. It follows that

---

Model Surrogacy Act which makes surrogacy contracts enforceable and overrides the common-law presumption that a mother is the woman who bears the child. 74 ABA J. 137 (March 1, 1988). The term, surrogate mother, is demeaning. The mother of the child is the mother, not a stand in, and using the term, "surrogate" takes away her personhood, her connectedness to her child).

151. *See*, Taub and Parles, *Amicus Brief: In the Matter of Baby M*, 10 WOMEN'S RIGHTS L. REP. 7, 9-11 (1987) (discusses cases applying prohibitions against the sale of children in adoption or related proceeding to the surrogacy contract). *Doe v. Kelly*, 106 Mich. App. 169, 307 N.W. 2d 438 (1981) (upheld a statute prohibiting the exchange or sale for money or other considerations of children in adoption and related proceedings as applied to a surrogate contract. In the Michigan case, the Court stated the child's rights were protected by the statute). To the contrary, *Surrogate Parenting Associates, Inc. v. Commonwealth ex rel. Armstrong*, 704 S.W. 2d 209 (Ky. 1986) (held a statute prohibiting the sale or purchase of a child for sale or purchase through adoption did not apply to a surrogate contract. The reasoning of the Court in the Kentucky case seems inappropriate to the issue of the child's rights of personhood. The court held the contract revocation feature protected the mother's right of choice).

sanctioned sexual relations are generally those within these (or auxiliary) institutions, while unsanctioned relations are those outside them.[152]

The literature suggests that prostitution is not an aberration of our culture or our criminal law. Rather it is a method of dealing with women's sexuality and sex role. It depicts the role of woman in society. Women are presumed to be inferior in every way, but when it comes to sex, the entire responsibility is placed on them. Men are allowed free sexuality with no moral or social limits. Women are controlled through the family and through punishment for deviation from social or legal norms about sexuality and sex role.

F. *Conclusion*

1. Stories

In an essay on historical methodology by R.G. Walters, "Sexual Matters as Historical Problems: A Framework of Analysis," the author set forth guidelines for researching the sexual history of prostitution. Walters asserted that sex roles— prescribed social behavior—and sexuality—erotic impulses expressed through behavior or rhetoric—were two separate phenomena, although interaction between the two might be the key to historical interpretation. He suggests that sexual history should be placed in a historical context of cultural values, norms, and practices.[153]

In the context of prostitution, Walters set forth six different questions, each relating to sex roles or sexuality as well as to a value, a norm, or a practice. Walters suggested the differences in a society among values espoused by a society, its legal norms, and actual practices would be much sharper than the differences between sex roles and sexuality. For example, nineteenth century female hysteria could be linked both to a restricted sex role and a repressive sexual morality. Walters also suggested that looking at larger societal values such as the nineteenth century value of redirecting sexual energy to economic production allows us to note instances where a value such as thrift as parsimony may have been a major reason for counseling sexual restraint rather than the narrower value of sexual repression.[154]

Sexual matters are a part of social structure, and it must be determined how different societies use sexuality and sex roles to define power relationships. For example, it is clear that nineteenth century sexual mo-

---

152. Davis *supra* note 131, at 746-747.

153. Walters, *Sexual Matters as Historical Problems: A Framework of Analysis*, 6 SOCIETAS 157-175, 158 (1976); To the contrary, R. BLEIER, *supra* note 2, at 167-68 suggests that there is nothing about desire or arousal that comes naturally. Instead we are conditioned from childhood to respond sexually to certain stimuli, whether that stimulus is a person or a physical experience such as violence or pornography. This suggests that sex roles and sexuality are cultural constructions in which we play out issues of control, dependency and vulnerability through sexual responses based on preconditioned sex roles.

154. Walters, *supra* note 153, at 159-163.

rality and sex roles limited women to the home and excluded them from the male dominated world of economics and politics. But one must also ask the question, Walters stated, of whether sexual control or more general values such as power, authority, and civilization were at stake. If so, than a transformation of sexual attitudes or a change in sex roles will not change the status of women.[155]

The literature I have surveyed tells a different story about the history of sexual matters. Sexuality for women has been what men have wanted as sexual gratification or as a sexual ideal.[156] Walter's questions on prostitution describe a male model of prostitution based on female responses to male demands.[157] More problematically, it presumes the actions of free agents and does not take into account domination and subjugation. Walters' model does not ask the right question, which is, who is doing what to whom and why do they have that power?[158]

I would argue that the literature shows sexuality and sex roles not to be separate or to merely interact but, rather, to be one and the same. Women's sexuality is defined by what men expect as sex and a woman's sex role is defined and restricted by a male dominated society. Gender is a little bit of biology and a lot of social construction. Researchers have taken Walter's lead and looked at a specific city, segmented the classes within that area, determined what male groups frequented prostitutes and what female groups became prostitutes. All of the research tells much of the same story. Women primarily became prostitutes for lack of viable alternatives to economic independence. Women's sex role restrictions and male-defined sexuality have made prostitution a women's economic alternative in the marketplace, albeit the underground or shadow economy.

---

155. *Id.* at 169-172. (The question, however, should be why is women's domination seen as a less general value than authority or civilization? Why should civilization be dependent on women's domination or on domination at all?). *See*, e.g., R. Bleier *supra* note 2, at 115-136 (on flawed theories of evolutionary "man as the hunter" scenarios used to justify women's domination).

156. C. MacKinnon, *supra* note 2, at 6-10.

157. Walter's analytical model divides prostitution into a study of sex roles and sexuality and asks six questions about values, norms, and behavior concerning sex roles and sexuality with reference to prostitution. The sex role questions are:

a. Values: How does promiscuity affect a woman's or man's social standing.

b. Norms: Whether it is condoned for males to go to prostitutes.

c. Behavior: What groups of men are most likely to frequent prostitutes and what groups of women are most likely to become prostitutes.

The sexuality questions are:

a. Values: Whether it is commonly regarded as moral to engage in sexual activity with people who are relative strangers.

b. Norms: Whether prostitution is socially sanctioned.

c. Behavior: Whether prostitution is a frequent source of gratification for males. *See*, Walters, *supra* note 153, at 159-163.

158. C. MacKinnon, *supra* note 2, at 6-10.

Legitimate and illegitimate sexual activity divides women into accepted and stigmatized classes. It keeps us in our place.[159]

2. More stories

"My great-great-great grandfather Austin Miller, a thirty-five-year-old lawyer, bought my eleven-year-old great-great-grandmother, Sophie, and her parents (being "family Negroes," the previous owner sold them as a matched set.) By the time she was twelve, Austin Miller had made Sophie the mother of a child, my great-grandmother Mary. He did so, according to family lore, out of his desire to have a family. Not of course, a family with my great-great grandmother, but with a wealthy white widow whom he in fact married shortly thereafter. He wanted to practice his sexual talents on my great-great-grandmother. In the bargain, Sophie

---

159. *See* West, "Jurisprudence and Gender," 55 UNIV. OF CHI. L. REV. 1 (1988) for a thoughtful analysis of masculine and feminist jurisprudence. Professor West contrasts the dominant masculine liberal legal theory of jurisprudence which is based on a minimalist state that ensures order and autonomy (represented by Rawls, R. Dworkin, Ackerman, Nozick) with the masculine critical legal theory of a longing for community (Kennedy, Unger, Gabel). Both, Professor West contends, are based on the separation thesis, which holds that all humans are distinct and not essentially connected with each other.

Feminist jurisprudence holds a contrary vision of human existence premised on the material fact that women are actually or potentially connected to other human life. The dominant feminist theory, cultural feminism, stresses connectedness as engendering nuturing and the ethic of care (Gilligan, Chordorow, Sherry) whereas radical feminist theory sees connectedness as penetration and invasion (A. Dworkin, MacKinnon, Estrich). Thus neither the dominant worlds nor the radical worlds can ever meet. Liberal males value autonomy while liberal females value connectedness. Crits value association which radical feminists see as oppressive invasion.

In an exchange over these contrary visions of the social order, Professor West compared Professor Richard (now Judge) Posner's liberal economic order to the literature of Franz Kafka. West, "Authority, Autonomy, and Choice: The Role of Consent in the Moral and Political Visions of Franz Kafka and Richard Posner," 99 HARV. L. REV. 384 (1985); Posner, in turn, attacked West's reading of Kafka as reductionist and her world view as critical legal theory, a romantic world of Dionysian disorder, opposed to the liberal Apollonian Rule of Law. Posner, "Significance of Free Choice: A Reply to Professor West," 99 HARV. L. REV. 1431 (1985); R. POSNER, LAW AND LITERATURE 176-205 (1988).

Not so. Perhaps women, as readers, bring a different perspective to Kafka. THE HUNGER ARTIST and THE TRIAL may remind us of ourselves—or lack of self. We are in a world we do not control. We are asking "to be", not the liberal autonomy or association desired by males, who know they "are". But as denizens of this world, we are also seeking otherness, because we must have something. And so the hunger artist cries out that she would eat if only she could find the food she liked. The bulimic and anorexic struggle between fear of invasion and fear of nothingness. In THE TRIAL, we struggle to find out what is going on, how to survive in a world not of our own making. But Posner sees K, and thus all of us, as equal aggressors seeking autonomy. Posner dismisses the washerwomans's rape as opportunistic flirtation and deception of K, just as the critics dismissed Lolita as a prepubescent fallen woman.

Posner ends by stating, "But if she [Professor West] believes these things [that we can be attracted to punishment] then she lives in a different world than yours and mine. And we say, yes we do, your "yours" excludes us.

bore Mary, who was taken away from her and raised in the Big House as a house servant, an attendant to his wife Mary (after whom Sophie's Mary, my great-grandmother, had been named) and to his legitimated white children."[160]

"The third argument is that to produce or deal with a child for money denigrates human dignity. To that premise, this court urgently agrees. The thirteenth amendment to the United States Constitution is still valid law. The law of adoption in New Jersey does prohibit the exchange of any consideration for obtaining a child. The fact is, however, that the money to be paid to the surrogate is not being paid for the surrender of the child to the father. And that is just the point—at birth, mother and father have equal rights to the child absent any other agreement. *The biological father pays the surrogate for her willingness to be impregnated and carry his child to term. At birth, the father does not purchase the child* (Italics added). It is his own biological genetically related child. He cannot purchase what is already his."[161]

"This court holds therefore that in New Jersey, although the surrogacy contract is signed, the surrogate may nevertheless renounce and terminate the contract until the time of conception. She may be subject then for such monetary damages as may be proven. Specific performance to compel the promised conception, gestation, and birth shall not be available to the male promisor. However, once conception has occurred the parties rights are fixed, the terms of the contract are firm and performance will be anticipated with the joy that only a newborn can bring."[162]

"Now having found that the best interest of the child will be enhanced and served in paternal custody, that there is no evidence of fraud overreaching or violation of any other principle of equity by Mr. Stern, [the biological father] this court having evaluated the equities finds them weighted in favor of Mr. Stern. Enforcing the contract will leave Mr. & Mrs. Whitehead [the "surrogate" biological mother] in the same position that they were in when the contract was made. To not enforce the contract will give them the child and deprive Mr. Stern of his promised benefits. This court therefore will specifically enforce the surrogate parenting agreement to compel delivery of the child to the father and to terminate the mother's parental rights."[163]

---

160. Williams, *Alchemical Notes: Reconstructing Ideals from Deconstructed Rights*, 22 HARV. C.R.-C.L. L. REV. 401, 418-19 (1987).

161. *In re* Baby M, *supra* note 150, at 2018.

162. *Id.* at 2019.

163. *Id.* at 2026. The New Jersey Supreme Court, *In re Baby M*, 56 U.S.L.W. 2442-2443 (Sup. Ct. A-39, 2/3/88) reversed in part and affirmed in part the lower court decision. (The Supreme Court invalidated the surrogacy contract as conflicting with statutes prohibiting the use of money in connection with adoption, statutes requiring proof of unfitness or abandonment before termination of parental rights, and statutes making surrender of custody revocable in private placement adoptions. The Court, however, upheld the custody decision of the lower court as in the best interests of the child but remanded for reinstatement of the mother's visitation rights).

"In reviewing those powerfully impersonal documents, [the contract of my great-great-grandmother Sophie's sale] I realized that both she and the fox [in Pierson v. Post][164] shared a common lot, were either owned or unowned, never the owner. And whether owned or unowned, rights over them never filtered down *to* them; rights to their persons never vested in them. When owned, issues of physical, mental and emotional abuse or cruelty were assigned by the law to the private tolerance, whimsy, or insanity of an external master. And when unowned—i.e., free, freed, or escaped—again their situation was uncomfortably precarious, for as objects to be owned, they and the game of their conquest were seen only as potential enhancements to some other self. They were fair game from the perspective of those who had rights, but from their own point of view, they were objects of a murderous hunt.[165]

---

164. *Pierson v. Post*, 3 Caines 175 (N.Y. Sup. Ct. 1805). (In *Pierson v. Post*, the issue was who was the rightful owner of the dead fox, the hunter of the fox who cornered it or the killer of the fox).

165. Williams, *supra* note 160, at 420-421.

BRIEF AMICI CURIAE OF FEMINIST ANTI-CENSORSHIP TASKFORCE, ET AL., IN *AMERICAN BOOKSELLERS ASSOCIATION v. HUDNUT*

Nan D. Hunter* and Sylvia A. Law**

The document that follows represents both a legal brief and a political statement. It was written for two purposes: to mobilize, in a highly visible way, a broad spectrum of feminist opposition to the enactment of laws expanding state suppression of sexually explicit material; and to place before the Court of Appeals for the Seventh Circuit a cogent legal argument for the constitutional invalidity of an Indianapolis municipal ordinance that would have permitted private civil suits to ban such material, purportedly to protect women.[1] Drafting this brief was one of

---

* Director, American Civil Liberties Union Projects on Lesbian and Gay Rights, and on AIDS and Civil Liberties. B.A., Northwestern University, 1971; J.D., Georgetown University Law Center, 1975.
** Director, Arthur Garfield Hays Civil Liberties Program and Professor of Law, New York University School of Law. B.A., Antioch College, 1964; J.D., New York University School of Law, 1968. MacArthur Prize Fellow.

1. The ordinance states:

Pornography shall mean the sexually explicit subordination of women, graphically depicted, whether in pictures or in words, that also includes one or more of the following:

 (1) Women are presented as sexual objects who enjoy pain or humiliation; or
 (2) Women are presented as sexual objects who experience sexual pleasure in being raped; or
 (3) Women are presented as sexual objects tied up or cut up or mutilated or bruised or physically hurt, or as dismembered or truncated or fragmented or severed into body parts; or
 (4) Women are presented being penetrated by objects or animals; or
 (5) Women are presented in scenarios of degredation [sic], injury, abasement, torture, shown as filthy or inferior, bleeding, bruised, or hurt in a context that makes these conditions sexual; [or]
 (6) Women are presented as sexual objects for domination, conquest, violation, exploitation, possession, or use, or through postures or positions of servility or submission or display.

INDIANAPOLIS, IND., CODE § 16-3(q) (1984).

The Court of Appeals held that the Indianapolis ordinance violated the first amendment, and the Supreme Court affirmed that ruling without issuing an opinion. American Booksellers Ass'n v. Hudnut, 771 F.2d 323 (7th Cir. 1985), *aff'd*, 475 U.S. 1001 (1986). It appears that the Feminist Anti-Censorship Taskforce (FACT) analysis had some influence on Judge Easterbrook's approach to the constitutional issues presented. The opin-

the most demanding and exhilarating assignments either author has yet undertaken.

The brief was written on behalf of the Feminist Anti-Censorship Taskforce (FACT) and was co-signed by the Women's Legal Defense Fund (WLDF) and eighty individual feminists. The analysis of sexuality underlying the brief flows directly from a long tradition of nineteenth-century women's rights activists who sought sexual self-determination as an essential aspect of full liberation. From the beginning, others within the early feminist movement opposed this understanding of feminism because they viewed sexuality as a realm in which women often suffered. To protect women, they sought to restrict male sexual freedom by imposing on men the standard of sexual purity already applied to women.[2]

The modern feminist movement has continued this divergence of viewpoint. Simone de Beauvoir, for example, saw the erotic as an aspect of human liberty and insisted that sexual self-determination constitutes a fundamental part of women's liberation.[3] Since 1966, women's demands have included calls for greater sexual freedom for women and an end to double standards.[4] At the same time, the movement has fought for and won a number of reforms to curb rape and other violence directed pointedly at women.[5] A part of the feminist antiviolence movement evolved first into a campaign aimed at depictions of violence against women in a variety of media and then into a campaign aimed at all pornographic imagery, whether violent or not.[6]

---

ion discusses concrete examples illustrating the difficulty of distinguishing images that liberate women from those that subordinate women. *Id.* at 330. It addresses the relationship between images, ideas, and behavior, and the distinction between fantasy and reality, in terms that are unusually rich and thoughtful for a judicial opinion. *Id.* The court rightly rejects the state's claim that pornography is "low value" speech, entitled to lesser constitutional protection than "serious" talk about public issues. *Id.* at 331.

2. DuBois & Gordon, *Seeking Ecstasy on the Battlefield: Danger and Pleasure in Nineteenth-Century Feminist Sexual Thought*, in PLEASURE AND DANGER: EXPLORING FEMALE SEXUALITY 31 (C. Vance ed. 1984) [hereinafter PLEASURE AND DANGER].

3. S. DE BEAUVOIR, THE SECOND SEX 202-03, 366-413 (H. Parshley trans., 5th printing 1968).

4. *See* Hunter, *The Pornography Debate in Context: A Chronology of Sexuality, Media & Violence Issues in Feminism*, in CAUGHT LOOKING: FEMINISM, PORNOGRAPHY & CENSORSHIP 26 (1986) [hereinafter CAUGHT LOOKING]; Snitow, Stansell & Thompson, *Introduction*, in POWERS OF DESIRE: THE POLITICS OF SEXUALITY 9 (A. Snitow, C. Stansell & S. Thompson eds. 1983) [hereinafter POWERS OF DESIRE].

5. *See* S. SCHECHTER, WOMEN AND MALE VIOLENCE: THE VISIONS AND STRUGGLES OF THE BATTERED WOMEN'S MOVEMENT (1982).

6. *See* Snitow, *Retrenchment Versus Transformation: The Politics of the Anti-pornography Movement*, in CAUGHT LOOKING, *supra* note 4, at 10, and in WOMEN AGAINST CENSORSHIP 107 (V. Burstyn ed. 1985).

Meanwhile, as feminist discourse on issues of sexuality became more elaborate, conservative forces also mobilized around issues of sexual imagery. An alliance of traditional moralists, the New Right, and some feminists promoted and defended the Indianapolis ordinance.[7] In the current political environment, the conservative voices are plainly more powerful than those of the feminists. For conservatives, the current interest in suppression of pornography forms part of a larger agenda to reverse recent feminist gains through a moral crusade against abortion, lesbian and gay rights, contraceptive education and services, and women's fragile economic achievements. Conservatives and religious fundamentalists oppose pornography because it appears to depict and approve of sex outside marriage and procreation. The Right seeks to use legitimate feminist concern about sexual violence and oppression to reinstate traditional sexual arrangements and the formerly inexorable link between reproduction and sexuality.

In 1985, conservative efforts to focus attention on suppression of sexual imagery culminated in Attorney General William French Smith's establishment of a Commission on Pornography charged to find "more effective ways in which the spread of pornography could be contained."[8] Because most Americans do not share the moral view that confines sex to a solely procreative role, the Commission's mission was to modernize the assault on sexually explicit images by demonstrating that pornography causes violence. Despite the number of members chosen with a history of vehement opposition to sexually explicit material[9] and

---

7. Duggan, *Censorship in the Name of Feminism*, Village Voice, Oct. 16, 1984, at 11, col. 1. The ordinance was introduced in the Indianapolis City Council by a member whose career was founded on anti-ERA organizing. *Id.* at 12, col. 1. The central popular support for its passage came from fundamentalists who attended the meetings at which the Council voted on the ordinance. The Reverend Greg Dixon of the Indianapolis Baptist Temple, a former Moral Majority official, organized the fundamentalist presence. *Id.* at 16, col. 1.

8. 2 ATTORNEY GENERAL'S COMM'N ON PORNOGRAPHY, U.S. DEP'T OF JUST., FINAL REPORT app. A, at 1957 (1986) [hereinafter COMM'N ON PORNOGRAPHY].

9. The Commission was chaired by Henry Hudson, a prosecutor whom President Reagan praised for closing down every adult bookstore in Arlington, Va. At least six of the 11 Commission members had previously taken strong public stands opposing pornography and supporting obscenity laws as a means of control. B. LYNN, POLLUTING THE CENSORSHIP DEBATE: A SUMMARY AND CRITIQUE OF THE FINAL REPORT OF THE ATTORNEY GENERAL'S COMMISSION ON PORNOGRAPHY 14-16 (1986) (ACLU Public Policy Report); Vance, *The Meese Commission on the Road*, NATION, Aug. 2, 1986, at 76 (also listing Commission member Frederick Schauer as having taken a public stand opposing pornography). For example, Commission member Dr. James Dobson is President of Focus on the Family, an organization that is "dedicated to the preservation of the home and the family and the traditional values growing out of the Judeo-Christian ethic." B. LYNN,

tight control of the witness list,[10] the Commission was unable to "prove" that pornography causes violence.

Social scientists, whose work the antipornography movement had previously utilized, refused in their testimony to draw the simple connections between pornography and violence that the Commission sought.[11] Like FACT, these researchers urged the use of caution in the extension of artificial laboratory findings to naturalistic settings. Further, they testified that aggressive imagery and the mainstream media present more worrisome concerns than sexual imagery and X-rated channels.[12] Unable to marshal systemic evidence that pornography causes concrete injury, the Commission was forced to rely upon the anecdotal testimony of carefully selected and well-prepared individual victims[13] and to invoke a vastly broadened concept of "harm."[14]

Perhaps the most significant and most telling aspect of the Commission's work was its inability to agree on a definition of pornography.[15] Undaunted, the Commission concluded that most commercially available pornography is "degrading" and contains "characteristics of degradation, domination, subordination, and humiliation," particularly of women.[16] An earlier draft

---

supra, at 15. In addition, Commission member Frederick Schauer had previously argued for a highly restricted application of the first amendment. *Id.* at 17; Schauer, *Speech and "Speech"—Obscenity and "Obscenity": An Exercise in the Interpretation of Constitutional Language*, 67 GEO. L.J. 899, 922-23 (1979).

The three people without prior established positions on pornography frequently resisted the staff's agenda. They endorsed a statement that said that while they abhorred "the exploitation of vulnerable people" in pornography, they also rejected "judgmental and condescending efforts to speak on women's behalf as though they were helpless, mindless children." 1 COMM'N ON PORNOGRAPHY, *supra* note 8, at 194 (statement of Dr. Judith Becker, Ellen Levine, and Deanne Tilton-Durfee). Two of these three women dissented from the final report. *See id.* at 195-212 (statement of Dr. Judith Becker and Ellen Levine).

10. Over three-fourths of the witnesses urged tighter controls over sexually explicit materials. B. LYNN, *supra* note 9, at 7.

11. *See generally id.* at 57-88. Prof. Edward Donnerstein has denounced as "bizarre" the Commission's effort to use his research to buttress a claim that sexually violent material causes criminal behavior. Goleman, *Researchers Dispute Pornography Report on Its Use of Data*, N.Y. Times, May 17, 1986, at A1, col. 1.

12. Vance, *supra* note 9, at 79.

13. *See* 1 COMM'N ON PORNOGRAPHY, *supra* note 8, at 322-49. With respect to materials regarded by the Commission as nonviolent but degrading, the Commission acknowledged that there was little concrete evidence "causally linking the material with sexual aggression" but nonetheless concluded that the "absence of evidence should by no means be taken to deny the existence of the causal link." *Id.* at 332.

14. "[T]he most important harms must be seen in moral terms, and the action of moral condemnation of that which is immoral is not merely important but essential." *Id.* at 303.

15. *Id.* at 227-32.

16. *See id.* at 331.

of the Commission report had even offered examples of such material.[17] For the final report, however, the Commission also found itself unable to agree on examples of "degradation."[18]

The Meese Commission recommended new federal and state legislation and increased prosecution to suppress sexually explicit materials to the maximum extent constitutionally possible.[19] Unfortunately, it failed to embrace the recommendation of the 1970 Commission on Obscenity and Pornography[20] to commence a serious sex education effort to empower young people to develop a healthy and balanced view of sexuality that would enable them to avoid unwanted pregnancy and sexually transmitted diseases. The Meese Commission did not recommend strengthening federal law to prohibit sexual harassment in the workplace.[21] It did not call for legislation to remove spousal immunity in sexual assault cases or for funding to improve law enforcement against domestic violence.

At the level of popular opinion, little support seems to exist for either conservative or feminist campaigns against sexual imagery. Press reaction to the Meese Commission report was uniformly negative.[22] In 1985, voters in Cambridge, Massachusetts,

---

17. B. LYNN, *supra* note 9, at 71-72. These examples included:

[D]epictions of a woman lying on the ground while two standing men ejaculate on her; two women engaged in sexual activity with each other while a man looks on and masturbates; a woman non-physically coerced into engaging in sexual activity with a male authority figure, such as a boss, teacher, or priest, and then begs for more; . . . a woman with legs spread wide open holding her labia open with her fingers; a man shaving the hair from the pubic area of a woman; a woman dressed in a dog costume being penetrated from the rear by a man . . . .

Id. at 71-72.

18. *Id.* at 72.

19. Two Commission members, both women, filed a sharp and cogent dissent. 1 COMM'N ON PORNOGRAPHY, *supra* note 8, at 195-212 (statement of Dr. Judith Becker and Ellen Levine).

20. COMMISSION ON OBSCENITY & PORNOGRAPHY, THE REPORT OF THE COMMISSION ON OBSCENITY AND PORNOGRAPHY (1970).

21. For a case illustrating an inadequacy of the present antidiscrimination law, see *Rabidue v. Osceola Refining Co.*, 805 F.2d 611, 622 (1986) (holding that posters of nude women on workplace walls and supervisors' obscene comments do not constitute actionable sexual harassment).

22. P. NOBILE & E. NADLER, UNITED STATES OF AMERICA VS. SEX: HOW THE MEESE COMMISSION LIED ABOUT PORNOGRAPHY 224-25 (1986). The *New York Times* opined, "[T]he report, widely circulated without formal publication, must be faulted for relying on questionable evidence and recklessly encouraging censorship." *Defeated by Pornography*, N.Y. Times, June 21, 1986, at A16, col. 1. *Washington Post* columnist William Raspberry praised the dissenting Commissioners for their "intellectual honesty, professional integrity and guts," and their refusal to be "buffaloed into unsupported conclusions." Raspberry, *Pornography Report*, Wash. Post, May 26, 1986, at A21, col. 4. Another *Washington Post* columnist, Richard Cohen, ridiculed the Commission's discovery of a causal link between pornography and violence as "more a wish than a scientific

rejected, by a wide margin, a public referendum on an ordinance similar to the one adopted in Indianapolis.[23] A broad range of feminist organizations opposed the ordinance.[24] In 1986, citizens of Maine voted nearly three-to-one against adoption of an obscenity law;[25] women's organizations in Maine strongly opposed the proposal.[26]

The feminists of FACT have helped to transform the contemporary dialogue about pornography. That debate no longer pits victimized women and conventional moralists against pornographers and civil libertarians. FACT affirms that sexuality is, for women, a source of pleasure and power, as well as a realm of danger and oppression. As a consequence, discussion of pornography and sexuality is more intricately contextualized and appropriately complex. The brief that follows aspires to keep open the discussion about sexual explicitness and to assert that sexually explicit materials have both liberating and repressive qualities. The feminist analysis of these issues remains far from complete. As Carole S. Vance, one of the founders of FACT, observes, "The hallmark of sexuality is its complexity: its multiple meanings, sensations, and connections."[27]

Despite the contradictory strands in the feminist approach, the empirical and intellectual exploration of sexuality remains a

---

finding." Cohen, *Pornography: The 'Causal Link,'* Wash. Post, June 3, 1986, at A19, col. 2. *Chicago Tribune* columnist Mike Royko observed:

> [I]n recent years there have been more than 220 bombings of abortion clinics. . . . Those who have been arrested have expressed deep religious convictions. . . .
>
> . . . .
>
> [E]xtremist groups shoot rural sheriffs, talk show hosts and lawyers they suspect of being liberal. They, too, spout religious devotion.
>
> So maybe we should begin considering the outlawing of religion because it is the root cause of so much violence.

Royko, *Nobody Ever Got Raped by a Book,* Chicago Trib., June 11, 1986, at 1, col. 3.

23. *Anti-Pornography Law Defeated in Cambridge,* N.Y. Times, Nov. 12, 1985, at A16, col. 6.

24. FACT, Boston Chapter; The Boston Women's Health Book Collective; Boston NOW; Women Against Violence Against Women, Boston Chapter; Cambridge Commission on the Status of Women; No Bad Women, Just Bad Laws (statements on file with the U. MICH. J.L. REF.).

25. Wald, *Voters in Maine Defeat Anti-Obscenity Plan,* N.Y. Times, June 11, 1986, at A32, col. 4. For ballot purposes, the four-and-a-half-page statute was reduced to the proposition, "Do you want to make it a crime to make, sell, give for value or otherwise promote obscene material in Maine?" *Id.*

26. Wald, *Obscenity Debate Focuses Attention on Maine, Where Voters Weigh Issue,* N.Y. Times, June 10, 1986, at A18, col. 1.

27. Vance, *Pleasure and Danger: Toward a Politics of Sexuality,* in PLEASURE AND DANGER, *supra* note 2, at 5.

central enterprise for the contemporary feminist movement.[28] Sexual ideas, images, and practices have been dominated by and oriented toward men and are often not responsive to women.[29] Many women experience sexual failure and frustration, rather than ecstasy and pleasure. Furthermore, feminism's core insight emphasizes that gender is socially defined. Social and sexual role acculturation largely determine gender differences; accordingly, these differences are not natural or immutable. In Simone de Beauvoir's classic words, "One is not born, but rather becomes, a woman."[30] Social ideas and material arrangements give deep meaning to masculinity and femininity. The social significance of gender is fabricated to favor men systematically through economic, political, and legal structures that rest upon and reinforce gender. Sexual desire, both powerful and pliable, forms a part of that gender system. Discovering, describing, and analyzing the complex interaction of gender and sexuality, of representation and reality, thus remains a key project of feminist theory and lives.

---

28. For three excellent feminist collections, see POWERS OF DESIRE, *supra* note 4; PLEASURE AND DANGER, *supra* note 2; WOMEN AGAINST CENSORSHIP, *supra* note 6.

29. *See* Keodt, *The Myth of the Vaginal Orgasm*, in NOTES FROM THE SECOND YEAR: WOMEN'S LIBERATION 37 (S. Firestone ed. 1970), and in VOICES FROM WOMEN'S LIBERATION 158 (L. Tanner ed. 1971); M. SHERFEY, THE NATURE AND EVOLUTION OF FEMALE SEXUALITY (1972); L. BARBACH, FOR YOURSELF: THE FULFILLMENT OF FEMALE SEXUALITY (1971).

30. S. DE BEAUVOIR, *supra* note 3, at 273.

IN THE
UNITED STATES COURT OF APPEALS
FOR THE SEVENTH CIRCUIT

No. 84-3147

AMERICAN BOOKSELLERS ASSOCIATION, INC., et al.,
Plaintiffs-Appellees,
v.
WILLIAM H. HUDNUT III, et al.,
Defendants-Appellants.

On Appeal from the United States District Court
for the Southern District of Indiana

BRIEF AMICI CURIAE OF
FEMINIST ANTI-CENSORSHIP TASKFORCE, et al.

NAN D. HUNTER
132 W. 43rd Street
New York, N.Y. 10036
(212) 944-9800

SYLVIA A. LAW
40 Washington Square South
New York, N.Y. 10003
(212) 598-7642

April 8, 1985

CERTIFICATE OF INTEREST

The undersigned counsel of record for Amici furnishes the following list in compliance with Circuit Rule 5(b).

1. The full name of each amicus curiae signing this brief is as follows:

Feminist Anti-Censorship Taskforce
Women's Legal Defense Fund

Roberta Achtenberg	Long Hall Press
Dennis Altman	Phyllis Lyon
Nancy K. Bereano	Del Martin
Joan E. Biren	Judith McDaniel
Betty Brooks	Kate Millett
Rita Mae Brown	Joan Nestle
Arlene Carmen	Esther Newton
Denise S. Carty-Bennia	Lynn M. Paltrow
Cheryl L. Clarke	Randolph J. Peritz
Michelle Cliff	Rosalind Petchesky
The Editors of Conditions	Felice Picano
Magazine	Minnie Bruce Pratt
Rhonda Copelon	Jane B. Ransom
Rosemary Daniell	Rayna Rapp
Peggy C. Davis	Judith Resnick
John D'Emilio	Adrienne Rich
Betty Dodson	David A.J. Richards
Mary C. Dunlap	Rand E. Rosenblatt
Thomas I. Emerson	Sue Deller Ross
Susan Estrich	Abby R. Rubenfeld
Mary L. Farmer	Gayle S. Rubin
Ann E. Freedman	Vito Russo
Estelle B. Freedman	Kathy Sarris
Betty Friedan	Karen Sauvigne
Jewelle L. Gomez	Susan Schechter
Bette Gordon	Elizabeth Schneider
Linda Gordon	Annamay Sheppard
Vivian Gornick	Susan Sherman
Lynn A. Haanen	Alix Kates Shulman
Carolyn Heilbrun	Barbara Smith
Donna J. Hitchens	Judith Stacey
Amber Hollibaugh	Catherine R. Stimpson

Joan W. Howarth	Amy Swerdlow
David Kairys	Nadine Taub
E. Ann Kaplan	Judith R. Walkowitz
Jonathan N. Katz	Wendy Webster Williams
Virginia Kerr	Ellen Willis
Norman Laurila	Sara Wunsch
Howard Lesnick	Diane L. Zimmerman

2. The Women's Legal Defense Fund is a not-for-profit corporation incorporated in Washington, D.C.

3. The following attorneys, not affiliated with a law firm, represent the Amici in this Court:

Nan D. Hunter
Sylvia A. Law

Nan D. Hunter
Sylvia A. Law
Attorneys for amici curiae
Feminist Anti-Censorship
Taskforce, et al.

TABLE OF CONTENTS

TABLE OF AUTHORITIES

LEGISLATIVE MATERIALS

OTHER AUTHORITIES

157

S. Schechter, Women and Male Violence: The Visions and
Struggles of the Battered Women's Movement (1982) . . . 34, 35

Shulman, A Story of a Girl and Her Dog, in Powers of
Desire: The Politics of Sexuality 410 (A. Snitow, C.
Stansell & S. Thompson eds. 1983)   23

Smith, The Social Content of Pornography, 26 J. Comm.
16 (1976)   2

Take Back the Night: Women and Pornography (L.
Lederer ed. 1980)   20

Toward an Anthropology of Women (R. Reiter ed. 1975) . .   25

Turan, Not Swept Away, The Progressive, May 1976, at
39   8

U.S. Commission on Civil Rights, Women and Poverty
(1974); Women Still in Poverty (1979); and Child Care
and Equal Opportunity for Women (1981)   25

Vance & Snitow, Toward a Conversation About Sex in
Feminism: A Modest Proposal, 10 Signs: J. Women in
Culture and Soc'y 126 (1984)   36

Williams, Reflections on Culture, Courts and Feminism, 7
Women's Rts. L. Rep. 175 (1982)   33

Willis, Feminism, Moralism and Pornography, in Powers
of Desire: The Politics of Sexuality 460 (A. Snitow, C.
Stansell & S. Thompson eds. 1983)   22

Interest of Amici

Amici are feminists who sign this brief as a statement of our opposition to the Indianapolis ordinance. We believe that the ordinance reinforces rather than undercuts central sexist stereotypes in our society and would result in state suppression of sexually explicit speech, including feminist images and literature, which does not in any way encourage violence against women. We condemn acts of violence against women; incitement to that violence; and misogyny, racism, and anti-semitism in all media. We believe, however, that the Indianapolis ordinance will not reduce violence against women and will censor speech and imagery that properly belong in the public realm. Some proponents of this ordinance genuinely believed that it would assist women to overcome disabling sex role stereotypes and promote greater equality for women. We who sign this brief are deeply concerned that it will have precisely the opposite effect.

THE FEMINIST ANTI-CENSORSHIP TASKFORCE (FACT) is a group of women long active in the feminist movement who organized in 1984 to oppose the enactment of Indianapolis-style antipornography laws. It is composed of community activists, writers, artists and teachers.

THE WOMEN'S LEGAL DEFENSE FUND, Inc. (WLDF) is a non-profit tax-exempt organization of over 1500 members founded to further women's rights and to challenge sex-based inequities through the law, especially in the area of employment discrimination and domestic relations. WLDF volunteer and staff attorneys conduct public education about women's rights and sex discrimination; counsel thousands of individual women annually about their rights; represent victims of sex discrimination in selected precedent-setting cases; and advocate on behalf of laws guaranteeing sex-based equality before legislative and executive branch policymakers and as amicus curiae in numerous court cases.

ROBERTA ACHTENBERG is the Directing Attorney of the Lesbian Rights Project in San Francisco and the Editor of Sexual Orientation and the Law (Clark Boardman 1985). She was formerly Dean of New College of California School of Law.

DENNIS ALTMAN is a Policy Fellow, University of California at San Francisco, in the Institute for Health Policy Studies and is the author of four books. He was Regents lecturer, University of California at Santa Cruz, 1983.

NANCY K. BEREANO is Editor and Publisher of Firebrand Books. Prior to that position, she was Editor of the Feminist Series for Crossing Press.

JOAN E. BIREN (JEB) is a freelance photographer and the author of Eye to Eye: Portraits of Lesbians. She has been a feminist activist for fifteen years.

BETTY BROOKS, Ed. D., is the Director of the Southern California Rape Hotline Alliance Self-Defense Certification Program, a member of the American College of Sexologists, and founder of Women Against Sexual Abuse. She recently organized a FACT chapter in Los Angeles.

RITA MAE BROWN is a well-known author whose works include Rubyfruit Jungle, Southern Discomfort, and Sudden Death.

ARLENE CARMEN is Program Associate at Judson Memorial Church in New York City, where she directs a ministry to street prostitutes. She is co-author of Abortion Counseling and Social Change (Judson Press 1973) and Working Women: The Subterranean World of Street Prostitution, scheduled to be published in August 1985.

DENISE S. CARTY-BENNIA is a Professor of Law, Northeastern University School of Law, and an active participant in movements opposing sex and race discrimination in the United States.

CHERYL L. CLARKE is a Black feminist lesbian poet, writer, and member of the editorial collective of Conditions Magazine.

MICHELLE CLIFF is the author of Claiming an Identity They Taught Me to Despise and Abeng. She is a member of Poets & Writers and The Authors Guild.

THE EDITORS OF CONDITIONS MAGAZINE—Founded in 1976, Conditions magazine is a feminist magazine of writing by women with an emphasis on writing by lesbians. The current editors are Dorothy Allison, Cheryl Clarke, Nancy Clarke Otter, and Debby Schaubman.

RHONDA COPELON is an Associate Professor of Law, City University of New York Law School at Queens College. For the past fifteen years, she has litigated civil rights and women's rights cases as an attorney with the Center for Constitutional Rights.

ROSEMARY DANIELL is a full-time writer. Her books include A Sexual Tour of the Deep South (poetry, 1975); Fatal Flowers: On Sin, Sex, and Suicide in the Deep South (non-fiction, 1980); and Sleeping with Soldiers (non-fiction, 1985).

PEGGY C. DAVIS, Assistant Professor, New York University Law School, is a former Judge of the New York Family Court and has worked in many efforts for racial and gender equality.

JOHN D'EMILIO, Ph. D., is an Assistant Professor of History at the University of North Carolina in Greensboro and the author of Sexual Politics, Sexual Communities (University of Chicago Press 1983).

BETTY DODSON is an artist, writer, publisher, and teacher. She has spent eleven years organizing sexual enhancement workshops for women. Her book, Self-Love and Orgasm, has sold 200,000 copies.

MARY C. DUNLAP is a law teacher and solo practitioner of civil law. She was co-founder and attorney-teacher at Equal Right Advocates, Inc., San Francisco, from 1973 to 1978. She is co-author of a chapter on the First Amendment in Sexual Orientation and the Law (Clark Boardman 1985).

THOMAS I. EMERSON, Lines Professor of Law, Emeritus, Yale University School of Law, has written extensively on the First Amendment and is co-author of The Equal Rights Amendment: A Constitutional Basis for Equal Rights for Women, 80 Yale L.J. 871 (1971).

SUSAN ESTRICH, Assistant Professor of Law, Harvard Law School, has written in the area of sex discrimination.

MARY L. FARMER is a lesbian feminist activist and bookstore owner in Washington, D.C.

ANN E. FREEDMAN, Professor of Law, Rutgers Law School, Camden, was a co-founder of the Women's Law Project, Philadelphia. She is co-author of The Equal Rights Amendment: A Constitutional Basis for Equal Rights for Women, 80 Yale L.J. 871 (1971), and of Sex Discrimination and the Law: Causes and Remedies (1975).

ESTELLE B. FREEDMAN is Associate Professor of History at Stanford University and Director of the Feminist Studies Program there. She is the author of Their Sisters' Keepers, a history of women's prison reform, and of articles on the history of sexuality.

BETTY FRIEDAN is the author of The Feminine Mystique and The Second Stage. She was founding president of the National Organization for Women, a founding member of the National Women's Political Caucus, and is presently co-chair of the National Commission for Women's Equality of the American Jewish Congress.

JEWELLE L. GOMEZ is a critic for the Village Voice, Wellesley Women's Review of Books, and Hurricane Alice (in Minneapolis). She is a Program Associate for the New York State Council on the Arts.

BETTE GORDON is an Assistant Professor of Film at Hofstra University in New York and an independent filmmaker. Her work has been exhibited at international film festivals in Cannes, Berlin, Florence, and Los Angeles, and is currently featured in New York, Paris, and Sydney, Australia.

LINDA GORDON is a Professor of History at the University of Wisconsin—Madison. She is the author of Woman's Body, Woman's Right: A History of Birth Control in the US, America's Working Women, and of numerous articles on the history of feminism and on family violence and the feminist response.

VIVIAN GORNICK is a feminist author and journalist whose works include Woman in Sexist Society: Essays in Feminism, In Search of Ali Mahmoud: An American Woman in Egypt, and Women in Science.

LYNN A. HAANEN is serving her third term on the Dane County (Wisconsin) Board of Supervisors and is a co-founder of FACT in Madison, Wisconsin, formed to raise concerns about antipornography and censorship measures.

CAROLYN HEILBRUN is Professor of English at Columbia University and an author.

DONNA J. HITCHENS is an attorney now in private practice in San Francisco, formerly the Directing Attorney of the Lesbian Rights Project and a staff attorney with Equal Rights Advocates.

AMBER HOLLIBAUGH was a founding member of the first Boston battered women's shelter and an organizer with Californians for Education Against the Briggs Initiative/Prop 6.

JOAN W. HOWARTH is currently the police practices attorney for the ACLU Foundation of Southern California. In 1976, she helped to establish Women Against Violence Against Women (WAVAW) and was active in that group until 1982.

DAVID KAIRYS is a writer, teacher, and attorney in Philadelphia and editor of The Politics of Law.

E. ANN KAPLAN is an Associate Professor at Rutgers University, where she teaches literature and film. She is the author of Women and Film: Both Sides of the Camera (Methuen 1983) and of other books and articles dealing with women's studies.

JONATHAN N. KATZ is the author of Gay American History and the Gay/Lesbian Almanac.

VIRGINIA KERR is Assistant Professor of Law at the University of Pennsylvania Law School.

NORMAN LAURILA co-owns and manages a gay and lesbian bookstore in New York City called "A Different Light," which also has a branch in Los Angeles.

HOWARD LESNICK is a Distinguished Professor of Law, City University of New York Law School at Queens College.

LONG HAUL PRESS is a lesbian-feminist press in New York.

PHYLLIS LYON, Ed. D., is co-author of Lesbian/Woman. She is a Human Rights Commissioner in San Francisco and a professor at the Institute for Advanced Study in Human Sexuality.

DEL MARTIN is the author of Battered Wives. She is also a member of the California Commission on Crime Control and Violence Prevention.

JUDITH McDANIEL, Ph. D., is a poet, novelist, teacher, and political activist. She is Program Director for the Albany, N.Y. Non-Violence Project.

KATE MILLETT is the author of Sexual Politics, The Prostitution Papers, Flying, and Sita.

JOAN NESTLE is a writer and co-founder of the Lesbian Herstory Educational Foundation, Inc./The Lesbian Herstory Archives. For the last nineteen years she has taught writing in the SEEK Program at Queens College and at the City University of New York.

ESTHER NEWTON, Ph. D., is an Associate Professor of Anthropology and Coordinator of Women's Studies, State University of New York College at Purchase.

LYNN M. PALTROW is an attorney working at the National Abortion Rights Action League through the Georgetown University Women's Law and Public Policy Fellowship Program.

RANDOLPH J. PERITZ is a Professor of Law at Rutgers Law School, Camden.

ROSALIND PETCHESKY is an Associate Professor of Political Theory at Ramapo College of New Jersey. She is the author of Abortion and Woman's Choice (Northeastern University Press 1984) and has published numerous articles on women's reproductive rights and feminist theory.

FELICE PICANO is founder and publisher of The SeaHorse Press and co-founder and publisher of Gay Presses of New York. He is the author of ten books, including Eyes, The Lure, and Slashed to Ribbons & Other Stories.

MINNIE BRUCE PRATT teaches in the Women's Studies Program, University of Maryland—College Park. She is the author of two books of poetry, The Sound of One Fork and We Say We Love Each Other, and co-author of Yours in Struggle: Three Feminist Perspectives on Anti-Semitism and Racism.

JANE B. RANSOM has been active in reproductive rights issues as a member of the Committee for Abortion Rights and Against Sterilization Abuse, of the staff of the Center for Constitutional Rights, and of the board of the Brooklyn Teen Pregnancy Network.

RAYNA RAPP, Ph. D., is an Associate Professor and Chair of the Department of Anthropology Graduate Faculty at the New School for Social Research. She is editor of Toward an Anthropology of Women (1975) and co-author, with Ellen Ross, of Sex and Society: A Research Note from Cultural Anthropology and Social History (1981).

JUDITH RESNICK is Associate Professor of Law at the University of Southern California Law Center and author of articles on the role of federal courts and on the problems faced by women in prison.

ADRIENNE RICH is widely known as a lesbian feminist poet and writer. Her books include Of Woman Born: Motherhood as Experience and Institution (1974); On Lies, Secrets and Silence (essays, 1979); and The Fact of a Doorframe: Poems 1950-1984. She is an A.D. White Professor-at-Large at Cornell University (1981-1987) and has been a part-time lecturer in English at San Jose State University since 1984. Ms. Rich is a member of P.E.N. and The Authors Guild.

DAVID A.J. RICHARDS, Professor of Law, New York University Law School, has written prolifically on issues of morality and jurisprudence. His most recent work, Toleration and the Constitution (New York: Oxford University Press), is scheduled for publication in the near future.

RAND E. ROSENBLATT, Professor of Law, Rutgers Law School, Camden, teaches constitutional law.

SUE DELLER ROSS, Clinical Professor of Law, Georgetown University Law Center, has litigated women's rights issues on the staff of the EEOC, the ACLU, and the United States Justice Department. She is co-author of Sex Discrimination and the Law: Causes and Remedies (1975) and The Rights of Women (1984).

ABBY R. RUBENFELD is Managing Attorney, Lambda Legal Defense and Education Fund, Inc.

GAYLE S. RUBIN, Department of Anthropology at the University of Michigan, is the author of The Traffic in Women (1975); Introduction, in A Woman Appeared to Me (1976); The Leather Menace (1981); and Thinking Sex (1984).

VITO RUSSO is a freelance writer and publicist. He is the author of The Celluloid Closet: Homosexuality in the Movies (Harper and Row 1981).

KATHY SARRIS is President of Justice, Inc., the only statewide gay and lesbian civil rights organization in Indiana.

KAREN SAUVIGNE was a co-founder of Working Women's Institute, a national research, resource, and action center that focuses on sexual harassment.

SUSAN SCHECHTER is the author of Women and Male Violence: The Visions and Struggles of the Battered Women's Movement and is a consultant to many organizations serving battered women.

ELIZABETH SCHNEIDER, Associate Professor, Brooklyn Law School, teaches Women and the Law and has litigated and written extensively on behalf of women's rights for over a decade.

ANNAMAY SHEPPARD is a Professor of Law at Rutgers Law School, Newark.

SUSAN SHERMAN is a poet and editor of IKON Magazine.

ALIX KATES SHULMAN is a Visiting Writer-in-Residence at the University of Colorado—Boulder. She is the author of three novels published by Knopf: Memoirs of an Ex-Prom Queen (1972); Burning Questions (1978); and On the Stroll (1981). She has also written two works on the anarchist-feminist Emma Goldman, entitled To the Barricades (Crowell 1971) and Red Emma Speaks (Schocken 1983), in addition to numerous essays and stories on feminist themes.

BARBARA SMITH is a Black feminist activist and writer. She is co-founder of the Combahee River Collective in Boston, which does community organizing on issues such as sterilization abuse, reproductive freedom, violence against women, battering, and the murders of twelve Black women in Boston from January to May, 1979. Ms. Smith is the author of All the Women Are White, All the Blacks Are Men, But Some of Us Are Brave and Home Girls: A Black Feminist Anthology.

JUDITH STACEY is an Associate Professor of Sociology at the University of California at Davis. She is the author of Patriarchy and Socialist Revolution in China, editor of And Jill Came Tumbling After: Sexism in American Education, and on the editorial boards of Feminist Studies and Signs.

CATHERINE R. STIMPSON is Professor of English and Director of the Institute for Research on Women at Rutgers University. She also edits a scholarly book series on women in culture and society for the University of Chicago Press.

NADINE STROSSEN, Assistant Clinical Professor, New York University Law School, has worked actively in antidiscrimination and free speech.

AMY SWERDLOW, Ph. D., is Director of the Graduate Program in Women's History at Sarah Lawrence College. She is the editor and co-author of Households and Kin: Families in Flux and co-editor of Race, Class and Sex: The Dynamics of Control.

NADINE TAUB is a Professor of Law and Director of the Women's Rights Litigation Clinic at Rutgers Law School, Newark, where she teaches constitutional law, civil liberties, and social welfare legislation. She has written widely in the field of women's rights on topics involving battered women, sexual harassment, and reproductive freedom.

JUDITH R. WALKOWITZ, Professor of History at Rutgers University, is the author of Prostitution and Victorian Society: Women, Class and the State (Cambridge University Press 1980) and a specialist on the history of commercialized sex, popular culture, and themes of sexual violence. She is also the history editor of Feminist Studies.

WENDY WEBSTER WILLIAMS, Professor of Law, Georgetown University Law Center, was a founding partner of Equal Rights Advocates and has written and litigated on women's rights issues for more than a decade. She has taught sex discrimination law at several law schools, including University of California at Berkeley and Harvard.

ELLEN WILLIS is Senior Editor of the Village Voice and the author of Beginning to See the Light (Knopf 1981).

SARAH WUNSCH is a staff attorney at the Center for Constitutional Rights, where her work has included challenging laws restricting access to birth control and abortion rights, laws creating marital rape exemptions, and laws restricting the expression of gay sexuality.

DIANE L. ZIMMERMAN, Professor of Law, New York University Law School, has written extensively in the areas of First Amendment, defamation, and privacy.

INTRODUCTION

The instant case involves the constitutionality of an anti-pornography ordinance enacted by the City Council of Indianapolis, City-County Ordinance No. 35, 1984. The ordinance was ruled unconstitutional by the U.S. District Court on a motion for summary judgment. American Booksellers Ass'n v. Hudnut, 598 F. Supp. 1316 (S.D. Ind. 1984).

Amici believe that the ordinance violates both the First Amendment guarantee of freedom of speech and the Fourteenth Amendment guarantee of equal treatment under the law. Under its trafficking provision, the ordinance would allow injunctions to issue against the distribution, sale, exhibition or production of any sexually explicit materials which fall within its definition of pornography. No showing of harm to the plaintiff (individual or class) is required as proof prior to the issuance of such an injunction. Because the trafficking provision and the definition most flagrantly violate constitutional principles, this brief concentrates its focus on those two aspects of the ordinance.

I. THE ORDINANCE SUPPRESSES CONSTITUTIONALLY PROTECTED
SPEECH IN A MANNER PARTICULARLY DETRIMENTAL TO WOMEN.

Although Appellants argue that the ordinance is designed to
restrict images which legitimate violence and coercion against
women, the definition of pornography in the ordinance is not
limited to images of violence or of coercion, or to images produced by women who were coerced. Nor is it limited to materials
which advocate or depict the torture or rape of women as a form
of sexual pleasure. It extends to any sexually explicit material
which an agency or court finds to be "subordinating" to a claimant acting on behalf of women and which fits within one of the
descriptive categories which complete the definition of
pornography.

For purposes of the trafficking cause of action, the ordinance
defines pornography as the "graphic sexually explicit subordination of women, whether in pictures or in words, that also includes one or more" of the depictions described in six categories.[1] The violent and brutal images which Appellants use as
illustrative examples[2] cannot obscure the fact that the ordinance

---

1. (1) Women are presented as sexual objects who enjoy pain or humiliation; or
   (2) Women are presented as sexual objects who experience sexual pleasure in be-
       ing raped; or
   (3) Women are presented as sexual objects tied up or cut up or mutilated or
       bruised or physically hurt, or as dismembered or truncated or fragmented or
       severed into body parts; or
   (4) Women are presented being penetrated by objects or animals; or
   (5) Women are presented in scenarios of degradation, injury, abasement, torture,
       shown as filthy or inferior, bleeding, bruised, or hurt in a context that makes
       these conditions sexual; or
   (6) Women are presented as sexual objects for domination, conquest, violation,
       exploitation, possession, or use, or through postures or positions of servility or
       submission or display.

Indianapolis, Ind., Code § 16-3(q) (1984).

2. By the use of highly selected examples, Appellants and supporting amici convey
the impression that the great majority of materials considered pornographic are brutal.
Although most commercial pornography, like much of all media, is sexist, most is not
violent. A study of pictorials and cartoons in Playboy and Penthouse between 1973 and
1977 found that, by 1977, about 5% of the pictorials were rated as sexually violent. "No
significant changes in the percentage of sexually violent cartoons were found over the
years." Malamuth & Spinner, A Longitudinal Content Analysis of Sexual Violence in the
Best-Selling Erotic Magazines, 16 J. Sex. Research 226, 237 (1980). The Women Against
Pornography (W.A.P.) amicus brief, in particular, totally mischaracterizes content analyses of pornography. It asserts, at p. 8 n.14, that one study found the depictions of rape in
"adults only" paperbacks had doubled from 1968 to 1974, a statement which is simply
false. The study found that the amount of explicit sexual content had doubled, but also

authorizes suppression of material that is sexually explicit, but in no way violent. The language of the definition mixes phrases that have clear meanings and thus ascertainable applications (e.g., "cut up or mutilated") with others which are sufficiently elastic to encompass almost any sexually explicit image that someone might find offensive (e.g., "scenarios of degradation" or "abasement"). The material that could be suppressed under the latter category is virtually limitless.

While the sweep of the ordinance is breathtaking, it does not address (nor would Amici support state suppression of) the far more pervasive commercial images depicting women as primarily concerned with the whiteness of their wash, the softness of their toilet tissue, and whether the lines of their panties show when wearing tight slacks. Commercial images, available to the most impressionable young children during prime time, depict women as people interested in inconsequential matters who are incapable of taking significant, serious roles in societal decision-making.

The constitutionality of the ordinance depends on the assumption that state agencies and courts can develop clear legal definitions of terms like "sexually explicit subordination," "sexual object," and "scenarios of degradation" and "abasement." In truth, these terms are highly contextual and of varying meanings. Worse, many of their most commonly accepted meanings would, if applied in the context of this ordinance, reinforce rather than erode archaic and untrue stereotypes about women's sexuality.

"that the plots, themes, and stories have remained much the same in these books throughout the years measured in this study." Smith, The Social Content of Pornography, 26 J. Comm. 16, 23 (1976). The brief then cites a study finding that depictions of bondage and domination in Times Square pornography stores "had increased dramatically in frequency by 1982," but neglects to mention that the increase was to 17.2%. The same study also concluded that "many bondage and domination magazines do not depict suffering or bodily injury." Dietz & Evans, Pornographic Imagery and Prevalence of Paraphilia, 139 Am. J. Psychiatry 1493, 1495 (1982). That some pornography would be found by amici on both sides to be offensive to women does not support this legislative approach to curtailing that pornography, which is overbroad and dependent on suppression of speech.

173

A. Historically the Law Has Incorporated a Sexual Double
    Standard Denying Women's Interest in Sexual Expression.

Traditionally, laws regulating sexual activity were premised
upon and reinforced a gender-based double standard which
assumed:

> that women are delicate, that voluntary sexual inter-
> course may harm them in certain circumstances and that
> they may be seriously injured by words as well as deeds.
> The statutes also suggest that, despite the generally deli-
> cate nature of most women, there exists a class of women
> who are not delicate or who are not worthy of protection.
> [By contrast, the law's treatment of male sexuality re-
> flected] the underlying assumption that only males have
> aggressive sexual desires [and] hence they must be re-
> strained . . . . The detail and comprehensiveness of
> [such] laws suggest that men are considered almost
> crazed by sex.

K. Davidson, R. Ginsburg & H. Kay, Sex-Based Discrimination
892 (1st ed. 1974).
    The Indianapolis ordinance is squarely within the tradition of
the sexual double standard. It allows little room for women to
openly express certain sexual desires and resurrects the notion
that sexually explicit materials are subordinating and degrading
to women. Because the "trafficking" cause of action allows one
woman to obtain a court order suppressing images which fall
within the ordinance's definition of pornography, it implies that
individual women are incapable of choosing for themselves what
they consider to be enjoyable, sexually arousing material without
being degraded or humiliated.
    The legal system has used many vehicles to enforce the sexual
double standard which protected "good" women from both sexual activity and explicit speech about sex. For example, the common law of libel held that "an oral imputation of unchastity to a
woman is actionable without proof of damage. . . . Such a rule
never has been applied to a man, since the damage to his reputation is assumed not to be as great." W. Prosser, Law of Torts,
759-60 (1971).
    The common law also reinforced the image of "good" women
as asexual and vulnerable by providing the husband, but not the

wife, remedies for "interference" with his right to sole possession of his wife's body and services. The early writ of "ravishment" listed the wife with the husband's chattels. To this day, the action for criminal conversation allows the husband to maintain an action for trespass, not only when his wife is raped

> but also even though the wife had consented to it, or was herself the seducer and had invited and procured it, since it was considered that she was no more capable of giving a consent which would prejudice the husband's interests than was his horse . . . .

Id. at 874-77.

While denying the possibility that "good" women could be sexual, the common law dealt harshly with the "bad" women who were. Prostitution laws often penalized only the woman, and not the man, and even facially neutral laws were and are enforced primarily against women. See, e.g., Jennings, The Victim as Criminal: A Consideration of California's Prostitution Law, 64 Calif. L. Rev. 1235 (1976). Prostitution is defined as "the practice of a female offering her body to indiscriminate sexual intercourse with men," 63 Am. Jur. 2d Prostitution § 1 (1972), or submitting "to indiscriminate sexual intercourse which she invites or solicits." Id. A woman who has sexual relations with many men is a "common prostitute" and a criminal while a sexually active man is considered normal.

The sexual double standard is applied with particular force to young people. Statutory rape laws often punished men for consensual intercourse with a female under a certain age. Comment, The Constitutionality of Statutory Rape Laws, 27 UCLA L. Rev. 757, 762 (1980). Such laws reinforce the stereotype that in sex the man is the offender and the woman the victim, and that young men may legitimately engage in sex, at least with older people, while a young woman may not legally have sex with anyone.

The suppression of sexually explicit material most devastating to women was the restriction on dissemination of birth control information, common until 1971. In that year, the Supreme Court held that the constitutional right to privacy protects an unmarried person's right to access to birth control information. Eisenstadt v. Baird, 405 U.S. 438 (1972). To deny women access to contraception "prescribe[s] pregnancy and the birth of an unwanted child as punishment for fornication." Id. at 448. For the previous century, the federal Comstock law, passed in 1873, had prohibited mailing, transporting or importing "obscene, lewd or lascivious" items, specifically including all devices and information pertaining to "preventing contraception and producing abortion."[3] Women were jailed for distributing educational materials regarding birth control to other women because the materials were deemed sexually explicit in that they "contain[ed] pictures of certain organs of women" and because the materials were found to be "detrimental to public morals and welfare." People v. Byrne, 99 Misc. 1, 6 (N.Y. 1917).

The Mann Act also was premised on the notion that women require special protection from sexual activity. 35 Stat. 825 (1910), 18 U.S.C. §§ 2421-2422. It forbids interstate transportation of women for purposes of "prostitution, debauchery, or any other immoral purposes," and was enacted to protect women from reportedly widespread abduction by bands of "white slavers" coercing them into prostitution. As the legislative history reveals, the Act reflects the assumption that women have no will of their own and must be protected against themselves. See H.R. Rep. No. 47, 61st Cong., 2d Sess. (1910), at 10-11. Like the premises underlying this ordinance, the Mann Act assumed

> that women were naturally chaste and virtuous, and that no woman became a whore unless she had first been raped, seduced, drugged or deserted. [Its] image of the prostitute . . . was of a lonely and confused female . . . . [Its proponents] maintained that prostitutes were the passive victims of social disequilibrium and the brutality of men . . . . [Its] conception of female weakness and male domination left no room for the possibility that prostitutes might consciously choose their activities.

---

3. 18 U.S.C.A. §§ 1461-1462 (West 1984); 19 U.S.C.A. § 1305 (West 1980 & Supp. 1984); see United States v. One Obscene Book Entitled "Married Love", 48 F.2d 821 (S.D.N.Y. 1931); United States v. One Book Entitled "Contraceptions", 51 F.2d 525 (S.D.N.Y. 1931) (prosecution for distribution of books by Marie Stopes on contraception); United States v. Dennett, 39 F.2d 564 (2d Cir. 1930) (prosecution of Mary Ware Dennett for publication of pamphlet explaining sexual physiology and functions to children); and Bours v. United States, 229 F. 960 (7th Cir. 1915) (prosecution of physician for mailing a letter indicating that he might perform a therapeutic abortion). It was not until 1971 that an amendment was passed deleting the prohibition as to contraception, Pub. L. No. 91-662, 84 Stat. 1973 (1971); and the ban as to abortion remains in the current codification of the law.

Note, The White Slave Traffic Act: The Historical Impact of a Criminal Law Policy on Women, 72 Geo. L.J. 1111 (1984).

The Mann Act initially defined a "white slave" to include "only those women or girls who are literally slaves—those women who are owned and held as property and chattels . . . those women and girls who, if given a fair chance, would, in all human probability, have been good wives and mothers," H.R. Rep. No. 47, 61st Cong., 2d Sess., at 9-10 (1910). Over the years, the interpretation and use of the Act changed drastically to punish voluntary "immoral" acts even when no commercial intention or business profit was involved. See Caminetti v. United States, 242 U.S. 470 (1917); Cleveland v. United States, 329 U.S. 14 (1946).

> The term 'other immoral acts' was held to apply to a variety of activities: the interstate transportation of a woman to work as a chorus girl in a theatre where the woman was exposed to smoking, drinking, and cursing; a dentist who met his young lover in a neighboring state and shared a hotel room to discuss her pregnancy; two students at the University of Puerto Rico who had sexual intercourse on the way home from a date; and a man and woman who had lived together for four years and traveled around the country as man and wife while the man sold securities.

Note, supra, at 1119.

Society's attempts to "protect" women's chastity through criminal and civil laws have resulted in restrictions on women's freedom to engage in sexual activity, to discuss it publicly, and to protect themselves from the risk of pregnancy. These disabling restrictions reinforced the gender roles which have oppressed women for centuries. The Indianapolis ordinance resonates with the traditional concept that sex itself degrades women, and its enforcement would reinvigorate those discriminatory moral standards which have limited women's equality in the past.

B. The Ordinance Is Unconstitutionally Vague Because Context Inescapably Determines the Effect of Sexual Texts and Images.

The ordinance authorizes court orders removing from public or private availability "graphic sexually explicit" words and images which "subordinate" women. A judge presented with a civil complaint filed pursuant to this law would be required to determine whether the material in question "subordinated" women. To equate pornography with conduct having the power to "subordinate" living human beings, whatever its value as a rhetorical device, requires a "certain sleight of hand" to be incorporated as a doctrine of law. American Booksellers Ass'n v. Hudnut, 598 F. Supp. 1316, 1330 (S.D. Ind. 1984). Words and images do influence what people think, how they feel, and what they do, both positively and negatively. Thus pornography may have such influence. But the connection between fantasy or symbolic representation and actions in the real world is not direct or linear. Sexual imagery is not so simple to assess. In the sexual realm, perhaps more so than in any other, messages and their impact on the viewer or reader are often multiple, contradictory, layered and highly contextual.

The film Swept Away illustrates that serious problems of context and interpretation confound even the categories which on first reading might seem reasonably easy to apply. Made in 1975 by Italian director Lina Wertmuller, Swept Away tells a powerful story of dominance and submission. A rich attractive woman and a younger working class man are first shown as class antagonists during a yachting trip on which the man is a deckhand and the woman a viciously rude boss, and then as sexual antagonists when they are stranded on a Mediterranean island and the man exacts his revenge. During the second part of the film, the man rapes the woman and repeatedly assaults her. She initially resists, then falls in love with him, and he with her.

Scenes in Swept Away clearly present the woman character as "experienc[ing] sexual pleasure" during rape. In addition, she is humiliated, graphically and sexually, and appears to grow to enjoy it. Although sexually explicit depictions are not the majority of scenes, the film as a whole has an active sexual dynamic. Given the overall and pervasive theme of sexual dominance and submission, it is improbable that the explicit scenes could be deemed "isolated." It is virtually certain that the film could be suppressed under the ordinance since it was shown in laboratory studies cited by Appellants to measure negative impact of aggressive erotic materials.[4]

Swept Away is an example of graphic, sexually explicit images and characterizations used to treat themes of power imbalance, to push at the edges of what is thought to be acceptable or desirable, and to shock. Critical and popular opinions of the film varied, ranging from admiration to repulsion.[5] Whatever one's interpretation of the film, however, its profoundly important themes entitle it to a place in the realm of public discourse.

Context often determines meaning. Whether a specific image could be found to "subordinate" or "degrade" women may depend entirely on such factors as the purpose of the presentation; the size and nature of the audience; the surrounding messages; the expectation and attitude of the viewer; and where the presentation takes place, among others.[6] Yet the trafficking provision allows blanket suppression of images based on highly subjective criteria which masquerade as simple, delineating definitions.

---

4. See Appellants' Exh. S. at 114-15.

5. The reviewer for Ms. Magazine wrote:

> At several points I was very offended by the idea of love won by brute force. . . . I'd like to explain this away by stressing that this is an allegory of class war, not sex war. But that is not true. For the brilliance of "Swept Away" is that it is everything at once. As a description of what capitalism does to us it is sophisticated and deep. At the same time, it comes to grips with the "war" between the sexes better than anything I've seen or read. . . . It has shocking scenes linking sex and violence and yet it is about tenderness. . . . [It] is a funny, beautiful, emotional movie about a somber, ugly, intellectual subject.

Garson, A Reviewer Under the Influence, Ms. Magazine, Dec. 1975, at 37, 38. Other reviewers strongly disagreed:

> I really don't know what is more distasteful about this film—its slavish adherence to the barroom credo that all women really want is to be beaten, to be shown who's boss, or the readiness with which it has been accepted by the critics. Yes, it is effective enough in parts, but strictly on the level of slick pornography.

Turan, Not Swept Away, The Progressive, May 1976, at 39, 40.

6. The same theme may be perceived very differently in different contexts. In her novel, A Sea Change, feminist author Lois Gould repeatedly invokes fantasies and images of rape and submission in order to make more dramatic her story of women transforming their sexual lives. One striking passage narrates the main female character being stroked and then entered by the gun held by a fantasy male character, B.G. L. Gould, A Sea Change 95 (1977). At the end of the novel, the woman character becomes B.G. This graphic depiction of penetration by an object, undoubtedly suppressible under the ordinance, especially since there are several scenes in the book which could meet the definition of pornography, is one of the fantasies Gould explores and uses in her treatment of the theme of sexual power.

C. The Ordinance Is Unconstitutionally Vague Because Its Central Terms Have No Fixed Meaning, and the Most Common Meanings of These Terms Are Sexist and Damaging to Women.

The ordinance's definition of pornography, essential to each cause of action, is fatally flawed. It relies on words often defined in ways that reinforce a constricted and constricting view of women's sexuality. Thus Amici fear that experimentations in feminist art which deal openly and explicitly with sexual themes will be easily targeted for suppression under this ordinance.

The central term "sexually explicit subordination" is not defined.[7] Appellants argue that "subordination" means that which "places women in positions of inferiority, loss of power, degradation and submission, among other things." Appellants' brief at 26. The core question, however, is left begging: what kinds of sexually explicit acts place a woman in an inferior status? Appellants argued in their brief to the District Court that "[t]he mere existence of pornography in society degrades and demeans all women." Defendants' memorandum at 10. To some observers, any graphic image of sexual acts is "degrading" to women and hence would subordinate them. To some, the required element of subordination or "positions of . . . submission" might be satisfied by the image of a woman lying on her back inviting intercourse, while others might view the same image as affirming women's sexual pleasure and initiative. Some might draw the line at acts outside the bounds of marriage or with multiple partners. Others might see a simple image of the most traditional heterosexual act as subordinating in presenting the man in a physical position of superiority and the woman in a position of inferiority.

In any of these contexts, it is not clear whether the ordinance is to be interpreted with a subjective or an objective standard. If a subjective interpretation of "subordination" is contemplated, the ordinance vests in individual women a power to impose their views of politically or morally correct sexuality upon other women by calling for repression of images consistent with those

---

7. To define "pornography" as that which subordinates women, and then prohibit as pornographic that which subordinates, makes the claim that pornography subordinates either circular or logically trivial.

views. The evaluative terms—subordination, degradation, abasement—are initially within the definitional control of the plaintiff, whose interpretation, if colorable, must be accepted by the court. An objective standard would require a court to determine whether plaintiff's reaction to the material comports with some generalized notion of which images do or do not degrade women. It would require the judiciary to impose its views of correct sexuality on a diverse community. The inevitable result would be to disapprove those images that are least conventional and privilege those that are closest to majoritarian beliefs about proper sexuality.

Whether subjective or objective, the inquiry is one that plainly and profoundly threatens First Amendment freedoms and is totally inconsistent with feminist principles, as they are understood by Amici. Sexuality is particularly susceptible to extremely charged emotions, including feelings of vulnerability and power. The realm of image judgment opened by the ordinance is too contested and sensitive to be entrusted to legislative categorization and judicial enforcement.

The danger of discrimination is illustrated by the probability that some women would consider any explicit lesbian scene as subordinating, or as causing "[their] dignity [to] suffer," Appellants' brief at 36. Appellants plainly intend to include same-sex depictions, since their carefully selected trial court exhibits include such materials.[8] Lesbians and gay men[9] encounter massive discrimination based on prejudice related to their sexuality.[10] The trafficking provision of the ordinance virtually invites new manifestations of this prejudice by means of civil litigation against the erotica of sexual minorities.

---

8. See, e.g., Appellants' Exhs. N., M., and W. These exhibits, like most commercial pornography which depicts sex between women, were not produced by or primarily for lesbians. Yet part of the shock value of such images in contemporary society may be attributable to their depiction of sexual explicitness between women. When the door is opened to suppress "scenarios of degradation," for example, there is no guarantee that this shock value of any graphic depiction of homosexual acts will not spill over to images and texts which authentically express lesbian sexuality.

9. The provision that "the use of men . . . in the place of women . . . shall also constitute pornography" makes clear that same-sex male images and texts could fall within the scope of the ordinance, especially so, one supposes, if one male partner is depicted as effeminate.

10. See, e.g., Baker v. Wade, 553 F. Supp. 1121 (N.D. Tex. 1982), on appeal; People v. Onofre, 51 N.Y.2d 476 (1980), cert. denied, 451 U.S. 987 (1980); National Gay Task Force v. Board of Educ., 729 F.2d 1270 (10th Cir. 1984), aff'd per curiam, 53 U.S.L.W. 4408 (U.S. Mar. 26, 1985).

The six subsections of the definition applicable to a trafficking complaint provide no clarification. The term "sexual object," for example, appears frequently in the definition. Appellants are confident that "the common man knows a sex object when he sees one." Appellants' brief at 40. Yet, although "sex object" may be a phrase which has begun to enjoy widened popular usage, its precise meaning is far from clear. Some persons maintain that any detachment of women's sexuality from procreation, marriage, and family objectifies it, removing it from its "natural" web of association and context. When sex is detached from its traditional moorings, men allegedly benefit and women are the victims.[11] Feminists, on the other hand, generally use the term "sex object" to mean the absence of any indicia of personhood, a very different interpretation.

Appellants argue that the meaning of "subordination" and "degradation" can be determined in relation to "common usage and understanding." Appellants' brief at 33. But as we have seen, the common understanding of sexuality is one that incorporates a sexual double standard. Historically, virtually all sexually explicit literature and imagery has been thought to be degrading or abasing or humiliating, especially to women.

The interpretation of such morally charged terms has varied notoriously over time and place. A state supreme court thirty years ago ruled that the words "obscene, lewd, licentious, indecent, lascivious, immoral, [and] scandalous" were "neither vague nor indefinite" and had "a meaning understood by all." State v. Becker, 364 Mo. 1079, 1087, 272 S.E.2d 283, 288 (1954). See also Winters v. New York, 333 U.S. 507, 518 (1948). In Kansas v. Great American Theatre Co., the court accepted as a definition for "prurient interest," "an unhealthy, unwholesome, morbid, degrading, and shameful interest in sex," 227 Kan. 633, 633, 608 P.2d 951, 952 (1980) (emphasis added). A Florida obscenity statute which declared it to be "unlawful to publish, sell[, etc.] any obscene, lewd, lascivious, filthy, indecent, immoral, degrading, sadistic, masochistic or disgusting book"[12] was found to be no longer adequate after the decision in Roth v. United States, 354 U.S. 476 (1957), absent both a contemporary definition of those terms and a standard based on the materials' overall value and

---

11. See, e.g., G. Gilder, Sexual Suicide (1973).

12. Act of June 20, 1957 ch. 57-779, § 1, 1957 Fla. Laws vol. 1, pt. 1, 1102, 1103-04 (amending Fla. Stat. § 847.01) (amended 1959, repealed 1961) (emphasis added).

not just their explicitness.[13] After Roth and subsequent decisions, the statute was amended three times to incorporate these
additional elements.[14] Upon amending the statute in 1961, the
word "degrading" was dropped. Words like "degradation,"
"abasement," and "humiliation" have been used in the past syn-
onymously with subjective, moralistic terms. There is no reason
to believe that the language in this ordinance will be magically
resistant to that kind of interpretation.

The First Amendment prohibits any law regulating expression
which would of necessity result in such unpredictable and arbitrary interpretations. This ordinance transgresses all three of the
measures of impermissible vagueness. A person of ordinary intelligence would be at a loss to predict how any of a huge range of
sexually explicit materials would be interpreted by a court.
Grayned v. City of Rockford, 408 U.S. 104, 108 (1972); Smith v.
Goguen, 415 U.S. 566, 572-73 (1974); Kolender v. Lawson, 461
U.S. 352, 357 (1983). Protected expression would be chilled because the makers, distributors, and exhibitors of sexually explicit works would be induced to practice self-censorship rather
than risk potentially endless lawsuits under this ordinance.
Buckley v. Valeo, 424 U.S. 1, 41 (1976); Smith v. Goguen, 415
U.S. at 573. Lastly, the absence of reasonably clear guidelines
for triers of fact would open the door to arbitrary and discriminatory enforcement of the ordinance. Id.; Grayned v. City of
Rockford, 408 U.S. at 108; Kolender v. Lawson, 461 U.S. at 358;
Papachristou v. City of Jacksonville, 405 U.S. 156, 168-69 (1972).

The ordinance requires enforcement of "common understandings" of culturally loaded terms. It perpetuates beliefs which undermine the principle that women are full, equal, and active
agents in every realm of life, including the sexual.

---

13. See State v. Cohen, 125 So. 2d 560 (Fla. 1960); State v. Reese, 222 So. 2d 732
(Fla. 1969); and Rhodes v. State, 283 So. 2d 351 (Fla. 1973).

14. See Act of May 5, 1961, ch. 61-7, 1961 Fla. Laws vol. 1, pt. 1, 13; Act of June 3,
1969, ch. 69-41, 1969 Fla. Laws vol. 1, pt.1, 164; Act of June 7, 1973, ch. 73-120, 1973 Fla.
Laws 185.

D. Sexually Explicit Speech Does Not Cause or Incite Violence in a Manner Sufficiently Direct to Justify Its Suppression Under the First Amendment.

To uphold this ordinance and the potential suppression of all speech which could be found to fall within its definition of pornography, this court must invent a new exception to the First Amendment. To justify that, Appellants must show that the speech to be suppressed will lead to immediate and concrete harm. Brandenburg v. Ohio, 395 U.S. 444 (1969); Collin v. Smith, 578 F.2d 1197 (7th Cir.), cert. denied, 439 U.S. 916 (1978). Only a small number of social science studies which purport to show a connection between violent pornography and negative attitudes and behavior toward women have been offered to support this position. For many reasons, their effort must fail.

Substantively, the studies relied upon do not justify the sweeping suppression authorized by the ordinance. Appellants cite the social science data in highly selective and grossly distorting ways. They fail to acknowledge that most of it is limited to studies of a narrow class of violent imagery. The ordinance, by contrast, both leaves untouched most of the images which may be said to cause negative effects and would allow the suppression of many images which have not been shown to have any harmful effect. Appellants also fail to mention that the "debriefing" phase of the cited experiments suggests that negative changes in attitudes may be corrected through further speech. They seek to create the false impression that new social science data have completely refuted the finding in 1971 by the Presidential Commission on Obscenity and Pornography that pornography was not harmful. However, as Professor Edward Donnerstein wrote in the study placed before the District Court by Appellants as Exh. T. at 127-28,

One should not assume . . . that all the research since the commission's time has indicated negative effects [of pornographic materials] on individuals. In fact, this is quite to the contrary. . . . [A] good amount of research strongly supports the position that exposure to certain types of erotica can reduce aggressive responses in people who are predisposed to aggression. The reader should keep in mind the fact that erotica has been shown to have many types of effects.

Lastly, whatever Appellants' claims, numerous methodological problems make these studies too unreliable as predictors of real world behavior to sustain the withdrawal of constitutional protection from what is now permitted speech.

Although the ordinance authorizes suppression of far more than simply violent images, the limited findings of a linkage between sexually explicit materials and a willingness to aggress against women under laboratory conditions have occurred only in studies of "aggressive pornography," defined as a particular scenario: "depictions in which physical force is used or threatened to coerce a woman to engage in sexual acts (e.g. rape)." Appellants' Exh. S. at 105. This limiting definition is used by both Professor Donnerstein and Professor Neil Malamuth in the recently published book, Pornography and Sexual Aggression. See Malamuth, Aggression Against Women: Cultural and Individual Causes, in Pornography and Sexual Aggression 19, 29-30 (N. Malamuth & E. Donnerstein eds. 1984); Donnerstein, Pornography: Its Effect on Violence Against Women, in Pornography and Sexual Aggression, supra, at 53, 63. Where nonaggressive pornography is studied, no effect on aggression against women has been found; it is the violent, and not the sexual, content of the depiction that is said to produce the effects.[15] Further, all of the aggression studies have used visual imagery; none has studied the impact of only words. Finally, even as to violent "aggressive pornography," the results of the studies are not uniform.[16]

15.
   Studies have indicated that if you take out the explicit sexual content from aggressive pornographic films, leaving just the violence (which could be shown on any network television show), you find desensitization to violent acts in some subjects. However, if you take out the aggressive component and leave just the sexual, you do not seem to observe negative effects of desensitization to violence against women. Thus, violence is at issue here. That is why restrictions or censorship solutions are problematical.
Donnerstein & Linz, Debate on Pornography, Film Comment, Dec. 1984, at 34, 35.
   16.   Malamuth describes a study he did in which no evidence was found of changes in perceptions or attitudes following exposure to this type of pornography:
   One group of male and female subjects looked at issues of Penthouse and Playboy magazines that showed incidents of sadomasochism and rape. A second group examined issues of these magazines that contained only non-aggressive pornography and a third group was given only neutral materials. Shortly afterward, subjects watched an actual videotaped interview with a rape victim and

Violent and misogynist images are pervasive in our culture. Nothing in the research cited by Appellants proves their hypothesis that these messages are believed in a qualitatively different way when they are communicated through the medium of sexually explicit material. Both Professors Donnerstein and Malamuth have noted that regulation of imagery targeted at the sexually explicit misses the core of the problem:

> Images of violence against women are not the sole property of aggressive or violent pornography. Such images are quite pervasive in our society. Images outside of the pornographic or X-rated market may in fact be of more concern, since they are imbued with a certain "legitimacy" surrounding them and tend to have much wider acceptance.
>
> Sexist attitudes, callous attitudes about rape, and other misogynist values are just as likely to be reinforced by non-sexualized violent symbols as they are by violent pornography.

Donnerstein & Linz, supra p. 14, at 35 (emphasis added).

> Attempts to alter the content of mass media . . . cannot be limited to pornography, since research has documented similar effects from mainstream movies. In addition, other mass media forms, such as advertisements, television soap operas, and detective magazines, to name a few, also contain undesirable images of violence against women. The most pertinent question on the issue of changing mass media content may not be where we draw the line between pornography and non-pornography but how we can best combat violence against women in its myriad forms.

Malamuth & Lindstrom, Debate on Pornography, Film Comment, Dec. 1984, at 39, 40.

---

responded to a questionnaire assessing their perceptions of a rape victim and her experience. Weeks later . . . subjects indicated their views on rape in response to a newspaper article. Exposure to the aggressive pornography did not affect perceptions of rape either in response to the videotaped interview with a rape victim or to the newspaper article.
Appellants' Exh. S. at 113.

When "more speech" can be an effective means of countering
prejudicial and discriminatory messages, the First Amendment
forbids the use of censorship to suppress even the most hateful
content. Collin v. Smith, 578 F.2d 1197 (7th Cir.), cert. denied,
439 U.S. 916 (1978). The social science data upon which Appellants rely so heavily indicate that further speech can remove the
negative effects on attitude registered after viewing certain kinds
of violent pornography. Malamuth and Donnerstein both conduct "debriefing" sessions at the conclusion of their experiments. In these sessions, the purposes of the studies are explained to the subjects, and information is presented to dispel
rape myths. The effectiveness of the debriefing sessions is then
tested up to four months later. "The findings of these studies
indicated consistently that the education interventions were successful in counteracting the effects of aggressive pornography
and in reducing beliefs in rape myths." Malamuth, supra p. 14,
at 46.

> Censorship is not the solution. Education, however, is a
> viable alternative. Early sex education programs which
> dispel myths about sexual violence and early training in
> critical viewing skills could mitigate the influence of
> these films.

Donnerstein & Linz, supra p. 14, at 35.
This debriefing effect demonstrates that the changes in attitude
shown from pornography are not permanent or, as Appellants
contend, conditioned.

The substance of the social science data provides no support
for the broad suppression of speech authorized by the ordinance.
Further, even if the ordinance were narrowly limited to the "aggressive pornography" which has been studied, limits in the
methodology fatally undermine Appellants' claims that even this
violent material causes the sort of concrete, immediate harm
that could justify creating a new exception to the First
Amendment.

Behavior under laboratory conditions cannot predict behavior
in life with the degree of accuracy and specificity required to
justify a censorship law. The college students being studied in
these laboratory tests knew that their actions would have no actual negative impact on real people. Indeed, the experimental

setting may induce conduct in subjects that they would not otherwise exhibit. In the words of one theorist:

> Laboratory studies that deliberately lower restraints against aggression . . . may be seen as representing a reversal of the normal socialization process. After a subject has been angered, he is allowed (actually told) to attack his adversary. The victim emits no pain cues . . . and the subject not only feels better but learns that, in this laboratory situation, aggression is permissible and socially approved (i.e. condoned by the experimenter).

Donnerstein, supra p. 14, at 60.

Moreover, most of the reported willingness to aggress occurs only in subjects who are previously angered as part of the experiment shortly before they are asked to administer shocks. See generally Donnerstein, supra p. 14. Some researchers believe that the anger is the primary factor producing the manifestation of aggression. See Gray, Exposure to Pornography and Aggression Toward Women: The Case of the Angry Male, 29 Soc. Probs. 387 (1982).

Additionally, in most studies cited, aggressive behavior occurs only when the experimenter gives subjects disinhibitory cues indicating that such behavior is acceptable, and not when the experimenter provides an inhibitory communication.

> These data highlight the important role of situational factors in affecting aggression against women and suggest that, while cultural factors such as aggressive pornography may increase some males' aggressive tendencies, the actual expression of aggressive responses may be strongly regulated by varied internal and external (i.e., situational) variables.

Malamuth, supra p. 14, at 35.

In life, more than in a laboratory, a multitude of interacting factors shape behavior, including early childhood experiences, family dynamics, religious training, formal education, and one's perceived relation to governmental structures and the legal system, as well as the entire range of media stimuli.[17] It is difficult

---

17. See also Abramson & Hayashi, Pornography in Japan: Cross-Cultural and Theoretical Considerations, in Pornography and Sexual Aggression 173 (N. Malamuth & E.

even in the laboratory to identify a single "cause" for behavior.[18] Every study finding a negative effect under laboratory conditions from viewing an image cannot be grounds for rewriting the First Amendment.

Appellants and supporting amici also claim a causal connection between the availability of pornography and rape. Such a claim is implausible on its face. Acts of rape and coercion long preceded the mass distribution of pornography, and in many cultures pornography is unavailable, yet the incidence of rape,

---

Donnerstein eds. 1984). Japanese pornography contains more depictions of rape and bondage than does American pornography and is also more readily available in popular magazines and on television. Yet, Japan has a substantially lower incidence of rape than any western country and a lower incidence of violent crime generally. The authors attribute the lower crime rate to cultural factors unrelated to pornography.

18. A good example of the limitations of laboratory studies is provided by the study described in Appellants' Exh. R. Male subjects viewed violent "slasher" movies, one a day for five consecutive days, and answered questions each day about the extent to which the film was degrading to women. The subjects clearly knew that attitudes related to sexual violence against women were being measured. On the last day of the experiment, subjects were informed that the sixth and final film had not arrived. They were told since their original film did not arrive they would watch a law school documentary about a rape trial. After viewing the rape documentary, subjects completed questionnaires. The authors concluded that "exposed subjects later judged the victim of a violent assault and rape to be significantly less injured and generally more worthless than a control group of subjects who saw no films." Appellants' Exh. R., abstract.

Appellants cite this study in support of their claim that "pornography" makes men "less able to perceive that an account of rape is an account of rape." Appellants' brief at 20. The study is of limited value. First, the images used in the slasher films are not within the ordinance's definition of pornography. Second, there is a high probability that "demand characteristics"—where subjects understand the purpose of a study and give the experimenter what he or she is thought to be looking for—skewed the responses. Third, the term "worthless" did not occur spontaneously to the subjects, but was suggested by a question asking, "I felt [the victim] was: valuable 1 2 3 4 5 6 7 8 9 worthless." Thus, when the authors state that subjects who viewed the films found the victim "more worthless," they mean that the subjects circled the number 6, say, instead of the number 4. The question regarding the perception of the victim's injury was presented in a similar manner. What is being measured in studies of this type are not complex sets of attitudes, such as all of us have in real life, but gross responses on a questionnaire. Fourth, although the authors found "significant differences" between subjects who had viewed the films and those who had not on the "injury" and "worthlessness" measures, they did not find significant differences on other measures including defendant intention, victim resistance, victim responsibility, victim sympathy, and victim unattractiveness. Finally, an hypothesized correlation between perception of violence and perception of degradation proved to be non-significant, as did the expected correlation between perception of degradation and enjoyment of the film. The point is not that this is poor social science research, but that this kind of research does not produce evidence sufficiently strong to justify censorship.

and of discrimination against women generally, is high.[19] The converse is also true; that is, there are places where pornography is widely available, and the incidence of rape is low compared to the United States.

Many studies have focused on Denmark to discern whether their abolition of the laws restricting pornography in the mid-1960's could be linked to any changes in behavior. Numerous conflicting arguments have been made as to the implications of the Danish experience. In 1979, the British Committee on Obscenity and Film Censorship published a report critically reviewing extensive data on the asserted linkage between pornography and sexual violence. Because it was done a decade after the American report, it includes much of the recent work published on this topic. The Committee found "no support at all" for the thesis that the availability of pornography in Denmark could be linked to an increase in sexual offenses. "It is impossible to discern a significant trend in rape which could be linked in any way to the free availability of pornography since the late 1960s." Obscenity and Film Censorship 83 (B. Williams ed. 1979).

Appellants' argument that pornography should be precluded from First Amendment protection would require this Court to find that it causes harm in the direct, immediate way that falsely shouting fire in a crowded theater does. The social science data upon which they rely lend no support to such a claim. The findings relate to only a small portion of the material which the ordinance would suppress, results of the studies are mixed, and even the data which report laboratory findings of aggression cannot be used blithely to predict behavior in the real world.

E. Constitutional Protection for Sexually Explicit Speech Should Be Enhanced, Not Diminished.

Sexually explicit speech which is judged "obscene" is not protected under the First Amendment. Miller v. California, 413

---

19. Even the Baron and Strauss chapter, Sexual Stratification, Pornography, and Rape in the United States, in Pornography and Sexual Aggression, cited by the W.A.P. amicus brief at 16, which found, in a state-by-state analysis, a positive correlation between circulation rates for mainstream pornographic magazines (e.g., Playboy) and incidents of rape, could not explain some strikingly anomalous results, such as, for example, Utah, which ranked 51st (last) in per capita readership of sex magazines, but 25th in per capita rate of rape.

U.S. 15 (1973). Appellants seek to vitiate the protection currently afforded non-obscene sexual speech on the ground that any expression falling within the scope of this ordinance "is not the free exchange of ideas." Appellants' brief at 12. They ask this Court to rule that all sexually explicit speech is disfavored:

> It is essential to look at the nature of the material regulated to measure the importance of the chilling effect. . . . [T]he ordinance reaches 'sexually explicit activity.' . . . The Supreme Court has determined that "there is . . . a less vital interest in the uninhibited exhibition of material that is on the borderline between pornography and artistic expression than in the free dissemination of ideas of social and political significance." The message of Young is that it is constitutional for anyone who steps too close to the line to take the risk of crossing it when sexually explicit material is involved. The chilling effect is simply not entitled to great weight in this context.

Appellants' brief at 53 (citations omitted).

The argument that the First Amendment provides less protection for sexual images than for speech which is "political" misunderstands both the value of free expression and the political content of sexually explicit speech. Many justifications support free expression: our incapacity to determine truth without open discussion; the need for people to communicate to express self identity and determine how to live their lives; the inability of the censor to wield power wisely.

Further, sexual speech is political. One core insight of modern feminism is that the personal is political. The question of who does the dishes and rocks the cradle affects both the nature of the home and the composition of the legislature. The dynamics of intimate relations are likewise political, both to the individuals involved and by their multiplied effects to the wider society.[20] To argue, as Appellants do, that sexually explicit speech is less important than other categories of discourse reinforces the conceptual structures that have identified women's concerns

---

20. Even clearly misogynist pornography is political speech. Indeed, antipornography activists have often argued that pornography is political propaganda for male dominance. One lawyer then associated with Women Against Pornography pointed out that the political message of pornography hostile to women results in its entitlement to heightened,

with relationships and intimacy as less significant and valuable precisely because those concerns are falsely regarded as having no bearing on the structure of social and political life.

Depictions of ways of living and acting that are radically different from our own can enlarge the range of human possibilities open to us and help us grasp the potentialities of human behavior, both good and bad. Rich fantasy imagery allows us to experience in imagination ways of being that we may not wish to experience in real life. Such an enlarged vision of possible realities enhances our human potential and is highly relevant to our decision-making as citizens on a wide range of social and ethical issues.

For sexual minorities, speech describing conduct can be a means of self-affirmation in a generally hostile world. Constrictions on that speech can deny fundamental aspects of self-identity. Cf. Gay Law Students Ass'n v. Pacific Tel. & Tel., 24 Cal. 3d 458, 488, 594 P.2d 592, 611, 156 Cal. Rptr. 14, 33 (1979). In Rowland v. Mad River Local School District, 730 F.2d 444 (6th Cir. 1984), cert. denied, 53 U.S.L.W. 3614 (U.S. Feb. 26, 1985), a public employee was fired from her job because she confided in coworkers that she was bisexual. Although her statement resulted in no disruption of the workplace, the Court of Appeals ruled that it was constitutionally permissible to fire her "for talking about it." Id. at 450. Yet, as in Gay Law Students Association, the speech should have been considered political:

> I think it is impossible not to note that a . . . public debate is currently ongoing regarding the rights of homosexuals. The fact of petitioner's bisexuality, once spoken, necessarily and ineluctably involved her in that debate. Speech that "touches upon" this explosive issue is no less deserving of constitutional attention than speech relating to more widely condemned forms of discrimination.

Rowland v. Mad River Local School Dist., 53 U.S.L.W. at 3615 (Brennan and Marshall, JJ., dissenting from denial of certiorari).

---

not lesser, First Amendment protection as a form of advocacy, albeit of noxious ideas. Kaminer, Pornography and the First Amendment: Prior Restraints and Private Action, in Take Back the Night: Women and Pornography 239-46 (1980).

Thus, sexually explicit expression, including much that is covered by the ordinance, carries many more messages than simply the misogyny described by Appellants. It may convey the message that sexuality need not be tied to reproduction, men, or domesticity. It may contain themes of sex for no reason other than pleasure, sex without commitment, and sexual adventure—all of which are surely ideas. Cf. Kingsley Corp. v. Regents, 360 U.S. 684 (1959).

Even pornography which is problematic for women can be experienced as affirming of women's desires and of women's equality:

> Pornography can be a psychic assault, both in its content and in its public intrusions on our attention, but for women as for men it can also be a source of erotic pleasure. A woman who is raped is a victim; a woman who enjoys pornography (even if that means enjoying a rape fantasy) is in a sense a rebel, insisting on an aspect of her sexuality that has been defined as a male preserve. Insofar as pornography glorifies male supremacy and sexual alienation, it is deeply reactionary. But in rejecting sexual repression and hypocrisy—which have inflicted even more damage on women than on men—it expresses a radical impulse.

Willis, Feminism, Moralism and Pornography, in Powers of Desire: The Politics of Sexuality 460, 464 (A. Snitow, C. Stansell & S. Thompson eds. 1983). Fantasy is not the same as wish fulfillment. See N. Friday, My Secret Garden: Women's Secret Fantasies (1973) and Forbidden Flowers: More Women's Sexual Fantasies (1975). But one cannot fully discuss or analyze fantasy if the use of explicit language is precluded.

The range of feminist imagination and expression in the realm of sexuality has barely begun to find voice. Women need the freedom and the socially recognized space to appropriate for themselves the robustness of what traditionally has been male language. Laws such as the one under challenge here would constrict that freedom. See Blakely, Is One Woman's Sexuality Another Woman's Pornography?, Ms. Magazine, Apr. 1985, at 37. Amici fear that as more women's writing and art on sexual themes[21] emerge which are unladylike, unfeminine, aggressive, power-charged, pushy, vulgar, urgent, confident, and intense, the traditional foes of women's attempts to step out of their "proper place" will find an effective tool of repression in the Indianapolis ordinance.

II. THE ORDINANCE UNCONSTITUTIONALLY DISCRIMINATES ON THE BASIS OF SEX AND REINFORCES SEXIST STEREOTYPES.

The challenged ordinance posits a great chasm—a categorical difference—between the make-up and needs of men and of women. It goes far beyond acknowledgment of the differences in life experiences which are inevitably produced by social structures of gender inequality. The ordinance presumes women as a class (and only women) are subordinated by virtually any sexually explicit image. It presumes women as a class (and only women) are incapable of making a binding agreement to participate in the creation of sexually explicit material. And it presumes men as a class (and only men) are conditioned by sexually explicit depictions to commit acts of aggression and to believe misogynist myths.

Such assumptions reinforce and perpetuate central sexist stereotypes; they weaken, rather than enhance, women's struggles to free themselves of archaic notions of gender roles. In so doing, this ordinance itself violates the equal protection clause of the Fourteenth Amendment. In treating women as a special class, it repeats the error of earlier protectionist legislation which gave women no significant benefits and denied their equality.

---

21. The following are among the works which could fall within the scope of the ordinance's definition and thus be suppressed pursuant to the trafficking cause of action: K. Acker, Blood and Guts in High School (1984); Bad Attitude (Quarterly, Boston); L. Barbach, Pleasures: Women Write Erotica (1984); A Woman's Touch (Cedar & Nelly eds. 1979); J. Chicago, The Dinner Party (1979); T. Corinne & J. Lapidus, Yantras of Women Love (1982); N. Friday, My Secret Garden: Women's Sexual Fantasies (1973) and Forbidden Flowers: More Women's Sexual Fantasies (1975); L. Gould, A Sea Change (1977); E. Jong, Fear of Flying (1973) and How to Save Your Own Life (1976); Kensington Ladies Erotica Society, Ladies Home Erotica (1984); S. Kitzinger, Women's Experience of Sex (1983); R. Mapplethorpe, Lady Lisa Lyon (1983); K. Millett, Sita (1976); A. Nin, Delta of Venus (1977); Olds, Bestiary, in Powers of Desire: The Politics of Sexuality supra p. 22, at 409; A. Oakgrove, The Raging Peace (1984); J. Rechy, City of Night (1963); Coming to Power (Samois ed. 1982); Shulman, A Story of a Girl and Her Dog, in Powers of Desire: The Politics of Sexuality, supra, p. 22 at 410.

A. The District Court Erred in Accepting Appellants' Assertion
    That Pornography Is a Discriminatory Practice Based on
    Sex.

The ordinance is predicated on a finding that:

> Pornography is a discriminatory practice based on sex
> which denies women equal opportunities in society. Por-
> nography is central in creating and maintaining sex as a
> basis for discrimination. . . . [It harms] women's oppor-
> tunities for equality of rights in employment, education,
> access to and use of public accommodations, and acquisi-
> tion of real property; promote[s] rape, battery, child
> abuse, kidnapping and prostitution and inhibit[s] just
> enforcement of laws against such acts . . . .

Indianapolis, Ind., Code § 16-1(a)(2).

The District Court accepted that finding, but held that First
Amendment values outweighed the asserted interest in protecting women. American Booksellers Ass'n v. Hudnut, 598 F. Supp.
1316, 1335-37 (S.D. Ind. 1984).

Amici dispute the City and County's "finding" that "pornography is central in creating and maintaining sex as a basis for
discrimination." There was no formal, or indeed informal, legislative fact-finding process leading to this conclusion. Rather, legislators who had previously opposed obscenity on more traditional and moralistic grounds adopted a "model bill"
incorporating this finding.[22] The model bill was in turn based on
legislative hearings, held in Minneapolis, which did not, in fair-
ness, reflect a reasoned attempt to understand the factors "central" in maintaining "sex as a basis for discrimination."[23] See
Appellants' brief at 15 n.6.

It is true that sex discrimination takes multiple forms, which
are reflected in the media. But the finding that "pornography is
central in creating and maintaining sex as a basis for discrimina-

---

22. Duggan, Censorship in the Name of Feminism, Village Voice, Oct. 16, 1984, at 15,
col. 1.

23. Courts may not defer to legislative determination of fact when the supposed
"facts" are marshaled to suppress free speech or to justify sex discrimination. "Deference
to a legislative finding cannot limit judicial inquiry when First Amendment rights are at
stake," Landmark Communications, Inc. v. Virginia, 435 U.S. 829, 843 (1978). See also
Craig v. Boren, 429 U.S. 190 (1976).

tion" does not represent our best understanding of the complex, deep-seated and structural causes of gender inequality. In the past decade, many people have grappled with the question of causation. Feminist law professors and scholars have published and revised collections of cases and materials. K. Davidson, R. Ginsberg & H. Kay, supra p. 3 (1974 & 2d ed. 1981); B. Babcock, A. Freedman, E. Norton & S. Ross, Sex Discrimination and the Law: Causes and Remedies (1974 & Supp. 1978). The factors they find most significant include: the sex segregated wage labor market; systematic devaluation of work traditionally done by women; sexist concepts of marriage and family; inadequate income maintenance programs for women unable to find wage work; lack of day care services and the premise that child care is an exclusively female responsibility; barriers to reproductive freedom; and discrimination and segregation in education and athletics.[24] Numerous feminist scholars have written major works tracing the cultural, economic, and psychosocial roots of women's oppression.[25]

Misogynist images, both those which are sexually explicit and the far more pervasive ones which are not, reflect and may help to reinforce the inferior social and economic status of women. But none of these studies and analyses identifies sexually explicit material as the central factor in the oppression of women. History teaches us that the answer is not so simple. Factors far more complex than pornography produced the English common law treatment of women as chattel property and the enactment of statutes allowing a husband to rape or beat his wife with impunity. In short, the claim that "pornography is central in creating and maintaining sex as a basis of discrimination" is flatly inconsistent with the conclusions of most who have studied the question.

Amici also dispute the "finding" that pornography, as defined by the ordinance, is "a discriminatory practice . . . which denies

---

24. See also U.S. Commission on Civil Rights, Women and Poverty (1974); Women Still in Poverty (1979); and Child Care and Equal Opportunity for Women (1981) and National Advisory Council on Economic Opportunity, Final Report: The American Promise: Equal Justice and Economic Opportunity (1981).

25. See, e.g., Toward an Anthropology of Women (R. Reiter ed. 1975); M. Rosaldo & L. Lamphere, Women, Culture and Society (1974); M. Ryan, Womanhood in America: From Colonial Times to the Present (1979); N. Chodorow, The Reproduction of Mothering: Psychoanalysis and the Sociology of Gender (1978); D. Dinnerstein, The Mermaid and the Minotaur: Sexual Arrangements and Human Malaise (1976); J. Mitchell, Women's Estate (1972).

women equal opportunities." Images and fictional text are not the same thing as subordinating conduct. The ordinance does not target discriminatory actions denying access to jobs, education, public accommodations, or real property. It prohibits images. Although ideas have impact, images of discrimination are not the discrimination.

Further, the ordinance is cast in a form very different from the traditional antidiscrimination principles embodied in the Constitution and federal civil rights laws. Antidiscrimination laws demand equality of treatment for men and women, blacks and whites. The ordinance, by contrast, purports to protect women. It assumes that women are subordinated by sexual images and that men act uncontrollably if exposed to them. Sexist stereotypes are thus built into its very premises, and, as we demonstrate infra, its effect will be to reinforce those stereotypes.

Hence, the District Court misperceived this case as one requiring the assignment of rank in a constitutional hierarchy. It is not necessary to rule that either gender equality or free speech is more important. The ordinance is fatally flawed not only because it authorizes suppression of speech protected by the First Amendment but also because it violates the constitutional guarantee of sex-based equality.

B. The Ordinance Classifies on the Basis of Sex and Perpetuates Sexist Stereotypes.

The ordinance defines pornography in gender specific terms as "the graphic sexually explicit subordination of women" that also presents "women" in particular ways proscribed by the law. The District Court found:

> [t]he Ordinance seeks to protect adult women, as a group, from the diminution of the legal and sociological status as women, that is from the discriminatory stigma which befalls women as women as a result of 'pornography.'

American Booksellers Ass'n v. Hudnut, 598 F. Supp. at 1335 (emphasis supplied).

The heart of the ordinance is the suppression of sexually explicit images of women, based on a finding of "subordination," a term which is not defined. The ordinance implies that sexually explicit images of women necessarily subordinate and degrade women and perpetuates stereotypes of women as helpless victims and people who could not seek or enjoy sex.

The ordinance also reinforces sexist stereotypes of men. It denies the possibility that graphic sexually explicit images of a man could ever subordinate or degrade him. It provides no remedy for sexually explicit images showing men as "dismembered, truncated or fragmented" or "shown as filthy or inferior, bleeding, bruised or hurt."

The stereotype that sex degrades women, but not men, is underscored by the proviso that "the use of men, children, or transsexuals in the place of women . . . also constitutes pornography." Indianapolis, Ind., Code § 16-3(q). The proviso does not allow men to claim that they, as men, are injured by sexually explicit images of them. Rather men are degraded only when they are used "in place of women." The ordinance assumes that in sexuality, degradation is a condition that attaches to women.[26]

The ordinance authorizes any woman to file a complaint against those trafficking in pornography "as a woman acting against the subordination of women." A man, by contrast, may obtain relief only if he can "prove injury in the same way that a woman is injured." Indianapolis, Ind., Code § 16-17(a)(7)(b). Again the ordinance assumes that women as a class are subordinated and hurt by depictions of sex, and men are not.

The ordinance reinforces yet another sexist stereotype of men as aggressive beasts. Appellants assert:

> By conditioning the male orgasm to female subordination, pornography . . . makes the subordination of women pleasurable and seemingly legitimate. Each time men are sexually aroused by pornography, they learn to connect a woman's sexual pleasure to abuse and a woman's sexual nature to inferiority. They learn this in their bodies, not just their minds, so that it becomes a

---

26. Appellants explain that the proviso is needed because "without it, pornographers could circumvent the ordinance by producing the exact same material using models other than adult biological females, i.e., men, children, and transsexuals, to portray women." Appellants' brief at 45.

natural physiological response. At this point pornography leaves no more room for further debate than does shouting "kill" to an attack dog.

Appellants' brief at 21.

Men are not attack dogs, but morally responsible human beings. The ordinance reinforces a destructive sexist stereotype of men as irresponsible beasts, with "natural physiological responses" which can be triggered by sexually explicit images of women, and for which the men cannot be held accountable. Thus, men are conditioned into violent acts or negative beliefs by sexual images; women are not. Further, the ordinance is wholly blind to the possibility that men could be hurt and degraded by images presenting them as violent or sadistic.

The ordinance also reinforces sexist images of women as incapable of consent. It creates a remedy for people "coerced" to participate in the production of pornography. Unlike existing criminal, tort, and contract remedies against coercion, the ordinance provides:

> proof of the following facts or conditions shall not constitute a defense: that the person actually consented . . .; or, knew that the purpose of the acts or events in question was to make pornography; or demonstrated no resistance or appeared to cooperate actively in the photographic sessions or in the sexual events that produced the pornography; or . . . signed a contract, or made statements affirming a willingness to cooperate in the production of pornography.

Indianapolis, Ind., Code § 16-3.(5)(A) VIII-XI.

In effect, the ordinance creates a strong presumption that women who participate in the creation of sexually explicit material are coerced.[27] A woman's manifestation of consent—no matter how plain, informed, or even self-initiated—does not constitute a defense to her subsequent claim of coercion. Women are judged incompetent to consent to participation in the creation of sexually explicit material and condemned as "bad" if they do so.

---

27. The provisions negating common law defenses to coercion are cast in facially neutral terms. But since "pornography" is defined in gender specific terms, the provisions abrogating defenses to coercion also apply to women or to others used "in the place of women."

Appellants argue that this provision is justified by Supreme Court precedent allowing suppression of sexually explicit material involving children. They assert that women, like children, "are incapable of consenting to engage in pornographic conduct, even absent a showing of physical coercion and therefore require special protection. . . . The coercive conditions under which most pornographic models work make this part of the law one effective address to the industry." [Sic.] Appellants' brief at 17.

This provision does far more than simply provide a remedy to women who are pressured into the creation of pornography which they subsequently seek to suppress. It functions to make all women incompetent to enter into legally binding contracts for the production of sexually explicit material. When women are legally disabled from making binding agreements, they are denied power to negotiate for fair treatment and decent pay. Enforcement of the ordinance would drive production of sexually explicit material even further into an underground economy, where the working conditions of women in the sex industry would worsen, not improve.

C.   The Ordinance Is Unconstitutional Because It Reinforces Sexist Stereotypes and Classifies on the Basis of Sex.

In recent years, the Supreme Court has firmly and repeatedly rejected gender-based classifications, such as that embodied in the ordinance. The constitutionally protected right to sex-based equality under law demands that:

> the party seeking to uphold a statute that classifies individuals on the basis of their gender must carry the burden of showing an "exceedingly persuasive justification" for the classification. . . . The burden is met only by showing at least that the classification serves "important governmental objectives and that the discriminatory means employed" are "substantially related to the achievement of those objectives."

Mississippi Univ. for Women v. Hogan, 458 U.S. 718, 724-25 (1982).

The sex-based classifications embodied in the statute are justified on the basis of stereotypical assumptions about women's vulnerability to sexually explicit images and their production and men's latent uncontrollability. But the Supreme Court has held that, "[This standard] must be applied free of fixed notions concerning the roles and abilities of males and females. Care must be taken in ascertaining whether the statutory objective itself reflects archaic and stereotypic notions." Id. Gender-based classifications cannot be upheld if they are premised on "'old notions' and 'archaic and overbroad' generalizations" about the roles and relative abilities of men and women." Califano v. Goldfarb, 430 U.S. 199, 217 (1977).

The ordinance damages individuals who do not fit the stereotypes it embodies. It delegitimates and makes socially invisible women who find sexually explicit images of women "in positions of display" or "penetrated by objects" to be erotic, liberating, or educational. These women are told that their perceptions are a product of "false consciousness" and that such images are so inherently degrading that they may be suppressed by the state. At the same time, it stamps the imprimatur of state approval on the belief that men are attack dogs triggered to violence by the sight of a sexually explicit image of a woman. It delegitimates and makes socially invisible those men who consider themselves gentle, respectful of women, or inhibited about expressing their sexuality.

Even worse, the stereotypes of the ordinance perpetuate traditional social views of sex-based difference. By defining sexually explicit images of woman as subordinating and degrading to them, the ordinance reinforces the stereotypical view that "good" women do not seek and enjoy sex.[28] As applied, it would deny women access to sexually explicit material at a time in our

---

28. Perpetuating the stereotype that "good girls" do not enjoy sex, and suppressing images of women's sexuality, is particularly tragic for teenagers. A recent study by the prestigious Alan Guttmacher Institute identifies factors explaining why teenagers in the United States experience unwanted pregnancy at rates significantly higher than those in any other developed nation. This extensive study found that the single most important factor associated with low rates of unwanted pregnancy is "openness about sex (defined on the basis of four items: media presentations of female nudity, the extent of nudity on public beaches, sales of sexually explicit literature and media advertising of condoms)." The researchers conclude:

American teenagers seem to have inherited the worst of all possible worlds regarding their exposure to messages about sex: Movies, music, radio and TV tell them that sex is romantic, exciting, titillating. . . . Yet, at the same time, young people get the message good girls should say no. Almost nothing that they see or hear about sex informs them about contraception or the importance of avoiding pregnancy. . . . Such messages lead to an ambivalence about sex that stifles

history when women have just begun to acquire the social and economic power to develop our own images of sexuality. Stereotypes of hair-trigger male susceptibility to violent imagery can be invoked as an excuse to avoid directly blaming the men who commit violent acts.

Finally, the ordinance perpetuates a stereotype of women as helpless victims, incapable of consent, and in need of protection. A core premise of contemporary sex equality doctrine is that if the objective of the law is to " 'protect' members of one gender because they are presumed to suffer from an inherent handicap or to be innately inferior, the objective itself is illegitimate." Mississippi Univ. for Women v. Hogan, 458 U.S. at 725. We have learned through hard experience that gender-based classifications protecting women from their own presumed innate vulnerability reflect "an attitude of 'romantic paternalism' which, in practical effect, puts women not on a pedestal but in a cage." Frontiero v. Richardson, 411 U.S. 677, 684 (1973).

The coercion provisions of the ordinance "protect" by denying women's capacity to voluntarily agree to participate in the creation of sexually explicit images. The trafficking provisions "protect" by allowing women to suppress sexually explicit speech which the ordinance presumes is damaging to them. The claim that women need protection and are incapable of voluntary action is familiar. Historically, the presumed "natural and proper timidity and delicacy" of women made them unfit "for many of the occupations of civil life," and justified denying them the power to contract. Bradwell v. Illinois, 83 U.S. (16 Wall.) 130, 141-42 (1872).

Until quite recently, the law commonly provided women special protections against exploitation. In 1936, the Supreme Court upheld a law establishing minimum wages for women saying, "What can be closer to the public interest than the health of women and their protection from unscrupulous and overreaching employers?" West Coast Hotel v. Parrish, 300 U.S. 379, 398 (1936). In 1948, the Court approved a law banning women from work as bartenders as a legitimate measure to combat the

---

communication and exposes young people to increased risk of pregnancy, out-of-wedlock births and abortions.

Jones, Forrest, Goldman, Heusbaw, Livecloer, Rosoff, Westoff, & Wolf, Teenage Pregnancy in Developed Countries: Determinants and Policy Implications, 17 Family Plan. Persp., Mar.-Apr. 1985, at 53, 61.

"moral and social problems" to which bartending by women might give rise. Goesaert v. Cleary, 335 U.S. 464, 466 (1948). The protectionist premise of these cases is now discredited and their holdings repudiated.

Women were, and continue to be, in a position of social and economic vulnerability that inhibits their ability to negotiate fair terms and conditions of wage labor. Further, the pervasive sexism and violence of our culture make women vulnerable to exploitation and inhibit their ability to enter into sexual or other relationships on a free and voluntary basis.

Slavery and free self-actualization are opposite poles on a continuum. Both free agency and response to external pressure are simultaneous aspects of human action. In the 1930's, employers challenged minimum wage and hour laws saying that laborers "freely consented" to work twelve hours a day, under dangerous and harmful conditions, for wages that did not provide minimal subsistence. We understand today that this concept of voluntary consent is self-serving and empty. Similarly, many women engage in sex or in the production of sexually explicit materials in response to pressures so powerful that it would be cynical to characterize their actions as simply voluntary and consensual.

Still, the laws that "protected" only women from exploitation in wage labor hurt them. B. Babcock, A. Freedman, E. Norton & S. Ross, supra p. 25, at 48, 191-217. Many employers responded by barring women from the best paying jobs with the greatest opportunity for advancement. Further, the protective labor laws reinforced general beliefs about women's vulnerability and incompetence. Similarly here, the protection of the ordinance reinforces the idea that women are incompetent, particularly in relation to sex.

The pervasive sexism and violence of our culture create a social climate—in the home, workplace, and street—that is different for women than for men. But even accurate generalizations about women's need for help do not justify sex-based classifications such as those in this ordinance. It is also true that women generally are still the ones who nurture young children. Yet we understand that laws giving mothers an irrebuttable "tender years" presumption for custody, or offering child rearing leaves only to mothers but not to fathers, ultimately hurt women and are unconstitutional.[29]

Some of the proponents of the ordinance believe that it will empower women, while others support it for more traditional, patriarchal reasons. Supra note 22. But many gender-based classifications are premised on a good faith intent to help or protect women. Good intent does not justify an otherwise invidious gender-based law. "Our nation has had a long and unfortunate history of sex discrimination." Frontiero v. Richardson, 411 U.S. at 684. The clearest lesson of that history is that sex-based classifications hurt women.

Thus, the District Court was correct to reject Appellants' claim that women are like children who need special protection from sexually explicit material. The Court found that:

adult women as a group do not, as a matter of public policy or applicable law, stand in need of the same type of protection which has long been afforded children. . . . Adult women generally have the capacity to protect themselves from participating in and being personally victimized by pornography . . . .

American Booksellers Ass'n v. Hudnut, 598 F. Supp. at 1333-34.

The gender-based classification embodied in the ordinance is unconstitutional because it assumes and perpetuates classic sexist concepts of separate gender-defined roles, which carry "the inherent risk of reinforcing the stereotypes about the 'proper place' of women and their need for special protection." Orr v. Orr, 440 U.S. 268, 283 (1979).

---

29. On the dangers and unconstitutionality of a blanket "tender years" presumption, see Devine v. Devine, 398 So. 2d 686 (Ala. 1981); Developments in the Law: The Constitution and the Family, 93 Harv. L. Rev. 1156, 1334-38 (1980); S. Ross & A. Barcher, The Rights of Women 229-30 (1983). On the danger and illegality of a mother-only child rearing leave, see Danielson v. Board of Higher Educ., 358 F. Supp. 22 (S.D.N.Y. 1972). See also Phillips v. Martin Marietta Corp., 400 U.S. 542 (1971) (company policy prohibiting the hiring of mothers, but not fathers, of preschool-aged children violates section 703(a) of Title VII of the Civil Rights Act of 1964). Williams, Reflections on Culture, Courts and Feminism, 7 Women's Rts. L. Rep. 175, 198 (1982).

D. The Sex-Based Classification and Stereotypes Created by the Ordinance Are Not Carefully Tailored to Serve Important State Purposes.

Appellants claim that the ordinance serves the "governmental interest in promoting sex equality." Appellants' brief at 23. Certainly preventing the violent subordination of women is the sort of compelling public purpose that might justify sex-based classification. But, as is often true of classifications justified on grounds that they protect women, the benefits actually provided are minimal. The ordinance thus also fails the requirement for a "substantial relationship" between its classification and the achievement of its asserted goal. Mississippi Univ. for Women v. Hogan, 458 U.S. at 724.

Supporters of the ordinance describe acts of violence against women and claim that the ordinance would provide a remedy for those injuries. But the only new remedy it provides is suppression of sexually explicit materials, a wholly inadequate and misdirected response to real violence.

Amicus Marchiano, for example, has written of her marriage to a man who beat her, raped her, forced her into prostitution, and terrorized her. L. Lovelace, Ordeal (1980). For several years prior to the making of Deep Throat, she was virtually imprisoned by her husband through brute force, control of economic resources, and the fact that she believed his claim that a wife could not charge her husband with a crime. Id. at 82. Had this ordinance existed then, it would not have helped her. There is a compelling social need to provide more effective remedies for victims of violence and sexual coercion. But the ordinance does not protect vulnerable people against those actions already prohibited by the criminal law. Those who have worked to empower battered women and children understand that effective enforcement of existing criminal sanctions demands a multipronged effort. Police and prosecutors must be trained, required to take complaints seriously, and given the resources to do so. Bruno v. McGuire, 4 Fam. L. Rep. (BNA) 3095 (1978). Help must be available on a continuous and prompt basis. A. Boylan & N. Taub, Adult Domestic Violence: Constitutional, Legislative and Equitable Issues (1981). Vulnerable people must be educated and provided support by community groups and shelters. L. Bowker, Beating Wife Beating (1982). See generally S.

Schechter, Women and Male Violence: The Visions and Struggles of the Battered Women's Movement (1982); Marcus, Conjugal Violence: The Law of Force and the Force of Law, 69 Calif. L. Rev. 1657 (1981). The remedy this ordinance provides for violence and sexual coercion is illusory.

Individuals who commit acts of violence must be held legally and morally accountable. The law should not displace responsibility onto imagery. Amicus Women Against Pornography describe as victims of pornography married women coerced to perform sexual acts depicted in pornographic works, working women harassed on the job with pornographic images, and children who have pornography forced on them during acts of child abuse. Appellants' brief at 13. Each of these examples describes victims of violence and coercion, not of images. The acts are wrong, whether or not the perpetrator refers to an image. The most wholesome sex education materials, if shown to a young child as an example of what people do with those they love, could be used in a viciously harmful way. The law should punish the abuser, not the image. Title VII of the Civil Rights Act provides remedies for working women injured by sexual taunts or slurs, including sexually explicit pictures, e.g., Barnes v. Costle, 561 F.2d 983 (D.C. Cir. 1977), and for those injured by misogynist imagery. See, e.g., Kyriazi v. Western Elec. Co., 461 F. Supp. 892 (D.N.J. 1978). These legal principles apply to any images or texts which people put to discriminatory use, whether pornography or the Bible. But no law has or should assume that the same woman harassed by pornographic images in the work place might not enjoy those very images if given the opportunity to put them to her own use.

To resist forced sex and violence, women need the material resources to enable them to reject jobs or marriages in which they are abused or assaulted and the internal and collective strength to fight the conditions of abuse. The ordinance does nothing to enhance the concrete economic and social power of women. Further, its stereotype of women as powerless victims undermines women's ability to act affirmatively to protect themselves.

Suppression of sexually explicit material will not eliminate the pervasive sexist images of the mainstream culture or the discriminatory economic and social treatment that maintains women's second class status. Such suppression will not empower women to enter into sexual relationships on a voluntary, consensual basis. Empowering women requires something more than suppression of texts and images. It demands "concrete material changes that enable women and men to experience sexuality less attached to and formed by gender."[30] These changes include social and economic equality; access to jobs, day care and education; more equal sharing of responsibility for children; recognition of the social and economic value of the work that women have traditionally done in the home; and access to birth control, abortion, and sex education.

III. CONCLUSION

Sexually explicit speech is not per se sexist or harmful to women. Like any mode of expression, it can be used to attack women's struggle for equal rights, but it is also a category of speech from which women have been excluded. The suppression authorized by the Indianapolis ordinance of a potentially enormous range of sexual imagery and texts reinforces the notion that women are too fragile, and men too uncontrollable, absent the aid of the censor, to be trusted to reject or enjoy sexually explicit speech for themselves. By identifying "subordination of women" as the concept that distinguishes sexually explicit material which is tolerable from that to be condemned, the ordinance incorporates a vague and asymmetric standard for censorship that can as readily be used to curtail feminist speech about sexuality, or to target the speech of sexual minorities, as to halt hateful speech about women. Worse, perpetuation of the concept of gender-determined roles in regard to sexuality strengthens one of the main obstacles to achieving real change and ending sexual violence.

---

30. Vance & Snitow, Toward a Conversation About Sex in Feminism: A Modest Proposal, 10 Signs: J. of Women in Culture and Soc. 126, 131 (1984).

Amici therefore ask this Court to affirm the judgment below.

April 8, 1985   Respectfully submitted,

_____

NAN D. HUNTER
132 West 43rd Street
New York, New York 10036
(212) 944-9800

_____

SYLVIA A. LAW
40 Washington Square South
New York, New York 10003
(212) 598-7642

The Feminist Debate Over Prostitution Reform:

Prostitutes' Rights Groups, Radical Feminists, and the (Im)possibility of Consent

Jody Freeman†

INTRODUCTION

This article has two purposes. The first is to identify the theoretical basis for the divergence between prostitutes' rights groups and radical feminists over prostitution reform.[1] I will argue that the crux of the divergence is different understandings of consent and coercion. The second purpose is to argue that despite their deep differences, both groups should support decriminalization as the only acceptable short-term option.

Throughout the article, I treat prostitutes' rights groups as having the same ideological base as those we might call liberal feminists.[2] They see sex-trade workers as respectable women doing dignified work. Radical feminists, in contrast, assume that prostitutes are victims of coercion in a society that services men by objectifying and subordinating women. Because their visions of the world are incompatible, it is hard to imagine both groups on the same side of the prostitution debate. I will argue, however, that they should agree on short-term reform proposals in the service of their very different long-term aspirations.

† B.A., Stanford University, 1985; LL.B., University of Toronto, 1989. I would like to thank Denise Réaume for her role in inspiring this article and overseeing its birth, Ruth Colker for her support and substantive suggestions, and Shirley Netten for courageously criticizing everything I write and always knowing what I want to say.

[1] To the extent that I use labels in the paper, such as radical feminist or liberal feminist, it is because I think they distinguish feminists and help locate them in a theoretical tradition and along a spectrum of belief in the possibility of choice. I realize that some of the individuals or groups I refer to would never call themselves either liberal or radical feminists.

[2] I will argue later that liberal feminism is a misnomer: to the extent that it is rooted in classic liberalism it cannot be feminist. It will become clear that I see prostitutes' rights groups as essentially liberal.

Despite their differences, both prostitutes' rights groups and radical feminists can be distinguished from anti-feminists in the sense that neither claims that prostitution is obscene, immoral, or offensive in isolation from its context. Neither group seeks to criminalize prostitution because it is an affront to heterosexual monogamy and, therefore, dangerous to traditional morality. This latter perspective is more properly attributable to anti-feminist groups.[3] Analyzing the reasons behind the prostitutes' rights groups' and radical feminist approaches to prostitution makes it possible to highlight how they differ from anti-feminists with whom neither wants to be associated. It is an obvious irony that radical feminists and conservative anti-feminist groups are both anti-pornography and anti-prostitution, despite their completely different world views.[4]

I am more sympathetic to the long-term view of radical feminists that prostitution should be eradicated, than to what I perceive to be the liberal (and only reluctantly feminist) position of prostitutes' rights groups. I do not claim, therefore, that decriminalization alone is the answer to the problem of prostitution. Only broad social and economic reforms, coupled with profound changes in our most deeply entrenched cultural norms, would eliminate the causes of prostitution. Because that amount of structural change is an unrealistic immediate goal, I think it is important to support decriminalization as an interim measure, without abandoning the purpose of eradicating prostitution.

The challenge of reforming prostitution laws poses an inescapable dilemma: to resist the commodification of women's sexuality, which requires circumscribing choices that some women themselves insist are voluntary, or to support the right of women to do the work they say they want to do, at the cost of reinforcing male dominance. The first approach is interventionist: it can be condescending, patronizing, and insensitive. The second is permissive: it appears to endorse the objectification of women and is, therefore, counterproductive if one is interested in dismantling gender hierarchy. This dilemma seems to recur whenever feminists try to remedy social inequality and empower women as a class, without punishing individual women in the process. It is a problem of transition from an unequal to an equal world.

---

[3] By anti-feminist, I mean those groups which do not seek power or equality for women but instead promote women as traditional appendages of men and as suited to certain activities (child-raising and homemaking for instance) for biological reasons. They seek to preserve the status quo or revert to the more traditional roles for men and women. All of this is inimical to feminism as it is understood in this essay.

[4] Robin West describes the conservative condemnation of pornography as:
> squarely based on a celebration of conservative social institutions of family, marriage, monogamy, and mandatory heterosexuality, and the conservative values of sexual privacy, sexual decency, and dignity. As feminists have strenuously argued, those institutions, that conception of virtue, and those particular values have done women in this culture and elsewhere tremendous harm.

Robin West, *The Feminist-Conservative AntiPornography Alliance and the 1986 Attorney General's Commission on Pornography Report*, Am Bar Found Res J 681, 707 (1987).

Two more introductory notes are necessary. This article is concerned with women prostitutes catering to a male clientele. I understand, of course, that prostitution may refer to a much broader spectrum of activity, and some of the arguments in this article may apply to men as well as to women. Nonetheless, the application of radical feminist and liberal theory will be made under the assumption that the sex-trade workers concerned are women. I do not think that male prostitutes are in an analogous situation because they have not endured a history of objectification and subjugation based on their gender. However, to the extent that the criticisms in the paper are about the objectification and commercialization of sex in general, they would apply to male prostitutes as well as to women. Also, I have tried to present the opinions of prostitutes in a way that is true to what they say about their condition. To that end, the reader will find many direct quotations. I have tried to clarify the prostitution debate for an audience that I hope will include prostitutes. I realize, however, that this article will probably be inaccessible or irrelevant to most prostitutes. Nonetheless, exposing the divergence in opinion on issues like this one is important because it helps feminists create coherent theory, which makes consistent and effective practice. It also clarifies the debate for those struggling to make political choices about reform.

ALTERNATIVE MODELS FOR REGULATING PROSTITUTION

In North America, there are three prevalent models for regulating prostitution. The first is criminalizing prostitution per se, as well as all the activities surrounding it, such as procuring, living off the avails, and keeping a bawdy-house. The second is legalization, which requires a licensing scheme that could entail fingerprinting, registration, and mandatory health checks. The final option involves criminalizing virtually every activity surrounding prostitution, but not prostitution per se. The Canadian scheme represents this last option. I will briefly discuss criminalization and legalization, taking New York and Nevada as examples. Both of these regimes have been criticized at length in the American literature on prostitution.[5] I will focus on the Canadian approach because it has received less attention and appears to be a good compromise. However, it too is flawed.

New York

American prostitution laws are more draconian than those in Can-

---

[5] For a summary and critique of the variety of legal regimes, see Kathleen Barry, *Female Sexual Slavery* 124-34 (NYU Press, 1979) ("*Sexual Slavery*").

ada and Britain, with prostitution per se being illegal in 46 states.[6] Generally, state criminal laws in the United States treat prostitution as a misdemeanor and pimping as a felony.[7] If states penalize clients at all, it is usually less severely than prostitutes.[8] In New York, the act of prostitution is a misdemeanor,[9] while patronizing a prostitute is criminal in varying degrees, depending on the prostitute's age.[10] Promoting or "advancing" prostitution is also criminal.[11] This prohibition encompasses profiting from "participating" in the proceeds of prostitution,[12] running a house of prostitution,[13] and compelling a person by force or coercion to engage in prostitution.[14] Penalties for each offense increase in severity as the age of the prostitute decreases.[15]

Nevada

Nevada's legislative scheme is unique in the United States because it permits legalization of prostitution in counties with populations of less than 250,000.[16] Individual counties can choose whether to license, tax, and regulate bawdy-houses.[17] Prostitution per se is not illegal, but soliciting for sex is.[18] Under the legalization regime, prostitutes are photographed, issued a work permit, fingerprinted, and forced to submit to a medical check-up before beginning work.[19] In addition, they are prohib-

---

[6] Pornography and Prostitution in Canada: Report of the Special Committee on Pornography and Prostitution 473-74 (Ottawa: Ministry of Supply and Services, 1985) ("Fraser Report").

[7] In Michigan, for instance, soliciting is a misdemeanor but is defined so broadly that it covers any invitation to engage in an immoral act: "Any person, male or female, 17 years of age or older, who shall accost, solicit or invite another in any public place, or in or from any building or vehicle, by word, gesture or any other means, to commit prostitution or to do any other lewd or immoral act, shall be guilty of a misdemeanor." Mich Comp Laws Ann § 750.448 (West 1970).

[8] Pasqua Scibelli, *Empowering Prostitutes: A Proposal for International Reform*, 10 Harv Women's L J 117, 121 (1987).

[9] NY Penal Law § 230.00 (McKinney 1969). "A person is guilty of prostitution when such person engages or agrees or offers to engage in sexual conduct with another person in return for a fee. Prostitution is a class B Misdemeanor."

[10] NY Penal Law §§ 230.03-230.06 (McKinney 1978).

[11] NY Penal Law § 230.15 (McKinney 1965).

[12] Id. This section is so vaguely worded as to include lovers and friends who "profit" from the work of a prostitute. "A person 'profits from prostitution' when, acting other than as a prostitute receiving compensation for personally rendered prostitution services, he accepts or receives money or other property pursuant to an agreement or understanding with any person whereby he participates or is to participate in the proceeds of prostitution activity."

[13] NY Penal Law § 230.25 (McKinney 1978).

[14] NY Penal Law § 230.30 (McKinney 1978).

[15] NY Penal Law §§ 230.25, 230.30, 230.32, and 230.04-230.06 (McKinney 1978). See also Commission Staff Notes following § 230.15 noting the changes in penalties according to age that were made after 1964.

[16] Nev Rev Stat § 244.345(8) (1986). When the Secretary of Commerce reports the 1990 census of the population to the President, the 1989 amendment to this act will become effective. Prositution will then be legal only in counties with populations of less than 400,000 people. Nev Rev Stat § 244.345(8) (1989).

[17] Nev Rev Stat § 244.345(3) (1989).

[18] Nev Rev Stat § 207.030(1)(b) (1986).

[19] Scibelli, 10 Harv Women's L J at 145-46 (cited in note 8).

ited from entering bars and gaming houses, from renting rooms in the town center, and they may even be prohibited from living in the same areas where their families reside. The hours when they are permitted outside the prostitution houses may be regulated, as might their dress and hygiene.[20]

Legalization is problematic because it allows the state effectively to control prostitutes' lives. Nevada's system is an example of how restrictive and coercive legalization can be. Not only does the licensing scheme restrict prostitutes' mobility, but many aspects of their private lives are monitored.[21] Prostitutes are dependent on their employers at the bawdyhouses and may be victims of abuse by police or other officials who have the power to grant or revoke their permits. Thus, although prostitutes are not subject to criminal prosecution, the disadvantages of legalization make it an unsatisfactory alternative.

Canada

Prostitution is currently legal in Canada. However, solicitation, living off the avails of prostitution, keeping a common bawdy-house, and communication for the purposes of obtaining the sexual services of a prostitute are all illegal.[22] Prostitution reform in Canada began with *Hutt v R.*, a case in which a conviction was quashed on the basis that the accused's conduct did not amount to solicitation within the meaning of then section 195 of the Criminal Code.[23] Solicitation was not explicitly defined in the Code and the Court held that the alleged solicitation had to be "pressing and persistent" for it to constitute a criminal offense.[24] In the wake of *Hutt*, law enforcement officials argued that Canada's prostitution laws were in need of serious reform. Feminists and prostitutes also supported the idea of reform, although for obviously different reasons. The Minister of Justice for the Liberal Government created a special legislative committee on pornography and prostitution which culminated in the publication of the Fraser Report.[25]

In the words of one legal scholar, the recommendations contained in the report were "liberal with healthy doses of feminism."[26] Much to the

---

[20] Id.

[21] See Barry, *Sexual Slavery* at 131-32 (cited in note 5) (recounting her visit to one prison-like prostitution house in Nevada called "Mustang Ranch").

[22] Rev Stat Canada 1985, c C-46, §§ 210-213 ("Criminal Code"). In Canada, the Criminal Code applies uniformly to all provinces because under the division of powers in the Constitution, criminal legislation falls within the jurisdiction of the federal government.

[23] *Hutt v R.*, 2 SCR 476 (1978).

[24] Id at 477-78.

[25] Fraser Report at 5-12 (cited in note 6).

[26] Michael Kanter, *Prohibit or Regulate? The Fraser Report and New Approaches to Pornography and Prostitution*, 23 Osgoode Hall L J 171, 178 (1983). Kanter criticizes the report's recommendations as being too vague and suggests that more positive steps be taken towards displacing male power and control in society including pay equity, day care, and family law reform.

chagrin of law enforcement officials, the committee advocated non-legal, social, and economic responses to prostitution, including a commitment from both the federal and provincial governments to removing economic and social inequities between men and women.[27] In terms of more specific measures, the committee recommended that prostitutes be able to work out of their own homes and that the offences of soliciting and operating a prostitution establishment be decriminalized.[28] This report thoroughly canvassed feminist and other viewpoints in a painstaking effort to reflect the diversity of Canadian opinion on the subject.

The recommendations attempted to respond to feminist concerns about the subordination of women, prostitutes' concerns about the right to work, and societal concerns about nuisance and moral decline. The report provided a thoughtful account of the causes and effects of prostitution, which was reflected in its proposals.[29] When a new Conservative government came into office it shelved the Fraser Report and instead enacted section 213, which criminalized communication "for the purposes of obtaining the sexual services of a prostitute."[30] More recently, the re-elected Conservative government passed an amendment to the Criminal Code, an act which arms the police with sweeping powers to seize anything they suspect has been obtained through the proceeds of

---

He further argues for women's increased access to media in order to create non-sexist depictions of women in film and on radio. Id at 186-89.

[27] Fraser Report at 699-703 (cited in note 6).

[28] Id at 27-28. The committee summarized many of its conclusions:

The adult prostitute is accorded by our proposed regime, some leeway to conduct his or her business in privacy and dignity. We would permit one or two prostitutes to receive customers in their own home, hoping thereby to provide people with a safe alternative to the street and parked cars. . . .

. . . We acknowledge that allowing full play to the concept of the responsibility and dignity of the adult prostitute may well require active consideration of treating prostitution like any other business. There is, indeed, an argument that this course is the only way of ensuring that the sexual and other subordination of women who are prostitutes will come to an end. . . .

. . . Only procuring which is effected by coercion or threats will be criminalized in the case of an adult. So, too, we stipulate that receiving financial support from an adult prostitute should be criminal only when that support is exacted by means of coercion or threats. Where young persons are concerned, the emphasis of our recommendation is to provide strong protection against exploitation. . . . We have recommended adding to the *Criminal Code* a specific prohibition against engaging, or offering or attempting to engage, in sexual activity with a young person. However, we do not recommend criminalizing the behaviour of young persons . . . .

[29] The committee explained that the following principles informed their recommendations: equality, responsibility, individual liberty, human dignity, and appreciation of sexuality.

The full working out of these principles will in some cases require considerable social adjustment. In particular, the equality principle, even if accepted at the theoretical level, will still need for its full implementation, substantial reallocation of economic and social resources. There remains, too, a formidable task in re-education and reshaping of attitudes in certain sectors of society. These long range [sic] tasks cannot be accomplished by means of legislation. They require social will and commitment. Id at 28.

[30] Criminal Code § 213 (cited in note 22).

crime.[31] Although the act is seen as part of an anti-drug campaign similar to RICO, the Racketeer Influenced and Corrupt Organizations statute passed in 1970 in the United States,[32] its potential effects on prostitutes are devastating.[33] The Act would conceivably permit the seizure of a prostitute's earnings and everything purchased with money earned through prostitution, including her home and all its contents— even if she is not involved with organized crime and operates privately from her own home. This move toward broader police powers over morality offences directly contradicts the recommendations contained in the abandoned Fraser Report.[34]

The fact that prostitution per se is not illegal in Canada is a limited reform when all the activities that make it possible are criminal. Criminalizing prostitution's companion activities makes prostitution impractical and dangerous for women because it drives the trade underground. The current regime keeps prostitutes on the streets by prohibiting bawdy-houses. It exposes them to more violence from both pimps and johns than they would experience in a controlled environment, and it contradicts the legislature's stated desire to remove the public nuisance created by street prostitution. The provision against living off the avails is indiscriminate such that anyone supported by a prostitute, including children, lovers, husbands, and even parents, may be criminally charged.

The law also isolates prostitutes by criminalizing communication and living off the avails. If prostitutes speak or even gesture to each other, or to johns, in a way that can be interpreted as "for the purposes of engaging the services of a prostitute" they can be prosecuted. Section 213 may be an infringement of freedom of expression under section 2(b) of the Canadian Charter of Rights and Freedoms.[35] Appeal Courts have

---

[31] An Act to Amend the Criminal Code, the Food and Drugs Act and the Narcotic Control Act, SC 1988, C-51.

[32] Racketeer Influenced and Corrupt Organizations, 18 USC §§ 1961-1968 (1982).

[33] The Act to Amend the Criminal Code defines an "enterprise crime" to include keeping a common bawdy-house and procuring (§ 420.1). The Act further provides that where an offender is convicted of an enterprise crime offence,
 and the court imposing sentence on the offender, on application of the Attorney General, is satisfied, on a balance of probabilities, that any property is proceeds of crime and that the enterprise crime offence was committed in relation to that property, the court shall order that the property be forfeited to Her Majesty to be disposed of as the Attorney General directs or otherwise dealt with in accordance with law [§ 420.17(1)].
Section 420.12 also authorizes a judge to issue a search warrant with respect to any property subject to forfeiture under § 420.17(1).

[34] Fraser Report at 507 (cited in note 6).
 [I]t seems that those countries, the majority, which have ignored the importance of non-legal, social responses to prostitution have experienced less success in controlling prostitution than those, such as Sweden, Denmark and Holland, which have recognized the value of social strategies in changing attitudes and responding to the human problems associated with prostitution. . . . [T]here is no necessary correlation between the existence of harsh criminal law provisions and effective control of prostitution.

[35] Canadian Charter of Rights and Freedoms, § 2(b): "Everyone has the following fundamental freedoms: . . . (b) freedom of thought, belief, opinion and expression, including freedom of the press and other media of communication . . . ."

made conflicting rulings on the section's constitutionality, however, and the issue is currently pending before the Supreme Court.[36]

Since section 213 came into effect, the Metropolitan Toronto police force has hired 90 constables to increase patrols in the local "strolls," resulting in a 150% increase in the number of charges brought against prostitutes, johns, and pimps.[37] In 1988 alone, the city spent $6.3 million fighting prostitution.[38] Yet, "despite more patrols, dramatically higher conviction rates, and the ongoing massive sweeps (something no other Canadian city had tried before), the police acknowledge that unless there is a raging blizzard the hookers will be out on the street tomorrow."[39]

The harassment takes its toll, however. The threat of prosecution and the stigma attached to prostitution undoubtedly make it difficult for prostitutes to organize and impossible for them to seek the protection of the police when they are victims of crime. Instead, it drives them to pimps for protection from both customers and police. Canada's approach enables the government to feel permissive while still treating prostitutes like criminals. The regime does nothing to improve the conditions under which prostitutes work, and it has failed to quiet the public's objections to the "unattractive features" of the sex trade.

In fact, none of the three North American regimes described above responds to feminist arguments about prostitution. Criminalizing prostitution per se, or its companion activities alone, subjects sex-trade workers to the arbitrary enforcement of the justice system and the physical and psychological violence of abusive pimps and customers. Prostitutes are beaten, raped, robbed, arrested, and, if they complain, ignored because they are perceived as "sluts" who deserve whatever treatment they get. Many are young girls with limited options and a history of victimization at the hands of rapists and child abusers.[40] Others are women trying to make a living in a society where the feminization of poverty is a documented phenomenon.[41] Economic desperation often

---

[36] See *R. v Skinner*, 79 NSR 2d 8 (NSCA 1987), reserved, 1988 SCC Bul 2029-30 (holding that § 195.1 [now § 213] infringes section 2(b) of the Charter and is not justified as a reasonable limit under section 1 of the Charter). See also *R. v Jahelka*, 79 AR 44 (Alta CA 1987) (holding that section 1 of the Charter saves § 195.1); *Reference Re §§ 193 & 195(1)(c) of the Criminal Code*, 6 WWR 289 (Man CA 1987). Rights are guaranteed in the substantive sections of the Charter and the State's power to reasonably limit rights is provided in section 1, where the limit is demonstrably justified in a free and democratic society. This structure is fundamentally different from that of the American Bill of Rights. In the United States, prostitution is not protected by the right to privacy. See *Paris Adult Theatre I v Slaton*, 413 US 49, 68-69 (1973) (holding that privacy does not protect commercialized obscenity). Prostitution is also not protected by the First Amendment right to free speech. *United States v Moses*, 399 A2d 46, 53 (DC Cir 1975), cert denied, 426 US 920 (1976).

[37] Wendy Dennis, *Street Fight*, Toronto Life 85, 130 (Nov 1988).

[38] Id.

[39] Id.

[40] Barry, *Sexual Slavery* at 119-20, 273 (cited in note 5).

[41] Lenore Weitzman, *The Divorce Revolution: The Unexpected Social and Economic Consequences for Women and Children in America* (Free Press, 1985).

puts them on the street; a combination of factors, ranging from coercive pimps to profitable male demand, keeps them there. Criminalization addresses none of these causes and effects of prostitution, and despite many attempts at legal reform, governments still seem reluctant to propose decriminalization. Perhaps that is partly because no clear consensus has yet emerged on the best approach to the problem.

What Sex-Trade Workers Think—Not a United Front

Women who have been, or are presently, in the sex trade disagree over many contentious issues: whether their work is chosen, whether they participate in their own oppression, and whether their economic self-interest should outweigh the concern that prostitution contributes to women's subordination. Prostitutes' rights groups, such as Cast Off Your Old Tired Ethics (COYOTE)[42] and the Canadian Organization for the Rights of Prostitutes (CORP),[43] demand that prostitution be decriminalized because it is dignified, respectable work. CORP's leadership says prostitutes should be entitled to organize, advertise, pay taxes, and receive unemployment insurance.

Our ideal situation is like anyone else's—that we have control over our work environment, we have control over our prices, we make our own compromises. . . . Let our businesses have the support of the medical profession, the legal profession. Let us set professional standards.[44]

CORP actually views prostitution as superior to many other jobs since it has distinct advantages: women set their hours and wages, work where they want to, and service only customers they choose. Prostitutes' rights groups say prostitution empowers women because it enables them to earn a living in an environment they control, or would control but for state interference. Margo St. James, of COYOTE, objects to the double standard inherent in the criminalization of prostitution: "The state's idea is that these are deviant women and normal men. But they are doing the same thing; they're engaging in the same act."[45] CORP's spokesperson, Valerie Scott, makes prostitution sound as mundane as anything else: "Ever since I was five, I dreamed of getting into the sex industry."[46]

The National Task Force on Prostitution (NTFP),[47] an American

---

[42] COYOTE was the first American prostitutes' rights group founded by Margo St. James.

[43] Founded in Toronto in 1983 and headed by Valerie Scott, CORP includes both male and female sex-trade workers.

[44] *Realistic Feminists*, in Laurie Bell, ed, *Good Girls/Bad Girls* 204, 209 (The Women's Press, 1987) ("*Good Girls*").

[45] Margo St. James, *The Reclamation of Whores*, in *Good Girls* 81, 83 (cited in note 44).

[46] Dennis, Toronto Life at 130 (cited in note 37).

[47] The NTFP and its affiliates have evolved from COYOTE and other prostitutes' rights organizations. *Coyote/National Task Force on Prostitution*, in Frédérique Delacoste and Priscilla Alexander, eds, *Sex Work* 290, 291-93 (Cleis, 1987).

organization promoting prostitutes' rights, argues that despite some exceptions, prostitution amounts to a voluntary exchange of sexual services for money. The NTFP seeks to empower prostitutes to bargain with employers and improve their working conditions.[48] The NTFP is similar to COYOTE and CORP in its support of prostitution as legitimate work, as is the English Collective of Prostitutes, which argues that "for some women to get paid for what all women are expected to do for free is a source of power for all women to refuse *any* free sex."[49]

The Charter for the International Committee for Prostitutes Rights (ICPR), which sponsored the first and second World Whores' Congress, calls for the decriminalization of all aspects of adult prostitution and affirms the basic human rights of prostitutes to work, immigrate, and claim unemployment and health insurance.[50] The Draft Statement from the second Congress reads in part,

> [P]rostitutes reject support that requires them to leave prostitution; they object to being treated as symbols of oppression and demand recognition as workers. . . . Financial autonomy is basic to female survival, self-determination, self-respect, and self-development. . . . The ICPR affirms the right of women to financial initiative and financial gain, including the right to commercialize sexual service or sexual illusion (such as erotic media), and to save and spend their earnings according to their own needs and priorities.[51]

Dolores French, another outspoken representative of prostitutes' rights, says that she loves being a prostitute and that "[i]t's the most honest, rewarding work I've ever done."[52] She recounts how she became a prostitute shortly after a life-threatening experience made her regret "all the things I hadn't done."[53] She decided to "grab every appealing opportunity that came along and to experience as much about living as possible."[54] Her husband, the vice-president of the Georgia Civil Liberties Union, understands her job. He says, "[O]ur jobs are quite similar: We both free-lance, we both get paid in advance, we both try to get our clients off."[55] French served on the Mayor's Task Force on Prostitution in Atlanta and recommended legalization.[56]

Before accepting the CORP/ICPR position as the definitive word on what prostitutes think, one should consider that women in the indus-

---

[48] Id at 290.
[49] Nina Lopez-Jones, *Workers: Introducing the English Collective of Prostitutes*, in *Sex Work* 271, 273 (cited in note 47) (emphasis in the original).
[50] International Committee for Prostitutes' Rights, *International Committee for Prostitutes' Rights World Charter and World Whores' Congress Statements*, in *Sex Work* 305, 305 (cited in note 47).
[51] Id at 307-08.
[52] Dolores French with Linda Lee, *Working: My Life as a Prostitute* 162 (EP Dutton, 1988).
[53] Id at 9.
[54] Id.
[55] Id at 266.
[56] Id at 248.

try have not yet reached a consensus on whether prostitution is empowering for women. Some align themselves with Scott and French: the money is attractive and their husbands support their decision to work as prostitutes. One woman, for example, describes how prostitution enabled her to support a seriously ill son. She also says it enriched her life and that she befriended most of her clients.[57] "Prostitution served me very well indeed. It was a most useful tool. I have no regrets, no shame, no remorse."[58]

However, others testify to the harmful aspects of the trade. They recall emerging from years of denial or guilt and finally realizing that they had been oppressed by prostitution. For example, Judy Helfand says that she used to think turning men on sexually was an affirmation of her sexual power, but later changed her mind:

> What I never saw was that in basing my self worth on men's desire I was far from developing a true sense of worth based on self love.
>
> I see this false sense of power as one way internalized oppression keeps us down. . . . I see that wanting men to want you sexually is what men want.[59]

In an exchange at a conference on prostitution and pornography, one participant asked, "What's so terrible about fucking for a living? I like it, I can live out my fantasies."[60] Another replied,

> I don't know how you can possibly say, as busy as you are as a lady of the evening, that you like every sexual act, that you work out your fantasies! Come on, get serious! . . . Can you count how many tricks you've had? You mean you have that many fantasies? Isn't it about having money to survive? . . . Can't we teach women some skills so they can survive? I know that's your opinion, you like it, but prostitution to me was degrading. I grew to hate it. If I had had to fuck one more of them—boy, I would have killed him![61]

There are also organizations that work in direct opposition to CORP, COYOTE and the NTPF. Sarah Wynter, founder and editor of Women Hurt in Systems of Prostitution Engaged in Revolt (WHISPER), argues,

> There has been a deliberate attempt to validate men's perceived need, and self-proclaimed right, to buy and sell women's bodies for sexual use. This has been accomplished, in part, by euphemizing prostitution as an occupa-

---

[57] Sunny Carter, *A Most Useful Tool*, in *Sex Work* 159, 164 (cited in note 47).

[58] Id at 165.

[59] Judy Helfand, *Silence Again*, in *Sex Work* 99, 101 (cited in note 47).

[60] *From the Floor*, in *Good Girls* 48 (cited in note 44). In 1985, feminists and prostitutes met face-to-face at a conference in Toronto called Challenging Our Images: The Politics of Pornography and Prostitution, to discuss the problems of sexuality and the law. Sponsored by the Ontario Public Interest Group (OPIRG), the conference provided a rare opportunity for academics, activists, and sex trade workers to confront their misunderstandings of each other. Not only is this healthy for the feminist movement as a whole, but it is the most practical way of tackling the divisive questions raised by prostitution.

[61] Id at 49-50.

tion. Men have promoted the cultural myth that women actively seek out prostitution as a pleasurable economic alternative to low-paying, low-skilled, monotonous labor, conveniently ignoring the conditions that insure women's inequality and the preconditions which make women vulnerable to prostitution.[62]

Wynter maintains that prostitution is not a "valid," freely chosen occupation. She wants us "to stop defining prostitution as a victimless crime, and acknowledge it for what it is—a crime committed against women by men."[63]

Despite their disagreement over whether prostitution is a legitimate occupation, virtually all those with experience inside the industry agree that the current conditions under which prostitutes must work are intolerable. Nearly universal support exists among sex-trade workers for decriminalization as a necessary first step toward (in CORP and COYOTE's case) finally seeing prostitution as valid employment or (in WHISPER's case) finally eradicating it as a means of oppressing women. Despite their different ultimate goals, all sex-trade workers want control of their lives. As long as prostitution is criminalized, they say, they will not have it.

THE "CONSENT IS POSSIBLE APPROACH" (LIBERAL FEMINISM)

The assumptions about consent and coercion that inform the prostitutes' rights groups' position can be traced to traditional liberal theory, which is committed to autonomy, individualism, and minimal state interference in private choice. Liberal theory is premised on an assumption that individuals are atomistic, pre-social beings who exist independent of their community.[64] The justification for state power in the liberal paradigm is the notion of implied consent: individuals surrender a certain amount of authority to the state in order to protect the autonomy of

---

[62] Sarah Wynter, *Whisper: Women Hurt in Systems of Prostitution Engaged in Revolt*, in *Sex Work* 266, 266 (cited in note 47).

[63] Id at 270.

[64] John Locke, *Two Treatises of Government*, Peter Laslett, ed 287 (Cambridge U Press, 2d ed 1967). Locke describes the State of Nature which all men are naturally in as "a *State of perfect Freedom* to order their Actions, and dispose of their Possessions, and Persons as they think fit, within the bounds of the Law of Nature, without asking leave, or depending upon the Will of any other Man." Id (emphasis in the original). He describes the consent contemplated by liberal theory: " 'tis not every Compact that puts an end to the State of Nature between Men, but only this one of agreeing together mutually to enter into one Community, and make one Body Politick." Id at 294-95. He describes political power, which he distinguishes from both paternal and despotic power, as "that Power which every Man, having in the state of Nature, has given up into the hands of the Society . . . in all such cases, where the Society can secure him, is, to use such means for the preserving of his own Property, as he thinks good, and Nature allows him; and to punish the Breach of the Law of Nature in others so, as (according to the best of his Reason) may most conduce to the preservation of himself, and the rest of Mankind. . . . And this *Power has its Original only from Compact* and Agreement, and the mutual Consent of those who make up the Community." Id at 399-400 (emphasis in the original).

everyone.[65]

Feminist theory and critical legal studies have attempted to expose the inability of liberal theory to account for our connections to others, or our "social constitutiveness." The central features of liberalism—the public/private distinction, a highly individualistic conception of rights— are commonly attacked as inappropriate for, and unresponsive to, feminist demands for equality and freedom.[66]

To the extent that liberal feminism is traceable to liberalism, it too accepts the notion of a pre-social autonomous individual capable of consent and choice. I understand liberal feminism to be "mainstream" feminism, the popular feminism that Zillah Eisenstein attributes to Betty Friedan.[67] In my view, members of CORP and COYOTE and those feminists that support their position are essentially liberal and only reluctantly feminist. Their vision is one of equal access to an equality defined and perpetuated by men; it is not concerned with the sexual subordination of women as a "class" and the need for structural change.

Liberal theory has traditionally advocated formal equality, without attempting to significantly restructure society or question the assumption of choice and consent that informs liberal theory. It has been concerned with eliminating the legal constraints on women's access to the world of men by levelling the "playing field" so that the sexes can compete more fairly. Liberal feminism directs our attention to dismantling false perceptions about women's "difference" in order to maximize women's options, and it attempts to educate men about the negative consequences of stereotyping and generalizing about women. As Robin West points out,

> The "liberal-legal feminist" would characterize the legal culture's discriminatory treatment of women's suffering as the reflection of "perceptual error" committed by that culture. Women are in fact *the same as*—and therefore *equal to*—men, in the only sense which should matter to liberal legal theory. Women, like men, are autonomous individuals who, if free to

---

65 Thomas Hobbes, *Leviathan*, Michael Oakeshott, ed 56 (MacMillan, 1962): "The greatest of human powers, is that which is compounded of the powers of most men, united by consent, in one person, natural, or civil, that has the use of all their powers depending on his will; such is the power of a commonwealth." To Hobbes, the state of nature is a state of war in which men are driven by passion to pursue their private interests. Id at 98-102. Man consents to be governed by a sovereign to avoid a life of misery. Otherwise man lives in "continual fear, and danger of violent death; and the life of man, [is] solitary, poor, nasty, brutish, and short." Id at 100. Men have also made "artificial chains, called *civil laws*, which they themselves, by mutual covenants, have fastened at one end, to the lips of that man, or assembly, to whom they have given the sovereign power . . . ." Id at 160 (emphasis in the original). Since one consents, one cannot claim to be harmed by the sovereign. Hobbes writes, "[N]othing the sovereign representative can do to a subject, on what pretence soever, can properly be called injustice, or injury; because every subject is author of every act the sovereign doth . . . ." Id at 161.·

66 See, for example, Judy Fudge, *The Public/Private Distinction: The Possiblities of and the Limits to the Use of Charter Litigation to Further Feminist Struggles*, 25 Osgoode Hall L J 485 (1989).

67 Zillah Eisenstein, *The Radical Future of Liberal Feminism* 177 (Northeastern Press, 1981) ("*Radical Future*").

do so, will choose among proffered alternatives so as to fashion their own "good life," and thereby create social value.[68]

Because it assumes that people are autonomous, self-interested actors, I understand liberal feminist analysis to begin with a presumption of consent. That is, in the absence of clear evidence to the contrary, a woman who says "yes" consents, regardless of the social context, the woman's past experience, or the constraints of ascribing meaning to language. Because the liberal feminist is committed to maximizing autonomy and individual choice, she presumptively sees individual expressions of sexuality as implicitly consensual, liberating, and empowering. Commercializing sex per se does not bother her; it is up to the individual woman to decide if she wants to use her body in a way that brings her money and satisfaction, even if that means trading in sex.

Zillah Eisenstein describes liberal feminism as more sophisticated than a sum of liberalism and feminism. This is because she believes that liberal individualism is incompatible with feminist sex-class consciousness since the former depends on atomistic actors completely divorced from social influence, and the latter depends on connections amongst individuals.[69] Liberal theory is inadequate for feminist practice, according to Eisenstein, because it lacks a theory of sex-class consciousness. She argues that the challenge facing feminists is to realize the radical potential of liberal feminism which lies in devising a theory of sex-class based oppression, without abandoning the value of individuality adopted from liberalism. I understand Eisenstein's point to be that liberal feminism has sown the seeds of its own radicalization because, "the ideology of liberal individualism and the social reality of sex-class oppression . . . cannot be fully contained within the same politics successfully."[70]

Eisenstein envisions all feminism, from socialist to radical to lesbian, as rooted in a notion of individuality (which she says makes it "liberal" in origin), but distinguishes individuality from liberal individualism:

By "liberal individualism," I mean the view of the individual pictured as atomized and disconnected from the social relations that actually affect his or her choices and options; by "individuality," I refer to the capacities of the individual conceptualized as part of a social structure that can either enhance or constrain his or her individual potential for human development.[71]

I agree with Eisenstein to the extent that she rejects liberal theory as ill-suited to contemporary feminist practice and thought. Her conception of individuality has nothing to do with the liberal view of autonomy because the latter depends on a notion of individuals disconnected from

---

[68] Robin West, *The Difference in Women's Hedonic Lives: A Phenomenological Critique of Feminist Legal Theory*, 3 Wis Women's L J 81, 83 (1987) (emphasis in the original).

[69] Eisenstein, *Radical Future* at 116 (cited in note 67).

[70] Id at 179.

[71] Id at 114.

the social context which creates them and which they help create. Without explicitly saying so, and by distinguishing between liberal individualism (understood as separateness from social structure) and individuality (understood as independence within a potentially limiting social structure), Eisenstein redefines autonomy. Her version of individuality is quite different from liberalism's autonomy: "Feminism uses the individualist stance against men because men inhibit women's self and collective development; it need not extend this vision to premise women's isolation from one another."[72] It is true that Eisenstein's individuality and liberalism's autonomy contain some common features such as independence, but in general they are fundamentally and critically different.

If Eisenstein's purpose is to rescue liberal feminism as a viable feminist "category," I think she fails. Feminism stands in direct opposition to the central tenets of liberal theory, and the crux of the divergence is the meaning of autonomy. When she says that liberal feminism is more than the sum of liberalism and feminism because of her definition of individuality, she essentially reformulates liberal feminism to make it something non-liberal. I take from her work that we need to abandon liberalism and embrace feminism fully.[73]

However, Eisenstein's endorsement of individuality is a valuable acknowledgment that a conception of autonomy is something important for feminist theory.[74] What matters to me about autonomy is that one's view of it can account for whether or not one believes consent is possible. If, as Eisenstein proposes, individuality is socially contingent, then consent must be relative and free choice always limited by social structure. The autonomy posited by liberal individualism is, by contrast, absolute and unrestrained by social influence. Herein lies the root of the disagreement over consent between liberals and radical feminists. Liberals do not envision socially structured, subjectively mediated consent, while radicals do. Radical feminists criticize the simplistic liberal assumption that "yes," or even silence, is consent. Liberals resist the language of victimization used by radical feminists to describe a complete absence of consent.

If liberal feminism realizes its radical potential to develop a sex-class theory of oppression in the way Eisenstein suggests, how will it resolve the debate between those who support the right to choose prostitution as an exercise of autonomy and those who believe prostitution subordinates

---

[72] Id at 154.
[73] MacKinnon agrees that liberal feminism is a misnomer: "Feminism has been widely thought to contain tendencies of liberal feminism, radical feminism, and socialist feminism. But just as socialist feminism has often amounted to traditional Marxism . . . liberal feminism has been liberalism applied to women. Radical feminism is feminism." Catharine A. MacKinnon, *Toward a Feminist Theory of the State* 117 (Harv U Press, 1989) ("*Feminist Theory*").
[74] See Jennifer Nedelsky, *Reconceiving Autonomy: Sources, Thoughts and Possibilities*, 1 Yale J of L & Fem 7 (1989).

women as a class? The answer depends on what autonomy would look like post-radicalization. A concept of autonomy that fits both Eisenstein's notion of individuality and a theory of sex-class oppression cannot be the same as the autonomy of liberal individualism which places individual license to do as one pleases ahead of community interests.[75] It will inevitably be a conception of autonomy that understands and responds to group harm. Adopting such a notion of autonomy reinforces the idea that prostitutes do not exist in isolation from their social context. Adopting this view of autonomy reinforces the claim that the harm prostitution causes to women as a class matters, and that consent is socially contingent.

Prostitutes' rights groups do not acknowledge the contradiction in their politics that Eisenstein points out is inherent in liberal feminism, and they do not fit within her reformulation because they minimize the harmful impact that prostitution has on women as a class. In many cases, prostitutes' rights groups see feminism as another enemy, along with the police and government. Feminists are either self-righteous puritans or unrealistic academics. Valerie Scott of CORP says,

> The feminist vision is unhealthy because it is cloning sexuality. What they're trying to do is set up a structure around people's sexuality. . . . So the vision to us really calls a lot of things into question.
>
> First of all, it calls into question the feminist understanding of what being human is all about. Second, it is so presumptuous and arrogant to think that we can really clearly imagine an egalitarian society and protect it from today's fuck-ups. What are they doing talking about it?[76]

CORP and COYOTE's essentially liberal argument is that women and men should be permitted to use their bodies and express their sexuality as they see fit. Underlying this position is an assumption that choice is possible and that prostitutes are entitled to determine for themselves whether selling sex is harmful. They encourage prostitution as sexual expression, even if it is considered "deviant," because it is private, freely chosen, and harmless to those not involved in the transaction. Harm is defined restrictively so that contributing to the subordination of women as a class does not count.

Although prostitutes' rights groups are fairly clear on their analysis of harm, their position on the possibility of choice is more confusing. I think they must be saying one of two things: either that choice exists (without really analyzing to what extent that is true, and whether this

---

[75] Such a concept of autonomy would not permit what Kathleen Barry calls "valueless individualism." Barry, *Sexual Slavery* at 262-66 (cited in note 5).

[76] *Realistic Feminists* in *Good Girls* at 208-09 (cited in note 44). Although they may see feminists as the enemy, prostitutes' rights groups are not "anti-feminist" in the sense discussed earlier. They are not opposed to feminism as an idea or equality and empowerment as goals. They do, however, oppose the feminism that seeks the eradication of prostitution, the feminism they perceive to be dominant in our culture. Id at 204-05.

choice varies among "classes" of prostitutes)[77] or that hookers have as little real choice as all women and they are trying to make the best of their situation in a world of coercion. These two statements mean very different things in terms of the presumption of consent. I understand CORP to be arguing the former: that prostitutes have and make choices and, furthermore, that other women should not criticize prostitution as harmful when they are guilty of "commercializing" sex themselves, by choice, in more subtle ways.

Prostitution is largely a response to a lack of economic alternatives. It is not surprising that women do it for the money. As Simone de Beauvoir remarks,

> It is naive to wonder what motives drive woman to prostitution. . . . The truth is that in a world where misery and unemployment prevail, there will be people to enter any profession that is open. . . . It is often asked: why does she choose it? The question is, rather: why has she not chosen it?[78]

However, despite the obvious constraints that economic need imposes on women, prostitutes' rights groups refuse to acknowledge the relativity of choice. The only situations they acknowledge as coercive are those in which the use of force is extremely obvious, such as when pimps use threats and violence to keep teenage runaways in the trade.

Even if prostitutes' rights groups would agree that a presumption of coercion is appropriate in cases where the activity in question is incompatible with individual freedom (slavery is an example), they would insist that prostitution enhances freedom. Rather than extinguish autonomy, prostitution enables it to flourish. Prostitutes may surrender themselves to the desires of others, but only for discrete periods and ideally under conditions they control. They can withdraw their services at their discretion. Their autonomy is never irretrievable. This is, of course, just one picture of prostitution, and the one portrayed by CORP to be most accurate.[79]

CORP does not seem concerned with the extent to which authentic choice depends on the context in which it is exercised. CORP's leadership argues that decriminalizing and legitimizing prostitution promotes autonomy and is also the only effective way of minimizing the coercion

---

[77] It is impossible to avoid the class implications of COYOTE's or CORP's defense of prostitution. High class call-girls with some control over their working environment and clientele obviously have a different quality of "choice" than teenagers faced with the threats of street life. Prostitution reform should not be designed with only the high class "businesswoman" hooker in mind—to think they represent the prostitution trade is to gloss over the majority of women working under conditions that are considerably less safe.

[78] Simone de Beauvoir, *The Second Sex*, H.M. Parshely, ed & trans 524-25 (Bantam Books, 1952).

[79] The other picture, described by Kathleen Barry, portrays prostitution as inherently coercive. To Barry, prostitution is synonymous with sexual slavery and the constituency that CORP seems to represent—self-possessed, college educated, and high class hookers—is really a small minority of the huge numbers of women coerced into selling sex. See Barry, *Sexual Slavery* at 39-40 (cited in note 5).

present in "exceptional" cases. If prostitutes are permitted to organize, form support groups, and run self-help networks, they will then be able to exert some control over the coercive elements of the sex-trade. Putting power into the hands of the women in the industry will enable them to prevent the worst abuses of the system. Obviously, the "consent is possible" approach is fuelled by the claim that prostitutes make free choices. Many feminists have challenged that claim by questioning the accuracy of the liberal version of freedom. Radical feminists have directed their attention, instead, to coercion.

THE "CONSENT IS NOT POSSIBLE" APPROACH

Contrary to liberal feminism, radical feminism focuses on sexuality as the mechanism of women's oppression. It has the sex-class consciousness that Eisenstein says liberalism lacks and, because it rejects the central tenets of liberalism, it does not assume that individuals exist in isolation from social context. Radical feminism has traditionally sought to expose and change the fact that we live in a male-defined, male-centered world in which women are objectified through sexuality. It seeks to displace the ubiquitous male voice with a multiplicity of female voices. It places value on subjectivity over objectivity, intuition over proof, community over individuality.[80] Consciousness-raising is its method and epistemology. Radical feminists have historically seen heterosexuality, pregnancy, and childrearing as institutions forced by men on women and used by men to reinforce male dominance.[81]

Radical feminists reject the notion that women are empowered by fulfilling male desire, and they see the desire for prostitution as male. They would likely dismiss Scott and French as having internalized male justifications for exploiting women and would treat prostitutes as victims, even if some insist that they enjoy their work and have freely chosen it.[82] Radical feminists say that prostitution is not a harmless, "private" transaction but a powerful means of creating, reinforcing, and perpetuating the objectification of women through sexuality.[83] They do not take the criminalization of prostitution to mean that society is committed to undoing the subordination of women. Rather, it serves as proof that female sexuality is not only manufactured by men, but also legally controlled through the exercise of authority in order to keep women isolated and powerless.[84] Society's acceptance of the persistent male demand for

---

[80] Alison M. Jaggar, *Feminist Politics and Human Nature* (Rowman & Allanheld, 1983).
[81] See generally, Catharine A. MacKinnon, *Feminism Unmodified* (Harv U Press, 1987); Catharine A. MacKinnon, *Feminism, Marxism, Method and the State: An Agenda for Theory*, 7 Signs 515 (1982).
[82] Barry, *Sexual Slavery* at 119-20 (cited in note 5).
[83] Id at 135-36.
[84] Andrea Dworkin, *Letters from a War Zone* 120 (Secker & Warburg, 1988). Dworkin writes: Hard-working prostitutes earn enormous gross sums of money (compared to gross

prostitutes only reminds us that all women are thought to be accessible (for a price) and that their commodification is natural.

Carole Pateman points out that in all traditional theories of the state women have never been seen as "individuals" capable of making contracts; rather, they are the subject of them. She criticizes classic social contract theory as incomplete because it represses one of its most central elements—the sexual contract. She explains the relationship between women and contract:

> Women are not party to the original contract through which men transform their natural freedom into the security of civil freedom. Women are the subject of the contract. The (sexual) contract is the vehicle through which men transform their natural right over women into the security of civil patriarchal right.[85]

The difference between men and women is constructed through contract, she says, into the difference between freedom and subjection. She calls the liberal justification of prostitution a "contractarian defence" because it attributes "the lack of acceptance of the prostitute . . . to the hypocrisy and distorted attitudes surrounding sexual activity," without addressing the role that prostitution plays in the political subordination of women.[86]

Radical feminism understands prostitution to be a microcosm of gender hierarchy. It not only encapsulates but reinforces the objectification of women. Even an argument that prostitution has "therapeutic" potential for providing sex to those who are socially or sexually dysfunctional cannot, to the radical feminist, redeem an institution that is so central to male dominance. In the story of the sexual contract, argues Pateman, "[P]rostitution is part of the exercise of the law of male sex-right, one of the ways in which men are ensured access to women's bodies . . . ."[87] She goes on to say that male access to females, "is part of the construction of what it means to be a man, part of the contemporary expression of masculine sexuality."[88]

The liberal would criticize the radical feminist approach as patronizing. It tells women who hold a positive view of prostituting themselves

---

sums typically earned by other women), but they do not go on to become financiers or founders of universitites. Instead, their money goes to men, because men control, profit from, and perpetuate female prostitution. The men their money goes to are pimps, racketeers, lawyers, police, and the like, all of whom, because they are men and not women, can turn that money into more money, social status, and influence. The prostitute herself is marked with a scarlet "W"—stigmatized as whore, ostracized as whore, exiled as whore into a world circumscribed by organized crime, narcotics, and the notorious brutality of pimps. The prostitute's utterly degraded social status functions to punish her for daring to make money at all. The abuse that accrues to her prevents her from translating money into dignity or self-determination; it serves to keep her in her place, female, cunt, at the mercy of the men who profit from her flesh.

[85] Carole Pateman, *The Sexual Contract* 6 (Stanford U Press, 1988).
[86] Id at 200.
[87] Id.
[88] Id at 199.

that they are deluded. It denies the reality and validity of their experience. The radical approach to the prostitution debate, with its condemnation of the subordination inherent in prostitution and its emphasis on power relations at a macro level, is not helpful for prostitutes who feel that state regulation, not male-defined sexuality, is responsible for the lack of control over their lives.[89]

Catharine MacKinnon, who I take as an example of a radical feminist, argues that sexuality defines gender through the eroticization of submission and dominance. Prostitution and pornography are central to that process. The power differential between men and women is socially and sexually constructed and so pervasive that it usually goes unnoticed. MacKinnon writes, "The perspective from the male standpoint enforces woman's definition, encircles her body, circumlocutes her speech, and describes her life. The male perspective is systemic and hegemonic."[90] The world MacKinnon sees is one in which "female" and "feminine" attributes correspond directly to what society does not value, or values only as objects, while male and masculine attributes are highly prized. MacKinnon argues that it is impossible to conceive of an alternative female sexuality until men get their feet "off our necks."[91]

Unlike liberalism, which is premised on the notion of an autonomous self, MacKinnon's analysis leads us to question whether we have a "self" at all.

> If women are socially defined such that female sexuality cannot be lived or spoken or felt or even somatically sensed apart from its enforced definition, so that it *is* its own lack, then there is no such thing as a woman as such, there are only walking embodiments of men's projected needs. For feminism, asking whether there is, socially, a female sexuality is the same as asking whether women exist.[92]

MacKinnon's analysis begins with a presumption of coercion. If we have no "self," it is difficult to imagine how we can consent to anything. The presumption of coercion forces us to confront the fact that our ability to consent is always socially constrained. MacKinnon offers the law of rape as an example of the illusion of consent:

> The law of rape presents consent as free exercise of sexual choice under

---

[89] One feminist issued this warning:
> As feminists we cannot disregard the suffering of individual women or groups of women. Our experience of being told to place our legitimate demands on the back burner until "more important" problems were solved should make us especially sensitive to the dangers of ignoring immediate human pain in the service of theoretical revolution.

Christine Littleton, *In Search of a Feminist Jurisprudence*, 10 Harv Women's L J 1, 5 (1987) (discussing necessity of including both individual women and groups in feminist jurisprudence).

[90] Catharine A. MacKinnon, *Feminism, Marxism, Method and the State: Toward Feminist Jurisprudence*, 8 Signs 635, 636 (1983).

[91] Ellen DuBois, et al, *Feminist Discourse, Moral Values and the Law: A Conversation* (James McCormick Mitchell Lecture, 1984), 34 Buff L Rev 11, 28 (1985).

[92] MacKinnon, 7 Signs at 534 (cited in note 81).

conditions of equality of power without exposing the underlying structure of constraint and disparity. Fundamentally, desirability to men is supposed a woman's form of power because she can both arouse it and deny its fulfillment. To woman is attributed both the cause of man's initiative and the denial of his satisfaction. This rationalizes force. Consent in this model becomes more a metaphysical quality of a woman's being than a choice she makes and communicates. Exercise of women's so-called power presupposes more fundamental social powerlessness.[93]

The pervasiveness of coercion should be a signal that women have not participated in the definition of their own sexuality. Although it is difficult to "prove" that MacKinnon's picture of the world is true, if one looks at how women are treated in this society, there is ample evidence that the male construction of women's sexuality serves male purposes exclusively.[94] Men manufacture pornography for a male audience and traffic in women to feed male consumption. Women are seen as sexual objects and victims. Their vulnerability to male violence makes them dependent on some men to protect them from other men. Under current conditions, women are overwhelmingly victims of male violence—not the other way around. These observations should lead one to suspect that the socially constructed view of women's sexuality may be "inauthentic" for women and that the possibility of real choice is limited at best.

A central argument in MacKinnon's critique is that women participate in their own subordination. They internalize dominance and submission as "normal" sexuality and, therefore, find accounts of oppression incompatible with their perception of their own experience. MacKinnon implies that women are not aware of what is in their own self-interest, since they perceive their needs only as a reflection of male desire.[95]

The circularity of that argument makes it difficult to refute. If one denies being subordinated, the disagreement itself is illustrative of collaborating in one's oppression. MacKinnon's analysis is frequently criticized as a betrayal of feminist methodology because it distrusts women and discounts the possibility of consensual submission. West has critiqued the radical feminist conclusion that women suffer from false consciousness:

> The judgment of falsehood is almost always against the will as well as the opinion of the woman who has the desire [for erotic submission]. This truly is a profound departure from feminist methodology which is also truly offensive—consciousness-raising is not about the imposition of judgments of truth or falsity on the desires of others.[96]

MacKinnon herself is a glaring example of why her analysis, if taken literally, cannot be true. How does she know this? What is the epis-

---

[93] MacKinnon, *Feminist Theory* at 175 (cited in note 73).
[94] MacKinnon, *Feminism Unmodified* at 23 (cited in note 81).
[95] See MacKinnon, 7 Signs at 534 (cited in note 81).
[96] West, 3 Wis Women's L J at 123 (cited in note 68).

tomological value of her critique if one never knows the difference between "glimpsing freedom"[97] and living male fantasies?

At least one feminist has criticized MacKinnon for failing to provide a theory of consciousness. Ruth Colker says that a woman has no basis for knowing whether or not to agree with MacKinnon because she must distrust her own perceptions of her condition. Colker maintains that without a theory of consciousness to explain what women should believe, MacKinnon's theory is "pure assertion."[98] Whether one thinks that women can "know" their own sexuality, or at least recognize it, has to do with the degree to which one believes women can tell the difference between engaging in their own pleasure and collaborating in their oppression.[99]

MacKinnon and radical feminists, like liberal feminists, do not pay enough attention to the relativity of consent. Liberal feminism assumes without explanation that choice is possible. MacKinnon resolves the matter in an equally unsatisfying way by assuming that choice is not possible for women under current conditions of male dominance, where, "[f]orce is exercised as consent, its authority as participation."[100] In my view, the notion that consent is relative and socially contingent makes sense within a feminist framework. It fits well with the value feminists place on subjectivity and community, but MacKinnon seems not to acknowledge the possibility of consent in a world where women's sexual-

---

[97] MacKinnon, *Feminism Unmodified* at 218 (cited in note 81). "Sex feeling good may mean . . . that one has glimpsed freedom, a rare and valuable and contradictory event."

[98] Conversation with Ruth Colker, Nov 17, 1988, during Feminist Bridge Week at the University of Toronto Faculty of Law.

[99] Colker argues that the first step in addressing this problem of consciousness is trying to discover one's authentic self, the self that is removed from patriarchy. This would be a positive, constructive process through which women would glimpse their freedom as well as their brokenness.

> The search for authenticity can be a dynamic feminist-spiritual journey. We can try to create a space of inner peace where we can catch a glimpse of ourselves removed from patriarchy and the other limiting influences of modern society. In this state of inner peace we can attempt to discover our selves behind and beyond our selves—what I call our 'authentic' selves.

Ruth Colker, *Feminism, Sexuality and Self: A Preliminary Inquiry into the Politics of Authenticity* (Book Review), 68 Boston U L Rev 217, 219-20 (1988) (footnotes omitted).

> Colker's vision clearly emanates from a radical perspective but her preoccupation with articulating how to arrive at an alternative to gender hierarchy departs from the radical position that we should focus on our current oppressive reality. Because prostitution embodies and perpetuates that oppressive reality, the radical feminist finds prostitution unacceptable. MacKinnon would likely argue that imagining what an authentic self would be like in a different world distracts us from the very real problem of dismantling gender hierarchy. In my view, Colker is also subject to the criticism that the idea of an authentic self is essentialist and unrealistic in a world in which the "self" is constructed.

[100] MacKinnon, 8 Signs at 683 (cited in note 90).

> That consent rather than nonmutuality is the line between rape and intercourse further exposes the inequality in normal social expectations. So does the substantial amount of male force allowed in the focus on the woman's resistance, which tends to be disabled by socialization to passivity. If sex is ordinarily accepted as something men do *to* women, the better question would be whether consent is a meaningful concept.

MacKinnon, 7 Signs at 532 (cited in note 81) (emphasis in the original).

ity is not their own. This refusal to acknowledge the possibility of consent is ironic since her vision of a truly "female" sexuality (implied by her critique of the male colonization of female sexuality) depends, in my view, on a fluid notion of consent. Admittedly, in MacKinnon's most recent work, she has explained the underlying constraints on consent more fully, but this analysis leads to the conclusion that genuine consent does not exist. She writes,

Consent is supposed to be women's form of control over intercourse, different from but equal to the custom of male initiative. Man proposes, woman disposes. Even the ideal is not mutual. Apart from the disparate consequences of refusal, this model does not envision a situation the woman controls being placed in, or choices she frames.[101]

CONSENT AND CONSCIOUSNESS

Neither radical feminism nor liberalism offers an account of the complexity of the underlying structural constraints on the meaning of consent. In liberal discourse, consent is assumed as a constant. If MacKinnon is right about the inevitability of collaborating in our own oppression, there is no hope for consent. Her critique denies the subjective ability of individuals to participate in its construction. For the radical feminist then, even saying "yes" in a given situation does not guarantee an absence of coercion. Neither does it incorporate the structure and fluidity of consent into the interaction. Rather, as Judith Vega argues, it assumes a "moment of choice" and allows women to believe in "the illusion of their own autonomy."[102] I cannot accept, however, that there is no possibility of women's self-determination and self-definition. MacKinnon does not claim that women are incapable of self-knowledge, and I would argue that her critique assumes that possibility. There must be hope for consent; if it is subjective and fluid, it must have transitional potential.

Proponents of critical legal theory argue that individuals determine what consent means in any given situation within the context of their own past experience and present knowledge; they mediate structure through a complex process of sifting and internalizing dominant social norms and contextual factors.[103] Consent is structural and changeable. Interpreting what consent means in a given situation is partly objective, and partly subjective. One is constrained to a certain extent by socially determined meanings (for instance, the common definition of intercourse versus rape), but interpreting one's experience of an event is always sub-

---

[101] MacKinnon, *Feminist Theory* at 174 (cited in note 73).
[102] Judith Vega, *Coercion and Consent: Classic Liberal Concepts in Texts on Sexual Violence*, 16 Intl J Soc L 75, 81 (1988).
[103] Rosemary J. Coombe, *Room For Manoeuver: Towards a Theory of Practice in Critical Legal Studies*, L & Soc Inq 69, 79-83 (1989).

jective. So when one consents, one is both responding to and creating the meaning of the term at a particular time in a particular context. A woman's past experience, her socialized self-image, her fears and expectations about sexuality—all of these are in play when she says yes, no, or remains silent.

Given the complexity of such an analysis of consent, I am skeptical about the liberal feminist assumption that choice is the norm and that it is absent only in extreme circumstances which we "objectively" recognize as coercion (i.e., the rapist is using a gun). The fixed nature of liberal consent fails to appreciate the importance of social context and human mediation. If consent and coercion are two ends of a spectrum, and if most decisions are to some extent constrained by structure and subjectivity, it becomes more difficult to accept as the norm the autonomy on which the liberal prostitutes' rights approach is premised. If consent really exists (and there are those who doubt that it is "ontologically" possible[104]), we must look at the factors that minimize, undermine, or extinguish it in order to work toward authentic consent.

If our common understanding of rape is at one end of the spectrum under "absence of consent" and a fully mutual, chosen, equal sexual interaction is at the other end under "presence of consent," we must determine what fits the definition of mutual, chosen, and equal and inquire whether those are even things that we want sex to be. If it does not matter to us that sex be equal or mutual, or if we think, in fact, that pleasurable and satisfying sex depends on inequality, non-mutuality, and power imbalance, then we have to adjust our criteria for consent accordingly.

The relationship between coercion and consent is not new to feminist theory, but it has yet to be fully explored. Vega argues that "[f]eminist politics as well as theory have declared the incompatibility of coercion and genuine consent. It is precisely this thinking in opposites . . . that paralyzes feminist thought about sexual violence."[105] She supports the restoration of the concept of consent as something socially constructed and capable of new meaning and believes consent reconceived should replace self-determination as the central feature of liberation.[106] When one begins to see consent as structural, two possibilities arise. As Vega describes it, "Either women's lives are ruled by force and all sexual relationships are variations on this, or one acknowledges an area of sexuality ruled by freedom of choice, set apart from the area of force."[107] I would argue that both of these propositions are true to women's experi-

---

[104] Margaret Hunt, *Report of a Conference on Feminism, Sexuality and Power: The Elect Clash with the Perverse* ("*Conf on Feminism*") in SAMOIS, eds, *Coming to Power* 81, 87-88 (Alyson, 3d ed 1987).
[105] Vega, 16 Intl J Soc L at 84 (cited in note 102).
[106] Id at 86-87.
[107] Id at 77.

ence of their sexuality. The difficulty lies in recognizing what feels free and working towards it.

Interestingly, Vega thinks MacKinnon's critique does contain a concept of authenticity in that MacKinnon identifies consciousness-raising as "the" feminist method and epistomology and bases her argument on women's reports of their own experience.[108] Vega says that in MacKinnon's work, "A female authenticity appears, which, in miraculous ways, turns out to be void of both passion and rationality, coercion and consent, dominance and submission."[109]

Vega goes on to criticize MacKinnon's concept of authenticity because it relies on an essentialist, liberal notion of the subject. This analysis would pose problems for MacKinnon since she clearly repudiates liberal theory.[110] I think the bigger problem is that MacKinnon validates only women's reports of subordination and not their reports of autonomy through submission. She is willing to acknowledge only victimization as legitimate, without providing a satisfying theoretical basis for doing so.[111]

One obstacle to developing a theory of consciousness or exploring

---

[108] Id at 83.

[109] Id. Of course, even if we could determine what "authentic" consent felt like, it would be impossible to ignore the structures of language and meaning by which it is constrained.

[110] MacKinnon only has this to say about the feminist unconscious, or what others have called the concept of authenticity:

> There may be a feminist unconscious, but it is not the Freudian one. Perhaps equality lives there. Its laws, rather than a priori, objective, or universal, might as well be a response to the historical regularities of sexual subordination, which under bourgeois ideological conditions require that the truth of male dominance be concealed in order to preserve the belief that women are sexually self-acting: that women want it. The feminist psychic universe certainly recognizes that people do not always know what they want, have hidden desires and inaccessible needs, lack awareness of motivation, have contorted and opaque interactions, and have an interest in obscuring what is really going on.

MacKinnon, *Feminist Theory* at 153 (cited in note 73).

[111] As far as I can tell, MacKinnon's justification for not pursuing the concept of authenticity further is that we are too constrained by male ideology to imagine ourselves outside it, and trying to do so diverts our energy from effecting political change.

> So long as sexual inequality remains unequal and sexual, attempts to value sexuality as women's, possessive as if women possess it, will remain part of limiting women to it, to what women are now defined as being. Outside of truly rare and contrapuntal glimpses (which most people think they live almost their entire sex life within), to seek an equal sexuality without political transformation is to seek equality under conditions of inequality.

Id at 153-54.

> In order to account for women's consciousness (much less propagate it) feminism must grasp that male power produces the world before it distorts it. Women's acceptance of their condition does not contradict its fundamental unacceptability if women have little choice but to *become* persons who freely choose women's roles. For this reason, the reality of women's oppression is, finally, neither demonstrable nor refutable empirically. Until this is confronted on the level of method, criticsm of what exists can be undercut by pointing to the reality to be criticized. Women's bondage, degradation, damage, complicity, and inferiority—together with the possibility of resistance, movement, or exceptions—will operate as barriers to consciousness rather than as means of access to what women need to become conscious of in order to change.

MacKinnon, 7 Signs at 542 (cited in note 81) (emphasis in the original).

the possibility of authenticity is the degree to which our culture is immersed in liberal ideology. Having internalized liberalism, we may not even realize that consent has limitations at all. Eisenstein explains the dialectic between ideology[112] and women's consciousness:

Ideology can intervene and limit one's consciousness of one's real conditions. Consciousness can obstruct the affects [sic] of ideology. Life conditions can obstruct consciousness. As such, the realms merge, and actual conditions come to include individual consciousness and ideology. Ideology becomes a part of the relations of power. . . . If consciousness is central to the understanding of ideology and its political force, and hence politics and political change, then we need to give the role of consciousness its due importance when we think about social change.[113]

The liberal individualist understanding of consent is an example of how ideology affects consciousness. Much of women's misery could be thought of as voluntary. To the extent that women marry, seek employment, and engage in heterosexual sex, they expose themselves to abuse, sexual harassment, and male expectations of their sexuality, all of which are often pleasurable for men and painful for women. And yet, to some extent all of these social arrangements are consensual. Liberal theory does not reflect the fact that choice and consent mean different things for men and women and that women's "choices" usually reinforce male power. In the liberal paradigm, when subjects do not explicitly choose to submit to state authority, tacit consent is imputed to them. As Vega points out, "Freedom includes submission, and submission includes freedom. Within the liberal theory, this is . . . never considered to be a serious dilemma for the autonomous subject: he survives without hesitation."[114]

Some feminists would argue that it is exactly this kind of contradiction that feminism should acknowledge and embrace. West, for example, defends sadomasochism as an example of voluntary submission.[115] Sadomasochists emphasize, "S/M is . . . freely chosen by people fully in command of their faculties."[116] West wants feminism to start paying attention to the contradictions in women's reports of what they experience as pleasure. According to West, both liberal and radical theory are inadequate because they fundamentally conflict with the traditional values and methodology of feminism:

[I]n both cases the theory does not pay enough attention to feminism: liberal feminist legal theory owes more to liberalism than to feminism and radical feminist legal theory owes more to radicalism than it does to femi-

---

112 Ideology is defined here as a system of ideas or beliefs that reflects social relations and also creates them. Eisenstein says ideology "mystifies" reality. Eisenstein, *Radical Future* at 10 (cited in note 67).
113 Id.
114 Vega, 16 Intl J Soc L at 79 (cited in note 102).
115 West, 3 Wis Women's L J at 129 (cited in note 68).
116 Hunt, *Conf on Feminism*, in *Coming to Power* at 87 (cited in note 104).

nism. Both models accept a depiction of human nature which is simply untrue of women.[117]

West argues that the radical goal of increasing women's power fails to ask the more important question: what will increase women's pleasure?[118]

Quite apart from my discomfort with making maximum pleasure the primary feminist goal, the problem with West's permissive approach to consent is that it purports to describe both the freedom and the submission of the subject simultaneously. This description is unacceptable to feminists who reject that possibility as a rationalization for male dominance and who daily confront society's insistence that women have consented to their subordination.

ANOTHER PERSPECTIVE

In contrast to the maximum pleasure approach, the concept of human dignity or personhood can provide the basis for an argument for decriminalizing prostitution while criminalizing its companion activities without resort to the liberal or radical feminist arguments presented above. For example, Margaret Radin has argued that the universal commodification of sexuality would be damaging to human flourishing.[119] I take Radin to mean that prostitution under any circumstances is damaging to women and society in general. Radin's opposition to prostitution does not strike me as particularly feminist; she just thinks there is something wrong with commercializing sexuality. She argues that there are certain things so closely connected to our personhood that they are "market-inalienable."[120] That is, they cannot be commodified, bought, and sold, or conceived of in market terms without harming the way we think about our sexuality and spirituality—things that are central to human flourishing.[121]

Some critics might challenge her proposition that there is something wrong with universal commodification, but I will assume for the moment

---

[117] West, 3 Wis Women's L J at 89 (cited in note 68).

[118] West thinks both liberal and radical theory miss the mark for feminism.

> [L]iberal-legal feminist theorists—true to their liberalism—want women to have more choices, and . . . radical-legal feminist theorists—true to their radicalism—want women to have more power. Both models direct our critical attention outward—liberalism to the number of choices we have, radicalism to the amount of power. Neither model of legal criticism, and therefore, derivatively, of feminist legal criticism, posits subjective happiness as the direct goal of legal reform, or subjective suffering as the direct evil to be eradicated. Neither model directs our critical attention inward. Consequently, and unsurprisingly, neither liberal nor radical feminist legal critics have committed themselves to the task of determining the measure of women's happiness or suffering.

Id at 87 (emphasis in the original).

[119] Margaret J. Radin, Market Inalienability, 100 Harv L Rev 1849, 1903-05, 1922 (1987).

[120] Id at 1903.

[121] Id at 1903-09.

that most of us would find it offensive to conceive of everything, from our work to our sexuality, entirely in market terms. To me, the idea that certain things belong outside the market realm is an intuitive one. Radin devotes much of her paper to explaining this intuition through an analysis of how commodification stifles human development and results in a "divided self"—the result of seeing one's attributes as separate, severable, and marketable commodities.[122]

Ideally we think of sexuality as something we experience consensually, mutually, and equally. Conceiving of sexuality in market terms dehumanizes how we think and act about something extremely important to our conception of self.[123] It would reduce sexuality to just another fungible good because commodification leads to "the domino effect"—the tendency in our society to completely commodify in all respects and for all purposes that which is commodified at all.[124] The existence of some commodified sexual interactions threatens to contaminate everyone's sexuality.[125] Under ideal conditions, to avoid the domino effect, we must reject prostitution as a valid occupation. Its effect on human flourishing is devastating because it objectifies women as a class and encourages a view of sexuality as a severable, tradeable good.[126]

Radin points out the difficulty in determining which goods should be commodified at all and to what extent.[127] She suggests, "One way to mediate the dilemma is through . . . incomplete commodification. . . . [I]ncomplete commodification . . . can sometimes substitute for a complete noncommodification that might accord with our ideals but cause too much harm in our nonideal world."[128] The approach could be seen as a compromise because it supports the radical feminist goal of eliminating prostitution while acknowledging the harm that criminalization does to women under current conditions.[129] Although the ideal of human flourishing supports the market-inalienability of certain "goods," criminalizing the sale of those goods may itself deny that ideal.[130] Still, " . . . despite the double bind and the harms of the black market to prostitutes, fear of a domino effect could perhaps warrant market-inalienability as an effort to ward off conceiving of all sexuality as fungible."[131]

But as Radin herself points out, the fundamental assumption that sex is an equal and consensual sharing may be false in a society where

---

122 Id at 1916.
123 Id at 1922.
124 Id at 1912-13.
125 Id at 1922.
126 Id.
127 Id at 1916-17.
128 Id at 1917-18.
129 Id at 1923. However, at first glance, her argument suggests that the state should mobilize its coercive power to prevent the commodification of sex because it threatens "personhood" in a very fundamental way.
130 Radin calls this the "double bind." Id at 1915-17.
131 Id at 1922.

women are already commodified.[132] Since sexuality is already incompletely commodified (in the sense that there are some aspects of it that are already conceived of and accepted in market terms, i.e., prostitution), she argues that we should adopt a legislative approach that reflects incomplete commodification.[133] Women should not be punished by repressive laws, but any activity that encourages trafficking in women's bodies, such as pimping, advertising, and recruitment should be criminal.[134] Radin wants, in effect, to cut our losses by adopting a principle that does not saddle women who are already victims of commodification with more pain, but which at the same time does not encourage an institution that offends human flourishing. In the end, Radin prefers to work toward the ideal by opting for that which does the least amount of harm to the victims of our nonideal society. In effect, she opts for Canada's status quo.[135]

I think Radin understands, at some level, the limitations on women's consent and tries to accommodate them. However, her approach would satisfy neither prostitutes' rights groups nor radical feminists. CORP and COYOTE would argue that women often freely choose pimps as business representatives. Advertising is essential to doing business and recruitment should be permissible since prostitution is respectable work, like any other work. They would reject Radin's pragmatic approach because many of the sanctions she wants to retain still directly or indirectly punish prostitutes. Liberal prostitutes' rights groups might say that Radin's theory does not enhance women's choices but rather takes steps to minimize some imagined harm to women as a concession to the radical feminist notion that women are merely victims of a patriarchal society.

Radical feminists would say that sexuality is in fact completely commodified and would ask how Radin's ideal can still be attainable by a theory that incorrectly describes social reality. Though Radin's ideal may be an unmonetized "free" exchange of sexuality, the reality of women's social condition precludes it. Many heterosexual relationships are reducible to an exchange of sex for money. As Radin herself points out, "[A]ttempted noncommodification means that prostitutes are being singled out for punishment for something pervasive in women's condition, and that they are being singled out because their class or race forecloses more socially accepted forms of sexual bargaining."[136]

I am not sure that I agree with Radin that the only way out of this "ideological bondage" is to maintain the ideal of noncommodified sexual-

---

[132] Id at 1923.
[133] Id at 1924-25.
[134] Id at 1923-25.
[135] See the Canadian legislative approach, cited in note 22, and accompanying text.
[136] Radin, 100 Harv L Rev at 1923 (cited in note 119).

ity. Perhaps the ideal is what keeps women locked into misconceptions about their sexuality and gender. They are socialized to believe sex is an equal exchange without ever inquiring whether it actually is. Radin even admits that the ideal might be the reason women continue to try to understand their relationships without recognizing their reality.[137]

WHY THE RADICAL FEMINISTS ARE RIGHT

There is a certain amount of hostility between prostitutes' rights groups and feminists, although both purport to be working to benefit women. The following is an exchange between Valerie Scott and an interviewer:

> Laurie Bell: Do you believe feminists have colluded with the rest of society to corrupt what is essentially a good profession, a necessary service?
> CORP: Very much so. That comes into where they're pimping us. They're hiding again behind all that facade and all the little fears to make us work in a really dangerous environment to keep our scores down. We think that feminists are right in there with the Moral Majority . . .[138]

I would argue that CORP misunderstands the radical feminist opposition to prostitution since, as I argued earlier, it is not rooted in a desire to revert to traditional, monogamous, heterosexual sexuality. It is, however, fair to say that radical feminists oppose ostensibly sexual activities, such as pornography, prostitution, and sadomasochism, and this is the attitude characterized by prostitutes' rights groups as "good-girl" morality. Prostitutes are clearly tired of being subjected to other people's views of appropriate sexuality. For them, the issue is sex. For feminists it is power. As Ti-Grace Atkinson put it,

> I do not know any feminist worthy of that name who, if forced to choose between freedom and sex, would choose sex. She'd choose freedom every time.
>   . . . By no stretch of the imagination is the Women's Movement a movement for sexual liberation.[139]

By contrast, COYOTE and CORP advocate a liberal acceptance of any "consensual" sexual behavior, regardless of the harm it does to women as a class. Their argument implies that mutual objectification might not be demeaning under certain circumstances. One returns to West's claim that sexual submission has erotic appeal and value when it is an expression of trust and not of fear.[140] As long as women have control over the situation, they can legitimately enjoy submission. The submissive person in sadomasochist activity can control the situation by

---

137 Id.
138 *Realistic Feminists*, in *Good Girls* at 211-12 (cited in note 44).
139 Ti-Grace Atkinson, *Why I'm Against S/M Liberation*, in Robin Ruth Linden et al, eds, *Against Sadomasochism: A Radical Feminist Analysis* 90, 91 (Frog in the Well, 1982).
140 West, 3 Wis Women's L J at 129 (cited in note 68).

saying a "single, pre-arranged word."[141] In this situation, consent can be given and withdrawn by the masochist at any time.

I think the defense by West and others of sadomasochism among both lesbians and heterosexuals is rooted in what Eisenstein calls the ideology of liberal individualism; it also fits Barry's description of valueless individualism:

> Valuelessness is of course itself a value statement in negation. It is a declaration of nonresponsibility and a proclamation: self-interest above all else. It creates a social atmosphere in which distinctions between good and bad are not only not desirable, they are wrong—that is the value implicit in valuelessness. It is the negative sanction against moral judgment, moral conviction. It states simply: it is wrong to determine right or wrong.[142]

I agree with Barry that we need to reclaim values that affirm and enhance, not demean human beings. Feminism that is unwilling or unable to choose among an assortment of behaviors may be tolerant, but to me it is apathetic and apolitical. Barry proposes a redefinition of perversion to describe sexuality that is unacceptable to her: "[S]exuality . . . which objectifies, forces, and violates . . . is perversion. . . . [W]here there is any attempt to separate the sexual experience from the total person, that first act of objectification is perversion."[143] My only apprehension about endorsing Barry's prescription for reclaiming values is that there is no way to know whether objectification *is* separable from the sexual experience. Barry obviously believes it is:

> Sexual values and the positive, constructive experience of sex *must be based in intimacy*. Sexual experience involves the most personal, private, erotic, sensitive parts of our physical and psychic being . . .
>
>   Intimacy is destroyed by depersonalization of this private, sensitive aspect of our being; the self is devalued into an object and deprived of respect, honor, and dignity. That is the living hell of female sexual slavery . . . .[144]

West's insistence that masochists can consent to submission as an act of liberation is anathema to feminists who believe that sadomasochism merely reinforces unequal power relationships and eroticizes the inequality. For the radical feminist, the masochist never consents because she has internalized heterosexual role-playing; submission is simply incompatible with freedom.

Disagreement over what is acceptable sexuality—the fact that what one feminist calls "valueless individualism"[145] another calls freedom—stems from incompatible understandings of consent. However, since we do not know whether consent is possible, I am partial to the radical femi-

---

141 Barbara Rose, *Reasons*, in *Coming to Power* 14, 15 (cited in note 104).

142 Barry, *Sexual Slavery* at 264 (cited in note 5).

143 Id at 266 (emphasis omitted).

144 Id at 267-68 (emphasis in the original).

145 Id at 262.

nist presumption of coercion and the implications that flow from it. MacKinnon's account of the relationship between gender and sexuality makes sense to me. Given the overwhelming abuse of women by men and the extent to which sexuality is used to keep women subservient, a presumption of coercion appears not only logical but healthy. MacKinnon's treatment of sexuality as a social construct has influenced my thinking about the self and was the genesis of my understanding of consent as something fluid. Even though, in my mind, she does not go far enough to acknowledge that fluidity, she has asked all the questions about sexuality that we need to pursue in order to understand consent.[146]

I am also convinced that feminists must look beyond their individual experience. This approach does not require women to negate their individuality; it simply means having a sex-class orientation and a broad, flexible notion of harm. Radical feminist theory, unlike liberal theory, analyzes a woman's perception of her experience within a social context. Radical feminists seek to understand the process of sexualizing dominance which depends upon the objectification of the individual woman, even if she "consents" to prostitution for what seem to her good reasons. Despite the argument that women "choose" to be prostitutes, I agree with Pateman's succinct condemnation of the sex-trade:

> When women's bodies are on sale as commodities in the capitalist market, the terms of the original contract cannot be forgotten; the law of male sex-right is publicly affirmed, and men gain public acknowledgement as women's sexual masters—that is what is wrong with prostitution.[147]

For me, the key to liberation is not an "anything goes" morality propped up by arguments about consent. I think it is important to retain a healthy skepticism toward the possibility of consent and to struggle against forces that undermine human dignity. As Dworkin describes it,

> A universal standard of human dignity is the only principle that completely repudiates sex-class exploitation and also propels all of us into a future where the fundamental political question is the quality of life for all human beings.[148]

Because radical feminists see prostitution as an impediment to such a universal standard, it is understandable that they would not support reform that seems to legitimize prostitution as a valid occupation. They

---

[146] See MacKinnon, *Feminist Theory* at 129-30 (cited in note 73).

> The gender issue, in this analysis, becomes the issue of what is taken to be 'sexuality'; what sex means and what is meant by sex, when, how, with whom, and with what consequences to whom. Such questions are almost never systematically confronted, even in discourses that purport feminist awareness. What sex is—how it comes to be attached and attributed to what it is, embodied and practiced as it is, contextualized in the ways it is, signifying and referring to what it does—is taken as a baseline, a given, except in explanations of what happened when it is thought to have gone wrong. . . . To suggest that the sexual might be continuous with something other than sex itself— something like politics—is seldom done, is treated as detumescent, even by feminists.
> Id.

[147] Pateman, *The Sexual Contract* at 208 (cited in note 85).

[148] Andrea Dworkin, *Right Wing Women* 220 (Putnam, 1983).

would prefer to advocate the radical political and economic change necessary to eliminate the causes of prostitution.

If equal opportunity were a reality, if women were not excluded from or ghettoized in the employment market, if they were not sexually harassed on the job, and if they were not socialized to be dependent and submissive, then arguably prostitution would not embody male dominance and female submission. However, I find it difficult to imagine a society of equality in which commercial sex were still sought after; commercial sex seems inextricably linked to gender hierarchy. I doubt whether radical feminists could envision circumstances where prostitution would not be harmful to women. As one woman said at the Toronto conference,

> I'll buy it under two conditions. First of all, let's have perfect economic equality between the sexes so that we're absolutely certain that nobody's going into this business out of economic desperation of any form. Second, I'll buy it if there are as many women buying as there are men, and I'm not sure that's ever going to happen.[149]

THE ARGUMENT FOR DECRIMINALIZATION

Criminalization only makes life more difficult for prostitutes, minimizing their chances of leaving the trade. The way to empower women is not to punish them for being powerless. Anything that pushes prostitution further underground and makes it more dangerous also makes it more profitable to pimps. If prostitution were decriminalized it would not necessarily be unregulated. Prostitutes would still be subject to sections of the relevant criminal code pertaining to nuisance, indecency, and causing a public disturbance. They would also have to abide by municipal zoning laws.

Even though I am sympathetic to the radical presumption of coercion, CORP's argument should be given some weight not because prostitution is legitimate and fully consensual, but rather because everyone's choices are limited in this world, and prostitutes should be entitled to make the best of a bad situation.[150] However, not all aspects of the trade should be decriminalized. As the Fraser Report suggests, procuring and living off the avails of prostitution should still be criminal where this is effected through threats and coercion.

The best short-term approach to reform entails removing prostitution from the criminal realm (subject to exceptions for pimping through coercion) so that it becomes an issue of gender equality and, at the same time, taking affirmative steps to destroy the conditions that create male

---

149 *From the Floor*, in *Good Girls* at 57 (cited in note 44).

150 As I said earlier, I do not think CORP is making this argument, because it insists that equality of opportunity *is* the reality for most prostitutes.

consumption and drive women to the trade. We should decriminalize prostitution per se, permit small groups to operate out of their own homes, provide education and information programs for those trying to leave the trade, and devote the money presently used for criminal law enforcement to prostitute self-help networks, havens, and halfway houses.[151]

Reform should also include provisions for vigorously prosecuting pimps who coerce women, particularly juveniles, into the trade. We should initiate training programs for women with little or no education, increase the minimum wage, finance businesses run by and for women, and design cooperative living and working arrangements for runaways and those with no place to go. Special police task forces should be devoted to prosecuting pimps but should be trained to treat prostitutes humanely. Public funds should be spent on the street and in the schools to raise awareness about equality, sexual abuse, and incest, as well as sexuality in general.

These proposals cost money and require a commitment from government and law enforcement agencies. If put into effect, they could dispel any notion that decriminalization was meant to legitimize prostitution. Rather they would be seen as the best alternative to a frustrating social problem.

CONCLUSION

I suspect that the law punishes prostitutes for reasons that have little to do with the interests of either prostitutes or women in general. Criminalization is clearly not informed by a conception of women as victims, because it punishes women who are already at a social and economic disadvantage. Rather, criminalization is likely intended to keep property values from dropping (as they would were brothels permitted in residential districts), prevent public nuisance, and keep children from being morally corrupted by witnessing the transaction between prostitute and customer.[152] The jurisdictions that have licensed prostitution, Nevada for example, seem to have chosen this solution in response to primarily liberal arguments that prostitution is a valid occupation and that it is "victimless." It seems that no North American scheme has adequately addressed the role prostitution plays in the subordination of women. The best proposal I have seen thus far, and the only one that attempts to respond to feminist concerns, is the Canadian Fraser Report which recommends broad social and economic reforms coupled with decriminalization.

---

[151] I am not suggesting supporting organizations like CORP who want to legitimize the trade but rather those groups that offer alternatives to women.
[152] See Dennis, Toronto Life at 86 (cited in note 37).

While we develop a theory of consciousness and wonder about consent, and while we dream of a world free of paid sex, real prostitutes face daily abuse. If radical feminists seek to eliminate prostitution, they should align themselves with liberal prostitutes' rights groups and support decriminalization, while simultaneously undermining gender hierarchy with every means at their disposal.[153] What separates radical feminists and prostitutes' rights groups is that for the former, decriminalization is not enough. It is, however, a necessary part of a holistic approach which I believe we must embrace. This is not a concession to valueless individualism. It is an admission that the world radical feminists seek remains elusive and that a policy of reform must respond to the reality of women's lives. It is a step we must take without abandoning our aspirations for a world in which choice is more possible and consent truly authentic.

---

[153] Aligning themselves with prostitutes' rights groups in support of decriminalization does not mean adopting the same approach or endorsing their rationale.

Pornography and the Traffic in Women: Brief on Behalf of Trudee Able-Peterson, et al., Amici Curiae in Support of Defendant and Intervenor-Defendants, *Village Books v. City of Bellingham*

Margaret A. Baldwin†

Introduction

Some nights ago, while I was struggling with how to introduce this piece, I decided that the only reasonable course was to reread John Steinbeck's *The Grapes of Wrath*. There they all were, Tom and Ma Joad, Preacher Casy, Rose of Sharon, Uncle John, Ruthie and Winfield, the bank agents, the truck, Route 66, California. The little story, the story in the story, is about what they learn from each other, what becomes of this sharecropper family evicted from their land in Oklahoma, battered by wind, poverty and exploitation. Then there is the story surrounding the story, the historical story of the Depression Dust Bowl, of labor resistance, of human suffering and death. That larger story is both roots and atmosphere of the novel, elevating the story of the small Joad family into an act of political exegesis. Then there are the stories but half-told in the novel, the stories of the characters not placed on center stage like Tom and Ma Joad, but who move in and out of the story only as they have meaning for Tom or Ma. If *The Grapes of Wrath* were Rose's story, or Winfield's, we would know them all differently.

What follows is a legal brief on prostitution, and the relationship between pornography and prostitution. It was written for and filed in a real

† Assistant Professor of Law, Florida State University College of Law.

For Toby Summer, survivor, poet, gardener, resister.

I wish to thank the amici, whose work and lives made sayable what is said in this brief, Annie McCombs, whose organizing skills, tenacity, wisdom and friendship made it possible, Washington Women for Civil Rights, Jane Doe, Mary Moe, Linda Marchiano, Catharine MacKinnon, Andrea Dworkin, and Deborah Maranville, who made it audible, and Arizona Luciano, Patricia Leary, Angela Hatcher, Beverly Perkins and Marlene Guerrieri, who made it material. I would also like to express my gratitude to Jeanne Barkey, Pauline Bart, Rhea Becker, Evelina Kane, Nikki Craft, Dorchen Leidholdt, Norma Ramos, Penelope Seator, Therese Stanton, Dorothy Teer, Melinda Vadas, Julie Vobosa and all women and men who work in this movement for the inspiration of their courage and dedication.

lawsuit.[a] Like a novel peopled with many characters, whom we come to know and understand as they live and eat and talk together, this lawsuit had many actors. This brief was just one. To read it, standing alone, necessarily conveys an incomplete account both of itself and of the litigation of which it was a part, as if all we read in *The Grapes of Wrath* were only Preacher Casy's speech to Tom at Keene's Ranch, or Ma Joad's rejoinders to Tom in their farewell conversation. I will try here, then, to provide a more complete account of the entire lawsuit than the text of the brief provides. This lawsuit, too, had its roots in a particular political and legal landscape, linking Minneapolis and Indianapolis and Cambridge, Massachusetts and New York City and Los Angeles and Bellingham, Washington. That is the story surrounding the story, which I can only suggest here. Finally, this brief and the interests it represents was, legally, a secondary character in this lawsuit, a Rose of Sharon to other Tom Joads, a half-told story. In very real ways, the story of this litigation is the story, too, of why that became true.

On November 8, 1988, sixty-two percent of the voters in Bellingham, Washington, voted to adopt an anti-discrimination ordinance, drafted by scholars Andrea Dworkin and Catharine MacKinnon, creating civil causes of action for sex-based injuries caused by pornography.[b] This electoral victory followed a sustained educational and organizational effort by local feminists and progressive organizations in Bellingham. Providing a legal tool for victims of pornography to seek remedial actions on their own behalf, the Bellingham ordinance was inspired by similar measures enacted by the city councils of Minneapolis and Indianapolis in recent years.[c] The ordinance creates five civil causes of action for damages or an injunction: (1) coercion of any person into performing for pornography; (2) trafficking in pornography; (3) forcing pornography on a person; (4) assaulting any person in a way that is directly caused by specific pornography; or (5) defaming any person through the unauthorized use in pornography of their name or likeness.[d] The ordinance also sets forth, as the operant definition of pornography, "the graphic sexually explicit subordi-

---

[a] *Village Books v. City of Bellingham*, No. 88-1470 (W.D. Wash. Feb. 9, 1989). (Alphabetical footnoting is used here, and to designate additional footnotes in the text of the brief, to distinguish them from the footnotes contained in the original text. The original footnotes are designated by conventional numerals.)

[b] Bellingham Herald, Nov. 9, 1988, § B, at 1; Chicago Tribune, Dec. 18, 1988, "Tempowoman" Section, at 7. The complete text of the Bellingham ordinance is set forth in an appendix to this piece.

[c] Amendment to the Minneapolis, Minn., Code of Ordinances, tit. 7, ch. 139 (December 30, 1983) (vetoed by the mayor January 5, 1984; reenacted in amended form on July 13, 1984; vetoed by the mayor on the same day); Indianapolis, Ind., City-County General Ordinance No. 24, ch. 16 (amended May 1, 1984); amended again by Indianapolis, Ind., City-County General Ordinance No. 35 (June 15, 1984). The City of Los Angeles has considered a similar version of the ordinance, and a referendum on the ordinance was rejected by less than 4,000 votes in Cambridge, Massachusetts in November, 1985. New York Times, Nov. 12, 1985, at A16, col. 6.

[d] See Appendix, *infra*, Bellingham Initiative 1C, § 3.

nation of women through pictures and/or words," that also includes specific presentations of women as inferior and degraded.[e]

Shortly after the effective date of the ordinance, focus shifted from the voting booths in Bellingham to the federal courthouse in Seattle. On November 23, 1988, a lawsuit was filed in federal district court against the City of Bellingham challenging the constitutionality of the new ordinance.[f] The lawsuit was initiated by two bookstore trade organizations, a library association, a local bookstore, and several Bellingham residents.[g] The plaintiffs sought declaratory and injunctive relief against enforcement of the ordinance on several legal theories.[h]

The plaintiffs relied heavily on the outcome of a legal challenge to the anti-pornography ordinance passed in Indianapolis in a suit brought by similar plaintiffs.[i] In that case, the plaintiffs had prevailed before both the federal district court and the court of appeals; the Supreme Court summarily affirmed the disposition.[j] Alleging that the provisions of the Bellingham ordinance are materially similar to those invalidated in the Indianapolis case, the plaintiffs here argued that the Supreme Court's disposition was binding precedent in this lawsuit. The plaintiffs further alleged that the ordinance was a "content-based" and "viewpoint-based" restriction on speech impermissible under the First Amendment, as the lower courts in *Hudnut* had concluded. In addition, the plaintiffs asserted that the ordinance was unconstitutionally vague and overbroad, failing to give residents and business persons fair notice of what materials constitute pornography under its provisions. These allegations were further elaborated in the plaintiffs' memorandum in support of their motion for summary judgment.[k]

The City of Bellingham, the formal defendant in the lawsuit, declined to defend.[l] Women in Bellingham filled the breach, successfully intervening Washington Women for Civil Rights and two individual women, all

---

[e] *Id.* at § 2.

[f] Complaint, *Village Books, supra* note a.

[g] *Id.*

[h] I hope that this will be as accessible as possible to people who are not lawyers and thus will try to keep legal jargon to a minimum. "Declaratory and injunctive relief," in this context, means that the plaintiffs asked the court to void the ordinance before it was actually used by anyone.

[i] *American Booksellers Association, Inc. v. Hudnut,* 598 F.Supp. 1316 (S.D.Ind. 1984), *aff'd* 771 F.2d 323 (7th Cir. 1985), *aff'd mem.,* 475 U.S. 1001 (1986), *reh'g denied,* 475 U.S. 1132 (1986). One of the plaintiffs in this case was the same American Booksellers Association. In both cases, the plaintiffs were represented by the American Civil Liberties Union.

[j] *Id.* The summary affirmance was rendered without full briefing, without argument, and with no citation to existing case law.

[k] For non-lawyer readers: A motion for summary judgment asks the court to decide the case based on the documents before it. In this case, those documents included legal arguments on the questions by both sides, sworn statements by parties and experts, as well as additional written documents submitted by both sides. The effect of granting a motion for summary judgment is to preclude any further hearings or consideration of additional evidence.

[l] This was not the first time the city balked at this ordinance and the wishes of its citizens to have it enacted as law. Prior to the vote, the city had attempted to keep the ordinance off the ballot altogether, requiring legal action to assure that the measure would be placed on the ballot.

of whom asserted legal interests in the enforcement of the ordinance, as intervenor-defendants. In extensive memoranda, the women challenged the plaintiffs' characterization of the ordinance as either a "viewpoint-based" or "content-based" restriction on protected speech. Rather, they argued, the ordinance is predicated, not on what pornographic material says or looks like, but on what it does and how it is used: to subordinate women. Thus, under this construction of the ordinance, the ordinance is "harm-based," tailored to provide redress for demonstrable injuries to women, not to suppress the content of the material.[m]

The intervenor-defendants further argued that, even if the ordinance were construed as content-based, its provisions nevertheless meet constitutional requirements in that a compelling interest in prohibiting discrimination against women justifies them. Similar arguments were raised by Linda Marchiano, who as "Linda Lovelace" was coerced into making the film "Deep Throat," in her memorandum in support of her motion to intervene as an intervenor-defendant. The intervenor-defendants also moved for summary judgment in their favor, or, in the alternative, for the court to deny summary judgment for the plaintiffs and to proceed to trial on the factual question of the sufficiency of the showing of harm to women to sustain the ordinance. Several other briefs *amicus curiae*,[n] including this one, were also filed at this juncture, representing the interests of diverse groups and individuals in the legal redress available under the ordinance.[o]

On January 18, 1989, the court denied Linda Marchiano's motion to intervene; she subsequently filed an amicus brief in the case. This order was the final substantive ruling by the court prior to its disposition of the parties' motions for summary judgment. As this lawsuit was structured, the presentation of the issues seemed strangely skewed in the absence of those persons most likely to be affected by the ordinance itself. Ultimately,

---

[m] This brief analysis of the arguments presented in the case cannot, I am afraid, do any of them justice. For an exposition of the legal theories supporting the constitutionality of the ordinance outlined here, *see* MacKinnon, *Pornography, Civil Rights, and Speech*, 20 HARV. C.R.-C.L. L. REV. 1 (1985); Sunstein, *Pornography and the First Amendment*, 1986 DUKE L.J. 589; Seator, *Judicial Indifference to Pornography's Harms: American Booksellers v. Hudnut*, 17 GOLDEN GATE U.L. REV. 297 (1987). For elaboration of the opposing view, *see Hudnut, supra* note f, Stone, *Comment: Anti-Pornography Legislation as Viewpoint Discrimination*, 9 HARV. J.L & PUB. POL'Y 461 (1986); Emerson, *Pornography and the First Amendment: A Reply to Professor MacKinnon*, 3 YALE L. & POL'Y REV. 130 (1984).

[n] "Amicus curiae" literally means "friend of the court." Unlike formal parties to a lawsuit, "amici" participate only as "advisors" to the court on issues about which they may claim special expertise.

[o] Articulating the interest in the litigation of sexually exploited children were amici Institute for Youth Advocacy, Voices in Action, Anne Burgess and Flora Colao, represented by Kent Harvey. Amici Andrea Dworkin, Gloria Steinem, and Susan Brownmiller, represented by Penelope Seator, expressed their interest in gaining redress for defamation in pornography. The Seventh Circuit's opinion in *Hudnut, supra* note i, was criticized for its broad negative effect on efforts to gain equality for women by amici Women's Institute for Freedom of the Press and Seattle National Organization for Women, represented by Cass Sunstein.

I would here like to acknowledge the incisive advocacy of Deborah Maranville, counsel for the intervenor-defendants, and Catharine MacKinnon, counsel for Linda Marchiano.

none of the plaintiffs in the case asserted that they in fact sold, distributed, or trafficked in pornography, or were subject to enforcement actions, under any plausible application of the ordinance. The initial defendant, the City, whose citizens had endorsed the ordinance, refused to defend the suit. Although the intervenors eloquently and cogently asserted the interests of women in the relief afforded under the ordinance, women and children whose lives have been deeply brutalized or destroyed by exploitation by pornography were largely confined to amici status. Women and children in prostitution, children subjected to sexual exploitation, Linda Marchiano, women whose reputations and integrity as women have been twisted in pornography, became secondary actors in a legal arena reserved for the least culpable on the plaintiffs' side, the least injured on the defendants'. This was *The Grapes of Wrath* written by Herbert Hoover.

The women whose lives you will read in this brief are women for whom this ordinance was written. I can say nothing more than what is before you about why that is true. For women who read this who are or have been in prostitution: I have tried here, with all I had, to tell the truth as best I understand it.

BRIEF ON BEHALF OF TRUDEE ABLE-PETERSON, ET AL., AMICI
CURIAE IN SUPPORT OF DEFENDANT AND INTERVENOR-DEFENDANTS[P]

Interest of Amici

Amici are organizations and individuals expert in the effect of pornography on women and girls in prostitution. Amici represent a spectrum of experience in this work, including scholarly contribution, provision of social services, advocacy, and personal knowledge. Amici include organizations of prostitution survivors such as amicus WHISPER, as well as social service agencies providing aid to women in prostitution and assistance in escaping prostitution. Those agencies include Genesis House in Chicago, Project Off Streets and the PRIDE program in Minneapolis, and Project RESPECT in Madison, Wisconsin. Numerous directors and staff of other such agencies, such as Trudee Able-Peterson of the New York Streetwork Project, Teri Lynch of the Delancey Street Foundation in San Francisco, Susan Hunter, Patricia French, Vicki Neland, Barb Sussex, and Susan Tisdale in Portland, Oregon, are also represented. Agencies and individuals providing shelter and assistance to victims of sexual violence are among the amici, as well as individuals and groups in advocacy roles. Former Minneapolis Council member Charlee Hoyt was an initial sponsor of the Minneapolis anti-pornography ordinance and is broadly experienced in the injuries to women caused by pornography. Amicus Professor Kathleen Barry has written a definitive account of prostitution as a system in her important and influential work, *Female Sexual Slavery*. Amicus Professor Jane Caputi has contributed an important study of serial sexual murders, murders in which prostituted women are often targeted. Several amici are themselves survivors of prostitution and pornography.

From this wide range of expertise and insight, amici all concur that women in prostitution are primary victims of pornography. The Bellingham anti-pornography ordinance, in amici's experienced judgment, is crucial to affording women in prostitution a means of redress and of enabling them to initiate protective action on their own behalf. For amici's work in dismantling systems of sexual exploitation and abuse and supporting individual survivors to succeed, this ordinance is a necessary tool.

The Amici[q]

Trudee Able-Peterson is the Director of the Streetwork Project, an outreach program for homeless children in Times Square. She is the author

---

[P] The text of the brief as reprinted here is identical to the text submitted to the court, with minor corrections of citation form and typographical errors. Patricia Leary co-signed the brief; I am responsible for it. James Dean patiently assisted in the preparation of the text for publication. The consent of each of the amici was obtained for republication of the document here.

[q] Annie McCombs deserves all credit for making this list a reality.

of *Children of the Evening*, and a survivor of pornography and prostitution.

Dr. Kathleen Barry is a sociologist and associate professor of Human Development at Pennsylvania State University. She is the author of *Female Sexual Slavery*. Her research reveals that women in prostitution are among the groups of women most endangered by pornography.

Professor Jane Caputi is an assistant professor of American Studies at the University of New Mexico. She is the author of *The Age of Sex Crime*, an investigation of serial sex murderers. Her research has shown that pornography played a significant role in the lives of serial sex killers and that many serial sex killers target prostitutes.

Challenging Media Images of Women is an organization that contests degrading and abusive images of women in the media.

Patricia A. French is a Portland, Oregon social service agency case manager who works with victims of pornography.

Frogtown Neighborhood Services/Catholic Charities, of St. Paul, Minnesota provides individual counseling, advocacy and crisis intervention to adult women in prostitution. Of particular concern to the agency is the use of "homemade" and commercial pornography in trapping women in prostitution.

Genesis House has provided services to over 4,000 women in prostitution in Chicago, primarily women in street prostitution, in the last four years; the vast majority of these women did not *choose* to be involved in prostitution.

Charlee Hoyt is a former Minneapolis, Minnesota City Council member and the cosponsor before that body of the first anti-pornography civil rights ordinance to be considered by a legislative body.

Alma Goddard is the Outreach Coordinator and counselor at the Bradley-Angle House, Inc. in Portland, Oregon, a shelter program for victims of domestic and sexual violence.

Susan Kay Hunter has worked for five years as the Executive Director of an organization which has provided social services and hope to over 450 women and children in Portland, Oregon, all of whom are survivors of prostitution.

Becky Ann Jones is a survivor of pornography and prostitution.

Teri Lynch is a member of the Delancey Street Foundation, San Francisco, and has been involved in working with women in prostitution for fifteen years.

Minnesota Coalition for Battered Women is a 70 member organization in Minnesota offering technical assistance and training to programs statewide addressing the needs of battered women and their families, including women escaping prostitution.

Amelia Moore is a survivor of prostitution. She is a member of the

Board of Directors of an Oregon social service agency providing services to survivors of prostitution.

Vicki Neland is a case manager in a social service agency in Portland, Oregon who works with victims of pornography.

Organizing Against Pornography (OAP) is a community-based organization in Minneapolis, Minnesota which seeks to raise awareness about the pornography-related victimization of women. OAP advocates for many women survivors of prostitution and pornography.

Aloha Palmer is a coordinator of rape education and rape support groups in Portland, Oregon.

Pornography Awareness, Inc. is a nonprofit feminist organization. The objectives of the organization include ending both prostitution and pornography.

PRIDE (People Reaching Out In a Determined Effort to End Prostitution) Program of Family and Children's Services, Minneapolis, Minnesota, has for ten years been helping women and children to leave prostitution.

Project RESPECT is a private nonprofit publicly funded outpatient agency for women involved in systems of prostitution, women trying to leave prostitution, and women trying to stay out of such systems who need support to do so. The program is also in some cases an alternative to criminal fines for women arrested on prostitution charges. The agency provides services to between eight and fifteen women at any given time.

Project Off Streets works with male and female youth in the Minneapolis-St. Paul area who have been sexually exploited. Workers there have seen hundreds of children who have been involved in the sex industry as young as age eleven, and they believe that prostitution and pornography devastate the lives of young boys, girls, and women.

ReSisters is an activist group in Albany, New York committed to opposing the harms of pornography.

Toby Summer is a survivor of prostitution and other forms of sexual abuse and knows that the remedies in this ordinance would have changed her life.

Barb Sussex is a social worker who works with prostitution survivors and people trying to leave prostitution. She is a member of the Board of Directors of a social service agency that works with survivors in Portland, Oregon.

Betsy Warrior is the Director of the Battered Women's Directory and supports the ordinance based on her work with battered women.

Tess Wiseheart is the Executive Director of a social organization providing services to women and children who are victims of domestic violence and sexual assault.

Sarah Wynter is a survivor of prostitution.

Women Hurt in Systems of Prostitution Engaged in Revolt

(WHISPER) is an organization of survivors of prostitution devoted to ending prostitution.

Women Organizing Against Pornography and Prostitution (WOAPP), Oakland, California, is an organization comprised of activists and survivors of many forms of sexual abuse working to stop the harm done to women and children by pornography and prostitution.

Chris Womendez is the president of the Prostitutes Union of Massachusetts (PUMA).

Women's Alliance Against Pornography Education Projects, Cambridge, Massachusetts, is a feminist organization dedicated to educating the public to the harms of pornography.

Wyoming Coalition Against Domestic Violence and Sexual Assault, Laramie, Wyoming supports the Bellingham ordinance.

Wyoming State Office on Family Violence & Sexual Assault, a unit of the Division of Community Programs, Department of Health and Social Services, Cheyenne, Wyoming, supports the Bellingham ordinance.

Argument

Amici urge this court to deny plaintiffs' motion for summary judgment and grant intervenors' motions opposing summary judgment and cross motions for summary judgment. Intervenors have ably argued the city's need for a factual hearing and its interest in providing civil redress for the sex discriminatory practices giving rise to claims under the ordinance, and the ordinance's constitutional validity. Amici will here direct the court's attention to the importance of the availability of those remedies to women enmeshed in systems of prostitution and to those women most vulnerable to sexual abuse, exploitation and discrimination through prostitution. The documentation relied on by amici here includes sociological studies, empirical analysis, and survivors testimony.[1] Those data, together with the record developed by intervenors, are material to the sufficiency of the city's justification for this law. Even viewed in the light most favorable to the plaintiffs, this showing, uncontested by the plaintiffs, of the severity of the injury to women caused by the practices prohibited by the ordinance, compels summary judgment in defendant's favor.

INTRODUCTION

Amici's argument is structured, in what follows, by reference to the substantive claims described in the ordinance. We urge this court, for the following reasons, to adopt a similar analytic approach to the issues presented in this case. The federal district and appeals court in *American Booksellers Association, Inc. v. Hudnut*, 598 F.Supp. 1316 (S.D. Ind. 1984), *aff'd* 771 F.2d 323 (7th Cir. 1985), *aff'd mem.* 106 S.Ct. 1172 (1986), from which this court may seek guidance in construing the substantially similar provisions of the ordinance at issue in this litigation, reached their legal conclusions based largely on an analysis of the definition of pornography contained in the ordinance. Both courts, then, proceeded on the assumption that *definitions* "regulate speech."

Legal definitions, in civil contexts, do not and cannot regulate anything. Nor do they, in and of themselves, describe an injury worthy of redress. This unfortunate analytic error, in amici's view, ineluctably led to each court's result. The courts' definition-bound approach, applied in other legal contexts, would have decided *New York v. Ferber*, 458 U.S. 747 (1982)[2] solely on the issue whether "sexual conduct" as defined in the statute described, in the abstract, "protected expression" without regard to

---

1. All of this material is plainly relevant to this court's determination of the facts. The Supreme Court in *New York v. Ferber*, 458 U.S. 747 (1982) based its conclusion that prohibition of juvenile sexual exploitation in pornography is a compelling interest both on the judgment of the state legislature and "the judgment found in all the relevant literature." *Ferber*, 458 U.S. at 758.

2. *Ferber* upheld a New York criminal statute subjecting to penal sanctions makers or distributors of visual depictions of "sexual conduct" by minors under the age of 15. *Ferber* is analyzed extensively *infra*.

the sexual exploitation the statute was designed to ameliorate; or *Gertz v. Robert Welch, Inc.*, 418 U.S. 323 (1974)[3] on the issue whether "defamatory statements" were entitled to constitutional protection regardless of the identity of the person defamed; or *Stanley v. Georgia*, 394 U.S. 557 (1969)[4] on the issue whether the material at issue was "obscene" without considering the particular factual context in which possession of the material was criminalized. Each of these cases, consistent with ordinary First Amendment doctrine, required the Court to evaluate the scope of First Amendment interests implicated, in view of the concrete injuries sought to be redressed under the statutory scheme, by actual people, under particular enforcement mechanisms. Indeed, the balancing of competing interests formed the doctrinal core of these opinions. None was or could have been resolved by analysis of the definition of the expressive communication alone. The *Hudnut* courts, however, by seizing on the definition of pornography as dispositive of the case, wholly abstracted from the scope of the legal claims in which the definition operates, and the sex-based character of those injuries, simply sidestepped the substantive doctrinal issues presented.

Amici are perhaps especially attentive to the implications of the courts' approach. Just as the courts in *Hudnut*, by focusing on the definition of pornography independently of the substantive injuries for which the ordinance would permit redress, rendered those harms largely irrelevant to their analyses, so too is the reality of prostitution for women commonly trivialized and, by sleight of hand, made invisible by the *social* definition of "prostitute": a woman who is so debased she will voluntarily exchange sex for money. This "definition," too, obscures and distorts the systems of sex-based coercion, violence and despair which is the common lived experience of prostitution for women. In what follows, amici will attempt to clarify for this court the means by which the pornography industry collaborates in the victimization of prostituted women, and the consequent importance of the availability of the legal claims created by the ordinance in remedying those conditions.

---

3. *Gertz* established a sliding scale of constitutional protection for libel defendants depending on the status of the libel plaintiff. *Cf. New York Times v. Sullivan, Inc. v. Greenmoss Builders, Inc.*, 472 U.S. 749 (1985) (sliding scale approach depending on whether defamatory statement dealt with a "matter of public concern"). The status of the plaintiff as well as the subject matter of the statement are now each to be taken into account in assessing the First Amendment protection due the speaker.
4. *Stanley* held that the possession of obscene literature in the home could not be criminalized consistent with First Amendment and privacy doctrine, even though "obscenity" had been declared in prior opinions of the court to be categorically without First Amendment protection. *See, e.g., Roth v. United States*, 354 U.S. 476, 485 (1957) ("obscenity is not within the area of constitutionally protected speech or press").

II. The Interests of the City in Inhibiting Sex Discriminatory, Sexually Exploitative, and Abusive Practices of Prostitution are Constitutionally Furthered by the Ordinance

Amici concur in the argument advanced by the intervenors that pornographic materials, as legally effective in the ordinance, are not entitled to First Amendment protection.[r] Amici contend, however, that the ordinance in any case addresses a compelling state interest in inhibiting sex discriminatory and sexually exploitative practices of prostitution. It is established that government may regulate speech directly, even based on its content, if the regulation is justified by an interest of compelling importance and is narrowly drawn to meet that end. *Boos v. Barry*, 108 S.Ct. 1157, 1164 (1988); *Roberts v. U.S. Jaycees*, 468 U.S. 609 (1984); *Perry Education Assn. v. Perry Local Educator's Assn.*, 460 U.S. 37 (1983); *New York v. Ferber*, 458 U.S. 747 (1982). In evaluating the weight of the governmental interest, the proximity of the expression regulated to the "core values" of the First Amendment is also taken into account. *Compare Meyer v. Grant*, 108 S.Ct. 1886, 1894 (1988) (regulation of ballot initiative, core political speech, requires state to overcome "well-nigh insurmountable" burden of justification) *with Roberts*, 104 U.S. at 618-623 (justifying burden on expressive association less onerous than justifying burden on intimate association) *and with Ferber*, 458 U.S. at 762-63 (*de minimus* speech value of expression in child pornography relevant to weight of state's burden of justification). To clarify for the court the full dimensions and impact of the discriminatory practices redressable under the ordinance on this group of women in particular, and because the condition of prostituted women is so little understood, amici will initially describe those conditions in broad outline. Amici contend that, so understood, promotion of the equality, freedom and safety of these women is a compelling interest. Amici will then demonstrate the means by which the causes of action described in the ordinance further that interest. Finally, we will show that those provisions are narrowly drawn to meet that end.

A.   *The promotion of equality, safety and freedom of prostituted women is a legitimate governmental objective furthered by the ordinance.*

Like the pornography industry, the institution of prostitution is an enormous economic enterprise. By one estimate, forty million dollars *per day* is spent on prostitution in the United States, or over $14 billion dollars a year. This figure excludes receipts from pornography and so-called "live sex." C. Pateman, *The Sexual Contract* 190 (1988). The total num-

---

[r] I would like to stress again here that the intervenors' principal argument was that the ordinance is neither a viewpoint nor content-based restriction on protected materials. *See supra* note m. and accompanying text.

ber of customers each week across the country has been conservatively estimated at 1,500,000 men. Jennings, *The Victim as Criminal: A Consideration of California's Prostitution Law*, 64 Cal. L. Rev. 1235, 1251 (1976). The commodity exchanged in these transactions is women's bodies. According to one estimate, the "average street prostitute sees 1,500 men a year." Alexander, *Prostitutes Are Being Scapegoated For Heterosexual AIDS*, in Sex Work: Writings by Women in the Sex Industry 249 (F. Delacoste & P. Alexander ed. 1987) (hereinafter *Sex Work*).

This vast "industry" is of course fueled and maintained by the demand by men that it exist, requiring a continuous supply of women who are consumed by it. These women tend to share some common characteristics. The average age of starting prostitution is fourteen years old. Weisberg, *Children of the Night: The Adequacy of Statutory Treatment of Juvenile Prostitution*, 12 Am. J. Crim. Law 1, 5-6 (1984); *see also* Silbert & Pines, *Entrance into Prostitution*, 13 Youth & Soc'y. 471, 483 (1982) (hereinafter Silbert & Pines, *Entrance*); Gray, *Turning-Out: A Study of Teenage Prostitution*, 1 Urb. Life & Culture 401 (1973). Some evidence suggests that the average age is declining. A study of 200 prostituted women in San Francisco revealed that among juveniles, the mean age for beginning prostitution was thirteen years. Silbert & Pines, *Entrance, supra*, at 483. A number were under nine, ten, eleven, and twelve.[5]

A majority of these young women and girls were victims of sexual, emotional, and other forms of physical abuse within the home. Research on incidence of sexual abuse indicates that between sixty and seventy percent of women entering prostitution were sexually abused as children. Silbert & Pines, *Entrance, supra*, at 479; Weisberg, *supra*, at 4 n.12. Sexual abuse by family members—ordinarily fathers, stepfathers and foster fathers—is the most common form of sexual assault; the average age of victimization is ten years of age. Silbert & Pines, *Entrance, supra*, at 479; Weisberg, *supra*, at 4; Enablers Inc., Study of Juvenile Prostitution in Minnesota (1978). Patterns of beatings and emotional abuse demonstrate similar rates of injury. *See* Silbert & Pines, *Entrance, supra*, at 479 (forty-five percent of girls beaten regularly while growing up; in over seventy-five percent of cases, the beater was a male in a position of authority over the girl); J. James, Entrance into Juvenile Prostitution, Final Report 48 (NIMH study, 1980)(sixty-two percent reported severe physical abuse)..

Moreover, in one study, the production and use of pornography were shown to have been instrumental in substantial percentages of the sexually exploitative acts inflicted on girls prior to entry into prostitution. The Sil-

---

5. Some accounts mention juvenile prostitution involving children as young as three years old. *See, e.g.,* Densen-Gerber & Hutchinson, *Medical-legal and Societal Problems Involving Child Prostitution, Child Pornography and Drug-related Abuse*, in The Maltreatment of Children 318 (1978).

bert and Pines survey of 200 prostituted women revealed, *in unsolicited comments*, that ten percent of the women had been used as children in pornographic films and magazines. All of the women were under the age of thirteen when they were victimized in this way. Silbert & Pines, *Pornography and Sexual Abuse of Women*, 10 Sex Roles 857, 865 (1984) (hereinafter Silbert & Pines, *Pornography*). A much higher number, thirty-eight percent, reported that they had had pornographic pictures taken of them as children before they were sixteen. *Id.* at 866. For example,[6] one fifteen year old girl, later prostituted, was taken by her mother's boyfriend to a house outfitted with cameras, lights, and a set where he took photographs of her. Interview with "M.D.", Minneapolis, Minnesota, WHISPER Oral History Project 39 (1987). She did not speak of this incident to anyone for twenty years. *Id.* Another woman reports having been offered a ride home by a stranger when she was thirteen or fourteen years old. "[I]nstead of taking me home, he took me to this park and took off my clothes, and started taking pictures, and tied me up." Interview with "R.M.", Portland, Oregon, WHISPER Oral History Project 22. The man apparently had a time-shuttered camera, and took photographs of himself touching the girl's breasts and digitally penetrating her. The incident was reported to the police; the police believed the man and dismissed the girl's statements. *Id.*

In addition, twenty-two percent of the 178 cases of sexual exploitation studied by Silbert and Pines involved the use of pornography by the adult

---

6. The following accounts were given by women not among the subjects in the Silbert and Pines research. They were among women interviewed for an oral history project of prostituted women conducted by amicus WHISPER. Subsequent citations to the WHISPER Oral History Project refer to this body of research.

As to the relevance to this case of the experience of women outside the city of Bellingham, the Supreme Court in *City of Renton v. Playtime Theaters, Inc.*, 475 U.S. 41 (1986) addressed a similar issue holding that the city of Renton could rely on empirical evidence of the deleterious effects of "adult theaters" in other municipalities in enacting its own zoning ordinance. The Court stated that evidence generated in other cities may be relied upon, so long as that evidence "is reasonably believed to be relevant to the problem that the city addresses." *Id.* at 51-52. Amici are aware of no demographic divergences suggesting prostituted women are differentially treated among locales. *Cf.* Weisberg, *supra*, at 3 no.7, 8 (noting demographic similarity in socioeconomic, racial patterns in different geographic locales). *See also Kirksey v. City of Jackson*, 506 F.Supp. 491, 517 (S.D. Miss. 1981) (interest of referendum discerned from experience of other communities); *11126 Baltimore Blvd. v. Prince George's County*, 684 F.Supp. 884, 894 n.16 (D.Md. 1988) (collecting cases regarding legislative reliance on experiences elsewhere).

Amici are also aware that testimony of individual women or accounts of particular cases of abuse of prostituted women are often dismissed with some impatience as melodramatic attempts at emotional manipulation, with little or no empirical value. However, in amici's experience, the accounts rendered here describe typical, rather than aberrant, or unusually grotesque, or merely anecdotal, incidents. The relative dearth of thorough-going empirical studies in this area reveals intense and real needs of prostituted women for safety, comprehension, and confidentiality as conditions of participating in sociological studies. The care required in meeting those needs is often acknowledged by researchers in the area. *See* M. Silbert, Sexual Assault of Prostitutes 6-7 (Nov. 1980) (research report to the National Center for the Prevention and Control of Rape); E. Miller, *Street Woman* 183-190 (1986). Thus, in reading these accounts, amici urge the court to recognize that each woman's voice represents hundreds more who require anonymity to speak at all. *See, e.g.,* Summer, *Women, Lesbians and Prostitution*, Lesbian Ethics n.1, Summer 1987, at 33 (explaining need to write pseudononymously).

prior to the sexual act. Some abusers used the pornography to persuade the children to "cooperate," or legitimize their actions, or to arouse themselves prior to abusing the child. Silbert & Pines, *Pornography, supra*, at 865. The researchers describe one example of this latter technique:

> [O]ne of the subjects in the study described a primitive movie projector her father had set up in the garage. He used to show himself and his friends pornographic movies to get them sexually aroused before they would rape her. (She was 9 at the time.) Her brother would also watch the movies when the father was gone; then he also abused her sexually.

Id. at 865-866. Moreover, the "line" between coercion into pornography by a family member, sexual assault within the family, and prostitution may be all but invisible in some instances.

> A mother and father in South Oklahoma City forced their four daughters, ages ten to seventeen, to engage in family sex while pornographic pictures were being filmed. This mother also drove the girls to dates with men where she would watch while the girls had sex, then she would collect fees of thirty to fifty dollars.

Attorney General's Commission on Pornography, U.S. Dept. of Justice, Final Report 780 (1986) (hereinafter cited as Attorney General's Commission, Final Report) (quoting letter to the Commission from Oklahomans Against Pornography).

The effects of these forms of sexual abuse and exploitation on young women have, in recent years, become better understood and more widely publicized. Indeed, the Supreme Court's disposition in *Ferber* is largely attributable to the enhanced public appreciation of the injury of juvenile sexual exploitation. The weight of clinical evidence "suggests that for any child, sexual contact with an adult, especially a trusted relative, is a significant trauma which may have long-lasting deleterious effects." J. Herman, *Father-Daughter Incest* 33 (1981); *See also* D. Russell, *The Secret Trauma: Incest in the Lives of Girls and Women* (1986). Their treatment often left them with the feeling "that they were good for little else besides sex." J. Herman, *supra*, at 100; *see generally* D. Russell, *supra*; D. Finkelhor, *A Sourcebook on Child Sexual Abuse* 143-79 (1986).

Many of these young women and girls run away from home in a courageous and desperate attempt to escape these conditions of abuse, neglect and abandonment. Silbert & Pines, *Entrance, supra*, at 485; Weisberg, *supra*, at 5. The extreme vulnerability of these women to further sexual exploitation is difficult to overstate. As detailed above, the "market" for women in prostitution is immense; once these young women "hit bottom," alone, without economic resources, and typically, in an extremely depressed mental state, they are again targeted for sexual exploitation by pimps.[7]

Over ninety percent of street prostitutes are controlled by pimps; K. Barry, *Female Sexual Slavery* 6 (1979); while approximately eighty percent of women prostituted from hotels are controlled by pimps. R. Prus & S. Irini, *Hookers, Rounders, and Desk Clerks* 11 (1980). Women are typically "procured" by pimps for prostitution and pornography by several different, sometimes concurrently practiced, strategies:

> 1) the use of befriending or "love" to feign a relationship, create an emotional dependency and exploit a young woman's vulnerabilities until she can be "turned out" for prostitution; 2) fraudulent employment agencies . . . which the [woman] finds after she [arrives] are only covers for prostitution; [and] 3) kidnapping.

Barry, *Social Etiology of Crimes Against Women*, 10 Victimology 164, 166 (1985) (hereinafter Barry, *Social Etiology*); *see generally* K. Barry, *Female Sexual Slavery, supra,* ch. 5. The initial object of these tactics is to gain immediate control, psychological or physical, of the woman. In many instances, immediate physical force is preferred.

> Pimp kidnapped me. He got me loaded and kept me on drugs for two weeks. Then he turned me out in exchange for drugs. Once I was hooked I was too scared.

Silbert & Pines, *Entrance, supra,* at 488.

> Late in 1976, Blood Stewart picked up 14-year-old Jennifer in the vicinity of Penn Station . . . [H]e beat, raped, and tortured her for three days. . . . He then informed her that she was going to work the streets for him.

K. Barry, *Female Sexual Slavery, supra,* at 78. A sixteen year old girl was kidnapped by four men while she was walking home from school. She was taken to a pimp's apartment where she was held for two weeks. Toward the end of the second week she deliberately took an overdose of sleeping pills so that she would be hospitalized, hoping thereby to escape him. The pimp told the hospital personnel he was her guardian and they released her to his care. The pimp later stabbed her repeatedly when she refused sex with him. *People v. McNutt*, 146 Ill.App.3d 357, 361–62, 496 N.E.2d 1089, 1092–93 (1986) (conviction for kidnapping and coercion). These are not anecdotal aberrations. One study of juvenile prostitutes re-

---

7. This is not to say that child sexual abuse "causes" prostitution. As will be clear in the discussion of procurement strategies, and other circumstances compelling initiation into prostitution, *infra,* the *demand for sexual access to women* causes prostitution. These young women are not "causing" anything by being vulnerable to abuse.

ports that seventeen percent of young women were directly forced into prostitution by their pimps. Harlan, Rodgers, Slattery, Male and Female Adolescent Prostitution: Huckleberry House Sexual Minority Youth Services Project 34 (1981).

Other women are exploited while attempting to meet immediate survival needs. One woman, for example, reported that she became involved with a pimp when he offered to take care of her baby. She was thirteen years old at the time. Silbert & Pines, *Entrance, supra,* at 488. Most young women are initially "won over" by attention and apparent affection under conditions where they have little leeway to refuse or question the direction of the "relationship." K. Barry, *Female Sexual Slavery, supra,* at 77. Another tactic is for a pimp to provide bail money to an impoverished, isolated woman on the condition that she prostitute for him.

> I tried maid's work but when they found out I wasn't living with my parents and not going to school they fired me. I was begging and shoplifting to live and got busted for shoplifting. Pimp came and got me off and told me I could pay him back by working the street.

Silbert & Pines, *Entrance, supra,* at 488. Women who believe they can outwit the pimp on this strategem may be wrong. One woman reports having been taken to the pimps' apartment at knifepoint. She continuously refused to be prostituted, and was beaten, threatened with a knife, and burned on the leg with a curling iron. *Davis v. State,* 635 S.W.2d 737, 738 (Tex.Crim.App. 1982).

Forcing women to perform in pornography is another means by which pimps achieve control over women they prostitute. The pornography is used to threaten blackmail, inspire terror, and to break a woman's resistance to prostitution within a relationship promising "protection". Alone, friendless, and broke, a woman may be used in pornography by a pimp who otherwise appears harmless to her, and the only person who cares for her welfare:

> The third night I was away from home I was wandering around the streets in a sort of daze when I was befriended by a man about twenty years my senior. I confided my problems to him and he offered to take me in. During my stay with him he treated me relatively well. He was kind to me, he fed me, and he said he cared about me. He also kept me drugged, spoke glowingly about prostitution and took nude photographs of me.

Attorney General's Commission, Final Report, *supra,* at 823 (footnote omitted). Similarly, photographs may be taken in circumstances where the woman believes her privacy will be respected by a "boyfriend", only to be confronted later with the "choice" between publication of the photographs or prostituting for him. *See, e.g.*, *Dula v. State*, 679 S.W. 2d 601, 602 (Tex.Ct.App. 1984).

In some instances, however, the pimp may forego reliance on deceit. He may prefer to force a woman into performing in pornography as a direct means of sexually brutalizing her and controlling her by terror.

> This pimp made pornography of all of us. He also made tape recordings of us having sex with him and recordings of our screams and pleading when he gave us brutal beatings. It was not unusual for him to threaten us with death. He would later use these recordings to humiliate us by playing them for his friends in our presence, for his own sexual arousal, and to terrorize us and other women he brought home.

Attorney General's Commission, Final Report, *supra*, at 810 (footnote omitted). The pimp may conjoin strategies of systematic blackmail, sexual degradation and abuse, and coercion into pornography in a single efficient episode.

> I was the main woman of a pimp who filmed sexual acts almost every night in our home . . . [He and another man] arranged to have women, who I assumed were forced to be there, have sex with dogs and filmed those acts. There were stacks of films all over the house, which my pimp used to blackmail people with.

Testimony, *Public Hearings on an Ordinance to Add Pornography As Discrimination Against Women Before the Minneapolis City Council*, Government Operations Committee, Session II, 48 (Dec. 12 and 13, 1983) (hereinafter cited as Testimony, *Minneapolis Public Hearings*).

Pornography is routinely "introduced" to women as a means of effecting a "transition" to prostitution. The pornography is intended to normalize the practices depicted in sex with the pimp and ultimately with customers.

> My last pimp was a pornographer and the most brutal of all. He owned, on the average, three women and girls at any given time. There was always pornography in our apartment. Every night he would set up the projector and run a series of stag films. When he was sufficiently aroused he would choose one of us for sex. The sex that happened always duplicated the pornography. He used it to teach us how to service him. In retrospect the only sex I knew until I was well into my twenties was coercive sex taught me through pictures of women coerced into pornographic performances.

Attorney General's Commission, Final Report, *supra*, at 784–85. Another woman, speaking for a group of former prostitutes, has reported: .

One of the very first commonalities we discovered as a group, we were all introduced to prostitution through pornography, there were no exceptions in our group, and we were all under eighteen . . . Pornography was our textbook, we learned the tricks of the trade by men exposing us to pornography and us trying to mimic what we saw. I could not stress enough what a huge influence we feel this was.

Testimony, *Minneapolis Public Hearings, supra,* at 46.

Once the pimp has achieved some measure of control or influence over the woman, a vast repertoire of practices may be used to compel her into prostitution, and keep her there. These techniques, commonly known as "seasoning" practices, include verbal and physical abuse intended to break the woman's will, restructure her social and psychological identity, and create paranoia of the outside world while simultaneously cutting off outside ties.[8] *See* Barry, *Social Etiology, supra,* at 167. She is given a new name and new identity papers which both serve as cover from the police and separate the woman from her past. K. Barry, *Female Sexual Slavery, supra,* at 79. In one field research study of pimps, these practices were explained, by pimps themselves, as follows:

You create a different environment. It's a brainwashing process; the whole thing is creativity. When you turn a chick out, you take away every set of values and morality she had previously and create a different environment. You give her different friends.

She must cut all family ties, because, you see, she can't be with her family and ho [whore], too. You can't cope with bringing disgrace upon your mother or father, your sister or whoever it is. You have to get away from them.

Turning out a square broad means that you must literally change her mind.

C. Milner & R. Milner, *Black Players* 94-95 (1972). *See generally,* L. Lovelace, *supra* note 8. Pimps use pornography to inculcate an acceptance of the role the women are to play as prostitutes as one means of transforming the women's identity:

He used pornography to give me role models to follow, you know, women to try and portray. He'd say, "This is what I want you to look like."

---

8. Linda Marchiano states that "Strangely enough, what bothered me the most was the endless verbal abuse. He never let up: I was *so* dumb; I was *so* ugly; I was *so* fat; I was *so* thin; I was *so* flat-chested; and I was *so* lucky to have him taking care of me." L. Lovelace, *Ordeal* 51 (1980).

Interview with "A.D.", New York City, New York, WHISPER Oral History Project 24.

In addition, the woman may be raped, her children may be threatened, she may be systematically beaten and threatened with murder, and kept in a continuous state of poverty and indebtedness. *See, e.g.,* Barry, *Social Etiology, supra,* at 167, Erbe, *Prostitutes: Victims of Men's Exploitation and Abuse,* 2 Law & Inequality 609, 612-13 (1984); G. Geis, *One-Eyed Justice* 215-16 (1974). As described above, the woman may be used in pornographic performances to provide leverage for blackmail, to habituate her to sexual objectification and abuse, and to *produce* pornography.

When asked why young women don't leave their pimps when the pimps' intention to prostitute them becomes clear, the director of a prostitution outreach program replied:

> The pimp will take out a razor and say "Bitch, you gonna leave me? I bought you all these clothes, food, gave you a place to stay. Bitch, you owe me fucking money." Sometimes they take photographs of her naked and threaten to send these to her high school. A pimp will always steal a girl's purse and get her home address. He'll threaten her family, threaten to send the nude photos.

Interview with T. Able-Peterson, *quoted in* 1 WHISPER, Spring 1986, at 6.

Another researcher described the following incident as a "not uncommon" dynamic in the "relationship" between a pimp and a prostituted woman:

> He had a six-foot bullwhip and he hit me in the head with it. He told me he was going to take me home and kick my ass . . . It scared me so bad that I said to myself, "Slick, you are in for it now." We got home and he beat me with that bullwhip and told me to go to sleep.

Gray, *supra,* at 416. The outcome of these practices is that the woman "finds herself in a situation she has neither the physical nor psychological power to change." Barry, *Social Etiology, supra,* at 167.

And then there is the "work," itself. Bought and sold for change, women who are prostituted are reduced to sexual commodities. The result is a collapse in the woman's identity and destruction of her self-worth. One woman has described her experience in prostitution as follows:

> The worst part about prostitution is that you're obliged not to sell sex only, but your humanity. That's the worst part of it: that what you're selling is your human dignity . . . When I really felt like a whore was when I had to talk to them . . .

That's the most humiliating thing—having to agree with them all the time because you're bought. That's why it's not as easy as just saying "prostitution is selling a service." That's why it's selling your soul and not selling a service. . . It involves a kind of contempt, a kind of disdain, and a kind of triumph over another human being.

Interview with "J." in K. Millett, *Prostitution: A Quartet for Female Voices*, in Woman in Sexist Society 104, 106 (V. Gornick & B. Moran ed. 1971). Initial customer encounters are described by some women as terrible, traumatic experiences. C. Jaget, *Prostitutes: Our Life* 59, 121, 143 (1975). Even after a number of sexual transactions with customers, women experience enormous pain from being sexually used, combined with guilt, self-disgust, and a sense of worthlessness. T. Able-Peterson, *Children of the Evening* 28-29, 58-59 and *passim* (1981); *see also* Enablers, Inc., *supra*, at 125. The resulting confusion of identity marks a transition to further isolation for the women. *Id.*[9]

Once a woman is initiated into prostitution,[10] transactions with customers often involve the added dimension of the creation of a photographic record. One women has estimated that one half of her customers wanted to take photographs of her, including requests that she have intercourse with a dog, that she be tied up and spanked. Interview with "J", Chicago, Illinois, WHISPER Oral History Project 61-62 (1987). Another woman estimates that she was photographed by tricks at least 20 times, the first time when she was fourteen years old. She was photographed, sometimes while bound, in various acts including masturbation, intercourse, penetration with pop bottles, sausages, dildoes. Interview with "R.M.", Portland, Oregon, WHISPER Oral History Project 54-56 (1987). Yet another woman reports having been photographed engaging in intercourse, with a Halloween mask covering her face. Interview with "C.D.", Minneapolis, Minnesota, WHISPER Oral History Project 57 (1987). For some men, the process of taking the pictures itself was the principal "sex act" involved in the transaction. One woman reports having been tied with rope on a bed, gagged and blindfolded, while the customer took pictures and masturbated. Interview with "L.C.", Minneapolis, Minnesota, WHISPER Oral History Project 75-76 (1987).

Of course, it is impossible to determine how many of the photographs

---

9. The abuse entailed in the "servicing" of clients of course extends to women who are not individually coerced by pimps, almost all of whom report having no other options for feeding themselves upon entering prostitution. Silbert & Pines, *Entrance, supra,* at 486.

10. It is a difficult matter to distinguish between a woman's entry into prostitution and into performing in pornography. The incidence of customers demanding that a woman perform for a camera is quite high, rendering the categories of behavior indistinguishable. *See infra.* Moreover, commercial institutions such as nude modeling studios and massage parlors similarly "merge" the practices. For example, women who are prostituted in massage parlors may be required to pose for pornographic pictures for advertising brochures and leaflets distributed on the street. *See* Interview with "R.C.", Portland, Oregon, WHISPER Oral History Project 20 (1987).

taken of women under these circumstances are marketed in commercial pornography. Although the production of commercial pornography is often described and analyzed separately from pornography fabricated by pimps and customers of prostituted women, for the women involved the distinction may be a meaningless one.

> He had video equipment in his home long before it was mass pro-duced. Every time my pimp sent me to him he would take porno-graphic pictures of me and a second woman. He also made video tapes of the sex that took place under his direction. This continued on the average of once a week for about a year.

> There was an apartment that I was sent to often. There were usu-ally two to three men there. After I had sex with them, they would take pictures of me in various pornographic poses. When I was a young girl I didn't have the vocabulary to call them pornographers. I used to refer to them as "the photographers."

> On another occasion another young girl and myself were taken to an apartment in [sic] to meet some men. We were told that they were gangsters and that we should be nice to them. When we arrived we were taken into a room that had a large bed at its center surrounded by lighting and film equipment. We were told to act out a "lesbian scene". After about fifteen minutes we were told to get dressed, that they couldn't use us. We were returned to [our city] unpaid. Again, it was only in retrospect as an adult that I realized I had been used in a commercial pornographic film loop.

Attorney General's Commission, Final Report, *supra*, at 780–81 (footnote omitted).

Pornography is also forced on prostituted women by their customers both to describe the sexual acts they demand of the woman and to ration-alize the demand.

> [A] trick first showed me how to do bondage and discipline acts. I had numerous customers who would have pornographic material with them. I was asked to shave my pubic hairs because it reminded them of a child or engage in specific sex acts they had seen in a magazine. Having me urinate on them, commonly referred to as golden showers, was a popular request.

> Again my customers, who were mostly professional types, would bring examples in magazines or books of the types of bondage they wanted or of other acts they thought would satisfy their sexual desires, like me acting like their mother, enemas, spanking or cross dressing (men dressing in women's undergarments or clothing).

Attorney General's Commission, Final Report, *supra*, at 793.

Prostituted women often develop strategies of distancing themselves from their bodies, splitting their affective selves from their physical selves as a mechanism for coping with the use to which their bodies are put. *See* Barry, *The Network Defines Its Issues: Theory, Evidence and Analysis of Female Sexual Slavery,* in *International Feminism: Networking Against Female Sexual Slavery* 42 (K. Barry, C. Bunch, S. Castley ed. 1984) (reporting presentation of Hanna Olsson). Women have repeatedly reported resorting to this attempt at self-protection.

> When [the johns] touch my breasts, I tell myself they're not really touching me . . . [a]nd sometimes I wonder how I can let the men do that. I wonder what is left for me. I wonder where *I* am.

Edelstein, *In the Massage Parlor* 62, 63 in *Sex Work, supra.*

> We did as we were told . . . as that was happening, I made myself go numb. I thought of myself as a metal robot, no human feelings at all, and that worked for a while. I was feeling nothing.

L. Lovelace, *supra* note 8, at 57. After several months of being prostituted, the same woman reported:

> I was no longer experiencing things that made me feel good or bad. I felt as if my self had been taken away from me. I was not a person anymore. I was a robot, a vegetable, a wind up toy, a fucking-and-sucking doll. I had become someone else's thing.

Id. at 91.

However, this very survival strategy can entail serious adverse consequences for the woman. This attempt to resist, to refuse total submission to object status imposes a split in the self, Olsson, *supra*, at 42, which may further "season" a woman to exploitation. One former prostitute describes this outcome of this conditioning cogently.

> The removing of oneself from one's body is a strategy for immediate survival; many prostitutes acknowledge this. This numbing . . . is flight from that which is intolerable. Numbing mechanisms become reflex quickly . . . It is my belief that numbing in sexual assault situations sets women up for tolerating abuse, especially prostitution and sado-masochism.

Summer, *supra* note 6, at 36.[11]

---

11. Research on sexually abused children suggests that use of this tactic may ultimately result in the woman experiencing dissociative symptoms apart from her conscious control. Researchers theorize that dissociation was used as a strategy to avoid the experience of abuse and that later this becomes an autonomous symptom. Briere & Runtz, *Symptomatology Associated With Prior Sexual Abuse in a*

Women also seek to blunt the experience of prostitution by drug and alcohol abuse, which then becomes another economic "hook" into the practice and yet another barrier to being able to leave:

> It's important for you to know that most women who turn tricks have to be loaded on something. You don't have any woman out there selling this commodity and doing this trading who's not loaded on something. They're not that hip to business. *And they're not that void* . . . There's a price a woman pays.

Interview with "M", in K. Millett, *supra*, at 65 (emphasis added). Another woman has reported:

> When I first started to work the street my 11 month old girl was murdered by my pimp, and this started me using drugs so I wouldn't have to face the reality of what happened. It got to the point where drugs didn't help me anymore so I joined a drug program . . . Sure it helped me kick drugs, but all of a sudden I was awake and can see what I have become—which is nothing.

Letter from a woman prostituted for eight years, to Genesis House, a support program for prostituted women, *quoted in* 1 WHISPER, Winter 1986/87 at 7.

Further, in addition to the abuse incurred in "ordinary" sexual transactions with customers, prostituted women are subject to grave acts of violence by customers, including rape, beatings, customer-forced perversion and murder. Two hundred prostitutes were murdered in New York City in 1978. R. Rosen, *The Lost Sisterhood* 174 (1981). Forty prostituted women were murdered in the Seattle area between 1982 and 1984. Washington Post, Sept. 20, 1988, at § 1, A6. In one study of street prostitute victimization, seventy-eight percent of the women reported customer-forced perversion; an average of seventeen times per woman. Silbert & Pines, *Occupational Hazards of Street Prostitutes*, 8 Crim. Just. & Behav. 397 (1981) (hereinafter Silbert & Pines, *Occupational Hazards*). Seventy percent of the prostitutes reported customer rape or similar customer behavior, an average of thirty-one times per woman. *Id.* Sixty-five percent were physically abused and beaten by customers; an average of four times per woman. *Id. See also* Gray, *supra*, at 421. In the same study, approximately forty-one percent of the women reported assaults by police officers, including rapes and beatings. Silbert & Pines, *Occupational Hazards, supra*, at 367.

The rape, beating and torture promoted by pornography, together with the readiness of male customers to model their sexual demands on porno-

---

Non-Clinical Sample (1985) (unpublished paper) *cited in* D. Finkelhor, *supra*, at 155-56.

graphy, greatly enhances a woman's vulnerability to those forms of sexual abuse. Prostituted women, typically deprived of any means of effective resistance to sexual assault, become the "cathartic" instruments of sexual fascination with these acts, often at very high levels of violence and physical injury. *See* M. Silbert, *supra* note 6, at 61-69 (reporting extemely high levels of violence in almost every rape of prostitute subjects; seventy-three percent of subjects had been raped).[12]

> He stripped me, tied me up, spread-eagled on the bed so that I could not move and then began to caress me very gently. Then, when he thought that I was relaxed, he squeezed my nipple really hard. I did not react. He held up a porn magazine with a picture of a beaten woman and said, "I want you to look like that. I want you to hurt." He then began beating me, and when I didn't cry fast enough, he lit a cigarette and held it right above my breast for a long time before he burned me.

Attorney General's Commission, Final Report, *supra*, at 789. Another former prostitute describes the following incident:

> The man returned with two other men. They burned her with cigarettes and attached nipple clips to her breasts. They had many S and M magazines with them and showed her many pictures of women appearing to consent, enjoy, and encourage this abuse. She was held for twelve hours, continuously raped and beaten.

Testimony, *Minneapolis Public Hearings*, at 47. As the testimony of these women suggest, pornography may motivate the assault and be invoked to justify it. Prostituted women are, of course, no more immune generally from rape inspired by pornography than any other woman. One prostituted woman reports the following rape by a "non-customer":

> They were cutting me and kicking me and I kept saying I was pregnant but they thought it was funny. They said all kinds of pornographic things about pornographic pictures of doing it to a pregnant women [sic].

---

12.   The experience of prostituted women raped outside of their "work" suggests the sexual reasons why the assault of women within sexual transactions with customers is epidemic. Women sometimes attempt to defuse the levels of violence in non-customer rapes by telling the rapist that they are prostitutes; some data indicate that there was more violence involved in the rape when the woman disclosed this fact. For example, one woman reported:
   I thought he knew I was a prostitute but he didn't. When I told him he got real mad and kept beating me and punching me.
M. Silbert, *supra* note 6, at 62. Where a customer seeks the sexual "kick" of a rape by raping a prostitute, he may be motivated to inflict other severe violence on her in order to achieve the sensation of having overcome her resistance. Thus, the danger to women generally posed by the eroticization of rape in pornography is yet more threatening to prostituted women, both because of their curtailed capacity to resist and because of their "stepping up" of physical violence required to fulfill the "demands" of the sexual dynamic for the man.

M. Silbert, *supra* note 6, at 63.

The suicide rate among prostitutes confirms the intolerable conditions under which these women are compelled to exist. Seventy-five percent of a sampling of "call girls" reported suicide attempts. G. Geis, *supra*, at 174. Reports from public hospitals indicate that fifteen percent of all suicide victims are prostitutes. *Id.*; *see generally* Erbe, *supra*, at 618–619 (prostitutes as victims of customer exploitation and abuse).

In a 1983 study submitted to the United Nations on the institution of prostitution, the reporter made several findings which sum up the description presented by amici of the oppression and exploitation of prostituted women. As to the "blame" due the victims, the reporter concluded that the causes of prostitution, including "poverty, frustration or lack of affection, trickery, and coercion on the part of procurers, makes it unnecessary to invoke any kind of mental weakness or supposed vicious inclination to explain why women fall into prostitution." Further, the reporter continues,

> Once embarked on that course, they enter a state of servitude. Denied any independence, . . . subjected by the procurer to a very effective discipline that metes out punishment with an infrequent admixture of reward, they immediately find themselves in a marginal situation and undergo a psychological conditioning such as may be experienced by someone living in a community within a sect. When able to judge objectively, those women who have been able to escape from this environment realized that they were deprived not only of their name, but of their very identity. . . . Those few prostitutes who are not controlled by a procurer do not find it much easier to break free of their environment, so profoundly have they been marked by it and so strongly do they feel themselves rejected, as in fact they often are, by the "normal" society to which they wish to return. It would not be an exaggeration to say that, if she is to be successfully reintegrated into that society, a prostitute requires heroic courage.

U.N. Dept of Int'l Economic and Social Affairs, Report of J. Fernaud-Laurent, Special Rapporteur on the Suppression of the Traffic in Persons and the Exploitation of the Prostitution of Others, at 12-13, U.N. Doc. ST/ESA/174, U.N. Sales No. E. 85. IV. 11 (1983).

Finally, we must question why it is true that prostituted women are "rejected" by "normal" society. The American hostages in Iran were filmed at Christmas, telling us they were well treated, well fed, and under no physical threat. Those films were not used to undermine them later, as evidence that they *were* well treated, contrary to their subsequent descriptions. Rather, the films were understood as evidence of *further* mistreatment and coercion. The experience of women coerced into making pornographic films while in prostitution is quite the opposite:

It was clear to me that in the years I was in prostitution that all of the women I met were systematically coerced into prostitution and pornography the same way a prisoner of war is systematically imprisoned, tortured and starved into compliance by his captors. The difference is that prisoners of war are not held responsible for coerced statements and acts but when a girl or woman is coerced in this very manner into prostitution and for use in pornography, she is held responsible.

Attorney General's Commission, Final Report, *supra*, at 809–810.

In the arena of First Amendment jurisprudence, arguments to the "slippery slope" are sometimes invoked to support the need for bright line rules in the doctrine, *see, e.g., Boos v. Barry*, 108 S. Ct. 1157, 1171–72 (1988) (Brennan, J., dissenting) or to explain the inevitability of certain results. Indeed, both the district and appeals courts in *Hudnut* set forth such arguments in their opinions. *Hudnut*, 598 F. Supp. at 1335–36; 771 F.2d at 327, 328, 330. Such arguments are often criticized as relying on irreal "parades of horribles" for rhetorical impact and as hypothetical to the point of absurdity. "Slippery slope" arguments can, of course, sometimes assist in sharpening analysis of the presence or absence of logical toeholds and limits to a particular legal rule. On the slippery slope of gender inequality, there is, however, no need to speculate as to the grade of the terrain or the risk of a fall to the bottom. For all women, prostitution *is* the bottom. Hundreds of thousands of real women have been pushed and kept there by the social avalanche of the demand that a class of women be available for sexual use by men. We already know because these women are already living it, or have already lost their lives for it. For these women, there were no toeholds, logical, legal, social, or sexual, to define the "limit" beyond which they could not be abused. We therefore urge this court, in pondering whether "Leda and The Swan" might be considered pornography under the ordinance, as postulated in *Hudnut*, in some fantasized future law suit, brought by some unidentified party, before an as-yet nameless judge, to bear in mind simultaneously that prostitution is not an hypothesized condition.[13]

In amici's view, the remedial provisions afforded in the ordinance would provide such a toehold, by means uniquely effective for prostitution victims. Section 3, subdivision 1 of the ordinance creates a cause of action for women coerced, intimidated, or fraudulently induced into performing in pornography. Like a refracted image in a kaleidoscope, coercion into

---

13. If the English language has any claim to being a language at all, rather than a tonal system of plosives and glottal stops, Yeats' poem is no more "pornography" under the ordinance than it is "obscenity," or, for that matter, a "frying pan." For an analysis of the application of the definition of pornography to this particular work, *see* Seator, *supra* note m, at 310 n.77 (1987). This article also cogently contrasts the use of "slippery slope" arguments in First Amendment doctrine with their application in equality analysis. *See id.* at 323 n.140

pornographic performances emerges as a repeated practice in the cycle of prostitution, inseparable from the panoply of coercive and exploitative means by which women are prostituted, from early sexual abuse to sexual transactions with customers to the production of commercial pornography. Moreover, short of the remedies in the ordinance, the permanent record created in the pornography renders it impossible for a woman ever wholly to escape prostitution. As long as the pornography is consumed, the material permits ongoing sexual access to the woman by anyone who can afford it, multiplied to limits set only by the constraints of available technology. So long as the pictures of her still exist as sexual commodities for exchange, she is being prostituted. The continued consumption of the pornography reinflicts the injury experienced in its production.

The Final Report of the Attorney General's Commission on Pornography reaches a similar conclusion in its summary of the effects of performing in pornography:

> During the course of our review of the position of performers in pornography, we have encountered evidence that they suffer physical coercion, damage to health, serious economic exploitation, and virtually complete loss of reputation. The pornography which they helped to create will live on to plague them long after they have extricated themselves from modeling. Its effects subject performers to long-term effects potentially worse than any other form of sexual abuse, a fact noted tellingly by Dr. Ulrich Schoettle in the context of child pornography:
>
>> Pornography is a graphic form of exhibitionism . . . . Pornography literally makes the child's body "available" for anyone willing to pay the price anywhere in the world.
>
> The "privacy interest" of performers in pornography seem to us real and compelling, while the value of the material itself is often indisputably minimal.

Attorney General's Commission, Final Report, *supra*, at 898. These conclusions were based on testimonial and documentary evidence of injury sustained by *all* performers, including those who did not themselves directly identify their participation as "coerced", or report that they were otherwise engaged in prostitution.

As the Commission itself asserted, prostitution and performing in pornography from the point of the women used in each are not distinct activities. The Commission noted, in its study of the use of performers in pornography generally, the "similarity of backgrounds of many of these models to those of prostitutes," *id.* at 859 n. 983, finding the following characteristics to be generally true of commercial pornography's use of performers:

(1) that they are normally young, previously abused, and financially strapped; (2) that on the job they find exploitative economic arrangements, . . . serious health hazards, strong temptations to drug use, and little chance of career advancement; and (3) that in their personal lives they will often suffer substantial injuries to relationships, reputation, and self-image.

Id. at 888. The Commission further speculated that "[b]ecause pornography and prostitution are so strongly linked, it may of course be inferred that the coercion which historically and currently afflicts the latter will play some role in the former." *Id.* at 867 n.1009. Certainly, when the woman *is* coerced, into the immediate performance as well as exploited as a prostitute, the effects may be yet more damaging than even those the Commission found "potentially worse than any other form of sexual abuse."[14]

Moreover, the continued availability of the pornography stands as an enduring threat of shame and humiliation against a woman already severely abused. The pornography can be used at any time to topple whatever security and safety the woman may have been able to achieve, already against considerable odds. One woman who escaped prostitution and pornography states:

> But there still exists the pornography that was made of me. I know the men who made it, I know where they are, and there is nothing I can do about it. I live knowing that at any time it could surface and could be used to humiliate me and my family. I know that it can be used to ruin my professional life in the future. I know because some of it was produced within months before my eighteenth birthday that it is protected under current law.

Attorney General's Commission, Final Report, *supra*, at 808 (footnote omitted). When men who have seen pornography made of a woman then see her, she is targeted for physical injury and sexual assault. There is no "putting the abuse behind her," because the abuse simply doesn't end, so long as the material remains available for consumption. Again, unlike films made of prisoners of war, the pornography stands as testament that

---

14. Some prosecutors have also drawn a connection between prostitution and the production of pornography, seeking pandering convictions of producers of pornography on the theory that hiring persons to perform for such films or pictures is promotion of prostitution. *See, e.g., People v. Souter,* 120 Cal. App. 3d 1039, 178 Cal. Rptr. 111 (1981); *People v. Fixler,* 56 Cal. App. 3d 321, 128 Cal. Rptr. 363 (1976); *but see People ex rel. Van De Kamp v. American Art Enterprises, Inc.,* 75 Cal. App. 3d 523, 142 Cal. Rptr. 598, 758 P.2d 1128 (1988) (en banc) (disapproving *Fixler* and *American Art Enterprises* on First Amendment grounds); *People v. Kovner,* 96 Misc. 2d 414, 409 N.Y.S.2d 349 (Sup. Ct. 1978). *See Arcara v. Cloud Books, Inc.,* 106 S. Ct. 3172, 3177 (1986) (closure of bookstore under nuisance statute permissible where acts of prostitution transpired on the premises, rejecting First Amendment challenge) ("First Amendment values may not be invoked by merely linking the words 'sex' and 'books' ", *Arcara,* 106 S. Ct. at 3177.). For reasons discussed *infra,* amici do not support this approach to the problem of coercion in pornographic performances, subjecting as it does the woman herself to prosecution for prostitution. However, amici are sympathetic to the view implied by this prosecutorial design that perceives prostitution and pornographic performances as overlapping descriptive categories.

she wanted all this, that she wasn't forced at all, that she wasn't injured, that she *is* the object the pornography depicts her to be.[15]

The ordinance affords monetary and injunctive relief to persons coerced into performing in pornography against makers, sellers, exhibitors and distributors of pornography produced by force. These remedial provisions could provide substantial redress to prostituted women so injured. The deterrent effect of the damages remedy may impede the open season practiced on women too naive, vulnerable, or sexually coerced to avoid being used in this way. The necessity of the injunctive remedy in perfecting the relief, and, in some cases, in providing a meaningful remedy at all, cannot be overemphasized. As shown above, the continued availability of the pornography operates as an ongoing grievous injury which is not and cannot be redressed by monetary damages alone.

The provisions of the ordinance which prohibit forcing pornography on a person, and create a cause of action for assault, physical attack, or injuring a person in a way directly caused by specific pornography, similarly describe injuries immediately linked to exploitative and abusive practices in prostitution. As amici have attempted to demonstrate, the lives of women in prostitution are defined by two major influences: the sexual demands of strangers, and the economic and sexual incentive of those who profit from providing women to meet those demands. These provisions of the ordinance at least place a legal floor on the means by which this exploitation can be accomplished. Forcing pornography on women emerges as the *sine qua non* of "seasoning" young girls to prostitution, battering them into compliance, fear, and a posture of hopelessness. The availability of the claim the ordinance provides could achieve some measure of "breathing space" to young women in resisting prostitution. Pimps are placed on notice that they must devise some other means of indoctrinating young women and silencing their refusals, confusion and shock.

Similarly, both provisions would provide redress for egregious customer abuse of prostitutes, especially rape and torture modeled on explicitly sadistic (often euphemistically referred to as "sado-masochistic") pornography. Amici would emphasize the need for injunctive remedies in meeting these ends. For women already under the control of a pimp or a customer, *post hoc* claims for damages against perpetrators, although important, are no substitute for removal of the pornography itself, and the consequent diminution of the supply of the material available for such use.

---

15. The pornographic record created of the woman, too, materially celebrates the "self-objectifying" mechanism women employ to avoid the experience of abuse. As she dissociates from her body, the pornography renders her an object for sexual consumption. The cruelty of this process lies in the fact that what is, for her, an attempt to maintain some sense of integrity by leaving her body behind, the pornography confirms as her identity. The "success" of the pornography, then, may be in direct inverse relation to her psychological and emotional trauma. Reconsider the "naturalism" of *Playboy* magazine. As will be described in what follows, pornography is "perfected" prostitution: an accessible woman transformed into a sexual object for consumption.

The ordinance also creates a claim against persons who traffic in pornography. This provision,\ in amici's view, is of greatest potential significance in curbing the traffic in women in prostitution. The traffic in pornography directly contributes to the immediate sexual demand for prostituted women. Promoters of prostitution often supply customers with pornography to arouse them sexually and to ensure a demand for their "product": live women, or more precisely perhaps, "animated pornography".

When I worked at massage studios, the owners had subscriptions to *Playboy, Penthouse, Penthouse Forum* and the like. These magazines were arranged in the waiting area of most of the massage places which I worked in. If a girl was not inside with a trick, she was expected to sit out front with the men who were waiting or who were undecided and to look at the magazines with them in order to get them titillated . . .

They used the soft porn to help them work up the courage to try the acts described in the magazine with the prostitutes at the massage studio.

Testimony, *Minneapolis Public Hearings, supra*, at 48.

I was also forced to work conventions. These were weekend affairs held at major hotels in New York attended by hundreds of professional men. The series of events was the same. Pornographic films followed by myself and other women having sex with the men. The films that were shown most often set the tone for the kinds of acts we were expected to perform.

Attorney General's Commission, Final Report, *supra*, at 784. Further, amici have already detailed the frequency with which customers make specific sexual demands on women patterned after the scenarios in pornography.

Even in instances where pornography may not be materially present, stimulating the customer and providing a script for his behavior, the effect of pornography in modeling the transaction is often apparent. One woman, formerly prostituted, reported the following events as an example of the common practice of using pornography as a sexual benchmark:

If pornography was not actually in the room with the client, there would be constant reference. One example is that a woman was in a room with two clients. One man told the other that he had seen some pictures of women who had shaved their pubic hair and that it had turned him on. They then proceeded with a jackknife to remove the woman's pubic hairs, plucking and burning what the knife missed. They made comments of how her hairless vagina reminded them of their young daughter's genitals. They then, of course, engaged in intercourse.

Testimony, *Minneapolis Public Hearings, supra*, at 47. In sum, the traffic in pornography both creates a sexual incentive for prostitution and defines the conduct which will meet the sexual agenda so created.

The confirmation of this description rests squarely in the practices of pimps in training women for prostitution. Pimps are in the business of understanding the "market" in prostitutes, of meeting the sexual demands and preferences of customers, as well as creating a market for prostitutes by creating traffic in pornography—by the use of those same women. Their judgment on the quality of those demands cannot be bettered. It is plain that the conditioning and indoctrination of women to prostitution by pimps, as examined above, is dictated by the scenarios of pornography. Thus, in their judgment, selling customers "live" pornography describes the market, unerringly.

And what is the product? In amici's experience, and as the data presented here suggests, it is a woman who is available for sexual use as the ordinance defines pornography: an explicitly sexually subordinated woman, dehumanized as a sexual object, thing or commodity, treated as a sexual object who enjoys pain or humiliation, used as a sexual object who experiences sexual pleasure in rape, presented as a sexual object tied up or cut up or mutilated or bruised, or physically hurt, etc.[16] These conditions precisely define how women are injured in prostitution, as well as why women are demanded in prostitution. Pornography, so defined, is "perfected" prostitution, which live women are coerced, violated, drugged, and turned into sexual robots to "enact" as well as they are capable, as many of the women were treated in order to produce it in the first place. Thus, the traffic in pornography, constructing as it does the sexual demand and specific "sexuality" of prostitution, is a direct causal factor in the victimization of women in prostitution.

---

16. This connection between the meaning of prostitution and the definition of pornography contained in the ordinance was analyzed by Professor Kathleen Barry, in her presentation at a recent conference on prostitution, *Trafficking in Women*, organized by The Coalition Against Trafficking in Women, Oct. 22, 1988, New York City, New York (unpublished paper).

The remaining definitional elements include:

(v). women are presented in postures or positions of sexual submission, servility, or display; or

(vi). women's body parts—including but not limited to vaginas, breasts or buttocks—are exhibited such that women are reduced to those parts; or

(vii). women are presented as whores by nature; or

(viii). women are presented being penetrated by objects or animals; or

(ix). women are presented in scenarios of degradation, humiliation, injury, torture, shown as filthy or inferior, bleeding, bruised or hurt in a context that makes these conditions sexual.

B. *The City's interests in providing these remedies to prostituted women are compelling.*

By whatever measure this court may employ, redress of the injuries here described constitutes a compelling interest. The Supreme Court's holdings in *New York v. Ferber*, 458 U.S. 747 (1982) and *Roberts v. U.S. Jaycees*, 468 U.S. 609 (1984) plainly support this result. *See also Rotary International v. Rotary Club*, 107 S. Ct. 1742 (1987) (relying on *Roberts, supra*). In each case, the Court held an asserted infringement of First Amendment guarantees outweighed by a countervailing interest, specifically, impeding juvenile sexual exploitation, *see Ferber*, 458 U.S. at 756-64, and prohibiting discrimination against women. *See Roberts*, 468 U.S. at 624-27. Taken together, these same concerns describe those advanced by the ordinance. Intervenors have already ably argued the application of those cases to this case. Amici will here argue the particular application of the Court's reasoning in *Ferber* and *Roberts*, in holding these interests compelling, to the condition of prostituted women.[17]

The most cogent facial distinction between *Ferber* and this case is, of course, that the statute at issue in *Ferber* criminalized "sexually explicit" performances by minors under the age of 16, *see Ferber*, 458 U.S. at 750-51, while the remedies contained in the ordinance are available to claimants without regard to age. However, parsing the urgency of the need for redress for injury by pornography experienced by women, and experienced by children, is both distorting as a matter of fact and legally irrelevant. As discussed above, the average age of women initiated into prostitution is sixteen or younger. The injuries amici have documented here do, in fact, substantially befall minor women, rendering this legislation supplemental to, and not exclusive of, the criminal sanctions upheld in *Ferber*. Nor do these injuries evaporate or disappear or subside once a girl passes the statutory age of majority. A sixteenth birthday, for her, likely means but one more day of the same abuse she endured the day before. The day she turns sixteen may be a day she is raped; the day after, she may be forced to perform in pornography. Turning eighteen may be significant only in that she is, by twenty-four hours, that much more likely to have sustained injury, and that much less likely to be able to escape prostitution.[18]

---

17. *A fortiori*, the City's justification for this regulation is also sufficiently "substantial" to satisfy the intermediate level of scrutiny applied to content-neutral legislation.

18. The Court in *Ferber* in fact showed some equivocation about the constitutional meaning of the age line drawn in the New York statute. Although the statute upheld in *Ferber* criminalized the production and distribution of "sexually explicit" material using a child younger than sixteen, *Ferber*, 458 U.S. at 750-51, the Court did not suggest that the age of sixteen had talismanic significance to its result. The Court noted, without suggesting possible constitutional infirmity, that sixteen state pornography statutes in effect at the time of the Court's decision defined "child" as a person under the age of eighteen, while four more placed the statutory age at seventeen. *Id.* at 764 n.18. Presumably, those statutes too would be constitutional directly under the *Ferber* holding. Thus, the *Ferber* balance

Further, the assumption made by the district court in *Hudnut* that "adult women generally have the capacity to protect themselves" from exploitation in pornography is contradicted in reality. *Hudnut*, 598 F. Supp. at 1334. Some women may be equipped with more durable social "buffers" than others, like money, a safer place to live, a secure job. However, as the data on the use of force in procuring women in prostitution presented above shows, where there is a demand for women prostituted for pornography, that demand will be met, by any means possible. Individual women can "protect themselves" only insofar as they are not, for the moment, demanded. The implicit assumption in the district court's statement therefore must be that the women exploited in pornography had the capacity to protect themselves, and chose not to exercise it. The documentation presented by amici hopefully puts that assumption to rest.

To the extent that the Supreme Court's opinion in *Ferber* is construed to turn on a presumed incapacity of minors meaningfully to consent to participation in sexually explicit performances, the scope of the substantive provisions in the ordinance renders that difference legally irrelevant. Four of the five causes of action in the ordinance require an explicit or implicit *showing* of lack of consent to sustain a prima facie case. Thus, the "presumptive" incapacity to consent implied as a predicate to the *Ferber* rationale is, under the ordinance, substituted with a required element of proof of coercion. Although the trafficking provision, by its terms, does not require a direct showing of force, it does mandate proof that the material subordinates women, in specified ways. As intervenors and other amici have shown, subordination itself is force. Moreover, as amici here have demonstrated, the traffic in pornography is both cause and effect in the victimization of women in prostitution, inseparable from the violence and duress to which they are subjected. Therefore, distinctions based on the degree of volition exercised by the victims in *Ferber* and women aggrieved under the ordinance cannot endure scrutiny.

The Court in *Ferber* also based its conclusion on its view that "[t]he value of permitting live performances and photographic reproductions of children engaged in lewd sexual conduct is exceedingly modest, if not *de minimus.*" *Ferber*, 458 U.S. at 762. In support of this conclusion, the Court found it unlikely that such material would constitute an important part of a literary or scientific work, which could not be conveyed through alternative means. *Id.* It is similarly rare for materials which meet the definition of pornography in the ordinance to constitute an important part of such a work, contrary to the overblown assertions often raised against this legislation. In addition, the countervailing social commitment to

---

of harms is struck in favor of protecting women at least to the age of eighteen. The Washington child pornography statute criminalizes such conduct at different severity levels, depending on whether the child is younger than eighteen or younger than sixteen. Wash. Rev. Code §9.68A.040 (1988).

prohibiting discrimination against women further diminishes the claim to serious value made for material described in the ordinance.

Roberts v. U.S. Jaycees, 468 U.S. 609 (1984) struck a similar balance in holding the state's interest in curbing discrimination against women by exclusion from all-male professional clubs outweighed the male membership's First Amendment rights to freedom of expression. To the extent that the plaintiffs' expressive interests are arguably burdened to a greater degree under the ordinance than were the First Amendment interests asserted by the Jaycees in *Roberts, see id.* at 626–27 (finding Jaycees' interests little impeded by application of challenged regulation), amici contend that the competing interest in prohibiting those sex discriminatory practices described in the ordinance are of comparably enhanced significance. To state the point delicately, while exclusion from membership to all-male social club may significantly impede a woman's career development, women consumed in prostitution and pornography have somewhat more at stake than this.[19]

Prostitution and pornography are such entrenched institutions, so long touted as rooted in the free choice of women, normative and (therefore) harmless outcomes of male sexuality, and in any case inevitable, that the sex discriminatory purpose and effect of these practices becomes simultaneously obscured. The testimony of women and empirical evidence cited here clarifies the sex-based character and discriminatory result of these practices. Sexual harassment law also affords an appropriate legal framework for analysis. In concluding that sexual harassment in employment is "based on sex," the D.C. Circuit Court, in an early and influential opinion reasoned that "[b]ut for her womanhood, from aught that appears, her participation in sexual activity would never have been solicited." *Barnes v. Costle*, 561 F.2d 983, 990 (D.C. Cir. 1977)[20] *see also Meritor Savings Bank v. Vinson*, 477 U.S. 57, 64 (1986) ("Without question, when a supervisor sexually harasses a subordinate because of the subordinate's sex, that supervisor 'discriminate[s]' on the basis of sex," quoting 42 U.S.C.

---

19. Including rape, murder, beating, torture, and other acts criminalized under Washington law. *See, e.g.,* Wash.Rev.Code § 9A.44 (1988) (rape); Wash.Rev. Code § 9A.46 (1988) (harassment, including threats to cause bodily injury in the future or threats of physical confinement); Wash.Rev.Code § 9A40.020 (1988) (kidnapping in the first degree). Given the indivisibility of prostitution and pornography as institutions, and the emerging, clear evidence of the violent criminal conduct necessarily entailed in maintaining both, the rationale, if not the precise legal standard, excluding advocacy which incites lawless action from First Amendment protection lends weight to amici's argument here. *See Brandenburg v. Ohio*, 395 U.S. 444, 447 (1969); *Hess v. Indiana*, 414 U.S. 105, 107–09 (1973). Certainly the evidence of systematic coercion, intimidation and sexual terror necessary to the viability of the pornography industry qualifies the likelihood of such conduct more probable than a "general fear" of commission of future crime, *Tinker v. Des Moines Indep. Community School Dist.*, 393 U.S. 503, 508 (1969), or "[m]ere speculation . . . that individuals might at some time engage in illegal activity." *San Diego Comm. Against Registration and the Draft v. Governing Bd.*, 790 F.2d 1471, 1479 (9th Cir. 1986), citing *Gay Student Orgs. v. Bonner*, 509 F.2d 652, 662 (1st Cir. 1974).

20. The court also noted that its analysis on this point was no less applicable to, nor defeated by, the use of men as sexual victims by other men or women. *See Barnes*, 561 F.2d at 990 n.55.

2000e-2(a)(1), Title VII of the Civil Rights Act of 1964). It also goes without saying that but for a prostituted woman's "womanhood," she would not have been coerced into prostitution in the first place, beaten, used and raped by customers and pimps, and terrorized, exploited and sold in pornography.[21]

Moreover, the injuries afforded redress under the ordinance lie at the heart of the prohibitions against sex discrimination elaborated in current law. Sexual harassment law proscribes any "requirement that a man or woman run a gauntlet of sexual abuse in return for the privilege of being allowed to work and make a living." *Vinson*, 477 U.S. at 67 (quoting *Henson*, 682 F.2d at 902). Clearly, the City's interest in affording remedies to women discriminated against in pornography and prostitution far exceed those interests advanced by legal prohibitions against sexual discrimination in employment.[22] Here, the "employment" is better understood as a condition of sex discriminatory involuntary servitude, the "services" themselves "run[ning] the gauntlet of sexual abuse." *See United States v. Kozminski*, 108 S. Ct. 2751, 2765, 101 L.Ed.2d 788 (1988) (defining "involuntary servitude" as a condition of servitude in which the victim is forced to work for the defendant by the use or threat of physical restraint or physical injury, or by the use or threat of coercion through law or the legal process); *see also United States v. Lewis*, 649 F. Supp. 1109 (W.D. Mich. 1986) (involuntary servitude plainly applied to defendant's conduct in frequently and severely beating children and forcing them to view the wounds of others); *United States v. Mussry*, 726 F.2d 1448 (9th Cir. 1984) (involuntary servitude indictment sufficient where facts alleged include transporting indigent foreign workers to U.S., keeping them in conditions of poverty and indebtedness, and withholding passports); *United States v. Warren*, 772 F.2d 827 (11th Cir. 1985).[23]

---

21. This is not to suggest that boys and young men are not also used in prostitution and pornography. The point is that for a *woman* so used, *she* is use because she is a woman, and for no other reason.

22. Describing the use of women in pornography and prostitution as sex discrimination is not inconsistent with case law holding that enforcement of criminal prostitution statutes against women only does not violate equal protection principles. *See, e.g., State v. Wilbur*, 110 Wash. 2d 16, 749 P.2d 1295 (1988); *People v. Nelson*, 103 Misc. 2d 847, 427 N.Y.S.2d 194 (1980); *People v. Superior Court*, 138 Cal. Rptr. 66, 562 P.2d 1315 (1977). In *Wilbur*, the Washington Supreme Court denied an equal protection challenge to the facial terms of the Washington prostitution statute, which at that time criminalized *receiving* a fee for "sexual services" but not "*paying*" a fee. The court reasoned that the facial gender neutrality of the statute was sufficient to satisfy equality norms. The defendant did not raise an "as applied" challenge. In cases alleging discriminatory enforcement of prostitution statutes against women only, the claims typically founder on an insufficient showing of discriminatory intent on the part of law enforcement officers. *Nelson, supra; People v. Superior Court, supra*. In each class of case, the allegedly culpable party was the state or a state actor: the facial legislative design in *Wilbur*, the intent of police personnel in the discriminatory enforcement cases. Here, by contrast, it is the conduct of the parties *to* the transactions which constitute the sex discriminatory practices described here, a wholly distinct legal configuration for purposes of equal protection analysis.

23. Declaring these interests compelling is also consistent with constitutional norms of the state of Washington. Washington's state Equal Rights Amendment (ERA) mandates that "Equality of rights

Furthermore, an invidious sex discriminatory practice is discernible by its enforcement of "outmoded and archaic stereotypes" of female subservient roles. See *Mississippi University for Women v. Hogan*, 458 U.S. 718 (1982); *Frontiero v. Richardson*, 411 U.S. 677 (1973). The "stereotypes" promoted and enforced by the demands of the pornography industry are not limited to assumptions that males are breadwinners and heads of households, see *Frontiero*, 411 U.S. at 680; *Bobb v. Municipal Court*, 143 Cal. App.3d 860, 192 Cal. Rptr. 270 (1983), or that women are properly confined to certain traditional occupations, *Hogan*, 458 U.S. at 729–730, or physically incapable of participating in certain sports, *Yellow Springs Exempted Village School Dist. Bd. of Educ. v. Ohio High School Athletic Assn.*, 647 F.2d 651 (6th Cir. 1981), or less able competently to control family wealth, *Kirchberg v. Feenstra*, 450 U.S. 455 (1981). In each of the cited cases, courts concluded that enforcement of such stereotypes stigmatized and humiliated women, impeding their full participation in civil life.

What men buy, trade or take in prostitution and pornography is their stereotype of a woman. Whatever "woman" means to him, she must be; whatever he wants from a "woman", she must want, or not, as he wishes. From the customers' point of view, what is bought, traded or taken is an object which is gender-female. This is a modest law. It does not claim that using women as sexual objects for consumption is invidious sex discrimination. Rather, only the use of women as subordinate sexual objects who enjoy pain, take pleasure in sexual assault, who exist as body parts, or are mutilated and cut so qualifies. Stereotyping women as economically dependent in a marriage, so as to require them to rebut a legal presumption to that effect, is sex discrimination. *Frontiero*, 411 U.S. at 680. Amici respectfully submit that if that is sex discrimination, the sexual commodity exchange of women, requiring women to *live* the "stereotypes" demanded by men, as limited to the practices defined in the ordinance, is something more. If sex discrimination exists, this is sex discrimination. If sex discrimination harms women, this is the length and breadth and width of that harm. If securing equality for women can ever be deemed a compelling interest, by any means, this is the means.

---

and responsibilities under the law shall not be denied or abridged on account of sex." Wash. Const. Art XXXI, § 1. The state ERA has been construed to secure substantive sex equality, in excess of that vested under a "strict scrutiny" analysis for gender classifications. *Darrin v. Gould*, 85 Wash. 2d 859, 871, 540 P.2d 487, 492 (1978) (en banc), superseding an "equality of opportunity" rationale with an "equality of outcome" analysis. Thus, the state of Washington, placing even stronger constitutional weight on equality for women than the federal equal protection clause exerts against racial classifications, confirms the compelling nature of the interests asserted by intervenors and amici. The United States Supreme Court has reserved the question whether a state interest afforded under a state constitutional provision may outweigh free speech interests protected by the federal constitution. *Widmar v. Vincent*, 102 S. Ct. 269, 277 (1981). Amici do not here assert that the state ERA alone, however, mandates a result in intervenors' favor.

C. *The remedies afforded by the ordinance are narrowly tailored to
provide prostituted women a means to escape.*

The substantive remedies provided by the ordinance extend no further
than necessary to redress the injuries cognized by the law. Thus, the ordinance meets the final element justifying content-based restrictions on expression. *See, e.g., Riley v. National Fed'n of the Blind*, 108 S. Ct. 2667,
2679 (1988); *Boos v. Barry*, 108 S. Ct. 1157, 1164 (1988). As amici have
discussed above, each of the remedial provisions interdicts conduct essential and crucial to the "task" of exploiting women in prostitution and sus-
taining the institution of pornography. Amici here will address two common objections to the scope of the remedies afforded by the ordinance:
first, that the trafficking provision sweeps too broadly; second, that existing state criminal law sufficiently advances the interests protected under
the ordinance so as to render the ordinance superfluous.

The traffic in women in prostitution and the traffic in pornography
cannot, as amici have shown, be meaningfully distinguished, in life or
logic. The trafficking remedy strikes at the core of the victimization of
women by pornography. The remedy impedes the cycle of prostitution
and pornography: by diminishing the incentive to produce pornography,
the incentive to prostitute women to produce pornography is lessened; by
slaking the sexual demand for prostituted women, the incentive to prostitute women to meet that demand is reduced. A similar rationale was relied upon by the Court in *Ferber* in upholding prohibitions on distribution of child pornography. There, the Court stated that "[t]he distribution
network for child pornography must be closed if the production of material which requires the sexual exploitation of children is to be effectively
controlled." *Ferber*, 458 U.S. at 759. Conversely, "the advertising and
selling of child pornography provide an economic motive for and are thus
an integral part of the production of such materials." *Ferber*, 458 U.S. at
761. Amici urge this court to adopt the *Ferber* court's reasoning in this
case, presenting as it does an identical nexus between production, distribution, and sexual exploitation.

In addition, enforcement of the trafficking provision is crucial in effecting actual redress of the injuries described in the other substantive provisions. Amici are aware that proving a prima facie case establishing liability under any of these provisions would present difficult evidentiary
hurdles for plaintiffs. To establish a claim for relief for a coerced pornographic performance, in addition to proving coercion, the woman of course
must be able to name a defendant. In instances where the maker of the
pornography was a customer, the anonymity of the transaction may
render that effort futile. Where the maker was a pimp, and thus more
readily identified by the woman, he may evade the jurisdiction of the court
or take his chances in failing to make an appearance. In either case, the

material may be wholly unrecoverable, mooting a claim for injunctive relief and jeopardizing even a claim for damages. Claims against distributors would, for identical reasons, be fragile from the outset. In addition,
proof of force under the prohibition against forcing pornography on a person, and proving legal causation under the assault provision place strin-
gent constraints on the scope of liability under these sections. Establishing
the ordinary elements permitting injunctive relief, i.e., the inadequacy of a
legal remedy and irreparable injury (including the probability of continuing harm), under the facts often to be presented in such a case, would
likely present very difficult obstacles to securing equitable remedies. *See,
e.g., City of Los Angeles v. Lyons*, 461 U.S. 95 (1983). Thus, insofar as
the other provisions describe injuries mandating redress, the trafficking
provision is incontestably necessary to effect them.

The argument is sometimes made that enforcement of existing criminal
sanctions against rape, prostitution, distribution of obscenity and related
offenses will sufficiently curtail the "abuses" of pornography and adequately secure the safety of women, without resort to the remedies defined
in the ordinance. In amici's experience, however, enforcement of these
criminal prohibitions is both unresponsive to injuries sustained by prostituted women through pornography, and wholly impracticable. Enforcement of criminal laws pertaining to sexual assault depend almost entirely
on the willingness and capacity of victims to report them to the police. For
women in prostitution, the common reasons for not reporting sexual assault, that is, suspicion of police, fear, belief that the report will not be
believed or taken seriously, are multiplied.[24] Moreover, the rate of police
officer assault of prostituted women may be extremely high. As stated
above, forty-one percent of prostituted women in one study reported assaults by police, including rapes and beatings. Silbert & Pines, *Occupational Hazards, supra*, at 397. These same personnel would be the recip-
ients of complaints of rape, coercion, harassment, and kidnapping. It is
unlikely that a woman in prostitution would find availing herself of criminal remedies, as suggested, a sufficient alternative remedy.

Moreover, the scope and effect of criminal sanctions against distribution
of obscenity and prostitution do not adequately further the interests protected under the ordinance. Obscenity statutes, tailored to conform to the
Miller standard, *Miller v. California*, 413 U.S. 15, 24 (1973), do not
even address the injuries sustained by women coerced into performing in
pornography, much less afford women meaningful remedies. The Court in
Ferber eloquently rejected the argument that "it is enough" for a state to

---

24. Thus, in the Silbert & Pines study, eighty-one percent of the women who had been raped did
not report the offense to the police. The most common reasons included embarrassment and fear that
the rape would not be taken seriously. Of those women who *did* report, forty-nine percent found the
police negative in their response, while twenty-three percent found them indifferent. M. Silbert, *supra*
note 6, at 67–68.

prohibit the distribution of obscene materials to halt the exploitation of children in pornography. The Court concluded that the "prurient interest" prong of the *Miller* test bore no relation to the degree of harm suffered by the child. Moreover, whether work was patently offensive, did or did not have other value, and would be or not be tolerated under contemporary community standards were questions also deemed irrelevant to the likelihood of injury to a child performer. *Ferber*, 458 U.S. at 761.

Those same considerations, likewise, concern not at all whether a woman was coerced into performing for pornography and the remedies appropriate to redress those injuries. The numerous obscenity prosecutions for distribution of *Deep Throat* nevertheless left Linda Marchiano without remedy for the sexual humiliation, torture and rape necessary for its production and the harm of its continued distribution. Nor does the *Miller* test address the sexual terrorism effected by forcing pornography on a woman to show her what she's good for, or the trafficking in women caused by the distribution of pornography. If the given is the norm, all of these practices, apparently, conform to "contemporary community standards," in any event. Finally, enforcement of criminal prostitution statutes will not advance the purposes of the ordinance. Arresting, charging, fining or sentencing a woman for prostitution plainly does not provide her any more security from, or legal relief for, the injuries specifically described in the ordinance.

Conclusion

All women need this law. Prostituted women need it desperately. Because the ordinance promotes a compelling state interest, by means narrowly tailored to bring it about, amici urge this court to grant intervenors' cross-motion for summary judgment, and deny plaintiff's motion for summary judgment.

EPILOGUE

On February 9, 1989, the court granted plaintiffs' motion for summary judgment, concluding that the ordinance is unconstitutional.[r] In reaching that conclusion, the court relied on its construction of the precedential effect of the Supreme Court's summary affirmance in *Hudnut*, stating the general rule that a summary affirmance may be disregarded only "if the statute under constitutional scrutiny presents issues that are different than the one previously reviewed."[s] Here, the court found the Bellingham ordinance "virtually identical"[t] to the ordinance declared unconstitutional in *Hudnut*, and therefore concluded that it was bound by that earlier ruling. The court reached this conclusion despite differences in the facial language and scope of the two ordinances, in the factual records before the courts, and changes in legal doctrine on the issues developed in the intervening years since *Hudnut* had been decided.

Speaking briefly to the injuries to women redressable under the ordinance, the court explicitly stated that "it is undisputed that many societal harms are caused by pornography."[u] The court also quoted extensively from the *Hudnut* court of appeals opinion reaching the same conclusion.[v] These words may have been inspired by authentic sorrow. Nevertheless, when coupled with a shrug, as in *Hudnut*, or a sigh, as in this case, recognition is no balm. The case will not be appealed.

---

[r] *Village Books v. City of Bellingham, supra* note a.
[s] *Id.* at 7.
[t] *Id.* at 7-8.
[u] *Id.* at 9-10.
[v] *Id.* at 10, n.8. The court reiterated the following language from *Hudnut*:
Therefore we accept the premises of this legislation. Depictions of subordination tend to perpetuate subordination. The subordinate status of women in turn leads to affront and lower pay at work, insult and injury at home, battery and rape on the streets. In the language of the legislature, "[p]ornography is central in creating and maintaining sex as a basis of discrimination. Pornography is a systematic practice of exploitation and subordination based on sex which differentially harms women. The bigotry and contempt it produces, with the acts of aggression it fosters, harm women's opportunities for equality and rights [of all kinds]."
771 F.2d at 329, quoting Indianapolis Code § 16-1(a)(2).

APPENDIX

BELLINGHAM INITIATIVE 1C

Section 1. STATEMENT OF POLICY

Pornography is sex discrimination. It exists in Bellingham, Washington, posing a substantial threat to the health, safety, peace, welfare, and equality of citizens in the community. Existing state and federal laws are inadequate to solve these problems in Bellingham.

Pornography is a systematic practice of exploitation and subordination based on sex that differentially harms women. The harm of pornography includes dehumanization, sexual exploitation, forced sex, forced prostitution, physical injury, and social and sexual terrorism and inferiority presented as entertainment. The bigotry and contempt pornography promotes, with the acts of aggression it fosters, diminish opportunities for equality of rights in employment, education, property, public and private harassment, persecution and denigration; expose individuals who appear in pornography against their will to contempt, ridicule, hatred, humiliation and embarrassment and target such women in particular for abuse and physical aggression; demean the reputations and diminish the occupational opportunities of individuals and groups on the basis of sex; promote injury and degradation such as rape, battery, child sexual abuse, and prostitution and inhibit just enforcement of laws against these acts; contribute significantly to restricting women in particular from full exercise of citizenship and participation in public life, including in neighborhoods; damage relations between the sexes; and undermine women's equal exercise of rights to speech and action guaranteed to all citizens under the Constitutions and laws of the United States and the State of Washington.

Section 2. DEFINITIONS

1. Pornography is the graphic sexually explicit subordination of women through pictures and/or words that also includes one or more of the following:

(i) women are presented dehumanized as sexual objects, things, or commodities; or

(ii) women are presented as sexual objects who enjoy pain or humiliation; or

(iii) women are presented as sexual objects who experience sexual pleasure in being raped; or

(iv) women are presented as sexual objects tied up or cut up or mutilated or bruised or physically hurt; or

(v) women are presented in postures or positions of sexual submission, servility, or display; or

(vi) women's body parts—including but not limited to vaginas, breasts, or buttocks—are exhibited such that women are reduced to those parts; or

(vii) women are presented as whores by nature; or

(viii) women are presented being penetrated by objects or animals; or

(ix) women are presented in scenarios of degradation, injury, torture, shown as filthy or inferior, bleeding, bruised, or hurt in a context that makes these conditions sexual.

2. The use of men, children, or transsexuals in the place of women in (1) above is also pornography.

Section 3. UNLAWFUL PRACTICES

1. Coercion into pornography: It shall be sex discrimination to coerce, intimidate, or fraudulently induce (thereafter, "coerce") any person, including transsexuals, into performing for pornography, which injury may date from any appearance or sale of any product(s), of such performance(s). The maker(s), seller(s), exhibitor(s), and/or distributor(s) of said pornography may be sued for damages and for an injunction, including to eliminate the product(s) of the performance(s) from the public view.

2. Trafficking in pornography: It shall be sex discrimination to produce, sell, exhibit, or distribute pornography, including through private clubs.

(i) City, state, and federally funded public libraries or private and public university and college libraries in which pornography is available for study, including on open shelves but excluding special display presentations, shall not be construed to be trafficking in pornography.

(ii) Isolated passages or isolated parts shall not be actionable under this section.

(iii) Any woman may file a complaint hereunder as a woman acting against the subordination of women. Any man, child, or transsexual who alleges injury by pornography in the way women are injured by it may also file a complaint.

3. Forcing pornography on a person: It shall be sex discrimination to force pornography on a person, including child or transsexual, in any place of employment, education, home, or public place. Only the perpetrator of the force or institution responsible for the force may be sued.

4. Assault or physical attack due to pornography: It shall be sex discrimination to assault, physically attack, or injure any person, including child or transsexual, in a way that is directly caused by specific pornography. Complaint(s) may be made against the perpetrator of the assault or attack and/or against the maker(s), distributor(s), seller(s), and/or exhibitor(s) of the specific pornography.

5. Defamation through pornography: It shall be sex discrimination to defame any person through the unauthorized use in pornography of their proper name, image, likeness, or recognizable personal evocation. For purposes of this section, public figures shall be treated as private persons. Authorization once given can be revoked in writing at any time prior to any publication.

Section 4. DEFENSES

1. It shall not be a defense that the defendant in an action under this law did not know or intend that the materials were pornography or sex discrimination, except that in an action for damages under Section 3(2), and in an action for damages against a publisher, seller, exhibitor, or distributor under Section 3(4), it shall be a defense that the defendant did not know or have reason to know that the materials were pornography.

2. It shall not, without more, constitute a defense to a complaint under Section 3(1) that:

(i) the person is a woman; or

(ii) the person is or has been a prostitute; or

(iii) the person has attained the age of majority; or

(iv) the person is connected by blood or marriage to any one involved in or related to the making of the pornography; or

(v) the person has previously had, or been thought to have had, sexual relations with anyone, including anyone involved in or related to the making of the pornography; or

(vi) the person has previously posed for sexually explicit pictures with or for anyone, including anyone involved in or related to the pornography at issue; or

(vii) anyone else, including a spouse or other relative, has given or purported to give permission on the person's behalf; or

(viii) the person actually consented to a use of a performance that is later changed into pornography; or

(ix) the person knew that the purpose of the acts or events in question was to make pornography; or

(x) the person showed no resistance or appeared to cooperate actively in the photographic sessions or in the events that produced the pornography; or

(xi) the person signed a contract, or made statements affirming a willingness to cooperate in the production of pornography; or

(xii) no physical force, threats, or weapons were used in the making of the pornography; or

(xiii) the person was paid or otherwise compensated.

Section 5. ENFORCEMENT

1. Civil Action: Any person aggrieved by violations of this law may enforce its provisions by means of a civil action filed in a court of competent jurisdiction. No criminal penalties shall attach for any violation of this law.

2. Injunctions: Complaints under this law may request such temporary or permanent injunctive relief as may be constitutional, specifically appropriate, and equitable in order to effectuate the purposes of this law within the powers and jurisdiction of the court.

3. Relief: Civil damages may include punitive and compensatory relief; damages for suffering and emotional distress, and reasonable attorneys' fees, costs, and disbursements within the discretion of the court.

Section 6. SEVERABILITY

Should any part(s) of this law be found legally invalid, the remaining part(s) remain valid, consistent with the overall intent of this law.

Section 7. LIMITATION OF ACTION

Complaints under this law must be filed within six years of the discriminatory acts alleged.

FEMINIST JURISPRUDENCE

CHRISTINA BROOKS WHITMAN

Real Rape. By Susan Estrich. Cambridge: Harvard University Press, 1987.

"Statutory Rape: A Feminist Critique of Rights Analysis." By Frances Olsen. *Texas Law Review* 63 (October 1984): 387-432.

"Jurisprudence and Gender." By Robin West. *University of Chicago Law Review* 55 (Winter 1988): 1-72.

"The Difference in Women's Hedonic Lives: A Phenomenological Critique of Feminist Legal Theory." By Robin West. *Wisconsin Women's Law Journal* 3 (1987): 81-145.

Making All the Difference: Inclusion, Exclusion, and American Law. By Martha Minow. Ithaca, N.Y., and London: Cornell University Press, 1990.

Justice and Gender. By Deborah L. Rhode. Cambridge: Harvard University Press, 1989.

"Telling Stories about Women and Work: Judicial Interpretations of Sex Segregation in the Workplace in Title VII Cases Raising the Lack of Interest Argument." By Vicki Schultz. *Harvard Law Review* 103 (June 1990): 1750-1843.

"Sapphire Bound!" By Regina Austin. *Wisconsin Law Review* 1989 (May 1989): 539-578.

"On Being the Object of Property." By Patricia Williams. *Signs* 14 (Autumn 1988): 5-24.

Feminist Studies 17, no. 3 (Fall 1991). © 1991 by Feminist Studies, Inc.

In the 1970s feminist legal theory furthered feminist legal practice. Feminist lawyers saw themselves as advocates of "women's rights," interested in winning legal victories in particular cases. Because their attention was focused on reform through legislation or litigation, the theory they developed was deliberately, if uncritically, grounded in what would be persuasive to those who held power in government institutions. They built directly upon the precedent made in race cases, precedent which assumed that the appropriate goal for social change was equality and defined equality as the similar treatment of similarly situated individuals. The key to the early legal victories[1] of the second wave was the assertion that women and men are similarly situated for all legally relevant purposes.

In the last decade, however, feminist jurisprudence has become less interested in arguing to judges. Instead, its attention has turned to the critique of law itself as a construct of patriarchy. As a practical matter this shift was provoked by the apparent deficiencies of the ostensibly neutral, formal equality strategy in cases involving problems, like pregnancy, that judges thought reflected bedrock biological differences between women and men.[2] Legal scholars, influenced by feminist critical theory in other disciplines, began to ask whether the standard methods of legal analysis necessarily distort what is at stake for women. In a move that parallels the feminist criticism of science, these scholars challenge the assumption that law establishes a neutral procedural framework that provides a fair hearing for all points of view.

One significant body of work within this critical movement argues that sex is not an issue that can be made to disappear through gender-neutral methods of analysis. This scholarship builds on the insights of Catharine MacKinnon, the only feminist legal theorist to come up with a unifying theory independent from legal precedent and the only one whose work has had a wide readership beyond the profession.[3] MacKinnon challenges the assumption that answers are to be found by comparing women to men. She argues that discrimination against women is based on dominance, rather than distinction, and that the key to understanding male dominance lies in the social construction of sexuality from a male perspective. The social meaning of sex as pleasurable for both sexes when men dominate and women submit justifies gender hierarchy. Women are seen as naturally subordinate in this most basic of biological activities and, by extension, naturally subordinate as political beings. Sex between women and men, which MacKinnon sees as coerced in fact but socially described as consensual, becomes for her the central subject of jurisprudential inquiry because it explains why sex inequality can be seen by law as the consequence of free individual choice.[4]

Examples of the way in which MacKinnon's work has influenced legal scholarship can be found in the legal reform work of Susan Estrich, the deconstructive work of Frances Olsen, and the more ambivalent, personally exploratory work of Robin West. Estrich fits within the tradition of the 1970s in that she argues for specific changes in legal rules, but when she writes about rape her central theme is the way in which criminal law has constructed sexual coercion as consent. Estrich also departs from earlier strategies for legal reform in her explicit rejection of objectivity and abstraction. She begins her discussions with a description of her own rape, and she goes beyond legal doctrinal analysis to the wider context of the reporting, investigation, prosecution, and disposition of rape cases. Unlike MacKinnon, Estrich is willing to adopt the language of consent. She would have the law find lack of consent when a woman has expressly refused to engage in intercourse ("No means no") or when her consent was coerced by threats or misrepresentation. This would leave unpunished those rapes in which consent or silence was coerced by more subtle means, but it would go beyond what is currently possible in the prosecution of rape by nonstrangers. Because Estrich is primarily interested in legal change, she has written her basic argument in two forms to two audiences, neither of which is the larger feminist community. Her work on rape initially appeared as a lengthy law review article addressed to lawyers[5] and was subsequently repackaged as a book, *Real Rape*, addressed to a lay audience. Although the article adopts the standard law-review format in that it consists of an extended discussion of cases and legislation, Estrich uses these materials to create a powerful narrative of the exclusion of the woman victim's perspective. Her theme throughout is that consent and coercion are defined from a male point of view. Criminal law has required, for example, that force be resisted in the way that men would respond to male aggression. And the due process concern that a defendant not be unfairly punished is exaggerated inappropriately by the male fear that women will cry rape. Although the book is addressed to a lay audience, it is in some ways less exciting than the article. The argument is more tightly written, focused on the problem of date rape, and Estrich carefully avoids the explicit feminism and anger that permeates the article. *Real Rape* is designed to persuade legislators to make changes that will facilitate the prosecution of date rape without requiring that they accept Estrich's more fundamental challenges to the way in which male perspectives are embedded in the criminal justice system.

Frances Olsen writes within the tradition of critical legal studies, which has challenged the consistency and coherence of the rights-based analysis·that was used to achieve the early victories of the "women's rights" movement. Olsen's most powerful article may be "Statutory Rape: A Feminist Critique of Rights Analysis," which analyzes *Michael M. v. Superior Court of Sonoma County*.[6] In that case the Supreme Court upheld a sex-based statutory rape statute against an equal protection challenge. Olsen demonstrates how any approach to the case threatens women: upholding statutory rape law provides security for some women while intruding on the autonomy of others who are not allowed to consent to sex; striking the laws down furthers autonomy at the expense of security when consent is coerced. The trouble, Olsen suggests, is that, under present circumstances, the interests of some women would be best served by stressing autonomy, but other women would be best served by stressing security. Indeed, a particular woman might well be oppressed by both sexual freedom and societal control of her sexuality. She might be subject to coerced sex that does not fit the legal definition of rape and yet be prohibited from other activities on the grounds of her sexual vulnerability.[7] To treat women as autonomous bearers of legal rights ignores MacKinnon's insight into the way consent is coerced. *Michael M.* provides a case study that demonstrates how legal argument forces advocates to reach premature foreclosure. The answer, according to Olsen, is not to give up on law but to give up on the effort to achieve credibility with judges by articulating principles that purport to decide all cases for all time. Feminist lawyers should make explicitly political choices and challenge those particular rules that have most pernicious effects at any given time.

Olsen's work demonstrates that feminist insights, the introduction of the perspectives of women, can be done in a way that is compatible with and continuous with the best sort of legal analytic reasoning. Lawyers have always dealt with precedent through close textual reading that searches for unsupported assumptions and suppressed inconsistencies. Olsen turns these techniques to self-consciously political purposes in her critique of the arguments made by the Supreme Court, by lawyers, by feminists, and by feminist lawyers. She demonstrates not only that each argument leaves some important interests out but also that a particular position may actually interfere with the ability of the advocate to see what has happened to the real woman in the real case. She points out, for example, that another feminist scholar, who advocates gender-neutral laws, characterizes the rape in *Michael M.* as a "victimless crime" even though the adolescent defendant in that case sought the consent of the victim by slugging her in the face.

Olsen's work builds explicitly on MacKinnon's. Robin West's scholarship is more deeply ambivalent about MacKinnon's contribution, but its very preoccupations demonstrate the way in which issues of sexuality and dominance have become central to feminist jurisprudence. West, like Olsen, has been very prolific. I will discuss only two of her articles here. In "Jurisprudence and Gender," West argues that both liberal rights-based theory and critical legal theory are premised upon a definition of "human being" that is inapplicable to women. Both theories regard humans as fundamentally separate from each other, but women, West claims, are not in fact physically individuated from other people. Women, unlike men, "are in some sense 'connected' to life and to other human beings during at least four recurrent and critical material experiences": pregnancy, heterosexual penetration, menstruation, and breastfeeding. Although West acknowledges that not all women have all these experiences, she argues that most women are forced into them by male power disguised as biological imperative. In this respect she builds on MacKinnon, and, perhaps more than MacKinnon,[8] West appears to assume that these fundamental experiences are the same for all women despite race, class, and even sexual preference. West differs from MacKinnon in that she has a positive as well as a negative view of sexuality: the "potentiality for physical connection with others that uniquely characterizes women's lives has within it the seeds of *both* intimacy and invasion" (p. 53). MacKinnon accurately describes women's experience, West says, but so do her opponents who describe sex as pleasurable and affirming; each describes one side of the fundamental contradiction inherent in the material condition of women.

West's approach is reassuring to those who feel uncomfortable with MacKinnon's emphasis on sex as inevitably coerced. It provides a less political way to understand the strategic tensions described by Olsen. And it is particularly powerful in describing why a woman's perspective on such issues as rape and abortion may not be captured by legal concepts of autonomy and independence: "The fear of sexual and fetal invasion and intrusion is the fear of being occupied *from within,* not annihilated from without . . . of having one's own physical and material life taken over by the pressing physical urgency of another, not ended by conflicting interests of another. . . " (p. 41). West claims to provide a means of reconciling "cultural feminists" like Carol Gilligan and "radical feminists" like Catharine MacKinnon. But much of the apparent force of her approach is attributable to the reductive way in which she describes the positions of others, and the reconciliation she claims to achieve may be simply schizophrenic. That possibility becomes apparent in a second, more personal, and very thought-provoking article ponderously titled "The Difference in Women's Hedonic Lives: A Phenomenological Critique of Feminist Legal Theory."

"The Difference in Women's Hedonic Lives" is divided into two parts. In the first part, West uses examples from her own life to demonstrate that women's suffering is invisible to men because men lack similar experiences and because women are taught either to deny pain or to regard it as inevitable or pleasurable. The examples West uses are promiscuity, physically abusive relationships, and street harassment. Much of this material is powerfully supportive of MacKinnon's point that sex is socially constructed in ways that are destructive to women. But the second part of West's essay takes MacKinnon to task for silencing women who experience pleasure in sexual submission. West takes *The Story of O* as illustrative of the way in which giving men power can further women's pleasure. MacKinnon's approach, West argues, leads to a feminism that ignores the "experiential reality" that some women feel pleasure in pain and thus diminishes the "hedonic" content of women's lives. West's article is so consistently interesting and so obviously an effort to speak honestly and directly on matters that are seldom discussed in legal literature that it cannot be easily dismissed. Yet it doesn't form a coherent whole. The author of part 2 seems not to have learned from the author of part 1, and vice versa. If women are taught to lie to men and to themselves about the existence of pain, as West argues in part 1, how are we to use their experience of pleasure in pain as a basis for feminist theory?

West's attempt to reconcile MacKinnon with the insights of cultural feminism reflects the importance of Carol Gilligan, who has been the other major influence on feminist work challenging the accepted discourse of law. In fact, Gilligan has had an impact on feminist jurisprudence that may be more powerful and more enduring than her impact on any other discipline. Legal feminists came late to the question of difference. The constraints of litigation led them to continue to focus on what women and men have in common at a time when feminists elsewhere were beginning to be preoccupied with difference. Gilligan's *In a Different Voice: Psychological Theory and Women's Development*[9] was published just at the time when legal scholars were looking for an alternative to the gender-neutral jurisprudence of the 1970s. It seemed to provide an explanation for the alienation that many women feel while in law school and legal practice, while suggesting that an alternative jurisprudence could be built around themes of caring, relationships, and responsibility.

Yet Gilligan's "ethic of care" has not proven to be very useful for deciding particular cases or generating legal theory. West's effort to bridge MacKinnon's emphasis on invasion and Gilligan's emphasis on intimacy is provocative but unsuccessful. Another ambitious but ultimately unsatisfying attempt to build from Gilligan is Suzanna Sherry's "Civic Virtue and the Feminine Voice in Constitutional Adjudication."[10] Sherry identifies Gilligan's "different voice" with the tradition of civic republicanism currently enjoying a vogue among constitutional scholars and then argues that the opinions of Justice Sandra Day O'Connor, at least when compared to the opinions of other conservative Justices, exhibit relational thinking in that O'Connor is particularly sensitive to the claims of community. The result is a rather dazzling but very strained exhibition of how unlike can be made to seem (a little bit) alike. In order to make the comparisons work to even a limited extent, Sherry is forced to describe not only civic republicanism, but also O'Connor and Gilligan, in the most abstract and ummodulated terms.

A more successful, because less ambitious, effort to apply Gilligan's insights can be found in the work of Carrie Menkel-Meadow. Menkel-Meadow, who writes about alternative dispute resolution and the legal profession, focuses not on the substance of law but on the role of women in legal practice. In an article written in 1985 she speculated, on the basis of Gilligan's work, that a significant increase in the numbers of women lawyers might lead to changes in the practice and values of the law.[11] Menkel-Meadow thought women might become "innovators and critics of the profession," creating, for example, a "more cooperative, less war-like" alternative to the "advocacy-adversarial model" of law and a non-hierarchical, participatory structure of law firm organization. More recently, Menkel-Meadow admits that her own research and that of others "seems to indicate that women in law are being assimilated into the traditional culture of the profession rather than bringing . . . innovations" (p. 313).[12] A major strength of Menkel-Meadow's work is her care not to claim too much. She is not insensitive to the dangers of perpetuating stereotypes and takes pains to stress that she is talking about socially created differences between women and men, but she is committed as "an act of faith" to the proposition that women will make a difference. Her work is aspirational, self-described as an agenda for future research and an effort to encourage the development of more caring methods of lawyering. Because it has so little upon which to build, it is also frustratingly vague.

Menkel-Meadow does not, except in the most general sense, try to use Gilligan's work to decide substantive questions. Martha Minow's recent book, *Making All the Difference: Inclusion, Exclusion, and American Law* does exactly that. It is an ambitious effort at synthesis. Minow combines Gilligan's insights with American pragmatism, and other work in philosophy, social science, and literary criticism, to suggest that a wide range of legal questions involving difference ought to be resolved by "attention to relationships – relationships between people, between concepts, and between the observer and the observed." Minow does not limit herself to issues of gender difference but explores the ways in which cases involving race, ethnicity, religious minorities, children, the mentally and physically disabled, and even the separation of governmental powers can be productively resolved by attention to relationships. Her theme is that problems of difference have seemed intractable because difference has been thought to inhere in the "different" individual rather than to be a product of social construction. This mistake has led courts to ask how "special" needs can be accommodated into essentially unchanging environments rather than to observe how environments create difference by unnecessary failure to be inclusive. Minow argues that we can restructure relationships to include difference. The standard feminist example of this point would-be the adoption of workplace structures and practices which assume workers have obligations to dependent family members. Minow generates others: developing hospital procedures that treat every patient as potentially HIV-positive; teaching sign language to the hearing students in a deaf child's class; finding another family to care for a Down's syndrome child whose parents are unable or unwilling to provide emotional support.

Minow does an effective job of explaining how pragmatist and feminist thinking can be used to challenge the "individual rights" analysis that has dominated law. Refreshingly undogmatic, she does not reject rights theory in favor of relational strategies but redefines rights as "communally recognized rituals for securing attention in a continuing struggle over boundaries between people" (p. 383). Despite the strength of her critique, however, Minow does not ultimately succeed in formulating an alternative decisional strategy. She herself sees the problem. It is one shared by many who have tried to articulate a theory of value based on caring: "This all sounds lovely, you may say, but awfully abstract, What actually happens?" (p. 381). Minow's response is to generate a series of actual case studies. They are all individually interesting but difficult to understand as part of a common strategy. Minow's "relational" solutions to particular problems–like, ironically, so many of the solutions generated by economic approaches to law – seem possible only because she makes factual assumptions that facilitate resolution. She assumes, for example, that there are enough resources to treat all hospital patients with extraordinary care. The deaf child appears to be in a class that is taught by a teacher who knows or can easily learn sign language and one in which no other disabled or disruptive students compete for accommodation; this ideal environment will apparently be re-created year after year. In the Down's syndrome example, which is based on actual litigation, the court has before it a family eager to be emotional parents to the child. Every case seems to turn on fortuities. Perhaps all Minow means to say is that the legal system ought to be open to taking advantage of those opportunities to restructure relationships that happen to exist. That is an important point but not one that promises a dramatic transformation in how law deals with difference.

The great temptation of legal thinking is the hope that the interests of women, like those of other groups, can be captured in a single narrative, or formula, or three- or four-part test to be applied to all cases. This would give litigators confidence that they are truly representing their clients' interests, and judges would be able to tell themselves that they are acting with appropriate neutrality. Cases, after all, must be decided, so lawyers must reach conclusions and come up with answers. Provisional, contingent solutions seem too political, too likely to be the result of unconscious or conscious bias. Yet feminist scholars, who have undergone their own temptation with unitary, foundational theory, have not been able to describe a theory that benefits some women without hurting others. There are real differences among women, and some of these have been exacerbated by the women's movement and its legal victories, which achieved access to power for some while removing traditional protections for others.[13] As Deborah L. Rhode puts it, "we need theory without Theory."

In her recent book, *Justice and Gender*, Rhode, like Minow, emphasizes the broader context in which legal rules are created. But unlike Minow, she addresses only questions involving gender and she reaches for no overarching method of analysis. Instead, Rhode discusses the full range of particular legal problems involving women, placing each one in its historical, social, and economic context before discussing the relevant judicial opinions and current legal arguments. Rhode herself makes very few suggestions for legal change, at least as ultimate solutions. There are aspects of this approach which are extremely frustrating. Rhode is so thorough in explicating the full range of arguments that she seems excessively balanced. Again and again she responds to hard questions with a simple call for more research. But Rhode has created the first true legal treatise on gender, and unlike most legal treatises, hers does not limit itself to doctrine. The book is crammed with information from secondary sources and exhaustive in describing the range of possible legal positions. It is not a comfortable book to read from cover to cover, largely because of its lack of a distinctive point of view, but it is a splendid resource.

Some of the most exciting scholarship now being produced

creates partial narratives. Much of it is innovative in its use of non-legal methods of analysis, and some departs dramatically from traditional approaches to legal inquiry. In one recent article, for example, Vicki Schultz uses statistical methods to analyze the role in Title VII cases of employers' arguments that women are overrepresented in low-paying, low-status jobs because they are not interested in more highly rewarded work. Instead of considering each judicial opinion as an independent, self-contained text, Schultz looks at a data set of fifty-four cases and makes a quantitative analysis of the relationship between argument, evidence, and outcome. She finds that courts are more willing to credit the lack of interest argument when employers show that they have made special efforts to attract women and less likely to credit it when plaintiffs produce individual victims who can offer anecdotal evidence of discrimination. Schultz concludes that courts assume that patterns of sex segregation are attributable either to women's choices or to employer coercion. Judges believe that discrimination exists only where employers refuse to hire those women who enter the work world with the desire to take on nontraditional jobs. They overlook the possibility that women's choices are evolving, formed in part in reaction to structural features of employment that affect women's experience in the workplace. Relying on sociological research which supports this latter interpretation, Schultz proposes a new story which implicates employment practices in women's choices even when employers do not engage in deliberate exclusion or coercion. Because she does not focus on doctrinal argument but on underlying judicial assumptions about the nonlegal world, Schultz does not discuss whether Title VII provides an adequate vehicle for remedies against individual employers when segregation is caused by structural and cultural features of workplace organization. But she makes a powerful case that, if it does not provide such remedies, the statute is not responsive to the most serious and enduring problems of employment discrimination against women.

Schultz's work suggests that no single legal approach is adequate because workplace exclusion operates in different ways for different women. Narratives by Black feminist scholars pose a more fundamental challenge, not only to the perspective of white feminist jurisprudence,[14] but also to its lack of passion. In "Sapphire Bound!" Regina Austin, a writer who has been particularly in-

terested in tactics of resistance,[15] calls for a jurisprudence that
would "preach the justness of the direct, participatory, grass-roots
opposition Black women undertake" (p. 544). She takes as her text
Chambers v. Omaha Girls Club,[16] in which a court held that Title
VII was not violated when a girls' club, administered primarily by
whites for Black teenage girls, fired its arts and crafts instructor, an
unmarried Black woman, because she became pregnant. The dismissal was found to be justified because Chambers was a "negative
role model" for her students. Austin points out the irony of an employment practice that replicates the very condition the organization claims to address: club administrators hoped to discourage
teenage pregnancy because of the economic hardship and social
prejudice it entails, but Chambers's pregnancy was not "problematic" in this sense until she was fired. Like Schultz, Austin relies on sociological and cultural studies of the way in which structure affects individual choice. She describes adolescent pregnancy
as a response to the material conditions in which many Black teenagers live, and Chambers's adult decision to become a mother as
"an alternative social form that one might choose deliberately, rationally, and proudly" (p. 576). Role models, Austin argues, ought
to be Sapphires, affirming the perspective of less powerful Black
women rather than projecting "an assimilated person that is . . . un-
threatening to white people" (p. 574).

Other Black scholars have refused to conform to traditional legal
standards of politeness and coherence. Some of the most powerful
work is by Patricia Williams, who is more explicitly autobio-
graphical than Austin. Williams's recent essays are written in a
fragmented, postmodern style that captures the contradictions of
her life as a descendant of slaves and of slaveowners who has
graduated from Harvard Law School and now teaches commercial
transactions. In "On Being the Object of Property," Williams challenges conventional legal discourse by wrenching legal concepts
away from their established meanings and using them evocatively
and metaphorically. An illusory contract, for example, becomes
not a contract in which consideration fails because it is nonexistent or unavailable but a metaphor for the way in which contract law is used to justify the brutal parting of a mother from her
children – Mary Beth Whitehead, a "surrogate" mother, from her
baby daughter; Williams's twelve-year-old great-great-grandmother, a slave raped by her owner, from her daughter, Williams's

great-grandmother, Mary. Williams's essay is disturbing because it is open-ended and evolving. It doesn't end with a solution. It doesn't even formulate a problem in a form that a court could answer. Perhaps it therefore isn't "law." But it certainly should speak to lawyers.

Law has a tendency to marginalize, and even exclude, theories that are tentative, ambiguous, provisional. Yet some of the most exciting feminist jurisprudence, as well as some of the most banal, has been explicitly open-ended. Formal rules and structured analyses are the ways in which law protects itself against favoritism and arbitrary decision making. But feminist scholarship has found that the dangers of legal power lie not only in bias and interest but also in the false confidence that bias and interest have been eliminated. Feminist jurisprudence has developed a group of theories that can be used to critique results in particular cases and be a powerful challenge to the rhetorical claims of the law. It has complicated and challenged legal discussion. Its interdisciplinary reach is impressive, although little of it is, perhaps as a consequence, strikingly original.

Yet there is a sense in which much of current feminist jurisprudence seems unmoored, directionless. Perhaps more than anywhere else, the strains of the debate over essentialism have disrupted feminist strategies in the law. The formal equality model that accomplished so much through litigation in the 1970s cannot be reconciled with what feminists have come to know about the dangers of assuming similarity within gender as well as across gender lines. However, no alternative model has emerged that avoids these dangers and successfully appeals to the constitutive principles of our Constitution and laws. Courts are just beginning to accept the full implications of the view that groups, as well as individuals, can be holders of legal rights. The next, and more difficult, stage will be to retain the force of that understanding while making a legal space for more nuanced claims about the way that disadvantage varies within groups.

NOTES

1. In cases such as those challenging the legality under Title VII of policies that prohibit all fertile women from certain high-paying jobs on the ground that working conditions

are harmful to fetuses, International Union, UAW v. Johnson Controls, 111 S. Ct. 1196 (1991), some of these victories have come under attack. Important work is being done by scholars such as Mary Becker, who has demonstrated the powerful similarities between these policies and early-twentieth-century protective legislation held unconstitutional in the 1970s. See Becker, "From *Muller v. Oregon* to Fetal Vulnerability Policies," *University of Chicago Law Review* 53 (Fall 1986): 1219-73.

2. See Joan Williams, "Deconstructing Gender," *Michigan Law Review* 87 (February 1989): 797-845; Lise Vogel, "Debating Difference: Feminism, Pregnancy, and the Workplace," *Feminist Studies* 16 (Spring 1990): 9-32.

3. Catharine MacKinnon's work over the last decade has been influenced by her collaboration with Andrea Dworkin, who is not a lawyer. A representative sample of MacKinnon's speeches can be found in *Feminism Unmodified* (Cambridge: Harvard University Press, 1987); her most recent work in political theory is *Toward a Feminist Theory of the State* (Cambridge: Harvard University Press, 1989).

For reviews in the legal literature, both positive and negative, see Angela Harris, "Categorical Discourse and Dominance Theory," *Berkeley Women's Law Journal* 5 (January 1990): 181-96; Frances Olsen, "Feminist Theory in Grand Style," *Columbia Law Review* 89 (June 1989): 1147-78; Christina B. Whitman, "Law and Sex," *Michigan Law Review* 86 (May 1988): 1388-1403; and Katherine T. Bartlett, "MacKinnon's Feminism: Power on Whose Terms?" *California Law Review* 75 (July 1987): 1559-70.

4. Perhaps because MacKinnon's framework has so dominated the discussion of sexuality in feminist jurisprudence (as both inspiration and focus of attack), there has been very little development of a lesbian perspective. See Patricia A. Cain, "Feminist Jurisprudence: Grounding the Theories," *Berkeley Women's Law Journal* 4 (January 1989): 191-214.

5. Susan R. Estrich, "Rape," *Yale Law Journal* 95 (May 1986): 1087-1184. Estrich has continued to write as an advocate for legal reform to a specific professional audience. A recent article on abortion doctrine, coauthored with Kathleen Sullivan, is explicitly directed to Justice Sandra Day O'Connor, whom the authors describe as "in the position single-handedly to decide the future of abortion rights." Susan R. Estrich and Kathleen M. Sullivan, "Abortion Politics: Writing for an Audience of One," *University of Pennsylvania Law Review* 138 (November 1989): 119-55.

6. See Michael M. v. Superior Court of Sonoma County, 450 U.S. 464 (1981).

7. For example, in Dothard v. Rawlinson, 433 U.S. 321 (1977), the Supreme Court held that the exclusion of women from employment as prison guards in all-male maximum security prisons that housed sex offenders did not violate Title VII of the Civil Rights Act because the "unique" vulnerability of women to rape created an increased security risk that justified their exclusion.

8. Angela Harris, "Race and Essentialism in Feminist Legal Theory," *Stanford Law Review* 42 (January 1990): 581-616, criticizes both West and MacKinnon as privileging white experience and ignoring Black women. Harris argues that MacKinnon's emphasis on the sexual domination of women by men ignores the way in which social constructions of sexuality (for example, the response to rape) have been used to oppress Black men as well as women. Harris's attack on West goes directly to the core of West's theory. By making gendered experiences primary in the formation of women's sense of self, West overlooks the lives of Black women, for whom "the web of race and gender" cannot be disentangled.

9. Carol Gilligan, *In a Different Voice: Psychological Theory and Women's Development* (Cambridge: Harvard University Press, 1982).

10. Suzanna Sherry, "Civic Virtue and the Feminine Voice in Constitutional Adjudication," *Virginia Law Review* 72 (April 1986): 543-616.

11. Carrie Menkel-Meadow, "Portia in a Different Voice: Speculation on a Women's

Lawyering Process," *Berkeley Women's Law Journal* 1 (Fall 1985): 39-63.

12. Ibid., "Exploring a Research Agenda of the Feminization of the Legal Profession: Theories of Gender and Social Change," *Law and Social Inquiry* 14 (Spring 1989): 289-319.

13. See, for example, the impact on women of gender neutrality in divorce law described in Lenore J. Weitzman, *The Divorce Revolution* (New York: Free Press 1985) and Kristen Luker's description of the abortion controversy as a dispute among women ignited by the Supreme Court's decision in Roe v. Wade, 410 U.S. 113 (1973). Kristen Luker, *Abortion: The Politics of Motherhood* (Berkeley: University of California Press, 1984).

14. For example, Patricia J. Williams, in "Alchemical Notes: Reconstructing Ideals from Deconstructed Rights," *Harvard Civil Rights-Civil Liberties Law Review* 22 (Spring 1987): 401-33, and Kimberle Crenshaw, in "Race, Reform, and Retrenchment: Transformation and Legitimation in Antidiscrimination Law," *Harvard Law Review* 101 (April 1988): 1331-87, have argued that some white feminists, and male critical legal scholars, have been too quick to jettison rights-based theory. Legal discourse of rights has, they argue, been a powerful tool for minorities, who do not consider its work complete.

15. In addition to the article under review here, also see Regina Austin, "Employer Abuse, Worker Resistance, and the Tort of Intentional Infliction of Emotional Distress," *Stanford Law Review* 41 (July 1988): 1-59; and Regina Austin, "Resistance Tactics for Tokens," *Harvard BlackLetter Journal* 3 (Spring 1986): 52-53.

16. 629 F. Supp. 925 (D. Neb. 1986), *affirmed*, 834 F.2d 697 (8th Cir. 1987), *rehearing denied*, 840 F.2d 583 (1988).

Split at the Root:

Prostitution and Feminist Discourses

of Law Reform

Margaret A. Baldwin[†]

> My case is not unique.
>
> Violette Leduc[1]
>
> Today, adjustment to what is possible no longer means adjustment, it means making the possible real.
>
> Theodor Adorno[2]

This article originated in some years of feminist activism, and a sustained effort to understand two sentences spoken by Evelina Giobbe, an anti-prostitution activist and educator, at a radical feminist conference in 1987. She said: "Prostitution isn't like anything else. Rather, everything else is like prostitution because it is the model for women's condition."[3] Since that time,

---

† Assistant Professor of Law, Florida State University College of Law.

For my family: Mother Marge, Bob, Tim, John, Scharl, Marilynne, Jim, Robert, and in memory of my father, James.

This article was supported by summer research grants from Florida State University College of Law. Otherwise, it is a woman-made product. Thanks to Rhoda Kibler, Mary LaFrance, Sheryl Walter, Annie McCombs, Dorothy Teer, Susan Mooney, Marybeth Carter, Susan Hunter, K.C. Reed, Margy Gast, and Christine Jones for the encouragement, confidence, and love. Evelina Giobbe, Kathleen Barry, K.C. Reed, Susan Hunter, and Toby Summer, whose contributions to work on prostitution have made mine possible, let me know I had something to say. The NCASA Basement Drafting Committee was a turning point. Catharine MacKinnon gave me the first opportunity to get something down on paper; she and Andrea Dworkin let me know the effort counted. Mimi Wilkinson and Stacey Dougan ably assisted in the research and in commenting on drafts. Mimi Wilkinson also found me a tenor saxophone at a crucial moment. Brenda Ellis, Millie Poulos, Elzy Williams, and Beverly Perkins worked intelligently and patiently on the manuscript. Cheers and love to all from your Meg.

1. VIOLETTE LEDUC, LA BATARDE 3 (1964).

2. THEODOR ADORNO, *Veblen's Attack on Culture, in* PRISMS 73, 94 (Samuel & Shierry Weber trans., 1981).

3. Evelina Giobbe, *Confronting the Liberal Lies About Prostitution, in* THE SEXUAL LIBERALS AND THE ATTACK ON FEMINISM 67, 76 (Dorchen Leidholdt & Janice Raymond, eds., 1990). Evelina Giobbe has written and worked in the past under the name Sarah Wynter. In 1989, she took back her birth name. This is part of what she has said about that decision:

> I, quite frankly, am tired of having my name taken from me by the pimps who stole my youth or due to my fear of retaliation by the pornographers. This year I am taking my name back. I consider it as much a political act as a personal choice. I choose to give up the illusion of safety that a pseudonym gave me, understanding now that no woman is safe as long as the traffic of women and children is allowed to continue. I take this action in defiance of the pimps and pornographers who sell women's bodies

I have listened to those sentences echo in my mind, as if they wanted to teach me something I could not yet understand but needed to. I believe now that my perplexity arose, perversely, from my own commitments as a lawyer and activist in support of women in prostitution: not, it seemed, from the commitment part, but from the lawyer part. Thinking from within prevailing discourses of feminist legal theory and law reform strategies, I found myself precluded from any adequate engagement with, much less response to, Giobbe's analysis. That is something to notice. A sister suggests that you take a look at her car, as something seems to be rattling. You stand befuddled, gazing at the saw and hammer in your hands.

This paper attempts to begin a response to Giobbe's insight. The fundamental inquiry I pursue is how the relationship between "prostitutes" and "other women" is given meaning in the sexual abuse of women and girls, in the legal response to that abuse, and in feminist reform strategies. In the design of existing law, in the behavior of individual men, and in the leading strategies of feminist law reform, the relationship is cast in oppositional terms: whoever a "prostitute" is, "other women" are not. In substance, the distinction provides a handy means of identifying appropriate female objects of punishment and contempt. To be deemed a "prostitute," whether by the state, by a john, or by any other man for that matter, immediately targets a girl or woman for arrest, for sexual assault, for murder, or, at the very least, dismissive scorn. Victims of rape, of incest, of domestic battery, of sexual harassment, are quite familiar with this difficulty. Declared to be "whores" and "sluts" by the men who abuse them, women then confront a legal system which puts the same issue in the form of a question: was she in fact a "slut" who deserved it, as the perpetrator claims, or not-a-slut, deserving of some redress? (The outcome of this interrogation is commonly referred to as "justice.")

I am not alone in this analysis. Feminist legal reformers have long challenged the legal relegation of "other women" to the status of prostitutes, in rape law reform, in representation of battered women in court, and in anti-sexual harassment advocacy. However, as I further contend, these strategies have less undermined the dichotomy between "prostitutes" and "other women" than they have further entrenched it. The core assertion advanced by this work has been the claim that "other women" are not "really" prostitutes, after all, and, therefore, denied justice by evidentiary standards and uneducated inferences yielding the contrary conclusion. Abusers, judges, and legal feminists seem agreed on the proper significance of the distinction between

---

and steal their souls, and the johns who think that they can turn child sexual abuse and rape into a job by throwing money at their victims. I hope that this public/private act will contribute to ending our silence, and I have one other personal reason. It's a fine name, my mother gave it to me because it was my grandmother's name. I reclaim it in memory of her struggles.

Evelina Giobbe, *From the Editors*, WHISPER 3 (Summer 1989). WHISPER is the newsletter of the prostitution activist organization of the same name. Giobbe is a founder and the executive director of the organization.

prostitutes and other women, but disagree on the finer points of identification and definition.

In the second part of this paper, I discuss where this approach leaves women who "are" prostitutes. In short, in some difficulty. In the seeming absence of other alternatives, feminist advocates for prostitutes have attempted to establish that prostitutes, too, are "other women" in the same sense in which "other women" have employed the term to distance themselves from prostitutes. Needless to say, these assimilation attempts have not proceeded smoothly. In part three, I argue that "distancing" oneself from prostitution, while representing oneself as an "other woman," the political position adopted by all of these advocates, is both the sexual demand made of women *in* prostitution, and the political demand made of all women vis á vis the state.

Such is the map this paper seeks to draw. Such, too, is the grammar in which it speaks, the conventional procession of the "If this/Then that; Because/Therefore; Not only/But also"[4] rhetorics of argument and justification. As conventionally, it is here that an author seeks the generosity of her reader, beseeching or demanding or cajoling acquiescence to the limitations of the announced agenda. This appeal, to a meta-agenda of "reading rules," often proceeds in two steps; the first humble, the second insistent. First, acknowledgment of deficiencies in the discussion to follow: of the unaddressed or insufficiently engaged or otherwise lingering issues, or the methodological or theoretical limitations of the claims asserted. Then, an analytic rescue of the importance of the work notwithstanding, by argument to the immateriality of those deficiencies to the integrity and usefulness of the overall approach. The quality of generosity sought from the reader is passive: a promise to keep still, to accept the author's project on its own terms, to banish for the moment all concerns disruptive to the orderly unfolding of the author's exposition.[5]

If my appeal is conventional, the quality of readerly sympathy I seek perhaps is not. The deficiencies which I believe most deeply mar this paper cannot be masked by vigorous defense, as they betray my intention and undermine the possibility of communicating what most needs hearing on the subject of prostitution. I mean the carnage: the scale of it, the dailiness of it, the seeming inevitability of it; the torture, the rapes, the murders, the beatings, the despair, the hollowing out of the personality, the near extinguishment of hope commonly suffered by women in prostitution. For the imperative of "If this/Then that" is the command to *move on*, from the dumb datum of "this"

---

4. The phrase is Christa Wolf's, from a discussion of poet and novelist Ingeborg Bachmann's work. Christa Wolf, *A Letter, about Unequivocal and Ambiguous Meaning, Definiteness and Indefiniteness; about Ancient Conditions and New View-Scopes; About Objectivity, in* CASSANDRA: A NOVEL AND FOUR ESSAYS 272, 301 (1984) [hereinafter, *A Letter*].

5. The sexual inference is of course intended. *See* LAURENCE STERNE, TRISTRAM SHANDY, *in* 36 GREAT BOOKS OF THE WESTERN WORLD 191-92 (Robert Maynard Hutchens ed., 1952) (Tristram's mother accused of disrupting Tristram's homuncular development when, at the crucial moment of Tristram's conception, she interrupted the proceedings to ask if his father had remembered to wind the clocks).

to the voluble authorial "that," to engage in the proper displays of mastery in drawing the finer distinction, executing the wittier hypothesis, solving the third riddle yielding the maiden's hand of the conclusion.

Although I speak archly of those satisfactions here, I do so in some bad faith as they are familiar to me, and treasured. Yet, after reading about, documenting, and classifying the murders, disappearances, tortures, fast or slow suicides of women in prostitution, I have often questioned the intellectual integrity of any stance but the hortatory and confrontational: This must end. See this. This must stop. I hear the protagonist in Andrea Dworkin's *Mercy*, after 27 years as a woman, imploring: "Stop them. They don't stop themselves, do they?"[6] To render this slaughter of women a matter to be assessed by analytic argument, even "dialogue," has at times seemed to me an act of barbarism. This work of mine, then, however beset with "thats," is not intended solely as argument, but as a meditation upon witnessing brutality. And what I ask of you is simple, but engaged: where my logic fails, please remember these women and do better than I have done.

There is a further complication. Brutality, written about, is different from brutality, lived. Writing, especially theoretical writing, is a practice which requires and maintains a certain distance; perhaps roughly the same distance necessary for pain's infliction. That tidy gap habilitates the entire field of aesthetics, and the much defended (when not asserted as natural) distinction between literature and life. As Christa Wolf notes:

> aesthetics, I say, like philosophy and science, is invented not
> so much to enable us to get closer to reality as for the purpose
> of warding it off, of protecting against it.[7]

Champions of pornography assert this principle with some complacency. For me the attempt to render women's pain into words, cast to the kindness of strangers, has caused great anguish and frustration. I had been both warned of and instructed about this trouble by feminist theorists, pedagogically through the feminist legal critique of objectivity,[8] and more immediately by the

---

6. ANDREA DWORKIN, MERCY 333 (1990).

7. Wolf, *A Letter, supra* note 4, at 300. *See also* ROBIN MORGAN, THE DEMON LOVER: ON THE SEXUALITY OF TERRORISM 51 (1989) ("If I had to name one quality as the genius of patriarchy, it would be compartmentalization, the capacity for institutionalizing disconnection."); *cf.* ELAINE SCARRY, THE BODY IN PAIN: THE MAKING AND UNMAKING OF THE WORLD (1985) (on the linguistic unexpressability of physical pain).

8. The germinal work in law is Catharine A. MacKinnon's pair of articles in SIGNS. *See* MacKinnon, *Feminism, Marxism, Method, and the State: An Agenda for Theory,* 7 SIGNS 515 (1982) and MacKinnon, *Feminism, Marxism, Method, and the State: Toward a Feminist Jurisprudence,* 8 SIGNS 635 (1983). The arguments which are refined and elaborated in MACKINNON, TOWARD A FEMINIST THEORY OF THE STATE (1989). *See also* Ann C. Scales, *The Emergence of Feminist Jurisprudence: An Essay,* 95 YALE L. J. 1373 (1986); Martha Minow, *Feminist Reason: Getting It and Losing It,* 38 J. LEGAL EDUC. 47 (1988); Robin West, *The Difference in Women's Hedonic Lives: A Phenomenological Critique of Feminist Legal Theory,* 3 WISC. WOM. L. J. 81 (1987) (hereinafter, *Phenomenology*); Lynne N. Henderson, *Legality and Empathy,* 85 MICH. L. REV. 1574 (1987). A related discourse is the emerging jurisprudence of "legal storytelling."

authorial examples of scholars who with brilliance have subverted or abandoned syllogistic compulsions in their own work.[9] More than once I read Kathleen Barry's description of her heartbreak, "an emotion men condemn as a failure of objectivity,"[10] while writing her landmark book on sexual slavery:

> And yet I realize that it is the stifling of such emotion that creates the conditions of violence and slavery. I've come to recognize in a way I've never before known so deeply and powerfully the extent to which emotionless objectivity leads directly to objectification—the starting point of violence, particularly sexual violence.[11]

As is the case with all "knowing," though, I too have come to understand this critique at a new level in challenging myself to live out what I had learned. Because I am a woman, this meant long stretches of believing my floundering to be my fault, demonstrating merely my stupidity, torpor or craziness. I was too angry, insufficiently detached to traverse from "this" to "that." However trivial the insight, I finally came to understand that one cannot write objectively from the victim's point of view; she must be abandoned as one pulls chair to table. The urgent collaboration, rather, is between the author and the reader, a collaboration wherein the sufferings of the victims "are used to create something, works of art, that are thrown to the consumption of a world which destroyed them."[12]

See Symposium, Legal Storytelling, 87 MICH. L. REV. 2073 (1989); Robert M. Cover, *The Supreme Court, 1982 Term-Forward: Nomos and Narrative,* 97 HARV. L. REV. 4 (1983); Robin West, *Jurisprudence as Narrative: An Aesthetic Analysis of Modern Legal Theory,* 60 N.Y.U. L. REV. 146 (1985); Richard K. Sherwin, *A Matter of Voice and Plot: Belief and Suspicion in Legal Storytelling,* 87 MICH. L. REV. 543 (1988).

9. *See, e.g.,* PATRICIA J. WILLIAMS, THE ALCHEMY OF RACE AND RIGHTS (1991); West, *Phenomenology, supra* note 8; Ann C. Scales, *Feminists in the Field of Time,* 42 FLA. L. REV. 95 (1990); DERRICK BELL, AND WE ARE NOT SAVED: THE ELUSIVE QUEST FOR RACIAL JUSTICE (1987). Robin West argues for an anti-objectivist legal scholarship in her *Love, Rage and Legal Theory,* 1 YALE J.L. & FEMINISM 101 (1989), an article which gave me an added measure of determination in writing this introduction and for which I thank her. While West in the just-cited article speaks to the subversive possibilities of writing directly from the first person singular, other authorial approaches are similarly disruptive though they are less facially challenging. For example, although Catharine MacKinnon's style is typically deemed "difficult," the quality of that difficulty from a rhetorical standpoint is seldom squarely addressed. I think the challenge she poses to her readers is to think from a "doubled" perspective, a perspective which she theorizes substantively by writing in near-allegorical mode. Frances Olsen's work also, I think, is formally "doubled" by an incisive humor scarcely visible on a first reading, but which flourishes on the third or fourth, levitating and unbalancing her formal style of argument.

10. KATHLEEN BARRY, FEMALE SEXUAL SLAVERY 215 (1979).

11. *Id.*

12. Theodor Adorno, *Commitment, in* THE ESSENTIAL FRANKFURT SCHOOL READER 300, 312 (Andrew Arato & Eike Gebhardt eds., 1982). James Agee's famous preamble to LET US NOW PRAISE FAMOUS MEN invokes a similar contradiction:

> It seems to me curious, not to say obscene and thoroughly terrifying, that it could occur to an association of human beings drawn together through need and chance and for profit into a company, an organ of journalism, to pry intimately into the lives of an undefended and appallingly damaged group of human beings . . . for the purpose of parading the nakedness, disadvantage and humiliation of these lives before another

In a paper about prostitution, it is difficult to avoid the inference that this collaboration shares certain features with that between pimp and john, the "prostitute" shaped by the author into a representation suitable and desirable for the anonymous reader's temporary, fleeting engagement. Again, the "prostitute" is but a species of exchange in a transaction through which her value is debated, quarreled over, but to which she remains a stranger. This dilemma, the revictimization of the sufferer in the very act of the writing that renders her visible, can perhaps only finally, securely be overcome by the eradication of the suffering such writing seeks to disclose. That will require a new form of communication among us, one which does not depend on the exchange of represented "women," in words and by commerce and as sex, for the false communion of author and reader (false because I speak to you as not-a-prostitute but as an author who objectifies "them," false because you read as a member of a general audience and not as yourself until you become yourself an author in another place).[13] Thus, the very themes of this essay I may describe, but I cannot yet enact. It is with sad irony, then, that I here "move on" to the first question I would like to explore; that is, the political significance of the dichotomy drawn between "prostitutes" and "other women," in life and then again in law, a dichotomy exactly founded on the

---

group of human beings, in the name of science, of "honest journalism" (whatever that paradox may mean), of humanity, of social fearlessness, for money, and for a reputation for crusading and for unbias which, when skillfully enough qualified, is exchangeable at any bank for money . . . .
JAMES AGEE & WALKER EVANS, LET US NOW PRAISE FAMOUS MEN 7 (1939).
   An alternative aesthetic premise is poet Laurie Sheck's visionary, and feminist, definition of beauty: "How beautiful, what is not made by fear." Laurie Sheck, *Almond Flowers*, in IO AT NIGHT 62 (1990).
   13. These problems are brilliantly explored by Susanne Kappeler in THE PORNOGRAPHY OF REPRESENTATION (1986). Kappeler's argument is densely layered and formally subversive, thus difficult to summarize fairly or excerpt. Her critique, like Wolf's, centers on the colonializing egoism of Kantian aesthetic apprehension, but focusses principally on the experiential benefits of that relation to the perceiver and its political consequences to the perceived:
      Under his aesthetic gaze any woman, known or unknown, turns into the 'stranger,' that object of no interest except for its capacity to stimulate the subject's feeling of life . . . .

            . . . .

      . . . The subject-object relation is at the core of this dominant way of seeing. The individualistic perspective of our culture has insistently focused on the necessity of this pair, denying any capacity of the human individual for collectivity and intersubjectivity. It is the fundamental axiom of the justification of inequality, domination and power.
Id. at 61, 212. *See also* DEBORAH CAMERON & ELIZABETH FRAZER, THE LUST TO KILL: A FEMINIST INVESTIGATION OF SEXUAL MURDER 166-70 (1987) (on the identification of freedom with actual killing of "objects" of sexual desire); for related explorations of the relationship between representation and domination, *see generally* LAURA MULVEY, VISUAL AND OTHER PLEASURES (1989) (especially her now classic *Visual Pleasures and Narrative Cinema*, in *id.* at 14, 16: "It is said that analyzing pleasure, or beauty, destroys it. That is the intention of this article."); TERESA DE LAURETIS, TECHNOLOGIES OF GENDER: ESSAYS ON THEORY, FILM AND FICTION (1987); Rosalind Coward, *Sexual Violence and Sexuality*, in SEXUALITY: A READER 307 (Feminist Review ed., 1987); Dee Dee Glass *et al.*, *Feminist Film Practice and Pleasure: A Discussion*, in FORMATIONS OF PLEASURE 156 (Formations Editorial Collective ed., 1983). An originating text, upon which Kappeler's argument builds, is JOHN BERGER, WAYS OF SEEING (1972).

assumption that "prostitution isn't like anything else."

I begin with a story.

I. A TWICE TOLD TALE

My activist colleague, K.C. Reed, is a strong woman. She was raped by her father and then sexually abused by her grandfather from the age of two, and prostituted for over 20 years, first at age 13.[14] She is now trying to remember her life as a way of beginning to live it in her own self. She needs to remember where she has lived, whether she did or did not attend a community college sometime in the 1970's, when and where she was in prison. This is difficult work. Her life's witnesses—family, friends, lovers, children, even the shreds of paper we rely on to remind us who we are and who we have been—number few. Many of the men are dangerous to her. Her children are far away. One of them, a daughter, is dead. K.C. believes she was murdered by a trick. Her sons are in the care of others. K.C. hopes for them but has no direct contact with them. Other family members know little. The facts have faded. The feelings were always wrapped tightly, or foregone by numbness, or dreamed in hard drugs that can make you feel a tenderness inside. Her memory is complex, kaleidoscoped, fluid. She is smart and vivid and full of devotion. She organizes on behalf of herself and other women in prostitution for support and for help in ending prostitution.

K.C. recently wrote down what happened to her during one night in prostitution when she was 15 years old. She and two other women had run away from a state hospital. They were picked up by some men and taken to a hotel room where about 25 other men had assembled. She describes how the men talked and acted, how many men penetrated her (15), in what positions, and with what objects after the penises gave out, how the men insisted that the women have sex with each other when the men wanted to watch, how the pictures were taken, how she moved to the next gang of men, the next road. She mailed her testimony to the newsletter of a feminist anti-rape organization for publication. One of the members of the board questioned whether her piece should be printed, objecting to formal deficiencies: "It just goes on and on and there's no point to it." The author's response, arguing to mimetic virtuosity, was simple. "Yes, that's right. It went on and on and there was no point to it."[15]

I have just now told you a story of my own. Mine too may seem simply

---

14. K.C. Reed, *There Isn't No Easy Way* 1-2 (July 6, 1990) (unpublished pamphlet on file with author).

15. Thankfully, with the support of other board members, Reed's piece was ultimately published. *See* K.C. Reed, *A Former Prostitute Speaks*, NCASA NEWS, Fall/Winter 1990, at 24. NCASA has now adopted a policy position defining prostitution as sexual violence, requiring member agencies to afford appropriate services to women in prostitution, "including services for rape, battery, and incest." Sandi Belote, *Seven Resolutions Passed at NCASA '90*, NCASA NEWS, Fall/Winter 1990, at 12-13. K.C. Reed was among the women who drafted, spoke in support of, and organized for this resolution.

an overlong account of a mere episode, and a needlessly pointed description of a fleeting, embarrassing moment of inadvertence and failed attention. In substance, in other words, an isolated incident. In form, however, my story occupies the status of creation myth in modern feminism: a story about a woman telling another woman a story about herself.[16] As "consciousness-raising," it is feminism's tale of origin;[17] as "feminist epistemology," it is feminism's claim to coherence;[18] as "woman identification," it is the basis of our self-understanding.[19] In substance, our stories, our activism and our

---

16. The great Blake scholar Northrop Frye defines the narrative form of myth as the "imitation of actions at or near the conceivable limits of desire." NORTHROP FRYE, ANATOMY OF CRITICISM 136 (1957). I intend Frye's understanding of myth as aspirational ideal in this context, rather than its commonplace usage as an institutionalized structure of misplaced belief.

17. Catharine A. MacKinnon explicitly theorizes consciousness-raising in these terms. See MACKINNON, TOWARD A FEMINIST THEORY OF THE STATE, supra note 8, at 83-105 ("Consciousness-raising is the process through which the contemporary radical feminist analysis of the situation of women has been shaped and shared," id. at 84). Historical accounts of contemporary feminism characteristically posit the formation of consciousness-raising groups as its constitutive event. See SARAH EVANS, PERSONAL POLITICS 212-32 (1980); ELIZABETH FOX-GENOVESE, FEMINISM WITHOUT ILLUSIONS: A CRITIQUE OF INDIVIDUALISM 13-15 (1991); MARY KING, FREEDOM SONG (1987); Alix Kates Schulman, Sex and Power: Sexual Bases of Radical Feminism, in WOMEN: SEX AND SEXUALITY 21, 23-27 (Catherine Stimpson & Ethel Person eds., 1980). Contemporaneous texts include Pamela Allen, Free Space, in RADICAL FEMINISM 271 (Anne Koedt, Ellen Levine, & Anita Rapone eds., 1973); Kathie Sarachild, Consciousness-Raising: A Radical Weapon in FEMINIST REVOLUTION 144 (1979). For a retrospective account of the impact of formal consciousness-raising on the members of one group, see ANITA SHREVE, WOMEN TOGETHER, WOMEN ALONE: THE LEGACY OF THE CONSCIOUSNESS-RAISING MOVEMENT (1989).

18. See, e.g., MACKINNON, TOWARD A FEMINIST THEORY OF THE STATE, supra note 8, at 106-25; Nancy Hartsock, The Feminist Standpoint: Developing the Ground for a Specifically Feminist Historical Materialism, in FEMINISM AND METHODOLOGY, 157 (Sandra Harding, ed., 1987); Theresa de Lauretis, Feminist Studies/Critical Studies: Issues, Terms and Contexts, in FEMINIST STUDIES/CRITICAL STUDIES 1 (de Lauretis ed., 1986); Dorothy Smith, Women's Perspective as a Radical Critique of Sociology, in FEMINISM & METHODOLOGY 84 (Sandra Harding ed., 1987). Catharine MacKinnon, Robin West and Christine Littleton each emphasizes the role of consciousness-raising as a standpoint for evaluating norms informing feminist legal practice, if from varying theoretical accounts of its political intention. See MACKINNON, TOWARD A FEMINIST THEORY OF THE STATE, supra note 8; Christine Littleton, Women's Experience and the Problem of Transition: Perspectives on Male Battering of Women, CHIC. LEGAL FOR. 23 (1989); West, Phenomenology, supra note 8, at 122-29.

19. As Teresa de Lauretis puts the point, at the bottom of feminist interpretive practices is the simple commitment to "reading, speaking, and listening to one another." De Lauretis, supra note 18, at 8. See also TERESA DE LAURETIS, ALICE DOESN'T: FEMINISM, SEMIOTICS, CINEMA (1984). Catharine MacKinnon stresses the same precondition in her analysis of consciousness-raising. See MACKINNON, TOWARD A FEMINIST THEORY OF THE STATE, supra note 8, at 84-88. See also BETTINA APTHEKER, TAPESTRIES OF LIFE: WOMEN'S WORK, WOMEN'S CONSCIOUSNESS AND THE MEANING OF DAILY EXPERIENCE (1989); MARILYN FRYE, To See and Be Seen: The Politics of Reality, in THE POLITICS OF REALITY: ESSAYS IN FEMINIST THEORY 152 (1983) AUDRE LORDE, Eye to Eye: Black Women, Hatred, and Anger, in SISTER OUTSIDER 145 (1984); JANICE RAYMOND, A PASSION FOR FRIENDS: TOWARD A PHILOSOPHY OF FEMALE AFFECTION (1985). Paulo Friere's model of education in liberation among oppressed people, too, posits such a shift in authority and accountability as the necessary origination moment of revolutionary perception. "The oppressed," Friere insists, "must be their own example in the struggle for their redemption." PAOLO FRIERE, PEDAGOGY OF THE OPPRESSED 39 (Myra Bergman Ramos trans., 1972).

The implications for both theory construction and practical politics of feminism's epistemological and ethical commitments of women to each other is often suppressed in feminist discussion. It is my fear that this ellipsis is in part a consequence of old-fashioned lesbophobia and fear of acknowledging the experiential significance of woman-identification explicitly before audiences which include men. I hope that we will begin to investigate the explanatory possibilities of this perspective with more attention in our work. For example, in debates on the transformative value of "empathy" in constructing norms and practices of community-building in the public sphere, and in the political consequences to women's status of elevating the civic value of women's capacity for empathy, much discussion revolves around the question whether women "really are" more empathic than men, and, if so, the significance of women's oppressed political

theoretical interventions are grounded principally in women's struggles for representational authority, in both senses of the term "representational": for the authorial power over the meaning of our experience, and for the political strength to make those meanings count for something reliably real.[20]

Compared to the typical arsenals of masculine political firepower, these may seem diminished pursuits indeed. As a political movement, feminism has not so far sought to mobilize territorial disputes for land, or for economic markets, or for a political system *per se* properly spectacularized by military force.[21] Perhaps we are too intimately aware of the consequences of these

---

condition to that ontological outcome. *See, e.g.*, Symposium, *Feminist Discourse, Moral Values and the Law—A Conversation*, 34 BUFF. L. REV. 11 (1985); Toni M. Massaro, *Empathy, Legal Storytelling, and the Rule of Law: New Words, Old Wounds?*, 87 MICH. L. REV. 2099 (1989); Deborah L. Rhode, *The Woman's Point of View*, 30 J. LEGAL EDUC. 39 (1988); Joan M. Shaughnessy, *Gilligan's Travels*, 7 LAW & INEQ. 1 (1988). Rarely addressed in these discussions is the significance of women's choice of *beneficiary* of that empathy, a choice which under conditions of male dominance has been channelled toward everyone and everything but other women.

I would hypothesize that the disruptive, rather than dutiful and defensive, practices of empathy and care-giving responsibility emerging from feminism do so as consequence of perceiving other women as deserving of our loving attention, and as entitled to survival, as men, children, pets, and the planet. The backbone of feminist activism is women's willingness to enact devotion to their sisters and what constitutes its distinctive "voice." Ruthann Robson's project of materializing a lesbian jurisprudence may provide further visibility to this issue. *See* Ruthann Robson, *Lesbian Jurisprudence?*, 8 LAW & INEQ. 443 (1990). *See also* Nancy Fraser, *What's Critical About Critical Theory? The Case of Habermas and Gender*, in FEMINISM AS CRITIQUE 31, 54 (Seyla Benhabib & Drucilla Cornell eds., 1987) (stressing the significance of an autonomous women's community in generating reinterpretations of women's experience). In concrete terms, the visibility and endurance of radical rape crisis services, battered women's shelters, and feminist abortion clinics, all philosophically separatist organizations, have been the most reliable, safe and militant presences of the feminist movement in the social landscape and constitute its essential institutional base. They exist because women need them, and need them this way. As these institutions come under continued political attack and struggle with economic erosion, it behooves us to develop a strong theoretical voice in their support.

20. Feminism thus tends to fuse and confound the conventional liberal democratic dichotomy between the protection of individual rights and the fostering of majoritarian representation. In liberal thought, these interests are typically conceived both as distinct and antagonistic, the former to be barricaded from the overreaching of the latter. Women's political situation, in contrast, presents the uncontemplated conjunction of the representational "silencing" of individual women as part and parcel of the political subordination of a numerical demographic majority. Thus, Justice Scalia's confusion as to whether abortion is an "individual" right fastidiously to be protected by the courts, or a "political" issue to be debated through the franchise. *See* Webster v. Reproductive Health Service, 492 U.S. 490, 502 (1989) (Scalia, J., dissenting). A similar raggedness is also expressed in the embarrassment I hear articulated by liberal professors on the applicability of the *Carolene Products* heightened scrutiny test to women, *see* United States v. Carolene Products Co., 304 U.S. 144, 152 n.4 (1938). The phrase "discrete and insular minority" scarcely seems readily descriptive of a majority seemingly wholly dispersed socially among men. *Id.*

21. An important exception is the struggle of Native American women for tribal sovereignty, conducted simultaneously with work for sex equality within tribal communities. *See* PAULA GUNN ALLEN, THE SACRED HOOP: RECOVERING THE FEMININE IN AMERICAN INDIAN TRADITIONS 189-193 (1986) (struggle for tribal survival continuous with and inextricable from combatting violence against Indian women by Indian men); MARY CROW DOG & RICHARD ERDOES, LAKOTA WOMAN 242-60 (1990) (describing Leonard Crow Dog's affirmation of women's spiritual participation in the Lakota tradition as a result of Mary Crow Dog's intervention); Kate Shanley, *Thoughts on Indian Feminism, in* A GATHERING OF SPIRIT: A COLLECTION BY NORTH AMERICAN INDIAN WOMEN 213, 215 (Beth Brant ed., 1988) (discussing the significance of tribal sovereignty to feminism for Indian women). The development of strategies for the empowerment of Indian women in fashioning the terms of tribal sovereignty seems the urgent task for feminism. This thesis seems to me to be the import of Catharine MacKinnon's essay on the subject. *See* CATHARINE A. MACKINNON, *Whose Culture? A Case Note on* Martinez v. Santa Clara Pueblo, *in* FEMINISM UNMODIFIED: DISCOURSES ON LIFE AND LAW 63 (1987).

Thus, while I am grateful for Robert A. Williams Jr.'s recent article on the necessity of situating

displays of bravado on women and children and other politically dependent people, who never seem to emerge substantially empowered upon the successful *coup d'etat*. As Michele Wallace puts the point, this is no accident; "it comes automatically to nationalist struggles to devalue the contributions of women, as well as gays or anybody else who doesn't fit the profile of the noble warrior or the elder statesman."[22] Perhaps too, we suffer from a failure of expectation. Women's structural homelessness does not readily yield a felt entitlement to territory. We have little money, much less markets to preserve or control. We have no army, or police force, or guerrilla squads to act in our behalf.[23] For better or worse, feminism's consistent strategy has been to seek to *explain* ourselves; our primary goal to be *understood* as deserving of a respected human life, whatever "human" comes to mean once women are considered instances of the species.[24]

Yet, despite these shared commitments, K.C. Reed told a story that another woman, a feminist, could not hear. She heard words, "on and on," but not a proper "story." She heard some representational version of nagging, incoherencies within the conceptual grid, the linguistic equivalent of insanity. These are the charges we conventionally associate with the suppression of women's voices within masculinist systems of meaning: less that we do not or cannot *talk* (although women's occupation of verbal space remains a controversial entitlement), than that we do not make *sense* (a conclusion further weakening our claim to verbal space).[25] If there exists a diagnostic consensus

---

analyses of Indian sexual politics within their originating cultural contexts, it is not clear to me how his approach concretely empowers Indian women to speak or act for themselves with respect to tribal sovereignty, or otherwise. Robert A. Williams, Jr., *Gendered Checks and Balances: Understanding the Legacy of White Patriarchy in an American Indian Cultural Context*, 24 GA. L. REV. 1019 (1990). Perhaps that issue was simply beyond the scope of his essay as he envisioned his immediate project, differentiating the expressive conventions of Indian gender relations from those characteristic of colonial white patriarchy. I am sure he is aware that such arguments, standing alone, tend to merge in theme with a whole history of cultural defenses, advanced by men, to silence feminist objections to culturally specific misogynist practices from *suttee* to clitoridectomy to marital rape. I hope, in short, that he will ultimately address the question how the cultural specificity of Indian misogyny can inform the specificity of an Indian feminism, and along the way address the problematics of his "speaking for" Indian women. In that endeavor, he may benefit from a rereading of MacKinnon's essay cited above, which takes these latter issues as central. William's dismissal of MacKinnon's essay as "ultimately crippled," seems to turn on his own failure to take these questions seriously. *See* Williams, *id.*, at 1023 n.9, *quoting* Angela Harris, *Race and Essentialism in Feminist Legal Theory*, 42 STAN. L. REV. 581, 594 (1990); *see also* e. christi cunningham, *Unmaddening: A Response to Angela Harris*, 4 YALE J.L. & FEMINISM 155, 161-63 (1991).

22. MICHELE WALLACE, *Introduction: How I Saw It Then, How I See It Now, in* BLACK MACHO AND THE MYTH OF THE SUPERWOMAN xx (1990 ed.,).

23. Even *Thelma and Louise* is, after all, only a movie, right?

24. My language here echoes Richard Rorty's on the import of Catharine MacKinnon's analysis of the status of women under male dominance: "MacKinnon's central point, as I read her, is that 'a woman' is not yet the name of a way of being human—not yet the name of a moral identity, but, at most, the name of a disability." Richard Rorty, *Feminism and Pragmatism*, 30 MICH. Q. REV. 231, 234 (1991).

25. Mary Daly put the point early, and succinctly, in these terms: "[I]t is necessary to grasp the fundamental fact that women have had the power of naming stolen from us." MARY DALY, BEYOND GOD THE FATHER: TOWARD A PHILOSOPHY OF WOMEN'S LIBERATION 8 (1974). *See also* Ruth Ginzberg, *Uncovering Gynocentric Science*, 2 HYPATIA 89 (1987); DOROTHY SMITH, THE CONCEPTUAL PRACTICES OF POWER (1990); Beverly Thiele, *Vanishing Acts in Social and Political Thought: Tricks of the Trade, in* FEMINIST CHALLENGES: SOCIAL AND POLITICAL THEORY 30 (Carole Pateman & Elizabeth Gross eds.,

point among feminist theorists on any issue, I would suggest this is the one, for it bridges gaps as wide as those among Carol Gilligan, whose argument with Kohlberg is this one,[26] Catharine MacKinnon, whose argument with masculinist epistemology is this one,[27] and Wendy Williams, whose argument with stereotypes of women as "irrational" is this one.[28] The editor is a fine woman, clear-headed, smart, dedicated; she is neither cruel nor insensitive. But what K.C. had to say about one night of prostitution didn't yield meaning to her on its own terms.

I am compelled by this story, and wanted to tell it to you, for a number of reasons in addition to witnessing to the anguish of my friend. I am haunted by the fear that this story is less anecdote than synecdoche, characteristic of a profound incomprehensibility of prostitution to feminism. Certainly I need search neither long nor hard to discover myself in K.C.'s editor. For a long time in my life, not one woman ever talked to me about being prostituted. That was a deafening silence, given that during the same period many women spoke to me about rapes, incest, abuse-related substance dependency, and beatings, and given that, as Catharine MacKinnon reports, some 20% of women engage in prostitution at some time in their lives.[29] Then, a 20% estimate would have seemed impossibly high. Now, it seems low.[30] It seems plain to me now that, however trustworthy I seemed as I listened respectfully to what women had to say about other violence and shame and fear in their lives, they did not feel safe talking about prostitution.[31] This is especially curious since a few of the women in my life at the time *were* prostituted. We just never talked about "that."

Seven or eight years ago, after I had worked visibly with Catharine MacKinnon, Andrea Dworkin, and many other non-conforming women on the Minneapolis anti-pornography ordinance, something shifted. Some women with whom I worked closely and whom I love told me of their histories in prostitution, carefully and from a distance. Sometimes in writing, sometimes

---

1986); and sources cited *supra* note 18. No summary of the conclusions of these investigations surpasses Andrea Dworkin's: "This power of naming enables men to define experience, to articulate boundaries and values, to designate each thing its realm and qualities, to determine what can and cannot be expressed, to control perception itself." ANDREA DWORKIN, PORNOGRAPHY: MEN POSSESSING WOMEN 17 (1983).

26. *See* CAROL GILLIGAN, IN A DIFFERENT VOICE (1982) (arguing that conventional measures of ethical development render incoherent forms of moral reasoning characteristic of girls).

27. *See* MACKINNON, TOWARD A FEMINIST THEORY OF THE STATE, *supra* note 8, at 106-25 (analyzing the impact of objectivist knowledge claims on women, rendering women "known" but never "knowing").

28. *See* Wendy Williams, *The Equality Crisis: Some Reflections on Culture, Courts and Feminism*, 7 WOMEN'S. RTS. L. REP. 175 (1982) (women's categorical exclusion from participation in public life commonly jusitified by our "tribalist," non-disinterested commitments within a universalized public order).

29. MACKINNON, TOWARD A FEMINIST THEORY OF THE STATE, *supra* note 8, at 143.

30. Robin West and Lucinda Finley similarly describe the statistical bewilderment gap between men and women in the measure of credence given to sexual assault prevalence rates. *See* West, *Phenomenology, supra* note 8, at 96; Lucinda Finley, *The Nature of Domination and the Nature of Women: Reflections on Feminism Unmodified*, 82 NW. U.L. REV. 352, 358-359 (1988).

31. One possible explanation is that the women with histories in prostitution were off talking with all the lesbians I didn't meet for a while, either. But I doubt it.

by unexpected announcement in a public place, sometimes as if they had already told me and nothing more needed to be said. Even approached this obliquely, I had to force myself to listen; they knew it and I knew it. It was a brutal time, much more for them than for me. I was part of the brutality. I didn't know how to hear, and I resisted learning. My friends, usually composed and compressed in expression, seemed disoriented, too. Uncertain, it appeared, of what to say, how to say it, why, even, to continue to speak. "On and on." Usually, the first conversation was about the johns, about the men. Tucked behind a corner, in the next conversation perhaps, a slightly different theme: how she betrayed another woman as a way to get out, or to placate a pimp, or to keep a john quiet. Sometimes, too, a resolve not to give over her own daughter to be prostituted as she had been.

Now I believe I hear better. More women talk to me. I work on issues of prostitution in the feminist movement. Women call. I feel, perhaps wrongly, that when the woman begins to speak I already know some of it: about the tricks, the drugs, the cops, the welfare, how things come to be after 3 weeks, after 3 months, after 3 years, after 30 years. In these conversations I hear a quality of uncontained contempt for men, for johns in particular, that is new to me in its conviction. Sometimes I think to ask about the other women, the renounced women, if she seems to want to talk about it. There is great grief there. I wonder if *she* is the other woman, to me: the one I will renounce. I pray that it isn't true, but know it has been. "There is no point to it."

I begin, too, to wonder if these women are telling me something about all the *other* "other" women, the women who haven't been prostituted, and the stories we tell. These days, we more readily recount to each other all kinds of stories about how we have lived our women's lives. Those stories, too, now seem familiar, yet they are shapelier than the prostitution stories, more formally precise, more modulated, tuned to the finer Aristotelian graces of beginning, middle and end. I wonder where the ease comes from, where the "form" comes from. I wonder if it comes from omission, elliding pieces that fall tangentially, pointlessly, out of the story, or which did not feel like "experiences" which could be given shape. I wonder if the missing pieces are *about* prostitution, somehow. Could we be suppressing stories about johns, or about contempt, or about money? Are we suppressing the stories in which we renounce a woman more vulnerable than ourselves, in our own defense? Do our stories *participate* in prostitution, operating as rehearsals for telling men the stories they want to hear from us, so that we can use them as best we can while we renounce prostitutes as part of the bargain? I am not sure, any more, about many tales I believed in once. What is the point to *them*?

One of feminism's stories, entrenched deeply in the history and political landscape of the contemporary movement, is that prostitution is indeed not "like anything else." The theme was often sounded in the early movement that prostitution is *only* a story, a representational overlay masking and justifying real abuse and sex-based inequality suffered by (other?) women. "Prostitution" was conceived as a symbol, a groundless stereotype, a cancerous, run-amok ideological construct; "the prostitute" was the embodied cultural sign representing the sum of depravations suffered by "all women" (real women?). For Jackie MacMillian, "[p]rostitution is an important issue for feminists because prostitutes [sic] most clearly express the cultural valuation and image of women as primarily sexual beings;"[32] for Susan Brownmiller, prostitution represents a "concept," a component of a "psychology," contributing to and rendering invisible male violence against women, especially rape.[33] As Deborah Rhode has recently pointed out, these accounts share less a concern with the pervasiveness of prostitution, or with its effect on or meaning to women involved directly in the practice, than with its "ideological significance;" specifically, the significance of our "cultural understandings about the sale of sexuality."[34] Patricia Hill Collins emphasizes the same theme in her analysis of the import of prostitution for Black women. With Angela Davis, Collins argues that "the myth of the Black prostitute" constitutes an ideological vehicle and justification for the social control of Black women, legitimizing rape and other sexual violence against Black women.[35]

The problem of prostitution to feminist reform, in consequence, comes to be posed as the problem the *idea* of prostitution poses for women's authority to tell our own, authentic stories of our own experiences. This form of analysis similarly inspires Margaret Radin's treatment of prostitution in her analysis proposing a pragmatic approach to sexual commodification. She concedes that prostitution likely entails a hard and dangerous life for women, yet for many women provides their only realistic means of survival.[36] In her view, women in prostitution thus confront a profound double-bind, for they are placed at serious risk by engaging in prostitution, while materially powerless to leave it. She argues that neither "pro-commodification" legal philosophies, nor "anti-

---

32. Jackie MacMillian, *Prostitution as Sexual Politics*, 4 QUEST (No. 1, 1977) at 41.
33. Brownmiller elaborates:
    [M]y horror at the idea of legalized prostitution is not that it institutionalizes a female service that should not be denied the civilized male. Perpetuation of the concept that the "powerful male impulse" must be satisfied with immediacy by a co-operative class of women, set aside and licensed for the purpose, is part and parcel of the mass psychology of rape.
SUSAN BROWNMILLER, AGAINST OUR WILL: MEN, WOMEN AND RAPE 392 (1975). Exceptions to this approach include TI-GRACE ATKINSON, AMAZON ODYSSEY 117-130 (1974); BARRY, *supra* note 10; INTERNATIONAL FEMINISM: NETWORKING AGAINST SEXUAL SLAVERY (Kathleen Barry, Charlotte Bunch, & Shirley Castlely eds., 1979); KATE MILLETT, THE PROSTITUTION PAPERS (1974); Ellen Strong, *The Hooker, in* SISTERHOOD IS POWERFUL: AN ANTHOLOGY OF WRITINGS FROM THE WOMEN'S LIBERATION MOVEMENT 289 (Robin Morgan ed., 1970). Robin Morgan, in her smart and poorly read 1974 essay, challenged the distinction between "other women" and prostitutes by arguing to the "whorification" of all women in the practice of pornographic sexuality. ROBIN MORGAN, *Theory and Practice: Pornography and Rape, in* GOING TOO FAR: THE PERSONAL CHRONICLE OF A FEMINIST 163, 167-68 (1978).
34. DEBORAH L. RHODE, JUSTICE AND GENDER: SEX DISCRIMINATION AND THE LAW 257 (1989).
35. PATRICIA HILL COLLINS, BLACK FEMINIST THOUGHT: KNOWLEDGE, CONSCIOUSNESS, AND THE POLITICS OF EMPOWERMENT 177 (1991); *see also* ANGELA DAVIS, WOMEN, RACE AND CLASS (1981).
36. Margaret J. Radin, *Market-Inalienability*, 100 HARV. L. REV. 1849, 1856, 1921-25 (1987).

commodification" positions adequately address this difficulty. The former ignore the violence; the latter, the need. Ultimately, however, Professor Radin counsels us to ignore both, so long as the "cultural discourse" of the problem of sexual commodification remains confined to prostitution.[37] Concluding that that ideology is unlikely to "trickle up" over its present discursive sea wall and contagiously threaten the comfort of other women, Professor Radin leaves prostitutes to fend as best they can, with all sympathy and good wishes for the future.

At least for women who are not publicly identified as "prostitutes," this understanding of prostitution as a false and dangerous idea nevertheless seems well enough supported in the experience of many women, despite Professor Radin's confidence in its effective containment. Especially on occasions of sexually exploitative and violent episodes, the characterization of women as "sluts" by assaultive men runs like a sturdy thread through women's accounts of sexual victimization. The epithet is apparently intended to humiliate, to eroticize, and to satisfy an urge for self-justification. In contemporary empirical research, the apparent irrationality of the charge threatens to render its content invisible, abstracted away in subsuming conclusions. The empirical preference too, it seems, is to perceive the allegation as "just a story," not a concrete explanatory or descriptive datum. Yet the charge is near-universally to be found, in the particular, if untheorized, event.

For example, investigators of wife beating commonly recite "jealousy" as an asserted motivation for men to beat and torture women with whom they are intimate.[38] Submerged in this conclusion are the allegations of prostitution which repeatedly emerge as the stated origin of that jealousy. In one collection of thirty-three women's accounts of their experience of being battered, nearly one third had been accused of prostitution or labelled as "whores" during the course of beatings and rapes. Exemplary are the following:

> After my mom died we went East for the funeral . . . At the funeral home everyone was hugging and kissing. Gerry went off mad and came back drunk, saying, "You want your uncle's in you." He grabs me and calls me a slut. "I'm going to tell your uncles you're out here waiting with your legs wide open."[39]

---

37. *Id.* at 1922-23 (analyzing whether the "domino effect" of commodified sexuality "might make the ideal of nonmonetized sharing impossible").

38. *See, e.g.*, LENORE WALKER, THE BATTERED WOMAN 114-15 (1979) ("Sexual jealousy is almost universally present in the battering relationship."); DEL MARTIN, BATTERED WIVES 58-61 (1976); ERIN PIZZEY, SCREAM QUIETLY OR THE NEIGHBORS WILL HEAR 85 (1974).

39. GINA NICARTHY, THE ONES WHO GOT AWAY: WOMEN WHO LEFT ABUSIVE PARTNERS 290 (1987). Where prostitution is not explicitly alluded to by batterers, these accounts universally recite accusations of promiscuity and secret affairs as reasons given for the battery. Two battered mothers report that their husbands beat them, doubting the children were theirs. *Id.* at 79 ("Lou became pregnant and Barry threatened to 'beat it out of her' insisting the baby wasn't his."), 96 ("You dirty whore, why don't you go drag men in off the street? Jay probably isn't even my son.").

He also humiliated her by telling her that other men thought she was a prostitute, and occasionally they did make that assumption and offered Matthew money for her sexual services . . . "Slowly," she says, "everything edged away from me."[40]

Similar recitations figure obsessively in prosecutions for men's murders of wives and girlfriends. As one defendant put the point, the victim was "just a slut" and he "had to kill her."[41] The same theme arises repeatedly in divorce actions, commonly where the husband beat and tortured his wife during the course of the marriage, and explains his behavior by reference to her whorish behavior.[42]

---

40. *Id.* at 120. These accounts corroborate Andrea Dworkin's conclusion that:

[T]he reality is that you can do everything in the world to be a good woman in this society, but when you are in the private house with the private husband whom you've attracted through your conformity to being what is on the surface a good woman, when that man starts hitting you, he hits you because you are bad.

Andrea Dworkin, *Woman-Hating Right and Left, in* THE SEXUAL LIBERALS AND THE ATTACK ON FEMINISM *supra* note 3, at 28, 33 (1990). Margo St. James, the founder of COYOTE, a pro-prostitution organization, on this point uncharacteristically agrees with Dworkin. "[W]hen a man slugs his wife, he precedes the abuse with, 'You slut! You whore!'" Margo St. James, (*Comment) From the Floor, in* GOOD GIRLS/BAD GIRLS: FEMINISM AND SEX TRADE WORKERS FACE TO FACE 114, 130 (Laurie Bell ed., 1987).

41. People v. Carroll, 180 Cal. Rptr. 327 (Cal. Ct. App. 1983). *See also* People v. District Court, 595 P.2d 1945 (Colo. 1979) (defendant, who lived with pregnant victim, commented during an argument with her that he was going to "smash her face in." He shouted at her, calling her a "bitch, whore, and a slut," while he beat her to death); People v. Bennett, 129 Cal. Rptr. 679, 682 (Cal. Ct. App. 1976) (defendant convicted of first-degree murder of his wife; he had told psychiatrist that he hated her; that she shouldn't live, "that she was a bad housekeeper, a slut, and an immoral woman;" that such "a terrible person ought not to live" and "ought not to be allowed to raise his child;" that his wife and child would be better off if his wife were dead); People v. Cooley, 27 Cal. Rptr. 543 (Cal. Ct. App. 1963) (defendant convicted of first-degree murder in the beating and torture death of his wife. Over 15 years of marriage, defendant had inflicted numerous severe beatings on her, resulting in many broken bones, choked her, threatened to kill her and the children, accused her of having extramarital affairs with two homosexual men, burned her nipples with cigarettes while she was semi-conscious, ripped out clumps of her hair, told his daughter that her mother was a "whore" and a "slut", and kicked her mother in the stomach, saying to the daughter, "See, she only cries when you hit her, she doesn't care what's happening"); People v. Hulsing, 825 P.2d 1027, 1032 (Colo. App. 1991) (husband convicted of murdering his wife had complained to a coworker beforehand that "she was screwing around on him," and that "she's a slut, a fucking slut"); State v. Pruitt, 506 N.E.2d 696 (Ill. App. 1987) (defendant convicted of murder after finding wife in partial state of undress in parked car with the victim; wife testified defendant "grabbed me by the hair of the head and threw me on the ground . . . calling me all kinds of names like slut and whore"); State v. Underwood, 1988 WL 37058 (Ohio App.) (estranged husband convicted of murdering his wife; he testified that he was jealous and angry at the thought of her seeing other men, and after arrest had told police, "I surely am a manly son of a bitch doing what I did . . . that slut just ruined my life, didn't she?"); State v. Smith, 791 P.2d 836 (Or. 1990) (defendant convicted of aggravated felony-murder of his wife; court found that throughout his ten-year marriage to the victim, defendant beat her, tortured her, and threatened to kill her, referring to her as a "whore" and a "slut," and repeatedly promised to tie her up and leave her somewhere to die); State v. Unsworth, 402 P.2d 507 (Or. 1965) (defendant convicted of second-degree murder in the shooting death of a friend; a deputy testified that while he was at defendant's cabin, defendant called his wife a "dirty son of a bitch and a slut," and said, "You're the one that I intended to kill anyway"). On and on.

42. Parker v. Parker, 519 So.2d 1232 (Miss. 1988) (husband had a vision in which the Lord told him that if his wife went out on a certain weekend, her face "would not be fit to be seen anymore on the earth . . . ," and that when he saw her dancing with another man at a birthday party, he shoved her into their car, bruising her leg in the process, calling her a "sorry low-down slut"); *In re* the Marriage of Ruby Elizabeth Walls, 743 S.W.2d 137 (Mo. Ct. App. 1988) (wife testified that defendant struck and kicked

These claims of punitive entitlement may extend beyond the situational to the structural. As women gain increased economic importance within families, it appears to at least one sociological researcher that the dynamics of battery increasingly mirror the familiar violence and economic exploitation typical of pimping. Ann Jones explains:

> [I] meet more and more battered women—severely battered women and women who have struck back—who were not being supported by the men who were their abusers. Rather, the economic arrangement is often the other way around: the man lives off the woman, off her wages or her welfare check or off the proceeds of her prostitution. He dominates and exploits her economically, just as he does physically and sexually. The parties may be husband and wife or a cohabiting couple, but the arrangement is the classic one of pimp and prostitute.[43]

---

her on numerous occasions, called her a "fuckin' slut" and a whore, and threatened to ". . . just tell your mother you're sick and I'll tie you up in the basement and just kill you a little each day"); Rollyson v. Rollyson, 294 S.E.2d 131 (W. Va. 1982) (wife testified that her husband had struck her on several occasions during their marriage, frequently called her a slut and a whore, accused her of "slutting around," and threatened her on several occasions, saying if he "caught her down on the street slutting around with those sluts and whores that they would be picking her up off the street, dead;" husband corroborated this testimony); Stillwell v. Stillwell, 357 So.2d 355 (Ala. Civ. App. 1978) (wife testified as to frequent screaming battles where he called her such names as "whore," "slut," "bitch," "motherfucker," "stupid, dumb-assed woman;" on several occasions searching for her around town with a gun); Ross v. Ross, 235 S.E.2d 405 (N.C. Ct. App. 1977) (defendant frequently assaulted and beat, kicked, and punched wife while in violent rages, cursing her calling her a "whore," "slut," and a "bitch"); Mezoff v. Mezoff, 307 N.E.2d 857 (Mass. Ct. App. 1974) (husband called petitioner a "dirty rotten slut" in front of their children, threw an object at her, and told her to go live in a slum); Deahl v. Deahl, 300 N.E.2d 497 (Ill. App. Ct. 1973) (wife testified that husband beat her up; that he regularly called her a bitch and a slut in front of others; that on one occasion he asked her if she had made any money, and when she replied she hadn't, said, "You could have went and sold yourself and made some money that way; that's all you're good for;" and with all the children present, told her that he didn't think the kids were his and that she was a slut like her mother); D.J.H. v. J.D.S., 481 S.W.2d 539 (Mo. Ct. App. 1972) (man threatened to kill himself and his daughters, tried to burn down the house with the daughters in it, and told his ex-wife's present father-in-law, "I'm going to kill them damn kids to get even with that slut"); Carpenter v. Carpenter, 262 A.2d 564 (Md. Ct. App. 1970) (husband beat wife "many times" and raped her; he suggested she have sexual relations with "some of the important people" so that he could "get a promotion;" he asked her to be a prostitute and he called her a "slut" and a "pig").

43. Ann Jones, *Family Matters, in* THE SEXUAL LIBERALS AND THE ATTACK ON FEMINISM, *supra* note 3, at 61, 63.

Evelina Giobbe explains how some of the sexual dynamics of prostitution are extended within marriage:

> The line between wife and prostitute—madonna and whore—has become increasingly blurred . . . With the invasion of the home by pornographic cable programs and video cassettes, the "good wife" has become equated with the "good whore," as more and more women are pressured into emulating the scenes in pornography. In this context, the wife is pressured, seduced, and/or forced into the role of prostitute while her husband adopts the role of the "john." Contests promoted by pornographers, like Hustler's "Beaver Hunt" and pornographic computer bulletin boards like High Society's "Sex-Tex," have resulted in a proliferation of homemade pornography. In this situation the wife is compelled to assume the role of "porn queen" when her husband adopts the role of the pornographer. The growth of "swingers' magazines" and "wife-swapping clubs" have allowed men to assume simultaneously the role of john and pimp, paying for the use of another man's partner by making his wife available in exchange. The last barrier separating the roles of wife and prostitute is smashed when men engineer sexual encounters which include their wives.

Since, at the same time, contemporary analyses of pimping practices frequently discern parallels between those arrangements and those characteristic of the traditional family, it becomes increasingly difficult to discern who is mimicking whom.[44]

Nor is the charge of prostitution limited to errant wives. While again little accounted for theoretically, it is by now a sad therapeutic commonplace that female victims of incest tend to identify as "prostitutes" as adult women, and to feel irrevocably separated from other, "normal" women.[45] In her comprehensive study of father-daughter incest, Judith Herman details the quality of that self-perceived difference: "Many women felt that what set them apart from others was their own evilness. With depressing regularity, these women referred to themselves as bitches, witches and whores."[46] Child sexual abuse researchers David Finkelhor and Angela Browne's analysis of the "traumatic sexualization" consequent to childhood sexual abuse suggests a social dynamic underlying this self-identification. "Traumatic sexualization . . . occurs through the exchange of affection, attention, privileges, and gifts for sexual behavior, so that a child learns sexual behavior as a strategy for manipulating [sic] others to get his or her other developmentally appropriate needs met."[47] Abusers may directly label their victims as "sluts" to enforce the girls' silence, to explain their compliance, and to reinforce their sense of complicity.[48] Those who learn of the abuse may make similar predictions,

---

Giobbe, *supra* note 3, at 67, 76-77. Giobbe explains that "Sex-Tex" is a computer service of HIGH SOCIETY magazine which "provides an unregulated market through which pornographic material can be distributed." *Id.* at 77. "Beaver Hunt" is a regular feature in HUSTLER magazine which elicits and publishes full genitalia photographs of women purported to be a reader's girlfriend or wife. Giobbe further quotes a survivor of prostitution describing such experiences in detail:

> A lot of men enjoyed bringing me in as third party with their wives. Usually what would end up happening is we'd watch some pornographic film, say, and then he'd say, "All right, I want you to do that to my wife." Now, in these instances, I felt the wife was the victim, and I was there to hurt the wife. I felt there was a real power play there, where the man was obviously saying to the wife, "If you don't do this, I'm going to leave you." I mean there were great overtones of manipulation and coercion.

Id. at 77.

44. The most thorough of these analyses is Kim Romanesko & Eleanor Miller, *The Second Step in Double Jeopardy: Appropriating the Labor of Female Street Hustlers*, 35 CRIME & DELINQUENCY 109 (1989). *See also* Hanna Olsen, *The Women, The Love, and The Power, in* INTERNATIONAL FEMINISM, *supra* note 33, at 73 (analyzing the parallels between the power dynamics of "seasoning" a woman for prostitution and those common to ordinary romantic seduction).

45. JUDITH HERMAN, FATHER-DAUGHTER INCEST 96-98 (1981); DIANA RUSSELL, THE SECRET TRAUMA: INCEST IN THE LIVES OF GIRLS AND WOMEN 167-170 (1986). David Finkelhor and Angela Browne's conceptual model of the distinctive trauma of childhood sexual abuse, entailing simultaneous infliction of traumatic sexualization, stigmatization, betrayal, and enforcement of the child's belief in her own powerlessness, has been influential in providing a framework for understanding these symptoms. *See* David Finkelhor & Angela Browne, *Initial and Long-Term Effects: A Conceptual Framework, in* A SOURCEBOOK ON CHILD SEXUAL ABUSE 180 (David Finkelhor ed., 1986). *See also* David Finkelhor, *Early and Long-Term Effects of Child Sexual Abuse: An Update*, 21 PROF. PSYCH. RES. & PRAC. 325 (1990).

46. HERMAN, *supra* note 45, at 97. Herman quotes one survivor describing herself as "nothing but a dressed up little whore." *Id.* Some girls are prostituted by their own families. *See infra* note 128 and accompanying text.

47. Finkelhor & Browne, *supra* note 45, at 181.

48. *See* Lazarowicz v. State, 561 So.2d 392 (Fla. 3d Dist. Ct. App. 1990) (new trial ordered for

excusing the father's behavior and furnishing justification for further punishment of the girl.[49] Girls may engage in bargains with their fathers for food, clothing, or some regulation of their father's sexual access to them.[50] Certainly a girl's self-understanding as a "prostitute" converges with that of the juvenile justice system, should she become enmeshed with that institution as a consequence of engaging in non-conforming behavior. As Meda Chesney-Lind has pointed out, "delinquency" in girls is commonly concluded to orginate in "sexual deviance," seamlessly assimilated to a diagnosis of prostitution or prostitution-prone behavior.[51]

Similar patterns are discernible in less intimate relationships such as sexual harassment and rape. In substance, as Catharine A. MacKinnon points out, "a great many instances of sexual harassment in essence amount to solicitation for prostitution."[52] Some years later the Eighth Circuit Court of Appeal made

defendant convicted of sexual battery of his seventeen-year-old daughter. In court, the daughter testified that her father forced her to engage in sexual intercourse and fellatio with him in 1985. When he began to suspect that she was having sexual relations with her boyfriend, he "punched me, knocked my head into the wall, threw me around the room, took me into the bedroom and laid me on the bed and punched me in the face, kicked me, and gave me a black eye, put bruises over other eye,"called her a "slut" and a "whore," and every time he walked by her he would punch her in the face); Commonwealth v. LaSota, 557 N.E.2d 34 (Mass. App. Ct. 1990) (defendant denied allegations by his sixteen-year-old daughter that he had sexually abused her continuously since she was in kindergarten, and claimed that when he discovered pornographic photographs of her in her closet, he slapped her and called her a "slut"); State v. Moore, 690 S.W.2d 453 (Mo. Ct. App. 1985) (defendant acquitted on incest charge but convicted of rape of his daughter, when she was thirteen and fourteen years old. Victim testified that defendant warned her not to tell anyone, or she would be called a "slut"); In re B.B., Juvenile, 584 A.2d 1126 (Vt. 1990) (twelve-year-old child, who was sent to live with her aunt because of escalated family tension, and who subsequently refused to return home, told SRS caseworker that her father "had mentally and physically abused her . . . [h]e's called her a slut, he's called her a lazy fucking bitch . . . he's kicked her"); Janke v. State, 692 P.2d 911 (Wy. 1984) (where defendant was convicted of aiding and abetting voluntary manslaughter of her abusive father, the record clearly showed history of abuse and humiliation by father including sexual assaults, severe beatings twice a week beginning at age four, and calling her a slut); Reed, supra note 14 (after being raped by her stepfather, at age nine, "He ordered me to take a shower and keep my mouth shut. Laughing, he said no one would believe a whore anyway.").

49. Herman reports that among the punitive responses of mothers to daughters' reports of abuse by fathers is sending their daughters away from home. One woman reported: "[My mother] was afraid I would become a lesbian or a whore. So she put me in a mental hospital. It was a good excuse to get rid of me." HERMAN, supra note 45, at 90. A woman who was the victim of attempted rape by her stepsister's husband was told that her stepmother "predicted she would be a prostitute." Her stepmother believed that the attempted rape was instead evidence of an "affair" between them. NICARTHY, supra note 39, at 267. See also id. at 75 ("My mother would keep track of my periods in a notebook . . . [E]ach time I went forty days or so she would think I was pregnant and would say things like 'you slut, who did you sleep with?'").

50. See, e.g., LOUISE ARMSTRONG, KISS DADDY GOODNIGHT 74, 75 (1978) (father agreed that he wouldn't touch her anymore, providing she went along with any decisions he made whenever she asked for anything; daughter could stay out until 8:30 at the Homecoming Parade if she had sex with father); KATHLEEN BRADY, FATHER'S DAYS 87 (1979) (among many examples of "bargaining" between father and daughter, Brady reports that when she wanted to get a job at age 16, her father agreed to sign her application form, but only if she would "be nicer" to him, threatening to make her quit if she didn't "keep her end").

51. See Meda Chesney-Lind, Girl's Crime and Women's Place: Toward a Feminist Model of Female Delinquency, 35 CRIME & DELINQ. 5 (1989); Meda Chesney-Lind, Judicial Enforcement of the Female Sex Role: The Family Court and the Female Delinquent, 8 ISSUES IN CRIMINOLOGY 51 (1973); Meda Chesney-Lind, Rediscovering Lilith: Misogyny and the "New" Female Criminal, in THE FEMALE OFFENDER 117-21 (Curt Griffiths & Margit Nance eds., 1980).

52. CATHARINE A. MACKINNON, SEXUAL HARASSMENT OF WORKING WOMEN: A CASE OF SEX DISCRIMINATION 159 (1979); see also Dierdre Silverman, Sexual Harassment: Working Women's Dilemma, 3 QUEST 15, 15-17 (no. 3, 1976/77) (links sexual harassment with prostitution, based on her "contention

the same connection, observing that "[a] woman invited to trade herself for a job is in effect being asked to become a prostitute."[53] In hostile work environment claims, the presumption of a working woman's ardent sexual availability to her co-workers, inferred either from her presence in the "wrong" workplace (that is, in male dominated trades and professions, where she can make a living wage), or from the assumption that sexual availability *is* her work (that is, in female dominated jobs, where she cannot), echoes throughout the reported cases.[54] The same presumption of a woman's exploitative "sluttish" sexual enticement of a rapist, summed up neatly by one defendant's view that "all women were whores and sluts and they all deserved what [the victim] was getting,"[55] persists *ad nauseum*.[56] In discussing this

---

that the paradigm for interaction between men and women in our society is that of the prostitute and her customer." *Id.* at 15); LYNN FARLEY, SEXUAL SHAKEDOWN (1978) (detailing social consequence of sexual harassment as prostitution in nineteenth and early twentieth century America); Mary Bularzik, *Sexual Harassment at the Workplace: Historical Notes*, 12 RADICAL AM. 25 (1978) (common condition of working women in nineteenth century America included both prostitution and sexual harassment).

53. Lucas v. Brown & Root, Inc., 736 F.2d 1202 (8th Cir. 1984) (sexual harassment violates public policy against prostitution, abrogating the "at will" employment doctrine as a defense to the discharge of a women who refused sex with her foreman); *see also* Kim Vance, *Wrongful Discharge—Sexual Harassment Equated With Prostitution to Find Public Policy Exception*, 8 U. ARK. LITTLE ROCK L.J. 49 (1985/86).

54. *See, e.g.*, Waltman v. International Paper Co., 875 F. 2d 468 (5th Cir. 1989) (pornographic graffiti on walls; "Sue is a whore" written on elevators; one employee told plaintiff he would cut her breast off and shove it down her throat, then suspended her over a stairwell more than thirty feet from the floor); Hansel v. Public Service Co. of Colorado, 778 F. Supp. 1126 (D. Colo. 1991) (harrassment included graffiti like "VH sucks all cocks," rape, co-worker facing her with a hangman's noose and suggesting she commit suicide; court believed conduct designed to drive her out to preserve an all-male plant); Jew v. Univ. of Iowa, 749 F. Supp. 946 (S.D. Iowa 1990) (woman professor called "slut" and "whore" by another faculty member in front of students; another faculty member referred to her as a "chink"; on-going rumors that she "slept her way to the top"); Zabkowicz v. West Bend Co., 589 F. Supp. 780 (E.D. Wisc. 1984) (woman warehouse worker called, among other names, "slut"; pornographic pictures posted with her initials written on them); Travi-Care Corp. v. Hospital and Institutional Worker's Union, 211 Cal. Rptr. 550 (Cal. Ct. App. 1985) (union appealed provision of preliminary injunction prohibiting picketers from intimidating other workers and visitors into staying away from the hospital; picketers shouted terms such as "bitch," "cocksucker," "cunt," "whore" at female employees attempting to enter the hospital, and yelled obscene accusations at one female employee, including allusions to sexual acts between the employee and her daughter, her supervisor, and the security guards); Continental Can Co. v. State, 297 N.W.2d 241 (Minn. 1980) (court found employer had failed to take action in response to complainant's allegations of sexual harassment including repeated verbal sexual advances and sexually derogatory remarks made to complainant by male co-workers, a male co-worker's comment that he wished slavery days would return so that he could sexually train her and she would be his bitch; two male co-workers informing her that women who worked at factories were tramps); United States Fire Insurance Co. v. St. Paul Fire and Marine Insurance Co., 511 N.E.2d 127 (Ohio App. 1986) (two female plaintiffs in sexual harassment suit alleged damage to their reputations by manger's false and defamatory remarks, including such statements that one plaintiff was "a whore and a slut," the other a "fucking jew broad"); Hussa v. Employment Security Dept., 664 P.2d 1286 (Wash. Ct. App. 1983) (claimant filed suit against employer after being subjected to sexual harassment by male co-workers, such as male employee patting her buttocks and grabbing another women's breast; being addressed as "bitch" by a co-worker who told her he felt women should not be employed as millwrights; and male co-workers routinely referring to female workers as "slut," "bitch," and "cunt").

This account has recently been inverted by two sociological investigators, who have "discovered" new types of *prostitution* in office environments in behavior readily identifable as sexual harassment. *See* Craig J. Forsyth & Lee Fournet, *A Typology of Office Harlots: Mistresses, Party Girls and Career Climbers*, 8 DEVIANT BEH. 319 (1987).

55. Fuget v. State, 522 A.2d 1371 (Md. App. 1987) (victim testified that after she and defendant drove to wooded area, defendant struck her jaw with his fist and said that if she refused to perform fellatio on him, he would kill her; after informing her of his opinion, quoted above, he raped and sodomized her).

56. Diana Scully reports that, among her sample of 114 convicted rapists, 69% of those who denied

---

paper with women around the country, I have been told repeatedly that rapists threw $20, or $50, at them after the attack, conduct which at the time confused them. Is the ploy now, like the old rape consent rule, that a woman can be made a whore "before or after the act"?

Given the enormous prevalence rates of each of these forms of sexual violence, it may be the rare woman who has not encountered a charge of prostitution or heard a justification for abusive behavior couched in related terms. As an ascriptive matter, the terms "prostitute" and "prostitution" seem to expand boundlessly, applied whenever we are punished for sexual behavior, fantasized or real, or for simply occupying the body of a woman, for which the punishment takes the form of sexualized terrorism. At least where a victim is designated "not a prostitute," the problem of prostitution seems to abide in the falsity of the man's belief about her, and in the over-pervasiveness generally of the "whore" stigma: a "specifically female gender stigma which can be defined as a mark of shame or disease on an unchaste woman."[57] As a prescriptive matter, on this view of the problem feminists might thus see fit to devote some cultural attention to educational campaigns deepening men's sensitivities to the distinction, as in: "This is a prostitute. This is *not*." Legal reform campaigns might be committed to the same ends. Aggressive strategies against overinclusion could be pursued, perhaps with the aid of identifying tattoos.

I *am* being facetious. Yet much feminist legal reform work against sexual violence has explicitly or implicitly advanced similar strategies of lawyerly separation, distinguishing with great delicacy and equal urgency between

---

having committed a "real" rape justified their behavior "by claiming that the victim was known to be a prostitute, or a 'loose' woman, or to have had a lot of affairs, or to have had a child out of wedlock." DIANA SCULLY, UNDERSTANDING SEXUAL VIOLENCE: A STUDY OF CONVICTED RAPISTS 108 (1990). *See also* Justice v. State, 1986 WL 1505 (Ark. App.) (defendant convicted of raping an eight-year-old girl claimed she tried to seduce him on many occasions, characterizing her as a "wanton libertine"; prosecuting attorney responded by stating in closing argument that defendant was trying to "make out the victim . . . to be a slut"); State v. Girardier, 801 S.W.2d 793 (Mo. Ct. App. 1991) (after victim testified at preliminary hearing that defendant stole cash and jewelry from her apartment, defendant followed her outside the courtroom calling her a "slut" and a "fat whore"); State v. Koonce, 731 S.W.2d 431 (Mo. Ct. App. 1987) (rape victim testified that the defendant, a college classmate, drove her to his mother's house, where he vaginally raped her several times, then attempted fellatio and anal intercourse while calling her a "slut and a tramp"); State v. Macon, 173 S.E.2d 286 (N.C. 1970) (defendant convicted of second-degree murder in the shooting death of a woman with whom he had engaged in an extramarital affair; defendant told police investigator that he did not see why he had to suffer for her death because she was a slut and led him on and that she was not worth a tinker's damn"); State v. Wright, 470 N.W.2d 594 (N.D. 1991) (complainant testified that Wright, an acquaintance, grabbed, shook, and threw [her] to the floor . . . pounced on top of her, grabbed her by the throat/neck, hit her with his fists, and "banged" her forehead on the floor. While on top of her, he "socked" her in the face and said: "You women are all bitches and sluts and you all deserve what's comin' to you. And you all deserve to be raped."); State v. Clary, 1991 WL 54187, (Ohio App.) (victim testified that she was introduced by her boyfriend to defendant, who later became upset when he saw her dancing with a stranger, calling her a "slut," then later raping her and demanding fellatio while holding a knife at ther throat, threatening to kill her); Bunch v. Commonwealth, 304 S.E.2d (Va. 1983) (defendant convicted of murder made statement to police investigator that he killed the victim because "she was a slut and she reminded him too much of his wife and wanted her money").

57. Gail Pheterson, *The Social Consequences of Unchastity, in* SEX WORK: WRITINGS BY WOMEN IN THE SEX INDUSTRY 215 (Frederique Delacoste & Priscilla Alexander eds., 1987).

"prostitutes" and "other women." The political rescue of "real womanhood" from conditions of prostitution, within the spheres of life believed occupied by "normal women," has been the mainstream feminist tactic advanced within many of our campaigns. These reform strategies have sought to displace these false beliefs by persuasion to counter-representations of our own devising, for example, "sexual harassment," "pornography victims," and "battered women."[58] Each of these counter-stories constitutes an appeal to "more speech," the valid representation driving out the false. Each also promotes a predictable theme about prostitution: emphatically, that we are *not* prostitutes. A mistake has been made—a grievous failure to contour the proper distinctions between the prostitution with which we are charged and our own conduct, and a consequent failure to treat us with justice. This analysis initially notes the analogic relationship conventionally drawn between a woman's behavior and prostitution, usually to punish her, and proceeds, as a predicate for reform proposals, to criticize the appropriateness of the comparison.

The success of these distancing strategies relies in the first instance on a threshold agreement among all concerned that we know who a prostitute *is*, "truly," permitting a tidy boundary to be drawn between ourselves and those others, with some hope of agreement on the distinction. In this pursuit, we have been uncharacteristically assisted by the contributions of existing law, which has rendered a conveniently unambiguous definition of the type. Among statutory definitions, the New York law is typical, defining a woman as culpable of prostitution if she "engages or agrees or offers to engage in sexual conduct with another person in return for a fee."[59] A comforting assurance of definitional fixity accompanies this legal catalogue; constitutional vagueness challenges have proven overwhelmingly unsuccessful in challenging the legal validity of solicitation and prostitution laws.[60] A "prostitute," as "everyone"

---

58. Thus, "[a] major contribution of feminist social action around sexual violence has been to provide and create new words with which to describe and name our experience. For example, the terms *battered woman* and *sexual harassment* did not exist 20 years ago." Liz Kelly, *How Women Define Their Experience of Violence, in* FEMINIST PERSPECTIVES ON WIFE ABUSE 115 (Kersti Yllo & Michelle Bograd eds., 1988). For the originating feminist treatment of sexual harassment, see MACKINNON, *supra* note 52. As MacKinnon points out, prior to feminist intervention, "[s]exual harassment was a nonissue, even a nonexperience. . . ." MACKINNON, TOWARD A FEMINIST THEORY OF THE STATE, *supra* note 8, at 112. On the victimization of women by pornography, see *Ordinance to Add Pornography as Discrimination Against Women: Hearings Before the Gov't Operations Committee of the Minneapolis City Council*, 2d Session (1983); LINDA LOVELACE (with Mike McGrady), ORDEAL (1975); TAKE BACK THE NIGHT: WOMEN ON PORNOGRAPHY (Laura Lederer ed., 1980); Catharine A. MacKinnon, *Pornography, Civil Rights, and Speech*, 20 HARV. C.R. — C.L.L.REV. 1 (1985); Dworkin, *supra* note 25. On the battered women's movement, see *infra* notes 74-93 and accompanying text.

59. N.Y. PEN. LAW § 230.00 (McKinney's 1991); *See also* TEX. PENAL CODE ANN. §43.02(a)(1) (West 1984) (same language); N.M. STAT. ANN. §30-9-2 (Michie 1989) ("engaging in or offering to engage in a sexual act for hire"); N.H. REV. STAT. ANN. §645:2(I)(a) (1985) ("solicits or engages in sexual penetration . . . in return for consideration"); NEB. REV. STAT. §28-801(1) (1989) ("performs, offers or agrees to perform any act of sexual penetration . . . in exchange for money or other thing of value").

60. Modern opinions rejecting vagueness challenges include Morgan v. City of Detroit, 389 F. Supp. 922, 929 (E.D. Mass. 1975) (The terms "prostitution" and "fornication" are "on their face precise and give fair notice of what conduct is forbidden"); City of Seattle v. James, 488 P. 2d 750 (1970) (facial language of statute clear and unambiguous); Commonwealth v. King, 372 N.E. 2d 196 (Mass. 1977)

knows, is a woman who has sex with many men, who are strangers to her, who pay her for it (or who promise to pay, and if not her, someone). Lingering confusions, especially regarding form of payment, have been dispelled by legally explicit or implied marital exemptions to the scope of anti-prostitution laws.[61] Feminist legal reformers have concurred, enthusiastically if implicitly, in these definitional judgments. Each of our counter-representations, our "true" stories, seeks to disidentify any particular sexual violence victim from the status of "prostitute" by distinguishing her behavior from at least one of the legal elements of prostitution.

In rape law reform, for example, feminist lawyers have long labored to establish a victim's "discriminateness," both in articulating the injury rape entails and in the representation of the victim at trial. Our most significant work focuses on the habilitation of a woman's "no" as probative of her lack of consent. This commitment in turn locates the injury of rape in the disregard of a woman's sexual selectiveness.[62] The enforcement of rape shield evidentiary rules and the articulation of women's injury through testimony of rape trauma syndrome continue this theme. Rape shield rules limit the admissibility of a woman's prior sexual history for the purpose of proving consent, at least when the defendant has not had sex with her before.[63] This

---

("[C]onduct known as prostitution has existed since time immemorial, . . . traditionally [including] both performance of sexual acts as a business and public soliciation for such business."); McCarty v. State, 616 S.W. 2d 194 (Tex. Crim. App. 1981); U.S. v. Herrera, 584 F. 2d 1137 (2d Cir. 1978); People v. Costello, 395 N.Y.S. 2d 139 (1977); People v. Block, 337 N.Y.S. 2d 153 (1972); State v. Parker, 690 P. 2d 1353 (Kan. 1984); People v. Mason, 642 P. 2d 8 (Colo. 1982); Profit v. City of Tulsa, 574 P. 2d 1073 (Okla. 1973); Glenn v. State, 749 P. 2d 121 (Okla. Crim. App. 1988); Eissa v. U.S., 485 A. 2d 610 (App. D.C. 1984); State v. Forrest, 439 So. 2d 404 (La. 1983); People v. Johnson, 376 N.E. 2d 381 (Ill. App. 1978); Commonwealth v. Potts, 460 A. 2d 1127, 1134 (Pa. Super. 1983) ("It cannot be gainsaid that 'prostitution' has persisted since biblical times, and, as such, has acquired a traditional meaning."); State v. Olson, 297 N.W. 2d 297 (Minn. 1980) ("'[P]rostitution'" is a word with a commonly understood objective meaning about which intelligent people do not differ.). An uncommon exception is State v. Lopez, 570 P. 2d 259, 267 (Idaho 1977) (upholding vagueness challenge to state prostitution law).

In a related vein, my research has disclosed not one reported case in which a woman's conviction for a prostitution-related offense was vacated on a challenge based on a claim of insufficient evidence. See, e.g., King, supra (upholding conviction against sufficiency challenge). An exception, in dissent, is Justice Shirley Abramson's opinion in City of Milwaukee v. Wilson, 96 Wis. 2d 11 (1980), in which she questions the sufficiency of the evidence to support a woman's conviction for solicitation where the arresting officers "were not able to testify that it was the defendant who 'repeatedly beckoned' the men, rather than vice versa."

61. See, e.g., MICH. STAT. ANN §750.449(a) (Callaghan 1930) ("Any male person who engages or offers to engage the services of a female person, not his wife, for the purposes of prostitution, lewdness, or assignation, by the payment in money or other forms of consideration, is guilty of a misdemeanor.") (emphasis added); ILL. ANN. STAT. CH. 38, PARA 11-18 (Smith-Hood 1990); NEB. REV. STAT. § 28-801 (1977); see also Cherry v. Koch, 491 N.Y.S. 2d 934 (1985); Profit v. City of Tulsa, 574 P. 2d 1053 (Okla. 1978); Tisdale v. State, 640 S.W. 2d 409 (Tex. App. 1982). If you can't buy your wife, who can you buy?

62. See, e.g., SUSAN ESTRICH, REAL RAPE 102 (1987) ("'Consent' should be defined so that no means no."); Kristin Bumiller, Rape as a Legal Symbol: An Essay on Sexual Violence and Racism, 42 U. OF MIAMI L. REV. 75, 76-77 (1987) (emphasis in feminist rape reform is on taking a woman "for her word"). See generally Carolyn Shafer & Marilyn Frye, Rape and Respect, in WOMEN AND VALUES: READINGS IN RECENT FEMINIST PHILOSPHY 188, 190-94 (M. Pearsall ed., 1986)(regard for "personhood" fundamental to sexual integrity); Frances Olsen, Statutory Rape: A Feminist Critique of Rights Analysis, 63 TEX. L. REV. 387 (1984) (women's autonomy fundamental value to be promoted by regulation of sexual conduct).

63. For a fine discussion of the rationale and statutory variations among state and federal rape shield rules, see Harriet Galvin, Shielding Rape Victims in the State and Federal Courts: A Proposal for the

representational spin control seeks to sever in a jury's mind the inferential connection it might otherwise draw between a woman's sexual "promiscuity" and her conduct on a particular occasion.[64] Less politely, these rules of exclusion are designed to defeat the whore status her prior activity would ascribe to her.[65] The admissibility of evidence of rape trauma syndrome, cataloging the physical, psychological, and behavioral symptoms commonly consequent to sexual assault,[66] has also been advocated by feminist reformers both to corroborate a woman's testimony that she did not consent to the act, and to dispel juror misunderstanding that women "ask for it," by rendering plain the profound, complex, and enduring suffering that unwanted sex causes.[67]

Prostitutes, of course, say "yes" a great deal. Our threshold commitment to the dismissal of woman's "no" as the talismanic violation of rape both renders prostitution beyond the pale of our rape reforms and, praise be, prostitutes as the women we are not.[68] The courts have also apparently aptly understood the intended limits of these reforms, consistently holding that the fictionalizing protections of rape shield rules should give way to the "plain

---

Second Decade, 70 MINN. L. REV. 763 (1983).

64. *Id.* See *also* sources cited *infra* note 63.

65. The point is put bluntly in the Florida case law predating the enactment of the Florida shield statute. In that jurisdiction, evidence of prior sexual history was admissible to prove "promiscuous intercourse with men, or common prostitution." Rice v. State, 17 So. 286, 287 (Fla. 1895); *See also* Huffman v. State, 301 So. 2d 815, 816 (Fla. Dist. Ct. App. 1974). Insofar as the Florida shield rule now deems admissible testimony of specific instances of prior sexual conduct when probative of a pattern of behavior by the victim, see FLA. STAT. ANN. § 794.022(2) (West 1990), at least one commentator has argued that the reform provision is in fact regressive, permitting at least in theory any woman to be proven in effect "a common prostitute." *See* Note, *Florida's Sexual Battery Statute: Significant Reform But Bias Against the Victim Still Prevails*, 30 U. FLA. L. REV. 419, 438 (1978). *See also* Leigh Bienen, *Rape III: National Developments in Rape Reform Legislation*, 6 WOMEN'S. RTS. L. REP. 170, 202 (1980) (commenting on this critique).

66. The term, and the symptomology it substantiates, was first developed by Ann Burgess and Lynda Holstrom in 1974, based on their study of 146 women who entered the emergency room of Boston City Hospital alleging they had been raped. *See* Ann Burgess & Lynda Holstrom, *Rape Trauma Syndrome*, 131 AM. J. PSYCHIATRY 981 (1974); *see also* Ann Burgess & Lynda Holstrom, *Assessing Trauma in the Rape Victim*, in THE RAPE VICTIM 112 (D. Nass ed., 1977).

67. On the rationales for admissibility, see Patricia Frazier & Eugene Borgida, *Juror Common Understanding and the Admissibility of Rape Trauma Syndrome Evidence in Court*, 12 LAW & HUM. BEHAV. 101 (1988); Toni M. Massaro, *Experts, Psychology, Credibility and Rape: The Rape Trauma Syndrome Issue and Its Implications for Expert Psychological Testimony*, 69 MINN. L. REV. 395 (1985). On the effects of rape on women victims, see Burgess & Holstrom, *supra* note 66; C. Nadelson, et al., *A Follow-up Study of Rape Victims*, 139 AM. J. PSYCHIATRY 1266 (1982); J. Norns & S. Feldman-Summers, *Factors Related to the Psychological Impact of Rape on the Victim*, 90 J. ABNORMAL PSYCH. 562 (1981); L. Ruch & S. Chandler, *The Crisis Impact of Sexual Assault on Three Victim Groups: Adult Rape Victims, Child Rape Victims, and Incest Victims*, 5 J. SOC. SERVICES RES. 83 (1982); L. Ruch & S. Chandler, *Sexual Assault Trauma During the Acute Phase: An Exploratory Model and Multivariate Analysis*, 24 J. HEALTH & SOC. BEHAV. 174 (1983). On the impact of attempted rape, see Kim Scheppele & Pauline Bart, *Through Women's Eyes: Defining Danger in the Wake of Sexual Assault*, 39 J. SOC. ISSUES 63 (1983).

68. In the theoretical literature, this distinction in the intended beneficiaries of feminist rape law reform is most starkly put in Martha Chamallas' article on the transformation of sexual norms animating reform of legal regulation of sexual behavior. She raises prostitution as a problem of sexual imposition only to dismiss it as an inappropriate subject matter for her theory. *See* Martha Chamallas, *Consent, Equality, and the Legal Control of Sexual Conduct*, 61 S. CAL. L. REV. 777, 826-30 (1988).

truth" when the defendant can prove that the victim "really was" a prostitute or that financial arrangements were involved in the contested act.[69] This conclusion is echoed in the avoidance of the question of whether prostitutes might likely endure some form, perhaps extreme, of rape trauma syndrome.[70] It may seem to some the better part of discretion not to cheapen the significance of a woman's "no" by the potentially embarrassing display of women engaging in otherwise nonconsensual sex for twenty dollars, accepting what amounts to a pittance in liquidated damages for rape, while "other women" assert the deep and lasting trauma that difference twenty dollars makes. Our strategy of differentiating prostitutes from ourselves, begun by categorically distinguishing between "yes or no" sex, here seems elevated to an ontological divide between nice women who are hurt and not so nice women presumptively calloused or insensible to selling themselves for the equivalent of a parking fine.

Nor have we questioned deeply the exclusion of "non-stranger" assailants from the reach of the shield rules,[71] even as we urge the prosecution of "voluntary social companions," husband-rapists, and incestuous fathers for sexual assault. An exception in the theoretical literature is Steven Katz's advocacy for the expansion of shield rules to non-stranger cases.[72] Katz locates the academic hesitation to challenge the existing limitation in a vestigial intuition that prior sexual acts with the defendant are probative of a general willingness on the victim's part to engage in similar acts again, in particular on the contested occasion.[73] The more compelling explanation for this acquiescence, because it is more closely linked with the perspectives of feminist activists (who, after all, identified the *injuries* of marital and date rape in the first place) lies in the proximity, both experientially and conceptually,

---

69. *See, e.g.*, People v. Varona, 143 Cal. App. 2d 566 (1983) (abuse of discretion to exclude evidence that the complaining witness was a prostitute); People v. Randle, 130 Cal. App. 3d 286 (1982) (exclusion of evidence that complaining witness had solicited public sex for money, drugs and alcohol reversible error even though there was evidence of physical injury to the woman). *Cf.*, Commonwealth v. Joyce, 415 N.E. 2d 181, 187 (Mass. 1981); People v. Williams, 330 N.W. 2d 823 (Mich. 1982)(evidence of reputation for prostitution inadmissible, where there were no financial arrangements involved in the instance); People v. Slovinski, 420 N.W. 2d 145 (Mich. Ct. App. 1988); State v. Gardner, 391 N.E. 2d 337, 340-41 (Ohio Sup. Ct. 1979) (same).

70. None of the empirical literature cited at notes 67-68, *supra*, discusses the impact of prostitution on women involved in the practice.

71. As of 1989, 46 states and the federal courts deem evidence of a woman's sexual history with the defendant admissible on a "minimal showing" that its probativeness outweighs its prejudicial effect. Steven Katz, *Desire and Expectation in the Law of Forcible Rape*, 26 SAN DIEGO L. REV. 21, 38 (1989).

72. *See* Katz, *supra* note 71, at 37-43.

73. Vivian Berger, *Man's Trial, Woman's Tribulation: Rape Cases in the Courtroom*, 77 COLUM. L. REV., 58-59 (1977) (distinguishing use of prior sexual history to hypothesize the "kind of woman" the victim is, from its use in non-stranger cases to comprehend an actual relationship); Katz, *supra* note 71, citing Galvin, *supra* note 63, at 624 (endorsing non-stranger exception); Leon Lefwin, *Unchaste Character, Ideology, and the California Rape Evidence Laws*, 54 S. CAL. L. REV. 35, 72 (1980) (history of sexual relationship bears heavily on victim's probable conduct and her motives for accusing the defendant on this occasion); Kenneth Ordover, *Admissibility of Patterns of Similar Sexual Conduct: The Unlamented Death of Character for Chastity*, 63 CORNELL L. REV. 90, 113 (1977) (admissibility justified as probative of a pattern of conduct).

of non-stranger sexual assault to the paradigm of domestic battery. As a tactical matter, argument for the expansion of the shield rules to exclude evidence of the sexual history of a relationship between victim and assailant runs head on into the principal strategy feminists have elaborated in behalf of battered women: the representation of battered women via battered women's syndrome testimony. Rather than placing restrictions in the factual context available to juries, we have in that domain sought the *expansion* of the representational frame to include the emotional history of the relationship, the psychological consequences of serial battery to victims, and the default in social recognition, support, and material alternatives women battered by cohabitant men commonly confront.[74] The contrast in the scope of these explanations, with the freeze-frame, miniaturist portrait of the rape victim constructed under the shield rules, could not be more acute.

This strategic distinction in representational preference perhaps can be explained by the difference in the questions courts and juries typically have in mind for stranger rape victims and domestic battery victims. The question addressed to the stranger rape victim is some version of the "why were you *there*?" question (dressed as you were/drinking as you were/knowing what you did). The question the battery victim confronts is some version of the "why did you *stay*?" question (if you are telling the truth/if you didn't get something out of it). The presumption against the stranger rape victim is that she assumed the risk, against the domestic battery victim that she failed to exhaust her self-help remedies through separation or divorce. In the latter case, if the persistence of the relationship is the problem perceived by the law and by juries, we will explain it. The inference to be overcome is that she remained for her own motives, including a taste for pain or luxury, or that she was properly disciplined for real lapses in wifely devotion or fidelity.[75]

Feminist explanations of "why she stayed" have been of two orders. The first describes women's *responses* to battery, detailing a woman's

---

74. The classic and fundamental accounts of the dynamics of domestic battery are Lenore Walker's. *See* WALKER, *supra* note 38; LENORE E. WALKER, TERRIFYING LOVE: WHY BATTERED WOMEN KILL AND HOW SOCIETY RESPONDS (1990). Her work has been criticized, especially for some of its implications in legal practice, by women as devoted as she to feminist change. *See, e.g.*, Martha R. Mahoney, *Legal Images of Battered Women: Redefining the Issue of Separation*, 90 MICH. L. REV. 1 (1991); Elizabeth M. Schneider, *Describing and Changing: Women's Self-Defense Work and the Problem of Expert Testimony on Battering*, 9 WOMEN'S RTS. L. REP. 195 (1986); Phyllis L. Crocker, *The Meaning of Equality for Battered Women Who Kill Men in Self-Defense*, 8 HARV. WOMEN'S L.J. 121 (1985). Although each of these critiques, in my view, is trenchant and wise, it is hard to imagine *any* of this discussion without the contribution of Walker's important work.

75. As Julie Blackman states the "masochism" rendition, "[i]f she stays, she must like it. She must do something to provoke it." JULIE BLACKMAN, INTIMATE VIOLENCE 42 (1989); *see also* State v. Anaya, 438 A. 2d 892, 894 (Me. 1981)(injuries argued to be part of a "love game" between husband and wife); People v. Powell, 83 A.D. 2d 719, 720 (N.Y. App. Div. 1981)(woman characterized as willing partner in abuse). A husband's right of conjugal discipline for a wife's "infractions" is deeply embedded in the law of battery. *See* Elizabeth M. Schneider, *Equal Rights to Trial for Women: Sex Bias in the Law of Self-Defense*, 15 HARV. C.R.-C.L. L. REV. 623, 627-29 (1980). As entrenched is the belief that "good wives" adapt their behavior to suit their husbands' will, is the fact of his desire to "discipline" her *res ipsa* on the question of her spousal default. *See* WALKER, *supra* note 38, at 20.

"socialization" *by* the relationship to hope for the man's eventual change, within a downward spiral of collapsing self-esteem extinguishing her feeling that she is entitled to better treatment. This emphasis stresses the complexities of love, intimacy, and commitment to a man over time as the crucial explanatory lens for comprehending women's decisions to remain in abusive relationships. Thus, Lenore Walker's "cycle of violence" theory revolves around a woman's restored hope for the future of the relationship, founded in the man's "loving contrition" in the aftermath of a violent attack.[76] She stays as her love for him, and her sense of effectiveness *in* the relationship, is shored up by his protestations of love for her and his promises for reform. Christine Littleton expands Walker's psychological explanation to one founded on broader normative commitments commonly held by women favoring the maintenance of ongoing relationships, independent of the measures of pain *or* pleasure the relationship yields. Women battered by men may "stay," on Littleton's account, regardless of whether any promised changes are likely to ensue, "because they are trying to rescue something beyond themselves"—the relationship itself.[77] In origin, these values are asserted by numerous social science researchers to emerge in consequence of women's sex role socialization, orienting women toward a value system endorsing that "their expected role is to be the wife and mother and that keeping the family together is their responsibility and obligation,"[78] the passing of love and its spectacularized publicity in divorce the most bitter of diminishments.[79]

On each of these accounts, the woman's "problem," if she has one, abides in an overcommitment to monogamous fidelity, even at the risk of her own life.

Self-defense strategies urge a similar framework for comprehending the

---

76. *See* WALKER, *supra* note 38, at 55-70 (outlining the three stages of the cycle of violence, rotating from "tension-building" to violent attack to "loving . . . contrite behavior"). *See also* Lenore E. Walker, et al., *Beyond the Juror's Ken: Battered Women*, 7 VT. L. REV. 1, 9 (1982). State appellate opinions recognizing the "cycle of violence" theory include State v. Kelly, 478 A. 2d 364, 373 (N.J. 1984); Commonwealth v. Stonehouse, 555 A. 2d 772, 783 (Pa. 1983); People v. Emick, 103 A.D. 2d 643, 654 (N.Y. App. Div. 1984); People v. Torres, 488 N.Y.S. 2d 358, 361 (Crim. Ct. 1985); People v. Aris, 215 Cal. App. 3d 1178 (1989). *See generally* Schneider, *supra* note 74, at 197 n.10 (collecting cases, as of 1985, admitting battered women's syndrome testimony in homicide prosecutions).

77. *See* Littleton, *supra* note 18, at 46.

78. Lynne Bravo Rosewater, *The Clinical and Courtroom Application of Battered Women's Personality Assessments*, *in* DOMESTIC VIOLENCE ON TRIAL: PSYCHOLOGICAL AND LEGAL DIMENSIONS OF FAMILY VIOLENCE 86, 91 (Daniel Jay Sonkin ed., 1987).

79. Phyllis Crocker summarizes this view as follows: "A battered woman who does not leave her husband, seek help, or fight back is behaving according to societal expectations: the cultural perception of marriage as a lifelong bond and commitment instructs a woman to stay and work to improve—not abandon the marriage." Crocker, *supra* note 74, at 135. *See also* MARTIN, *supra* note 38, at 81-83; WALKER, *supra* note 38, at 31, 32-34 (1979); Moore [sic], *Editor's Introduction: An Overview of the Problem*, *in* BATTERED WOMEN (D. Moore ed., 1979); Mildred Pagelow, *Sex Roles, Power and Woman Battering*, *in* WOMEN AND CRIME IN AMERICA (Lee Bowker ed., 1981); Natalie Shainess, *Psychological Aspects of Wife Battering*, *in* BATTERED WOMEN: A PSYCHOSOCIOLOGICAL STUDY OF DOMESTIC VIOLENCE (M. Roy ed., 1977); *but see* Lenore E. Walker, *The Battered Woman Syndrome Study*, *in* THE DARK SIDE OF FAMILIES 31, 33 (David Finkelhor et al. eds., 1983) (battered woman as a group indicated self-perception as "more liberal" in views of roles of women than most women).

reduction of a woman's options for survival to killing her abuser and for explaining the validity of her perception of imminent danger in circumstances which might be understood by a jury as less than immediate. Although several commentators have remarked on the apparent contradiction between the love and hope motivating a woman's decision to remain in an abusive relationship, and the despair and violence of a woman's commission of a homicide,[80] the theme of intimate proximity bridges both. Her *familiarity* with the particular man's habits and patterns of violence, it is argued, yields her a special understanding of the risks he threatens. Phyllis Crocker explains:

> Battered women in particular may perceive danger and imminence differently from men. Because they become attuned to stages of violence from their husbands, they may interpret certain conduct to indicate an imminent attack or a more severe attack. A subtle gesture or a new method of abuse, insignificant to another person, may create a reasonable fear in a battered woman.[81]

The courts, too, have been sympathetic to this account of the objective reasonableness of her behavior, perhaps because the explanation reaffirms the traditional "domestic privacy" notion of the uniqueness and complexity of long-term sexual relationships, even as it states the conclusion in "objective" terms.[82] "Intimacy" will still have its privileges, even if they sometimes must accrue to women.

This representation, like that drawn of rape victims under the rape shield laws, benefits women little in encounters with "real" johns, or toward explaining why a woman "stays" in prostitution; even if, like most women in the life, she is raped, assaulted, and threatened with murder on a regular basis.[83] The ties and insights of persistent affection are not commonly present

---

80. *See* Crocker, *supra* note 74, at 136 (by taking action to kill her abuser, the battered defendant may be seen as an exception to the group of which she is a part); Mahoney, *supra* note 74, (resolving contradiction by recasting battery as a means of controlling a woman's separation from a relationship and recharacterizing woman as attempting to take action or her own behalf in both spheres of her conduct); Schneider, *supra* note 74, at 222 (suggesting a fuller description of women's agency required to better explain "why a battered woman doesn't leave the house *and* why she kills to save her own life").

81. Crocker, *supra* note 74, at 127, citing Schneider, *Equal Rights to Trial for Women*, *supra* note 75, at 634. *See also* CYNTHIA GILLESPIE, JUSTIFIABLE HOMICIDE: BATTERED WOMEN, SELF-DEFENSE AND THE LAW 69 (1989); Schneider, *supra* note 74, at 211 ("The jury needs expert testimony . . . that the battered woman's prediction of the likely extent and imminence of violence is particularly acute and accurate.")

82. *See, e.g.*, State v. Hundley, 693 P. 2d 475, 475-76 (Kan. 1985) (degree of imminence to be evaluated from perspective of "prudent battered woman"); State v. Kelly, 478 A. 2d 364, 378 (N.J. 1984) ("the expert's testimony might also enable the jury to find that the battered wife, because of the prior beatings, numerous beatings, as often as once a week, for seven years, from the day they were married to the day he died, is particularly able to predict accurately the likely extent of violence in any attack on her"); Commonwealth v. Stonehouse, 555 A. 2d 772, 784 (Pa. 1989) (reasonableness to be determined from perspective of "reasonable battered woman").

83. *See infra* notes 117-26, 140-55, and accompanying text.

between a prostitute and a john. "Loving contrition" is not a common behavior pattern in men who buy women for sex. Nor does the prostitute enjoy the tidy legal status of an otherwise socially conforming "victim." The "good woman" sex role of loyalty to intimate monogamous fidelity, while perhaps of tactical assistance in garnering sympathy for women battered by husbands, is but a tool of punishment of women in prostitution. A prostitute who kills a john cannot argue a specialized understanding of a particular john's habits of violence, at least so long as johns are not understood as men who pose particular perils to prostituted women. Nor are these theoretical distancing strategies only of academic significance. The inapplicability, even structural hostility, of battered women defenses to women in prostitution contributed strongly to Aileen Carol Wuornos's recent first degree murder convictions for killing several johns, for which she has been sentenced to death.

This focus on women's responses to battery by an intimate partner is a relative latecomer to feminist analyses of wife beating, although now the dominant one in the legal arena. The originating critiques questioned more directly how men have come to enjoy the privilege, how male power is enacted in families, how the structure of the family reproduces that power, how law and other institutions of social control remain complicit in male torture of women in the home, and under what political conditions women continue to live with and marry men.[84] The issue for these scholars and activists was not why some women "stayed," but how any woman escaped living in a violent household but by the grace of God or, less transcendentally, by a wholesale restructuring of her social options. These critiques bring to light the institutional controls rendering women targets for violence in marriage, including the social, sexual, and economic "channelling" of women into marital dependency to the near exclusion of other viable living arrangements. The feminist shelter movement was the "first line" mobilization of these insights, founded on the understanding that new feminist institutions and strategies for women's empowerment were necessary to provide women with options other than to "stay," or to move on to other domestic arrangements where she would be vulnerable to the same treatment.[85] Shelters were envisioned as the necessary first step; the overall vision the crafting of intervention politics intended structurally "to alter the power system which

---

84. The strongest contribution to this critique remains R. EMERSON DOBASH & RUSSELL DOBASH, VIOLENCE AGAINST WIVES: A CASE AGAINST THE PATRIARCHY (1979). *See also* MARTIN, *supra* note 38; SUSAN SCHECHTER, WOMEN AND MALE VIOLENCE: THE VISIONS AND STRUGGLES OF THE BATTERED WOMEN'S MOVEMENT (1982); Wini Breines & Linda Gordon, *The New Scholarship on Family Violence*, 8 SIGNS 490 (1983). For a collection of essays reviewing the development of these critique in the social sciences, some authored by their originators, see FEMINIST PERSPECTIVES ON WIFE ABUSE, *supra* note 58.

85. For a political history of the shelter movement in the United States, see generally SCHECHTER, *supra* note 84; in Canada, see generally GILLIAN A. WALKER, FAMILY VIOLENCE AND THE WOMEN'S MOVEMENT: THE CONCEPTUAL POLITICS OF STRUGGLE (1990).

creates the foundation of battering behavior."[86]

These broadly political critiques and agendas for change have in recent years become largely muffled. Within the shelter movement, the enormity of the struggle and necessary commitments of energy devoted to maintaining minimal resources to keep existing shelter services open and available explains much of the exhaustion.[87] Similar political pressures have contributed to the "professionalization" of the shelter movement, which in the view of some experienced movement leaders has narrowed its political vision and disempowers women who seek its support.[88] In this political environment, "get her out" shelter strategies have become concretized into a "time out" approach to patriarchy, the problem of intrafamilial sexual dominance confined to motivating "the couple" to "break up."[89] The social scientific emphasis, less accountably, has shifted in the same direction.[90]

In the legal representation of women, these structural insights have largely been compressed to one line mention of women's common economic dependency on husbands in marriage, ordinarily in the context of a court's explication of the necessity of expert testimony on battered women's syndrome. For example, in an extensively reasoned opinion holding that defense counsel's failure to present evidence on battered women's syndrome in a prosecution of a woman charged with involuntary manslaughter of her boyfriend constituted reversible error, a California appellate court mentioned the economic factor only once, while discussing at length the inconsistencies in a battered woman's report of events as a consequence of amnesiac denial.[91] Mention of specific

---

86. Ellen Pence & Melanie Shepard, *Integrating Feminist Theory and Practice: The Challenge of the Battered Women's Movement, in* FEMINIST PERSPECTIVES ON WIFE ABUSE, *supra* note 58, at 282 (quoting ELLEN PENCE, CRIMINAL JUSTICE RESPONSE TO DOMESTIC ASSAULT CASES: A GUIDE FOR POLICY DEVELOPMENT 2 (1985)). Pence has been a significant contributor to the crafting of community strategies against domestic violence in the United States.

87. Phyllis Crocker cites sources stating that existing shelters can provide for but 25-35% of women and children in need. Further, "one-half of these shelters are in the ten most populated states; some states have no shelters." Crocker, *supra* note 74, at 133 n.63. Some of the most divisive issues within the national anti-domestic violence movement concern the politics of accepting funding from sources which place limitations on the services provided or on advocacy naming male power as the "problem" of battery. The federal government has led the pack in exercising this form of political control.

88. *See* SCHECHTER, *supra* note 84; Pence & Shepard, *supra* note 86.

89. I would be mortified and angry if these comments were interpreted to suggest that battered women's shelters are somehow "unprogressive" for women. My criticism is only with a vision of the mission of the anti-battery movement implying that moving a few desperately embattered women out of their own homes "solves" the problem of battery. I also do not intend to suggest that "time outs" do nothing to save women's lives. One researcher has concluded that femicide rates correlate negatively with availability of shelter services, rape crisis support, and legislative reform of civil orders for protection. *See* Karen D. Stout, *"Intimate Femicide": Effect of Legislation and Social Services*, AFFILIA 21 (Summer 1989).

90. For a brilliant and glitteringly written critique of the tendencies of even pro-feminist social science research toward "interpersonal" explanations for battery, and the re-awakening of the "complicit female" as a consequence of those investigations, *see* Laurie Wardell, et al., *Science and Violence Against Wives, in* THE DARK SIDE OF FAMILIES *supra* note 79, at 69, 70-78. A popular example of the "new" social science literature is Jeanne P. Deschner's THE HITTING HABIT: ANGER CONTROL FOR BATTERING COUPLES (1986). The author articulates the "problem" of battery as an excess of hostile emotionalism within "battering couples," happily resolvable by properly administered psychotherapy.

91. *See* People v. Day, 1992 WL 828 (Cal. App. 5th Dist.).

economic motives for "staying" in the particular case is rarer still.[92] Nor have feminist legal critics much attended to this descriptive factor, even as the affinity of the heavily "psychologized" content of battered women's syndrome testimony with the stereotype of women as neurotic and helpless is critiqued.[93] At most, we "maternalize" the economic dimension, attending to the "special" economic pressures on battered women with children to support to remain in abusive marriages. Further, the economic interest of *men* in the women they control by violence, in the time-honored tradition of pimping, remains wholly uninterrogated. Of course, avoidance of the economic question also serves to maintain the "good woman" distance from the inference of prostitution, which the emphasis on intimacy and love in the construction of battered women's syndrome testimony further severs. Whatever we are there for, it isn't for the money. If he is no trick, she is no whore.

"Legitimate" work is, after all, the place where women are supposed to make money, an assumption which has fueled anti-sexual harassment legal initiatives and education efforts. Here, our advocacy stresses the *distinction* between a woman's willingness to work and her willingness to have sex as part of the bargain, or to be sexualized in her status as worker: "real women" do not combine sex with money. At the outset, this may seem a quite perverse distinction to draw in the context, as sexual harassment is defined in those conditions where that combination is women's lived employment experience. The underlying critical insight is that women are *injured* by that conjunction. As Chief Justice Rehnquist has so nicely acknowledged, sexual harassment prohibitions stand at the ready to sanction any "requirement that a man or a woman run a gauntlet of sexual abuse in return for the privilege of being allowed to work and earn a living."[94] By "sexual abuse", Justice Rehnquist seems here to mean any "unwelcome" sex imposed on a woman as a condition or entailment of her job.[95]

Thus, it would seem but a small step conceptually to hold all prostitution

---

92. Exceptions include State v. Felton, 329 N.W. 2d 161 (1983), where the court noted that the woman returned to a battering husband in part because "he was being nice to her and she was having financial problems," *id.* at 163, and Borders v. State, 433 So. 2d 1325 (Fla. 3rd Dist. Ct. App. 1983), where the court explains that although the woman was the household provider, "the victim on several occasions stole household funds and food stamps in order to purchase additonal alcoholic beverages." *Id.* at 1326.

93. *See* Schneider, *Describing and Changing, supra* note 74 (criticizing inference often raised from battered women's syndrome testimony that woman is "sick" and wholly passive). Relevant counsel have been less restrained. *See* State v. Anaya, 456 A. 2d 1255 (Me. 1983) (defense testimony that male batterer never had a steady job admissible to rebut expert testimony that battered women are often economically dependent); State v. Ciskee, 751 P.2d 1165, 1173 (Wash. 1988) (defense counsel in co-habitant rape prosecution opened with statement that the victim "was an independent woman; hardly a prisoner in her own home"; victim was a bookkeeper, defendant unemployed).

94. Meritor Savings Bank v. Vinson, 477 U.S. 57, 67 (1986) (holding sexual harassment to constitute sex discrimination prohibited under Title VII) (quoting Henson v. Dundee, 682 F.2d 897, 902 (11th Cir. 1982)).

95. *Id.*, at 65 (distinguishing "unwelcome" sex from "involuntary" sex and affirming unwelcomeness as the proper standard, as an involuntariness requirement would too narrowly confine sexual harassment to circumstances where the woman was "forced to participate against her will").

to be *per se* actionable as sexual harassment, as the demand for money in the transaction shows that a woman's sexual compliance in the acts were otherwise unwanted. Certainly, demand for payment, unequivocally delivered, might in most circumstances distinguish such transactions from the "romantic attractions" courts find so distressingly indistinguishable, at least in hypothethical contemplation, from unwanted workplace sexual attention.[96] Prostitution may also be fairly described as consistent with one of the two alternative strategies available to women in response to workplace sexualization:

> The sexualization of the workplace imposes burdens on women that are not borne by men. Women must constantly monitor their behavior to determine whether they are eliciting sexual attention. They must conform their behavior to the existence of the sexual stereotyping whether by becoming sexy and responsive to the men who flirt with them or by becoming rigid, standoffish and distant so as to make clear they are not interested in the status of sex object.[97]

Both in legal doctrine and in feminist theory, however, this coerced election is instead treated as if it instead defined one class of women who are injured by sexual harassment (the distant ones) and another, those who are not (the "welcoming" ones).

Even Catharine MacKinnon, while she acknowledges that prostitution represents in pure form the model of *quid pro quo* sex for money exchange prohibited in sexual harrassment law, nevertheless retreats from the conclusion that prostitution should be actionable as such, apparently even when "unwelcome." Her hesitation seems driven by the belief (affirmatively theorized in Margaret Radin's work[98]) that for women materially supported in the practice, prostitution may be better than nothing at all,[99] and more

---

96. For feminist critiques of this "problem," *see* MACKINNON, SEXUAL HARASSMENT, *supra* note 52, at 32, Wendy Pollack, *Sexual Harassment: Women's Experience vs. Legal Definitions*, 13 HARV. WOM. L.J. 35, 52 (1990)("much of the behavior that women find offensive is behavior that is accepted as normal heterosexual behavior by men"), Nancy S. Ehrenreich, *Pluralist Myths and Powerless Men: The Ideology of Reasonableness in Sexual Harassment Law*, 99 Yale L.J. 1177, 1201-10 (1990); Opinions that continue to wrestle with the romance incitement problem include Lipsett v. Rive-More, 669 F. Supp. 1188 (D.P.R. 1987)(supervising physician's "flattering remarks" to plaintiff were based on "romantic attraction"), Highlander v. K.F.C. National Management Co., 805 F.2d 644 (6th Cir. 1986) (plaintiff asked boss to go to a bar with her).

97. Robinson v. Jacksonville Shipyards, 760 F.Supp 1486, 1505 (M.D. Fla 1991) (finding based on expert testimony by Dr. Susan Fiske on the effects of sexual stereotyping in employment settings).

98. *See* Radin, *Market-Inalienability*, *supra* note 36.

99. MacKinnon argues:

> In these situations, more than is impermissibly the case for most women's jobs, without the sexual harassment, there *is* no job. Until all women *need* no longer sell their physical attractiveness, there is no point in the law prohibiting all such behavior in these contexts.

MACKINNON, SEXUAL HARASSMENT, *supra* note 52, at 209.

rewarding than "romantic" sexual compliance promising little by way of material benefits.[100] While prostitution may represent the "fundamental" economic and sexual "condition of women,"[101] it is, itself, deemed here by MacKinnon a condition too fundamental for redress.[102] Whatever the practical merits of MacKinnon's view,[103] as in the domestic violence arena, the "unwelcomeness" requirement is understood to founder where the woman is comprehended to "get something" out of it, in particular money. Even those millions of us who believed Anita Hill, and believed in her injury, largely did so not *because* she was prostituted, but because she was *not*.

Taken together, these boundary defenses form a solid wall against the imputation of prostitution to particular "other" women: she is not sexually promiscuous, does not subject herself to random treatment by strangers, and doesn't do it for cash. Beyond these defenses, is but silence. Domestic legal reform activity on prostitution is nearly nonexistent, both in feminist legislative projects[104] and feminist legal scholarship.[105] The recent legal scholarship

---

100. MacKinnon quotes Roberta Victor, a woman with history in prostitution, to the point:

> What I did was no different from what ninety-nine percent of American women are taught to do. I took the money from under the lamp instead of in Arpege. What would I do with 150 bottles of Arpege a week?

MACKINNON, SEXUAL HARASSMENT, *supra* note 52, at 217.

101. MACKINNON, TOWARD A FEMINIST THEORY OF THE STATE, *supra* note 8, at 243.

102. MacKinnon does declare in her later work that under a legal theory of equality sufficient for redress of women's subordination "prostitution . . . would become actionable." *Id.* at 248.

103. I actually find it a quite lovely thought that feminists could organize a national class action with women in prostitution against some well-placed johns, the pornography industry, the state of Nevada, every outcall and massage parlor and sauna and woman behind glass outfit for damages and injunctive relief. The return might be better than years of $20 blow jobs. *See* Thoreson v. Penthouse Int'l., 149 Misc. 2d 150 (1990), (recovery of $4,060,000 in actual and punitive damages for sexual slavery), *aff'd as modified*, 80 N.Y.2d 490 (1992)(reversing award of punitive damages). In any event, MacKinnon's account also leaves unaddressed why women wouldn't do better stealing cars, and such like, in the meantime.

104. Much of the legislative activity on behalf of women in recent years has been inspired and guided by state gender bias commission studies. *See* Lynn Hecht Shafran, *Gender and Justice: Florida and the Nation*, 42 FLA. L. REV. 181 (1990); Elizabeth M. Schneider, *Task Force Reports on Women in the Courts: The Challenge for Legal Education*, 38 J. LEGAL EDUC. 87 (1988). Only Florida's study has included prostitution as a subject matter for scrutiny, and is the only state to have enacted legislation affecting prostitution in consequence of those findings. *See* FLA. STAT. ANN. § 796.09 (West 1991 Supp.). I initiated that process in Florida and drafted the core provisions of our new state legislation. (I mention my involvement only to indicate that this article and that work are of a piece, rather than indicative of bodies of work supported by distinct constituencies.)

105. But a few law review articles on the legal treatment of prostitution have appeared since 1985, a remarkably slim bibliography given the relative robustness of feminist legal inquiry generally in the same period. Those pieces in addition to those cited *supra*, include Jody Freeman, *The Feminist Debate Over Prostitution Reform: Prostitutes' Rights Groups, Radical Feminists, and the (Im)possibility of Consent*, 5 BERKELEY WOMEN'S L.J. 75 (1989-90); Pasqua Scibelli, *Empowering Prostitutes: A Proposal for International Reform*, 10 HARV. WOMEN'S L.J. 117 (1987); Nancy Erbe, *Prostitutes: Victims of Men's Exploitation and Abuse*, 2 LAW & INEQUALITY 609 (1984); Belinda Cooper, *Prostitution: A Feminist Analysis*, 11 WOMEN'S RTS. L. REP. 98 (1989); P.R. Glazebrook, *Sexist Sex Law*, 44 CAMBRIDGE L.J. 42 (1985); Lori Douglass Hutchins, *Pornography: The Prosecution of Pornographers Under Prostitution Statutes — A New Approach*, 37 SYRACUSE L. REV. 977 (1986); Beth Bergman, *AIDS, Prostitution and the Use of Historical Stereotypes to Legislate Sexuality*, 21 J. MARSHALL L. REV. 777 (1988); Christine L.M. Boyle & Sheila Noonan, *Prostitution and Pornography: Beyond Formal Equality*, 10 DALHOUSIE L.J. 225 (1986); Lan Cao, *Illegal Traffic in Women: A Civil RICO Proposal*, 96 Yale L.J. 1297 (1987); Julie Pearl, *The Highest Paying Customers: America's Cities and the Costs of Prostitution Control*, 38 HASTINGS L.J. 769 (1987); Ina L. Potter, *Locking Out Prostitution*, 15 HASTINGS CONST. L.Q. 181 (1987);

on prostitution that exists is largely limited in vision to the rather narrow question of whether prostitution should or should not be decriminalized,[106] a discourse closely enmeshed with and perhaps as unproductive to feminist imagination as the never ending debates over the legal treatment of obscenity. Anti-discrimination litigation strategies have been confined to challenges to statutory schemes which criminalize the behavior of prostitutes but not the behavior of johns or impose sanctions at different severity levels, and to enforcement practices with the same effect. Advanced on formal equality theories, these challenge have largely foundered, either because prostitutes and johns are held dissimilarly situated, or because sufficient proof of discriminatory intent is deemed lacking.[107] Conceptually, these strategies exclude consideration of the experience of women in prostitution beyond the rather abstract injury of being jailed while her john takes a walk.[108] This insult, I would propose, pales in comparison to other relevant comparisons in life circumstances that might be made between them.

Our activism in providing support services and progessive organizing has done little better than our legal initiatives. Domestic violence shelters remain in effect inaccessible to women and girls in prostitution, for reasons as precise as express policies excluding drug and alcohol dependent women from admission to shelters, as well as denying access to women who engage in illegal activities of any kind. In addition to specific policy restraints, the invisibility of prostitution to service providers limits their awareness of prostituted women's access and safety needs, the urgency of maintaining confidentiality of the identities of minor girls when sought by police and social service agencies, and the requirement of long-term support for prostituted

---

Belinda M. Cheney, *Prostitution—A Feminist Jurisprudential Perspective*, 18 VICTORIA UNIV. OF WELLINGTON L. REV. 239 (1988).

106. *See, e.g.*, RHODE, JUSTICE AND GENDER, *supra* note 34, at 259 (criminalization asserted as origin of problems women in prostitution encounter), Freeman, *supra* note 105, at 77-83, 107-109 (analysis of consent, legal regulation focussed on question of decriminalization), Radin, *Market Inalienability*, *supra* note 36, at 1924-25 (arguing for decriminalization combined with regulation of advertising and promotion.), Scibelli, *supra* note 105 (same); Nancy Erbe's article pursues instead an analysis of the conditions of violence dominating the lives of women and girls in prostitution. *See generally* Erbe, *supra* note 105.

107. *See, e.g.*, People v. Superior Court, 562 P.2d 1315 (Cal. 1977) (prostitute and john not similarly situated insofar as prostitute is a "profiteer" and the john a mere user), Commonwealth v. King, note 60 (absence of statutory penalty for "customers" of prostitutes no violation of equal protection where solicitation statute gender neutral; evidence that arrests made only of female and not male prostitutes also insufficient to prove discriminatory enforcement where male prostitutes "could have" been charged under other offense ratings), Commonwealth v. Finnegan, 421 A.2d 1086 (Sup. Ct. Penn. 1980) (disparate sentencing scheme justified as parties not similarly situated); State v. Wilbur, 749 P.2d 1295 (Wash. 1988) (gender-neutral solicitation statute, even if johns' behavior is not prohibited, no violation of equal protection).

108. It is also not self-evidently clear to me that these strategies, designed ultimately to inhibit arrest of women, even serve women's immediate interests. At present, jail is the closest thing many women in prostitution have to a battered women's shelter. Among the reasons women have recited to me as why sometimes they seek "voluntary arrest" include to get a night's sleep, to escape a violent pimp or john, to detox, to get AZT therapy, to not have to fuck, and to eat a hot meal. I beg the civil libertarians among my readers who represent women in prostitution to please interview a woman carefully on these issues before deciding unilaterally what is "best" for her.

women and girls.[109] From my observation, once women are admitted to shelters, they often feel constrained to lie about their circumstances, reducing the possible benefits of proffered support to painful farce.[110] Her pimp becomes her husband, the cigarette burns on her thighs the consequence of a jealous outburst over her "seeing" other men, she is sexually harassed on the job, and on and on. Anti-pornography activism, which has mobilized the most visible contemporary feminist challenge to prostitution in the United States, has been largely pushed "underground," unlike pornography or prostitution.[111] Women's health agendas, to the extent that work has comprehended prostitution as a health issue at all, have limited the scope of their consideration of prostitution to the risks of AIDS transmission to and by prostitutes.[112] This emphasis obscures the significance of research indicating that chronic poor health among juvenile prostitutes is often a consequence of inadequate clothing,[113] that injuries from beatings and sexual assaults most commonly immobilize women in prostitution,[114] and the social targeting of

---

109. In public talks I refer to these patterns as shelter "June Cleaver triage." I hasten to note that some shelters *do* provide real support for women and girls in prostitution; the Harriet Tubman shelter in Minneapolis is one sterling example. Evelina Giobbe and WHISPER have begun a process of educating shelter services to the implications of these policies in excluding women in prostitution from service assistance. As a result of these efforts, the National Coalition Against Domestic Violence did enact a resolution in 1989 in support of full access for women in prostitution to battered women's shelters, as yet without great practical effect. The most active prostitute support and recovery services continue to be provided by the few committed and precariously funded organizations devoted specifically to women and girls in prostitution.

110. These comments are based on personal conversations with women in prostitution who have sought assistance from a variety of shelters. These reports are echoed in the responses of some service providers with whom I have discussed these concerns, who express fear that women in prostitution who are open about their circumstances will disturb and frighten the other women in the shelters. (It is uncontemplated that those "other women" might be prostitutes, too).

111. In my view, the suppression of anti-pornography work is part and parcel of the denial of prostitution I am describing here. As I noted above, my own involvement with anti-pornography work began my engagement with prostitution. Anti-prostitution work internationally has focussed principally, if not exclusively, on trafficking women across national borders and on the prostitution of indigenous women for use by foreign men. *See, e.g.,* ARLENE EISEN-BERGMAN, WOMEN OF VIET NAM (1975) (prostitution systems developed for American soldiers in Viet Nam); THANH-DAM TRUONG, SEX, MONEY AND MORALITY: PROSTITUTION AND TOURISM IN SOUTHEAST ASIA (1990); INTERNATIONAL FEMINISM, *supra* note 33; Siriporn Skrobanet, *Strategies Against Prostitution in Thailand, in* 2 THIRD WORLD/SECOND SEX 211 (Miranda Davies ed., 1987); Tonette Raguisa, *Prostitution: A Phillippine Experience in* 2 THIRD WORLD/SECOND SEX, *id.* at 218. U.S. scholars and activists Kathleen Barry and Charlotte Bunch, whose work has for many years centered on prostitution, are presently primarily engaged in reform at the international level against all forms of prostitution within the international human rights agenda. Kathleen Barry is now the executive director of The Coalition Against Trafficking in Women, an organization with consultative status to the United Nations Economic and Social Council. Charlotte Bunch recently authored *Women's Rights as Human Rights: Toward a Re-Vision of Human Rights,* 12 HUM. RTS. Q. 486 (1990).

112. *See* Gloria Lockett, *Prostitution, in* BLACK WOMEN'S HEALTH BOOK 189 (Ellen White ed., 1990). *See also* Priscilla Alexander, *Prostitutes are Being Scapegoated for Heterosexual AIDS, in* SEX WORK, *supra* note 57, at 241; A VINDICATION OF THE RIGHTS OF WHORES 109-140 (Gail Pheterson ed., 1989).

113. D. KELLY WEISBERG, CHILDREN OF THE NIGHT: A STUDY OF ADOLESCENT PROSTITUTION 116 (1985) (citing DOROTHY H. BRACEY, BABY-PROS: PRELIMINARY PROFILES OF JUVENILE PROSTITUTES 62-63 (1979)).

114. Eleanor Miller reports of her research on health conditions of "street women":
Health-related [concerns] . . . even more frequently mentioned as occasions for temporary withdrawal from street life than disease or pregnancy included the bruises, broken bones, cuts and abrasions that were the result of the ever-present risk of violence on the streets. The beatings and sexual assaults female street hustlers received

all prostitutes for murder.[115]

Prostitution, indeed, is not like "anything else," especially anything that we might be. The most brutal rendition of this theme may be Kate Millett's account, as recounted by Alice Echols, of an episode at a radical feminist conference on prostitution in 1971:

> The place finally erupted when a member of The Feminists declared herself an "honorable woman" because she lived in a tenement, worked as a secretary, and yet refused to sell her body. As Millett noted, "the accusation, so long buried in liberal good-will and radical rhetoric—'You're selling it, I could too, but I won't'—was finally heard. Said out loud at last.[116]

The form of this claim is also familiar, if usually more delicately expressed. Women make it all the time, especially before we identify as feminists or engage in experiences of feminist consciousness-raising. *It's not me*: if they say it is, I can recite sixteen reasons and change why they are wrong.

I have expressed a good deal of anger here, and mostly at the wrong people. In its legal expression, this feminist flight from prostitution seems largely reactive, driven by a tacit recognition that legal regulation of sexual violence and sex discrimination at bottom always functions as some form of judicial review of a man's conclusion that a complaining woman was, in fact, a whore, and therefore a permissible target of misogynist rage, contempt, and sexual use. The fate of a woman's claims on justice, we all seem to know somewhere, crucially depends on her success in proving that she is not, and never has been, a prostitute. As Andrea Dworkin puts the point, "The woman's effort to stay innocent, her efforts to prove innocence, her effort to prove that she was used against her will is always and unequivocally an effort to prove she is not a whore."[117]

"There is no point to it." The point, apparently, is to fix a point of departure from which to flee. With Freud's Dora, we may acknowledge the prostitute only to expel her.[118]

---

at the hands of their "men," their dates, their wives-in-law, former "women" of their "men," and other street people as well as the police were numerous and often brutal. ELEANOR MILLER, STREET WOMAN 138 (1986).

115. *See* Jane Caputi, *The Sexual Politics of Murder*, 3 GENDER & SOCIETY 437 (1989); *see also infra* notes 126-154 and accompanying text.

116. ALICE ECHOLS, DARING TO BE BAD: RADICAL FEMINISM IN AMERICA 1967-1975, 194 (1989). *See also* Gail Pheterson, *Not Repeating History*, in A VINDICATION OF THE RIGHTS OF WHORES, *supra* note 112, at 3, 18 ("Feminists who followed the anti-prostitution and anti-pornography line were often viewed by political prostitutes as naive or self-righteous agents of control and condemnation.").

117. DWORKIN, *supra* note 25, at 204.

118. I am here paraphrasing Jane Gallop:

> As a threatening representative of the symbolic, the economic, the extrafamilial, the maid must be both seduced (assimilated) and abandoned (expelled) . . . . Dora and Freud cannot bear to identify with the governess because they think there is still

II. THE GREATEST STORY NEVER TOLD

Some women find this business of fleeing somewhat more difficult to achieve. Prostitutes, for example. Some notice has been taken of this, both by prostitutes and by feminist scholars, via feminist prostitution activism and in some corners of feminist legal theory. Nevertheless, as I will detail in this section, the insight that some women "are" prostitutes, and as women are consequently of some interest to feminists, has curiously little disrupted the design of our "not a prostitute" reform strategies. The principle argument advanced on behalf of prostitutes in these activist circles indeed echoes in substance the identical tactic: that prostitutes, too, are "other women," and, therefore, "not prostitutes," either. On the surface of things, this may seem a problematic maneuver, assimilating prostitutes into a political discourse which depends on no one we care about being one. As a purely logical matter, certainly, the effectiveness of our "not a prostitute" negation strategies demands that we find one, somewhere, not to be. This structural requirement in fact remains intact on each of the arguments to assimilability offered by prostitution activists reinterating the good woman/bad woman dichotomy permeating mainstream feminist defenses of "other women." Within this discussion, however, the dichotomy is instead drawn among prostitutes. Some prostitutes (the assimilable ones), are deemed "good prostitutes," some others (the unassimilable), "bad" ones. The design of these arguments, and their implications for feminist strategy, are the themes I will pursue in this section.

The methodological foundations of these debates are implied in some recent feminist legal scholarship, which questions whether we have, or ever could have, a sufficient grasp of the "subject matter" of prostitution for scholarly consideration; that is, whether prostitution is suffiently "known" or "knowable" such that "a point to it" can meaningfully be discerned. These hesitations are feminist ones, and it matters that they are. Outside of feminism, it may seem a strange assertion that we "know" little about prostitutes, and display a peculiar fastidiousness to question whether "prostitution," as a discrete subject matter of inquiry, actually exists. Non-feminist historians, sociologists, psychologists, legal theorists, "ans" and "ists" of all descriptions, have long and avidly inquired of the prostitute and her doings, with a fervor at least as great as the enthusiasm with which similar attempts to capture "other women" have been pursued. Thus, when feminists question whether prostitution is a "knowable" phenomenon for feminist analysis, their doubt is

---

someplace where one can escape the structural exchange of women. They still believe there is some mother who is not a governess.

Jane Gallop, *Keys to Dora, in* IN DORA'S CASE: FREUD-HYSTERIA-FEMINISM 200, 216 (Charles Bernheimer & Claire Kahane eds., 1989). For further feminist discussion of Freud's severance of "servant girls" from "women," see HELENE CIXOUS & CLAIRE CLEMENT, THE NEWLY BORN WOMAN 153 (Betsy Wing trans., 1986); KAPPELER, *supra* note 13, at 201-206.

implicitly motivated by concern about whether prostitution is knowable in a feminist way.[119]

There are three routes by which "data" about women's lives have been made accessible to feminists in the position to be in the group called "we": they come to us, we go to them, or "they" become "we." Women "come to us" through data accumulated by existing sexual violence services or ongoing activism. Women participate, and tell the truth, in those arenas when they are welcome and recognized. As I have discussed earlier, feminism has created neither of those conditions for women in prostitution, in practical support or in the scope of our announced agendas. Our reform campaigns have little contributed little to the security or visibility of women in prostitution; indeed, they have been hostile to them. Needless to say, in that environment we find few "prostitutes," a state of affairs that explains Martha Chamallas' conclusion that the whole issue of prostitution is "difficult," because "we know very little about the lives of prostitutes."[120] Moreover, so long as feminist support and advocacy work continues its present stance toward prostitution, "we" are unlikely to know much more.

If "they" decline to come to us, we can "go to them." We "go to them," by first identifying a class of "them," and then asking "them" questions about which we have some curiosity. Those investigations have been constrained in two related dimensions: in the difficulties of finding "them," and in the matters about which we have seen fit to inquire. Those matters, as I will demonstrate more completely in the following discussion, have been largely limited to inquiry whether, and to what extent, the life histories of women in prostitution share features in common with those of "other women." To the extent they might not, that is, the extent to which prostitution is different from "everything else," our curiosity has tended to wane. Having confined our interest in prostitutes to what is "not prostitution," attention to what may be the distinctiveness of the practice itself, and its analytic usefulness, necessarily and rapidly wanders. This approach finds many "prostitutes," but little "prostitution."

---

119. However much feminists may debate whether feminism affords a unique angle of vision from which to comprehend women's experience, it effaces the achievements of twenty years of feminist activism, both scholarly and otherwise, to assume that "conventional" methods of investigation and interpretation have been fully equipped to perceive "the point" of women's lived realities. On this much, I hope, we can agree. For discussion of the debate within feminist legal theory on this issue, see Katharine T. Bartlett, *Feminist Legal Methods*, 103 HARV. L. REV. 829 (1990); Deborah L. Rhode, *Feminist Critical Theories*, 42 STAN. L. REV. 617 (1990); Martha Minow, *Beyond Universality*, U. CHI. LEGAL. F. 115 (1989).

120. Chamallas, *supra* note 68, at 826. I have been truly astounded by the different things my own law students talk to me about since I have been publicly identified with prostitute support work. Before "coming out" as a prostitution activist, not one student ever told me about her own history in prostitution, her present involvement in prostitution, her self-identification as a prostitute, her "fucking everybody" periods, about behaviors associated with prostitution like excessive drug and alcohol use as a way of "getting over" in the sex, "consenting" to oral and anal sex as a tactic to avoid vaginal intercourse, cutting herself with knives and razor blades in the crotch and thighs, and performing sex with men or women to please a husband or lover. Now, these are commonplace discussions, enabled, I believe, by students' impressions that I do not find these disclosures "abnormal," but all too ordinary occasions for grief.

In short order, the coherence of the category "prostitutes," descriptive of the unique experience of women *in* prostitution, falters as well. Thus, Deborah Rhode finds the data on the experience of women in prostitution inadequate to support reliable conclusions descriptive of prostitutes as a group, and questions whether such data could ever be generated given the range of circumstances under which women enter, practice, and leave prostitution.[121] That *prostitution* may forge a connecting link in the experience of "prostitutes" is a notion suppressed from the empirical get-go by the suppression of prostitution itself as a topic of analysis. Neither "come to us" nor "go to them" strategies of investigation, then, seem likely to cast much light on the subject. Rather, both (again) banish prostitution from feminist sight by causing prostitutes and prostitution to vanish from the realm of the "known."

These vanishing acts have motivated feminist prostitution activists, like "other women" before them, to engage in autonomous organizing of women in prostitution on their own behalf. This work has availed itself of the third, and perhaps most significant, method devised in feminism for feminist "investigation": that of "consciousness-raising," meshing practices of "naming" women's experience from "the inside," with the crafting of political strategies for change on the "outside." As I have noted earlier, consciousness-raising is the fundamental process by which feminist "stories" of women's experience have come to be told.[122] As a means of political investigation, consciousness-raising tends to diverge from conventional analytic methods in three ways I think relevant to this discussion. As a process, consciousness-raising relies on participatory, interactive dialogue, in sharp contrast with the distanced, "observational" techniques employed in the empirical social sciences. This procedural emphasis, in turn, mirrors the thematic focus in consciousness-raising on building a synthetic description of women's common life conditions. The participatory process of consciousness-raising echoes this discursive theme, *creating* such shared experience "in the act" of consciousness-raising itself.[123] Finally, this process, and these themes, are committed to a specific end: towards a political critique of existing gender relations which have both obscured women's political identities and inhibited collective action against the prevailing regime.[124]

---

121. RHODE, *supra* note 34, at 258.

122. *See* sources cited *supra* at notes 17-19, and accompanying text.

123. Catharine MacKinnon describes the relationship so enacted among women as "build[ing] a community frame of reference which recasts the perceived content of social life as it alters the relation between 'I,' the 'other' and the 'we'. . . creating a shared reality which 'clears a space in the world' within which women can begin to move." MACKINNON, TOWARD A FEMINIST THEORY OF THE STATE, *supra* note 8, at 101 (citing Allen, *Free Space, supra* note 17).

124. Kathie Sarachild, an originating theorist of feminist consciousness-raising, emphasizes the rootedness of consciousness-raising in the theme of "who or what has an *interest* in maintaining the oppression in our lives." Sarachild, *supra* note 17, at 144-45. *See also* Mari Matsuda, *Pragmatism Modified and the False Consciousness Problem,* 63 S. CAL. L. REV. 1763 (1990) (explaining the dialectic of experience and critical consciousness in developing a politics for and by the oppressed). This critical dimension distinguishes consciousness-raising, and feminist activism generally, from simple confession of "personal problems" or pursuit of whatever passes currently for "mental health." Kathie Sarachild early

It might seem a dubious proposition for women in prostitution to pursue a method of political action which in the hands of other women, crafting their "stories," has so threatened the integrity of prostituted women's lives. The following discussion attempts to chart the difficulties women in prostitution and their allies have encountered in organizing and "integrating" with the larger movement through practices of consciousness-raising. At the outset, though, I want to emphasize two crucial points which I hope will not be lost in the thicket of this analytic escapade. First, *without* feminist consciousness-raising, including, for example, Linda Marchiano's resistance to the pornography industry and the statements by women used in prostitution given to the Minneapolis City Council in support of the Dworkin/MacKinnon ordinance, none of this discussion would be possible at all. Second, as these examples suggest, the political possibilities *for* prostitution advocacy were in part enabled *within* the existing movement, if in some tension with its dominant programs and vision. Thus, the critique I offer here is intended to urge a greater commitment to consciousness-raising, not a recommendation that we abandon it. Nevertheless, insofar as the politics of consciousness-raising have constructed difficulties for women in prostitution to achieve a "voice" in feminism, these difficulties must be confronted.

The first difficulty is obvious, but especially in connection with prostitution, profoundly undercomprehended. The dead, the deeply incoherent, and those presently living in conditions of grave danger are not participants. Consciousness-raising is necessarily a practice for survivors, not casualties. As a method which relies on *participation* for its political analysis, consciousness-raising excludes the testimony of women who did not have enough luck to make it to the meeting, and not only for reasons of inadequate child care. Empirical evidence little assists in "completing the picture," although it helps a bit. Reliable rates of prostitute murders are not available, in part due to statistical reporting methods,[125] but also, and more importantly,

---

stressed the significance of activism and critique as essential components of feminist process. "The view of consciousness-raising as an end in itself—when consciousness-raising is made into a methodology, a psychology, is [a] severe and destructive . . . distortion of the original idea." Sarachild, *supra* note 17, at 148. bell hooks has also criticized tendencies towards "therapism" in feminist consciousness-raising, suggesting that "[w]hen women internalized the idea that describing their own woe was synonymous with developing a critical political consciousness, the progress of the feminist movement was stalled." BELL HOOKS, FEMINIST THEORY: FROM MARGIN TO CENTER 24-25 (1984). *See also* RAYMOND, *supra* note 19, at 156-60 (1986) (situating the "personification of the political" of "therapism" in "the dissociative context in which many women live"); Anna Lee, *Therapy: The Evil Within*, 9 TRIVIA 34, 43 (1986) ("Feminist analysis of rape did not come from the human potential movement. . . . Feminist analysis of racism didn't come from therapy. . . ."). The recuperation of feminist political critiques of sexual violence by the psychological disciplines in recent years back into the therapeutic realm of interpersonal disturbance by is the institutional analogue. Louise Armstrong, a feminist activist, author, and survivor of incest, has recently expressed, along with other feminists, a critique of the co-optation and de-politicization of feminist anti-incest work by the "helping professions" wherein the fodder of women's victimization becomes fuel for therapeutic incentive for "forgiveness" of victimizers. *See* Louise Armstrong, *Surviving the Incest Industry*, TROUBLE AND STRIFE 29 (Summer 1991).

125. The Uniform Crime Reports, published annually under the aegis of the FBI, analyzes victimization rates only by sex, age, and race and some circumstantial information, such as victim-offender

because of the "disappeared" status of women and girls involved in the practice.[126] They are "unaccounted for" females, from virtually every possible vantage point of observation, the whereabouts of migrating ducks are more devotedly attended. These unaccounted for females are often runaways or "throwaways" from families,[127] sometimes pimped by them.[128] Family members likely have no knowledge of or interest in a girl's whereabouts. Those more immediately present in a girl's life may readily assume she merely "moved on," fear compromising themselves to the police, be the killer, or simply not care.[129] Police may make similar assumptions,[130] while the vagaries of a prostituted woman's legal identity[131] render reports listing a woman under a possibly false name and a cursory description of little assistance in linking a corpse to an identifiable woman's life. Commenting on the difficulties of establishing prevalence rates for serial murder in particular, one team of researchers has hypothesized that many "missing persons" (a gender neutral term even though they document that all but a few known victims of serial murder are women) may be serial murder victims,[132] and even the number of victims reported by apprehended perpetrators may never adequately be established. "We will never know for certain, because the majority of [the victims] would have been prostitutes whose disappearance may

---

relationship. Such "relationships" as those a prostitute has with a john, pimp, or serial homicide perpetrator are not within the breakdowns. The National Center for Health Statistics publishes victimization rates only by sex and age. For a survey and critique of the statistical literature of homicide as it pertains to women, see William Wilbanks, *Murdered Women and Women Who Murder: A Critique of the Literature, in* JUDGE, LAWYER, VICTIM, THIEF: WOMEN, GENDER ROLES, AND CRIMINAL JUSTICE 157 (Nicole Hahn Rafter & Elizabeth A. Stanko eds., 1982).

126. *See generally* BARRY, *supra* note 10.

127. Running away from or being "shoved out" of families is the most common predicate for entry into prostitution among juveniles. *See, e.g.*, MILLER, *supra* note 114, at 87-108 (approximately half of her sample are either runaways or "pushouts"), WEISBERG, *supra* note 113 (summarizing research to date).

128. Two major studies of juvenile prostitution report that 4% of girls interviewed were either with a family member at the time of their first act of prostitution or a family member turned them out. *See* WEISBERG, *supra* note 113 (*citing* MIMI SILBERT, SEXUAL ASSAULT OF PROSTITUTES: PHASE ONE 40 (1980) and JENNIFER JAMES, ENTRANCE INTO JUVENILE PROSTITUTION 77 (1980)). *See also* MILLER, *supra* note 114, at 65-85 (prevalence of recruitment via "domestic networks"), James A. Inciardi, *Little Girls and Sex: A Glimpse at the World of the "Baby Pro"*, 5 DEV. BEHAVIOR 71 (1984) (study of girls age 8-12 prostituted by relatives).

129. Robert Keppel, chief investigator for the Washington state Attorney General's Office and consultant to the Green River investigation, stated, "Nobody keeps track of these women, monitors where they are going to be day by day. Often by the time the police get involved, it's a historical research project." Michael Hedges, *Prostitutes, Psychopaths Too Often a Deadly Match*, WASH. TIMES, June 12, 1990, at A10. Retired Los Angeles Police Department Captain Pierce Brooks deems prostitutes the "easiest victims to kill. All you have to do is drive up, wave a $5 or $20 bill. [She] hops in the car and off you go. No muss, no fuss." Lisa Faye Kaplan, *Someone is Killing U.S. Hookers*, GANNETT NEWS SERVICE, June 7, 1990.

130. Robert DePue, former administrator of the FBI National Center for the Analysis of Violent Crime, asserts that prostitutes are "easier" to murder than children. "Prostitutes can disappear, and there won't even be a missing person report filed. They're expendable people, unfortunately, in our society." Kaplan, *supra* note 129.

131. Women and girls commonly take on a series of assumed names, sometimes in the course of being seasoned for prostitution by pimps, see BARRY, *supra* note 10, at 94-95, and in an attempt to avoid an extensive police record under any one name.

132. JACK LEVIN & JAMES ALAN FOX, MASS MURDER: AMERICA'S GROWING MENACE 19 (1985).

not have been reported. Some may have ended up among the many "Jane Does" in the Los Angeles County Morgue."[133] Pornographic "snuff" films eroticize this ambiguity.

When the bodies are found and even tagged with names, the women even in death are still not "real women." An investigator of the "Green River" serial murders of 48 prostituted women in the Seattle area remarked, "There was wide public attention in the Ted [Bundy] case . . . because the victims resembled everyone's daughter . . . . But not everyone relates to prostitution on the Pacific Highway."[134] Prostitutes, apparently, are nobody's daughters; no longer even "victims" when murdered, but rather part of the flotsam of "prostitution on the Pacific Highway." The murdered spirits of women are contested, in doubt, tainted, interrogated. Were they good women or bad? Deserving dead or undeserving bystanders? During the investigation of the "Yorkshire Ripper" murders, Jim Hobson, police investigator, issued the following statement to the public, with a bit of hortation to the killer:

> He has made it clear that he hates prostitutes. Many people do. We, as a police force, will continue to arrest prostitutes . . . . But the Ripper is now killing innocent girls. That indicates your mental state and that you are in urgent need of medical attention. You have made your point. Give yourself up before another innocent woman dies.[135]

Murderers murder prostitutes, police arrest prostitutes. "Troubled" is but the murderer of "innocent girls." According to one reporter, the families of the "innocent girls" were also troubled by the possibility of contagion by those "others" of the purity of their daughters' deaths: "It is the main grief work for the families of [the Ripper's] non-professional victims to try to understand how their girls came under this man's hand. By having the same killer as the prostitutes, their daughters have somehow been tainted."[136]

To be a "prostitute" is to be rapable, beatable, killable, and *why* women are

---

133. *Id.* at 75.

134. JANE CAPUTI, THE AGE OF SEX CRIME 94 (1987) (quoting *The Random Killers*, NEWSWEEK, Nov. 26, 1984, at 100, 106).

135. *Id.* at 93 (quoting Joan Smith, *Getting Away with Murder*, NEW SOCIALIST, May/June 1982, at 10, 12). Peter Sutcliffe was ultimately charged as the "Yorkshire Ripper" with the attempted murder of nine women and the murder of thirteen others. The case was submitted to the jury on diminished capacity manslaughter instructions and was Sutcliffe convicted. For a feminist analysis of the competing (and equally misogynist) psychiatric and criminal deviancy discourses structuring the Sutcliffe trial, see Wendy Hollway, *"I Just Wanted to Kill a Woman." Why? The Ripper and Male Sexuality, in* SWEEPING STATEMENTS: WRITINGS FROM THE WOMEN'S LIBERATION MOVEMENT, 1981-83, 14 (Hannah Kanter, et al. eds., 1984). For a superb analysis and critique of the anti-feminism of prevailing criminological explanations of serial sexual murder, see CAMERON & FRAZER, *supra* note 13.

136. CAPUTI, *supra* note 134, at 95.

(righteously to non-controversially) raped, beaten and killed.[137] Many people do hate prostitutes. Good girls don't get murdered.

It thus seems the better part of prudence to suggest that the murder data that do exist be evaluated in light of whatever multiplier might fairly comprehend prostitutes' social invisibility, compounded yet again by the gendered specificity of their status as "safe" objects of eroticized violence and misogynist hatred.[138] Some numbers are available. Up to thirty-one women murdered in Miami over a three year period, most of them prostitutes;[139] fourteen in Denver; twenty-nine in Los Angeles;[140] seven in Oakland.[141] Forty-three in San Diego;[142] fourteen in Rochester;[143] eight in Arlington, Virginia; nine in New Bedford, Massachusetts, seventeen in Alaska, ten in Tampa.[144] Three girls, ages 3, 4, and 6, sold in Suffolk, New York.[145] Three prostitutes were reported dead in Spokane, Washington in 1990, leading some to speculate that the "Green River" murderer of 48 women and girls had once again become "active."[146]

We can spin tales with the national data. Jane Caputi reports an estimate by a Justice Department official that 4,118 serial murders were committed in

---

137. To date, the Green River murders have not been solved; there are no suspects and 48 women counted killed. The director of a support program for women in prostitution estimates that 23 women a year *she knows of* disappear from the streets of Portland, Oregon; she presumes them murdered. Interview with Susan Kay Hunter (July 13, 1990). For a "man vs. man" account of the Green River investigation, posing the intrepid police department of King County against the wily killer, see CARLTON SMITH & TOMAS GUILLEN, THE SEARCH FOR THE GREEN RIVER KILLER (1991). The book is worthwhile for the individual photographs of each of the women and girls who have been murdered. The impact these pictures, one after another, told me that I still hadn't believed in them, in the density and depth of their real existence, when even only partially reminded of them in these photographic traces.

138. Deborah Cameron and Elizabeth Frazer conclude in their study of sexual murder that "prostitute-killing is the clearest example of the lust to kill whose main component is misogyny." CAMERON & FRAZER, *supra* note 13, at 138. Serial murderer Peter Sutcliffe described his motives in killing his first "non-prostitute": "I realized Josephine was not a prostitute but at the same time I wasn't bothered. I just wanted to kill a woman." Hollway, *supra* note 135, at 131.

139. Hedges, *supra* note 129. Hedges estimates a "low-end" figure of eighteen. *See also* Barry Bearak, *Eerie Deaths of 17 Women Baffle Miami*, L.A. TIMES, May 14, 1989, Part 1, at 1.

140. Nieson Himmel & Edward J. Boyer, *2nd South-Central Wave of Prostitute Slayings Probed*, L. A. TIMES, Feb. 17, 1989, Part 2, at 3.

141. *Seventh Victim Tied to Serial Killer*, L.A. TIMES, Oct. 8, 1989, Part 1, at 2. Describing the circumstances of six of the women's deaths, the reporter recites that three were shot to death on the street, two were beaten to death, and one hung from a tree.

142. *Suspect in 2 Oakland Killings Probed in 42 San Diego County Murders*, L.A. TIMES, Oct. 13, 1989, at A34. For a time, police involvement with these murders was believed; two of the victims were police informants suspected to have been murdered by police officers. *See* Seth Mydans, *Police Criticized in San Diego Killings*, N.Y. TIMES, September 22, 1990, at A7.

143. *See Serial Killer Convicted of Second Degree Murder*, ROCHESTER TIMES UNION, Dec. 13, 1990 (9 prostitutes of 10 female victims, all strangled); Mills, *5 Killings Stir Talk of New Serial Killer*, ROCHESTER DEMOCRAT, July 12, 1991 (all 5 women prostitutes).

144. *See* Hedges, *supra* note 129, at A10. Regional distinctions fleetingly surface; the women in Alaska were allegedly killed after being taken into wilderness areas, stripped, and hunted with a high-powered rifle.

145. Carolyn Colwell, *4 Arraigned on Sexual Abuse of 3 Girls*, NEWSDAY (Suffolk Home Edition), May 31, 1991, at 33.

146. *Suspected Serial Killer Grips Seattle for 2nd Time in Six Years*, DURHAM MORNING HERALD, May 28, 1990, at B4.

the United States in 1982.[147] If a scant half of those victims were women,[148] and of those one third were prostitutes, we divine a low end figure of 600 women in prostitution murdered by serial killers *alone* in that year. In the same year, 4,922 women were reported murdered, approximately 30% by lovers, boyfriends, and husbands.[149] The latter statistic is often employed to support the inference that women are disproportionately targetted for death by "sexual partners." If that inference holds true for the remaining 70% of victims, stranger rape victims and women in prostitution would constitute a substantial percentage of that remainder. Evaluating the cause of death poses its own complications.[150] By whatever means, women in prostitution are dying quickly. One authority cited in the 1985 Canadian government report on prostitution and pornography concluded that women and girls in prostitution suffer a mortality rate 40 times the national average.[151]

These women are not telling their "prostitution stories." Nor do a great

---

147. CAPUTI, *supra* note 134, at 203 n.4 (citing Robert Lindsey, *Officials Cite Rise in Killers Who Roam U.S. for Victims*, N.Y. TIMES, Jan. 21, 1984, at A1). Caputi cites an increase of serial murders from 644 in 1966 to the 4,118 figure in 1982. *Id.* at 1-2. I have been unable to discover more recent statistics.

148. The estimate of half of victims being women is likely low; the majority of such victims are women. *See* Steven A. Egger, *A Working Definition of Serial Murder and the Reduction of Linkage Blindness*, 12 J. OF POL. SCI. & ADMIN. 348, 351 (1984).

149. *See* U.S. DEP'T OF COMMERCE, STATISTICAL ABSTRACT OF THE UNITED STATES: 1988 160 (108th ed. 1988) (tabulating total number); FEDERAL BUREAU OF INVESTIGATION, U.S. DEP'T OF JUSTICE, CRIME IN THE UNITED STATES: 1986, at 11 (1987) (analyzing relationship of perpetrators to victims).

150. Our conceptions of "cause" remain as politically contingent in this arena as they do in others. On the general problem, see Scales, *supra* note 9. On its complexities in this context, Robin Morgan is illuminating:

> [Lisa McElhaney's] seventeen year old body was found in a plastic bag in Columbus, Ohio in April 1987. Her father was an alcoholic, her mother had tried to get an abortion when pregnant with Lisa, but couldn't afford it. Lisa was raped as a child, became pregnant and miscarried at age fifteen, was thrown out by her family, became addicted to drugs, and worked in pornography and prostitution to support her habit. Each time she ran afoul of the law and was incarcerated in a home for delinquents, social workers noted on her file that she displayed an eagerness for relationships and was "starved for affection." But the system was set up to rehabilitate, not to provide relationships or affection, so Lisa withdrew and "would sit for hours and hours, staring into space." When photographs of her performing sexual acts were discovered by the police, she was subpoenaed to testify in a child pornography case against Larry Miller, the pornographer. Although Miller was a suspect in her murder, police believed the killer was a client of hers, Rob Roy Baker, a thirty-four-year-old truck driver who had been linked to similar attacks on other prostitutes. When police came to question him, Baker shot himself to death in a house filled with pictures of nude women cut from pornographic magazines.

> So I would ask myself, did Lisa die of assault? Which assault? The lack of affordable abortion for her mother? The beating from her john? Did she die of the disease called "family" or the disease called "rehabilitation," of poverty or drugs or pornography, of economic or sexual slavery or a broken body? Or a broken spirit? . . . .

> Perhaps she died of unknown causes.

MORGAN, *supra* note 7, at 316. Commenting on the death of Ingeborg Bachmann by burns sustained in a fire in her apartment, Karen Achberger finds the circumstances, in common with the deaths of other women, to "elude our customary distinctions between accident, murder, and suicide." Karen Achberger, *Introduction, in* INGEBORG BACHMANN, THE THIRTIETH YEAR (Michael Bullock trans., 1987).

151. SPECIAL COMMITTEE ON PORNOGRAPHY AND PROSTITUTION, PORNOGRAPHY AND PROSTITUTION IN CANADA 350 (1985).

many others want to chat. For storytelling, especially of past sexual abuse and humiliation, has a particular sexual significance to women in prostitution. Often a john's "tell me about yourself" gambit operates as a bid for verbal arousal in a prostitution transaction, a dynamic too often mirrored in conversation with self-proclaimed "sympathetic" others.[152] The recollection and articulation of a history in prostitution may bring with it the reliving of profound pain and anguish, experience which may seem better left abandoned.[153] While some stories and acts may "spirit murder" an audience, the relation of prostituted women to storytelling here described suggests that some stories may "spirit murder" their *narrators*.[154] The "acting" theme of the prostitution transaction itself is too closely echoed in the "self-performance" of disclosure; the proximity of persuasion to pleasing an audience, erotically and otherwise, verging on the too familiar dynamics of hooking, this time, of feminists. "Storytelling" also requires the ability to remember, to draw connections, to reflect. Among women in prostitution, researchers report a disproportionately high incidence of psychogenic amnesia, multiple personality disorder, clinical depression, and borderline personality

---

152. Similar dynamics have been depressingly detected by incest survivors seeking help from male therapists. *See* HERMAN, *supra* note 45, at 186-187. Herman reports the account of one survivor:

> When I began trying to find help, it was the beginning of a bitter education in human failings. As I went from therapist to therapist, it became terribly clear that the supposedly dispassionate professionals seemed just as titillated by my story of incestuous involvement with my father as my father had been excited by the actual experience with me.

SANDRA BUTLER, THE CONSPIRACY OF SILENCE: THE TRAUMA OF INCEST 170 (1978) (*cited in* Herman, *supra* note 45, at 186). Torture survivor therapists also grapple with the implications of "talking therapists" for successful recovery, as the conduct of the therapy so closely resembles the structure of inquisition and confession of the torture itself. *See* Shaun R. Whittaker, *Counseling Torture Victims,* COUNSELLING PSYCHOLOGIST 272, 276 (Apr. 1988). The relationship of battery survivor to therapist has been similarly critiqued. *See* Mary Ann Douglas, *The Battered Woman Syndrome, in* DOMESTIC VIOLENCE ON TRIAL *supra* note 78, at 39, 52 ("The professional, like the batterer, believes s/he knows what is best for the battered woman and attempts to control her behavior to conform with the mold in order not to feel like a failure.").

I am attentive to these difficulties in my own life. I am excruciatingly aware of the multitude of occasions when, in some act of self-disclosure of instances of abuse, I can see my interlocutor eroticize the "story," or begin to contemplate what it means that I have been sexually hurt in the past. Too often, it seems, the inferred meaning is that I can be sexually hurt *again* (perhaps by him?).

153. Organizers and prostitute support workers have emphasized to me the deep reluctance of women with histories in prostitution to relate their experience in prostitution in public, narration which often brings with it terrible psychic costs. Therapists who work with other victims of torture also caution against unnecessary narrative replication of the experience, suggesting less mimetic methods of communication. *See* Marianne Kastrup, et al., *Coping With the Exposure to Torture,* CONTEMP. FAM. THERAPY, 280, 284 (Winter 1988); Whittaker, *supra* note 152, at 272, 276. Some therapists promote one-time tape recording of testimony from the survivor to diminish the need for retelling and to channel the survivor's experience toward restoration of self-esteem through storytelling and social action. *See* Whittaker, *supra* note 152, at 276-277; Ana Julia Cienfuegos & Christina Monelli, *The Testimony of Political Repression as a Therapeutic Instrument,* 53 AMER. J. OF ORTHO-PSYCHIATRY. For an excellent selection of essays on the recovery process in torture victims, see generally PSYCHOLOGY AND TORTURE (Peter Suedfeld ed., 1985).

154. The term is Patricia Williams's. *See* Williams, *Spirit-Murdering the Messenger: The Discourse of Finger-Pointing as the Law's Response to Racism,* 42 U. MIAMI L. REV. 127, 151 (1987). In her conception, "spirit-murder" is the "disregard for others whose lives qualitatively depend on our regard," this is characteristic of racism (and, as Williams notes, of prostitution). *Id.* at 151. As I state in the text, I would extend her description of the damage done to targets of racist speech to those who are compelled to describe their injuries to potential victimizers.

disorder inhibiting those powers.[155] Care-givers commonly trace the origin of such disintegration of the self to an attempted defense against shattering and repetitive trauma, entailing the collapse of memory and profound fragmentation of linguistic cognition.[156] As Andrea Dworkin puts the "rhetorical" problem:

> The formal writing problem, frankly, is that the bait can't write the story . . . . I barely know any words for what happened to me yesterday, which doesn't make tomorrow some-thing I can conceive of in my own mind; I mean words I say to myself in my own head; not social words you use to explain to someone else. I barely know anything and if I deviate I am lost; I have to be literal, if I can remember, which mostly I cannot.[157]

The matter of one's entitlement to speak "as a prostitute" is also complex. If the theme of "commonality" is that to be pursued in feminist consciousness-raising, it is not one readily seized by women in prostitution, as a "prostitute" among "prostitutes." The label is not a self-identification readily or transparently taken as one's own; more frequently, it is copped as a pose, an expediency, or just a condition of being a woman. This may seem an odd equivocation, as the definitiveness of the term "prostitute," and of what counts as "prostitution," would seem to dispatch any uncertainty in a hurry. Indeed, the fixity of the boundary can urge its own imperatives. A woman who had for a period of time performed in pornographic films and as a stripper reports: "Within a month, I did my first job as a whore . . . . It was quicker, it was more money, and it was definite. I felt like: Okay, now, I am a whore and if

---

155. Colin A. Ross et al., *Dissociation and Abuse Among Multiple-Personality Patients, Prostitutes and Exotic Dancers*, 41 HOSP. & COMM. PSYCHIATRY. 328 (1990) (significant incidence of psychogenic amnesia, multiple personality disorder, clinical depression and borderline personality disorder among prostituted women and "dancers." Nineteen percent of sample of persons affected by multiple personality disorder had been prostituted); Colin A. Ross et al., *Multiple Personality Disorder: An Analysis of 236 Cases*, 34 CAN. J. OF PSYCHIATRY 413 (1989); Dirk De Schampheleire, *MMPI Characteristics of Professional Prostitutes: A Cross-Cultural Replication*, 54 J. OF PERS. ASSESS. 343 (1990) (serious mental health problems perceived among subjects).

156. *See* James A. Chu & Diana L. Dill, *Dissociative Symptoms in Relation to Childhood Physical and Sexual Abuse*, 147 AMER. J. OF PSYCHIATRY 887 (1990); Frank Putnam, et al., *The Clinical Phenomenology of Multiple Personality Disorder: Review of 100 Recent Cases*, 47 J. CLIN. PSYCHIATRY 285 (1986). *See generally* JUDITH LEWIS HERMAN, TRAUMA AND RECOVERY (1992).

157. DWORKIN, MERCY, *supra* note 6, at 229, 231. Primo Levi counts among the silences at the core of our knowledge of the conditions of torture in the Nazi concentration camps the accounts of the most deeply victimized. "At a distance of years one can today definitely affirm that the history of the Lagers has been written almost exclusively by those who, like myself, never fathomed them to the bottom. Those who did so did not return, or their capacity for observation was paralyzed by suffering and incomprehension." PRIMO LEVI, THE DROWNED AND THE SAVED 17 (1986).

Torture investigators have noted the same inevitable partiality of personal accounts in developing a descriptively adequate understanding of the effects of torture on human beings. Persons capable of such articulation, known in the literature as "the adapted afflicted," have already accomplished an unusual degree of recovery. "These accounts often suggest that individuals emerge as better people, having experienced personal growth, with firm identities and life goals," profoundly skewing comprehension of the more typical consequences. Engdahl & Eberly, *The Effects of Torture and Other Maltreatment: Implications for Psychology*, in PSYCHOLOGY AND TORTURE, *supra* note 153, at 31, 38.

anyone calls me that they are right."[158] Or the same certainty can be turned around defensively: one is not a "real prostitute" if the men don't seem like strangers, or the financial arrangement is indefinite, or the woman doesn't care for the sex.

> I never called myself a prostitute; I never called myself a porno actress either. I was a filmmaker. I didn't work the streets, I didn't work every day, my customers were repeats, referrals. I called them my friends . . . it was an easy lie. They didn't pay me, I would tell myself; they helped me out with my rent and bills, and they would land me film jobs. And I liked them; you're never a prostitute when you like them. Besides, I was a lesbian, and I was experimenting, and it was safe. . . . I could get out or stop anytime I wanted . . . . I was on top.[159]

> I wouldn't have thought of it as prostitution at the time. This was doing casual jobs in bars with a friend of mine, an airline pilot, picking up men in the bars. These guys would give me money to go out with them and sleep with them, but it was still a game to me and I didn't realize I was working. I didn't identify as a prostitute because I didn't say 'look, you've got to pay such and such an amount and I'll sleep with you'; they used to just take me out, give me dinner, and then I would sleep with them.[160]

Or as one woman, addicted to heroin, states: "Yeah, I've turned tricks, but I don't consider myself a prostitute. I always got pretty embarrassed about it. I'd tell the guy, 'Hey man, I'm not really into this, but I really do need the money.'"[161] Complying to the sex may be, for the woman, only a last ditch

---

158. Eva Rosta, *Comment in* A VINDICATION OF THE RIGHTS OF WHORES, *supra* note 117, at 144, 145.

159. Sharon Kaiser, *Coming Out of Denial, in* SEX WORK, *supra* note 57, at 104, 105. Another woman who had worked as a topless dancer writes of her ambivalence about her entitlement to submit a piece for publication in an anthology of writings by women in the "sex industry," doubting her "credentials:"

> Maybe my experiences weren't really "sex industry." I couldn't waste people's time with my writing because what I had done was too "tame" to be legitimate. And anyway, my experience didn't really count because I was a college student; I wasn't tied to it; I was really above it all, not part of it.

Judy Helfand, *Silence Again, in* SEX WORK, *supra* note 57, at 99.

160. Roberta Perkins & Garry Bennett, *Bonnie: International Prostitute, in* BEING A PROSTITUTE: PROSTITUTE WOMEN AND PROSTITUTE MEN 133, 134 (1985). At seventeen, Bonnie and another woman were taken from New Zealand to the Phillipines, then to Hong Kong and other locales to practice prostitution. At the time of the interview, she was prostituting in Australia, addicted to drugs, with no resources and about to lose custody of her son. *Id.*

161. Marsha Rosenbaum, *Work and the Addicted Prostitute, in* JUDGE, LAWYER, VICTIM, THIEF, *supra* note 125, at 131, 148. Women and girls who are addicted to cocaine sometimes refer to the exchanges

method of getting money, or only one of many strategies.[162] Or the distinction between prostitution and any other "work" or condition of proximity to men may seem, at least in prospect, wholly artificial and illusory. One isn't a "prostitute" if everyone else is, too. "When I was nineteen years old I made what seemed like a conscious decision to become a prostitute. Having experienced sexual harassment on the job, in the streets, and in virtually every area of life, it was not a particularly fantastic leap to take."[163] "No trick ever broke my ribs like my husband did."[164] This ordeal of self-definition, though, is also avoidable by anticipatory defense: "I had considered myself a whore from the time I had become sexually active, even before I became sexually active. From that time on, I had thought of myself as a whore, and it was like, well, I'm gonna make money at it."[165]

In our political critiques, we have less acknowledged these equivocations than reified them, within an array of contending and mutually exclusive advocacy positions. The tones of doubt, bravado, defensiveness, inevitability these women express about "being prostitutes" are dispersed and frozen politically in the competing terms of a political debate over what constitutes "prostitution" and what does not. Neither the fundamental design of this debate, nor its frozen quality has been "chosen" by its participants. For there is dignity in this discussion, but also an edge of desperation. As fractious as these debates have proven, uniting the visions of these advocates is a shared assumption that the particular case of prostitution can be assimilated into the general case of "women's oppression" as feminism has heretofore elaborated that condition. Each coalition of advocates has seized a different version of our "other woman" representations, and claims it as the salient description of *prostitution* from women's perspective. If "other women" seek to split from prostitution by disidentifying from one element of it, prostitute advocates have sought to identify *as* "other women" by identifying *with* one of the "not a prostitute" stories. Prostitutes thereby can "become" other women; prostitution is but one variant of a condition shared in common with those others. If other women aren't prostitutes, neither are prostitutes. On *all* of the contending

---

of sex for drugs as a "tossup," or as "strawberrying," deflecting the terms "prostitution" or "whoring" to define their behavior.

162. *See* Miller, *supra* note 114, at 6, 70-71 (describing repertoire of activities women engage in for money of which prostitution was but one). As one woman told me: "I didn't think I would ever have to actually fuck them. I thought I could just rob them."

163. Donna Marie Niles, *Confessions of a Priestesstute, in* SEX WORK, *supra* note 57, at 148. Niles ultimately left prostitution, stating that ". . . I simply no longer could justify working in an industry that profited from the sexual objectification of women." *Id.* at 149.

164. Phyllis Luman Metal, *One for Ripley's, in* SEX WORK, *supra* note 57, at 119, 120.

165. Priscilla Alexander, *Interview with Nell, in* SEX WORK, *supra* note 57, at 53, 55. For a discussion of the process of women's self-identification as "prostitutes," see Jennifer James & Jane Meyerding, *Early Sexual Experience and Prostitution,* 134 AMER. J. PSYCHOL. 1381 (1977) ("A woman who views herself as sexually debased or whose sexuality is more than normally objectified may see prostitution as a "natural"—or as the only—alternative.). *See also* Clifton D. Bryant & C. Eddie Palmer, *Massage Parlors and "Hand Whores:" Some Sociological Observations,* 11 J. OF SEX RES. 227, 241 (1975) (disidentification of massage parlor workers from label as "prostitutes").

perspectives, prostitution *is* "like everything else." The dispute turns on what the "else" is characterized to be. The dignity abides in the simple claim that no woman is a "prostitute," no woman is deserving of the violence and contempt women in prostitution routinely suffer. The desperation comes in the cost of "proving" it. In this public discussion, that effort, already a brutal demand, seems to require that prostitutes' lives be *justified*, rather than empathetically understood.

In this compelled endeavor of justification, prostitute advocates have been assisted both by the contributions and the theoretical disputes of liberal feminism, socialist feminism, and radical feminism. In theoretical emphasis and strategic design, these tendencies in feminism identify discrete political "locales" as fundamental to women's oppression. Liberal feminism, with its stress on the conditions of women's individual consent, has had principal influence in rape law reform, foundationally in the sex-with-strangers variety. Radical feminism, with its stress on the conditions of women's coercion in "private" intimacy with men, has had principal influence in domestic violence intervention. Socialist feminism, with its stress on women's economic exploitation in the family and in the workplace, has had principal influence in altering monetary conditions of women's employment. Aside from some turf skirmishes (most vituperatively fought among academics), these tendencies co-exist relatively calmly, perhaps because the "sphere of influence" attended to by each conforms with what is viewed as a "natural" division of the street, from the home, and from the workplace, in women's lives.

This same tripartite division habilitates, if less serenely, the splits among prostitution advocates, providing political precedent for the contention by each that prostitutes are "other women," after all. In the liberal advocates' view, prostitution "is" non-monogamous, consensual sex, again taking up the selectiveness component as fundamental. In the socialist view, prostitution is work, attending to the matter of money. In the radical feminist view, the woman's circumstances of intimate coercion occupies the essential territory. Having distilled the crucial problem, we each notice that other women share it. Other women, too, are stigmatized for apparent sexual independence and nonconformity. Other women, too, are economically exploited, reviled for making money at all, the value of their labor cheapened if they do. Other women, too, are "invisibly" sexually coerced, the realities of lifelong sexual abuse masked and perpetuated under an erotic regime which rewards the compliance of the hopeless and thrives in the possibilities which proliferate when no questions are asked.

Each of these positions, in turn, is also argued from the representational framework commonly advanced by their "other woman" counterparts. Liberal advocates favor the "shielded" version, limiting their "story" of prostitution to the immediate sexual component of the transaction, while arguing to the irrelevance of any other feature of the exchange (often including the money), and of any other surrounding conditions of a woman's life. Socialist feminist advocates favor the categorical divide between "sex" and "work," familiar from sexual harassment campaigns, holding prostitution unambiguously to fall in the productive realm of "work." Radical feminist advocates urge an expanded version of the domestic violence story, stressing the effect of serial, sometimes life-long, suffering of sexual abuse in prostitutes' lives as the relevant interpretive context. Having set the terms, however divergent, on the correspondence of the oppression of women in prostitution with that suffered by "other women," the (feminist) debate on prostitution thus seeks to merge in theme and strategic focus with those familiar from other feminist campaigns without rupture.

The most publicly visible of these positions is that advanced by prostitutes' rights organizations, who promote political demands for affirmative legal and social rights for women to practice prostitution.[166] These advocates advance this view under principles familiar from mainstream liberal feminism: the fostering of women's individual autonomy and sexual self-expression. In this normative emphasis, these campaigns follow themes familiar in mainstream feminist anti-rape work. The manifesto of the International Committee on Prostitutes' Rights, for example, states that it *"affirms the right of all women to determine their own sexual behavior, including commercial exchange, without stigmatization or punishment."*[167] A specific political parallel between the legal and social suppression of women's sexuality generally and the criminalization and loathing of prostitutes is explicitly drawn in support of this position. Each case constitutes a practice of female sexual nonconformity in a culture which punishes any female sexual behavior uncontained by legal monogamy or released from functions (re)productively beneficial to men.[168]

The strong version of this argument asserts that prostitution is a sexually progressive practice for women, yielding women both useful rewards in return for the sex we otherwise forfeit for no discernible benefit, and, for some women, a context for the felt exercise of control and power in sexual transactions. As Margo St. James, founder of COYOTE, states the points, "In private, the whore has power. She is in charge, setting the terms for the sexual

---

166. Those organizations include Call Off Your Old Tired Ethics (COYOTE), founded in 1973 by Margo St. James, the National Task Force on Prostitution (NTFP), and the International Committee for Prostitute's Rights (ICPR). *See* A VINDICATION OF THE RIGHTS OF WHORES, *supra* note 116, at 33-51 (on the organization of the ICPR); *COYOTE/National Task Force on Prostitution, in* SEX WORK, *supra* note 57, at 290 (organizing and policy statement of COYOTE); *id.* at 305 (charter of ICPR and statements from conferences).

167. *International Committee for Prostitutes' Rights World Chapter and World Whore's Congress Statements, in* SEX WORK, *supra* note 57, at 305, 310.

For negative assessments of the representative legitimacy of prostitutes' rights organizations, see Kathleen Barry, *The Opening Paper: International Politics of Female Sexual Slavery, in* INTERNATIONAL FEMINISM, *supra* note 33, at 21, 24-25.

168. *See, e.g.*, Joan Nestle, *Lesbians and Prostitutes: A Historical Sisterhood, in* SEX WORK, *supra* note 57, at 231. For a strong objection to this political correlation authored by a lesbian with a history in prostitution, see Toby Summer, *Women, Lesbians and Prostitution: A Workingclass Dyke Speaks Out Against Buying Women for Sex*, LESBIAN ETHICS 33 (Summer 1987).

exchange and the financial exchange."[169] Priscilla Alexander of the NTFP reports, too, that many women in prostitution assert that "the first time they felt powerful was the first time they turned a trick."[170] Prostitution, in this view, offers an alternative to the straitjacket of female sexual "respectability" and an opportunity for women and girls to experience the self-affirmation of outlaw rebellion and the fast thrill of feeling desired enough to part a man from what he likely covets most: his money.[171] The weaker version, less committed to wholesale endorsement of prostitution as a practice of sexual freedom for women, urges the decriminalization and social acceptance of prostitution consistent with the feminist program of state deregulation of women's sexual behavior.[172] If no means no, yes should mean yes under whatever conditions a woman chooses. Voluntariness may be inferred from ordinary indicia of age and capacity, confirmed in the receipt of cash.

These claims are legally articulated in the discourse of privacy doctrine. This argument asserts that the "sex" of prostitution differs in quality not at all from adult, heterosexual sex ordinarily deemed within the realm of the private. This premise profits from arguments long advanced in explanation of the "inevitability" of prostitution: a view of the practice as meeting natural, and urgent, "human" requirements for sex.[173] For example, philosopher Lars Ericsson argues that prostitution is a necessary feature of human life, as "sexual urges" are natural and therefore will be satisfied by whatever means necessary. He draws the analogy of sex to food, then, among food sources, of prostitution to restaurants, and concludes that bought meals are not always

---

169. Margo St. James, *The Reclamation of Whores*, in GOOD GIRLS/BAD GIRLS, *supra* note 40, at 82. *See also* M. Anne Jennings, *The Victim as Criminal: A Consideration of California's Prostitution Laws*, 64 CAL. L. REV. 1235, 1253 (1976) ("[Prostitution] may also be viewed as a choice by the prostitute to exercise control over her own sexuality, giving her greater economic and psychological independence than may otherwise be available.").

170. Priscilla Alexander, *Introduction*, in SEX WORK, *supra* note 57, at 15.

171. *See, e.g.*, Peggy Miller, *From the Floor*, in GOOD GIRLS/BAD GIRLS, *supra* note 40, at 48-49. Women who do not identify as prostitutes express similar motives for engaging in "risky" sexual behavior. One woman who regularly had sex with members of a fraternity known for gang raping women explains:

> I thought I could pick and choose whatever man I was going to sleep with and this gave me a feeling of power to be able to say to some guy, "No, I don't want to sleep with you," or "Yes, I do." . . . I also liked to court danger. Being warned against going to [the fraternity] was the incentive to make me go. There was a certain thrill in going someplace that I knew had a bad reputation, where it was hard to say what was going to happen next. I also liked going someplace where my name was known, where I would be recognized when I walked into the room—even if they were kind of jerks.

Comments by "Amy," in PEGGY REEVES SANDAY, FRATERNITY GANG RAPE: SEX, BROTHERHOOD AND PRIVILEGE ON CAMPUS, 100-01 (1990). Amy was later gang raped by the fraternity members. *Id.* at 98-100.

172. For another summary of these arguments, see Freeman, *supra* note 105, at 91 (prostitutes' rights groups contend that "prostitution enhances freedom . . . [and] enables [autonomy] to flourish").

173. The inevitability of prostitution is taken as a given in most work in the area, even that urging reform of the practice. *See, e.g.*, ARLENE CARMEN & HOWARD MOODY, WORKING WOMEN: THE SUBTERRANEAN WORLD OF STREET PROSTITUTION 195 (1985) ("It should be clear that in none of the alternatives that we look at, including the status quo, is it possible to abolish prostitution."); Jennings, *supra* note 169, at 1259 ("[B]ecause some amount of prostitution is likely to continue for the forseeable future, legislative reform should be aimed not at its abolition, but at minimizing the undesirable aspects of prostitution, particularly overt public solicitation.").

the worst.[174] David Richards continues the gourmet theme on a moral ground, arguing that affirmation of an array of "eating styles" is consistent with respect for individual autonomy and that "to compel by law any one style of eating would evince contempt for the dignity of individual self-determination." For Richards it then follows that "[l]egal enforcement of a particular sexual ideal fails equally to accord respect for individual autonomy."[175]

These justifications for the "naturalness" of prostitution are further aided by often-expressed perplexities over how to distinguish prostitution from other, socially conforming sexual transactions. Confusions articulated by men, including legislators, over the appropriate boundary to be drawn between prostitution and ordinary "courting" behavior reflect this definitional difficulty. For example, during public hearings on proposed revisions to the New York prostitution statute, language defining prostitution as sex exchanged "for a fee or for other compensation" was successfully challenged as impossibly broad. One witness persuaded the hearing commission that the term "or compensation" should be deleted, as "the whole concept of the male-female relationship in our culture . . . is based on compensation."[176] I heard similar uncertainties expressed while testifying before the Florida legislature in support of a bill affording civil remedies for women induced into prostitution.[177] Among other practices defined in the statute to constitute "inducement" to prostitution is a "promise of marriage," designed principally to reach "mail order bride" operations which motivate women and girls to enter the United States and which then turn them out to prostitution. Several legislators indicated concern that *all* marriage could be understood as prostitution, and therefore all husbands plausible defendants. In a related vein, some legislators were anxious to know if the statutory definition of prostitution in Florida requires cash payment, so as to distinguish the practice from the giving of gifts, dinners, and so forth, followed by sex. The legislators were not joking; they seemed deeply disturbed and anxious. I was, too, if for different reasons.

These men are hardly isolated in these views. Women often voice them, angrily. Men complain that the price of ordinary sex comes too high and without adequate assurance of performance. When sex researcher Shere Hite asked, "Have you ever had sex with a prostitute? How did you feel about paying for sex?," many of her male respondents, including men who answered

---

174. Lars Ericsson, *Charges Against Prostitution: An Attempt at a Philosophical Assessment*, 90 ETHICS 335, 341 (1980). For feminist responses to Ericsson, see Carole Pateman, *Defending Prostitution: Charges Against Ericsson*, 93 ETHICS 561 (1983); Laurie Shrage, *Should Feminists Oppose Prostitution?*, 99 ETHICS 347 (1989). *See also* CAROLE PATEMAN, THE SEXUAL CONTRACT 189-218 (1988) (prostitution is most adequately conceived as an institution which enables all men to affirm themselves as masters).

175. David A. J. Richards, *Commercial Sex and the Rights of the Person: A Moral Argument for the Decriminalization of Prostitution*, 127 U. PA. L. REV. 1195, 1239 (1979).

176. Pamela A. Roby, *Politics and Criminal Law: Revision of the New York State Penal Law on Prostitution*, 17 SOC. PROBS. 83, 91 (1969) (quoting testimony of Dr. Biegel).

177. *See* FLA. STAT. ANN. § 796.09 (West 1991 Supp.).

"no" to the first question, replied, "you always pay anyway."[178] Thus:

> I have had sex with a prostitute. I have no feeling about paying
> for sex. After all, marriage is paying for sex by contract.
> You pay for it one way or another—actually its cheaper with
> a whore! Also she's a pro, doesn't play coy games, and no
> pretenses.

> I don't like paying for sex, but really what's the difference if
> a guy pays twenty-five or thirty dollars on a date, then 'maybe'
> has intercourse, or just picks up a prostitute off the street and
> pays her the same? Actually a person is money ahead with a
> whore.[179]

Each of these arguments, whether to natural inevitability or to social convention, bolster the affirmative case in support of prostitution offered by liberal prostitution advocates: it's all just "sex," no more and no less, after all.

The case for decriminalization further proceeds by way of critique of the conventional justifications for state sanctions against prostitution. Those justifications include the control of venereal disease; the inhibition of other crimes related to prostitution, including theft, assault, and drug use; the protection of girls and women in prostitution; and the suppression of "public offense" caused by prostitution, taking either the form of neighborhood disruption or moral outrage. Analysis of those justifications is largely confined to challenging the empirical assumptions about prostitutes underlying them. Where those assumptions are factually corroborated, the causal connection between those conditions and the practice of prostitution itself is the site of contest. The empirical and causal "control group" explicitly or implicitly invoked in structuring these inquiries is "normal women." The empirical question becomes whether social dangers said to be posed by prostitutes are not similarly posed for or by "normal women." The causal question becomes whether it is prostitution or "womanhood" that brings them into being. Needless to say, with a control group like that, prostitution begins to look rather tame as a social problem, as criminalizing "womanhood" appears to be an unthinkable alternative. In structure, this strategy is also similar to our anti-rape campaigns. Like the representational minimalism pursued via rape shield legislation, these analyses seek to confine the significance of prostitution to the "four corners" of the transaction, slicing away any other conditions commonly

---

178. SHERE HITE, THE HITE REPORT ON MALE SEXUALITY 293-94 (1981). Hite found the frequency of this response "terrifying."
    179. *Id.*

experienced by women in the practice as accidental to "prostitution itself."
The role of prostitution in the spread of venereal diseases, for example,
is empirically tested by amassing data on the incidence of venereal diseases
among prostitutes. This data typically does not support the inference that
prostitution contributes substantially to the spread of those diseases in the
"general population."[180] Women in prostitution, thus, are no more or less
dangerous than "other women" for sex. The link between prostitution and the
commission of other crimes is similarly found overstated as a matter of
fact,[181] or causally distinguished from prostitution in origin. The causal
argument is that most vigorously pursued in contemporary advocacy, as the
statistics on the incidence of violence against prostitutes continues to mount.
The most detailed of those investigations is Mimi Silbert's analysis of
victimization rates among 200 street prostitutes in San Francisco. Silbert
summarizes her findings on victimization rates by johns:

> Of the subjects, 78% reported being victimized by forced
> perversion an average of 16.6 times each woman. Also, 70%
> were victimized by customer rape or clients similarly going
> beyond the prostitution contract, an average of 31.3 times . .
> . . Of the subjects, 41% were victimized in some other way,
> an average of 2.6 times (e.g., forced into sex for no pay with
> police, being beaten by police, being beaten by other
> prostitutes). Additionally, 65% of the prostitutes were
> physically abused and beaten by customers, an average of 4.3
> times . . . . More than three-fourths of the victims stated there
> was nothing they could do about customer abuse; only 1%
> mentioned reporting to the police.[182]

These data are consistent with other studies finding high sexual and physical
victimization rates among women engaged in prostitution in its various milieus,
inflicted by pimps, other women, and strangers other than johns.[183] The

---

180. *See, e.g.*, Priscilla Alexander, *Prostitutes Are Being Scapegoated for Heterosexual AIDS, in* SEX
WORK, *supra* note 57, at 248-263; Scibelli, *supra* note 105, at 129-131 (assembling data on incidence of
AIDS, syphilis, and gonorrhea in prostitutes); Barbara Milman, *New Rules for the Oldest Profession: Should
We Change Our Prostitution Laws?*, 3 HARV. WOMEN'S L.J. 1, 28-29 (1980); Jennings, *supra* note 169,
at 1242, 1243; Therese M. Wandling, *Decriminalization of Prostitution: The Limits of the Criminal Law*,
55 OR. L. REV. 553, 556 (1976).
181. *See, e.g.*, Charles Rosenbleet & Barbara J. Pariente, *The Prostitution of the Criminal Law*, 11
AM. CRIM. L. REV. 373, 418-19 (1973); Wandling, *supra* note 180, at 557; Jennings, *supra* note 169,
at 1244.
182. Mimi H. Silbert & Ayala M. Pines, *Occupational Hazards of Street Prostitutes*, 8 CRIM. JUST.
& BEHAV. 395, 397 (1981).
183. *See supra* notes 125-151 and accompanying text (on murder); Enablers, Juvenile Prostitution in
Minnesota: The Report of a Research Project 70, 75 (1978) [hereinafter Enablers] (more than half of girls
beaten by pimps; 20% report constant or regular beatings); (40% beaten by johns; 28% three or more
times); MILLER, *supra* note 114, at 138; PERKINS & BENNETT, *supra* note 160, at 238-41, 295-96 (33.99%
of women raped while engaging in prostitution); A VINDICATION OF THE RIGHTS OF WHORES, *supra* note

means of causal finesse of these numbers is illustrated by Barbara Milman's comments on the victimization of women in prostitution by pimps: "The prostitute who is regularly beaten by her pimp is, like a battered wife, certainly the victim of a violent crime. But is she a victim of prostitution?"[184]

The incidence of drug dependency among women in prostitution, as well as the massive incidence of childhood incest, sexual use and physical battery in the life histories of women in prostitution is similarly dispatched as accidental to the woman's situation as a prostitute. Like the issue of violence against prostitutes, the problem of drug use and addiction[185] is again scuttled on the business of cause.[186] The matter of childhood sexual abuse, especially incest, is less handily suppressed. The prevalence statistics suggest very high rates of incestuous sexual abuse, physical harm, and emotional brutalization in prostituted women's childhood histories.[187] Running away from home to escape these circumstances is a common precondition for entry into prostitution, a factor noted in earlier literature but dismissed with Freudian alacrity. One study published in 1969 reported:

> In a large proportion of cases, there is considerable indication that the girl runs away from home to ward off *the unconscious threat of an incestuous relation* with her father, the fear of the resultant dissolution of the family, and the concurrent depression.[188]

112, at 161-68 (routine violence reported by ICPR conference attendants); WEISBERG, *supra* note 113, at 108-110 (with few exceptions, girls reported that any pimp would beat a prostitute given "provocation" (citing DOROTHY H. BRACEY, BABY-PROS: PRELIMINARY PROFILES OF JUVENILE PROSTITUTES 37 (1979)); more than half of girls and women beaten regularly or constantly by pimps (citing MIMI SILBERT, SEXUAL ASSAULT OF PROSTITUTES: PHASE ONE 60 (1980)); rape by "non-customers" common and extremely violent (citing SILBERT, *id.* at 62)).

184. Milman, *supra* note 180, at 33.

185. For incidence rates of drug use and addiction, see, Mimi H. Silbert et al., *Substance Abuse and Prostitution*, 14 J. PSYCHOACTIVE DRUGS, 193 (1982); WEISBERG, *supra* note 113, at 99-100; PERKINS & BENNETT, *supra* note 160, at 241-42 (estimating 70-75% of women drug users). I am increasingly troubled generally by the emphasis placed on drug addiction as an index of trauma incurred by women and girls in prostitution. In no other arena is drug addiction considered a dispositive indication of whether trauma has been inflicted on a woman. Indicia of rape trauma syndrome, for example, do not suggest that a woman is injured only if she becomes an inveterate junkie as a consequence of sexual assault.

186. *See* Milman, *supra* note 180, at 25 ("[T]he literature suggests that drug addiction and prostitution are probably not causally related to each other."); Scibelli, *supra* note 105, at 128; MILLER, *supra* note 114, at 108 (few women in her study "describe substance abuse as the thing that caused them to be involved in deviant street networks").

187. For rates of incest, *see* Enablers, *supra* note 183, at 22-23 (31% of respondents reported incestuous abuse); WEISBERG, *supra* note 113, at 91-92 (66% of women sexually abused by father or father figures, including stepfathers, foster fathers, or mother's common law husband)(citing MIMI SILBERT, SEXUAL ASSAULT OF PROSTITUTES: PHASE ONE 85 (1980)). For sexual abuse by others, see James & Meyerding, *supra* note 165, at 38 (65% of respondents had been raped; 85% of those occurred when victim was under 15); Mimi Silbert & Ayala Pines, *Entrance Into Prostitution*, 13 YOUTH & SOC'Y 471, 479 (1982) (60-70% of women in prostitution sexually abused as children). For other physical and emotional abuse, see Silbert & Pines, *id.*, at 479 (45% of girls beaten regularly when growing up; 70% emotionally abused); Enablers, *supra* note 183, at 22 (66% beaten by family member).

188. Ames Roby, *The Runaway Girl*, in FAMILY DYNAMICS AND FEMALE SEXUAL DELINQUENCY 127, (Otto Pollack & Alfred S. Friedman eds., 1969) (emphasis added). It is now well known that Freud

Even in contemporary research, these data seem most relevant to investigators of juvenile prostitution. Eleanor Miller's otherwise detailed and astute interviews with a sample of Milwaukee "street women," excluded questions on the topic of incest until she began to note the high rates of unsolicited disclosure of incestuous sexual abuse from her subjects.[189] Even at that juncture, she decided only to inquire on the subject when the context seemed to warrant further interest in the matter, while asserting that the issue requires further study.[190] The empirical assumption appears to be that the effects or relevance of childhood abuse to adult prostituted women's experience wither away upon attainment of the age of majority.

The marginalization of issues of drug abuse and childhood abuse is aided by a further empirical split between juvenile and adult prostitutes and between drug-addicted and chemically clean women and girls in the practice of prostitution. In the literature, "juvenile prostitutes" and "addicted prostitutes" are treated as distinct populations, "special cases" within the cohort of ordinary prostitutes. These distinctions are maintained despite the fact that the median age for entry into prostitution is 14,[191] and, as noted above, regular use of drugs is widespread among women and girls used in the practice.[192] This adjectival sleight of hand is justified by the inference of involuntariness raised by youth and drug dependency,[193] and of the presumed greater recklessness among addicted women in conducting themselves.[194] The norm of an adult, "professional," and voluntary cadre of prostitutes may remain undisturbed by the existence of these discordant actors.

In sum, insofar as women in prostitution share the plight of all women, by rape, battery, sexual torture, self-destruction, humiliation and contempt,

---

knowingly suppressed the incidence of incestuous sexual abuse of girls in favor of an explanation of female "hysteria" generated by incest fantasies. See FLORENCE RUSH, THE BEST KEPT SECRET: SEXUAL ABUSE OF CHILDREN (1980); JEFFREY M. MASSON, THE ASSAULT ON TRUTH: FREUD'S SUPPRESSION OF THE SEDUCTION THEORY (1984).

189. MILLER, supra note 114, at 114-15.

190. Id.

191. See WEISBERG, supra note 113, at 94 (summarizing the available data). As Weisberg notes, Mimi Silbert's study found a median age of entry of 13. Id. at 137, n.130. The average age of entry seems to be dropping in recent years. Prostitute advocates link this decline to the greater sexualization of children culturally, as well as an increased demand for virgins or young girls thought less likely by johns to carry the AIDS virus.

192. See supra notes 185-186, and accompanying text.

193. On the social construction of juvenile prostitution as a social problem distinguishable from prostitution generally, see WEISBERG, supra note 113, at 1-17. Of addicted prostitutes, Marsha Rosenbaum observes: "[F]or the addicted prostitute [in contrast to others], there is no way out. She must utilize this form of work because of the desperation of her heroin habit." Rosenbaum, supra note 161, at 142.

194. See Milman, supra note 180, at 27 ("[T]here is a definite group of prostitute-addicts...[who] are often less professional, may take more risks, and may be arrested more often than other prostitutes."); MILLER, supra note 114, at 108-14 (analyzing marginal status of addicted women within street networks facilitating prostitution); Marsha Rosenbaum, Women Addicts' Experience of the Heroin World, URBAN LIFE 65 (Apr. 1981). I suspect the "addicted prostitute" will be the subject of increased attention with the rise of greater research interest in heterosexual AIDS transmission. Some research work is already in print on the rate of HIV exposure among women in prostitution. See S.E. Barton et al., HTLV-III Antibody in Prostitutes, 2 LANCET 1424 (1985); G. Papaevangelou et al., LAV/HTLV-III Infection in Female Prostitutes, 2 LANCET 1018 (1985).

prostitution is effaced as a significant factor in bringing about that treatment or in adding to it. As a story of origin, "normal womanhood" precedes prostitution; the significance of a woman's status as "prostitute" eroded insofar as her treatment conforms with treatment of "normal women."[195] Some advocates take this argument one step further: if prostitution creates particular risks for women, it is because prostitutes are identified *as* "other women" by men. The proper focus is thus to recognize the status of "other women" as the problem of prostitution. Marie Arrington explains:

> One of the issues that we hear constantly at our speaking engagements with the public is: "What are the effects of prostitution and pornography on society's perception of women?" One more time it is turned around. We think the real question is, "What effect does society's perception of women have on prostitution and pornography?" We think that is the *real* issue because the perception is there before the imagery of the trade comes into being.[196]

There are many who exploit, manipulate, and profit from the views expressed here. Pimps, johns, and pornographers are all enthusiastic promoters, as well as the husbands and boyfriends of "other women" emboldened by the promise that there is no great difference between the "prostitute" he imagines and the woman he lives with. For women in prostitution, there is another kind of promise held out by this rhetoric: perhaps the acknowledgement, however fleeting, that she *is* a person, that she may *have* a sexuality, and that she does not have to justify herself anymore, to anyone. The rhetoric of the pro-prostitution position promises to give her what the prostitution takes away, by validating the prostitution. This is not consciousness-raising. This is the exploitation of consciousness.

For what women and girls are enacting in prostitution is not their "self-determining sexuality," but paid sexual compliance to the demands of a consumer. In this "public" dimension, prostitution is reconceptualized by socialist feminist advocates as a form of work rather than libidinal

---

195. *See also* Richards, *supra* note 175, at 1268-69:
   Many accounts forcefully show how difficult and costly an occupation [prostitution] can be, but many recent accounts of women's traditional role show how difficult and costly that life can be as well . . . . When we look at these lives unsentimentally . . . . We cannot regard either as necessarily rational or irrational.
   196. Marie Arrington, *Under The Gun, in* GOOD GIRLS/BAD GIRLS, *supra* note 40, at 173. Nina Lopez-Jones of the English Collective of Prostitutes explicitly asserts this analysis in opposition to the traditional feminist view. "Most of Women's Liberation was hostile to prostitute women on the grounds that exchanging sex for money was uniquely degrading. They said it encouraged rape by leading men to believe that all women are available, conveniently forgetting that men already thought that." Nina Lopez-Jones, *Workers: Introducing the English Collective of Prostitutes, in* SEX WORK, *supra* note 57, at 271, 273.

adventure.[197] By a strategy familiar from our anti-sexual harassment campaigns, this position is founded on the categorical *divide* between "work" and "sex," and, in stark contrast with the liberal advocacy position, allocates prostitution to the former category. Thus, Rachel West, a spokeswoman for the United States Prostitutes Collective, emphatically severs the connection drawn between prostitution and a woman's experience of sexuality by the prostitutes' rights organizations. "Prostitution is about money, not about sex."[198] This account seeks to place prostitution squarely in the public realm of commerce and exchange as organized under capitalism, split conceptually and experientially from "sex" as a feature of corporeal or emotional identity. In contrast to the prostitutes' rights organizations, these advocates do not argue for an unqualified right to practice prostitution as a vindication of a basic human right to express one's sexuality in whatever form. Like any work organized under capitalism, the fundamental structure of this labor is not valorized, but its most exploitative features sought to be ameliorated in support of the interests of the workers themselves. "We are not interested in legitimizing prostitution, but in legitimizing all prostitute women."[199]

The institutional organization of prostitution into an economic enterprise might also be theorized to distinguish the practice from the more entrepreneurial "dating" and courting rituals held indistinguishable from prostitution by the prostitutes' rights advocates. One report asserts that 40 million dollars *per day* is spent on prostitution in the United States,[200] while in 1978, the French Ministry of the Interior reported that pimping and procuring constituted that country's third largest business, generating seven billion dollars in annual profit.[201] A 1986 report on prostitution commissioned by the United Nations Educational, Scientific and Cultural Organization concluded that some nations foster prostitution as a fruitful development strategy, elevating private economic incentive to the level of state economic policy. Distinguishing such "promotional" governments from those more inadvertently encouraging prostitution through less specific industrial development plans, the report explains:

---

197. Traditional arguments supporting the criminalization of prostitution echo this theme, insofar as they distinguish "public" and "private" sex under the rubric of "public morality." Privacy challenges to prostitution and other "public" sex have recently failed before the Supreme Court. *See* Barnes v. Glen Theatre, Inc., 111 S.Ct. 2456 (1990). Earlier privacy challenges to prostitution laws pursued in state courts have universally foundered on this justification. *See, e.g.,* In re Dora P., 418 N.Y.S.2d 597 (Sup. Ct. 1979).

198. Rachel West, *U.S. PROStitutes Collective, in* SEX WORK, *supra* note 57, at 279, 283. West deflects the entire subject of women's alleged sexual motivations for entering prostitution with a plain economic explanation. "If women's basic economic situation does not change, then women will continue to work as prostitutes." *Id.*

199. Lopez-Jones, *supra* note 196, at 275. *See generally* NO BAD WOMEN/JUST BAD LAWS (English Collective of Prostitutes ed., 1990).

200. *See* PATEMAN, THE SEXUAL CONTRACT, *supra* note 174, at 190 (citing SAN FRANCISCO EXAMINER (Feb. 3, 1985)). *See generally* HELEN REYNOLDS, THE ECONOMICS OF PROSTITUTION (1986).

201. This figure is reported in SISTERHOOD IS GLOBAL 226-27 (Robin Morgan ed., 1984). *See also* Kathleen Barry, *The Underground Economic System of Pimping,* 35 J. INT'L AFF. 117 (1981).

In certain parts of the world, however, prostitution is not a consequence of the national income but a 'planned' and 'institutionalized' part of it. In certain countries in South-East Asia and Europe, the existence of mass prostitution and the structure of the market, which makes use of the media, airlines, hotel chains, international communications and the banks, mean that it could neither exist nor develop without the tacit or implicit agreement of the institutions.[202]

Indeed, cash and incentive abound, as do reports of some women earning better than survival sums in the practice.[203]

Explanations for the source of the demand for prostitution have also long been couched in economic terms, even by feminists. The demand side, we are told, is a function of the persistent "sexual scarcity" suffered by men in the uncompensated market. For example, the Bullough history recites as one of the essential conditions supporting prostitution "a shortage of willing female sex partners."[204] Such "shortages" are said to exist for men living on military bases[205] or in environments where they are in the demographic gender majority,[206] lacking the opportunity for "a normal married life."[207] The notion of "scarcity" is also flexible enough to include desire for forms of sexual contact otherwise unavailable, or at rates deemed insufficiently frequent, e.g., fellatio,[208] sadistic sexuality, and a form of iconized masturbation reminiscent of "money shots" in pornographic films. Lars Ericsson further

---

202. UNESCO, DIVISION OF HUMAN RIGHTS AND PEACE, *Final Report: International Meeting of Experts on the Social and Cultural Causes of Prostitution and Strategies for the Struggle Against Procuring and the Sexual Exploitation of Women*, SHS-85/Conf. 608/14, 7 (1986). It is estimated that 60% of the two million tourists visiting Thailand each year are drawn by the availability of "cheap" sex. In 1982, more than one million Japanese men traveled to Thailand, the Philippines, South Korea, Taiwan and Hong Kong on "kisaeng" tours, expressly designed for access to prostitution. *See* Truong-Dam, *The Dynamics of Sex Tourism: The Case of Southeast Asia*, 14 DEVELOPMENT & CHANGE 533, 533 (Apr., 1983). Statistical information compiled in Sisterhood is Global reveals the following data regarding prostitution in Thailand: "A 1981 report estimated that 300,000 women worked in approx. 1157 places offering sex services in Bangkok alone . . . approx. 40% of women working in the Bangkok region are prostitutes (1980)." SISTERHOOD IS GLOBAL, *supra* note 201, at 670.
203. *See* SPECIAL COMMITTEE ON PORNOGRAPHY AND PROSTITUTION, *supra* note 151, at 386 (reports of gross incomes of over $40,000 a year heard by Committee).
204. VERN BULLOUGH & BONNIE BULLOUGH, WOMEN AND PROSTITUTION: A SOCIAL HISTORY 293 (rev. ed., 1987); *see also* Ericsson, *supra* note 174, at 347.
205. *See* BARRY, *supra* note 10, at 70-72 for a review of this literature; *see also* James A. Sandos, *Prostitution and Drugs: The United States Army on the Mexican-American Border, 1916-1917*, 1980 PAC. HIST. REV. 621.
206. *See, e.g.*, ALAIN CORBIN, WOMEN FOR HIRE: PROSTITUTION AND SEXUALITY IN FRANCE AFTER 1850, 186-213 (1990).
207. CHARLES WINICK & PAUL M. KINSIE, THE LIVELY COMMERCE: PROSTITUTION IN THE UNITED STATES 198-99 (1971) (dubbing such sexual restraints "ecological considerations," also including "the location of some cities," "the many beautiful women around Hollywood," and extensive travelling).
208. Some, perhaps outdated, academic research reports that fellatio is the most demanded sexual practice in prostitution. *See, e.g.*, HAROLD GREENWALD, THE ELEGANT PROSTITUTE 223 (1970) (75% to 90% of johns request fellatio); MARTHA L. STEIN, FRIENDS, LOVERS, SLAVES: NINE MALE SEXUAL TYPES 95 (1974) (85%); WINICK & KINSIE, *supra* note 207, at 207 (90%).

expands this litany of lacks to include the "scarcity" of reciprocity of sexual desire between individuals, describing as a condition of "scarcity" any sexual economy except one in which all persons are granted sexual access upon demand to all other persons.[209] That is the abstract argument. This is what it means: "My wife won't blow me and these girls are good at it. They'd rather suck cock than breathe."[210]

Despite the magnitude of the demand for prostitution, the economic circumstances of prostituted women and girls are commonly marginal to impoverished. The Canadian report on prostitution states that "[t]he best estimates put the net income of a female street prostitute at $12,000 to $15,000 per year."[211] Yet D. Kelly Weisberg's study of adolescent prostitution concludes that "[m]ost street walkers are constantly on the edge of financial crisis."[212] The annual report for 1990 of one prostitution support program recites that 90% of the women in the program had been transient for average of six years,[213] while 88% of the women who participated in Mimi Silbert's study "described themselves as poor."[214] Kim Romanesko and Eleanor Miller's study of street women in Milwaukee concludes that "although women do make a great deal of money from their work as street hustlers, they personally derive little benefit from the wealth they create."[215] The authors conclude generally that women and girls in prostitution suffer even greater economic marginalization as a consequence of their involvement in prostitution than in the "licit" market where they were already marginalized as workers.[216]

Advocates committed to the "prostitution as work" position accordingly locate their argument for reform in placing "ownership" control over prostitution in the women themselves, to the ends of greater economic empowerment and improved working conditions. Demands for reform take up themes familiar from the campaigns of organized labor for trade union status, government benefits, and collective organization. As members of the Canadian Organization for the Rights of Prostitutes (CORPS) explain:

> Our ideal situation is like anyone else's—that we have control
> over our work environment . . . We want the support systems
> everyone else has.[217]

---

209. Ericsson, *supra* note 174, at 341.

210. LEWIS DIANA, THE PROSTITUTE AND HER CLIENTS: YOUR PLEASURE IS HER BUSINESS 190 (1985).

211. SPECIAL COMMITTEE ON PORNOGRAPHY AND PROSTITUTION, *supra* note 151, at 385.

212. WEISBERG, *supra* note 113, at 112-113.

213. COUNCIL FOR PROSTITUTION ALTERNATIVES, ANNUAL REPORT 2 (1990) (data based on case histories of 72 women).

214. Silbert & Pines, *Occupational Hazards, supra* note 182, at 396.

215. Romanesko & Miller, *supra* note 44, at 131.

216. *Id.* at 109-10.

217. Valerie Scott, Peggy Miller, and Ryan Hotchkiss, *Realistic Feminists, in* GOOD GIRLS/BAD GIRLS, *supra* note 40, at 204, 209.

The design of these reforms mirror at a strategic level the identification of prostitution with any form of "work" engaged in by other women. The "most crucial truth" about prostitutes, states Nina Lopez-Jones, spokeswoman for the English Collective of Prostitutes, is that "prostitute women have poverty and overwork in common with each other and with most others, especially women. They also share the increasing criminalization of those who refuse this destiny."[218] Ultimately, this argument merges prostitution with a general critique of labor under capitalism. In accord with Karl Marx, prostitution is elevated as the paradigm of the alienation of all workers from their own labor, both in process and in capital accumulation,[219] and "at the very least, the argument implies that there is nothing wrong with prostitution that is not also wrong with other forms of work."[220] Consequently, if "other workers" are aided, if not wholly liberated, by trade unionist collective action, then this strategy fundamentally should assist in the empowerment of prostitutes.

The political determination crucial to the design of these strategies, again in common with a marxist political critique, is the identity of the "capitalist," or "owner" of the labor sold in prostitution. Women's economic disempowerment in prostitution, it is argued, is a consequence of the pervasiveness of economic exploitation of women in the practice by "third-party" pimps, massage parlors, brothels and outcall services. Like other "owners," these actors appropriate percentages of 50-100% of the cash taken in by the women, either in exchange for facilities, purported protection, displays of affection, or through simple brutality or its threat.[221] The economic interest of these actors in rationalizing the transaction itself in turn has increasingly proletarianized prostitution as a labor practice over the last century. As Rachel West points out, especially in highly regulated, state licenced prostitution, the practice is organized both for the john and for the woman into "assembly line" systems, each behavior sought by the john broken down into commodified units, each with a predetermined value:

Legalization in Nevada, in the United States, and in the Eros

---

218. Lopez-Jones, *supra* note 196, at 272.

219. KARL MARX, ECONOMIC AND PHILOSOPHICAL MANUSCRIPTS OF 1844, 133 (International Publishers ed., 1964) ("Prostitution is only a *specific* expression of the *general* prostitution of the *laborer*. . .") More recently, John Reiman has recited the same theme: "Prostitution is the incarnation of the degradation of the modern citizen as producer. . ." Jeffrey H. Reiman, *Prostitution, Addiction, and the Ideology of Liberalism*, 3 CONTEMP. CRISES 53, 66 (1979).

220. PATEMAN, *supra* note 174, at 191.

221. Romanesko & Miller, *supra* note 44, at 116-119, 123-128. The authors state that "[a]ccording to the women of this study, a prerequisite to working as a street hustler is that a woman must have a male sponsor, a 'man,' to act as a 'keep-away' from other 'men' who vie for a living on the street." *Id.* at 116. *See also* Sally Engle Merry, *Manipulating Anonymity: Streetwalkers' Strategies for Safety in the City*, 45 ETHNOS 157 (1980) (on the relation of pimps to street prostitutes); Silbert & Pines, *Occupational Hazards, supra* note 182, at 397 (more than half of adult and three-fourths of juvenile prostitutes had pimps; 41% reported "no advantage" to having a pimp).

> Centers of West Germany are basically the new sex assembly
> lines. The women have no control over working conditions,
> hours worked, the number of clients they see, tips they receive,
> etc. Women, when working, have to register with the police
> and therefore are registered as 'kno wn prostitute women.'
> They are also subject to health checks and are restricted in their
> movements outside the brothels."[222]

From the point of view of the john, the woman so "assembled" as product is
apotheosized in pornography, the women "restricted in their movements" to
a photographic freeze or celluloid zoo. Health checks are rendered obsolete
by the elimination of the risky business of skin contact, the product herself
consumable any time, anywhere, the price fixed wholly in advance along with
the promised repertoire, catalogued with bibliographic nicety at your local
pornography brothel.

   One difficulty at the heart of this critique is that its reform agenda collapses
the separation of sex from money, the very separation which forms the
predicate assumption of its analysis of prostitution as labor. The "reformed"
version of prostitution urged by these advocates anticipates the arrival of a
decentralized, individualized practice of prostitution: "deproletarianized,"
presumably, by an integration of the woman's personal choices, preferences,
and desires into the terms of the transaction. Thus, as the *economic* conditions
urged by these advocates approach the ideal, the entailed *sexual* conditions
approach the normatively non-economic. The better a "job" prostitution is, that
is, the less it looks like a job, or the less it looks like prostitution.

   More fundamentally, the entire "money not sex" critique avoids the whole
question of *what* the woman is selling, and the john buying, in the prostitution
transaction itself. The argument that prostitution *is* labor, it will be recalled,
relies on an analysis of the conditions of economic exploitation entailed in the
relationship of pimp to prostitute. The matter of consumption, of the social
interaction between prostitute and john which produces "prostitution" as a
commodity, is never addressed. The issue of gender is also suppressed, in
regard to both the pimp/prostitute relationship and the john/prostitute
relationship. The fact that both are typically male/female arrangements,
similarly economizing the prostitute's identity as a "sexed female," huddles
silently, inarticulable within an analysis rigorously distinguishing "sex" from

---

222. Rachel West, *U.S. PROStitutes Collectives, in* SEX WORK, *supra* note 57, at 279. West's analysis
is argued from an historical vantage point by Judith Walkowitz in her study of the impact of government
regulation of prostitution in Victorian England. According to Walkowitz, those regulation attempts had the
immediate effect of "professionalizing" prostitution for women to an extent unknown in modern society,
locking women into the practice while at the same time constructing them as a "problem" for the state.
"Third party" intermediaries, such as pimps and brothel owners, consequently emerged as institutional
buffers/exploiters of this newly created "class" of women, themselves rendered increasingly vulnerable
by their social isolation and public scrutiny. *See generally* JUDITH R. WALKOWITZ, PROSTITUTION AND
VICTORIAN SOCIETY: WOMEN, CLASS, AND THE STATE (1980).

"work."

Like the liberal position on prostitution, the socialist view, too, is subject to cynical exploitation, available to advance the interests of men and to maintain the institution of prostitution exactly as it is. Evelina Giobbe critiques the characterization of prostitution as a "job":

> There has been a deliberate attempt to validate men's perceived need, and self-proclaimed right, to buy and sell women's bodies for sexual use. This has been accomplished, in part, by euphemizing prostitution as an occupation. Men have promoted the cultural myth that women actively seek out prostitution as a pleasurable economic alternative to low-paying, low-skilled monotonous labor, conveniently ignoring the conditions which make women vulnerable to prostitution.[223]

In common with the liberal position, the "prostitution as work" campaign also holds out a promise to women in prostitution: that whoever her "self" is, she isn't in the prostitution. Prostitution is something she *does*, not something she *is*. Yet, for the woman used in this transaction, neither the money nor the sex may translate readily as anything her "own." In respect to both, she remains a stranger, neither worker nor "partner." As K.C. Reed once said to me, "I could never make it feel like a job, not once. I would go to COYOTE meetings; they would tell me it was a job. I would try to make it feel like a job. I felt like a failure, again. I couldn't make it feel like a job, when they were telling me it was." Evelina Giobbe reports, based on her oral history research among women with histories in prostitution, survivors have "testified repeatedly that they did not experience prostitution as a career."[224]

Devoted to making visible that experience is a third group of advocates, comprised of a loose collective of prostitution advocacy groups, prostitution survivors and academic activists, commonly umbrellaed under the label "radical feminist."[225] These advocates, including myself, have pursued what might be understood as a "two tier" analysis of prostitution, which seeks to sever, not the sex from the money, but the john from the prostitute. This analysis conceives of the prostitution transaction as one in which, if both parties are present, they are not to each other. On this account, the prostitute is present to the john literally and solely as a thing that produces an experience of sex for him, as he wishes it. These theorists identify the john as twice-

---

223. Sarah Wynter (Evelina Giobbe), *WHISPER: Women Hurt in Systems of Prostitution Engaged in Revolt, in* SEX WORK, *supra* note 57, at 266.

224. Giobbe, *supra* note 3, at 68.

225. For a rough-cut sampling of the organizations and individuals who have aligned themselves with this position, *see* Margaret A. Baldwin, *Pornography and the Traffic in Women*, 1 YALE J.L. & FEMINISM 111, 116 (listing of amici supporting radical feminist position on prostitution in pornography litigation). As implied by this citation, I am myself committed to the radical feminist position for reasons I hope this article makes clear.

blessed: both "owner" and "consumer" of the transaction, the john dominates both economically and sexually.[226]

Fundamental to the john's sexual experience is eroticized disregard of the woman. Developing Hanna Olsen's description of the "sex" of prostitution as "masturbation in a woman's body,"[227] Kathleen Barry accordingly has described the john's sexual agenda as the reduction of a woman to "body parts separated from the self and the woman's sexual experience. . . . This experience constitutes an essentially noninteractive, non-mutual sexual experience which establishes the basis for further demands of perversions and violence in the exchange."[228] Timothy Beneke refers to this sexual process as "pornographizing," the sexual experience of relating to a woman as a "low whore":

> In pornographizing, one anonymizes the woman and fails to

---

226. This analysis reverses a popular view of the quality of the prostitution transaction, which characterizes the woman's behavior as nearly a form of theft. Promoted some years ago by sociologist Kingsley Davis, this view holds that prostitution represents an arrangement of economic exploitation, this time of the *man*. The woman "gets" both money and sex, while the man "gets" only the sex and forfeits the money:

> It is even true that some women enjoy the intercourse they sell. From a purely economic point of view prostitution comes perilously near the situation of getting something for nothing. The woman may suffer no loss at all yet receive a generous reward, resembling the artist who, though paid for his work, loves it so well that he would paint anyway.

Kingsley Davis, *The Sociology of Prostitution*, 2 AMER. SOC. REV. 744, 750 (1937). The issue posed here, of course, is whether the "womanhood" which makes a woman marketable as a prostitute ought to divest her of a claim that she loses something in the transaction for which she should be compensated. That is, if prostitution is an economic system, it is not one for her. She is a woman with the job of *being* a woman; the distinctiveness of her job from her pleasure receding to the vanishing point. Insofar as her sexuality aligns with her job demands, the lingering issues of exploitation and the puzzle of prostitutes' impoverishment can thus be dispatched with speed. Rushing to meet these descriptive challenges is a small industry of social science investigators set on probing the sexual experience of women in prostitution with johns and others. Orgasm-counting is thought sufficient to capture the gist of the matter: Look! She *is* having sex, after all! (And is robbing us.) Recent contributions to this literature, commenced with vigor by Havelock Ellis, *see* 4 STUDIES IN THE PSYCHOLOGY OF SEX 275 (1936), include Exner, Wylie, Leura, & Parrill, *Some Psychological Characteristics of Prostitutes*, 41 J. PERSONALITY ASSESSMENT 474 (1977) ("sexual responsiveness" of prostituted women equal or greater than control in most categories); Paul H. Gebhard, *Misconceptions About Female Prostitutes*, 3 MEDICAL ASPECTS OF HUMAN SEXUALITY 24 (1969) (reaching similar conclusions); Wardell B. Pomeroy, *Some Aspects of Prostitution*, 1 J. SEX RES. 177 (1965) (finding women in prostitution more sexually responsive than women interviewed for major Kinsey study on female sexual behavior); Leonard Sovitz & Lawrence Rosen, *The Sexuality of Prostitutes: Sexual Enjoyment Reported by Streetwalkers*, 24 J. SEX RES. 200 (1988) (prostituted women report they usually derive pleasure from both lovers and customers); *but see* WINICK & KINSIE, *supra* note 207, at 26 ("many prostitutes are revolted if they are expected to respond"); Mimi Silbert & Ayala Pines, *Early Sexual Exploitation as an Influence in Prostitution*, SOCIAL WORK, Jul.-Aug. 1983, at 285, 288 (14% of subjects reported being asexual, close to 50% reported almost never reaching orgasm).

These largely "sex-positive" accounts (excepting Silbert and Pines) have displaced the older psychoanalytic conclusions, rooted in female illness explanations for prostitution, that women in prostitution, are sexually frigid, hostile to men, or "homosexually oriented." *See, e.g.*, KARL ABRAHAM, *Manifestations of the Female Castration Complex*, *in* KARL ABRAHAM, SELECTED PAPERS 361 (1942); FRANK CAPRIO & DONALD BRENNER, SEXUAL BEHAVIOR: PSYCHO-LEGAL ASPECTS 249 (1961).

227. Kathleen Barry, *Social Etiology of Crimes Against Women*, 10 VICTIMOLOGY 164, 171 (1985)(quoting Hanna Olsen).

228. *Id.* at 172.

acknowledge her moral, spiritual or emotional being. One relates to her as a thing without a soul. The woman as a locus of experience is denied. And, one often relates to her body as a fetish . . . Pornographizing is the perceptual counterpart to sex as the achievement of possession of a commodity and sex as aggressive degradation.[229]

The transfer of money from the john to the prostitute, on this view of his sexual interest, confirms and celebrates his entitlement to treat the woman this way (any way he wishes), situating him in the role of "owner." As Susanne Kappeler has observed, the transfer confirms his dominance, his power to control the value, the meaning, the script of the "exchange": "[I]t is the one with the surplus (capital) who decides what is 'like for like,' who fixes the price according to his demand. He decides what to buy, and what is a commodity. He writes the possible scenarios, and determines how they are viewed."[230] Among those possible scenarios, as Barry suggests,[231] are the rape scripts, the laceration scripts, the murder scripts—whatever "story" a john might have in mind for a woman whose status as human is for him to determine. That is the sexual authority men buy in prostitution: to fix the meaning of who or what a woman *is*.

According to research on customer satisfaction, this experience is said to confer considerable psychic benefit on the john, from enhanced self-esteem[232] to the unimpeded exercise of sexual ideational dissociation, sometimes called "fantasy." As the Kinsey researchers reported:

> As far as psychologic responses are concerned, the male in many instances may not be having coitus with the immediate sexual partner, but with all the other girls with whom he has ever had coitus, and with the entire genus Female with whom he would like to have coitus.[233]

Lewis Diana summarizes these findings as standing for the proposition that "[p]rostitution provides temporary relief from the obligations inherent in involved sexual and emotional relationships,"[234] while David Richards sees in the quotidian arrangement a modern form of "the best in romantic love":

---

229. TIMOTHY BENEKE, MEN ON RAPE 23-24 (1982). *See also* Katz, *supra* note 71, at 62 ("pornographizing" of women central predicate for men's felt entitlement to rape).

230. KAPPELER, *supra* note 13, at 159.

231. *See* Barry, *Social Etiology, supra* note 227, at 171.

232. *See* STEIN, *supra* note 208, at 316-317 (interaction with prostitute restored john's "battered self-worth"); WINICK & KINSIE, *supra* note 207, at 197 (61% of sample of johns said prostitute refurbished battered ego).

233. ALFRED C. KINSEY ET AL., SEXUAL BEHAVIOR IN THE HUMAN FEMALE 684 (1953). *See also* Harold R. Holzman & Sharon Pines, *Buying Sex: The Phenomenology of Being A John*, DEVIANT BEHAVIOR 89 (Oct.-Dec. 1982).

234. DIANA, *supra* note 210, at 191.

"when the relationship is most realistic, fair and reciprocal."[235] This is again the flavor of the empirical data relied on in reaching these conclusions: "This woman wants nothing, asks nothing, needs nothing. I don't need to please her or be concerned about whether she's enjoying it. I can do what I want and please myself."[236]

Kathleen Barry further suggests that women may experience deep ambivalence regarding their right to benefit from money received in prostitution which they nominally control, even absent direct economic exploitation by third parties. She reports:

> A former call girl, who is now working in a shelter trying to get young girls out of prostitution, told me that in her opinion one reason why she and all other call girls she knew went through their money so fast and couldn't save "for that boutique in the sky" was that to her it wasn't clean money. After six years in the life she left. "When I found myself crying as I turned tricks I knew that I couldn't take life that way anymore."[237]

Similarly, Eleanor Miller's study of street women in Milwaukee indicates that, for many women, the cash has a particular meaning as "fast money": as dead, as useless, as phony, as demeaning to hold, as the trick.[238] Moreover, life in prostitution is simply expensive: the cost of transience is very high in lodging, food, and the need for constant replacement of necessities.

If the cash is never quite hers, neither, exactly, is the sex. The sex is done to her, on her, in her; certainly never *with* her. Renditions of women's experience of the sex of prostitution, on these advocates' accounts, commonly proceed by way of flat, objective description of the acts performed by the women at the man's express or implied behest. Andrea Dworkin's narrative summaries of the content of pornography capture the tone;[239] K.C. Reed's "story" of one night in prostitution speaks in the same voice. The experience of prostitution profoundly conveyed by this narrative style is the fact of the woman's utter *irrelevance* to what happens, how it happens, why it happens, much less her subjective "feelings" toward the encounter. Her presence is marked by her availability as sexual apparatus, in a transaction to which her role is to be the perfect small appliance: useful, but beside the point, not the

---

235. Richards, *supra* note 175, at 1271. Psychiatrist Ethel Person also analyzes the relationship of john to prostitute as one of "erotic transference" similar to the transference phenomenon of psychotherapy, integrating both into an account of romantic love. *See* ETHEL PERSON, DREAMS OF LOVE AND FATEFUL ENCOUNTERS: THE POWER OF ROMANTIC PASSION 262-63 (1988).

236. DIANA, *supra* note 210, at 191.

237. BARRY, *supra* note 10, at 135-36.

238. MILLER, *supra* note 114, at 139-40 ("The women always corrected me when I asked if there was 'good money' to be made on the streets. They said that there was, rather, fast money.").

239. *See* DWORKIN, *supra* note 25 *passim*.

point, no point at all.

Yet for these advocates, too, who have devoted the closest attention of all prostitution advocates to comprehending the process and consequences of sexual commodification in the transaction to the woman, the point lies principally elsewhere. The principal explanatory emphasis urged by radical feminist advocates goes to the "why did she stay" question applied to prostitution, and, in common with the representational strategies advanced on behalf of battered women, opens up the descriptive frame of reference for addressing that question to include the significance of the incest, seasoning by pimps, battery, rape, humiliation, and torture conceded by all as the preconditions and conditions of life for vast numbers of women and girls involved in the practice.[240]

Of course, social scientific inquiry into prostitutes' motivations for entering and remaining in prostitution comprises a vast literature. The matter of girls' "flight from incestuous fantasies" has already been noted,[241] which is the more modern version of now somewhat outdated phrenological, medical, and psychoanalytic accounts of some women's innate will to prostitute themselves.[242] Like the masochistic battered woman, the prostitute on these analyses is exoticized, subject to self-destructive or erotic urges beyond ordinary ken. As Kathleen Barry states the thrust of these inquiries:

> To those who study the victims of the practice I have called female sexual slavery these women are the exceptions for whom exceptional behavior is normal; to sociologists they are deviants; to psychologists they are sadomasochists. Their life and experiences are construed as normal for them while they are supposedly different from the rest of us.[243]

The radical feminist position, instead, seeks to "normalize" women in prostitution by demonstrating the "normalcy" of her responses to systematic abuse and coercion which, in common with the battered woman, cause her to "stay."

The direction of this work was early charted by Kathleen Barry's groundbreaking investigations of domestic and international trafficking in women for prostitution, which she theorized as practices of female sexual

---

240. *See supra* nn. 187-195 and accompanying text.

241. *See supra* note 188 and accompanying text.

242. *See, e.g.*, ELLIS, *supra* note 226, at 275 ("there can be no doubt that moral imbecility of slight degree is very frequently found among prostitutes"); Edward Glover, 2 THE ROOTS OF CRIME: SELECTED PAPERS ON PSYCHOANALYSIS (1960) (prostitution constitutes acting out of oedipal conflicts); CAESAR LOMBROSCO & WILLIAM FERRERO, THE FEMALE OFFENDER 147 (1895); Clinton P. McCord, *One Hundred Female Offenders: A Study of the Mentality of Prostitutes and "Wayward" Girls*, 6 J. OF THE AM. INST. OF CRIM. L. & CRIMINOLOGY 385, 388 (1915) (half of women in study of intelligence indicators were of "phlegmatic, lazy, apathetic type" the other half "lack emotional control").

243. BARRY, *supra* note 10, at 9.

slavery. In her formulation, sexual slavery entails *"all* situations where women and girls cannot change the immediate conditions of their existence; where regardless of how they got into those conditions they cannot get out; and where they are subject to sexual violence and exploitation."[244] Prostitution induced under those conditions is thus, for Barry, but one form of an array of similar coercive sexual practices, including woman battery, incest and compulsory marriage.[245] Especially for United States prostitution, Barry emphasizes the central role played by pimping in creating those conditions of coercion for women in prostitution. In contrast with the economic exploitation entailed in pimping stressed by the prostitution-as-work advocates, Barry focuses on the effects of "seasoning" practices common to pimping, combining strategies of force, isolation, and emotional and physical dependency to gain control of the woman and to render her otherwise defenseless.[246] In this emphasis, Barry locates as a key feature of forced prostitution the dynamics of traumatic intimacy, now familiar from feminist accounts of domestic battery. Here, the pimp stands in the role of the controlling, battering, cajoling husband, a continuity, as I noted much earlier, often seized upon by (non-pimping) husbands as they shout "you slut" at their bewildered wives. The woman's prostitution adds but another means by which he can humiliate and injure her, with the added boot of a profit.

The overwhelming incidence of incest in the life histories of women in prostitution expands this basic framework for understanding "why she stayed." Among radical prostitution advocates, incest is understood as a *form* of seasoning, a practice of a father pimping his daughter to himself: isolating her in silence, from recognition or help, imposing as a condition of survival her sexual compliance, and delivering the deal in the names of love and protection. On this view, incest is less a "precondition" of prostitution than a practice of it. The common self-identification of incest victims as "whores" noted by Judith Herman,[247] and the "traumatic sexualization" suffered by them theorized by David Finkelhor,[248] trace this continuity symptomatically. Like the battering husband, the father rapist who calls his daughter a "slut" is simply missing the obvious point: that he is a pimp, turning his daughter out

---

244. *Id.* at 40.
245. *Id.* at 163. "Familial sexual slavery" Barry thus describes in these terms:
    Many girls and women directly experience female sexual slavery without ever going out of their homes. For them, home replaces brothel, they are the wives and daughters who are the victims of husbands or fathers instead of pimps. I am speaking of course, of wife battery and incest, practices which make the private family instead of the public street or "house" the location of female sexual slavery. In certain cultures, these practices take the form of forced marriage, polygyny, veiling and the seclusion of women.
    Id.
246. *See id.* at 77-79; BARRY, *Social Etiology, supra* note 227, at 167; *see also* Diana Gray, *Turning Out: A Study of Teenage Prostitution*, 1 URB. LIFE & CULTURE 401 (1973); Silbert & Pines, *supra* note 182, at 488.
247. *See* HERMAN, *infra* note 45.
248. *See* Finkelhor, *infra* note 45.

first to himself and later, if "passively," to others. For the girl, "[o]nce in prostitution, both pimps and johns replicate the abuse these girls endured in their families."[249]

The other prostitution "data," on this account, also rise above the footnote line and theorize the "you slut" epithets hurled at "other women" with such reckless abandon. The routine beatings, rapes, and humiliation of the woman by johns confirm her helplessness and reinforce her status as a woman born to be used, this time in the "workplace." The "solicitations" of sexual harassment, replete with insult and contempt, here receive their full expression. Drugs are good buffers, as "other women" know, too.

In sum, prostitution is here conceived as the obvious consequence of serial, unbounded, life-long sexual and emotional abuse. As Evelina Giobbe puts it, the act of prostitution represents a john's try at "turn[ing] child sexual abuse and rape into a job by throwing money at their victims."[250] I honor this story, because it acknowledges and respects women's pain. It knows the murdered women are out there, stuffed in garbage cans, floating in rivers, tossed by the roadside, because a john chose not to believe she was alive in the first place, or because killing her was his idea of a good time. It knows that the incest, the neglect, the beatings, the betrayals, have real and deep consequences that persist beyond the first date with a new boyfriend. It knows, too, that these women are the least likely to be recognized as injured, ever, because everyone is too busy fantasizing them, beyond the pale of suffering or empathy. It knows that prostitution is what happens to "other women" who are luckless, who are treated as nothing but cunt, relentlessly, their whole lives long.

The argumentative rejoinder is obvious, and, as I have already explored, often lodged by advocates of the opposing positions: all of this torture, humiliation, and exploitation may happen, and be truly terrible, but what does it have to do with prostitution? Are not the incest, the beatings, the rapes (on and on) but "ancillary" to prostitution, itself? Doesn't the radical feminist critique merely restate, if rather more grimly, the point made by all of these advocates: that prostitutes *are* "other women," and prostitution, *per se*, therefore unremarkable? And they would be right, as right as each of the advocacy groups is in making the identical criticism of each of the others. *For the purpose of each of these positions is to destroy itself,* and "prostitution" along with it. Each of us is more apt to savor this point in criticism of our opponents than reflect on its implications for ourselves, or for what it means toward advancing this debate. The measure of success we each set for our own accounts of prostitution is the ease with which our "other woman" story can swallow it whole. This same measure of success is, in turn, the measure of failure we use to castigate the failings of our opponents. The more persuasively

---

249. Evelina Giobbe, *The Vox Fights,* VOX MAGAZINE 29, 33 (Winter 1991).
250. Giobbe, *supra* note 3, at 3.

we argue the continuity of our accounts of prostitution with our renditions of "other women's" life conditions, the more vulnerable we are to the charge that we have failed to grasp the specificity, the "reality" of "prostitution itself." Since each of us is bent on "de-specifying" prostitution in our own terms, the charge begins to ring rather falsely as a criticism. If each of these positions is self-consuming in its own terms, the "debate" is as self-defeating.

The "real truth," I think, about this debate is its irreality *as* a debate, at least about *prostitution*, to all concerned. As no doubt my own rendition demonstrates, there is a vivisectionist's abstraction, a deadness, a feeling of being semantically distracted from insight, that imbues the entire discussion. There is an explanation for this. The "true" question in contest in the prostitution debate is not really prostitution at all. Rather, the debate is the site of contest over the representational expansion and dominance of our "other women's" stories beyond the zones of explanatory control each formerly more peaceably occupied. The struggle over prostitution, as it is presently argued, is a bid by each tendency in feminism for territory largely ceded to the others by each before prostitution entered the scene: a bid for a story of money by liberals, for a story of sex by socialists, and for a story of strange men by radicals.

Within a political movement founded on "explaining ourselves," these are some large stakes indeed. Yet, at least in the "larger movement," we have seemed about equally committed to winning them as we are to losing them. I notice this contradiction in the conditions of my own activism in the "larger movement." Sometimes, conference organizers and symposium planners call. They express enthusiasm for your "prostitution story." This enthusiasm is shown when the prostitution story you are telling is helpful toward advancing the position of some "other women" engaged in a jurisdictional conflict with some other "other women." Some factions within liberal feminism, for example, express enthusiasm for the liberal and socialist advocates' position on prostitution, because those advocates help shore up against radical feminist incursion certain views liberal feminists promote about "choice" and about "privacy." Those of us who identify as radical feminists, in turn, look to gain added leverage in our critiques of liberal theories of consent in the display of "our" prostitutes, whose stories we consume with satisfaction until we move on to the next workshop. Feminists of post-modern sensibility may marvel at the complexities, how "prostitution" can mean so many things, and, as they would argue, the more prolific the discursive possibilities, the freer we know we are. In all of this, we cast ourselves in the role of the john: It could be any way. This is how I want it. (And if we can have it lots of ways, so much the better.)

An added dimension of utility in this procedure is that all concerned can maintain the separation between "prostitutes" and "other women" which has proven so significant in all our reform strategies (if the latter category now includes some "good prostitutes," the former category is comprised of the "bad" ones, allied with our political adversaries). The distinction is also maintained in the degree of attention and support offered by "other women" to women in prostitution off the grander stages of our jurisdictional wars. When it's time for the dirty work, there are about a dozen women to call, fewer than would assemble a respectable workshop. The real struggle, most days, seems far from any conference paper — getting some money together for prostitution support programs; calling to see if there is one more space at the "good" juvenile detention center for another 15 year old; seeing the look on a woman's face which says that she will be calling tomorrow, or next year, to tell you about the prostitution; overcoming in myself again and again the flicker of despair just before I hear what I will hear when she calls (will it be *worse*? how *can* it be worse?); afterwards, losing some of the women and knowing it may be permanent. The "larger movement" at these times seems scarcely to exist, the "prostitution debate" of little aid in meeting these women's needs or in gaining further clarity for myself or them on how, ever, to get them met.

Sometimes these moments occur at feminist meetings. These are moments with "other women" who don't believe in the stories we tell about them, either: the woman whose father gave her money, maybe a lot of it; the woman who "stayed" because she wanted to prove she could beat him back; the woman who cuts herself after a couple of drinks; all the stories that don't quite fit the "other woman" stories we tell. They are "other women," too, who see how close they were, or are, to being prostituted; who were prostituted, and could never talk about it to anyone. All the "you whore! you slut!" stories wanting to be told. The pressure to speak, the pressure not to speak, is enormous. There is a fear of the boundaries eroding, and a fear of the boundaries not eroding.

What is lost in the prostitution debate, as we are all asked to justify the lives of prostitutes as just like those of other women, is what other women need to learn and know and appreciate and politicize about the conditions of their own existence *from* women in prostitution. That is the fundamental condition of consciousness-raising that has been forfeited by the larger movement: that women in prostitution have insight and knowledge that other women need to make sense of their *own* lives. The continued silence, shame, the formalistic appeals, the elevation of theorizing over action stifling the participation of woman in prostitution in our movement is supported by a political climate that wants prostitutes only to ask permission to join, not authority to direct. "Other women" don't want to hear, perhaps, that our boyfriends and husbands are buying sex from women in prostitution. "Other women" don't want to hear, perhaps, that the "straight" jobs we have are sexualized top to bottom. "Other women" don't want to hear, perhaps, that we are each one man from the street. But if our stories are to gain in boldness and integrity, we all need to be able to hear all of that, and find the "point to it."

I am not about to say, as you may think I am about to say, that "all women are prostitutes." That is a glib and silly, nearly insulting, thing to say. (I mean, insulting to women in prostitution.) There is a theme, though, that obviously links all of these stories. That is the story that *no one is a prostitute*, recited with utmost conviction, or with the passion of a final plea for help and justice. And perhaps *that* is the story that is the prostitution story itself: a woman declaring, with equal parts conviction and resignation, that she is not a prostitute, to please somebody else upon whom her survival depends.

[III. UNTITLED]

There is one more prostitution story I want to tell you. This is it:

> There you are, in a dump that's more or less clean, holding a towel in your hand, looking at somebody you've never seen before. The more you retreat, the more he advances; since the room is fairly cramped, you soon find yourself with your back against the wall. The guy's arms are around you, they're all over your body like slimy tentacles that grope you, strip you, and drag you down as he pulls you over the
> bed . . .

For an instant, you escape
from the nightmare: you
are back in the church play-
ground, playing hopscotch.
It seems like yesterday.
You almost feel good, and
you shut your eyes to make
the dream last. When
you reopen them, after a split second, reality blinds you.

> Reality has taken the form of a cock, a real family man's   wiener,   a   little   soft   but   still enterprising.[251]

This is not an isolated incident. It is a commonplace observation within prostitution support and advocacy circles that dissociative strategies of

---

251. JEANNE CORDELIER, THE LIFE: MEMOIRS OF A FRENCH HOOKER 69-70 (1978), *quoted in* Kathleen Barry, Prostitution, Sexual Violence, and Victimization: Feminist Perspectives on Women's Human Rights 7-8 (1991) (unpublished manuscript).

distancing the act, herself, and the john are routine tactics practiced by women in prostitution, described by Kathleen Barry as constructing a "split-identity" between "that" woman performing an act of prostitution and her "other" self.[252] "Disengagement," Barry explains, "is the up-front strategy of women in prostitution."[253] Nor is this a costless tactic. The terrible psychic injury absorbed as a consequence of these survival tactics is recorded in the litany of "splitting" disturbances suffered by prostitutes.[254] As is becoming better known, similar strategies of disengagement, of "not being there," are also commonly employed by women and girls to avoid trauma in incest and rape.[255] The term "denial," I think, but weakly and perhaps misleadingly conveys this experience. From the "inside," the feeling is less one of repression than of being released to someplace *else*, anywhere else, where it feels better, or doesn't feel at all. "It's not happening, no, this *other* thing is happening."[256] For women in prostitution, these other things may occur very frequently. Estimates of the frequency of sale of women in prostitution range from three or four to 80 tricks *a day*, over a course of days, months, or years.[257]

These disengagement strategies, though, as Barry further points out, are not only the last defenses of the used. "Disengagement" from her "real self" is the fundamental demand made of women in prostitution, the essential term of the transaction itself. What a john wants is for the woman to *act* like the woman he wants, and for the woman to maintain a credible performance as part of the bargain. She is to act as if she *is* the role he wants her to play. Barry explains:

> [C]ustomers generally require that prostitutes act as if they are
> engaged with the customer emotionally, psychically, affectively
> by entering into a fantasy or by feigning the role of a lover.

---

252. Barry, *supra* note 227, at 171. *See also* Summer, *supra* note 168, at 36; *see generally* Baldwin, *supra* note 225, at 133.

253. Barry, *supra* note 251, at 5. In the words of women Barry quotes:
   Dia says: "I have to be a little stoned to go through with it. I have to shove my emotions completely to the side. I get talkative and don't give a shit." Elizabeth reports: "You switch off your feelings, you have to do it." Brita reports "I've taught myself to switch off, to shove my feelings away. I don't give a damn, as long as there's money. It doesn't have anything to do with feelings."
Id. at 5. Former prostitute Rosie Summers describes the sexual experiences of prostitution as "a [woman] turning off her emotions, being psychically someplace else while someone who despises her is making love to her." Rosie Summers, *Prostitution, in* SEX WORK, *supra* note 57, at 117-18.

254. *See supra* notes 155-156 and accompanying text.

255. *See, e.g.*, WOMEN'S RESEARCH CENTRE, RECOLLECTING OUR LIVES: WOMEN'S EXPERIENCE OF CHILDHOOD SEXUAL ABUSE (1989); ELIZABETH A. STANKO, INTIMATE INTRUSIONS: WOMEN'S EXPERIENCE OF MALE VIOLENCE (1985).

256. For a powerful literary account of this experience, see SUSAN PALWICK, FLYING IN PLACE (1992).

257. *See, e.g.*, PERKINS & BENNETT, *supra* note 160, at 16 (Sydney, Australia sample averaged 40 to 50 johns per week); Matthew Freund et al., *Sexual Behavior of Resident Street Prostitutes With Their Clients in Camden, New Jersey*, 26 J. SEX RESEARCH 460, 465 (1989) (average of 4.13 johns per workday; 553 johns over a seven month period).

Either the prostitute is to *act* like a whore or she is to *act* like an affectionate lover. . . . In prostitution, what men expect from women is the *semblance* of emotional involvement, pleasure and consent, a *semblance that they can treat as if it is real* in the moment of the commodity exchange.[258]

This dynamic plainly exceeds in complexity the description of prostitution as "objectified sex," understood as a wholly unselfconscious, unilateral act of sexual consumption. Rather, the demand made of the woman is to demonstrate a happy complicity, to whatever role is demanded.[259]

I would suggest that a similar demand, and similar strategy in the fact of it, drives the design of our feminist strategies in our public advocacy. The disengagement tactic step, has, I hope, been demonstrated throughout this paper: whatever we are, wherever we are, it is not prostitution. It is love, or freedom, or work, or force, or fear; anything but prostitution. We can prove it by our arguments, over and over, from every possible angle that might be mustered in opposition. It is all a great mistake, and if no one else is convinced, we can at least convince ourselves. "I was never really into it." How many times a day do we turn this trick? How many years has feminism told this story, been "somewhere else" as a strategy of resisting what we are told we are?

And who are we talking to? Who is it, who cares so much, that we should care to convince? The men, it seems: the men who feel license to destroy us if we fail to convince them, the johns we hope at the risk of our lives will remember we are human beings. We are not prostitutes, and hope we can act well enough to fit the part of not being one. The law, too, we hope to convince. Our stories of "consent," of "work," of "intimacy," have been crafted with the law in mind, placating its demand that we not "really" be sluts. We deliver the goods, compliantly, now in the name of a self-determining, liberated feminism. "It was good for me, too, honest."

My further intuition is that this is a structural political requirement, not only a problem of bad men, silly laws, or short-sighted feminism. My belief, also my fear, is that within the existing political and legal order, and the possibilities for change afforded some women, is embedded a profound

---

258. BARRY, *supra* note 251, at 6-7.
259. *See also* Holzman & Pines, *supra* note 233, at 108-109:
    In every encounter discussed, the individual paying for sex engaged in social, courting behaviors that were often flavored with varying degrees of romance. According to the subjects in the study, these behaviors represented a conscious attempt to create a positive experience that would fulfill their fantasies, that is, the client via such devices as compliments tries to manipulate the prostitute into complying with his particular vision of a pleasant, satisfactory encounter . . . There existed a belief that by being pleasant or even amorous they could subtly seduce the prostitute into allowing their created illusion to play itself out. Even better, if their tactics worked, the prostitute might exceed mere tolerance of the fantasy - they might become a more energetic (as opposed to passive) participant, albeit still a paid professional.

bargain: take what you can, but it will always be at the price of abandoning prostitutes, of gaining your advantage at her expense. There is a term for women who accept bargains like that. It's called being a pimp's "bottom woman," the one who treasures his highest regard, and sometimes gets off the street herself, but only if she helps run the less lucky girls. There is also a term for the arrangement which makes this bargain compelling. It's called pimping, period. If my intuition is correct, this is the arrangement women presently have with the state, motivating the "not a prostitute" content of our legal stories as a condition of our legal citizenship. My question for all of us, in love and struggle, is this: if I am right, in this intuition, do we love our pimp so much, after all? What stories would we tell, if not for him?

Whores[†] In Court:

Judicial Processing of Prostitutes in the

Boston Municipal Court in 1990

Minouche Kandel[††]

Kay is a former prostitute.[1] She first started hooking to support her boyfriend's heroin addiction. Later, she worked the streets of Boston and New York to support her own drug habit. Once on the street, heroin helped make her experience more tolerable. Kay generally made between $200 and $300 a night, for roughly five hours' work,[2] but any money earned was immediately spent on drugs.

In time, Kay was arrested and sentenced to serve three months at the Massachusetts Correctional Institution at Framingham (MCI-Framingham). Incarceration cost her the job as a university administrator she had held for fourteen years. While in prison, Kay received no counseling for her drug addiction and her already low self-esteem dropped still further. Upon release, Kay again turned to drugs. Her addiction worsened. Out of work and out of money, she returned to prostitution.

In 1990 Boston police arrested more than two hundred fifty women for prostitution and common nightwalking/common streetwalking.[3] This number does not include arrests for disorderly conduct.[4] Counting prostitution-related disorderly conduct cases, the number of women arrested on prostitution-related

---

† Many street prostitutes self-identify as "whores," or more frequently the vernacular "ho." I mean to imply no disrespect in using the term.

†† J.D. Harvard Law School, 1991, B.A. Yale University 1987. Staff attorney with HomeBase, a public policy center for homelessness in the Bay Area of Northern California and member of the California Coalition for Battered Women in Prison. The Coalition helps battered women imprisoned for killing their abusers apply for clemency.

I wish to thank Professor Charles Ogletree for giving me the opportunity to pursue this research, and the clerks at the Boston Municipal Court (BMC) for their patience and help in providing court files. Most of all, I am grateful to Sally Hunt, for supplementing my cold data with passion and commitment.

1. Interview with Kay, in Somerville, Mass. (Mar. 28, 1991). I have used Kay's street name, as she wished to retain her anonymity.

2. The going rate seems to be from $20 to $50 for a blow job, the most common activity. If a prostitute is able to see ten men a night, she can earn from $200 to $500 for an evening's work. Each encounter generally runs no longer than twenty to thirty minutes. Interview with J.W. by Ayelet Waldman, in Boston Municipal Court, Boston, Mass. (Mar. 26, 1991).

3. This figure includes multiple arrests of some individuals in that year. See infra part I.

4. Despite the fact that the Massachusetts courts have specifically held the disorderly conduct statute inapplicable to prostitution-related activities, the police continue to arrest most prostitutes under this statute. See Commonwealth v. Blavackas, 419 N.E. 2d 856, 858-859 (Mass. App. Ct. 1981) discussed infra text accompanying notes 42-49.

charges in Boston each year would approach roughly one thousand.[5]

In Massachusetts, almost half the women chronically involved in the courts list prostitution as their usual illegal activity.[6] Studies show that nationwide, prostitutes may comprise more than fifty percent of the female prison population in large urban areas.[7] Every year, Boston and other cities spend hundreds of thousands of dollars on processing these women in court.

Based on a case study of the Boston Municipal Court's (BMC) treatment of prostitution-related crimes in the year 1990, this article will argue that prostitution should be decriminalized. First, the system has a minimal deterrent effect—women arrested and charged with this crime are more often than not released only to be arrested again. If this crime has any real victims, they are the prostitutes themselves, many of whom need drug counseling and safe haven, not punitive treatment.[8] This article recommends the removal of all state controls on prostitution and advocates the diversion of funds presently spent on court costs and incarceration to programs serving the needs of women who work as street prostitutes.[9]

In discussing the decriminalization of prostitution, it is important to

---

5. Interview with Sarah J. Hunt, Massachusetts criminal defense attorney, in Boston, Mass. (Mar. 26, 1991). Over 200,000 women are arrested for prostitution every year in the United States. Margo St. James, Address Before the 2nd World Whores' Congress at the European Parliament (Oct. 1, 1986) *in* A VINDICATION OF THE RIGHTS OF WHORES 78 (Gail Pheterson ed., 1989). Over the past decade, the number of people arrested for prostitution in the U.S. has increased by 20%. FEDERAL BUREAU OF INVESTIGATION, 1989 UNIFORM CRIME REPORTS, CRIME IN THE UNITED STATES 176 (1989). The FBI's 1989 report lists 107,400 estimated arrests for prostitution and commercialized vice. *Id.* at 172. This figure does not include arrests for loitering or disorderly conduct. In 1989, 119,786 women were arrested for disorderly conduct. *Id.* Many of these women were probably prostitutes as there was a 46% percent increase in the number of women arrested for disorderly conduct between 1980 and 1989. *Id.*

6. MARIAN KLAUSNER & BETSEY SMITH, OPENING DOORS FOR CHANGE: ALTERNATIVES TO INCARCERATION, A REPORT ON ALTERNATIVE SENTENCING FOR WOMEN 15 (1991). Between 1988-1990 the Boston-based organization Social Justice for Women conducted a survey among 65 of their alternative sentencing clients—women who are chronically involved in the courts and at risk of incarceration. The statistics cited in KLAUSNER & SMITH were based on this sample.

7. CORAMAE R. MANN, FEMALE CRIME AND DELINQUENCY 121-22 (1984). One-third of the women in jails and prisons throughout the United States are serving time for prostitution offenses.

8. This paper does not address the broader arguments of some feminists that: (1) prostitutes are inevitably victimized and dehumanized by selling their bodies to men for money, and that no matter what the working conditions, women should be discouraged/prevented from engaging in sex for money; and (2) prostitution harms all women in a social context where women are politically, economically and socially unequal, by reinforcing conceptions of female subordination and the commodification of women's bodies. *See generally* Jody Freeman, *The Feminist Debate Over Prostitution Reform: Prostitutes' Rights Groups, Radical Feminists, and the (Im)possibility of Consent*, 5 BERKELEY WOMEN'S L.J. 75 (1990); Laurie Shrage, *Should Feminists Oppose Prostitution?*, 99 ETHICS 352 (1989). However even if one believes that prostitution per se harms prostitutes and/or all women, the criminal justice system is not the place to redress that harm. No city has abolished prostitution through criminalization. Barbara Milman, *New Rules for the Oldest Profession: Should We Change Our Prostitution Laws?*, 3 HARV. WOMEN'S L.J. 37 (1980). In 1967 New York City instituted more lenient, non-criminal sanctions for prostitution. Two years into the experiment, the legislature again made prostitution a criminal offense. Throughout this period, the prevalence of street prostitution in New York remained unchanged. GILBERT GEIS, ONE EYED JUSTICE 198-200 (1974).

9. This article will focus on prostitutes who work on the street because they are the primary targets of prostitution laws. Ninety-nine percent of the prostitutes arrested in Boston were street-walkers. Nationwide, street prostitutes comprise 85-90% of arrested prostitutes. Priscilla Alexander, *Prostitution: A Difficult Issue for Feminists, in* SEX WORK 196 (Frédérique Delacoste & Priscilla Alexander eds., 1987).

distinguish decriminalization from legalization. Nevada is currently the only state in the U.S. where prostitution has been legalized in certain counties. Legalization, as it is understood in the United States, carries with it a full regime of government regulations and controls, similar to that for alcohol sales. In Nevada, prostitutes must work under the auspices of a brothel.[10] Women who wish to work independently may not legally do so.[11] Moreover, prostitutes must be tested for the HIV virus, and those who test positive are not permitted to continue their work at all.[12] In addition, the brothel system screens out prostitutes who use drugs.[13] This is not to say that drug-addicted or HIV-positive prostitutes change professions; these women are simply forced to work illegally.[14] Thus legalization may serve to make prostitution safer for some, but it does not eliminate the dangers of drug use and AIDS that plague most prostitutes on the street.

The first part of this article analyzes the disposition of prostitution-related cases in the BMC in 1990.[15] Parts II and III discuss the inconsistencies this system creates—the fact that most judges no longer treat prostitution as an act deserving criminal sanction, but police nonetheless continue to arrest women for selling sexual services. And despite evidence that judges are reluctant to treat prostitution as a serious crime, attempts to fully dismantle the prostitution laws have failed. Part IV outlines historical views of prostitution and female sexuality that may inform present day attitudes of judges and police officers. Part V attempts to demystify the link between prostitution and AIDS, the most pressing rationale for maintaining criminalization. Finally, Part VI looks briefly at the real dangers these women face and the protections they deserve.

I. RESULTS OF THE SURVEY

Many of the court officers, administrators, and judges interviewed by our staff expressed the belief that if not for prostitution cases, the Second Session of the BMC, as it currently functions, would not be necessary.[16]

---

10. Advantages for Nevada prostitutes include a safer environment in which to work, and freedom from fear of arrest. However, Nevada prostitutes are restricted from deciding how and when they will work. Brothels maintain a fixed work schedule, and prostitutes must yield as much as forty percent of their earnings to the brothel. Carole Campbell, *Prostitution, AIDS and Preventive Health Behavior*, 32 SOC. SCI. & MED. 1370, 1371-72 (1991).

11. Alexander, *supra* note 9, at 210.

12. Campbell, *supra* note 10, at 1370.

13. *Id.* at 1371.

14. *Id.* at 1372.

15. I examined a BMC computer generated list of all cases dealing with prostitution-related offenses disposed of in 1990.

16. Julie Pearl, *The Highest Paying Customers: American Cities and the Cost of Prostitution Control*, 38 HASTINGS L.J. 769, 777 (1987) (citing BOSTON UNIVERSITY LAW SCHOOL CENTER FOR CRIMINAL JUSTICE STUDY, IMPLICATIONS FOR THE CRIMINAL LAW AND ITS ENFORCEMENT 626 (1976) [hereinafter CJC STUDY]).

In order to analyze the processing of prostitutes in Boston's judicial system, I examined the court records of women charged with prostitution-related offenses in the BMC in 1990. I take the BMC as the focus of this analysis because it is there that the vast majority of Boston's prostitution cases are heard, given that it includes in its jurisdiction those districts of Boston where most street prostitution occurs.[17] In 1990, one hundred and sixty-three women were charged with two hundred and sixty-three prostitution-related offenses.[18] Of these, one hundred women were charged with prostitution; one hundred sixty with common nightwalking/streetwalking; and three with maintaining a house of prostitution. These numbers are not indicative of the actual number of prostitutes who work in Boston, or of the number of prostitutes arrested each year, due to the fact that most prostitutes are arrested under the disorderly conduct statute. Therefore, it is likely that the actual number of prostitution-related arrests is far larger.

While the police see prostitution as a law needing enforcement, and continue to arrest hundreds of prostitutes each year,[19] the majority of judges in Boston do not treat prostitution as a serious crime. In 1990, twenty percent of the prostitution-related cases against women in the BMC were dismissed outright (including findings of not guilty) and sixteen percent were continued without a finding (which operates as a dismissal unless the defendant commits a crime in the future).[20] Another thirty-eight percent of the women were given suspended sentences and/or probation. Six percent were fined; ten percent served time; and ten percent had cases pending or on appeal.[21] These dispositions appear to have little deterrent or rehabilitative effect; more than a third of the women whose cases I examined were arrested for a prostitution-related offense at least twice in the same year.[22]

---

17. Ninety-seven percent of prostitution in Boston occurs in District 1 (which includes the Combat Zone) and District 4 (which includes Back Bay). Milman, *supra* note 8, at 11. Most of these areas are under the jurisdiction of the BMC.

18. Thirty-five percent of the women were rearraigned on prostitution-related offenses at least once in 1990. Again, this does not account for prostitutes who had multiple arrests in the same year under the disorderly conduct laws. For the most part, I am not including in my discussion the cases of male prostitutes, as my focus is on how prostitution laws reinforce sexist conceptions of women. The factors of gender and sexual orientation that enter into male prostitution (male prostitutes generally service a gay clientele) warrant a separate article. However, a broad comparison of the sentencing fates of male and female prostitutes, discussed *infra* at text accompanying notes 24-26, helps to highlight prejudices against sexually promiscuous women.

19. In 1985, Boston police arrested twice as many persons for prostitution as for all homicides, rapes, robberies, and assaults combined. Pearl, *supra* note 16, at 769.

20. See *infra* text accompanying note 23 for a chart of sentencing patterns for female prostitutes in the BMC in 1990.

21. Imposing fines on prostitutes only forces them to work doubletime to earn money for the fine. A former inspector with the New York City Vice Squad referred to judges who fine prostitutes as "the biggest pimp[s] of all." ARLENE CARMEN & HOWARD MOODY, WORKING WOMEN: THE SUBTERRANEAN WORLD OF STREET PROSTITUTION 185 (1985) (quoting Inspector Richard Dillon).

22. The 1990 repeat offender rate would be higher if I had been able to include prostitutes charged under the disorderly conduct statute.

Sentencing Patterns for Female Prostitutes in the BMC (1990)[23]

	Number of Cases	Percent of Total
Dismissed/Not Guilty	51	19.5%
Continuance Without a Finding	43	16.2%
Probation Only	43	16.2%
Suspended Sentence	59	22.3%
Fine	16	6.0%
Time Served	27	10.4%
Pending/On Appeal	24	9.4%
Total	263	100%

Boston police fail to target the worst criminal offenders—pimps. In 1990, only five men were arraigned in the BMC for deriving support from the work of a prostitute, and only three for procuring/soliciting clients for a prostitute. Four of these cases were dismissed, and one was on appeal at the completion of the survey. One Boston police detective noted the difficulty of bringing charges against pimps—prostitutes are generally reluctant to testify against their "man" out of fear, love, or loyalty.[24]

Differences in the judicial treatment of cases against male and female prostitutes revealed a clear bias.[25] While judges dismissed outright forty-three percent of the charges against male prostitutes, they dismissed only nineteen percent of those brought against female prostitutes.[26] The failure of the BMC to arraign a single customer in all of 1990 further highlights a double standard. There was not a single case of a defendant being charged with buying sexual services. Although most of the female prostitutes ultimately receive insubstantial sentences, the lingering sexism implicit in the arrest and dismissal statistics may help to explain why judges continue to criminalize prostitution,

---

23. Time served includes those sentenced to jail, those sentenced to attend drug treatment programs and persons whose suspended sentences were revoked. Defendant is sentenced to and credited for the number of days she spent in jail awaiting trial.

24. Interview with Marvin R. Emery, Detective, Boston Police Department, in Boston, Mass. (Apr. 18, 1991) [hereinafter Interview with Detective Emery].

25. The male prostitutes were all charged with selling sexual services. Thus the difference between the treatment of male and female prostitutes can only be attributed to gender and sexual orientation, since they are being charged with exactly the same crime. Whatever biases may exist against men selling sexual services to other men, it is nevertheless curious that male prostitutes received markedly different treatment.

26. One study of judicial processing of 2859 male and female prostitutes in a large city in Texas from 1973-1985 found that judges were most likely to find defendants guilty of prostitution if they were female or repeat offenders, or if they belonged to a minority. Women and minorities were most likely to receive jail time and minorities most likely to receive the harshest sentences. John H. Lindquist et al., *Judicial Processing of Males and Females Charged with Prostitution*, 17 J. CRIM. JUST. 277 (1989).

and why they appear reluctant to treat prostitution as a public health, unemployment, or welfare problem.

II. THE POLICE

When men sell women's bodies, or images of women's bodies, it is called pornography and it is legal, its right to exist vehemently defended with the first amendment. But when women sell their own bodies, it is called prostitution, and we can see what an imperative it's been to protect the rights of prostitutes in our society.[27]

Even as judges dispose of prostitution cases with a slap on the wrist, the police as law enforcers continue to make arrests. Three basic arguments are used to justify police enforcement of prostitution laws. The most standard reason has little to do with the harm prostitution might cause. As long as prostitution remains a crime, police can claim, "It's on the books, so we enforce it." The other two justifications revolve around the perceived by-products of prostitution. Police accuse street prostitutes of frequently engaging in robbery or pickpocketing.[28] Thus, they justify arresting prostitutes on prostitution charges by arguing that they are preventing petty larceny in the process. The third reason police often give for targeting prostitutes in certain neighborhoods is that they are responding to complaints from residents who live in the areas where prostitution occurs. None of these justifications hold up under close scrutiny.

The argument that police are just upholding existing laws falls short because the law as written is so vague and broad that it would be just as easy to ignore as to enforce. Yet the police make a concerted effort to go after street prostitutes. The vast majority of prostitution arrests are made through the use of police decoys. This gives law enforcement officers unusually broad discretion over whom to target.[29] Arrest patterns in Boston reveal that the women targeted by the police decoys are the poorest, most vulnerable prostitutes—those who work on the street. Of the 263 women arraigned for prostitution related offenses in the BMC in 1990, all but three were arrested on the street.[30] The dearth of non-street walker arrests in Boston does not reflect a shortage of prostitutes working as call girls or masseuses. The Boston

---

27. Donna M. Niles, *Confessions of a Priestesstute*, in SEX WORK, *supra* note 9, at 149.

28. Interview with Detective Emery, *supra* note 23; Milman, *supra* note 8, at 9.

29. The personal values of individual police officers inevitably influence their application of the laws. This may lead to discriminatory arrest patterns. *See* Daniel Mendoza de Arce & Omar L. Peraza, *Institutional Discrimination in Criminal Justice Processes*, in DISCRIMINATION IN ORGANIZATIONS 296-97 (Rodolfo Alvarez & Kenneth G. Lutterman eds., 1979).

30. Two of the three off-street prostitutes were arrested for bringing clients to rooms in the Sheraton Hotel and charged with "maintaining a house of prostitution." The other was charged with "keeping a house of ill fame." (Arrest detail on file with author). Nationally, street prostitutes constitute only 10-20% of the prostitute workforce. Alexander, *supra* note 9, at 189.

Yellow Pages list numerous escort service with names like "Pussy Cat Escort Service" or "Allure Escort Referrals." The ads feature illustrations of bikini-clad women with the assurance "Sensitive young ladies always available." These businesses are cross-referenced in the "massage" section as "Pussy Cat Massage" and "Allure Massage" and provide the same telephone numbers.

Police who choose to arrest women under the prostitution laws engage in sexual stereotyping that criminalizes "indiscriminate" female sexuality (or, more cynically, women who dare to require payment for their sexual services) while ignoring the men who patronize prostitutes.[31] Police propensity to impose a double standard dovetails with a general disdain for streetwalkers. As one police detective put it: "The only guy who would go with an ugly whore at two in the morning has gotta be drunk."[32] In Massachusetts, the prostitution statutes apply equally to those selling and buying sexual services, but in 1990, not a single customer was arraigned in the BMC.[33] This is due in part to the use of undercover vice police to serve as "decoys" for prostitutes. Since most of the police officers are male, those arrested are generally women and a few male prostitutes. Of all the prostitution cases in the BMC in 1990, only eleven listed a "witness" (i.e., client) who was not a police officer.[34] Even when the witness was identified by name, however, there was only one complaint that specifically noted that the witness was issued a summons as well.

The prostitution statute in Massachusetts was specifically amended in 1983 to cover both the seller and buyer of sex for a fee.[35] Yet no cases involving clients actually showed up at the BMC in 1990. Boston police and a BMC judge noted that the police periodically conduct "sweeps" for prostitution

---

31. Under the Model Penal Code, for example, only the prostitute and not the customer violates the law. MODEL PENAL CODE § 251.2. As Margo St. James sees it:

> The great fear for men, who are running things, is that if whores have a voice, suddenly good women are going to find out how much their time is worth and how to ask for the money. I really think that women are being put in jail for asking for money.

Margo St. James, *The Reclamation of Whores, in* GOOD GIRLS/BAD GIRLS: FEMINISTS AND SEX TRADE WORKERS FACE TO FACE 82 (Laurie Bell ed., 1987).

32. Interview with Detective Emery, *supra* note 23.

33. Nationally, clients make up 5% of the persons arrested for violation of prostitution statutes. St. James, *supra* note 5, at 78.

34. Whenever police reports indicate a "witness" for a prostitution charge, they are referring to the client. Prostitution is defined as offering or engaging in sex for a fee. MASS. GEN. LAWS ANN. ch. 272 § 53A (West 1990). Therefore, witnesses of the crime are those who hear or see the women ask for money. In light of the fact that most prostitutes who work the streets of Boston are picked up by car to have sex there or in a hotel room, the only likely witness to the offer or demand for money is the client himself (or the police decoy).

35. Any person who engages, agrees to engage, or offers to engage in sexual conduct with another person in return for a fee, or any person who pays, agrees to pay or offers to pay another person to engage in sexual conduct, or to agree to engage in sexual conduct with another natural person may be punished by imprisonment in a jail or house of correction for not more than one year, or by a fine of not more than five hundred dollars, or by both such fine and imprisonment.

MASS GEN. LAWS ANN. ch. 272, § 53A (West 1990).

customers, arresting forty to fifty at a time, a few times a year.[36] However, the computer generated list of all prostitution related offenses in the BMC in 1990 did not include a single case of a client being arraigned.

Since the "sex for a fee" law was amended, the statistics for prostitution arrests show a marked decrease from 1241 in 1983 to 790 in 1984 to 389 in 1989.[37] This apparent slide is most likely *not* a reflection of a decreasing number of women working as prostitutes or being arrested for prostitution. Rather, the decrease can most likely be attributed to the elimination of a separate Boston Police Department vice squad in 1984, and the increasing tendency of the police to charge prostitutes with disorderly conduct, a crime not covered by the Boston Prostitution and Commercialized Vice statistics.[38]

Boston police currently arrest the majority of prostitutes under the disorderly conduct statute.[39] Detective Emery estimated that seventy percent of the prostitutes they arrest are brought in under a disorderly conduct charge.[40] A sample criminal complaint for a woman charged with disorderly conduct reads, "for being a disorderly person going into street, stopping motor vehicles causing a disturbance."[41] "Stopping motor vehicles" is also the activity most likely to appear in police complaints for common nightwalking. Police who do not have enough evidence to arrest prostitutes under the common nightwalking law rely on the vagueness of a disorderly conduct charge to justify the arrest, notwithstanding the fact that the disorderly conduct statute was written to apply to people who "disturb the peace," not prostitutes themselves.

Police use of the disorderly conduct statute against prostitutes persists despite a Massachusetts court ruling which held that the statute was not intended to be used against prostitutes. A 1981 case, *Commonwealth v. Blavackas*,[42] held that the disorderly conduct statute "is not primarily, if at all, directed at offensive sexual conduct."[43] The court relied on an earlier case, *Alegata v. Commonwealth*,[44] which had interpreted the disorderly

---

36. Interview with Detectives Marvin Emery and John Pumphret, Boston Police Department, Area A, in Boston, Mass. (Apr. 19, 1991); Interview with Judge Sally Kelly, Boston Municipal Court, in Boston, Mass. (Dec. 9, 1990).

37. BOSTON POLICE DEP'T, PROSTITUTION AND COMMERCIALIZED VICE RESEARCH AND ANALYSIS PRINTOUT (1990).

38. Interview with Detective Emery, *supra* note 23. Because the disorderly conduct law covers a broad range of activities, and is rather vague, it is easier to arrest people under that statute than under the prostitution laws.

39. *Id.*; Interview with Sarah Hunt, *supra* note 5. Hunt, a criminal defense attorney who represents roughly 250 prostitutes a year, confirmed that most of her clients are arrested under the disorderly conduct law.

40. Interview with Detective Emery, *supra* note 23.

41. Complaint (No. 256582), Boston Mun. Ct. (1990). The identities of the parties named in this complaint and those cited hereinafter were unavailable.

42. 419 N.E.2d 856 (Mass. App. Ct. 1981).

43. *Id.* at 858.

44. 231 N.E.2d 201 (Mass. 1967). A more recent case dealing with political protesters followed the *Alegata* interpretation of disorderly conduct:

A person is guilty of disorderly conduct if, with purpose to cause public inconvenience,

conduct law to require "proof at least of significant risk of violence or serious disturbance."[45] The *Blavackas* court threw out the conviction of a woman who had been found guilty of disorderly conduct after two police officers saw her:

> [A]s she stopped with hand signals four automobiles, each with a lone male operator. She engaged each operator in conversation for about a minute. Other traffic in significant volume was forced to go around the stopped automobiles. She stopped a fifth automobile . . . . After a brief conversation between her and the vehicle's operator, this vehicle was driven onto Murray Avenue where it stopped.[46]

The woman got into the car. The police followed and arrested her for disorderly conduct just as she was taking off the driver's pants in a nearby driveway. This fact pattern, short of catching them in the act, matches the criminal complaints filed by Boston police officers who arrest prostitutes for disorderly conduct. Some judges are beginning to throw out disorderly conduct cases against prostitutes.[47] However, judges are unlikely to dismiss such cases without the relevant legal arguments from defense counsel. Many defense attorneys are not familiar with the history of these laws, and do not raise the proper legal objections to the court.[48]

The argument that prostitution increases the level of street crime in the neighborhoods where prostitutes work was specifically addressed in Barbara Milman's 1976-77 study of prostitution in Boston. Milman compared street crime rates with prostitution rates in various areas of the city, and found that while prostitution and street crime often occur together, there is no evidence that prostitution causes or attracts street crime. In some neighborhoods, prostitution existed with no correspondingly higher level of street crime.[49]

Some people are upset by the presence of prostitutes in their neighborhood whether or not they believe prostitutes also engage in other street crimes. People object to seeing women sell themselves on their corner or are appalled that their children are witness to such activity. Many people do not like having to see homeless people on their sidewalk, but that is not a sufficient argument

---

annoyance or alarm, or recklessly creating a risk thereof, he: (a) engages in fighting or threatening, or in violent or tumultuous behavior; (b) makes unreasonable noise or offensively coarse utterance, gesture or display, or addresses abusive language to any person present; or (c) creates a hazardous or physically offensive condition by any act which serves no legitimate purpose of the actor.
Commonwealth v. Feigenbaum, 536 N.E.2d 325, 327 (Mass. 1989) (citing Alegata v. Commonwealth, 231 N.E.2d at 211). Most of the activities street prostitutes are arrested for under a disorderly conduct charge, such as waving down cars and talking to unknown men, do not fall into any of these three situations.

45. 419 N.E.2d at 858.
46. *Id.*
47. Interview with Sarah Hunt, *supra* note 5; Interview with Detective Emery, *supra* note 23.
48. Interview with Sarah Hunt, *supra* note 5.
49. Milman, *supra* note 8, at 17-18.

for criminalizing homelessness.[50] If prostitution were legal, neighbors would have no more right to call the police than they do to call the police about pornographic book stores or other legal businesses which nevertheless annoy and disturb nearby residents. Under the current regime, since prostitutes have no legal way of notifying clients of their whereabouts, high visibility in public places is the easiest way to meet clients. If prostitution were decriminalized, prostitutes would not have to rely on sidewalk solicitation, and the social problem of offending uninvolved parties would diminish.

III. IN COURT

Police discretion in arresting prostitutes is paralleled in the courtroom by the various judicial attitudes towards the crime.[51] As the 1990 BMC disposition statistics show, Boston's judges do not enforce prostitution laws with serious criminal penalties.[52] In only the rare case does a prostitute serve a sentence or pay a fine, but judges have not been willing to ignore the criminality of prostitution altogether. Even in the face of viable legal challenges, Massachusetts courts have refused to strike down prostitution laws. In 1977 the common nightwalking statute, chapter 272, section 53 of the Massachusetts General Laws, was challenged as unconstitutional on its face and as applied in *Commonwealth v. King*.[53] While the legal arguments against the law were based on discrimination theory and were not explicitly arguments for decriminalization, the case gave the court an opportunity to effectively decriminalize prostitution by striking down the law as discriminatory. The court upheld the law. The judge was not convinced by the argument that women were discriminated against when clients were not arrested, analogizing the situation to one which criminalizes the selling, but not the buying, of obscene goods.[54] The court also refused to find the enforcement of the laws discriminatory against women on the grounds that the police primarily arrested female and not male prostitutes, since no evidence was presented to the court that male prostitutes were not being arrested. The court noted that if such evidence did exist, a female prostitute could get her charges dismissed.[55]

In the wake of the *King* case, the Massachusetts Legislature passed Section 53A of the Criminal Code in 1983, making both the purchase and the sale of sexual services a crime.[56] A defendant successfully challenged discriminatory

---

50. Unfortunately, some cities are starting to act as if it were.

51. A New York City outreach group for prostitutes tried posting a weekly list of judges sitting in each session, the sentences they were giving to prostitutes, and how they were handling outstanding warrants for unpaid fines resulting from previous convictions, so that the women could "decide intelligently whether they wanted to risk arrest in light of the penalties being dispensed." CARMEN & MOODY, *supra* note 21, at 160.

52. *See supra* part I.

53. 372 N.E.2d 196 (Mass. 1977).

54. *Id.* at 204.

55. *Id.* at 205.

56. MASS. GEN. L. ch. 272, § 53A.

application of the law in *Commonwealth v. An Unnamed Defendant.*[57] The testimony of a Brockton police officer that it was department policy not to arrest male customers showed discriminatory enforcement of sections 53 and 53A (the common nightwalker and "sex for a fee laws") on the basis of sex, and the complaints were dismissed.[58] However, as the BMC statistics make abundantly clear, police in Boston continue to enforce the law in a discriminatory manner, as no clients were arraigned in 1990.[59]

The practice of convicting under the nightwalking statutes solely on the basis of circumstantial evidence was challenged in 1986 in *Commonwealth v. Proctor,*[60] but the challengers were as unsuccessful as the *King* defendants. The court held that evidence of a specific and express act of solicitation is not required to convict a defendant of walking the streets for the purposes of prostitution. Circumstances alone sufficed. In *Proctor,* the defendant was convicted based on the following:

[O]n repeated occasions, over a period of two or three months, arresting officer saw defendant on street corner in area frequented by prostitutes, conversing with male motorists and getting into their vehicles, and that on night of her arrest defendant talked to a man who had stopped his car, had started to enter his car, but walked away as police officer approached.[61]

In a typical common nightwalking case from this past year, police observed a woman "on several recent occassions [sic] in the 'Combat Zone' Area in conversation with different unknown males and told [her] on each occasion to vacate the area." When she refused to leave, she was arrested.[62] The ludicrousness of the "conversation with different unknown males" standard becomes obvious if we imagine it being applied in a bar or a nightclub.

Some judges take the paternalistic view that prostitutes themselves are the victims of prostitution and arrest is in their own best interest. One BMC judge who refused to grant bail to a prostitute last year wrote on the bail papers:

Four arrests in 1990—she defaulted on each one. . . . She is seven and a half months pregnant. Charged last night with prostitution. Appears high—major drug problem. She needs help. Please do not release her.[63]

---

57. 492 N.E.2d 1184 (Mass. App. Ct. 1986).
58. *Id.*
59. *See supra* text accompanying note 25.
60. 493 N.E.2d 879 (Mass. App. Ct. 1986).
61. *Id.* at 880 (quoting facts as described in headnote).
62. Complaint (No. 259775), Boston Mun. Ct. (1990).
63. Hearing on Motion to Grant Bail (No. 255721), Boston Mun. Ct. (1990).

One African-American female ex-judge at the BMC who heard prostitution cases daily described the tension this way:

> The pull is that it always seems as if you can do something when you are sitting there, that you can turn this life around—can get this woman off the street. The pull in the other direction is that criminalization only enhances the oppression of the institution, which is especially true for the black prostitutes. The race factor makes them more vulnerable to arrest, to police harassment, and to prejudice in the courts as black defendants.[64]

This judge made it her policy to refuse to hear cases against prostitutes unless the customer was arrested as well.[65]

In recent years, the outbreak of AIDS has created a new "justification" for enforcing prostitution laws. The concern that judges in the BMC reveal most frequently in the court papers I examined is that the AIDS epidemic has made prostitutes a public health threat, and that the judicial system should be mobilized to stem the spread of AIDS in this context. As one BMC judge put it, "There ought to be posters up in the Combat Zone that say "Prostitution = Death."[66] Some judges in the BMC will use the knowledge that a prostitute has AIDS to deny her or him bail or make bail exceptionally high. One judge hearing the bail argument for one female prostitute refused to set bail: "Three separate cases of prostitution, common nightwalking (2 cases). Defendant has AIDS. Defendant is a public health risk."[67]

One example of this mentality is the current trend in some states requiring mandatory HIV testing of people arrested for or convicted of prostitution. At least nine states currently have such laws.[68] Nevada has created a separate criminal offense for people who prostitute knowing they have AIDS.[69] Yet as Carole Campbell points out, using mandatory AIDS testing might not encourage these prostitutes to leave the streets.[70] The felony charge that accompanies these new laws might give a prostitute a more serious record, making it even more difficult for her to get a "straight" job. Furthermore, prostitutes have no support programs to help them change careers. Many women will continue to prostitute no matter what the criminal consequences

---

64. Barbara M. Hobson, Uneasy Virtue: The Politics of Prostitution and the American Reform Tradition 224 (1987) (quoting Margaret Burnham, former judge, Boston Mun. Ct.).

65. Interview with Sarah Hunt, *supra* note 5.

66. Interview with Judge Sally Kelly, *supra* note 36.

67. Hearing on Motion to Grant Bail (No. 255827), Boston Mun. Ct. (1990).

68. Larry O. Gostin, *Public Health Strategies for Confronting AIDS: Legislative and Regulatory Policy in the United States* 261 JAMA 1621, 1626 (1989).

69. *See* Larry Gostin, *The Politics of AIDS: Compulsory State Powers, Public Health, and Civil Liberties* 49 Ohio. St. L.J. 1017, 1041 n.128 (1989).

70. Campbell, *supra* note 10, at 1376.

because they have no occupational choices.[71]

IV. THE HISTORY OF PROSTITUTION LAWS

For two hundred years, prostitution was a common law offense in the colonies and later in the United States. It was not until the nineteenth century that states began to pass statutes specifically criminalizing prostitution.[72] Under the common law order, prostitution had been understood as the crime of selling one's body for gain. Under the statutory regime, however, judges began to penalize women who simply had "indiscriminate intercourse."[73] Many women who were simply on the street after dark were arrested for the crime of "nightwalking"—the assumption being that any woman on the street at that time intended to solicit money for sex.[74] The criminal law often treated prostitution as a status offense, and equated women's sexual non-conformity with criminal behavior.[75]

The criminal justice system placed considerable emphasis on, and used as a measure of women's criminality, the sexual histories of female offenders, often basing the sentence of the woman on this, rather than on the crime itself.[76] There was no parallel linking of male sexuality with male deviance. Indeed, the same acts committed by men were not even charged as crimes. In the beginning of the nineteenth century, one quarter of the persons arrested for public lewdness in Boston were men; by 1850, there were no such prosecutions.[77]

Conviction rates for accused prostitutes averaged eighty to ninety percent in the first half of the nineteenth century, while the average conviction rate for all crimes was sixty-five percent.[78] Prostitutes were also given longer sentences than persons convicted of other misdemeanors like drunkenness or vagrancy.[79]

Not all prostitutes were hounded by the police, however. Class and race bias influenced the enforcement of prostitution laws as much as gender.

---

71. Campbell, *supra* note 10, at 1373.

72. By 1900 all the states had anti-prostitution statutes on the books. THOMAS C. MACKEY, RED LIGHTS OUT: A LEGAL HISTORY OF PROSTITUTION, DISORDERLY HOUSES AND VICE DISTRICTS, 1870 - 1917, at 123 (1987).

73. *Id.* at 50-54.

74. HOBSON, *supra* note 64, at 33. The nightwalking statute was written to apply to "fiddlers, peddlers, and many others who in their speech or behavior disturbed the public peace," but engaging in the sale or offer of sexual services was not an element of the nightwalking crime. *Id.* at 32.

75. *Id.* at 17. In 19th century Boston, for example, unwed mothers who applied for public charity could be sentenced to the workhouse where people convicted of misdemeanors were incarcerated, simply because they had children and were unmarried. *Id.* at 19.

76. *Id.* at 112.

77. *Id.* at 34.

78. *Id.* at 36.

79. More than 90% of women convicted of nightwalking or lewdness received sentences of three to six months in prison, while persons convicted of other misdemeanors averaged two to three month sentences. *Id.* at 117.

Women who serviced wealthier clients in private clubs and brothels were left alone, while the police cracked down on those who worked on the street or in dance halls and "disorderly houses" frequented by the "lower" classes.[80] The police targeted areas where working class, recent immigrant and black families tended to live.[81]

Boston lawmakers took aim at prostitution as one way of attacking the flood of immigrants who came to the city in the first decades of the nineteenth century.[82] Immigrant women who worked as street prostitutes were particularly vulnerable to arrest.[83] The attack on prostitutes as a symbol of the poor, dirty invading immigrant was reinforced by public health laws which branded prostitutes as the cause of sexually transmitted disease. The tendency to link women to the spread of venereal disease had far more to do with characterizations of sexually active women as "dirty" and "diseased" than with scientific evidence. Beth Bergman points out that "nineteenth century scientists believed that women could spread gonorrhea without having the disease, while some thought women innately possessed the disease."[84] In 1910, the New York State Legislature passed the Page Law, which mandated that all prostitutes be tested for venereal disease upon arrest.[85] If infected, the woman was held until she was no longer contagious. There was no similar requirement for the male clients of prostitutes. Legislators completely ignored the role of men in spreading the disease.[86] This double standard impeded the effort to check the spread of sexually transmitted diseases.

During World War I, U.S. government officials depicted prostitutes as spreaders of venereal disease who could potentially threaten the fighting capacity of the U.S troops. Government pamphlets described prostitutes as "enemy agent[s] sent from Germany to debilitate the American forces."[87] Any woman walking alone "near a military base risked being labeled a 'suspected prostitute.'"[88] This label could have serious consequences since federal laws required the quarantining of civilians suspected of being infected with venereal disease. The suspicion did not have to be based on any act of

---

80. *Id.* at 33. *See also* CARMEN & MOODY, *supra* note 21, at 5.

81. HOBSON, *supra* note 64, at 35.

82. Boston's population rose from 18,000 to 43,000 from 1790-1820, and the city seemed more dangerous to its longer settled residents. *Id.* at 12.

83. In mid-19th century Boston, 36% of all women, but 55% of all convicted prostitutes, were foreign-born. *Id.* at 88. Most of the immigrants were from Ireland. Black women were two percent of the jailed prostitute population. *Id.*

84. Beth Bergman, *AIDS, Prostitution, and the Use of Historical Stereotypes to Legislate Sexuality,* 21 J. MARSHALL L. REV. 777, 793 (1988) (citing PRINCE ALBERT MORROW, SOCIAL DISEASES AND MARRIAGE, SOCIAL PROPHYLAXIS 84 (1904)).

85. Martha Vicinius, *Sexuality and Power: A Review of Current Work in the History of Sexuality,* 8 FEMINIST STUD. 133, 134 (1982). The move in some states to require that convicted prostitutes be tested for AIDS replicates the pattern of the Page Law.

86. Bergman, *supra* note 84, at 795 n.102.

87. HOBSON, *supra* note 64, at 180 (citing ALLAN M. BRANDT, NO MAGIC BULLET: A SOCIAL HISTORY OF VENEREAL DISEASE IN THE UNITED STATES SINCE 1880 85-111 (1985)).

88. HOBSON, *supra* note 64, at 167.

solicitation.[89] Local health boards were empowered to hold women suspected of carrying venereal disease until they had been tested and the results were known, acting in effect like courts and jails. If a woman tested positive she could be detained until cured, and a positive test result was seen as virtual proof of a chastity offense.[90] Eighteen-thousand women were held under quarantine during this period.[91] The current trend among judges to refuse bail to prostitutes with AIDS harbors elements of a quarantine mentality.[92]

The campaign against sexually transmitted disease during World War I focused on controlling women's sexuality through the quarantine system. Army doctors did not distribute condoms to troops until World War II, even though physicians at the time of World War I were aware of the effectiveness of condoms in preventing V.D. In the first half of this century, public health officials assumed that prostitutes, rather than their customers, were responsible for transmission of V.D.; that poor, sexually promiscuous women were for all purposes prostitutes; and that male sexuality was too "explosive" to be controlled.[93]

V. THE CASE OF AIDS

Some BMC judges maintain they are forcibly removing prostitutes from the streets either to protect them from contracting AIDS or to prevent them from spreading the disease to their customers. Admittedly, a significant number of street prostitutes test positive for the AIDS virus.[94] However, several recent epidemiological studies question the extent to which heterosexual prostitution is responsible for the spread AIDS in the United States.[95]

---

89. *Id.* at 167, 176.

90. *Id.* at 167.

91. *Id.* at 176. This number does not even include the large numbers of women who were inspected, held pending the results, and found to be uninfected. Forty-five percent of the cases of women suspected of being V.D. carriers were dismissed without arrest. *Id.*

92. Bergman, *supra* note 84, at 793. Some states have passed legislation which specifically allows for the quarantine of AIDS or HIV infected persons "who pose a serious threat to public health when less restrictive measures have failed to curtail their dangerous behavior." Gostin, *supra* note 68, at 1626 n. 108.

93. HOBSON, *supra* note 64, at 180.

94. Michael J. Rosenberg & Jodie M. Weiner, *Prostitutes and AIDS: A Health Department Priority?*, 78 AM. J. PUB. HEALTH 418 (1988).

95. *Id.* at 420; *See generally* Campbell, *supra* note 10. There is evidence that heterosexual prostitution is responsible for the spread of AIDS in some African countries. This trend is not necessarily applicable to the United States, and the CDC still does not consider prostitution as a recognized risk factor for AIDS. *Id.* For analyses of the risk to prostitutes, see Centers for Disease Control, *Antibody to Human Immunodeficiency Virus in Female Prostitutes*, 36 MORBIDITY & MORTALITY WEEKLY REP. 157 (1987) [hereinafter CDC, *Antibody to Human Immunodeficiency Virus*]; Centers for Disease Control, *Human Immunodeficiency Virus Infection in the United States: A Review of Current Knowledge*, 36 MORBIDITY & MORTALITY WEEKLY REP. 1, 8 (Supp. VI 1987) (summaries of 1987-88 studies showing prostitutes at risk for HIV infection).

While there is substantial data on HIV transmission from men to women, there are far fewer reported cases in the United States of women infecting men.[96] One reason is that, as compared to men, fewer women in the general population have the virus. A second explanation is the lower efficiency of female-to-male AIDS transmission.[97] As of April 1991, the Centers for Disease Control report women as the source of only thirty percent of all AIDS cases attributed to heterosexual contact.[98] This number may well be skewed given that some men refuse to admit to homosexual activity and falsely blame their AIDS infection on sex with a prostitute.[99] A New York City Department of Health study conducted from 1979-1989 showed only seven out of 17,000 men with AIDS whose risk factor was "sex with a woman."[100] One of the most recent studies of female-to-male transmission of AIDS looked at seventy-two male partners of HIV-infected women and found only one case in which the man had contracted HIV from his partner, as compared with a twenty percent transmission rate from men to women.[101] Even then, there is very little data indicating how many of the female-to-male AIDS transmission cases are due to sexual contact with a prostitute.[102]

Another factor which minimizes the risk of transmission is that the vast majority of street prostitutes provide oral sex rather than intercourse.[103] The chance of contracting AIDS from receiving unprotected oral sex is quite small.[104] Condom use further mitigates the risk of transmission.[105] In

---

96. Bergman, *supra* note 84, at 782 (citing Peterman, *Risk of HTLV-III/LAV Transmission to Household Contacts of Persons with Transfusion-Associated HTLV-III/LAV Infection,* Program and Abstracts of the 2d Int'l Conference on AIDS (1986)).

97. Nancy S. Padian, *Female-to-Male Transmission of Human Immunodeficiency Virus,* 266 JAMA 1664 (1991).

98. *Id.* at 1664 (citing CENTER FOR DISEASE CONTROL, HIV/AIDS SURVEILLANCE REPORT: YEAR-END EDITION (1991)); Campbell, *supra* note 10, at 1368.

99. One social worker who administered a questionnaire on AIDS transmission to people with AIDS (P.W.A.'s) in New York noted that after there had been media coverage on the role of Haitian prostitutes in spreading AIDS, she saw a noticeably larger number of persons with no identified risk attributing their infection to prostitutes. She noted that 63% of the P.W.A.'s who at first listed prostitutes as the source of their infection later changed their answers after she had gotten to know them and earned their trust. Bergman, *supra* note 84, at 784 n.34.

100. Donna King, *Prostitutes as Pariah in the Age of AIDS—A Content Analysis of Coverage of Women Prostitutes in The New York Times and The Washington Post, September 1985-April 1988,* 16 WOMEN & HEALTH 158 (1990) (citing AIDS Surveillance Unit, N.Y.C. Dep't of Health, AIDS Surveillance Update (1989)). *See also* Michael Bloor et. al., *Estimating Hidden Populations: A New Method of Calculating the Prevalence of Drug-Injecting and Non-Injecting Female Street Prostitution,* 86 BRIT. J. OF ADDICTION 1477, 1482 (1991).

101. Padian, *supra* note 97, at 1664. In the one case in which the male did contract the virus, he had repeated unprotected sexual contact with the same partner. If frequency of repeated contact is a factor in female-to-male transmission, this is another reason why prostitutes are less likely to transmit the disease to their clients, since most clients do not have frequent repeated sexual contact with the same streetwalker. *Id.*

102. Rosenberg & Weiner, *supra* note 94, at 421; *See generally* Campbell, *supra* note 10.

103. One estimate put oral sex at about 80% of the prostitution work in the United States. Lyn Hampton, *Health: Our First Concern, in* A VINDICATION OF THE RIGHTS OF WHORES, *supra* note 5, at 109, 127.

104. Alan R. Lifson, *Do Alternative Modes of Transmission of Human Immunodeficiency Virus Exist?,* 259 JAMA 1353, 1354 (1988) (oral-genital contact not independent risk factor for HIV infection and risk of HIV infection after extensive contact with infected saliva "extremely low").

short, recent data does not support the theory that prostitutes contribute significantly to the spread of AIDS in the United States.

Judges also see arrest/incarceration as a means of protecting prostitutes themselves from the risk of AIDS, a risk they view as inextricably tied to their work. Studies indicate, however, that in the United States prostitutes are at the greatest risk of contracting the HIV virus not from random intercourse with clients but through intravenous drug use. It is not surprising that a CDC study of prostitution in seven U.S. cities found that risk factors for AIDS in female prostitutes may be similar to those in other women living in the same geographic areas.[106] Prostitutes who do not use drugs tend not to be HIV-positive.[107] The 1987 CDC study found that approximately twenty percent of IV drug using prostitutes were HIV-positive, while only about five percent of non-IV drug using prostitutes also tested positive for the virus.[108] Fifty percent of the prostitutes in the 1987 study were IV drug users or had regular sex with boyfriends or lovers who took drugs intravenously.[109]

Nevertheless, even among drug using prostitutes who may be HIV-positive, there is no conclusive evidence that prostitutes in the United States are responsible for spreading AIDS to their clients. This is true even though HIV-infected women continue to work the streets. As Priscilla Alexander notes:

> If prostitutes were effectively transmitting the AIDS virus to their customers, there would be far more cases of white, heterosexual males diagnosed with AIDS than is reflected in the current statistics because some IV users in New York have been infected with the AIDS virus since at least 1976, and a third to a half of street prostitutes use IV drugs. . . . The average street prostitute sees 1,500 customers a year.[110]

---

105. Bergman, *supra* note 84, at 782; Campbell, *supra* note 10, at 1373. Prostitutes addicted to heroin and crack are less likely to insist on condom use, however, as they may be too high or too desperate for money to refuse a client who will not wear one. Alexander, *supra* note 9, at 204.

106. CDC, *Antibody to Human Immunodeficiency Virus, supra* note 95, at 158. This 1987 CDC study of AIDS and prostitutes surveyed 1396 prostitutes in Las Vegas, San Francisco, Los Angeles, Atlanta, Colorado Springs, Miami, Southern New Jersey and Northern New Jersey.

107. Rosenberg & Weiner, *supra* note 94, at 418; Campbell, *supra* note 10, at 1368.

108. Campbell, *supra* note 10, at 1368.

109. CDC, *Antibody to Human Immunodeficiency Virus, supra* note 95, at 157 *cited in* Campbell, *supra* note 10, at 1368. Approximately 54% of the MCI-Framingham women surveyed by Social Justice for Women between 1988-1990 had "a history of chronic intravenous drug abuse." KLAUSNER & SMITH, *supra* note 6, at 1. While many, but by no means all, of the women were incarcerated for prostitution, the report notes that many drug addicted women turn to prostitution to support their habit. *Id.* at 2, 9, 11. Drugs taken intravenously include heroin and crack-cocaine. *Id.* at 11.

110. Priscilla Alexander, *Prostitutes Are Being Scapegoated for Heterosexual AIDS*, in SEX WORK, *supra* note 9, at 248, 249. According to Alexander,

> a simple calculation, taking as its basis that perhaps five percent of 20,000 prostitutes in New York were infected in 1978, follows: 4,000 prostitutes x 1,500 customers x 3 years [to allow some time for incubation] x 20 percent [one estimate of the rate of female to male transmission] = 360,000 diagnosed cases of AIDS among the client population. However, only approximately seventy men [as of 1986] have been diagnosed with AIDS who claim contact with prostitutes as

As for the risk on the job, the 1987 CDC study found that female prostitutes are most likely to contract the HIV infection from their boyfriends or husbands, with whom they often do not employ safe sex practices.[111] Thus, overall, there is little scientific data to strengthen the claim of many judges that prostitutes must be kept off the streets to protect both their clients and themselves from the risk of AIDS.

VI. ON THE STREETS

I prefer to do this or else be on aid because regular jobs take all the money out, and if you got kids you got nothing left. Anyway, I gotta find me a house before I can get on aid. Having to work a job to get pay—it's too slow. But this is my job. I gotta work all the time. I worry about AIDS—very much so—and all the other diseases,too. I use condoms when I can get them. I also worry about the guys out there—they take your money, beat you up, kill you. I been hurt a bunch of times. A bunch of times. I had a knife pulled on me, they raped me, beat me up. My sister got a black eye the other day. . . . You work hard out there and they be trying to give you a hard time. The police say all the time, "Hey, you suck my dick and I won't arrest you." Even the lawyers and judges buy sex, I know some. It's bad out there.[112]

Some judges recognize that prison may serve little rehabilitative or deterrent purpose for prostitutes. Yet they see incarceration as a safe haven from the violence and drug use prostitutes face on the street. However, the criminal "justice" system itself, which allows judges to jail prostitutes "for their own good," may be contributing to the dangers faced by streetwalkers. Under a system of criminalization, both clients and pimps may abuse prostitutes without criminal sanction, as prostitutes' own illegal activity makes them fear complaining to the police. Countries like the United States which have the strictest criminal prohibitions against prostitution also have the largest incidence of pimping, juvenile prostitution, and violence against prostitutes.[113] More prostitutes are murdered in the United States than in any

---

their only risk factor, again indicating that prostitutes are not passing the disease as quickly as is commonly believed.
Id.

111. Rosenberg & Weiner, *supra* note 94, at 421. Condom use is often a way prostitutes distinguish sex with those they love from sex with clients. Sophie Day & Helen Ward, *The Praed Street Project: A Cohort of Prostitute Women in London, in* AIDS, DRUGS AND PROSTITUTION 61, 68 (Martin Plant ed., 1990).

112. Jane, *featured on* Carol Jacobson poster for *Street Sex: A Video Installation on Street Prostitution in Detroit* (on file with author).

113. Alexander, *supra* note 9, at 195-96.

other country.[114]

Mimi Silbert's study of sexual assault on street prostitutes revealed that seventy percent of the surveyed women reported that they had been raped while working the streets.[115] While these rapes occurred as often as eight to ten times a year, only four percent of the women reported their assault to the police.[116] Prostitutes are unlikely to report sexual assault because police departments tend to assume that rape is one of the "occupational hazards" of prostitution and do not follow up such complaints. A *San Francisco Examiner* study of police response to rape complaints in Oakland found a huge number of improperly investigated rape cases, many of which involved complainants who were prostitutes.[117] One out of four rape cases in Oakland were listed as "unfounded," although in many instances the police had not bothered to interview the complainant.[118] This dismissive attitude toward prostitute rape victims is not unique to Oakland's police force.[119]

The other major source of violence to prostitutes on the streets comes from pimps. Three different studies have concluded that physical abuse occurs in over half of the pimp-prostitute relationships.[120] More than half of the participants in one of the studies attested to being "beaten regularly or constantly."[121] The criminal complaint from one "deriving support" case brought against a pimp in the BMC last year suggests what form the violence can take:

> Victim reports that she has been working as a prostitute for the defendant from 1/19/90 till 2/5/90, turning over in excess of $1000 to the defendant. Victim also reports that the defendant did put a .38 caliber revolver to her head, at the corner of Church St. and Charles St. South, whereupon he took $20.00 in U.S. currency from her,

---

114. Margo St. James, *supra* note 5, at 79.

115. Alexander, *supra* note 9, at 201, 214 (citing MIMI SILBERT, SEXUAL ASSAULT OF PROSTITUTES (1981)).

116. *Id.*

117. Jane Gross, *203 Rape Cases Reopened in Oakland as the Police Chief Admits Mistakes*, N.Y. TIMES, Sept. 20, 1990 at A14. As a result of public outrage following the release of this article, the Oakland Police subsequently decided to review all the files for the cases that had been listed as "unfounded."

118. *Id.*

119. *See* Jane Gross, *To Some Rape Victims, Justice is Beyond Reach*, N.Y. TIMES, Oct. 12, 1990, at A14.

120. D. KELLY WEISBERG, CHILDREN OF THE NIGHT 108 (1985) (citing DOROTHY H. BRACEY, "BABY-PROS": PRELIMINARY PROFILES OF JUVENILE PROSTITUTES 37 (1979); MIMI H. SILBERT, NAT'L INST. OF MENTAL HEALTH, SEXUAL ASSAULT OF PROSTITUTES: PHASE ONE 60 (1980); ENABLERS, JUVENILE PROSTITUTION IN MINNESOTA: THE REPORT OF A RESEARCH PROJECT 70 (1978)). However, participants in a 1987 survey conducted by the Prostitutes Union of Massachusetts (PUMA), on the violence experienced by fifty female prostitutes, claimed that they were more likely to experience violence from a client or a family member upset with their prostitution than from a pimp. Only 20% of the women in the survey were streetwalkers. The remainder were "dirty mixers," women who work out of bars. Telephone Interview with Chris Womandez, Prostitutes Union of Massachusetts (PUMA), in Boston, Mass. (Apr. 12, 1991).

121. SILBERT, *supra* note 120, at 60.

telling her she had till 10:30 P.M. to come up with another $200.00, or she would be dead.[122]

It is difficult to determine the extent to which prostitutes are involved in pimp relationships because many women refuse to admit that they are relinquishing money to a pimp. Eleanor Miller's study of street prostitutes in Milwaukee found that women very rarely work on the street completely independent of pimps.[123] Women working alone were known as "outlaws," a term that itself points to the pimp relationship as the norm.[124] Most attempts at independent working were brief. According to Miller, "men would simply not permit women to hustle in this fashion," independent of male control.[125]

Younger prostitutes in particular seem to rely on pimps. The average age of females entering the profession is fourteen.[126] One study of juvenile prostitutes found that only ten percent had never worked for a pimp, as compared with twenty-eight percent of the adult prostitute population.[127] The lowest estimates still place the majority of street prostitutes (sixty percent) under a pimp's control.[128]

Pimps convince prostitutes to work for them by offering protection against other violent men and/or by physical coercion. As an eighteen year old prostitute in New York City who works independently describes it:

> [N]ot having a pimp does cause some problems because if the pimps on the streets know that a girl is renegading, they'll be on her ass. It's against their laws to not have a pimp. So if they know that a girl is renegading, they'll make it difficult for her to work. That's why almost every girl out there has one.[129]

While women themselves may make the initial decision to prostitute, they often find it difficult to survive alone on the street so long as prostitution remains illegal. The prostitutes in Miller's study gave all their proceeds to a pimp "in exchange for affection, an allowance, the status of their company,

---

122. Complaint (No. 254938), Boston Mun. Ct. (1990).
123. ELEANOR M. MILLER, STREET WOMAN 145 (1986).
124. *Id.* This same term is used in New York City and in Boston.
125. *Id.* Attorney Sarah Hunt related stories of Boston pimps who would send in clients to beat up women working on their own. Interview with Sarah Hunt, *supra* note 5.
126. D. Kelly Weisberg, *Children of the Night: The Adequacy of Statutory Treatment of Juvenile Prostitution,* 12 AM. J. CRIM. L. 1, 5-6 (1984); Margaret A. Baldwin, *Pornography and the Traffic in Women: Brief on Behalf of Trudee Able-Peterson, et. al., Amici Curiae in Support of Defendant and Intervenor-Defendants, Village Books v. City of Bellingham,* 1 YALE J.L. & FEMINISM 111, 123 (1989). One study of twenty street prostitutes in Camden, New Jersey found that half of the women started prostituting before they were eighteen. Matthew Freund et al., *Sexual Behavior of Resident Street Prostitutes with their clients in Camden, New Jersey,* 26 J. OF SEX RES. 467 (1989).
127. BRACEY, *supra* note 120, at 33.
128. Alexander, *supra* note 9, at 189.
129. MICHAEL ZAUSNER, THE STREETS: A FACTUAL PORTRAIT OF SIX PROSTITUTES AS TOLD IN THEIR OWN WORDS 35 (1986).

and some measure of protection, even if it is simply permission to use the man's name as a "keepaway" (from me) for other predatory men."[130]

If prostitution were not a crime, prostitutes would not be dependent upon pimps to protect them from police and clients. They would be free to press criminal charges against violent customers and against pimps who force women into working for them.[131] Under the current system, prostitutes correctly perceive that police will not investigate crimes committed against them, because officers treat these incidents as "hazards of the job," and do not bother to investigate them seriously.[132] Furthermore, were prostitution to be decriminalized, prostitutes could unionize and collectively demand safer working conditions from clients such as requiring all clients to wear condoms. Individually, prostitutes lack sufficient bargaining power to enforce such demands.

Decriminalization would have an unpredictable effect upon the other principal destructive force for streetwalkers: drug use. Currently, the majority of prostitutes who work the street use drugs.[133] It is difficult to determine whether drug use sends women onto the streets to earn money for their habit, or whether working the streets drives women to drugs.

One trait common among drug-using prostitutes is their relationship with drug-using men. According to Priscilla Damon, a counselor with Community Services for Women (a Boston-based alternative sentencing program for women), some prostitutes first venture into drug use in order to cement a relationship with an addicted lover.[134] Often it is not a pimp but a drug-addicted boyfriend who persuades a woman to begin selling her body.[135] One study found that women are most frequently introduced to drugs by men.[136] This is because "the control of the illegal distribution of drugs, especially heroin, is in the hands of men."[137] The same study also found that most women developed their drug addictions after being on the street.[138]

Putting prostitutes in prison, however, solves none of their problems. Prison is no cure for an addict. In Massachusetts, the women's prison at MCI-Framingham has no full-time drug counseling program. Thus, judges who jail prostitutes in the belief that they are rescuing addicts from drugs are not

---

130. MILLER, *supra* note 123, at 37.
131. *See* Alexander, *supra* note 9, at 184-214.
132. *See* Gross, *supra* note 119.
133. *See supra* note 109.
134. Interview with Priscilla Damon, Community Services for Women, in Boston, Mass. (Jan. 4, 1991).
135. Interview with Kay, *supra* note 1.
136. MILLER, *supra* note 123, at 109.
137. *Id.*
138. *Id.* Many streetwalkers suffer from extremely low self-esteem, and may take drugs, as Kay did, both to boost their confidence and to survive the less appealing aspects of their trade. WEISBERG, *supra* note 120, at 91-93. The self-image problems of female prostitutes are often the result of sexual, emotional, and other forms of physical abuse in the home. Female prostitutes are extremely likely to have suffered both physical and sexual abuse as children. Two-thirds of the participants in one study of juvenile prostitutes in Minnesota said they were beaten by a family member. *Id.* at 93.

sending addicted women to a place where they can receive help.[139] As Kay's story illustrates, incarceration proves mostly unsuccessful in rehabilitating women who pass through the BMC. The recidivism rate, defined as "the return to a state or federal correctional institution, a county house of correction, or a jail for a period of thirty days or more within one year of . . . release," is twenty-five percent at MCI-Framingham.[140] Thirty-five percent of the women arraigned for prostitution-related offenses in 1990, not even counting those charged with disorderly conduct, reappeared in court on another prostitution charge at least once in the same year.[141] In her study of street prostitution in Milwaukee, Eleanor Miller found that jailing prostitutes had no deterrent or rehabilitative impact on the women, other than only temporarily reducing or stopping their drug use.[142]

However, some former prostitutes credit their arrest and time in jail as finally enabling them to leave the street. Jennifer Colasuono, a battered woman who was forced by her abusive husband to prostitute for an escort agency, wishes she had been arrested by the police because this would have stopped her sooner.[143] Kay also admitted that her arrest may have helped her quit prostitution, "because I couldn't humble myself to go into a place and ask for help."[144] She stressed, however, that while the arrest may have helped to take her off the street, only a detoxification program that also dealt with her emotional issues helped to keep her off. Being sent to MCI-Framingham without any counseling only worsened her situation.

In both Kay's and Jennifer's cases, the criminalization of prostitution failed to address the underlying problems in their lives—drug abuse and violence. Jennifer was able to escape from her abusive relationship only by attempting to kill her husband. Kay successfully left the streets only after she was referred to a drug counseling program.

While some of the problems facing prostitutes on the street can be directly solved by decriminalization, other problems demand additional measures. Prostitutes caught in violent, controlling relationships need safe houses;[145]

---

139. MCI-Framingham, the only prison for women in Massachusetts, has only one part-time substance abuse counselor. About three to four hundred women go through MCI-Framingham each year, with about 475 there at any one time. High turnover also makes sustained drug treatment difficult. By the time a woman gets into a program, release from prison is imminent. Radio Interview by Tatiana Scheifer with Sister Jeannette Normandin, former chaplain, MCI-Framingham, and Marcie, inmate (Apr. 11, 1989). *See also* KLAUSNER & SMITH, *supra* note 6, at 3.

140. KLAUSNER & SMITH, *supra* note 6, at 5 (citing DANIEL P. LECLAIR, MASS. DEP'T OF CORRECTIONS, THE EFFECT OF COMMUNITY REINTEGRATION ON RATES OF RECIDIVISM: A STATISTICAL OVERVIEW OF DATA FOR THE YEARS 1971 THROUGH 1987, AT 8 (1990)).

141. *See supra* text accompanying note 22.

142. MILLER, *supra* note 123, at 133.

143. Jennifer Colasuonno, Address at Feminism in the 90s: Bridging the Gap Between Theory and Practice (Feb. 9-10, 1991) (tape on file with YALE J.L. & FEMINISM).

144. Interview with Kay, *supra* note 1.

145. Many battered women's shelters do not accept prostitutes because they fear her pimp might arrive and provoke a violent encounter. Shelters also do not want the women to continue working the streets during their stay. Telephone Interview with Chris Womandez, *supra* note 120.

prostitutes trapped by drug addiction need access to substance abuse counseling. Prostitutes who voluntarily choose their work should be given the power to protect themselves and control their working environments.

One study found that women coerced into drug treatment programs by the criminal justice system enjoyed greater rehabilitative success than women who sought treatment on their own:

> They do better, in part, because legal pressure keeps an addict in treatment for a longer period of time, and virtually all studies agree that the longer an addict receives treatment, the better his [or her] chances for long-term success. . . . For those referred to treatment by the courts, whose only other option is imprisonment or further legal sanctions, the incentive to complete treatment is even more powerful.[146]

But the study also found that women diverted into drug programs had a better rehabilitation rate than women sent to prison.[147] It cost at least $20,000 to maintain each of the 3,461 women prisoners at MCI-Framingham in 1990.[148] In contrast, it costs $8000 for a woman "to participate and complete an average residential recovery program" for drug abuse.[149]

VII. CONCLUSION

On February 11, 1991, two women in tight black leggings and hightop sneakers carried a cross down the aisle of the church at the Jesuit Urban Center in Boston. Following behind them was a draped coffin containing the body of Lori DeLury. DeLury was forty when she was stabbed to death while on the job. She was working as a prostitute to support her drug addiction, when one of her customers murdered her. Despite the fact that she had been arrested for prostitution and common streetwalking three times in the previous year, the intervention of the legal system which criminalizes prostitution did nothing to save her life.

Prostitution should be decriminalized. The endless shuffling of prostitutes through police stations and courtrooms serves no effective protective, rehabilitative or deterrent function. Efforts to jail prostitutes as temporary protection from pimps and drugs target the victim, not the danger. By way of example, it is difficult to imagine sending battered women to jail so as to protect them from their batterers, or to prevent them from going back into an

---

146. KLAUSNER & SMITH, *supra* note 6, at 13 (citing OFFICE OF NAT'L DRUG CONTROL POLICY, UNDERSTANDING DRUG TREATMENT (1989)).

147. *Id.*

148. KLAUSNER & SMITH, *supra* note 6, at 13.

149. *Id.* Women suffering from drug abuse should not be arrested for prostitution as a pretext for forced drug treatment.

abusive situation. Even when prostitutes are imprisoned, they are likely to return to the streets upon release because the Massachusetts prison system fails to adequately address the *reasons* why women choose to sell sex.

Given that prostitution-related cases may comprise as much as fifteen percent of the caseload at the BMC,[150] a tremendous sum is being spent on arresting, holding, and then simply releasing women charged with prostitution. A study by Julie Pearl of the amount spent on arresting and processing Boston prostitutes in 1985 estimated the cost at $1,196 *per case*.[151] Court costs alone for Boston prostitution cases totalled $1,225,224.[152] Altogether, Pearl calculated that in 1985 Boston spent $6,156,133 on the enforcement of its prostitution laws.[153] If judges and policy-makers are sincerely concerned about the violence, drug abuse and risk of disease threatening these women, funds presently spent on criminalization should be shifted to drug rehabilitation, counseling, and safe haven programs. At the very least, decriminalization will give prostitutes the chance to make choices, a possibility remote at best under the present system.

---

150. Interview with Sarah Hunt, *supra* note 5. A 1972-73 study of the BMC by the Boston University Law School Center for Criminal Justice found that one quarter of the complaints (excluding moving traffic violations) were for prostitution cases. Pearl, *supra* note 16, at 777.

151. Pearl, *supra* note 16, at 797.

152. *Id.*

153. *Id.* In 1985, half of the sixteen largest cities in the United States spent more on prostitution control than on either education or public welfare. *Id.* at 772 (citing U.S. BUREAU OF THE CENSUS, CITY GOVERNMENT FINANCES IN 1981-82, SERIES GF82, NO. 4 , at 1-3 (1984)).

HATE CRIME STATUTES: A PROMISING TOOL FOR FIGHTING VIOLENCE AGAINST WOMEN

MARGUERITE ANGELARI*

TABLE OF CONTENTS

* Court Law Clerk, District of Columbia Court of Appeals, 1993-1994. B.A. 1988, The George Washington University; J.D. 1993, The American University, Washington College of Law. I would like to thank Joan Williams for her guidance and support through numerous drafts. I would also like to express my gratitude to Jamin Raskin and Catherine Klein for their comments and to Anne Ruth for her editorial work.

INTRODUCTION

Many feminist theorists and advocates argue that numerous types of violent crime against women should be characterized as "hate crime"; that is, crime motivated by a hatred of women and a desire to control and terrorize women.[1] As early as 1975, Susan Brownmiller

---

1. *See* CENTER FOR WOMEN POLICY STUDIES, VIOLENCE AGAINST WOMEN AS BIAS MOTIVATED HATE CRIME: DEFINING THE ISSUES 1 (1991) (stating that "[t]hroughout these past two decades, feminist theorists have written extensively about violence against women, which is seen as the quintessential example of sex discrimination and sexual oppression—as the most powerful tool of male domination and patriarchal control"). The Center for Women Policy Studies relies on the following works to support its proposition: SUSAN BROWNMILLER, AGAINST OUR WILL: MEN, WOMEN, AND RAPE 14-15 (1975) (stating that "[m]an's discovery that his genitalia could serve as a weapon to generate fear must rank as one of the most important discoveries of prehistoric times, along with the use of fire and the first crude stone axe"); CATHARINE A. MACKINNON, TOWARD A FEMINIST THEORY OF THE STATE 245 (1989) [hereinafter MACKINNON, THEORY OF THE STATE] (asserting that the rape of women by men "is integral to the way inequality between the sexes occurs in life. Intimate violation with impunity is an ultimate index of social power. Rape both evidences and practices women's low status relative to men. . . . Threat of sexual assault is threat of punishment for being female."); KATE MILLETT, SEXUAL POLITICS 25, 44 (1970) (claiming that "[i]n rape, the emotions of aggression, hatred, contempt, and the desire to break or violate personality, take a form consummately appropriate to sexual politics"); and Charlotte Bunch, *Women's Rights as Human Rights: Toward a Re-Vision of Human Rights*, 12 HUM. RTS. Q. 486, 486 (1990) (arguing that gender-related abuse should be incorporated into human rights goals and that "many violations of women's human rights are distinctly connected to being

argued that rape is not a crime of sex, but rather a crime of violence that preserves male dominance and keeps all women in a state of terror.[2] This same analysis of violence against women is applied in the context of domestic violence.[3] Studies show that victims of rape

---

female—that is, women are discriminated against and abused on the basis of gender").

2. Brownmiller defines rape as "a conscious process of intimidation by which *all men* keep *all women* in a state of fear." BROWNMILLER, *supra* note 1, at 15 (emphasis in original). Catharine MacKinnon argues that "[r]ape is an act of dominance over women that works systemically to maintain a gender-stratified society in which women occupy a disadvantaged status as the appropriate victims and targets of sexual aggression." Catharine A. MacKinnon, *Reflections on Sex Equality Under Law*, 100 YALE L.J. 1281, 1302 (1991) [hereinafter MacKinnon, *Sex Equality*]; *accord* MACKINNON, THEORY OF THE STATE, *supra* note 1, at 126 (asserting that dominance and submission between women and men is eroticized, placing women in a dangerous position in relation to men); Susan Griffin, *Rape: The All-American Crime*, 10 RAMPARTS 26, 27 (1971) (emphasizing that all women are victims of rape even if they have not experienced a direct attack because "'rape and the fear of rape are a daily part of every woman's consciousness'"), *quoted in* Patricia L.N. Donat & John D'Emilio, *A Feminist Redefinition of Rape and Sexual Assault: Historical Foundations and Change*, 48 J. SOC. ISSUES 9, 15 (1992).

Dr. JoAnn Evans-Gardner, a founder of the Association for Women in Psychology, asserts that rape is "an act of political oppression," and that "[r]apists perform for sexist males the same function that the Ku Klux Klan performed for racist whites—they keep women in their 'place' through fear." NANCY GAGER & CATHLEEN SCHURR, SEXUAL ASSAULT: CONFRONTING RAPE IN AMERICA 209 (1976); *accord* MacKinnon, *Sex Equality*, *supra* at 1303 (stating that "sexual assault in the United States today resembles lynching prior to its recognition as a civil rights violation").

However, some African-American feminists argue that these theories about the functions of rape have been developed by caucasian feminists in response to their own particular experience of rape. *See infra* notes 162-196 and accompanying text (discussing the argument that mainstream feminism is essentialist). *But see* BELL HOOKS, *Reflections on Race and Sex, in* YEARNING 57, 59 (1990) ("both groups [caucasian men and African-American men] have been socialized to condone patriarchal affirmation of rape as an acceptable way to maintain male domination. It is the merging of sexuality with male domination within patriarchy that informs the construction of masculinity for men of all race and classes.").

3. *See* Edward W. Gondolf, *Anger and Oppression in Men Who Batter: Empiricist and Feminist Perspectives and Their Implications for Research*, 10 VICTIMOLOGY: AN INT'L J. 311 (1985). Gondolf asserts that "feminist researchers . . . analyze abuse as an expression of patriarchy. Men abuse women in the home as they do elsewhere in our society—as a means of maintaining power and exerting control over women. Wife abuse in this light is a kind of gender terrorism." *Id.* at 313. Gondolf further states that

feminists . . . consider male oppression to be fundamental to violence against women. The individual batterer abuses his wife not so much to release his anger as he has been taught to do, as the empiricists imply, but rather, for the same reason men exploit women in the larger society and have beaten and discriminated against them throughout history—to keep them in their place . . . . The man then uses abuse not to relieve or release anger but to exert his power and privilege.

Id. at 316.

Professor Elizabeth Schneider makes the same argument when she states that "[t]raditionally, feminist work on battering identified battering as a problem of sexism, of male domination within heterosexual relationships, shaped by the institution of marriage." Elizabeth M. Schneider, *Particularity and Generality: Challenges of Feminist Theory and Practice in Work on Woman-Abuse*, 67 N.Y.U. L. REV. 520, 539 (1992). She further notes that feminists have challenged "the traditional interpretive frameworks used by psychologists" in the field of wife-battering, and in doing so "have drawn analogies between battered women and other victims of terrorism." *Id.* at 541 n.81; *see also* Michele Bograd, *Feminist Perspectives on Wife Abuse: An Introduction, in* FEMINIST PERSPECTIVES ON WIFE ABUSE 11, 14 (Kersti Yllo & Michele Bograd eds., 1988) (stating that "[even] if individual men refrain from employing physical force against their partners, men as a class benefit from how women's lives are restricted and limited because of their fear of violence by husbands and lovers as well as strangers").

and domestic violence, like victims of other hate crimes, are inter-changeable in the eyes of their attackers.[4] Moreover, violent crimes against women are frequently devoid of any criminal motive and are excessively violent.[5] In similar fashion, advocates for victims of violent crimes motivated by racial and ethnic hatred argue that the intent of such hate-based crimes is to control and terrorize the members of racial and ethnic groups.[6] These crimes also lack criminal motive[7] and are excessively violent.[8]

Despite the similarities between race and ethnic hate-based crimes and violence against women, the development of the law concerning the two types of crimes has differed considerably. While many feminist theorists and women's rights advocates adopt the perspective that violence against women is often hate crime,[9] they have generally failed to have gender included in hate crime statutes.[10] Advocates for victims of ethnic, racial, and other hate-based violence, on the other hand, have successfully promoted legislation that treats such violent crimes differently from other violent crimes through the inclusion of these crimes in hate crime statutes.[11]

This article explores the legal and political issues surrounding the inclusion of gender in hate crime statutes. Part I discusses hate crime statutes in general and the constitutional constraints on the types of behavior that these statutes cover. Part II describes federal and state

---

4. See Elaine Hilberman, Overview: The "Wife-Beater's Wife" Reconsidered, 137 AM. J. PSYCHIATRY 1336, 1337 (1980) (arguing that "[t]he basic fact of the victim's femaleness is used by the offender to justify the assault"); Hate Crime Statistics Act of 1988: Hearing on S. 2000 Before the Subcomm. on the Constitution of the Senate Comm. on the Judiciary, 100th Cong., 2d Sess. 262, 268 (1988) (testimony of Molly Yard, President, National Organization for Women) [hereinafter Yard testimony] (stating that "in the eyes of the rapist, one woman could stand in for any other").

5. See CENTER FOR WOMEN POLICY STUDIES, supra note 1, at 10 (explaining that "[m]any crimes against women involve excessive violence, including mutilation, that characterizes bias-motivated hate crimes"); Peter Finn, Bias Crime: A Special Target for Prosecutors, THE PROSECUTOR, Spring 1988, at 9, 13 (explaining that crimes are identified as bias-motivated by considering the "severity of the attack (e.g., mutilation)").

6. See Peter Finn, supra note 5, at 10 (asserting that "crimes motivated by bias have a far more pervasive impact . . . because they are intended to intimidate an entire group") (emphasis in original).

7. See Finn, supra note 5, at 13-14 (stating that "[w]ith some hate violence incidents there seem to be no innocent victims—everyone appears compromised").

8. See supra note 5 and accompanying text.

9. See supra notes 1-5 and accompanying text (citing to proponents of the argument that violent crime against women is based upon the attacker's desire to control and intimidate women as a group).

10. See infra notes 110-137 and accompanying text (discussing the opposition of national advocacy groups to the inclusion of gender in hate crime statutes).

11. See infra notes 11-27 and accompanying text (discussing legislative efforts on the state and federal level to fight hate crime); see infra note 110 and accompanying text (discussing the success of national advocacy organizations in including a broad range of individuals in hate crime statutes).

hate crime legislation that includes gender. Part III examines the obstacles to the passage and implementation of these laws and the arguments against treating violence against women as hate crime. Part IV analyzes two potential benefits to treating violence against women as hate crime. The article concludes that these potential benefits outweigh the concerns raised in Part III, and that therefore women's advocacy groups should promote both the inclusion of gender in hate crime statutes and the effective implementation of these statutes.

I.   GUIDANCE FROM EXISTING LAW

A.   Hate Crime Statutes In General

1.   Federal Law

For over a century, the American legal system has recognized that individual members of some groups are the targets of violence merely because of their membership in a specific group. The Ku Klux Klan Act of 1871,[12] passed in response to violence against African-Americans following the Civil War and arguably the first federal hate crime statute, was the first federal effort to combat attacks motivated by a person's membership in a particular group.[13] Since the passage of this statute, federal hate crime statutes have expanded the scope of federal protection to include racial, religious, and ethnic minorities.[14] These statutes impose criminal penalties and/or civil remedies.

---

12. Ku Klux Klan Act of 1871, ch. 22, 17 Stat. 13 (codified as amended at 42 U.S.C. §§ 1985-1986 (1988)) (attempting to curtail the violence against African-American citizens from the Ku Klux Klan).

13. *See* S. REP. NO. 197, 102d Cong., 1st Sess. 42 (1991) (stating that Congress first barred discriminatory "attacks against persons because of their race, religion or political beliefs" in 1871).

14. For example, the following federal statutes provide criminal sanctions for those convicted of violating a person's civil rights on the basis of the person's race, religion, or ethnicity. These statutes address: (1) conspiracy to interfere with civil rights, 18 U.S.C. § 241 (1988); (2) deprivation of civil rights under color of law, 18 U.S.C. § 242 (1988); (3) forcible interference with civil rights, 18 U.S.C. § 245 (1988 & Supp. IV 1992); and (4) willful interference with civil rights under the Fair Housing Act, 42 U.S.C. § 3631 (1988). Although three statutes cover private acts, one requires a conspiracy, 18 U.S.C. § 241, and one is restricted to the housing context, 42 U.S.C. § 3631. Furthermore, the statute that addresses forcible interference with civil rights protects only specific civil rights: voting and election activities; participation in programs administered or financed by the United States; federal employment; and jury service in the federal courts. 18 U.S.C. § 245.

Additionally, at least four federal statutes offer civil remedies for victims of civil rights violations that are based upon the victim's race, religion, or ethnicity. 42 U.S.C. § 1983 (1988) (prohibiting an individual from depriving another person of equal protection of the law); 42

2. State Law

A majority of states have enacted hate crime statutes.[15] Many states provide for both criminal penalties and civil remedies in cases of hate crime.[16] Some states require data collection on hate crime.[17] Others train their police to handle hate crime cases.[18] Most importantly, state hate crime statutes extend protection to several traditionally disadvantaged groups not protected by federal

---

U.S.C. § 1985 (1988) (prohibiting two or more individuals from conspiring to deprive any person or class of persons of equal protection of the law); 42 U.S.C. § 1986 (1988) (providing a cause of action against any person who fails to prevent a conspiracy that deprives another person of his civil rights, where the person charged with violating the statute also has the power to prevent the commission of the conspiracy); 42 U.S.C. § 3617 (1988) (providing a cause of action for victims of interference, coercion, or intimidation in violation of the Fair Housing Act). *See generally* NATIONAL INSTITUTE AGAINST PREJUDICE AND VIOLENCE, STRIKING BACK AT BIGOTRY: REMEDIES UNDER FEDERAL AND STATE LAW FOR VIOLENCE MOTIVATED BY RACIAL, RELIGIOUS AND ETHNIC PREJUDICE 23-37 (1986) (discussing federal hate crime remedies, with a particular concentration on the legal remedies for violence motivated by race and religion).

15. The following hate crime statutes are in force: CAL. PENAL CODE § 422.6 (West Supp. 1993); COLO. REV. STAT. § 18-9-121 (Supp. 1992); CONN. GEN. STAT. ANN. § 46a-58 (West 1986); D.C. CODE ANN. § 22-4001 (1992); FLA. STAT. ANN. ch. 877.19 (Harrison 1991); IDAHO CODE § 18-7902 (1987); ILL. ANN. STAT. ch. 38, para. 12-7.1 (Smith-Hurd 1992); IOWA CODE ANN. § 729A.2 (West 1993); KY. REV. STAT. ANN. § 15.331 (Baldwin 1992); ME. REV. STAT. ANN. tit. 25, § 1544 (West 1988); MD. CODE ANN. art. 27, § 470A (1987 & Supp. 1991); MASS. GEN. LAWS ANN. ch. 22C, § 32 (West 1992); MICH. COMP. LAWS ANN. § 28.257 (West 1991); MINN. STAT. ANN. § 609.2231(4) (West Supp. 1993); MO. ANN. STAT. § 574.090 (Vernon 1992); MONT. CODE ANN. § 45-5-221 (1991); NEV. REV. STAT. § 207.185 (1991); N.H. REV. STAT. ANN. § 651:6(g) (1955 & Supp. 1992); N.J. STAT. ANN. § 2C:12-1(b)7e (West 1982 & Supp. 1993); N.Y. PENAL LAW § 240.30 (McKinney 1989 & Supp. 1993); N.C. GEN. STAT. § 14-401.14 (1992); OHIO REV. CODE ANN. § 2927.12 (Anderson 1993); OKLA. STAT. ANN. tit. 21, § 850 (West 1993); OR. REV. STAT. § 166.155, .165 (1991); PA. STAT. ANN. tit. 18, § 2710 (1983); R.I. GEN. LAWS §§ 9-1-35, 11-42-3 (1992); TENN. CODE ANN. § 39-17-309 (1991); UTAH CODE ANN. § 76-3-203.3 (Supp. 1993); VT. STAT. ANN. tit. 13, § 1455 (Supp. 1990); VA. CODE ANN. § 8.01-42.1 (Michie 1992); WASH. REV. CODE ANN. § 9A.36.080 (Supp. 1993); W. VA. CODE § 61-6-21 (1992); WIS. STAT. ANN. § 939.645 (West 1992).

16. The following hate crime statutes include both criminal and civil penalties: D.C. CODE ANN. § 22-4003, -4004 (1992); FLA. STAT. ANN. ch. 775.085 (Harrison 1992); IDAHO CODE § 18-7903 (1987); IOWA CODE ANN. §§ 716.7A, 729A.5 (West 1993); MICH. COMP. LAWS ANN. § 750.147b (West 1991); OR. REV. STAT. § 30.190 (1991); R.I. GEN. LAWS §§ 9-1-35, 11-42-3 (1992); VT. STAT. ANN. tit. 13, §§ 1455, 1457 (Supp. 1990).

17. The following statutes require the collection of hate crime statistics: CONN. GEN. STAT. ANN. § 29-27m (West 1986); D.C. CODE ANN. § 22-4002 (1992); FLA. STAT. ANN. ch. 877.19 (Harrison 1991); IDAHO CODE § 18-7902 (1987); IOWA CODE ANN. § 729A.2 (West 1993); KY. REV. STAT. ANN. § 17.1523 (Baldwin 1992); ME. REV. STAT. ANN. tit. 25, § 1544 (West 1988); MD. CODE ANN. art. 88B, § 9 (1991); MASS. GEN. LAWS ANN. ch. 22C, §§ 32-35 (West 1992); MICH. COMP. LAWS ANN. § 28.257 (West 1991); MINN. STAT. ANN. § 626.5531 (West Supp. 1994); OR. REV. STAT. § 181.550 (1991); R.I. GEN. LAWS § 44-28-46 (1992); TEX. GOV'T CODE ANN. § 441.046 (West Supp. 1993).

18. The following statutes mandate special police training for dealing with hate crimes: IOWA CODE ANN. § 80B.11 (West 1984 & Supp. 1993); KY. REV. STAT. ANN. § 15.331 (Baldwin 1992); MASS. GEN. LAWS ANN. ch. 6, § 116B (West 1992); MINN. STAT. ANN. § 609.8451 (West Supp. 1993).

hate crime statutes, such as gays and lesbians,[19] women,[20] the mentally and physically disabled,[21] the elderly,[22] and members of unpopular political groups.[23] The inclusion of such groups is a direct response to changing attitudes about who can be a victim of hate crime. Today, most hate crime originates not with organized hate groups such as the Ku Klux Klan, but instead with "individuals or small groups of people acting on their own."[24] By broadening the definition of the hate crime perpetrator, the definitions of hate crime and the hate crime victim are broadened as well.

Over half of all state hate crime statutes are based on, or are similar to, the model hate crime statute developed by the Anti-Defamation League of B'nai B'rith (ADL) in 1981.[25] The distinctive feature of this statute is its enhancement of penalties for criminal activities when the victim is a member of a protected group and the perpetrator

19. The following hate crime statutes include sexual orientation as a protected characteristic: CAL. PENAL CODE § 422.6 (West Supp. 1993); D.C. CODE ANN. § 22-4001 (1992); ILL. ANN. STAT. ch. 38, para. 12-7.1 (Smith-Hurd 1992); IOWA CODE ANN. § 729A.2 (West 1993); MASS. GEN. LAWS ANN. ch. 22C, § 32 (West Supp. 1992); MICH. COMP. LAWS ANN. § 28.257 (West 1992); MINN. STAT. ANN. § 609.2231(4) (West Supp. 1993); NEV. REV. STAT. § 207.185 (1991); N.H. REV. STAT. ANN. § 651:6(g) (1955 & Supp. 1992); N.J. STAT. ANN. § 2C:12-1(b)7e (West 1982 & Supp. 1993); OR. REV. STAT. § 166.165 (1991); VT. STAT. ANN. tit. 13, § 1455 (Supp. 1990); WIS. STAT. ANN. § 939.645 (West 1992).

20. The following hate crime statutes include gender as a protected characteristic: CAL. PENAL CODE § 422.6 (West Supp. 1993); CONN. GEN. STAT. ANN. § 46a-58 (West 1986); D.C. CODE ANN. § 22-4001 (1992); ILL. ANN. STAT. ch. 38, para. 12-7.1 (Smith-Hurd 1992); IOWA CODE ANN. § 729A.2 (West 1993); KY. REV. STAT. ANN. § 15.331 (Baldwin 1992); MICH. COMP. LAWS ANN. § 28.257 (West 1992); MINN. STAT. ANN. § 609.2231(4) (West Supp. 1993); N.H. REV. STAT. ANN. § 651:6(g) (1955 & Supp. 1992); VT. STAT. ANN. tit. 13, § 1455 (Supp. 1990); W. VA. CODE § 61-6-21 (1992).

21. The following hate crime statutes include physical and/or mental disability as a protected characteristic: CAL. PENAL CODE § 422.6 (West Supp. 1993); CONN. GEN. STAT. ANN. § 46a-58 (West 1986); D.C. CODE ANN. § 22-4001 (1992); ILL. ANN. STAT. ch. 38, para. 12-7.1 (Smith-Hurd 1992); IOWA CODE ANN. § 729A.2 (West 1993); MASS. GEN. LAWS ANN. ch. 22C, § 32 (West 1992); MINN. STAT. ANN. § 609.2231(4) (West Supp. 1993); OKLA. STAT. ANN., tit. 21, § 850 (West 1992-1993); VT. STAT. ANN. tit. 13, § 1455 (Supp. 1990); WASH. REV. CODE ANN. § 9A.36.080 (1988 & Supp. 1993); WIS. STAT. ANN. § 939.645 (West 1992).

22. The following hate crime statutes include age as a protected characteristic: D.C. CODE ANN. § 22-4001 (1992); IOWA CODE ANN. § 729A.2 (West 1993); MINN. STAT. ANN. § 609.2231(4) (West Supp. 1993); VT. STAT. ANN. tit. 13, § 1455 (1990).

23. The following hate crime statutes include political affiliation as a protected characteristic: D.C. CODE ANN. § 22-4001 (1992); IOWA CODE ANN. § 729A.2 (West 1993); MONT. CODE ANN. § 45-5-221 (1991); W. VA. CODE § 61-6-21 (1992).

24. Finn, supra note 5, at 9. In fact, "at least half" of all people who are arrested for bias crimes are between the ages of 16 and 25. Id. at 9-10. These individual perpetrators of hate crime may be encouraged by the rhetoric of hate groups and by the lack of an effective community response to hate crime. Id. at 9.

25. See ANTI-DEFAMATION LEAGUE OF B'NAI B'RITH, HATE CRIMES STATUTES: A 1991 STATUS REPORT 2-5 (1991) (setting forth model hate crime legislation intended to assist state and local legislatures that are considering enacting hate crime laws). The ADL stated that over half of all state hate crime statutes are based upon, or similar to, the ADL model statute. Id. at 1.

commits the crime because of the victim's membership in this group.[26] Like federal hate crime statutes, the ADL model statute also provides civil remedies for victims of hate crime.[27]

B. Enforcement Of Hate Crime Statutes In Race Cases

In general, the enforcement of hate crime statutes is problematic. The same prejudices that motivate people to commit hate crime may also influence the decisions of prosecutors and the actions of the police.[28] To combat these prejudices while assisting the enforcement of hate crime statutes, some jurisdictions have created special police and prosecutorial units that deal solely with hate crime cases.[29] Some of these special units coordinate police and prosecutorial action,[30] while others work directly with the community organizations of statutorily-protected groups.[31] Although data is limited, it appears that hate crime statutes are most effectively enforced in jurisdictions with these special units.[32] When the police know that they have community support and that prosecutors will actually prosecute hate

---

26. *Id.* at 2 (concluding that prosecutors would be more inclined to pursue convictions under hate crime statutes if the penalties were increased).

27. *Id.* at 3. In the ADL model statute, civil remedies include general tort damages, punitive damages, and attorney's fees. *Id.* In addition, the model ADL statute makes parents liable for their children's actions. *Id.*

28. *See* Finn, *supra* note 5, at 10 (stating that a "[l]ack of police and prosecutor attention to bias crime sometimes reflects the attitudes of local residents who do not want minorities in their community"); Tanya Katerí Hernández, Note, *Bias Crimes: Unconscious Racism in the Prosecution of "Racially Motivated Violence"*, 99 YALE L.J. 845, 851-55 (1990) (stating that "unconscious racism, ingrained in North American culture, makes it difficult for prosecutors to concede that racially motivated violence is indeed a crime").

29. *See* Finn, *supra* note 5, at 11-12. For example, in New York City, the Manhattan District Attorney's office has appointed a senior trial attorney to supervise cases involving crimes against gays and lesbians. *Id.* at 12. Sensitivity training regarding the unique problems of gay and lesbian crime victims is mandatory for new District Attorneys. *Id.* Prosecutors are to recommend the highest offense possible for persons charged with the commission of a bias crime and are to urge the judge to consider the bias when passing sentence. *Id.*

30. For example, the Queens County, New York, District Attorney's office has created an Anti-Bias Bureau that works through the Police Department's Bias Incident Investigating Unit. Finn, *supra* note 5, at 11-12. The Unit monitors and investigates hate violence that is allegedly based upon the victim's race, religion, ethnicity, or sexual orientation. *Id.* at 11. The Anti-Bias Bureau follows up with legal action where appropriate. *Id.* at 11. Very few of these bias cases are plea-bargained. *Id.* at 12.

In Boston, Massachusetts, the Police Department's Community Disorders Unit aggressively pursues bias-crime investigations, including ride-alongs with victims, surveillance, rapid response operation, and undercover operations. *Id.* Once satisfied that a hate crime has occurred, the case is forwarded directly to the Attorney General's Civil Rights Division for prosecution. *Id.*

31. For instance, a paralegal in the Manhattan, New York, District Attorney's Office also acts as a liaison to the gay and lesbian community. Finn, *supra* note 5, at 12.

32. In spite of the difficulties inherent in hate-crime investigation, the successes encountered by those states which have created special units suggests that "targeting these cases is both feasible and rewarding." Finn, *supra* note 5, at 14. For example, in 1986, Boston's Community Disorders Unit brought 155 charges, 93 criminal and 62 civil, and convicted nearly 90% of those charged. *Id.* at 12.

crime cases, the police have a strong incentive to treat hate crime seriously.[33] Unfortunately, most jurisdictions are not devoting special efforts to prosecuting hate crime.[34]

In addition, there are two particular problems with the enforcement of race-based hate crime statutes. First, caucasians appear to be using these statutes in surprisingly high numbers. For instance, in Minnesota, 49% of the victims who reported hate crimes between 1988 and 1991 were caucasian.[35] Some advocates maintain that hate crime statutes should only be available to minority victims.[36] The justification offered for this position is that hate-motivated violence against caucasians has less impact on the individual and the community than hate-motivated violence does against members of racial and ethnic minorities.[37]

Second, racial and other biases among prosecutors is believed to be a primary obstacle to the use of these statutes by minorities.[38] Two proposed solutions include revising the statute to create a presumption of racist motivation in all interracial crimes of violence[39] and

---

33. Finn, *supra* note 5, at 15 (stating that "unless it becomes office policy for all trial assistants to single out hate violence, police may stop arresting suspects for these offenses when equally aggressive prosecutorial action does not follow").

34. Finn, *supra* note 5, at 15.

35. MINNESOTA BOARD OF PEACE OFFICER STANDARDS AND TRAINING, BIAS MOTIVATED CRIMES: A SUMMARY REPORT OF MINNESOTA'S RESPONSE 38 (1990) [hereinafter SUMMARY REPORT] (noting that 49% and 51% of the victims of hate crimes in 1988 and 1989, respectively, were caucasian); Minnesota Department of Public Safety, Minnesota Bias Offense Summary 1990-1991 (1992) (unpublished manuscript, on file with *The American University Journal of Gender & the Law*) [hereinafter Bias Offense Summary] (noting that 48% of hate crime victims in both 1990 and 1991 were caucasian).

36. *See* Marc L. Fleischauer, Comment, *Teeth for a Paper Tiger: A Proposal to Add Enforceability to Florida's Hate Crimes Act*, 17 FLA. ST. U. L. REV. 697, 703, 706 (1990) (proposing that minority offenders be exempted from penalty enhancements and civil damages in racially motivated crimes).

37. *See* Hernández, *supra* note 28, at 861 (arguing that "white victims may feel threatened by criminals who happen to be people of color, but this is a concern to be distinguished from the fear of bias motivated attacks which contributes to the oppression of disfavored groups").

In the case of hate speech involving civil action, not criminal, advocates argue that expressions of hatred directed against members of historically dominant-groups are not the same as hate speech directed at a member of a historically subordinate group because the latter keeps "victim groups in an inferior position." Mari Matsuda, *Public Response to Racist Speech: Considering the Victim's Story*, 87 MICH. L. REV. 2320, 2362 (1989).

38. Hernández, *supra* note 28, at 851-52 (arguing that the lack of enforcement of state hate crime statutes is a result of "unchecked prosecutorial discretion," which is greatly affected by "unconscious racism of prosecutors"); Note, *Combatting Racial Violence: A Legislative Proposal*, 101 HARV. L. REV. 1270, 1275 (1988) (stating that prosecutors have wide discretion and can use their own racist sentiment to find that a criminal act was not racially motivated).

39. *See* Fleischauer, *supra* note 36, at 704 (proposing that the state legislatures create a presumption of bias in their hate crime statutes, while simultaneously creating an affirmative defense that places the burden on the defendant to prove that his actions were not racially-motivated); Note, *supra* note 38, at 1275 (concluding that the "Constitution permits states . . . to shift to the defendant the burden of proving a lack of racial motivation").

creating mechanisms for monitoring and challenging prosecutorial discretion.[40]

II.   LEGISLATION THAT TREATS VIOLENCE AGAINST WOMEN AS HATE CRIME

A.   *Federal Legislation*

The only federal statute that offers remedies to victims of violent acts that are motivated by gender bias is Title VII of the Civil Rights Act of 1964.[41] This statute only applies to cases of discrimination in an employment setting.[42] Congress, however, is currently considering the enactment of several pieces of legislation—the Violence Against Women Act of 1993 and the Hate Crimes Sentencing Enhancement Act of 1993—which would define bias-motivated crimes based upon the victim's gender as a type of hate crime.

1.   *The Violence Against Women Act of 1993*

The Violence Against Women Act of 1993 (VAWA)[43] was introduced in the Senate in January 1993 by Senator Joseph Biden.[44] A companion bill[45] was also introduced in the House of Representatives by Representative Patricia Schroeder in February 1993.[46] As amended, the bills share a number of important provisions.[47] Among other things, both provide federal funding to improve

---

40. One commentator recommends that each state establish a Bias Reporting Agency to aid in regulating prosecutorial discretion. Hernández, *supra* note 28, at 855. This agency, among other things, would require a "mandatory justification process" for prosecutors who plea bargained or failed to prosecute a bias crime case. *Id.* at 856. It would also assist victims who wished to challenge a prosecutor's decision not to prosecute a case. *Id.* at 856-58. The agency could also bring a class action against individual prosecutors who displayed a pattern of not prosecuting bias crimes. *Id.* at 860.

41. Civil Rights Act of 1964, Pub. L. No. 88-352, §§ 701-716, 78 Stat. 241, 253-66 (codified as amended at 42 U.S.C. § 2000e to 2000e-17 (1988 & Supp. III 1991)).

42. *Id.* § 703, 78 Stat. at 255 (prohibiting unlawful employment practices that result in discrimination on the basis of race, color, religion, gender, or national origin).

43. S. 11, 103d Cong., 1st Sess. (1993).

44. 139 CONG. REC. S190, S345 (daily ed. Jan. 21, 1993). As of the time that this article was written, the bill had been favorably reported by the Senate Judiciary Committee as amended, 139 CONG. REC. D597 (daily ed. May 27, 1993), and submitted to the Senate for consideration, *id.* at S11,444 (daily ed. Sept. 10, 1993).

45. H.R. 1133, 103d Cong., 1st Sess. (1993).

46. 139 CONG. REC. H877, E450 (daily ed. Feb. 24, 1993). As of the time that this article was written, the bill had passed the House of Representatives by a voice vote, *id.* at H10,370 (daily ed. Nov. 20, 1993), and was awaiting consideration by the Senate Judiciary Committee, *id.* at S16,935 (daily ed. Nov. 22, 1993) (referring the bill to committee).

47. The amended version of the Senate bill may be found in the Senate Judiciary Committee's Report, S. REP. NO. 138, 103d Cong., 1st Sess. 2-37 (1993). Similarly, the amended version of the House bill is located in the House Judiciary Committee's Report, H.R. REP. NO. 395, 103d Cong., 1st Sess. 1-24 (1993).

criminal law enforcement;[48] implement pro-arrest policies in domestic violence cases;[49] authorize education and training programs for judges of state and federal courts;[50] create a United States Department of Justice Task Force on Violence Against Women;[51] establish new federal criminal penalties for domestic violence;[52] and require that financial restitution be made to victims by their attackers when their attackers are convicted of federal sex offenses.[53]

In addition, the Senate bill contains several additional remedies that are not included in the House bill. First, Title III of the bill[54] allows for the recovery of damages[55] under federal civil rights law for violent crimes that are motivated by the victim's gender.[56] The effect of this provision is to offer women something entirely new—a federal civil rights remedy that is available outside of the employment setting.[57] Second, the Senate bill contains penalty increase and

---

48. S. 11, § 121 (authorizing grants to combat violent crimes against women through increased training of police officers and development of law enforcement programs specifically designed for fighting these crimes); H.R. 1133, §§ 126, 1701-1704 (authorizing grants to "develop law enforcement and prosecution strategies to combat violent crimes against women").
49. S. 11, §§ 231, 317; H.R. 1133, §§ 221, 1901-1904.
50. S. 11, §§ 501, 511-514, 521-522 (authorizing grants to train state judges on gender-motivated bias crimes, as well as grants to study gender bias in the federal courts); H.R. 1133, §§ 401-404, 411-412 (using the same language as the Senate bill).
51. S. 11, §§ 141-148; H.R. 1133, §§ 311-319. The purpose of the Task Force is to develop strategies for combatting and punishing violent crimes against women. S. 11, § 142; H.R. 1133, § 312.
52. S. 11, § 221 (creating new penalties for interstate domestic violence where a spouse or intimate partner is injured); H.R. 1133, § 211 (punishing interstate domestic violence where the victim suffers bodily injury).
53. S. 11, § 113; H.R. 1133, § 131.
54. S. 11, §§ 301-304.
55. *Id.* §§ 302(c), 303 (allowing the victim to recover compensatory and punitive damages, declaratory and injunctive relief, and attorney's fees, among other remedies).
56. *Id.* § 302(c). The term "motivated by gender" is borrowed from existing civil rights law, specifically, Title VII of the Civil Rights Act of 1964, 42 U.S.C. § 2000e to 2000e-17, which prohibits employment discrimination because of sex. *See* S. REP. NO. 138, *supra* note 47, at 52-53.
57. S. 11, § 302(a)(2) (stating a Congressional finding that "current law provides a civil rights remedy for gender crimes committed in the workplace, but not for gender crimes committed on the street or in the home").
However, certain organizations have voiced concerns about the potential impact of Title III on other civil rights laws. For example, Brenda Smith of the National Women's Law Center stated that, hypothetically, if the bill were to pass with a provision requiring a higher standard of proof for demonstrating gender bias, such as that the crime must be "overwhelmingly" because of gender bias, then perhaps there would be an attempt to move this standard over to other kinds of cases, such as employment discrimination. Telephone Interview with Brenda V. Smith, Senior Staff Attorney, National Women's Law Center (July 6, 1992). This issue is specifically addressed in October 1991 Senate Judiciary Committee Report, which states that the term "overwhelmingly" was specifically eliminated from the 1991 bill because there was "no counterpart to such language in any other civil rights remedy." *See* S. REP. NO. 197, *supra* note 13, at 51 (stating additionally that such a term would "pose an unnecessary and harmful burden on women"); *see also* S. REP. NO. 138, *supra* note 47, at 53 (noting that the 1993 bill does not require a higher standard of proof than in other civil rights cases and that it is not intended to undermine existing civil rights laws). As Ms. Smith suggested, however, the bill theoretically

enhancement provisions for certain defendants who are convicted of sexual assault.[58]

2. *The Hate Crimes Sentencing Enhancement Act of 1993*

Another recent effort to combat hate crimes on the federal level is the Hate Crimes Sentencing Enhancement Act of 1993 (HCSEA),[59] introduced in the House of Representatives by Representative Charles Schumer in March 1993.[60] A companion bill[61] was also introduced in the Senate by Senator Dianne Feinstein in October 1993.[62] Both the House bill as amended, and the Senate bill, direct the United States Sentencing Commission to create and/or amend guidelines to provide sentencing enhancements for hate crime.[63] Hate crime is defined in both bills as one in which the defendant intentionally "selects a victim . . . because of the [victim's] actual or perceived race, color, religion, national origin, ethnicity, gender, or sexual orientation . . . ."[64] The sentencing enhancements are to raise an offense by at least three "severity" levels, increasing, on average, the actual time served by one-third.[65]

It is expected that both of these bills will be able to withstand any challenges to their constitutionality. In *Wisconsin v. Mitchell*,[66] the U.S. Supreme Court recently upheld a Wisconsin hate crime statute that enhances criminal penalties where the defendant intentionally selects a victim based upon certain protected characteristics of the

---

could be amended to include a higher standard of proof.

58. S. 11, § 111 (increasing the prison term of a repeat sex offender up to twice that which is otherwise authorized); *id.* § 112 (directing the U.S. Sentencing Commission to enhance penalties for persons who are convicted of aggravated sexual abuse).

However, as discussed in Part III of this article, the bill's progress has been stalled in part because of concerns expressed by women's rights and other organizations about these provisions. *See infra* notes 144-161 (discussing the objections made by some organizations to increasing penalties for sex offenses).

59. H.R. 1152, 103d Cong., 1st Sess. (1993).

60. 139 CONG. REC. H911 (daily ed. Mar. 1, 1993). As of the time that this article was written, the bill had passed the House of Representatives by a voice vote, *id.* at H6795-96 (daily ed. Sept. 21, 1993), and was awaiting consideration by the Senate Judiciary Committee, *id.* at S12,241 (daily ed. Sept. 22, 1993) (referring the bill to committee).

61. S. 1522, 103d Cong., 1st Sess. (1993).

62. 139 CONG. REC. S13,172, S13,175-77 (daily ed. Oct. 6, 1993). As of the time that this article was written the bill was awaiting consideration by the Senate Judiciary Committee. *See id.* (referring the bill to committee).

63. S. 1522, § 2(b); H.R. 1152, § 2(a).

64. S. 1522, § 2(a); H.R. 1152, § 2(b). To date, it appears that there has been no controversy surrounding the inclusion of gender as a protected characteristic in the bill. However, the only women's organization that has endorsed the bill is the National Council of Jewish Women. List of Groups Supporting the Hate Crimes Sentencing Enhancement Act (as of Mar. 12, 1993) (on file with *The American University Journal of Gender & the Law*).

65. H.R. REP. NO. 244, 103d Cong., 1st Sess. 2 (1993).

66. Wisconsin v. Mitchell, ___ U.S. ___, 113 S. Ct. 2194 (1993).

victim, such as race.[67] The language of the penalty enhancement clause of the Wisconsin statute is substantially similar to that of the Senate and amended House bills.[68] *Wisconsin v. Mitchell* is consistent with the opinions expressed during the July 1992 hearing held by the Subcommittee on Crime and Criminal Justice of the House Committee on the Judiciary concerning the constitutionality of penalty enhancement statutes in light of *R.A.V. v. St. Paul.*[69] At this hearing, leading constitutional scholars testified that penalty enhancement provisions do not violate the First Amendment.[70]

B. State Statutes

There has been more progress at the state level than at the federal level in treating violence against women as hate crime. Eleven states and the District of Columbia now include gender in their hate crime

---

67. 113 S. Ct. at 2194. The Court found that the statute did not violate the defendant's First Amendment rights because it was not designed to punish his bigoted beliefs, but rather to redress special harms that are caused by hate crimes. *Id.* at 2199. Nor did the statute violate his Fourteenth Amendment rights because it was not overbroad and thus did not have a chilling effect on free speech. *Id.* at 2201.

68. Both the Wisconsin statute and the Congressional bills define hate crime as one in which the perpetrator intentionally selects his victim based upon a particular protected characteristic. *Compare id.* at 2197 n.1 (citing the Wisconsin hate crime statute) *with* S. 1522 *and* H.R. 1152. In fact, the House bill was deliberately amended to include language that "parallel[s] as much as possible" the Wisconsin statute's language. *See* 139 CONG. REC. H6793 (daily ed. Sept. 21, 1993) (statement of Rep. Hyde) (explaining that the purpose of the amendment was to avoid constitutional challenges to the statute by having it comport with the language upheld in Wisconsin v. Mitchell).

69. R.A.V. v. St. Paul, ___ U.S. ___, 112 S. Ct. 2538 (1992) (striking down an ordinance that prohibited bias-motivated disorderly conduct on the grounds that it violated the First Amendment).

The hearing concerned H.R. 4797, the Hate Crimes Sentencing Enhancement Act of 1992. H.R. 4797, 102d Cong., 2d Sess. (1992). *See Hate Crimes Sentencing Enhancement Act of 1992: Hearing on H.R. 4797 Before the Subcomm. on Crime and Criminal Justice of the House Comm. on the Judiciary,* 102d Cong., 2d Sess. (1992) [hereinafter *Hearing on H.R. 4797*]. H.R. 4797 is identical in form to H.R. 1152 as the latter was introduced in March 1993. *Compare* H.R. 4797 *with* H.R. 1152. H.R. 4797 passed the House of Representatives by voice vote in October 1992, 138 CONG. REC. H11,136 (daily ed. Oct. 3, 1992), but died in the Senate.

70. While these arguments were made with regard to H.R. 4797, they are also applicable to H.R. 1152 in spite of amendments to the latter; this means that H.R. 1152 will likely pass muster under the First Amendment. *See, e.g., Hearing on H.R. 4797, supra* note 69, at 18, 19 (statement of Floyd Abrams, Esq., Cahill, Gordon & Reindel, New York, New York) (stating that while the government may not punish evil thoughts or ideas per se, it may consider evil motive when fashioning a sentence); *id.* at 59, 64 (prepared statement of Bruce Fein, former Associate Deputy Attorney General of the United States) (stating that under *R.A.V. v. St. Paul,* a statute may proscribe fighting words directed at protected groups and not violate the First Amendment because the proscription is "ideologically neutral"); *id.* at 7, 10 (statement of Lawrence H. Tribe, Professor of Law, Harvard Law School) (stating that H.R. 4797 is neither overbroad nor void for vagueness); *see also* H.R. REP. NO. 981, 102d Cong., 2d Sess. 5 (1992) (asserting that the First Amendment is not "unduly burdened when otherwise protected statements are used at sentencing as evidence to show that illegal conduct was motivated by hatred, bias or prejudice").

statutes.[71]   Vermont's hate crime statute passed with virtually no discussion about the inclusion of gender as a protected characteristic.[72]   Similarly, a recent amendment to include gender[73] in an Illinois hate crime statute passed through the legislature by overwhelming margins in both legislative houses.[74]

The remedies offered to women victims by state hate crime statutes vary considerably.   Of the states that include gender in their hate crime statutes, six states and the District of Columbia offer civil

---

71. (1) CAL. PENAL CODE § 422.6(a)-(b) (West 1988 & Supp. 1993) (making it a crime to injure a person, or a person's real or personal property, because of that person's gender); CAL. CIV. CODE § 51.7(a) (West 1982) (providing that every person within the state has the right to be free from gender-based violence against his or her person or property).
(2) CONN. GEN. STAT. ANN. § 46a-58(a) (West 1986) (declaring it a crime to violate a person's constitutional rights based on that person's gender).
(3) D.C. CODE ANN. § 22-4001 (Supp. 1992) (defining a "bias-related crime" as a crime that is of a certain class of designated criminal acts and that demonstrates the offender's bias towards the victim's gender).
(4) ILL. ANN. STAT. ch. 38, para. 12-7.1(a) (Smith-Hurd Supp. 1992) (making it a crime for a person to commit certain offenses against another person or person's property because of gender).
(5) IOWA CODE ANN. § 729A.1 (West 1979 & Supp. 1993) (creating a civil rights provision that protects a person's right to be free from violence or intimidation because of the person's gender); id. § 729A.2 (defining "hate crime" as one where an offender commits certain types of public offenses against an individual because of gender).
(6) KY. REV. STAT. ANN. § 15.331(1) (Baldwin Supp. 1992) (defining bias-related crime as an offense which is either the result of or related to the victim's gender).
(7) MASS. GEN. LAWS ANN. ch. 22C, § 32 (West 1992) (defining "hate crime" as a criminal offense motivated by bias, which includes gender).
(8) MICH. COMP. LAWS ANN. § 750.147b(1) (West 1992) (making intimidation or harassment of a person because of that person's gender a crime).
(9) MINN. STAT. ANN. § 609.2231(4(a)) (West 1987 & Supp. 1993) (declaring it a crime to assault a person because of that person's sex); id. § 609.595(1a), (2) (criminalizing damage to property perpetuated because of the property owner's gender); id. 609.605(3) (prohibiting trespass that is motivated by gender bias); id. § 609.746(3) (criminalizing interference with a person's privacy because of that person's gender); id. § 609.79(1a(a)) (making it a crime to make obscene or harassing telephone calls which are motivated by the recipient's gender); id. § 609.795(2(a)) (declaring it a crime to use the mails in a harassing manner because of the recipient's gender).
(10) N.H. REV. STAT. ANN. § 651:6 (1955 & Supp. 1992) (allowing the state to extend the term of imprisonment if the victim's gender "substantially motivated" the offender to commit the crime).
(11) VT. STAT. ANN. tit. 13, § 1455 (Supp. 1990) (defining "hate crime" as a crime that is "maliciously motivated" by the victim's gender).
(12) W. VA. CODE § 61-6-21(a) to (c) (1992) (making it a felony to forcefully interfere with a person's constitutional rights because of the person's gender, or to conspire to interfere with those rights because of gender).
72. Telephone Interview with Judy Rex, Coordinator, Vermont Network Against Domestic Violence and Sexual Assault (July 6, 1992).
73. H. 2065, 87th Gen. Ass., 1991 Reg. Sess., 1991 Ill. Legis. Serv. 2210 (West) (codified at ILL. ANN. STAT. ch. 38, paras. 12-7.1, 1005-5-3.2 (Smith-Hurd 1982 & Supp. 1992)) (including as a hate crime the commission of certain criminal offenses by reason of the victim's gender).
74. Telephone Interview with Jan Schakowsky, Representative, State of Illinois General Assembly (July 20, 1992). Representative Schakowsky introduced H. 2065.

remedies.[75] Nine states and the District of Columbia have statutes that inflict criminal penalties: four states make the offense a misdemeanor[76] and five states classify crimes motivated by bias as felonies.[77] New Hampshire and Vermont extend the imprisonment term

---

75. (1) CAL. CIV. CODE § 52(b) (West 1982 & Supp. 1993) (awarding actual damages plus exemplary damages, a twenty-five thousand dollar civil penalty, and attorney's fees); *id.* § 52(c) (authorizing the state Attorney General, a District Attorney, City Attorney, or any aggrieved party to file a civil action requesting an injunction, restraining order, or other preventive relief); *id.* § 52(d) (allowing the state Attorney General, or a District or City Attorney, to intervene when a hate crime victim has filed a civil action alleging an equal protection violation under the Fourteenth Amendment and the case is of "general public importance").
(2) CONN. GEN. STAT. ANN. § 52-251b (West 1991) (allowing the recovery of costs and attorney's fees in a civil action, but declining to create a new cause of action).
(3) D.C. CODE ANN. § 22-4004(a) (Supp. 1992) (providing hate crime victims a cause of action for appropriate relief, including, but not limited to, an injunction, actual damages [including damages for emotional distress], punitive damages, attorney's fees, and costs).
(4) ILL. ANN. STAT. ch. 38, para. 12-7.1(c) (Smith-Hurd Supp. 1992) (providing for an independent civil action for actual and punitive damages [including emotional distress damages], and injunctive or other appropriate relief).
(5) IOWA CODE ANN. § 729A.5 (West 1979 & Supp. 1993) (authorizing a civil action for injunctive relief, general and special damages, attorney's fees, and costs for victims of hate crimes).
(6) MICH. COMP. LAWS ANN. § 750.147b(3) (West 1991) (creating a civil cause of action for injunctive relief, actual damages, damages for emotional distress, and other appropriate relief). Furthermore, a plaintiff who prevails in such an action may recover the greater of treble the actual damages or two thousand dollars, attorney's fees, and costs. *Id.*
(7) VT. STAT. ANN. tit. 13, § 1457 (Supp. 1990) (creating an independent civil cause of action for compensatory and punitive damages, injunctive relief, costs, attorney's fees, and other appropriate relief).
76. (1) CAL. PENAL CODE § 422.6(c) (West 1988 & Supp. 1993) (setting the punishment for a hate crime violation at imprisonment in a county jail for no more than one year, a fine of no more than five thousand dollars, or both).
(2) CONN. GEN. STAT. ANN. § 46a-58(d) (West 1986) (establishing the penalty for a hate crime that violates a person's civil rights and incurs no more than one thousand dollars in property damages as a misdemeanor).
(3) IOWA CODE ANN. § 716.8.3 (West 1993) (providing punishments for "serious misdemeanor" for trespass with the intent to commit a hate crime, and "aggravated misdemeanor" for trespass to commit a hate crime which results in injury to a person or in damage of more than one hundred dollars to any property).
(4) MINN. STAT. ANN. § 609.2231(4) (West 1987 & Supp. 1993) (setting the penalty for a bias-motivated assault in the fourth degree); *id.* § 609.595(2(b)) (establishing the penalty for criminal damage to property in the third degree that is bias-motivated); *id.* § 609.605(3) (making a bias-motivated trespass a misdemeanor); *id.* § 609.746(3) (adding the punishment of misdemeanor for a bias-related invasion of privacy); *id.* § 609.79(1a(a)) (setting the punishment for gender-based obscene or harassing telephone calls as a misdemeanor); *id.* § 609.795(2(a)) (establishing the penalty for using the mails for harassment purposes as a misdemeanor). The penalty for all of these misdemeanor offenses is no more than one year in jail, a three thousand dollar fine, or both.
77. (1) CONN. GEN. STAT. ANN. § 46a-58(d) (West 1986) (making a hate crime that violates a person's civil rights because of gender a felony where the violation results in more than one thousand dollars worth of property damage).
(2) ILL. ANN. STAT. ch. 38, para. 12-7.1(b) (Smith-Hurd 1992) (classifying hate crime as a Class 4 felony for a first offense, a Class 2 for subsequent offenses). Any probation or conditional discharge may include a minimum of an extra two hundred hours of community service. *Id.*
(3) MICH. COMP. LAWS ANN. § 750.147b(2) (West 1992) (setting the penalty for ethnic intimidation as a felony punishable by up to two years in jail, a five thousand dollar fine, or both).

for hate-motivated crime.[78] Four states increase penalties for repeat offenders.[79] Four states have penalty enhancement power: Iowa and the District of Columbia have penalty enhancement statutes,[80] while Illinois and West Virginia treat hate crime as an aggravating factor at the time of sentencing.[81] Two states define hate crime as a civil rights violation.[82]

Additionally, some state hate crime statutes contain provisions governing data collection and law enforcement training. Eight states and the District of Columbia mandate hate crimes data collection.[83]

---

(4) MINN. STAT. ANN. § 609.595(1a(a)) (establishing the punishment for criminal damage to property in the second degree as imprisonment for no more than one year and one day, payment of a three thousand dollar fine, or both).

(5) W. VA. CODE § 61-6-21(b)-(c) (1992) (making it a felony to forcefully interfere with a person's civil rights, the penalty for which is up to ten years in jail, a five thousand dollar fine, or both).

78. N.H. REV. STAT. ANN. § 651:6 (1955 & Supp. 1992) (extending the penalty for misdemeanor crime by two to five years); VT. STAT. ANN. tit. 13, § 1455(1) (Supp. 1990) (stating that where the imprisonment penalty for a hate crime is ordinarily no more than one year it shall be increased to no more than two years, a fine of no more than two thousand dollars, or both).

79. (1) CAL. PENAL CODE § 422.7(c) (West 1988 & Supp. 1993) (increasing the penalty for a person who has been previously convicted of committing, or conspiring to commit, a hate crime to no more than one year in jail, no more than a ten thousand dollar fine, or both).

(2) CONN. GEN. STAT. ANN. § 53a-40a (West 1985 & Supp. 1993) (increasing the penalty for "persistent offenders" by one offense level at the court's discretion). This means that if the offense would ordinarily be punished as the most serious type of misdemeanor that it will now be punished as the least serious type of felony. *Id.*

(3) ILL. ANN. STAT. ch. 38, para. 12-7.1(b) (Smith-Hurd Supp. 1992) (increasing the penalty by two offense levels for the commission of subsequent hate crime).

(4) MINN. STAT. ANN. § 609.2231(4(b)) (West 1987 & Supp. 1993) (creating a new punishment for a hate-motivated assault that is committed within five years of a prior assault by increasing the penalty to a maximum sentence of one year and one day, a three thousand dollar fine, or both); *id.* § 609.747 (West Supp. 1993) (making it a gross misdemeanor for a person to harass the same victim within six months of the first violation, where the harassment is bias-related).

80. (1) IOWA CODE ANN. § 712.9 (West 1979 & Supp. 1993) (classifying and punishing a hate crime which violates individual rights as an offense which is one level higher than the underlying offense); *id.* § 716.6A (classifying and punishing bias-motivated criminal mischief in violation of individual rights as an offense which is one level higher than the underlying offense).

(2) D.C. CODE ANN. § 22-4003 (Supp. 1992) (authorizing the court to sentence a hate crime offender to no more than one and one-half times the maximum imprisonment and fine allowed by the underlying offense).

81. ILL. ANN. STAT. ch. 38, para. 1005-5-3.2(a)(10) (Smith-Hurd 1982 & Supp. 1992) (making a bias-motivated hate crime a factor in aggravation to be considered when imposing an imprisonment term or when deciding whether to impose a more severe sentence); W. VA. CODE § 61-6-21(d) (1992) (authorizing the court to consider the fact that a crime is bias-related as an aggravating circumstance when the court imposes sentence).

82. CAL. PENAL CODE § 422.6 (West 1988 & Supp. 1993) (including hate crimes as a violation in the exercise of individual rights); IOWA CODE ANN. § 729A.2 (West Supp. 1993) (providing that hate crime offenses include violations of individual rights).

83. (1) CONN. GEN. STAT. ANN. § 29-7m (West 1990) (ordering the state police who are within the department of public safety to "monitor, record and classify" all bias-related crimes).

(2) D.C. CODE ANN. § 22-4002 (Supp. 1992) (ordering the Metropolitan Police force to afford all victims of bias-related crimes the opportunity to submit a written report). The reports are collected, compiled, and analyzed by the Mayor, who shall annually publish the results of this

Five states mandate police training in the identification of hate crime.[84] Iowa requires sensitivity training for police and prosecutors.[85] California suggests sensitivity training for offenders as a condition of probation,[86] and Illinois allows for a human relations program in all public universities.[87]

Interestingly, two states include gender in their hate crime statutes for some purposes but not for others. Connecticut includes gender in a civil rights statute that classifies bias crime as a misdemeanor,[88] but does not include gender in a criminal statute enacted in 1990 that

---

analysis. *Id.*

(3) Act of June 29, 1992, ch. 293, 1992 Haw. Sess. Laws 754 (authorizing the state Attorney General to develop a model for the specification and collection of data regarding hate crimes, and to submit any appropriate findings, recommendations, and implementing legislation).

(4) ILL. ANN. STAT. ch. 127, para. 55a(31) (Smith-Hurd 1993) (mandating the Department of State Police to "collect and disseminate information relating to 'hate crimes'").

(5) IOWA CODE ANN. § 692.15 (West 1993) (requiring all law enforcement agencies to report information on hate crimes to a bureau that generates crime statistics).

(6) KY. REV. STAT. ANN. § 17.1523 (Baldwin Supp. 1992) (creating the uniform offense report, which is to be completed by all officers when investigating a bias-related crime).

(7) MASS. GEN. LAWS ANN. ch. 22C, §§ 33-35 (West Supp. 1992) (establishing a comprehensive model for the collection of hate crime data).

(8) MICH. COMP. LAWS ANN. § 28.257a (West 1992) (authorizing the regional chiefs of police to report certain information regarding bias-motivated crime to the state police).

(9) MINN. STAT. ANN. § 626.5531 (West Supp. 1994) (establishing a comprehensive system for the collection of hate crime data. Investigating officers are required to complete reports on all bias crimes, which are discussed and analyzed in monthly reports by local law enforcement agency chiefs. The monthly reports are further summarized and analyzed in the annual report to be filed by the commissioner of public safety.).

84. (1) CAL. PENAL CODE § 13,519.6 (West 1988 & Supp. 1993) (instructing the Commission on Peace Officer Standards and Training to develop an instruction course related to hate crimes).

(2) IOWA CODE ANN. § 80B.11 (West 1984 & Supp. 1993) (requiring that all law enforcement officers complete a course on the "investigation, identification, and reporting" of all hate crime).

(3) KY. REV. STAT. ANN. § 15.331 (Baldwin Supp. 1992) (requiring biennial law enforcement training courses to include a unit on bias-related crimes).

(4) MASS. GEN. LAWS ANN. ch. 6, § 116B (West Supp. 1992) (authorizing the criminal justice training council to provide instruction for all law enforcement personnel in "identifying, responding to and reporting" all hate crime).

(5) MINN. STAT. ANN. § 626.8451 (West Supp. 1994) (establishing a comprehensive training system for all officers in identifying and responding to bias-motivated crimes). This system includes training courses on violent crimes, and pre-service and in-service training requirements. *Id.*

85. IOWA CODE ANN. § 729A.4 (West 1979 & Supp. 1993) (directing the prosecuting attorneys' training coordinator to develop a sensitivity training course for police and prosecutors to enable them to determine whether a civil rights violation has occurred).

86. CAL. PENAL CODE § 422.95(a) (West Supp. 1993) (deferring to the court's discretion to decide whether a sensitivity training class, or "similar training in the area of civil rights," should be a condition of probation for an offender).

87. ILL. ANN. STAT. ch. 144, para. 189.21(a)(3) (Smith-Hurd Supp. 1992) (requiring all public universities, among other things, to forward all reports of hate crime on their campuses to the local state's attorney).

88. CONN. GEN. STAT. ANN. § 46a-58(d) (West 1986) (making it a misdemeanor to deprive a person of their constitutional rights because of gender). However, if the violation results in property damage in excess of one thousand dollars, the violation is a felony. *Id.*

classifies intimidation based on bigotry or bias as a felony.[89] Massachusetts amended its Hate Crimes Reporting Act[90] to include gender-motivated hate crime in response to the murders of at least nineteen women by their estranged husbands, ex-spouses, or boyfriends in the first six months of 1992.[91] After signing the measure, Governor William Weld stated, "We are seeing a disturbing pattern of violent crime against women in Massachusetts. . . . By explicitly defining gender prejudice as a hate crime, we are helping law enforcement officials get a better handle on the dimensions of the problem and focus resources where they're needed."[92] Nevertheless, despite Governor Weld's intent to define violence against women as hate crime, the Massachusetts legislature did not amend the statutes providing civil and criminal remedies for hate crime to include gender.[93]

While eleven states and the District of Columbia include gender in their hate crime statutes, interviews with women's rights advocates, hate crime victims' advocates, and state attorney generals' offices in these jurisdictions revealed no knowledge of instances in which these statutes have actually been used in cases of violence against women.[94] Minnesota's evaluation of its hate crime statute may offer insight into why this is the case. In 1988, the Minnesota legislature mandated the development of a training course for police officers, which was to include written material to assist officers in distinguishing, under-standing, and reporting hate crime.[95] When Minnesota added gender to its hate crime statute in May 1989,[96] it also mandated the

---

89. *Id.* § 53a-181b(a) (classifying intimidation based on bigotry or bias against a person or property because of the person's race, religion, ethnicity, or sexual orientation as a crime).

90. MASS. GEN. LAWS ANN. ch. 265, § 39 (West 1992).

91. *Weld Signs Hate Crime Amendment,* UPI, June 3, 1992, *available in* LEXIS, Nexis Library, Curnws File.

92. *Id.*

93. MASS. GEN. LAWS ANN. ch. 265, § 39 (West 1992) (making intimidation of a person based on that person's race, religion, ethnicity, or national origin a felony punishable by up to two and one-half years imprisonment, a fine of at least five thousand dollars, or both).

94. Telephone Interview with Diane Alexander, Assistant Director of Library and Information Services, National Victim's Center (July 6, 1992); Telephone Interview with Loretta Frederick, Attorney, Minnesota Battered Women's Coalition (July 6, 1992); Telephone Interview with Ann Noel, Hearing Officer, California Fair Employment and Housing Commission and Bay Area Hate Crimes Investigating Association (July 21, 1992); Telephone Interview with Judy Rex, *supra* note 72; Telephone Interview with Elizabeth Shumann-Moore, Staff Attorney, Chicago Lawyer's Committee for Civil Rights Under Law (July 20, 1992); Telephone Interview with John Stein, Department Executive Director, National Organization for Victim Assistance (June 22, 1992).

95. MINN. STAT. ANN. § 626.5531, .8451 (West Supp. 1994) (mandating officer training courses, as well as pre-service and in-service training requirements).

96. Act of May 25, 1989, ch. 261, 1989 Minn. Laws 892 (codified at MINN. STAT. ANN. § 609.2231, .595, .605, .746, .79, .795 (West 1987 & Supp. 1993)) (amending sections of the code which increase penalties for crimes that are bias-motivated to include gender).

collection of data on all types of hate crime, including those crimes that were motivated by gender-bias.[97] However, the training materials that Minnesota developed and the actual data collected on hate crime indicate that the police have virtually ignored crimes motivated by gender-bias.[98] For instance, the information collected at hearings and from testimony, and submitted to the Governor's Task Force on Violence and Prejudice, indicated that through April 1988, gender-biased crimes constituted 38.08% of all hate crimes reported.[99] Yet gender accounted for only 2% of the bias crimes reported to police in 1988,[100] 1.2% of those reported in 1989,[101] and fewer than 1% of those reported in 1990 and 1991.[102] Moreover, at a May 1989 conference on bias-motivated crimes, over fifteen panelists from hate crime advocacy organizations, local and national police investigation units, and a gay and lesbian rights organization participated.[103] There were, however, no panelists representing victims of rape or domestic violence.[104] Nowhere in the Summary Report, which was prepared from presentations made at the conference, is there any mention of gender-motivated hate crimes.[105]

III. OBSTACLES TO TREATING VIOLENCE AGAINST WOMEN AS HATE CRIME

As discussed in Part II, while some states have included gender in their hate crime statutes, they have been either unwilling or unable to fully implement these statutes so as to provide women with the protection due to them under the statutes. Several possible reasons for this failure in implementation are examined below.

---

97. *Id.* (codified at MINN. STAT. ANN. § 626.5531 (West Supp. 1994)) (requiring the reporting by law enforcement personnel of bias-motivated crimes).

98. *See* MINNESOTA BOARD OF PEACE OFFICER STANDARDS AND TRAINING, BIAS-MOTIVATED CRIMES: INSTRUCTIONAL MATERIALS FOR LAW ENFORCEMENT 29-30, 35 (1990) (defining a bias-motivated crime as one which is motivated by the victim's race, religion, ethnicity, sexual orientation, or gender but failing to instruct law enforcement to ask questions regarding gender); SUMMARY REPORT, *supra* note 35, at 22, 35 (listing incidents of gender-based hate crime reported to the Governor's Task Force and to law enforcement personnel).

99. SUMMARY REPORT, *supra* note 35, at 22.

100. SUMMARY REPORT, *supra* note 35, at 35.

101. SUMMARY REPORT, *supra* note 35, at 35.

102. Bias Offense Summary, *supra* note 35.

103. SUMMARY REPORT, *supra* note 35, at 43-57 (summarizing the remarks made during the conference by the individual panelists).

104. SUMMARY REPORT, *supra* note 35, at 43-57.

105. SUMMARY REPORT, *supra* note 35, at 43-57. Additionally, not one of the sources listed in the Summary Report's bibliography appears to address violence against women. *Id.* at 83-87.

A.   Resistance From Hate Crime Victim Advocacy Groups And Judges

Advocates for victims of hate crime and judges often resist accepting the fact that rape, domestic violence, and other violent crimes against women should be treated as hate crime. The following discussion demonstrates the ways in which this resistance has been manifested.

1.   The Argument That Inclusion Of Gender Will Stall Passage Of Progressive Legislation And Implementation Of Hate Crime Statutes

The Hate Crime Statistics Act (HCSA)[106] directs the United States Attorney General to collect data on crimes that "manifest evidence of prejudice based on race, religion, sexual orientation, or ethnicity";[107] crimes motivated by gender bias are not included. The Senate Judiciary Committee Report on one of the Senate companion bills states that the purpose of this type of act is to provide information about the incidence of hate crime to "help law enforcement agencies and local communities combat hate crimes more effectively by identifying their frequency, location, and other patterns over time."[108] Advocates of the HCSA argue that it also raises public awareness of hate crime and encourages the police to develop greater "sensitivity to the particular needs of victims of hate crimes."[109]

The passage of the HCSA without the inclusion of gender as a counted category illustrates the resistance on the part of hate crime victim advocacy groups to recognizing violence against women as hate crime. The enactment of the HCSA in its present form is the result of strong lobbying efforts by the Coalition on Hate Crimes Prevention, a group composed of religious, civil rights, gay and lesbian, and law enforcement organizations.[110] Although some member groups of the Coalition wanted to lobby Congress to add gender as a catego-

---

106. *See* H.R. 1048, 101st Cong., 1st Sess. (1989) (codified at 28 U.S.C. § 534 (Supp. IV 1992)).

107. *Id.* These crimes include murder, non-negligent manslaughter, forcible rape, simple and aggravated assault, intimidation, arson, and destruction or vandalism of property. *Id.* The Attorney General is to develop guidelines for determining when such a crime is bias-motivated. *Id.* In addition, the Bias Crimes Programs Establishment Act, H.R. 1437, 103d Cong., 1st Sess. (1993), directs the Attorney General to appoint a National Director of bias crimes, who would develop instructions on how to comply with reporting requirements under the HCSA.

108. S. REP. NO. 21, 101st Cong., 1st Sess. 2 (1989), *reprinted in* 1990 U.S.C.C.A.N. 158, 158 (discussing S. 419, 101st Cong., 1st Sess. (1989)).

109. Joseph M. Fernandez, Recent Development, *Bringing Hate Crime Into Focus—The Hate Crime Statistics Act of 1990, Pub. L. No. 101-275*, 26 HARV. C.R.-C.L. L. REV. 261, 263 (1991).

110. CENTER FOR WOMEN POLICY STUDIES, *supra* note 1, at 12; *see* Fernandez, *supra* note 109, at 269-78 (discussing the efforts of the Coalition in pushing the Act through Congress, especially when various Members objected to inclusion of sexual orientation).

ry,[111] the Coalition eventually decided against taking such action for a number of reasons.[112]

First, some member groups were concerned that lobbying for such an addition would delay passage of the bill.[113] Additionally, it was argued that adding gender would "open the door" to other groups, such as the elderly or disabled,[114] and thereby delay the passage even further. In promoting these arguments to defeat the inclusion of gender, the Coalition acted in its own interest[115] and displayed a surprising lack of empathy for the victims of violence against women.

Second, most of the Coalition members felt that additional hearings were needed to determine whether existing gender-based crime data collection was deficient.[116] Adding gender as a counted category, it was argued, would not improve then-existing data collection of rape and domestic violence.[117] Some member groups even suggested that collecting any data on violence against women would be too difficult because it is so pervasive[118] and because, it was argued, such violence is not the same as other types of hate crime.[119] However, the Coalition should have known that the collection of data on rape and domestic violence is sorely inadequate in terms of both figures

---

111. At no time did the Act ever include gender. *See* Fernandez, *supra* note 109, at 275-81 (describing how H.R. 1048 was amended before being passed by Congress, but never to include gender). Those organizations that urged the addition of gender to it were predominantly women's advocacy groups. CENTER FOR WOMEN POLICY STUDIES, *supra* note 1, at 13.

112. Fernandez, *supra* note 109, at 275 (stating that the Coalition considered and rejected expanding the statute to include gender).

113. CENTER FOR WOMEN POLICY STUDIES, *supra* note 1, at 13.

114. CENTER FOR WOMEN POLICY STUDIES, *supra* note 1, at 13.

115. The bill was largely supported and promoted by four distinct lobbying groups, all of which had their own interests and agendas in ensuring the passage of the bill. The first group was a loosely connected alliance of organizations that were expressly created to fight racial, ethnic, and religious hate crime, such as the Anti-Defamation League (ADL) and the Anti-Klan Network. Fernandez, *supra* note 109, at 269-70. The second group was a coalition of gay and lesbian organizations. *Id.* at 270-74. The third group consisted of unassociated civil liberties organizations, such as the ACLU. *Id.* at 272. The final group was a confederation of law enforcement agencies. *Id.* at 274. The exclusion of national multi-issue women's organizations was noticeable. *See* Marie de Santis, *Hate Crimes Bill Excludes Women,* OFF OUR BACKS, June 1990 (noting the "absence of any women's groups" from the Coalition).

116. *See* Fernandez, *supra* note 109, at 275 n.74 and accompanying text (summarizing Fernandez's telephone interviews with Sue Armsby, a Lobbyist for People for the American Way, and Kevin Berrill, Director of the Anti-Violence Project of the National Gay and Lesbian Task Force).

117. Fernandez, *supra* note 109, at 275.

118. CENTER FOR WOMEN POLICY STUDIES, *supra* note 1, at 13.

119. CENTER FOR WOMEN POLICY STUDIES, *supra* note 1, at 13. An example of the belief that gender-based hate crime differs from other hate crime is that, because female victims of hate crime sometimes have a prior relationship with their attacker, they are not interchangeable in the way that other hate crime victims are. *Id.* (citing an argument made by the ADL against including gender in hate crime statutes). The issue of a victim's interchangeability is explored further in Part III, *infra* notes 128-137 and accompanying text.

and methods used.[120]   Moreover, rape and domestic violence are not the only crimes against women that are motivated by gender hatred. Like racial minorities and gays and lesbians, women are the victims of such crimes as murder, assault, battery, and intimidation, simply because they are women.[121]

Third, women's rights groups in Washington could not agree whether including gender in the statute would be "the appropriate way to count gender-based crime."[122]   However, almost two years before the HCSA was enacted, the National Organization for Women (NOW) had come out strongly in favor of including gender as a enumerated category.[123]   NOW and the National Coalition Against Domestic Violence (NCADV) even met several times with the Coalition to discuss the inclusion of gender in the bill.[124]   Even eight months prior to the bill's enactment, the two groups had sponsored several meetings of various organizations to discuss gender inclusion.[125]   Clearly there was strong, well-organized support among these groups for including gender in the bill.

---

120. To begin with, it is difficult to determine the actual number of violent crimes that are committed against women every year, because women often fail to report them to police. CENTER FOR WOMEN POLICY STUDIES, *supra* note 1, at 6 (stating that statistics on reported crime "represent a substantial undercount of actual violence against women"); *see* Finn, *supra* note 5, at 9 (explaining that many bias crime victims fail to report the crime to police because the victim distrusts the police, feels the crime was minor, believes that the police cannot "do anything" about the crime, has a language barrier, or fears retaliation from the perpetrator if the crime is reported).

But even if all violent crimes against women were reported to the police, the federal government is unable to compile meaningful statistical data on these crimes because of flaws in its data collection system. *See* CENTER FOR WOMEN POLICY STUDIES, *supra* note 1, at 6-8 (discussing problems with data collection on information concerning violence against women). Furthermore, at the time that the bill was passed, no "working models or police protocols" existed at the state or local level for identifying gender-motivated hate crimes as actually being hate crime. Fernandez, *supra* note 109, at 275 n.4.

121. CENTER FOR WOMEN POLICY STUDIES, *supra* note 1, at 8.

122. Fernandez, *supra* note 109, at 275.

123. *See* Yard testimony, *supra* note 4, at 264 (urging the amendment of S. 2000, one of the Senate companion bills to H.R. 1048, to include gender). Molly Yard testified before the Senate in June 1988. *Id.* However, Congress did not enact the bill until April 1990. 136 CONG. REC. H1460 (daily ed. Apr. 4, 1990) (concurring in the Senate amendment to H.R. 1048).

124. Memorandum from Nancy Buermeyer, Director, Lesbian Rights, NOW, to the NOW Executive Committee 1 (Dec. 15, 1988) (on file with *The American University Journal of Gender & the Law*) (discussing NOW and NCADV's December 1988 meeting with the Coalition). However, the Coalition notified NOW and NCADV that a poll had been taken and that the Coalition member-groups had decided unanimously to not include gender, thereby cancelling any future meetings. de Santis, *supra* note 115.

125. Letter from Nancy Buermeyer, Director, Lesbian Rights, NOW, and Janet Nudelman, Public Policy Advocate, NCADV, to organizations supporting the inclusion of gender in the bill (Aug. 28, 1989) (on file with *The American University Journal of Gender & the Law*) (referring to an August 1989 meeting of "feminist" organizations concerning the inclusion of gender in the bill, and inviting additional organizations to participate in a September 1989 forum on the same subject).

Ironically, the Coalition argued that "[w]ithout the inclusion of sexual orientation in the act, there would be two standards. Crimes against gays and lesbians would be viewed as less significant, less pervasive, and less reprehensible than crimes motivated by racial, religious, or ethnic prejudice."[126] That a coalition of religious, civil rights, and gay and lesbian organizations should fail to see that their actions relegated crimes against women to the same secondary position illustrates one of the major obstacles that women's advocates must overcome before violence against women will be treated as hate crime.

2. The Argument That Women Are Not Interchangeable In The Same Way As Other Hate Crime Victims

Interchangeability is important to hate crime victims' advocates. They argue that hate crime should be punished more severely, at least in part because such crime has a greater impact on the particular community to which the victim belongs.[127] A particular community is more affected by a hate crime that is motivated by the victim's membership in the community, because the victim could be interchanged with any other member of the group. Therefore, other members of the community may live in fear that such a crime could happen to them.[128] Similarly, women fear for their own safety when another woman in the community is the victim of a violent crime, whether the attacker is known to the woman or is a stranger.

Female victims of violent crime often have a prior relationship with their attackers.[129] For some commentators, the existence of a prior relationship between victim and perpetrator is the only factor that should determine how the legal system addresses violence against women.[130] If a woman has a prior relationship with her attacker, they would argue, then she is not "interchangeable" as are victims of racial and other hate crimes.

---

126. Fernandez, *supra* note 109, at 274 (citing John H. Buchanan, Chairman, People for the American Way Action Fund, from his remarks in a June 7, 1990 press release).

127. *See supra* note 6 and accompanying text (noting that bias crimes against an individual because of that person's membership in a particular group affect the entire group who share that immutable characteristic because such bias crime is intended to intimidate that particular group of people).

128. Finn, *supra* note 5, at 10 (finding that the fear that hate crimes generate can "victimize a whole class of people").

129. CENTER FOR WOMEN POLICY STUDIES, *supra* note 1, at 12 (stating that women who are victimized are often victimized by "close associates").

130. CENTER FOR WOMEN POLICY STUDIES, *supra* note 1, at 13 (citing a memo by the Civil Rights Division of the Anti-Defamation League, which says that crimes against racial and ethnic groups are interchangeable because a crime against a member of one of these groups sends a message to the entire group but that rape victims may not be interchangeable).

In an interview, Richard Cohen, the Legal Director of the Southern Poverty Law Center, the umbrella organization for Klanwatch, offered an explanation for the position that women are not perceived to be interchangeable in the same manner as victims of racial and other hate crime.[131] In his effort to illustrate that violence against women does not have the same effect on the community as violence against racial and ethnic minorities, Cohen asked me to compare two hypotheticals. In the first, a caucasian male writes "I'm going to get you nigger" on the door of an African-American's home. In the second, a male writes "I'm going to get you bitch" on the door of a woman's home. Cohen argued that the second example would not threaten women in the community because it is directed at a specific individual and not at women in general. I countered that it would threaten women in the community because "bitch," like "nigger," is a derogatory term that applies to a sub-group of the population. By using the term "nigger" or "bitch," the aggressor signifies that it is the victim's ethnicity or femaleness that he sees as prominent. If I were to see the statement "I'm going to get you bitch" on a door in my neighborhood, I would assume that there is a man in the vicinity who hates women and I would fear encountering him.

In a similar vein, the Anti-Defamation League of B'nai B'rith (ADL), a leader in the hate crime victims' movement, advocates that, because many women have a prior relationship with their attackers, they are not interchangeable like other victims of hate crime.[132] The ADL has stated that "the relationship between individual perpetrator and victim is the salient fact—whether the defendant is a women-hater in general is irrelevant."[133] The ADL has not only refused to support the inclusion of gender in hate crime statutes, but has actually testified against it.[134]

In conclusion, both Richard Cohen and the ADL assume that when women have a prior relationship with their assailants, they are neither interchangeable nor perceived to be interchangeable; therefore, violence against women does not have the same impact on the community as other hate crime. Remarkably, these advocates appear completely unaware of the arguments feminist advocates and theorists

---

131. Telephone Interview with Richard Cohen, Legal Director, Southern Poverty Law Center (Aug. 5, 1992).

132. CENTER FOR WOMEN POLICY STUDIES, *supra* note 1, at 13.

133. CENTER FOR WOMEN POLICY STUDIES, *supra* note 1, at 13.

134. Susan R. Boyle, *Legislative News*, MASS. LAW. WKLY., May 25, 1992, at 23 (noting that the ADL, one of the original drafters of the Massachusetts hate crime reporting law, testified against a proposal to modify the law to include gender because "domestic violence and rape cases would draw attention from crimes involving bias").

have been making for decades—that rape and domestic violence victims are interchangeable in the minds of their attackers[135] and that women alter their lifestyles in numerous ways to avoid male violence because they fear such violence happening to them.[136]

3. Persistent Sexism Among Judges

Another obstacle to treating violence against women as hate crime is the persistence of sexism among judges. This hurdle emerged in the debate about passage of the 1991 Senate version of the Violence Against Women Act.[137] In a statement opposing the civil rights remedy granted by the Act,[138] the Conference of Chief Justices stated, by implication, that granting legal remedies for family violence cases will allow women to misuse the law by making false legal claims, and that granting a federal civil rights remedy for hate violence against women will choke the federal courts with domestic relations issues.[139] The Chief Justice of the United States Supreme Court, William Rehnquist, shares this view.[140]

The Conference of Chief Justices maintains that family policy is a sensitive issue that should be reserved to the states, and that the remedies offered in the Violence Against Women Act would contra-

---

135. *See supra* note 4 (discussing the interchangeable nature of female victims of violent crime).

136. Margaret Gordon and Stephanie Riger interviewed women and men living in several large cities to assess how fear of violence affects their lives. The authors' study found that 68.4% of the women, but only 5.4% of the men, never go to bars and clubs alone. Further, 47% of the women, but only 7.5% of the men, said that they never go downtown alone after dark. MARGARET T. GORDON & STEPHANIE RIGER, THE FEMALE FEAR 15 (1989), *cited in* CENTER FOR WOMEN POLICY STUDIES, *supra* note 1, at 11.

137. S. 15, 102d Cong., 1st Sess. (1991); H.R. 1502, 102d Cong., 1st Sess. (1991).

138. The civil rights remedies contained in the 1991 version of the Act are substantially similar to those contained in the 1993 version. *Compare* S. 15, § 301 *with* S. 11, §§ 301-304 (providing, in both bills, victims of gender-based crimes of violence with the right to sue for compensatory and punitive damages and for injunctive or declaratory relief). Thus, arguments against these remedies apply to the 1993 Act as well.

139. *Violence Against Women: Victims of the System: Hearings on S. 15 Before the Senate Comm. on the Judiciary,* 102d Cong., 1st Sess. 314, 315 (1991) [hereinafter *Hearings on S. 15*] (prepared statement of Hon. Vincent L. McKusick, President, Conference of Chief Justices) [hereinafter McKusick statement]:

> If, as it appears to be the case, Section 301(c) permits civil suits against male relatives, particularly against husbands or intimate partners, it can be anticipated that this right will be invoked as a bargaining tool within the context of divorce negotiations and add a major complicating factor to an environment which is often acrimonious as it is.

Id.

This opinion demonstrates the gender bias of the Chief Justices. They ignore the fact that a civil rights remedy will allow women to pursue legitimate claims against their abusers. They also ignore a primary reason victims want to be in federal court—the unwillingness of state courts to remedy their wrongs.

140. *See* Jack Sirica, *Federal Protection of Women at Issue,* NEWSDAY, Feb. 16, 1992, at 17 (noting that Rehnquist told the American Bar Association that the "proposed civil rights protections for women would 'unnecessarily expand' the jurisdiction of federal courts").

dict state law.[141] This statement clearly reflects the assumption that family violence should be treated differently from other violence. The Justices fail to grasp that it is precisely because state remedies for victims of gender-motivated hate crime are inadequate, in both theory and practice, that a federal civil rights remedy was deemed necessary.[142]

B.   *The Debate Over Increased Penalties Versus Treatment For Sex Offenders*

As previously discussed in Part II, the Senate version of the Violence Against Women Act of 1993 (VAWA) contains a provision calling for penalty increases and enhancements for certain defendants that are convicted of sex offenses.[143] While a number of prominent multi-issue women's rights organizations endorse the Senate bill,[144] still other such organizations oppose the bill because of these penalty provisions.[145] Some of these opponents favor treatment programs for sex offenders over increased punishment.[146] The resulting debate over treatment versus incarceration has divided the women's advocacy community.

In September 1990, the Task Force on the Violence Against Women Act[147] began meeting to promote the Senate version of the Violence

---

141. McKusick statement, *supra* note 139, at 317 (arguing that Title III will override "state laws on damages and civil suits between spouses").

142. S. REP. NO. 138, *supra* note 47, at 49 (noting that "[t]raditional [s]tate law sources of protection have proved to be difficult avenues of redress for some of the most serious crimes against women"); S. REP. NO. 197, *supra* note 13, at 43 (noting that crimes that disproportionately affect women are often treated "less seriously" by the courts than comparable crimes against men). For example, certain court practices, such as the "prompt complaint" rule, deter victims from reporting and prosecuting crimes of violence and put the victim on trial. S. REP. NO. 197, *supra* note 13, at 45-46. Finally, stereotypes of crime victims prevent them from receiving equal treatment by the courts. *Id.* at 46-48 (discussing the problem of victim-blaming in rape cases).

143. S. 11, 103d Cong., 1st Sess. §§ 111-112 (1993); *see supra* note 58 and accompanying text (explaining the provisions of the bill).

144. Those organizations that support the bill include, among others, Center for Women Policy Studies, Ms. Foundation for Women, National Coalition Against Domestic Violence, NOW, National Women's Health Resource Center, and National Women's Political Caucus. *See* List of Organization Endorsements, Violence Against Women Act of 1993 (as of Oct. 13, 1993) (on file with *The American University Journal of Gender & the Law*).

145. For example, the National Women's Law Center and Women's Legal Defense Fund support neither the Senate nor the House version of the VAWA. *Id.*

146. Statement of NOMAS, VAWA Title I: Treating Sex Offenders: Concerns (on file with *The American University Journal of Gender & the Law*) [hereinafter Statement of NOMAS] (stating that "when we consider battery, rape, or child abuse, the thought quickly moves to the issues of treatment for the offenders").

147. The Task Force is a coalition of women's advocacy groups dedicated to crafting and promoting the bill. Letter from Sally F. Goldfarb, Senior Staff Attorney, NOW Legal Defense and Education Fund, to organizational supporters of the VAWA (Sept. 13, 1990) (on file with *The American University Journal of Gender & the Law*) (enclosing minutes from the Task Force's

Against Women Act of 1991.[148] Certain members of the Task Force immediately raised concerns about several provisions that increased penalties for convicted sex offenders;[149] such penalty increases, it was argued, would have a disproportionate effect on communities of color.[150] As a result, some Task Force member organizations refused to support the bill.[151] Despite this opposition, substantially similar penalty provisions were carried over to the succeeding bill, the Violence Against Women Act of 1993.[152]

In February 1993, Representative Patricia Schroeder introduced the House version of the Violence Against Women Act.[153] This bill does not contain a penalty increase provision; instead, it provides grants to develop treatment programs for sex offenders.[154] A similar provision in the 1991 House bill[155] received a great deal more support than the 1991 Senate bill.[156] As of the time that this article was written, it was too early to tell which 1993 version of the bill would

---

September 1990 that describe the Task Force and its function). Specifically, the Task Force assists in drafting the Act, mobilizes support for the bill and any amendments to it, and educates the public about the bill to ensure its passage. *Id.*

148. S. 15, 102d Cong., 1st Sess. (1991).

149. S. 15, §§ 111, 112. Section 111 provides that repeat sex offenders may receive up to twice the imprisonment and/or fine otherwise provided in the guidelines. Similarly, section 112 increases penalties for rape and aggravated rape by at least four offense levels.

150. *See* Minutes from the December 18, 1990 Meeting of the Task Force on the Violence Against Women Act 2-4 (Dec. 18, 1990) (on file with the *American University Journal of Gender & the Law*) [hereinafter Task Force Minutes] (suggesting that a number of Task Force members opposed the sentencing provisions because of their disproportionate effect on minorities). Two factors contribute to this disproportionate effect. First, because Indian reservations are the most populated areas subject to federal jurisdiction, Native Americans also are the largest group of people to be affected by the penalty increase provisions. *See Hearings on S. 15, supra* note 139, at 299, 300 (prepared statement of Peg Rogers, Attorney, Native American Rights Fund) (stating that Native Americans will "bear the weight" of the provisions). Second, the danger of selective prosecution means that members of minority groups would be punished in greater proportion than those of non-minority groups. *Id.* at 295, 295 (prepared statement of The Women's Circle) (noting that "the law is followed to the letter" when used against Native Americans and other minorities).

151. *See* Task Force Minutes, *supra* note 150, at 3 (noting that during one meeting of the Task Force, it was determined that "[i]f the Task Force supported increased sentences, many groups could not support the bill"). These groups also stated that they would "lobby against the sentencing provision and not support the bill as a whole" if the provision remained in the bill. *Id.* at 4.

152. *Compare* S. 15, § 111 *with* S. 11, § 111 (making, in both bills, a subsequent sexual offense punishable by a term of imprisonment up to twice that which is authorized by statute or by the sentencing guidelines).

153. H.R. 1133, 103d Cong., 1st Sess. (1993).

154. *Id.* § 121(a).

155. *Compare* H.R. 1502, § 112 (requiring that all federal sex offenders participate in a treatment program within 30 days of entering prison) *with* H.R. 1133, § 127 (requiring the United States Attorney General to ensure that community treatment information is made available to released sex offenders).

156. *See* List of Organization Endorsements, Violence Against Women Act of 1991 (as of Oct. 29, 1992) (on file with *The American University Journal of Gender & the Law*) (indicating that 34 organizations supported only the House version while twelve supported only the Senate version).

receive more support. However, it is conceivable that another such split could occur.

Concern about increasing incarceration for rapists has led the Task Force on the Violence Against Women Act to form a subcommittee to explore the possibility of treatment for sex offenders.[157] Interestingly, it is the sole men's group involved in the Task Force, the National Organization for Men Against Sexism (NOMAS), that has highlighted the apparent contradiction between labeling certain acts "hate crime" and maintaining that the perpetrators of such crime can be treated.[158] NOMAS argues that treating sex offenders from a healing perspective, rather than from a criminal justice perspective, reinforces the erroneous belief that sex offenders are different from other hate crime perpetrators and merely require treatment.[159] In fact, much of the work of anti-rape advocates has focused on countering the image of rapists as sick individuals who should spend time in therapy and, instead, promoting the notion that these individuals should be treated as perpetrators of violent crime who deserve to spend time in jail.[160]

Promoting treatment as a response to violence against women has distracted women's advocates from the task of promoting the VAWA. As a practical matter, the treatment/incarceration debate has split the women's advocacy community. The opposition that some women's organizations have toward the increased penalties provision signifies their discomfort with the underlying premise of hate crime statutes that contain penalty enhancement provisions—that is, that increased penalties are desirable.[161]

C.   The Argument That Male Violence Against Women Affects Women Differently

As discussed in Part III, concern exists that increased penalties for convicted sex offenders have a disproportionate effect on communi-

---

157. Telephone Interview with Rus Ervin Funk, Coordinator, Men's Anti-Rape Resource Center, National Organization for Men Against Sexism (NOMAS) (July 6, 1992). NOMAS is a member of the Task Force subcommittee.

158. Statement of NOMAS, *supra* note 146.

159. Statement of NOMAS, *supra* note 146 (stating that no other hate crime legislation mandates treatment of hate crime offenders, and suggesting that treatment for offenders of the Violence Against Women Act undermines its characterization as a hate crime).

160. Statement of NOMAS, *supra* note 146. A more acceptable option might be to permit "sensitivity training," the way that California does, as a condition of probation for all hate crimes. *See* CAL. PENAL CODE § 422.95 (West Supp. 1993). This option focuses on confronting the assailant's desire to dominate women as a whole rather than focusing on the assailant's individual problem of "controlling" his sexuality.

161. For example, national women's organizations have not endorsed the Hate Crimes Sentencing Enhancement Act. *See supra* note 64 and accompanying text.

ties of color.[162] Therefore, while it is tempting to assume that male violence against women plays the same role in all women's lives and that all women believe that an increased judicial response to violence against women is desirable and/or effective, such an assertion is essentialist.[163]

The anti-essentialist critique of feminism maintains that mainstream feminist legal theory assumes that there is an "essential 'woman'" beneath the race, class, and sexual orientation differences that distinguish women from one another.[164] Feminist theorists who speak of a single women's voice or experience view women's interests as the same and the fate of all women as being bound together.[165] However, it is argued, the single women's voice that is spoken is that of the caucasian woman.[166] In this way, mainstream feminism ignores the experiences of women of color.[167]

In particular, feminism has been charged with essentialism in its theories on rape. Some African-American feminists argue that African-American women and caucasian women have had, and continue to have, very different experiences of rape, giving rape a different meaning for the two groups.[168] For instance, Angela Harris asserts that for African-American women rape is a far more complex experience than it is for caucasian women, for it is rooted in racism.[169] On the one hand, while rape laws historically were used in a racist fashion to single out African-American men for the rape of

---

162. *See supra* note 150 and accompanying text (discussing the effect that penalty increase provisions have upon Native American communities).

163. The theory of gender essentialism asserts that a "monolithic 'women's experience'" exists that can be isolated and described independently of such factors as a woman's race, class, or sexual orientation. Angela P. Harris, *Race and Essentialism in Feminist Legal Theory*, 42 STAN. L. REV. 581, 588 (1990).

164. *See id.* at 591. Angela Harris also discusses the work of Robin West as an example of mainstream feminist legal theory that is based upon essentialism. *Id.* at 602-05.

165. For example, Catharine MacKinnon argues that society is constructed along gender lines, with women being dominated by men. CATHARINE A. MACKINNON, *Desire and Power, in* FEMINISM UNMODIFIED 46, 51 (1987) (stating that gender is "a matter of dominance, not difference"). Thus, in spite of their different situations, women are linked to each other by their membership in a subordinated gender class. *Id.* at 56.

166. ELIZABETH V. SPELMAN, INESSENTIAL WOMAN: PROBLEMS OF EXCLUSION IN FEMINIST THOUGHT 3-4 (1988) (asserting that mainstream feminism's description of women 'as women' is almost always a description of middle-class women from western industrialized countries); Harris, *supra* note 163, at 588 (stating that most feminist legal theorists who claim to speak for all women are caucasian, heterosexual, and from socio-economically advantaged backgrounds).

167. Angela Harris explains that essentialism requires that some voices be silenced to benefit the woman who speaks for all women. Harris, *supra* note 163, at 585. Those silenced voices are "the same voices silenced by the mainstream legal voice of [the country]—among them, the voices of black women." *Id.*

168. Harris, *supra* note 163, at 598.

169. Harris, *supra* note 163, at 598.

caucasian women,[170] the laws did at least provide formal protection to caucasian women.[171] On the other hand, the law did not even recognize the rape of an African-American woman as a crime until after the Civil War.[172] Even after the Civil War, the laws were seldom used to protect these women, because African-American women were considered to be naturally promiscuous.[173]

The intersection of rape and racism continues today.[174] Statistics show that African-American men are more likely to receive harsher penalties for rape than caucasian men,[175] and that all men are treated less harshly when the rape victim is African-American.[176] As a result, when an African-American woman is raped by an African-American man and reports her rape to the police, she is exposing herself, and her assailant, to a criminal justice system that is both

---

170. Harris, *supra* note 163, at 598 (quoting Catharine A. MacKinnon, *Feminism, Marxism, Method, and the State: Toward Feminist Jurisprudence*, 8 SIGNS 635, 646 n.22 (1983)); Jennifer Wriggins, *Rape, Racism, and the Law*, 6 HARV. WOMEN'S L.J. 103, 106 (1983) (discussing the "selective recognition" of only one type of rape—that of a caucasian woman by an African-American man). The mere allegation that an African-American man raped a caucasian woman sometimes led to his lynching by a mob; a conviction brought castration or death. Wriggins, *supra* at 105. Caucasian men accused of raping caucasian women were subjected to far less severe penalties. *Id.* at 106 n.15.

171. *But see* Wriggins, *supra* note 170, at 107 (noting that traditional common law barriers protected most caucasian rapists from prosecution for raping caucasian women).

172. Harris, *supra* note 163, at 599; Wriggins, *supra* note 170, at 118.

173. *See* Sharon A. Allard, *Rethinking Battered Woman Syndrome: A Black Feminist Perspective*, 1 UCLA WOMEN'S L.J. 191, 199-200 (1991) (stating that because African-American women were deemed to be "immoral," they were undeserving of legal protection from sexual exploitation).

174. This commingling extends into distant areas. For example, the myths and stereotypes about African-American women that justified their sexual abuse during slavery affects their experience of sexual harassment in the workplace. *See* Kimberlé Crenshaw, *Whose Story Is It Anyway? Feminist and Antiracist Appropriations of Anita Hill*, in RACE-ING JUSTICE, EN-GENDERING POWER 402 (Toni Morrison ed., 1992). The first result is that the sexual harassment of African-American women is often used to note the woman's "subordinate racial status." *Id.* at 412-14. For example, while both caucasian and African-American women may be objectified as "pieces," insults directed at African-American women may often be prefaced with "nigger," "black," or other words that call attention to the woman's race. *Id.* The second result is that courts may be less likely to believe African-American women's reports of harassment. *See id.* (noting that because an African-American woman was not expected to be chaste, she was considered less likely to be truthful and thus her testimony was less likely to be believed by judges and jurors). Therefore, mainstream feminism should recognize this difference in women's experiences, and develop alternative narratives of sexual harassment that are grounded in African-American women's experiences as well. *See id.* at 435 (stating that "[n]onwhite and working-class women . . . must see their own diverse experiences reflected in the practice and policy statements of these predominantly European-American middle-class groups").

175. For example, between 1930 and 1967, 89% of the men executed for rape in the United States were African-American. Harris, *supra* note 163, at 600 (citing SUSAN ESTRICH, REAL RAPE 107 n.2 (1982)).

176. African-American men continued to be treated more harshly "when charged with raping white women . . . [than] with raping black women." DIANA SCULLY, UNDERSTANDING SEXUAL VIOLENCE: A STUDY OF CONVICTED RAPISTS 145 (1990) (citing Gary D. LaFree, *The Effect of Sexual Stratification by Race on Official Reactions to Rape*, 45 AM. SOC. REV. 842 (1980)); *see also* Wriggins, *supra* note 170, at 121-22 (stating that both judges and caucasian jurors impose lighter sentences where the victim is African-American).

racist and sexist.[177] This reality has led some commentators to question the goal of mainstream feminism to increase the number of rape convictions, arguing that it would merely serve to reproduce the problem of disparate punishments between African-American and caucasian rapists.[178]

It has also been argued that mainstream feminism is essentialist in its treatment of domestic violence. Some feminists believe that African-American women experience male violence differently from caucasian women, giving violence against women a different meaning for the two groups.[179] This difference in meaning, it is argued, has been ignored by mainstream feminists.[180] Instead, the efforts of mainstream feminism on behalf of battered women have been based on caucasian women's experiences.[181] The resulting feminist legal theory on woman-battering issues, such as coercive intervention in

---

177. For example, many African-American women remain silent about experiences of sexual abuse out of fear that their stories will be used to "reinforce stereotypes of black men as sexually threatening." Crenshaw, *supra* note 174, at 415. Even African-American women who do not share this fear may choose not to testify against African-American men because they fear ostracism from those who do share this view. *Id.*

In addition, Crenshaw states that the African-American community has not fully addressed intra-racial rape and "other abusive practices," partly because of a reluctance to expose internal conflict that could, in turn, reflect negatively on the rest of the community. *Id.* at 420. The effect of this "code of silence" is to coerce women into keeping quiet for fear of being labeled a traitor to their race. *Id.* at 420-22 (noting that many accounts of the Anita Hill/Clarence Thomas Senate hearings portrayed Hill as a traitor to African-American people for testifying against Thomas).

178. Wriggins, *supra* note 170, at 138.

Angela Harris takes this argument one step further, arguing that caucasian feminists have not only ignored the racist use of rape, but in fact have perpetuated it as well. She relates an example where Susan Brownmiller, a caucasian feminist, describes the African-American defendants in a rape trial as "'pathetic, semiliterate fellows'" and the caucasian female accusers as "innocent pawns of white men." Harris, *supra* note 163, at 601 (quoting Brownmiller, *supra* note 1, at 237). Thus, the contemporary feminist analysis of rape explicitly relies on racist ideology to minimize caucasian women's complicity. *Id.*

179. *See* Crenshaw, *supra* note 174, at 414. Crenshaw states that "[b]lack women experience much of the sexual aggression that the feminist movement has articulated but in a form that represents simultaneously their subordinate racial status." *Id.*

180. *See* ANGELA Y. DAVIS, WOMEN, CULTURE AND POLITICS 45 (1990) (discussing the reluctance of African-American, Latina and Native American women to join the anti-rape movement of the early 1970s because the feminist theoretical foundations for the campaign failed to "develop an analysis of rape that acknowledged the social conditions that foster sexual violence as well as the centrality of racism in determining those social conditions"). Davis states that "since much of the early activism against rape was focused on delivering rapists into the hand of the judicial system, Afro-American women were understandably reluctant to become involved with a movement that might well lead to further repressive assaults on their families and their communities." *Id.* at 44.

181. *See* ANDREA DWORKIN, WOMAN HATING 21-22 (1974) (stating that most of the women who were involved in the early stages of feminism were caucasian and middle class). As a result, most of them, and hence the movement, failed to take any action that would harm their privileged lifestyle. *Id.*; *see* Schneider, *supra* note 3, at 532 (noting that, until recently, the battered women's movement, a sub-group of the feminist movement, was "largely shaped by the experiences and understanding of white women").

family matters[182] or battered woman syndrome,[183] may not address the experiences of African-American women at all.[184]

Despite the fact that women as a group suffer from male violence, a variety of factors influence a woman's decision to seek assistance from the criminal justice system. Obviously, race is one factor that should not be ignored.[185] However, it is essentialist to assert that

---

182. Catharine MacKinnon has argued that the privacy doctrine shields battery and marital rape when they occur inside the home. MacKinnon states that certain alternatives for women are precluded by conditions of sex, race, and class before a legal doctrine is chosen, ensuring that "the existing distribution of power and resources within the private sphere will be precisely what the law of privacy exists to protect." CATHARINE A. MACKINNON, *Roe v. Wade: A Study in Male Ideology*, in ABORTION: MORAL AND LEGAL PERSPECTIVES 45, 53 (Jay L. Garfield & Patricia Hennessey eds., 1984) [hereinafter MACKINNON, *Roe v. Wade*]. According to Dorothy Roberts, MacKinnon's argument is an example of how mainstream feminist legal theory "focuses on the private realm of the family as an institution of violence and subordination." Dorothy E. Roberts, *Punishing Drug Addicts Who Have Babies: Women of Color, Equality, and the Right of Privacy*, 104 HARV. L. REV. 1419, 1470 (1991) (citing MACKINNON, *Roe v. Wade*, *supra* at 51-53). However, Roberts argues, women of color often focus on the family as the "site of solace and resistance against racial oppression." *Id.* at 1470-71; *see also* ELMER P. MARTIN & JOANNE M. MARTIN, THE BLACK EXTENDED FAMILY 1 (1978) (noting the importance of the family to African-Americans for psychological and material support). Thus, women of color may view domestic violence less as a type of abuse within the private sphere (the battering) and more as a potential abuse in the public sphere (the government intervention); *cf.* Roberts, *supra* at 1471 (asserting that in the area of reproductive rights, many African-American women are more concerned about coercive government intervention than about abuse in the private sector).

183. Battered woman syndrome is characterized by a cyclical pattern of psychological and physical abuse which may be divided into three stages, those of tension-building, acute battering, and reconciliation. LENORE E. WALKER, THE BATTERED WOMAN 55-70 (1979). The syndrome is based upon the idea that the woman suffers from "learned helplessness," a state of psychological paralysis where she feels incapable of escaping the battering relationship. *Id.* at 47-48.

However, at least one commentator has noted that battered woman syndrome is built on a definition of woman which is based on "limited societal constructs of appropriate behavior for white women." Allard, *supra* note 173, at 192-94. Moreover, African-American women must hurdle the additional stereotype asserting that they do not deserve the protection under the syndrome because of their race. *See id.* at 199-200 (noting that in the Victorian era, African-American women were deemed to be "immoral." This stereotype was used to further the perception that these women did not deserve legal protection from sexual exploitation.).

184. For example, "[w]omen of color may believe that the means to ending their abuse is to end racial oppression, not gender subordination. The battered women's movement as it has been constructed may not speak to their experiences at all." Schneider, *supra* note 3, at 532 n.46.

185. In reality, most African-American women, like most caucasian women, are raped by men of the same race. Statistics show that 90% of rapes are intra-racial. MacKinnon, *Sex Equality*, *supra* note 2, at 1300 n.90 (citing MENACHEM AMIR, FORCIBLE RAPE 44 (1971)). A recent Department of Justice study shows that "in rapes with one offender, 7 of every 10 white victims were raped by a white offender, and 8 of every 10 Black victims were raped by a Black offender." *Id.* (citing CAROLINE WOLF HARLOW, FEMALE VICTIMS OF VIOLENT CRIME 10 (1991)).

Furthermore, the percentage of African-American women who experience sexual assault is similar to that of caucasian women. Note, for example, the percentage of women who reported being victimized at least once by rape or attempted rape: caucasian (non-Jewish), 45%; Jewish, 50%; African-American, 44%; Latina, 30%; Asian, 17%; Filipina, 17%; Native American, 55%; and other, 28%. DIANA E.H. RUSSELL, SEXUAL EXPLOITATION: RAPE, CHILD SEXUAL ABUSE, AND WORKPLACE HARASSMENT 84, tbl. 3.3 (1984).

Additionally, African-American women may be more likely than women of other racial and ethnic groups to report their rapes. In one study, 20% of rapes overall were reported. Out of

race is the only factor that influences women's decisions about whether to seek out judicial intervention[186] or to assert that all women of a particular race feel the same way about judicial intervention.[187] Feminists, in particular, should allow policy decisions to be guided by the voices of the women who have actually been the victims of male violence.[188] Through personal work experience, I have encountered many women of color who believed that their abuse should be treated as seriously as violent crime between strangers; who wanted their abusers to be prosecuted to the full extent of the law; and who chose to take advantage of all legal remedies, both civil and criminal.[189] Advocates should listen to the voices of women from diverse backgrounds to ensure the availability of all possible remedies. Individual women can then choose the appropriate remedy.

D.　The Argument That Domestic Violence Should Be Treated Differently From Other Hate Crime

The argument that the interests of domestic violence victims may be better served by training police and prosecutors to address the specific problems of domestic violence, rather than by treating domestic violence as the more general problem of hate crime, has some merit. Victims of domestic violence are different from victims of other hate crime in that they often maintain an intimate relation-

---

these, 17% of the rapes of African-American women were reported, 9% of the rapes of Jewish women, 8% of the rapes of Asian and Filipina women, 7% of the rapes of caucasian non-Jewish women, and 0% of the rapes of Native American women. *Id.* at 100.

　186.　For instance, one study found that, regardless of race, victims of rape were most likely to seek judicial intervention when their homes were broken into, they were raped by a stranger, they were threatened with a weapon, or they were subject to a "high degree of violence." RUSSELL, *supra* note 185, at 96-98.

　187.　Joan Williams has noted that the sameness/difference debate has divided the African-American community, as well as the feminist community. Joan C. Williams, *Dissolving the Sameness/Difference Debate: A Post-Modern Path Beyond Essentialism in Feminist and Critical Race Theory*, 1991 DUKE L.J. 296, 297. Williams offers a post-modern formulation of "difference" in which "[c]laims of difference simply mean that *in some contexts* gender or race may shape (or even determine) one's outlook. This reformulation of difference . . . avoids essentialism because it refuses to concede that race, gender—or, indeed, *any* given category—will always be determinative." *Id.* at 307 (emphasis in original).

　188.　The idea that women's voices are silenced under patriarchy and that feminism should therefore look to individual women's experiences is not new. *Id.* at 320 (advocating that women's "personal narrative" be used "to enable women to communicate what they see as basic realities").

　189.　My experiences include volunteering as a hotline counselor at a shelter for battered women; serving as the shelter's house manager; counseling women seeking Civil Protection Orders through the Civil Victim's Advocacy Project of the D.C. Coalition Against Domestic Violence; surveying over one thousand intrafamily offense cases for the D.C. Task Force on Gender Bias in the Courts; and representing battered women as a student attorney with The American University Women and the Law Clinic.

ship with their attackers following a battering incident.[190] Throughout my experiences working with police and prosecutors on behalf of battered women,[191] I found that this single factor completely guided the former's approach to reports of domestic violence. They responded with either disbelief—if she stayed then the alleged violence must not have occurred—or with the belief that the abused woman would not follow through with the prosecution of her case. This resistance by police, prosecutors, and judges to treating domestic violence as a crime has been, in fact, well documented.[192] Therefore, given their special biases against battered women, law enforcement personnel need to be educated about the dynamics of relationships in which domestic violence takes place. Only with this education will law enforcement officials be able to understand domestic violence as an expression of hatred toward women[193] and be motivated to prosecute domestic abusers to the full extent of the law.

It might appear that in those few jurisdictions that have already developed an adequate law enforcement response to domestic violence, including gender in hate crime statutes would not help, and might even harm, domestic violence victims. This issue recently arose in Connecticut, where domestic violence advocates have been training law enforcement officials on how to properly respond to domestic disturbances.[194] When the possibility of including gender in a pending hate crime statute arose, Connecticut NOW and the

---

190. Some victims choose to continue living with their batterers. Some reasons why a victim stays include: the batterer pleads and promises to reform; he threatens, and/or performs, further acts of violence if she leaves him; the victim has no place else to go; the children still live in the home; and the victim feels love or sorrow for the batterer. DEL MARTIN, BATTERED WIVES 72-86 (1976) (citing a 1975 survey of battered women). Even if the victim does leave her batterer, in some cases she will continue to maintain a contact with him. For example, the victim and batter may have a child in common and thus need to maintain a non-intimate relationship.

191. See supra note 189.

192. See S. REP. NO. 138, supra note 47, at 44 (stating that there is "widespread gender bias in the courts," especially regarding domestic violence cases). A California task force on gender bias in the courts has reported that every element of the California justice system, from police to judges, treats domestic violence victims "as though their complaints were trivial, exaggerated or somehow their own fault." Id. at 46 (citing to the findings of the Administrative Office of the Judicial Council of the Courts of California); cf. Carolyne R. Hathaway, Case Comment, Gender Based Discrimination in Police Reluctance to Respond to Domestic Assault Complaints, 75 GEO. L.J. 667, 672 (1986) (addressing the fact that prosecutors are slow in responding to domestic violence complaints and that judges do not impose meaningful sanctions in domestic violence cases).

193. CENTER FOR WOMEN POLICY STUDIES, supra note 1, at 10 (discussing wife abuse as a "motiveless" crime of domination and control. "In virtually all of these cases, the 'motive' is hatred and anger at women, and a desire to control [women], acted out on a particular woman.").

194. Telephone Interview with Betty Gallow, Lobbyist for the Connecticut Civil Liberties Union, Coalition for Gay and Lesbian Rights, and Connecticut Coalition Against Domestic Violence (Aug. 4, 1992).

Connecticut Coalition Against Domestic Violence decided not to advocate the inclusion of gender in the statute.[195] The group was concerned that the police, who had already been trained to respond to domestic violence calls in one manner, would become confused, and therefore less effective, if required to treat domestic disturbances as hate crime incidents.[196]

The inclusion of gender in hate crime statutes does not, however, preclude legislatures from offering more specific guidance to law enforcement officials about how to address domestic violence. Hate crime statutes already include special guidelines for addressing violence against gays and lesbians, women, the mentally and physically disabled, the elderly, and members of unpopular political groups.[197] Therefore, there is no reason why guidelines and training programs which states have already developed for fighting domestic violence cannot be incorporated into a state's program for addressing hate crime.

E.　The Argument That Hate Crime Statutes Will Be Used Against Women

Another argument against including gender in hate crime statutes is that these statutes may be used *against* domestic violence victims if not specifically restricted to crime against recognized subordinate groups. For instance, in some cases police have responded to mandatory arrest statutes[198] by arresting both parties; as a result, mandatory arrest statutes that were intended to protect the victim often become a second form of abuse for the victim.[199] Therefore, hate crime statutes that do not specifically state that they can only be used against a member of a dominant group by a member of a

---

195. *Id.*

196. *Id.*

197. *See supra* notes 19-23 and accompanying text (describing the groups that are covered by state hate crime statutes).

198. Mandatory arrest statutes require the police to arrest the primary physical aggressor when they have probable cause to believe that a felony or misdemeanor domestic assault has occurred. Sarah Mausolff Buel, *Mandatory Arrest for Domestic Violence,* 11 HARV. WOMEN'S L.J. 213, 214-15 (1988).

199. Professor Catherine Klein has stated that

> [a] major area of concern surrounding mandatory arrest laws has been dual arrests, which occur when the victim is arrested along with the abuser. A dual arrest is rarely appropriate in domestic violence cases: . . . [Nevertheless,] in some jurisdictions, usually during the initial implementation period of a mandatory arrest policy, dual arrests have occurred all too frequently. There appear to be two main reasons: some police officers, resenting the loss of some of their discretion, were trying to sabotage the mandatory arrest law; and some officers, because of inadequate training, genuinely misunderstood the provisions of the law.

Catherine F. Klein, *Domestic Violence: D.C.'s New Mandatory Arrest Law,* WASH. LAW., Nov./Dec. 1991, at 24, 27-28.

subordinate group may pose a particular threat to battered women, who are normally in a subordinate position to their batterers.[200] As previously discussed in the context of racial discrimination in Part I, if both dominant and subordinate groups can use these statutes, then statutes created to protect subordinate groups may in fact be used against them by dominant groups.[201]

One solution to this problem is to provide law enforcement officials with adequate training about the purpose of hate crime statutes and to explain the reasoning behind the legislature's decision to curtail their discretion by creating special reporting and arrest guidelines for hate crimes.[202] Another solution to this problem is to monitor prosecutorial decisions, as suggested in Part I.[203] Together these measures help ensure that the subordinate members of society are not further injured by the very laws that are designed to protect them.

F. The Argument That Proving Gender Bias Is Difficult

Another obstacle to progress in the states on treating violence against women as hate crime is confusion about how to prove motive.[204] Discussions with advocates in states that include gender in their hate crime statutes indicated that there is interest in using these statutes in cases involving violence against women.[205] However, these advocates expressed concern that there were no guidelines for demonstrating that a particular act of violence against a woman was motivated by gender bias.[206]

Concern about proving motive should not, however, be a barrier to using hate crime statutes to protect women. Motive can be difficult

---

200. See WALKER, supra note 183, at 34-35 (discussing the "traditionalist orientation" of the battered woman, and noting her subordination to her husband in the marriage, her home, her career, her financial position, and her other relationships).

201. See supra notes 36-38 and accompanying text (discussing problems associated with the enforcement of race-based hate crime statutes).

202. For example, some jurisdictions have amended mandatory arrest laws to ensure that the police arrest only the primary aggressor in situations where both parties have used violence, thus protecting the subordinate party. "In determining who was the primary aggressor, the officer was to take several factors into account, including the relative degree of injury inflicted by both parties and the existence of a prior history of violence." Klein, supra note 199, at 28.

203. See supra notes 38-40 and accompanying text (discussing bias among prosecutors as a primary obstacle to the use of race-based hate crime statutes by minorities, and offering two possible solutions).

204. See Finn, supra note 5, at 13-14 (listing proof of bias motive as the main problem in prosecuting hate violence).

205. Telephone interview with Loretta Frederick, supra note 94; telephone interview with Ann Noel, supra note 94; telephone interview with Judy Rex, supra note 72; telephone interview with Elizabeth Shumann-Moore, supra note 94.

206. Telephone interview with Loretta Frederick, supra note 94; telephone interview with Ann Noel, supra note 94; telephone interview with Judy Rex, supra note 72; telephone interview with Elizabeth Shumann-Moore, supra note 94.

to prove for any hate crime.[207] However, mere difficulty in proving motive has not prevented the legal system from punishing hate crime based on characteristics other than gender. For example, proving motive is perceived as a major obstacle in race-based hate crime prosecutions, yet race-based hate crime is successfully prosecuted.[208]

There are a number of sources of guidance for proving motive. One source is federal employment discrimination law. The Senate Judiciary Committee Report on the Violence Against Women Act of 1993 states that Title VII employment discrimination cases are to provide federal prosecutors with standards for establishing motive in gender-based hate crime.[209]

A second source is the National Institute of Justice of the United States Department of Justice's guidelines, which list factors to be considered in determining whether a crime is motivated by bias.[210] These factors include the following: common sense; language (for example, use of racial epithets); severity of harm; lack of provocation; previous history of similar events in the area; and absence of motive (for example, battery without robbery).[211] The guidelines could easily be applied in cases of gender bias: sexist slurs are often made during attacks on women; lack of provocation and severity of harm might be demonstrated in a case where a man pummels his wife for burning the dinner; and absence of motive is apparent when a woman is assaulted on the street or in her home and her assailant makes no attempt to rob her.[212]

---

207. Finn, *supra* note 5, at 13 (noting that a potential bias crime may lack the necessary "physical evidence, verification of bias language used by the alleged offender, or reliable witnesses" to prove that it is bias-motivated); Fleischauer, *supra* note 36, at 701 (arguing that "prosecutors face the difficult burden of proving not only the elements of the original crime and the disparate races . . . of the victim and the offender, but also that the reason or motivation for the crime itself was racist in nature").

208. Finn, *supra* note 5, at 11-13, 14 (describing the success of state task forces on bias crime and special prosecution units in prosecuting bias cases).

209. S. REP. NO. 138, *supra* note 47, at 52-53 (stating that because the "definition of gender-motivated crime is based on [T]itle VII," case law discussions of Title VII "will provide substantial guidance to the trier of fact in assessing whether the requisite discrimination was present").

210. CENTER FOR WOMEN POLICY STUDIES, *supra* note 1, at 9.

211. CENTER FOR WOMEN POLICY STUDIES, *supra* note 1, at 9.

212. A more difficult question is whether all rapes should be treated as hate crime. One commentator has suggested that there should be a presumption that every rape is a hate crime, but that the defendant can rebut this presumption by demonstrating some other motive for the rape. Wendy R. Willis, Note, *The Gun is Always Pointed: Sexual Violence and Title III of the Violence Against Women Act*, 80 GEO. L.J. 2197, 2206 (1992) (stating that rape is "almost always gender-motivated").

Under Willis' proposed scheme, the plaintiff has the initial burden of making a prima facie case that there was sexual contact with the defendant and that it occurred under coercive circumstances. *Id.* at 2217. Once met, the burden shifts to the defendant to raise voluntary consent as an affirmative defense. *Id.* If the plaintiff then proves sexual assault by a preponderance of the evidence, the court presumes that the assault was gender-motivated. *Id.*

In conclusion, while the application of these guidelines and the standards developed in Title VII cases might seem unusual at first, especially in domestic violence cases, difficulty in proving motive in gender-based hate crime should not deter advocates from pressuring prosecutors to use these statutes on behalf of women.

IV.   POTENTIAL BENEFITS TO TREATING VIOLENCE AGAINST WOMEN AS HATE CRIME

Two important benefits exist for treating violence against women as hate crime. Together they more than outweigh the arguments against such treatment discussed in Part III.

A.   *Valuable New Legal Remedies For Female Victims Of Violence*

The strongest argument for classifying violent acts against women that are motivated by gender bias as hate crime is that hate crime statutes offer legal remedies that are not presently available to women. For example, while rape and sexual assault statutes provide criminal remedies for crimes involving specified sexual acts between strangers, these statutes often offer less severe penalties when the victim and the assailant are acquainted, and perhaps offer no penalties when the victim and the assailant are married.[213]   Furthermore, domestic violence statutes offer injunctive relief to victims of violence who are either married to, or involved in long-term relationships with, their attacker, but do not offer relief to other female victims of male violence.[214]   Treating violence against women as hate crime would close these gaps.

Including gender in hate crime statutes offer women the following additional remedies. First, by upgrading assaults from misdemeanor to felony status, penalty enhancement statutes provide a much needed incentive for police and prosecutors to take violent crimes against women seriously.[215]   Second, including gender in hate crime statutes

---

213. *See* Robin West, *Equality Theory, Marital Rape, and the Promise of the Fourteenth Amendment,* 42 FLA. L. REV. 45, 46 (1990) (explaining that severe sexual assault laws that exempt, or provide lighter sentences for, marital rape, deny victims their Fourteenth Amendment right to equal protection of the law).

214. For instance, in the District of Columbia, Civil Protection Orders are only available for committed or threatened intrafamily offenses. D.C. CODE ANN. §§ 16-1003, -1004 (1989). Intrafamily offenses are limited to criminal acts committed upon a person "to whom the offender is related by blood, legal custody, marriage, having a child in common, or with whom the offender shares or has shared a mutual residence; and with whom the offender maintains or maintained an intimate relationship . . ." D.C. CODE ANN. § 16-1001(5)(A)-(5)(B) (1989 & Supp. 1993).

215. Arrest and prosecution rates in domestic violence cases are notoriously low. For instance, while over twelve hundred women petitioned for Civil Protection Orders in the District

offers women the opportunity to seek civil remedies and enhanced criminal penalties for bias-motivated acts of violence perpetrated by casual acquaintances and strangers, regardless of whether the acts are explicitly sexual. Third, damages awarded in civil suits provide the financial assistance that some victims of bias-motivated violence need. As the result of an attack, some victims suffer from emotional trauma so severe that they are temporarily or permanently unable to support themselves. In cases of sexual assault, victims collect damages in less than 1% of the cases.[216] There were only 255 trial verdicts over a ten-year period in civil rape cases.[217] It is even more difficult for women to seek civil damages if they are married to their attacker; not all states permit civil suits between spouses or permit them only in limited circumstances.[218] Fourth, civil suits offer an important

---

of Columbia in 1989, only 22 court jackets indicated that criminal cases were pending. District of Columbia Courts, Final Report of the Task Force on Racial and Ethnic Bias and Task Force on Gender Bias in the Courts 123-24 n.199 (1992) [hereinafter D.C. Gender Bias Task Force Report]. The District of Columbia police receive approximately nineteen thousand domestic violence calls each year. Sandra J. Sands, Karen Baker & Naomi Cahn, Report on District of Columbia Police Response to Domestic Violence 1, 54 (Nov. 3, 1989) (unpublished manuscript, on file with *The American University Journal of Gender & the Law*). Yet in 1986, only 42 written police reports were taken. *Id.* This means that there were no more than (and possibly less than) 42 arrests. *Id.*

216. Jury Verdict Research, Inc., *cited in* S. REP. NO. 197, *supra* note 13, at 44 n.43.
217. Jury Verdict Research, Inc., *cited in* S. REP. NO. 197, *supra* note 13, at 44 n.43.
218. The common law doctrine of interspousal tort immunity prohibited suits between a husband and wife, on the grounds that such suits

> disturb the harmony of the marital relationship; they involve the courts in 'trivial' disputes between spouses; they encourage fraud and collusion between spouses; criminal and divorce law provide adequate remedy; [and] the defendant is rewarded for his wrong, since he stands to recover some of the judgement if the parties cohabitate.

National Woman Abuse Prevention Project, *Victim Compensation: An Old Remedy Opens New Avenues for Battered Women,* 3 THE EXCHANGE 1, 4 (1989). The following states have abrogated this doctrine in whole, unless otherwise noted parenthetically:
(1) Penton v. Penton, 135 So. 481, 483-84 (Ala. 1931).
(2) Cramer v. Cramer, 379 P.2d 95, 97 (Alaska 1963).
(3) Fernandez v. Romo, 646 P.2d 878, 880-83 (Ariz. 1982) (en banc) (abrogating the doctrine for vehicular tort actions only).
(4) Leach v. Leach, 300 S.W.2d 15, 17 (Ark. 1957).
(5) Klein v. Klein, 376 P.2d 70, 71-72 (Cal. 1962) (en banc).
(6) Rains v. Rains, 46 P.2d 740, 742-44 (Colo. 1935).
(7) Brown v. Brown, 89 A. 889, 890-91 (Conn. 1914).
(8) Beattie v. Beattie, 630 A.2d 1096, 1098-101 (Del. 1993).
(9) FLA. STAT. ANN. ch. 741.235 (Harrison Supp. 1992); Waite v. Waite, 618 So. 2d 1360, 1361-62 (Fla. 1993).
(10) Harris v. Harris, 313 S.E.2d 88 (Ga. 1984) (abrogating the doctrine only in situations where there is "realistically speaking, no 'marital harmony' to be protected by application of the interspousal immunity rule . . . [nor] any hint of collusion between the [husband and wife] or of intent to defraud an insurance company").
(11) HAW. REV. STAT. § 572-28 (1993).
(12) Rogers v. Yellowstone Park Co., 539 P.2d 566, 571-72 (Idaho 1975) (abrogating the doctrine for vehicular tort actions only); Lorang v. Hays, 209 P.2d 733, 737 (Idaho 1949) (abrogating the doctrine in intentional tort actions only).

emotional reward for victims: establishing the "guilt" of their attacker.[219] Finally, statutes that define violent acts against women as civil rights violations offer victims of gender bias-motivated violence confirmation that their suffering is part of a greater, and regretfully unaddressed, social problem of violence against women. In this sense,

---

(13) ILL ANN. STAT. ch. 40, para. 1001 (Smith-Hurd 1993).

(14) Brooks v. Robinson, 284 N.E.2d 794, 798 (Ind. 1972).

(15) Shook v. Crabb, 281 N.W.2d 616, 619-20 (Iowa 1979) (abrogating the doctrine for personal injury actions only).

(16) Flagg v. Loy, 734 P.2d 1183, 1189-90 (Kan. 1987).

(17) Brown v. Gosser, 262 S.W.2d 480, 481-84 (Ky. 1953).

(18) MacDonald v. MacDonald, 412 A.2d 71, 75 (Me. 1980).

(19) Boblitz v. Boblitz, 462 A.2d 506, 522 (Md. 1983) (abrogating the doctrine for negligence actions only); Lusby v. Lusby, 390 A.2d 77, 89 (Md. 1978) (abrogating the doctrine for intentional tort actions only).

(20) Lewis v. Lewis, 351 N.E.2d 526, 532-33 (Mass. 1976) (abrogating the doctrine for vehicular tort actions only).

(21) Hosko v. Hosko, 187 N.W.2d 236, 237-38 (Mich. 1971).

(22) Beaudette v. Frana, 173 N.W.2d 416, 420 (Minn. 1969).

(23) Burns v. Burns, 518 So.2d 1205, 1209 (Miss. 1988).

(24) Townsend v. Townsend, 708 S.W.2d 646, 650 (Mo. 1986) (en banc) (abrogating the doctrine as to intentional tort actions only).

(25) MONT. CODE ANN. § 40-2-109 (1993); Noone v. Fink, 721 P.2d 1275, 1276 (Mont. 1986).

(26) Imig v. March, 279 N.W.2d 382, 386 (Neb. 1979).

(27) Rupert v. Stienne, 528 P.2d 1013, 1017 (Nev. 1974) (abrogating the doctrine for vehicular tort actions only).

(28) Gilman v. Gilman, 95 A. 657, 657 (N.H. 1915).

(29) Merenoff v. Merenoff, 388 A.2d 951, 960-62 (N.J. 1978).

(30) Maestas v. Overton, 531 P.2d 947, 948 (N.M. 1975).

(31) N.Y. GEN. OBLIG. LAW § 3-313 (McKinney 1989); State Farm Mut. Auto. Ins. Co. v. Westlake, 324 N.E.2d 137, 139 (N.Y. 1974).

(32) N.C. GEN. STAT. §§ 52-5, -5.1 (1991); Crowell v. Crowell, 105 S.E. 206, 208-10 (N.C. 1920).

(33) Fitzmaurice v. Fitzmaurice, 242 N.W. 526, 527-29 (N.D. 1932).

(34) Shearer v. Shearer, 480 N.E.2d 388, 392-94 (Ohio 1985).

(35) Courtney v. Courtney, 87 P.2d 660, 665-70 (Okla. 1938).

(36) Antonacci v. Davis, 816 P.2d 1202, 1203 (Or. Ct. App. 1991).

(37) Hack v. Hack, 433 A.2d 859, 868-69 (Pa. 1981).

(38) Digby v. Digby, 388 A.2d 1 (R.I. 1978) (abrogating the doctrine for vehicular tort actions only).

(39) Pardue v. Pardue, 166 S.E. 101, 103 (S.C. 1932).

(40) Scotvold v. Scotvold, 298 N.W. 266, 268-69 (S.D. 1941).

(41) Davis v. Davis, 657 S.W.2d 753, 759 (Tenn. 1983).

(42) Price v. Price, 732 S.W.2d 316, 319 (Tex. 1987).

(43) Stoker v. Stoker, 616 P.2d 590, 590-92 (Utah 1980).

(44) Richard v. Richard, 300 A.2d 637, 641 (Vt. 1973) (abrogating the doctrine for vehicular tort actions only).

(45) Surratt v. Thompson, 183 S.E.2d 200, 201-02 (Va. 1971) (abrogating the doctrine for vehicular tort actions only).

(46) Freehe v. Freehe, 500 P.2d 771, 773-76 (Wash. 1972) (en banc).

(47) Coffindaffer v. Coffindaffer, 244 S.E.2d 338, 343-44 (W. Va. 1978).

(48) Wait v. Pierce, 209 N.W. 475, 480-81 (Wis. 1926).

(49) Tader v. Tader, 737 P.2d 1065, 1069 (Wyo. 1987).

219. National Woman Abuse Prevention Project, *supra* note 216, at 5.

civil rights remedies promote one of the fundamental tenets of feminism—the personal is political.[220]

B. Increased Public Awareness Of The Seriousness And Prevalence Of Violence Against Women

The use of hate crime statutes in cases of violence against women focuses attention on the root of the crime—hatred. There are two potential benefits to focusing on the hatred involved in violence against women. First, treating violence against women as a hate crime may direct emphasis away from the sexual nature of certain bias-motivated acts of violence against women, such as rape. In the minds of many, rape is simply the result of a misguided sexual urge.[221] This perception is problematic because it immediately diverts attention away from the perpetrator and toward the victim.[222] The extent to which juries accept culturally supported "rape myths" demonstrates this problem.[223] Three of these myths—that rape is an expression of sexual desire; that women invite sexual assault by their dress, behavior, or decision to be alone in the "wrong" place; and that a woman's prior consensual sexual relations with the accused implies consent—confuse rape with sex. The effect of these myths is to "shift the focus from the perpetrator to the victim from the very moment the offense takes place."[224] Instead of looking for evidence that the rapist hates women, juries are led to look for indications that

---

220. MACKINNON, THEORY OF THE STATE, supra note 1, at 120. After explaining what "the personal is the political" does not mean, MacKinnon stresses women's powerlessness next to men. She states that it "means that gender as a division of power is discoverable and verifiable through women's intimate experience of sexual objectification, which is definitive of and synonymous with women's lives as gender female. Thus, to feminism, the personal is epistimologically the political, and its epistemology is its politics." Id.

221. Richard T. Andrias, Rape Myths, 7 A.B.A. Crim. Just. 3, 3 (1992).

222. Id.

223. Richard Andrias, a New York State Supreme Court Justice, lists seven common rape myths:

- The true victim of a rape will immediately seek out and complain to family, friends, or the police.
- Rape usually occurs at night, out of doors, and between strangers; the perpetrator uses a weapon and leaves the victim physically injured.
- Rape is an expression of sexual (albeit misplaced) desire.
- Women falsely accuse men of rape.
- The woman invited the sexual assault by her dress, behavior, or being alone in the wrong place.
- A woman's prior consensual sexual relations with the accused (or with others known to the accused) implies consent.
- A woman impaired by drugs or alcohol deserved to be raped.

Id.

224. Id.

the woman either consented or gave the appearance of consent.[225]
A logical step toward treating rape as an expression of power and
dominance[226] is to divorce sex from rape where possible.[227]

Second, viewing violence against women as hate crime might deflect
the emphasis away from the relationship between the perpetrator and
victim.[228] Just as the misperception that rape is a crime of sex
impedes the prosecution of sex crimes against women, the misperception about the significance of the relationship between victim and
assailant also serves as a barrier to effective prosecution.[229] Treating
violence against women as hate crime emphasizes the tremendous
significance of the violence.

CONCLUSION

Hate crime statutes offer a promising tool for fighting violence
against women. As discussed in Part I, gender is now included in
legislative efforts to combat hate crime on both the state and federal
levels. State statutes that provide women with civil rights remedies,
and mandate data collection and special police training, are becoming
increasingly prevalent.

Nevertheless, a variety of obstacles have stalled the inclusion of
gender in hate crime statutes and the implementation of hate crime
statutes in cases of violence against women. First, there is resistance
on the part of hate crime victims' advocates and others to the
inclusion of gender in hate crime statutes. In their efforts to keep
gender out of hate crime statutes, these advocates have overlooked
much feminist scholarship concerning violence against women.

---

225. *See* S. REP. NO. 138, *supra* note 47, at 45-46 (asserting that the "'pervasive suspicion of
rape victims' credibility,'" and persistent victim-blaming by court and law enforcement personnel,
move the focus in hate crime cases "from the attacker—where it should be—to the behavior of
the victim") (citation omitted).
226. GORDON & RIGER, *supra* note 136, at 45 (saying that feminists argue rape keeps women
afraid, dependent on men, and subservient).
227. One example of the effort to divide rape and sex is a recent movement on the part of
police and prosecutors to change the names of their specialized units from "sex crimes" to
"special victims." Andrias, *supra* note 223, at 4.
228. *See supra* note 130 and accompanying text (noting that opponents to treating hate
violence against women as hate crime believe that existence of a relationship between the victim
and perpetrator means that a victim is not interchangeable with other women). Focusing on
their relationship impedes focusing on the fact that rape is violence against women as a group.
Id.
229. In response to a survey by the D.C. Task Force on Gender Bias in the Courts, 50% of
respondents stated that they believed bail was set lower in domestic violence cases than in "other
cases of similar violence"; 70% of the respondents with an opinion stated that when the parties
are married, sentences are generally shorter than in "other similar cases"; and 50% of the
respondents with an opinion stated that sentences in domestic violence cases are shorter than
"other similar cases," even when the parties are not married. D.C. Gender Bias Task Force
Report, *supra* note 215, at 126.

Second, national multi-issue women's organizations have expressed ambivalence over whether lengthening incarceration periods is an appropriate response to male violence. This ambivalence is primarily the result of concern that lengthening incarceration periods will disproportionately impact communities of color due to racism in the American criminal justice system. Furthermore, it has been argued that increased judicial intervention in cases of violence against women may not be desirable to women of color. However, although sexual violence may have a different meaning for many African-American women due to the racist use of rape laws in this country, the argument that all African-American women do not want an effective criminal justice response to crimes of violence against them is essentialist and therefore ignores the individuality of these women. Feminist advocates should listen to the voices of victims of male violence to determine whether to support increased penalties for gender-based hate crime. In response to the claim that treating domestic violence as hate crime might be less effective, it cannot be denied that the inclusion of gender in hate crime statutes does not preclude legislatures from creating more specific responses to domestic violence. Finally, the confusion in the states about how to demonstrate motive in cases of hate-based violence against women should not preclude prosecution of these cases. Since motive is always difficult to demonstrate in hate crimes, advocates should lobby for application of pre-existing motive determination guidelines in cases involving women.

In conclusion, the potential benefits of the use of hate crime statutes for women outweigh the concerns that have arisen. Hate crime statutes offer completely new legal remedies for women. Moreover, by focusing attention on the general hatred of women that violent acts motivated by gender bias demonstrate, these statutes could help overcome the two major barriers to prosecuting hate-motivated violence against women by de-emphasizing the significance of the relationship between the victim and her assailant and directing attention away from the sexual nature of so many violent crimes against women. Now more than ever, it is critical that women's advocacy groups become, or remain, involved in the fight to include violence against women in hate crime statutes.

Acknowledgments

MacKinnon, Catherine A. "Not a Moral Issue." In *Feminism Unmodified: Discourses on Life and Law* (Cambridge: Harvard University Press, 1987): 146–62, 262–74. Reprinted by permission of the publisher. Copyright 1987 by the President and Fellows of Harvard College.

Beckman, Marlene D. "The White Slave Traffic Act: Historical Impact of a Federal Crime Policy on Women." *Women and Politics* 4 (1985): 85–101. Reprinted with the permission of Haworth Press, Inc. Copyright 1985.

Bernat, Frances P. "New York State's Prostitution Statute: Case Study of the Discriminatory Application of a Gender Neutral Law." *Women and Politics* 4 (1985): 103–20. Reprinted with the permission of Haworth Press, Inc. Copyright 1985.

Dworkin, Andrea. "Against the Male Flood: Censorship, Pornography, and Equality." *Harvard Women's Law Journal* 8 (1985): 1–29. Reprinted with the permission of the *Harvard Women's Law Journal*.

Morse, Anita L. "Pandora's Box: An Essay Review of American Law and Literature on Prostitution." *Wisconsin Women's Law Journal* 4 (1988): 21–62. Reprinted with the permission of the University of Wisconsin-Madison School of Law.

Hunter, Nan D. and Sylvia A. Law. "Brief Amici Curiae of Feminist Anti-Censorship Taskforce, et al., in *American Booksellers Association* v. *Hudnut.*" *University of Michigan Journal of Law Reform* 21 (1987–88): 69–136. Reprinted with the permission of the University of Michigan Law School.

Freeman, Jody. "The Feminist Debate Over Prostitution Reform: Prostitutes' Rights Groups, Radical Feminists, and the (Im)possibility of Consent." *Berkeley Women's Law Journal* 5 (1989–90): 75–109. Reprinted with the permission of the University of California Press.

Baldwin, Margaret A. "Pornography and the Traffic in Women: Brief on Behalf of Trudee Able-Peterson, et al., Amici Curiae in Support of Defendant and Intervenor-Defendants, *Village Books* v. *City of Bellingham.*" *Yale Journal of Law and Feminism* 1 (1989): 111–55. Reprinted with the permission of the *Yale Journal of Law and Feminism*.

Whitman, Christina Brooks. "Feminist Jurisprudence." *Feminist Studies* 17 (1991): 493–507. Reprinted with the permission of the publisher, FEMINIST

STUDIES, Inc., c/o Women's Studies Program, University of Maryland, College Park, MD 20742.

Baldwin, Margaret A. "Split at the Root: Prostitution and Feminist Discourses of Law Reform." *Yale Journal of Law and Feminism* 5 (1992): 47–120. Reprinted with the permission of the *Yale Journal of Law and Feminism*.

Kandel, Minouche. "Whores in Court: Judicial Processing of Prostitutes in the Boston Municipal Court in 1990." *Yale Journal of Law and Feminism* 4 (1992): 329–52. Reprinted with the permission of the *Yale Journal of Law and Feminism*.

Angelari, Marguerite. "Hate Crime Statutes: A Promising Tool for Fighting Violence Against Women." *American University Journal of Gender and the Law* 2 (1994): 63–105. Reprinted with the permission of the Washington College of Law.